Anthropology
Second Edition

Prentice-Hall, Inc.,
Englewood Cliffs, New Jersey

Library of Congress Cataloging in Publication Data

EMBER, CAROL R
    Anthropology.

    Bibliography: p. 477
    Includes indexes.
      1. Anthropology.   I. Ember, Melvin, joint author.
II. Title.
GN25.E45 1977   301.2   76-54977
ISBN 0-13-036962-4

Printed in the United States of America

10 9 8 7 6 5 4 3 2 1

Photo research by Ann Novotny and Rosemary Eakins, Research Reports, NYC

Cover photo of New Guinea dancer by Luis Villota

Part opening photo credits: Part I: Ian Berry, Magnum Photos. Part II: David Agee Horr/Anthro-Photo. Part III: The American Museum of Natural History. Part IV: Henri Cartier-Bresson, Magnum Photos.

Chapter opening photo credits: Chapter 1: Georg Gerster, Rapho/Photo Researchers. Chapter 2: Bruce Coleman. Chapter 3: Robert C. Hermes, National Audubon Society, Photo Researchers. Chapter 4: A. W. Ambler, National Audubon Society, Photo Researchers. Chapter 5: The American Museum of Natural History. Chapter 6: Ralph S. Solecki. Chapter 7: Ken Heyman. Chapter 8: Irven DeVore/Anthro-Photo. Chapter 9: René Millon. Chapter 10: Henri Cartier-Bresson, Magnum Photos. Chapter 11: Irven DeVore/Anthro-Photo. Chapter 12: Burk Uzzle, Magnum Photos. Chapter 13: Marc Riboud, Magnum Photos. Chapter 14: The American Museum of Natural History. Chapter 15: Marilyn Silverstone, Magnum Photos. Chapter 16: Marc and Evelyne Bernheim, Woodfin Camp and Associates. Chapter 17: Arthur Tress, Magnum Photos. Chapter 18: Film Study Center, Peabody Museum, Harvard University. Chapter 19: Hiroshi Hamaya, Magnum Photos. Chapter 20: The American Museum of Natural History. Chapter 21: The American Museum of Natural History. Chapter 22: Marc and Evelyne Bernheim, Woodfin Camp and Associates. Chapter 23: United Nations.

Prentice-Hall International, Inc., London
Prentice-Hall of Australia Pty. Ltd., Sydney
Prentice-Hall of Canada, Ltd., Toronto
Prentice-Hall of India Private Limited, New Delhi
Prentice-Hall of Japan, Inc., Tokyo
Prentice-Hall of Southeast Asia Pte. Ltd., Singapore
Whitehall Books Limited, Wellington, New Zealand

Outline

IV Culture and Anthropology in the Modern World

Introduction to Anthropology

Human Evolution: Biological and Cultural

Contents

Cultural Variation

Culture and Anthropology in the Modern World

One of the things that makes teaching introductory anthropology so much fun for us is the irrepressible curiosity of beginning students. Anthropology is largely new to them, and they seem to want very much to know about the world beyond their usual purview—to learn about it and to try to understand it. They ask innumerable questions, some that anthropologists can answer, others that cannot be answered as yet. In the second edition of our text, as in the first, we have tried to gear our presentation to the kinds of questions students as well as anthropologists have asked about human evolution and variation. Our aim is to capitalize on the curiosity of students about how and why human populations have come to be what they are.

We pay particular attention to theories and the evidence pertaining to them, even if there is no agreement in the field on a particular explanation. We believe it is important and exciting to convey not only what is known but also what is not known or only dimly suspected, so that students may acquire a feel for what anthropology is and what it could be. We think that this way of writing a textbook may heighten the interest and involvement of the student, because it conveys some of the pleasures, problems, and disappointments of researchers who are working on the frontiers of our discipline.

Plan of the Book

We have tried to integrate the materials in each chapter so that the sequence of presentation is ordered, rather than encyclopedic. We feel that this style of organization makes the content both more readable and easier to remember. It is for this reason that, at the beginning of each chapter, we highlight what is to come. After all, we want students to like and recall their exposure to anthropology. Sometimes, as in the chapters on biological and cultural evolution, we begin with an overview of the sequence of developments we will be discussing. Other times, as in the chapters on cultural variation,

Preface

we begin by trying to give a feeling for the particular range of variation we deal with in that chapter. Often a chapter on some aspect of cultural variation begins with a brief description of how our culture differs from others. We think that such contrasts make the anthropological materials more relevant to students, by arousing their natural curiosity about how and why their culture is different.

In Chapter 1, we discuss what is special and distinctive about anthropology as a whole, about each of the subfields in particular, and about how each of the subfields is related to the other disciplines such as biology, psychology, and sociology. In this edition, Chapter 1 also discusses the relevance of anthropology in the modern world.

Part II, "Human Evolution: Biological and Cultural," begins in Chapter 2 with a discussion of evolutionary theory as it applies to all forms of life, including humans; the chapter concludes with an enlarged section on how culture may also be viewed in terms of the theory of natural selection. In Chapter 3, we discuss the primates that survive in the modern world and their variable adaptations, as a background for understanding the evolution of primates in general and humans in particular. Chapters 4 through 6 discuss what is known or suspected about the evolutionary sequences—the biological as well as the cultural—from the earliest primates to the emergence of modern humans. In these chapters, which have been extensively revised, we focus on questions such as: What changes in the environment may have favored the earliest primates? What may have favored the distinctive hominid adaptation of bipedal locomotion? What are the places of the australopithecines and the Neandertals in human evolution? What were the life-styles of the various hominids? By orienting our discussion around such questions, we hope that students will better remember and appreciate the details of the fossil and archaeological records. Chapter 7 brings the discussion of human biological evolution into the present, dealing as it does with biological variation in living human populations. In Chapter 8 we deal

with the origins of food production and settled life; and in Chapter 9 we discuss the origins of the earliest cities and states. (The latter is, in this edition, a separate chapter—which we think is appropriate, given the enormous research efforts which have been devoted recently to explaining the emergence of cities and states.) Finally, in preparing Chapters 6, 8, and 9 for this edition, we have increased the global scope of our presentation by incorporating more materials from areas of the world outside Europe and the Near East.

Part III, "Cultural Variation," begins with a discussion of the concept of culture. We try first to give a feel for what culture is, before dealing more explicitly with the concept and some assumptions about it. We then proceed to discuss how and perhaps why recent populations vary culturally—in language; food getting; economic systems; social stratification; sex, marriage, and the family; marital residence and kinship; associations and interest groups; political organization; culture and personality; religion and magic; and the arts. In the chapters in Part III, we try to convey the range of variation, with ethnographic examples from all over the world, and we then discuss some possible explanations of why societies are similar or different. If anthropologists have no explanation as yet for some kind of variation, we say so. But if we have some idea of what kinds of conditions are related to some particular kind of variation, even if we do not know yet *why* they are related, we discuss that too. If we are to train students to go beyond what we know now, we have to tell them what we do not know as well as what we think we know.

Finally, in Part IV, "Culture and Anthropology in the Modern World," we discuss first (in Chapter 22) what we think are the major features of contemporary culture change, predominantly those that seem to have resulted from Western expansion and commercialization. And then we discuss some of the goals and problems involved in applying anthropological knowledge. The book concludes with a discussion of the effect of the modern world on the discipline of anthropology and how anthropology may be changing.

Features of the Book

Readability We have tried to minimize technical jargon, using only those terms that students must know to appreciate some of the achievements of anthropology and to go on to advanced courses. We think that clear and familiar language not only makes a book readable, but also makes it more enjoyable. When new terms are introduced, which of course they must be, they are set off in italics and defined right away. A glossary at the back of the book serves as a convenient reference in case the student needs to be reminded of definitions.

References Although we believe that a text should be as readable as possible, we also believe that interested readers should know the sources of our materials. And so we provide extensive references in footnotes, which the reader may consult to pursue a point further.

Summaries and Suggested Readings In addition to the overview provided at the beginning of each chapter, there is a detailed summary at the end of the chapter that will help the student review the major concepts and findings discussed therein. The suggested readings are included to provide some general references on the subject matter of the chapter.

Supplements A study guide for students and an instructor's manual have been prepared to accompany this text. The study guide is designed to help students review the important points of the text and test themselves on their understanding. The instructor's manual includes suggested discussion topics and ideas for students' essays. A test item file of multiple-choice and fill-in questions is also available to the instructor.

Acknowledgments

In order to prepare this second edition, we have had the benefit of many suggestions and criticisms from students and professionals. Some of this advice was solicited by us, some by Prentice-Hall which we received anonymously. In addition, there were some who were kind enough to write to us on their own. We thank all of those who gave us advice.

There are some people to whom we owe special thanks. First, we are grateful to our graduate assistants—Lenore Khan, Gary Feinman, and Dennis Werner. Second, we wish to thank our colleagues Frederick Szalay, John Speth, and Burton Pasternak for their extensive advice on how we could improve the first edition. Finally, we thank Ann Torbert, Patti Balassi, and Ed Stanford of Prentice-Hall for their help.

To all of the above we are grateful for their contributions to whatever completeness of coverage, clarity of expression, and felicity of style we may have achieved.

C.R.E. and M.E.

Anthropology

Introduction to Anthropology

I

What Is Anthropology?

1

Anthropology defines itself as a discipline of infinite curiosity about human beings. But this definition—which comes from the Greek *anthropos* for "man, human" and *logos* for "study"—is both accurate and inaccurate. It is accurate because anthropologists seek the answers to an enormous variety of questions about human evolution and existence. The questions range from, When and where and how did humans first appear on the earth? to, How and why did two thousand or more recent human societies develop such varying ways of life? However, defining anthropology as the study of human beings is also inaccurate, for according to this definition anthropology would appear to encompass a whole catalog of disciplines: sociology, psychology, political science, economics, history, human biology, and perhaps even the humanistic disciplines of philosophy and literature. Needless to say, the many other disciplines concerned with humans would not be happy to be regarded as subbranches of anthropology. (After all, most of them have been separate disciplines longer than anthropology, and each one considers its jurisdiction to be somewhat distinctive.) There must, then, be something unique about anthropology—a reason for its having developed as a separate discipline and for its having retained a separate identity over the approximately one hundred years since its inception.

The Scope of Anthropology

Anthropologists are generally envisioned as traveling to little-known corners of the world to study exotic peoples, or as digging deep into the earth to uncover the fossil remains or the tools and pots of people who lived long ago. These views, though clearly stereotyped, do indicate one way in which anthropology differs from other disciplines concerned with humans: anthropology is broader in scope than are these other fields of study. Anthropology is explicitly and directly concerned with all varieties of people throughout the world, not only those close at hand or within a limited area. It considers people of all periods, beginning with the emergence of humans over a million years ago and tracing their development until the present. Every part of the world that has ever contained a human population is of interest to anthropologists.

Anthropologists have not always been as broad and comprehensive in their concerns as they are today. Traditionally, they have concentrated upon non-Western cultures and have left the study of Western civilization and similarly complex societies, with their recorded histories, to other disciplines. In recent years, however, this general division of labor among the disciplines has begun to disappear. Now, anthropologists can be found at work in cities of the industrial world as well as in remote villages of the non-Western world.

What induces the anthropologist to choose so broad a subject for study? In part, he or she is motivated by the belief that any generalization which is made about human beings should be shown to be applicable to many times and places of human existence. For example, before Margaret Mead embarked on her famous field study of the people of Samoa (which was later reported in her *Coming of Age in Samoa*, 1928) many Americans believed that adolescence was necessarily a period of "storm and stress" because of the physiological changes that occur at puberty. However, on the basis of her observations of Samoan adolescents, who did not seem to show signs of emotional upheaval, Mead concluded that the Western belief about adolescence was not universally applicable and was therefore subject to question.[1] The clear implication to be drawn from her work was that emotional stress in adolescence is to some extent a function of the way that growing up is managed in Western societies. Anthropologists, then, are often in a position to correct or clarify beliefs and practices generally accepted by their contemporaries, for they are acquainted with

human life in a variety of geographical and historical settings.

Not only are anthropologists concerned with testing the accuracy of certain beliefs about human behavior; they are also interested in exploring the accuracy of certain beliefs about human biology. In our own society, for example, children are constantly told to drink milk because it will make them strong and healthy. Yet anthropologists have known for years that in many parts of the world where cows and goats are raised, people do not drink fresh milk. Recently, physicians and physiologists have found that many human populations generally lack an enzyme that facilitates the digestion of fresh milk. If these people should drink fresh milk, they would probably become ill. Therefore, in many areas, either people sour their milk to make it digestible or they do not drink milk at all. Human populations, then, vary in their biological characteristics; what is healthy for some persons is not necessarily healthy for all.

The Holistic Approach

Another distinguishing feature of anthropology is its holistic approach to the study of human beings. Anthropologists not only study all varieties of people, they also study many aspects of human experience. For example, when describing a group of people whom he or she has studied, an anthropologist might include a discussion of the history of the area in which the people live, the physical environment, the organization of their family life, the general features of their language, the group's settlement patterns, political and economic systems, religion, styles of art and dress, and so on.

In the past, individual anthropologists tried to be holistic and cover all aspects of the subject. Today, as in many other disciplines, the field of anthropology has become so broad and so much information has been assembled that anthropologists tend to specialize in one topic or area. Thus, one anthropologist may investi-

[1] Margaret Mead, *Coming of Age in Samoa*, 3rd ed. (New York: William Morrow, 1961). Originally published in 1928.

gate the physical characteristics of our pre-historic ancestors. Another may study the biological effect of the environment on a human population over time. Still another will concentrate upon the customs of a particular group of people. Despite this specialization, however, the discipline of anthropology retains its holistic orientation in that its specialty areas, taken together, describe many aspects of human existence, both past and present and on all levels of complexity.

The Anthropological Curiosity

Thus far we have described anthropology as being broader in scope, both historically and geographically, and more holistic in approach than other disciplines concerned with human beings. But this statement again implies that anthropology is the all-inclusive human science. How, then, is anthropology really different from these other disciplines? We suggest that anthropology's distinctiveness may lie principally in the particular kind of curiosity it arouses.

Anthropologists are concerned with many types of questions: Where, when, and why did people first begin living in cities? Why do some peoples have darker skin than others? Why do some languages contain more color terms than other languages? Why, in some societies, are men allowed to be married to several women simultaneously? Although these questions seem to deal with very different aspects of human existence, they do have at least one thing in common: they all deal with *typical characteristics* of particular populations. The typical characteristic of a people might be relatively dark skin, a language having many color terms, or the practice of having several wives. In fact, it could be almost any human trait or custom. This concern with typical characteristics of populations is perhaps the most distinguishing feature of anthropology. Thus, for example, where an economist might take a particular monetary system for granted and ask how that system operates,

the anthropologist might ask why only some societies during the last few thousand years used money. In short, anthropologists are curious about the typical characteristics of human populations—how and why such populations and their characteristics have varied—throughout the ages.

The Subfields of Anthropology

Different anthropologists may concentrate their attention upon different typical characteristics of societies. Some are concerned primarily with biological or physical characteristics of human populations; others are interested principally in what we call "cultural" characteristics. Hence, there are two broad classifications of subject matter in anthropology: *physical* (biological) *anthropology* and *cultural anthropology*. We shall consider archaeology and linguistics as subdisciplines of cultural anthropology, even though they are academic disciplines in their own right. A third subdiscipline, ethnology, encompasses so large an area that it is often referred to by the parent name, cultural anthropology.

PHYSICAL ANTHROPOLOGY

There are two distinctive sets of questions to which physical anthropology seeks to provide answers. The first set includes questions about the emergence of humans and their later evolution (an area of physical anthropology called *human paleontology*). The second set includes questions as to how and why contemporary human populations vary biologically (an area referred to as *human variation*).

In order to reconstruct human evolution, human paleontologists search for and study the buried, hardened bones and teeth of humans and prehumans, which are known as fossils. Paleontologists working in East Africa, for instance, have excavated the fossil remains of human-like beings who lived more than 3 million years ago. These findings have suggested

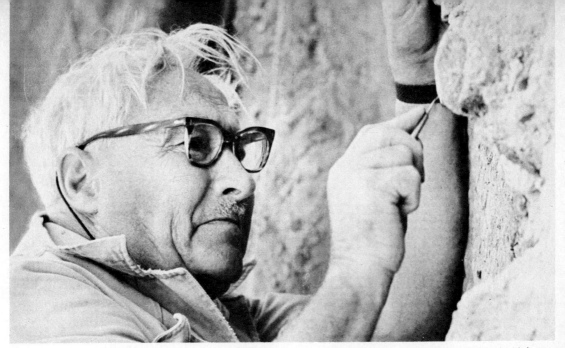

Paleontologist Louis Leakey, at Olduvai Gorge in East Africa, closely examines remains that may yield further information about the emergence and evolution of humans. (Ian Berry, Magnum Photos.)

the approximate dates when our ancestors began to develop an upright posture, flexible hands, and a larger brain.

To clarify the evolutionary sequence, the human paleontologist may make use not only of the fossil record but also of geological information on the succession of climates, environments, and plant and animal populations. Moreover, when reconstructing the past of humans, the paleontologist also is interested in the behavior and evolution of our closest relatives among the mammals—the apes and monkeys which, like ourselves, are members of the order of Primates. Species of primates are observed in the field and in the laboratory. One especially popular subject of study is the chimpanzee, which bears a close resemblance to humans in behavior and physical appearance, has similar bloodtypes, and is susceptible to many of the same diseases. From primate studies, physical anthropologists seek to distinguish those characteristics that are distinctly human from those that might be part of a generalized primate heritage. With this information, we may be able

to guess what our prehistoric ancestors were like. The inferences from primate studies are checked against the fossil record. Thus, the evidence from the earth, collected in bits and pieces, is correlated with scientific observations of our closest living relatives.

In short, physical anthropologists who are interested in human evolution are like detectives. They piece together bits of information obtained from a number of different sources. They construct theories to explain the changes observed in the fossil record and then attempt to evaluate these theories by cross-checking one kind of evidence against another. Human paleontology thus overlaps a great deal with other disciplines such as geology, general vertebrate (and particularly primate) paleontology, comparative anatomy, and the study of comparative primate behavior.

The second major area of physical anthropology—the study of human variation—investigates how and why contemporary human populations differ in physical or biological characteristics. All living peoples belong to one

Because of their similarities to humans, chimpanzees are among the most closely observed nonhuman primates. Here Jane Goodall, a primatologist, observes chimps in their natural habitat, hoping to shed some light on our understanding of what our prehistoric ancestors were like. (Baron Hugo von Lawick © National Geographic Society.)

species, *Homo sapiens,* for all can successfully interbreed. Yet there is much that varies among human populations. The investigators of human variation ask such questions as, Why are some peoples taller than others? Why do some peoples have more body hair than others? and so on.

To help them understand the biological variations observable among contemporary human populations, physical anthropologists make use of the principles, concepts, and techniques of three other disciplines: human genetics (the study of how human traits are inherited); population biology (the study of environmental effects on, and interaction with, population characteristics); and epidemiology (the study of how and why diseases affect dif-

ferent populations in different ways). Research in human variation, therefore, overlaps with research in other fields. Those who consider themselves physical anthropologists, however, are most centrally concerned with human populations and how those populations vary biologically.

For example, physical anthropologists interested in human variation might ask how human populations have adapted physically to their environmental conditions. Are Eskimos better equipped than other people to endure cold? Does darker skin pigmentation offer special protection against the tropical sun? Does the capacity of the lungs or the ability of the blood to carry oxygen increase among populations living at high altitudes?

CULTURAL ANTHROPOLOGY

To an anthropologist, the term "culture" generally refers to the customary ways of thinking and behaving that are characteristic of a particular population or society. The culture of a social group, therefore, is composed of its language, general knowledge, laws, religious beliefs, food preferences, music, work habits, taboos, and so forth. Archaeology, anthropological linguistics, and ethnology, the subdisciplines we shall consider next, are all directly concerned with human culture. Thus, they can be grouped under the broad classification of cultural anthropology.

Archaeology The archaeologist seeks not only to reconstruct the daily life and customs of prehistoric peoples, but also to trace cultural changes in their societies and to offer possible explanations as to why those changes occurred. This concern is similar to that of the historian, but the archaeologist reaches much farther back in time. The historian deals only with societies possessing written records and is therefore limited to the last 5,000 years of human history. For all past societies lacking a written record—and this includes many groups within the last 5,000 years which did not develop writing—the ar-

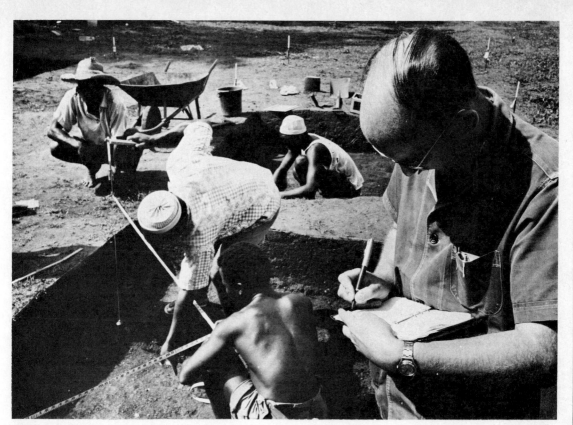

Archaeologist Frank Willett, at an excavation in Ife, Nigeria, supervises and notes the precise calculations and measurements of his assistants in an attempt to ascertain the daily life and customs of prehistoric peoples. (Copyright by Dr. Georg Gerster, Rapho/Photo Researchers.)

chaeologist serves as historian. Lacking written records for study, archaeologists are compelled to reconstruct history from the remains of human cultures which they find. Some of these remains are as grandiose as the Mayan temples discovered at Chichen Itza in Yucatan, Mexico. More often they are as ordinary as bits of broken pottery, stone tools, and even garbage heaps.

To recreate these histories is not easy. For one thing, because there are no written records to go by, the archaeologist cannot precisely date cultural patterns and changes. In contrast, the historian can often date particular conditions and events to the month and even day of the year. Archaeological chronologies deal with 50- to 100-year intervals at best. And the farther

back in time we attempt to date a particular set of archaeological materials, the more imprecise the date becomes. Moreover, archaeological materials are only the products of cultural behavior and therefore do not directly reveal the ways of life of a society. Literally, the remains are often fragmentary. For example, archaeologists may infer that a particular social group believed in an afterlife because they find tools and other objects in graves. Presumably, the objects were placed there to be used by persons after death. On the basis of this kind of evidence, archaeologists conclude that humans had religious beliefs as early as 100,000 years ago.

In trying to establish how and why ways of life have changed through time in different parts of the world, archaeologists collect materials from sites of human occupation found on the surface of the earth and, more usually, from sites that must be unearthed. On the basis of materials they have collected and excavated, they then ask various questions, such as, Where, approximately when, and why did the distinctive human characteristic of toolmaking first emerge? Where, approximately when, and why did agriculture first develop? Where, about when, and why did people first begin to live in cities? To collect the data needed to answer these and other questions, archaeologists make use of techniques and findings borrowed from a number of other disciplines, as well as what they already know from anthropological studies of recent and contemporary cultures. For example, to know where to dig for evidence of early toolmaking, archaeologists rely on geology to tell them where sites of early human occupation are likely to be found close to the existing surface of the earth. (The evidence available at the present time indicates that the earliest toolmakers lived in East Africa.) To infer when agriculture first developed, archaeologists date the relevant excavated materials by a process originally developed by chemists. And to understand why cities first emerged, archaeologists may need information from historians, geographers, and others explaining how recent and contemporary cities relate economically and politically to their hinterlands. If we can discover what recent and contemporary cities have in common, perhaps we can speculate why cities developed originally. Archaeologists could then test those speculations. Thus, archaeologists may use information from the present and the recent past to help them understand what happened in the distant past.

Anthropological Linguistics A second branch of cultural anthropology is linguistics, the study of languages. As a science, the study of language is somewhat older than anthropology. The two disciplines became closely associated in the early days of anthropological fieldwork, when anthropologists enlisted the help of linguists to study unwritten languages. In contrast to other linguists, however, anthropological linguists are primarily interested in the history and structure of languages. This focus requires a more extensive array of techniques of analysis and investigation than those used by earlier linguists.

Like the physical anthropologists, the linguists are interested both in changes that have taken place over time and in contemporary variation. Thus, anthropological linguists are concerned with the emergence of language and also with the divergence of languages over the centuries. This aspect of linguistics is known as *comparative* or *historical linguistics*. Anthropological linguists are also interested in how contemporary languages differ—especially in the way they differ in construction and use. This area of linguistics is generally called *descriptive linguistics*. More specifically, the study of how languages are constructed is called *structural linguistics*. The study of how language is used in actual speech is called *sociolinguistics* or *ethnolinguistics*.

In contrast to the human paleontologist and archaeologist, who have physical remains to help them reconstruct change over time, the historical linguist is dealing only with languages—and usually unwritten ones at that. Because an unwritten language must be heard in order to be studied, it does not leave any traces once its speakers have died off. Linguists interested in reconstructing the history of unwritten languages must begin in the present, with comparisons of contemporary languages. On the basis of these comparisons, they may draw inferences about the kinds of change in language which may have occurred in the past and which may account for similarities and differences observed in the present. The historical linguist typically asks such questions as, Did two or more contemporary languages diverge from a common ancestral language? If they are so related, how far back in time did they begin to become different?

Unlike the historical linguist, the descriptive (or structural) linguist is typically concerned with discovering and recording the rules which determine how sounds and words are put

Robert Russell, a linguist from the Summer Institute of Linguistics, uses a tape recorder to arrive at a permanent record of the unwritten language of the Amahuaca Indians of Peru. (Cornell Capa, Magnum Photos.)

together in speech. For example, a structural description of a particular language might tell us that the sounds *t* and *k* are interchangeable in a word without causing a difference in meaning. In the islands of American Samoa, one could say *Tutuila* or *Kukuila* as the name of the largest island and everyone, except perhaps the visiting anthropologist, would understand that the same island was being mentioned.

The sociolinguist is interested in determining how contemporary languages differ, and particularly how people speak differently in various social contexts. In English, for example, we do not address everyone we meet in the same way. "Hi, Joe" may be the customary way that a person greets a friend. But the same person would probably feel uncomfortable addressing a doctor by first name; instead, he or she would probably say, "Good morning, Dr. Smith." Such variations in language, which are determined by the social status of the persons being addressed, are significant for the sociolinguist.

Ethnology Ethnologists seek to understand how and why peoples today, and in the recent past, differ in their customary ways of thinking and acting. Ethnology, then, is concerned with patterns of thought and behavior such as marriage customs, kinship organization, political and economic systems, religion, folk art, music, and the like, and with the ways in which these patterns differ in contemporary societies. Ethnologists also study the dynamics of culture— that is, how various cultures develop and change, and how they interact with other cultures. In addition, ethnologists are interested in the interaction of diverse beliefs and practices within a culture and their effects on individual personalities. Thus, the aim of the ethnologists is largely the same as that of the archaeologists. However, the ethnologists generally use data which are collected firsthand by fieldworkers. Archaeologists, on the other hand, must work with fragmentary remains of past cultures, on the basis of which they can only make educated guesses about the actual customs of prehistoric peoples.

One type of ethnologist, the *ethnographer*, usually spends a year or so living with, talking to, and observing the people whose customs he or she is studying. This fieldwork provides the

Megan Biesele, an ethnographer, is studying the folklore and music of the !Kung Bushmen of Africa's Kalahari Desert. (Megan Biesele, Anthro-Photo File.)

data for a detailed description (an *ethnography*) of many aspects of the customary behavior and thought of those people. The ethnographer not only describes the general patterns of their life but also may provide possible answers to such questions as, How are economic and political behavior related? How may the customs of people be adapted to environmental conditions? Is there any relationship between beliefs about the supernatural and beliefs or practices in the natural world? In other words, the ethnographer depicts the ways of life of a particular group of people and may also suggest explanations for some of the customs he or she has observed.

Because so many cultures in the recent past have undergone extensive change, it is fortunate that another type of ethnologist, the *ethnohistorian*, is prepared to study how the ways of life of a particular group of people have changed over time. Ethnohistorians investigate written documents (which may or may not have been produced by anthropologists). They may spend many years going through documents, such as missionary accounts, reports by traders and explorers, and official government records, to establish a sequence of the cultural changes that have occurred. Unlike ethnographers who rely mostly on their own observations, ethnohistorians must rely on the reports of others. Often, they must attempt to piece together and make sense of widely scattered, and even apparently contradictory, information. Thus, the ethnohistorian's research is very much like that of the historian, except that the ethnohistorian is usually concerned with the history of a people who did not themselves leave written records. The ethnohistorian tries to reconstruct the recent history of a people and may also suggest reasons why certain changes in their way of life took place.

With data collected and analyzed by the ethnographer and ethnohistorian, the work of a third type of ethnologist, the *comparative*, or *cross-cultural, researcher*, can be done. Obviously, to understand how customs may be distributed and associated, we need to know what customs are characteristic of many peoples, both in the present and in the past. For example, how often, and in what places, do we find such customs as

FIGURE 1

The four major subdisciplines of anthropology (in bold letters) may be classified according to subject matter (physical or cultural) and according to the time period with which each is concerned (distant past versus recent past and present).

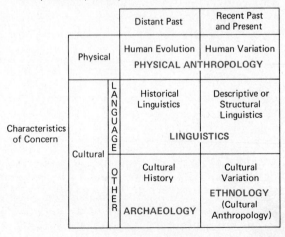

		Distant Past	Recent Past and Present
Physical		Human Evolution **PHYSICAL ANTHROPOLOGY**	Human Variation
Cultural	L A N G U A G E	Historical Linguistics	Descriptive or Structural Linguistics
		LINGUISTICS	
	O T H E R	Cultural History	Cultural Variation
		ARCHAEOLOGY	**ETHNOLOGY** (Cultural Anthropology)

Characteristics of Concern

plural marriages (one spouse of one sex and two or more spouses of the other sex), circumcision of adolescent boys, or the belief in a high god or Supreme Being? The cross-cultural researcher may also ask why a particular type of custom—witchcraft, for instance—is found in some societies but not in others. In such ways, cross-cultural research attempts to discover which of the explanations suggested to account for particular customs may be more generally applicable.

All types of cultural anthropologists may be interested in many aspects of customary behavior and thought, ranging from economic behavior to political behavior and to styles of art, music, and religion. Thus, cultural anthropology overlaps with other disciplines that concentrate on some particular aspect of human existence, such as sociology, psychology, economics, political science, art, music, and comparative religion. The distinctive feature of cultural anthropology is its interest in how all these aspects of human existence vary from society to society, in all historical periods and in all parts of the world.

The Relevance of Anthropology

For many centuries, the idea of traveling to the moon was only a dream. Yet, in 1969, the dream became a reality when an American Air Force officer gingerly planted his space boot in the moon dust. As the moon shot demonstrates, we know a great deal about the laws of nature in the physical world. If we did not understand so much, the technological achievements we are so proud of would not be possible.

In comparison, we know little about people, about how and why they behave as they do. When we consider the great number of social problems facing mankind, the importance and relevance of continuing research in cultural anthropology and the other social sciences becomes evident. Since social problems such as violence in the streets and wars between nations are products of human activity, we need to find out what conditions produce those problems. Once we gain such understanding, we may then be able to change the conditions and so solve the problems. The fact that anthropology and other sciences dealing with humans began to develop only relatively recently is not in itself a sufficient reason for our knowing so little. Why, in our quest for knowledge of all kinds, did we wait so long to study ourselves? Leslie White has pointed out that in the history of science, those phenomena most remote from us and the least significant as determinants of human behavior were the first to be studied. He suggests that this has been so because humans like to think of themselves as impregnable citadels of free will, subject to no laws of nature. Hence there is no need to see ourselves as objects to be explained.[2] Even today, society's unwillingness to accept the notion that human behavior is objectively explainable is reflected in the popularity of astrology as a determining factor in human behavior. It is highly improbable that the stars could account for human behavior, when there are no known mechanisms by which they could influence people. Yet, as long as such far-removed and improbable "causes" can pass for explanations of human behavior, no other, and more reasonable, explanations will be sought.

The belief that it is impossible to account for human behavior scientifically, either because our actions and beliefs are too individualistic and complex or because human beings are understandable only in other-worldly terms, is a self-fulfilling idea. We shall not be able to discover principles explaining human behavior if we neither believe there are such principles nor bother to look for them. The result is assured from the beginning: those who do not believe in principles of human nature will be reinforced by their finding none. If we are to increase our understanding of human beings, we first have to believe that it is possible to do so.

[2] Leslie A. White, "The Expansion of the Scope of Science," in *Readings in Anthropology*, ed. Morton H. Fried, 2d ed. (New York: Thomas Y. Crowell, 1968), vol. 1, pp. 15–24.

Why Study Anthropology?

The study of anthropology may help us become more tolerant of other peoples. If we can understand why other groups are different from ourselves, we may have less reason to condemn them for behavior which appears strange to us. We will realize that many differences among peoples may be physical and cultural adaptations to different environments.

For example, someone not very knowledgeable about the !Kung[3] Bushmen of the Kalahari Desert of South Africa might decide that these people are "inferior savages." The !Kung wear little clothing, have few possessions, live in meager shelters, and enjoy none of our technological niceties. But let us reflect on how well a typical American community might fare if it awoke to find itself in an environment similar to that in which the !Kung live. The Americans would undoubtedly find that the absence of arable and pasture land made both agriculture and animal husbandry impossible, and they would have to adopt a nomadic existence. They might then discard many of their material possessions so that they could travel easily, in order to take advantage of changing water and wild food supplies. Because of the extreme heat and the lack of extra water for doing laundry, they might find it more practical to be naked than to wear clothes. They would undoubtedly find it impossible to build elaborate homes. For social security, they might start to share the food that was brought into the group. Thus, if they survived at all, it is very likely that they would end up looking and acting far more like "ignorant savages" than like typical, middle-class Americans.

Physical differences, too, may be seen as adaptations to the environment. For example, in our society we admire people who are tall and slim. However, if these same individuals were forced to live above the Arctic Circle, they might wish that they could trade their tall bodies for short, compact ones, since stocky physiques appear to conserve body heat more effectively and may therefore be more adaptive in cold climates.

Exposure to anthropology might help to alleviate some of the misunderstandings that arise between people of different cultural groups. Some of these misunderstandings may result from very subtle causes operating below the level of consciousness. For example, different cultures have different conceptions of the gestures and interpersonal distances that are appropriate under various circumstances. Arabs consider it proper to stand close enough to another person to smell him.[4] Judging from the popularity of deodorants in our culture, Americans seem to prefer to keep the olfactory dimension out of interpersonal relations. When someone comes "too close," we may feel that he is being too intimate. However, we should remember that this person may only be acting according to his culturally conditioned conception of what is proper in a given situation. If our intolerance for others results in part from a lack of understanding of why peoples vary, then the knowledge of other peoples accumulated by anthropologists and passed on to us may help lessen our intolerance.

Knowledge of our past may bestow both a feeling of humility and a sense of accomplishment. If we are to attempt to deal with the problems of our world, we must be aware of our vulnerability, so that we do not think that the problems will solve themselves. But we also have to think enough of our prior accomplishments to believe that we can find solutions to our problems.

It may be that much of the trouble people get themselves into is a result of their exaggerated feeling of self-importance and invulnerability—in short, their lack of humility. Knowing something about our evolutionary past may help us to understand and accept our place in the biological world. Just as for any other form

---

[3] The exclamation point in the word *!Kung* signifies a clicking sound that is made with the tongue. This sound is a characteristic feature of the Bushman languages.

[4] Edward T. Hall, *The Hidden Dimension* (Garden City, N.Y.: Doubleday, 1966), pp. 144–53.

Throughout history, people have studied and learned more about the physical sciences than about human environment and experience. (NASA)

animals, we gained greater control over our food supply and were able to establish more permanent settlements. We mined and smelted ores to fashion more durable tools. We built cities and irrigation systems, monuments and ships. We made it possible to travel from one continent to another in a single day. We have prolonged human life. In short, human beings and their cultures have changed considerably over the course of history. It seems, then, that at least some human populations—though different ones at different times—have been able to adapt to changing circumstances. Let us hope that we will continue to be able to find the necessary adaptations to meet the challenges that face us.

Summary

1. Anthropology has often been called the "study of human beings." Anthropology differs from other disciplines concerned with people in that it is broader in scope. It is concerned with humans in all places of the world (not simply those places close to us), and it considers humans of all historical periods, beginning with the emergence of the first humans over a million years ago and tracing human development to the present day.

2. Another distinguishing feature of anthropology is its holistic approach to the study of human beings. Not only do anthropologists study all varieties of people, they also study all aspects of those peoples' experiences.

3. Anthropologists are concerned with identifying typical characteristics that are shared by particular human populations. The typical characteristic might be any human trait or custom; the population studied is most often a single society.

4. Physical anthropology is one of the broad classifications of subject matter included in

of life, there is no guarantee that any particular human population, or even the entire human species, will perpetuate itself indefinitely. The earth changes, the environment changes, and humanity itself changes, so that what survives and flourishes in the present may not do so in the future.

Yet our vulnerability should not make us feel powerless. There are many reasons to feel confident about the future. Consider what we human beings have accomplished so far. By means of tools and weapons that we fashioned from sticks and stones, we were able to hunt animals larger and more powerful than ourselves. We discovered how to make fire and we learned to use it to keep ourselves warm and to cook our food. As we domesticated plants and the discipline. Physical anthropology studies the emergence of humans and their later physical evolution (a subject area called human paleontology); it also studies how and why contemporary human populations vary biologically (a subject area referred to as human variation).

5. The second broad area of concern to anthropology is cultural anthropology. The three subdisciplines of archaeology, anthropological linguistics, and ethnology all deal with aspects of human culture—that is, with the customary ways of thinking and behaving that are characteristic of a particular society.

6. Archaeologists seek not only to reconstruct the daily life and customs of prehistoric peoples, but also to trace cultural changes and offer possible explanations as to why those changes occurred. Therefore, archaeologists must reconstruct history from the fragmentary remains of human cultures. Their search for these remains may be aided by the findings of other disciplines, as well as by what we know from anthropological studies of recent cultures.

7. Anthropological linguists are concerned with the emergence of language and with the divergence of languages over time (a subject matter known as comparative or historical linguistics). They also study how contemporary languages differ, both in construction (structural linguistics) and in use in actual speech (sociolinguistics or ethnolinguistics).

8. The ethnologist seeks to understand how and why peoples today, and in the recent past, differ in their customary ways of thinking and acting. One type of ethnologist, the ethnographer, usually spends a year or so living with, talking to, and observing the customs of a particular population; later, he or she may prepare a detailed report of the group's behavior, called an ethnography. Another type of ethnologist, the ethnohistorian, investigates written documents to determine how the ways of life of a particular group of people have changed over time. A third type of ethnologist—the comparative, or cross-cultural, researcher—studies the data collected by ethnographers and ethnohistorians for a large number of societies and attempts to discover which of the explanations suggested to account for particular customs may be more generally applicable.

9. Anthropology may help people to be more tolerant. Anthropological studies can show us why other peoples are the way they are, both culturally and physically. Customs or actions of theirs which appear improper or offensive to us may, in reality, be adaptations to particular environmental and social conditions.

10. Anthropology is also valuable in that knowledge of our past may bring us both a feeling of humility and a sense of accomplishment. Like any other form of life, we have no guarantee that any particular human population will perpetuate itself indefinitely. Yet, knowledge of our achievements in the past may give us confidence in our ability to solve the problems of the future.

Suggested Readings

Birdsell, J. *Human Evolution*. New York: Macmillan, 1972.
An up-to-date introductory text, covering many aspects of the subdiscipline of physical anthropology.

Burling, R. *Man's Many Voices*. New York: Holt, Rinehart and Winston, 1970.
A readable introduction to the subject of anthropological linguistics, focusing on how language is used within its cultural context.

Edgerton, R., and Langness, L. L. *Methods and Styles in the Study of Culture*. San Francisco: Chandler and Sharp, 1974.
This book gives introductory students a

broad overview of the various methods of gathering ethnographic data and the different ways of analyzing it.

Gillin, J. P. *For a Science of Social Man.* New York: Macmillan, 1954.

Seven prominent American social scientists discuss the ways in which their respective disciplines interrelate.

Hole, F., and Heizer, R. F. *An Introduction to Prehistoric Archaeology.* 2d ed. New York: Holt, Rinehart and Winston, 1969. Chapter 1.

An overview of the field of prehistoric archaeology, emphasizing the methods of inference employed in archaeological research.

Human Evolution: Biological and Cultural

Evolution

2

Astronomers estimate that the universe has been in existence for some 15 billion years. To make this awesome history more understandable, Carl Sagan has devised a calendar that condenses the 15-billion-year span into a single year.[1] Using as a scale 24 days for every billion years and 1 second for every 475 years, Sagan moves from the "Big Bang," or beginning of the universe, on January 1 to the origin of the Milky Way on May 1. September 9 marks the beginning of our solar system and September 25 the origin of life on earth. At 10:30 on the evening of December 31, the first humans appear. In this book, we are concerned with what happens in the last one and one-half hours of the year.

Sagan's compression of history provides us with a manageable way to compare the short span of human existence with the total time span of the universe: human beings have been around for only about ninety minutes out of a twelve-month period!

The first mammals appeared on earth about 225 million years ago—a fairly recent occurrence, if we keep in mind the 15 billion figure. They probably fed on insects at night and hid in nests during the day, in order to avoid the dinosaurs and reptiles which dominated the earth at that time.[2]

Some 90 million years ago, the first primates may have appeared. They are believed to be ancestral to all living primates, including monkeys, apes, and humans. With the growth of forests, the early primates began to live in trees. They developed fingers and a grasping reflex.[3] Later (about 35 million years ago) they began to be replaced by the first monkeys and apes.

Some 20 million years after the appearance of monkeys and apes, the first direct ancestors of humans probably emerged. About 40,000 years ago, "modern" humans evolved.

How do we account for the biological and

[1] Carl Sagan, "A Cosmic Calendar," *Natural History*, December 1975, pp. 70–73.
[2] John E. Pfeiffer, *The Emergence of Man*, rev. and enl. ed. (New York: Harper & Row, 1972), pp. 21–23.
[3] Ibid., pp. 30, 32.

2

cultural evolution of humans? The details of the emergence of primates and the evolution of humans and their cultures will be covered in subsequent chapters. In this chapter, we shall focus on how the modern theory of evolution developed and how it accounts for change over time.

The Evolution of Evolution

According to the Judaeo-Christian view of history, the world was only a few thousand years old. An eminent calculator of biblical events, Archbishop Ussher, even set the date of creation at precisely 4004 B.C. That was the year that God was supposed to have created Adam and, from Adam's rib, Eve. Man and woman, fashioned in God's image, were seen as "little lower than the angels." Given such a view, the acceptance of the theory of *evolution*—the idea that different species developed, one from another, over very long periods of time—was impossible.

The dominant Western view of the seventeenth and eighteenth centuries also held that God and all of his creations were locked into a natural hierarchy. This hierarchy was defined and perpetuated by the theological doctrine of the *Scala Naturae,* the Scale of Nature, also called the Chain of Being.[4] It placed humans above rocks, plants, and animals and below spiritual beings. Although the Scale of Nature placed humans close to the apes, society was not shocked, for each creature in the Chain of Being was said to be created separately by God's Divine art. The physical resemblances between human and ape were thus the result of separate acts of Divine creation.

Belief in the Scale of Nature was accompanied by the conviction that an animal species could not become extinct. The notion of extinction threatened people's trust in God; it was unthinkable that a whole group of God's crea-

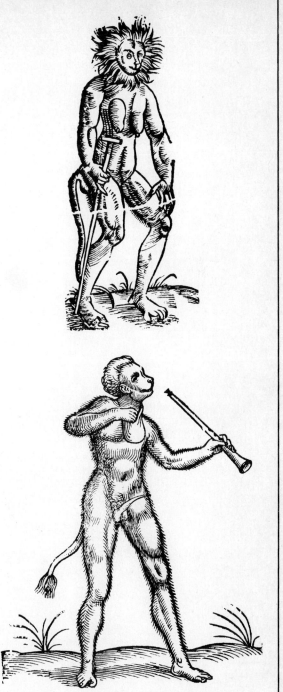

The etchings of Edward Topsell, published in 1658, illustrate a conception of early humans based more on imagination than science. (Courtesy Rare Book Division, the New York Public Library, Astor, Lenox, and Tilden Foundations.)

[4]See Loren C. Eiseley, "The Dawn of Evolutionary Theory," in *Darwin's Century: Evolution and the Men Who Discovered It* (Garden City, N.Y.: Doubleday, 1958), as reprinted in *Evolution of Man,* ed. Louise B. Young (New York: Oxford University Press, 1970), p. 10.

TABLE 1 An Overview of Human Evolution: Biological and Cultural

Time (years ago)	Geologic Epoch	Fossil Record (first appearance)	Archaeological Periods (Old World)	Major Cultural Developments (first appearance)
5,500 (3,500 B.C.)			Bronze Age	Cities and states; social inequality; full-time craft specialists
10,000 (8,000 B.C.)			Neolithic	Domesticated plants and animals; permanent villages
14,000 (12,000 B.C.)			Mesolithic	Broad spectrum food collecting; increasingly sedentary communities; many kinds of microliths
40,000		Earliest Humans in New World / Modern Humans *Homo sapiens sapiens*	Upper Paleolithic	Cave paintings; female figurines; many kinds of blade tools
	Pleistocene		Middle Paleolithic	Religious beliefs (?); burials; Mousterian tools
100,000		Neandertal *Homo sapiens*		
250,000		Earliest *Homo sapiens* (?) Fontéchevade Swanscombe Steinheim		
700,000		*Homo erectus*	Lower Paleolithic	Use of fire; big game hunting; Acheulean tools
1,800,000		*Homo erectus* (?)		Hunting and/or scavenging; seasonal campsites; division of labor by sex (?); Oldowan tools
5,000,000	Pliocene	Earliest Definite Hominids *Homo* (?) *Australopithecus*		Earliest stone tools
22,500,000	Miocene	Earliest Hominids (?) *Ramapithecus* *Dryopithecus*		
38,000,000	Oligocene	Earliest Apes and Monkeys *Aegyptopithecus* *Propliopithecus* *Parapithecus* *Apidium*		
53,500,000	Eocene	*Plesiadapis* *Tetonius*		
65,000,000	Paleocene			
90,000,000	Cretaceous	Earliest primates (?) *Purgatorius*		

Geological dates from W. A. Berggren and J. A. Van Couvering, "The Late Neogene: Biostratigraphy, Geochronology and Paleoclimatology of the Last 15 Million Years in Marine and Continental Sequences," *Palaeogeography, Palaeoclimatology, Palaeoecology* 16 (1974):13–16, 165.

tions could simply disappear. The irony of history is that although the Scale of Nature rejected and delayed an evolutionary theory, its concept of an order of all things in nature encouraged comparative anatomical studies of creatures and thus provided a stimulus for the development of evolutionary theory.

Early in the eighteenth century, one of the period's most influential scientists, Carl Linnaeus (1707–1778), classified plants and animals in a *Systema Naturae* which placed humans in the same order—primates—as apes and monkeys. However, Linnaeus did not suggest an evolutionary relationship between humans and apes. Although he classified both forms as primates, he initially accepted the notion that all species were created by God, fixed in their form. As his research progressed, though, Linnaeus appeared to be less certain about the fixity of species. Later, he recognized the possibility that new species might arise.[5]

The Comte de Buffon (1707–1788), a contemporary of Linnaeus, was more certain that species do not remain the same. As a matter of fact, he not only accepted the principle that species evolve from one another but also espoused most of the other tenets of later evolutionary theory as formulated by Wallace and Darwin.[6] However, either because his ideas were not organized or because he did not consistently espouse evolutionary theory, his work did not have the impact that Darwin's did.

If species evolve from one another, how can evolutionary change be explained? One explanation, most often associated with the name Jean Baptiste Lamarck (1744–1829), was that acquired characteristics could be inherited. According to this theory, individuals who in their lifetime developed characteristics helpful to their survival would pass those characteristics on to future generations, thereby changing the physical makeup of the species. For example, Lamarck explained the long neck of the giraffe as the result of successive generations of giraffes

[5] Ibid., pp. 13–15.
[6] Ibid., p. 18.

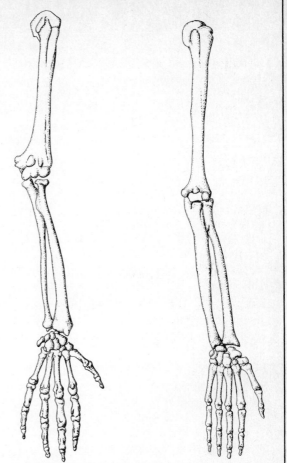

FIGURE 1
The idea that chimpanzees and humans descend from a common ancestor is suggested by anatomical similarities, such as in their forelimbs. Chimpanzee forelimb skeleton (*left*); human forelimb skeleton (*right*).

stretching their necks to reach the high leaves of trees. The stretched muscles and bones of the neck were somehow transmitted to the offspring of the neck-stretching giraffes, and eventually all giraffes came to have long necks. Erasmus Darwin (1731–1802), the grandfather of the celebrated Charles Darwin and a contemporary of Lamarck, also believed in the inheritance of acquired characteristics as a way of explaining evolutionary changes in life forms. But because Lamarck and later biologists failed to produce evidence to support the hypothesis that acquired characteristics can be inherited, this explanation of evolution is now generally dismissed.[7]

Although the mechanisms of evolutionary change were not understood in the early 1800s, more and more people were questioning the biblical conception of creation. For example, in the years 1830 to 1833 (in his *Principles of Geology*), Sir Charles Lyell (1797–1875) rejected the view of an unchanging earth. He suggested instead that the earth was constantly being shaped and reshaped by forces that had been operating since the beginning of time—far longer than previously had been supposed—and he presented fossil evidence in support of his thesis.

Lyell's progressive views were opposed not only by theologians but by his fellow naturalists and scientists. A rival theory, *catastrophism*, expounded chiefly by Georges Cuvier (1769–1832), proposed that previous cataclysms and upheavals, such as Noah's flood, had killed off all former living creatures and that new creatures had come to replace them. The fossils being discovered were taken, not as evidence of evolution, but as proof that catastrophes had destroyed all living things, which were then replaced by new Divine creations. The weight of fossil evidence, however, was great enough to discredit catastrophism. Only evolution could explain the presence of species significantly different in appearance although obviously related whose remains were preserved in different layers of rock.

The Theory of Natural Selection

In the mid-nineteenth century, another blow was struck at the orthodox interpretation of creation. After studying changes in plants, fossil animals, and varieties of domestic and wild pigeons, Charles Darwin (1809–1882) rejected the notion that each species was independently created. The results of his investigations pointed clearly, he thought, to the evolution of species through change. While Darwin was completing the work necessary to support his theory, he was sent a manuscript by Alfred Russell Wallace, a naturalist who had reached conclusions about the evolution of the species that matched his own. The two men presented their astonishing theory to their colleagues in 1858, at a meeting of the Linnaean Society of London.[8]

In 1859, when Darwin published *On the Origin of Species,* he wrote: "I am fully convinced that species are not immutable; but that those belonging to what are called the same genera are lineal descendants of some other and generally extinct species, in the same manner as the acknowledged varieties of any one species."[9] His revolutionary conclusions outraged those who believed, literally, in the biblical account of creation. Evolutionary evidence was sufficiently convincing to make some people interpret the Bible metaphorically or figuratively, but the fundamentalists who worshiped the literal word of "The Book" would not compromise their beliefs. Years of bitter controversy followed.

Until 1871 (when *The Descent of Man* was published), Darwin avoided stating categorically that humans were descended from subhuman forms, but the implications of his theory were clear. People began to take sides for and against Darwin. In June 1860, at the annual meeting of the British Association for the Advancement of Science, Bishop Wilberforce saw an opportunity to attack the Darwinists. Concluding his speech, he faced Thomas Huxley, one of the Darwinists' chief advocates, and inquired, "Was it through his grandfather or his grandmother that he claimed descent from a monkey?" Huxley responded, "If . . . the question is put to me would I rather have a miserable ape for a grandfather than a man highly endowed by nature and possessing great means

[7]G. Ledyard Stebbins, *Processes of Organic Evolution,* 2d ed. (Englewood Cliffs, N.J.: Prentice-Hall, 1971), p. 4.

[8]Ibid., p. 10.
[9]Charles Darwin, *On the Origin of Species,* as reprinted in *Evolution of Man,* ed. Louise B. Young, p. 78.

and influence and yet who employs those faculties and that influence for the mere purpose of introducing ridicule into a grave scientific discussion—I unhesitatingly affirm my preference for the ape." [10]

One of the most famous confrontations between fundamentalists and evolutionists occurred at the 1925 Scopes Monkey Trial in Tennessee. John Scopes, defended by the renowned lawyer Clarence Darrow, was convicted of teaching evolution. Scopes' opponents won the court decision, but the real victors were the proponents of Darwin's theory. The wide publicity given to the trial and the discussion it generated greatly increased the public's awareness and understanding of evolution—if not its total acceptance. But as late as 1968, a petition to the city of Wheeling, Illinois, protested the teaching of evolution as fact, rather than theory.

Darwin was not the first person to view the creation of new species as evolutionary, but he was the first to provide a comprehensive, well-documented explanation for the way evolution had occurred. He pointed out that each species is composed of a great variety of individuals, some better adapted to their environment than others. The better-adapted individuals generally survive longer and produce more numerous offspring than the poorer-adapted. Very gradually, the proportion of individuals with advantageous traits increases. Thus, this process of *natural selection* over appreciable time results in the evolution of better-adapted forms of a species in a particular environment. Changes in a species can be expected to occur as the environment changes or as some members of the species move into a new environment. With environmental change, different traits become adaptive. The forms of the species that possess the more adaptive traits will become more frequent whereas those forms whose characteristics make continued existence more difficult or impossible in the modified environment will eventually become extinct. According to Wallace, as expressed in the original presentation of his theory, environmental difficulties would mean that ". . . those forming the least numerous and most feebly organized variety would suffer first, and, were the pressure severe, must soon become extinct. . . . the parent species would next suffer, would gradually diminish in numbers, and with a recurrence of similar unfavorable conditions might also become extinct. The superior variety would then alone remain. . . ." [11]

Consider, in contrast to Lamarck, how the theory of natural selection would explain why giraffes became long-necked. Originally, the necks of giraffes varied in length, as happens with virtually any physical characteristic in a population. During a period when food was scarce, those giraffes with longer necks who could reach higher tree leaves might be better able to survive and suckle their offspring, and thus they would leave more offspring than shorter-necked giraffes. Eventually, the shorter-necked giraffes would diminish in number and the longer-necked giraffes would increase in number. The resultant population of giraffes would still have variation in neck length but, on the average, would be longer-necked than earlier forms.

Because the process of evolution occurs in small, nearly imperceptible gradations over many generations, it is difficult to observe directly. Although we possess fossilized remains of more ancient forms of the horse, no one living today can point to a modern horse and say, "I remember when you were the ancient *Eohippus.*" Nevertheless, because some life forms reproduce very rapidly, it is possible to observe some examples of natural selection operating over relatively short time periods in changing environments.

Within the last 100 years in England, for example, scientists have been able to observe natural selection in action. When certain areas

[10] From Ashley Montagu, Introduction to *Man's Place in Nature* by Thomas H. Huxley, in *Evolution of Man,* ed. Louise B. Young, pp. 183–84.

[11] Alfred Russell Wallace, "On the Tendency of Varieties to Depart Indefinitely from the Original Type," *Journal of the Proceedings of the Linnaean Society,* August, 1858, reprinted in *Evolution of Man,* ed. Louise B. Young, p. 75.

Long necks enable giraffes to reach the top branches of trees. Through natural selection, those animals with longer necks had a better chance of surviving and reproducing, thus transmitting their genes to offspring. (Photo by Leonard L. Rue, III; courtesy of Wildlife Photographers and Bruce Coleman, Inc.)

of the country became heavily industrialized, the pale bark of trees in those regions became coated with black soot. Light-colored moths, formerly well adapted to blend with their environment, became clearly visible against the sooty background of the trees and were easy prey for birds. Darker moths, previously at a disadvantage against the light bark, were now better adapted for survival. Their dark color became an advantage in industrial regions and subsequently the darker moths became the predominant variety.

Natural selection is also apparent in the newly acquired resistance of houseflies to the insecticide DDT. In the last twenty-five years,

since DDT use became common, a new, DDT-resistant strain of housefly has *evolved*. In the early DDT environment, many houseflies were killed. But the few that survived were the ones that reproduced—and their resistant characteristics became common to the housefly populations. To the chagrin of medical practitioners, similar resistances develop in bacteria. After it comes into wide use, a particular antibiotic drug may lose its effectiveness because new bacterial strains emerge which have resistance to the drug.

Natural selection can also operate on the behavioral or social characteristics of populations. For example, consider the lion. Although members of the cat family normally are solitary creatures, lions live in social groups known as "prides." Why? Schaller has suggested that lion social groups may have evolved primarily because group hunting is a more successful way to catch large mammals in open terrain than is solitary hunting. He has observed that not only are several lions more successful in catching prey than are solitary lions, but several lions are more likely to catch and kill large and dangerous prey such as giraffes. Then, too, young cubs are generally safer from predators in a social group than when they are alone with their mothers. Thus, the social behavior of lions probably evolved primarily because it provided selective advantages in the lions' open-country environment.[12]

The theory of natural selection answered many questions, but it also raised at least one question whose answer eluded even Darwin. The appearance of a beneficial trait may assist the survival of an organism, but what happens when the organism reproduces by mating with other members who do not possess this new variation? Will not the new adaptive trait eventually disappear if subsequent generations mate with individuals who lack this trait? Darwin knew variations were transmitted through heredity, but he could not explain the source of

---

[12] G. B. Schaller, as referred to in Edward O. Wilson, *Sociobiology* (Cambridge, Mass: Belknap Press, 1975), p. 504.

Prides of lions are more successful in catching large animals than are solitary lions. This social behavior probably evolved because it provided selective advantages in the lions' open-country environment. (Norman Myers, Bruce Coleman, Inc.)

new variations and the mode of inheritance. Gregor Mendel's pioneering studies in the science of genetics provided the foundations for the answers, but his discoveries were not widely known until 1900.

Heredity

GREGOR MENDEL'S EXPERIMENTS

Mendel (1822–1884), an Austrian monk and amateur botanist, bred several varieties of pea plants and made detailed observations of their offspring. He chose as breeding partners plants that differed by only one observable trait: tall plants were crossed with short ones and yellow ones with green, for example.

When the pollen from a yellow pea plant was transferred to a green pea plant, Mendel observed a curious phenomenon: all of the first generation offspring bore yellow peas. It seemed that the green trait had disappeared. But when seeds from this first generation were crossed, they produced both yellow and green pea plants in a ratio of three yellow to one green pea plant. Apparently, Mendel reasoned, the green trait had not been lost or altered; the yellow trait was simply *dominant* and the green trait was *recessive*. Mendel observed similar results with other traits. Tallness dominated shortness, and the factor for smooth-skinned peas dominated the factor for wrinkled ones. In each cross, the 3 to 1 ratio appeared in the second generation. Self-fertilization, however, produced different results. Green pea plants always yielded green pea plants, and short plants always produced short plants.

From his numerical results, Mendel concluded that some yellow pea plants were pure for that trait, whereas others also possessed a green factor. That is, although two plants might both have yellow peas, one of them might produce offspring with green peas. In such cases, the full complement of inherited traits, the *genotype*, differed from the observable appearance, or *phenotype*.

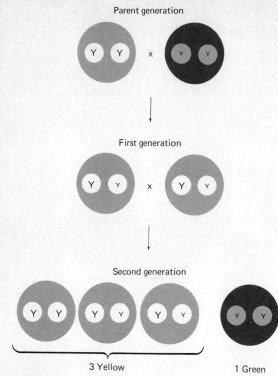

Parent generation

First generation

Second generation

3 Yellow   1 Green

FIGURE 2
When Mendel crossed a plant with two genes for yellow peas (YY) with a plant with two genes for green peas (yy), the peas of each offspring were yellow but carried one gene for yellow and one gene for green (Yy). The peas were yellow because the gene for yellow is dominant over the recessive gene for green. Crossing the first generation yielded three yellow pea plants and one green pea plant.

GENES: THE CONVEYORS OF INHERITED TRAITS

Mendel's units of heredity were what we now call *genes*. He concluded that these units occurred in pairs for each trait, and that offspring inherited one unit of the pair from each parent. (Today we call each member of a gene pair or group an *allele*.) If the two genes, or alleles, for a trait are the same, the organism is *homozygous* for that trait; if the two genes for a characteristic differ, the organism is *heterozygous* for that trait. A pea plant that contains a pair of genes for yellow is homozygous for the trait. A yellow pea plant with a dominant gene for yellow and a recessive gene for green, although phenotypi-

cally yellow, has a heterozygous genotype. As Mendel demonstrated, the recessive green gene can reappear in subsequent generations. But Mendel knew nothing of the composition of genes or the processes which transmit them from parent to offspring. Many years of scientific research have yielded much of the missing information.

The genes of an organism are located on rod-shaped bodies, called *chromosomes,* within the nucleus of every one of the organism's body cells. Chromosomes, like genes, occur in pairs. Each allele for a given trait is carried on the identical position of corresponding chromosomes. The two genes that determined the color of Mendel's peas, for example, were opposite each other on a pair of chromosomes.

Mitosis and Meiosis   The body cells of every plant or animal carry chromosome pairs in a number appropriate for its species. Humans have 23 pairs, a total of 46 chromosomes, each carrying many times that number of genes. Each new body cell receives this number of chromosomes during cellular reproduction, or *mitosis,* as each pair of chromosomes duplicates itself.

But the question then arises, What happens when a sperm cell and an egg cell unite to form a new organism? What prevents the human baby from receiving twice the number of chromosomes characteristic of its species—23 pairs from the sperm and 23 pairs from the egg? The process by which the reproductive cells are formed, *meiosis,* ensures that this will not happen. Each reproductive cell contains *half* the number of chromosomes appropriate for the species, Only one member of each chromosome pair is carried in every egg or sperm. At fertilization, the human embryo normally receives 23 separate chromosomes from its mother and the same number from its father, adding up to the 23 pairs.

DNA

As we have said, genes are located on the chromosomes, the rod-like structures discussed above. Each gene carries a set of instructions

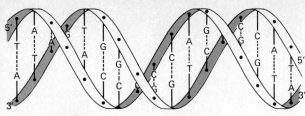

FIGURE 3

The DNA molecule consists of two spiral sugar-phosphate strands. The strands are linked by the nitrogenous bases adenine (A), guanine (G), thymine (T), and cytosine (C). When the DNA molecule reproduces, the bases separate and the spiral strands unwind. Each original strand serves as a mold along which a new complementary chain is formed. (From "A DNA Operator-Repressor System" by Tom Maniatis and Mark Ptashne. Copyright © 1976 by Scientific American, Inc. All rights reserved.)

encoded in its chemical structure. It is from this coded information carried in the genes that a cell makes all the rest of its structural parts and chemical machinery. In every living organism, it appears that heredity is controlled by the same chemical substance, DNA (deoxyribonucleic acid). An enormous amount of recent research has been directed toward understanding DNA—what its structure is how it duplicates itself in reproduction, and how it conveys or instructs the formation of a complete organism.

One of the most important keys to understanding human development and genetics is the structure and function of DNA. In 1951, biologist James Watson, with British chemist Francis Crick, proposed that DNA is a very long, two-stranded molecule, shaped as a double helix (see Figure 3). The model they proposed for DNA also suggested how it could reduplicate itself within minutes. Subsequent research has substantiated their model of both the structure and function of DNA.[13]

Additional research has focused on how DNA directs the making of an organism according to the instructions in its genetic code. It now appears that another nucleic acid, RNA (ribonucleic acid), copies the blueprint from DNA and "transmits" the instructions to the cytoplasm of a cell. Thus, DNA is the language of life. As George and Muriel Beadle put it, ". . . the deciphering of the DNA code has revealed our possession of a language much older than hieroglyphics, a language as old as life itself, a language that is the most living language of all—even if its letters are invisible and its words are buried deep in the cells of our bodies."[14]

Sources of Variability

Natural selection proceeds only when individuals within a population vary. There are two genetic sources of variation: genetic recombination and mutation.

GENETIC RECOMBINATION

The distribution of traits from parents to children varies from one offspring to another. Brothers and sisters, after all, do not look exactly alike, nor does each child resemble 50 percent of the mother and 50 percent of the father. This variation occurs because when a sperm cell or an egg cell is formed, the single member of each chromosome pair it receives is a matter of chance. Each reproductive cell, then, carries a *random assortment* of chromosomes and their respective genes. At fertilization, the egg and sperm that unite are different from every other egg carried by the mother and every other sperm carried by the father. A unique offspring is thus produced.

The traits displayed by each organism are not simply the result of combinations of dominant and recessive genes, as Mendel had hypothesized. In humans, most traits are influenced by the activity of many genes. Skin color, for example, is the result of several inherited characteristics. A brownish shade results from the presence of a pigment known as melanin; the degree of darkness in the hue depends largely on the amount of melanin present and how it is distributed in the layers of the skin. Another factor contributing to the color of all

[13] George and Muriel Beadle, *The Language of Life* (New York: Doubleday, 1966), pp. 173–99.

[14] Ibid., p. 216.

human skin is the blood that flows in blood vessels located in the superficial layers of the skin. Thus, skin color is determined by genes which bear various instructions. Humans carry at least five different genes for the manufacture of melanin, and many other genes for the other components of skin hue. In fact, almost all physical characteristics in humans are the result of the concerted action of many genes. Some traits are sex-linked. The so-called X chromosome, which, together with the presence or absence of a Y chromosome, determines sex, may also carry the gene for hemophilia or color blindness; the expression of these two characteristics depends on the sex of the organism.

Such processes of genetic recombination ensure that variety is achieved, and genetic variation within a species is essential for the operation of natural selection. Evolution and genetic variation, then, are inseparable.

At any given moment, the major source of variability in a population is genetic recombination. Ultimately, however, the major source of variability on which natural selection proceeds is mutation. For mutation replenishes the supply of variability which is constantly being reduced by the selective elimination of less-fit variants.

MUTATION

Mutation is a change in the molecular structure or DNA code of a gene. Such a change produces a new gene. Mutations occur randomly and are usually harmful to an individual, since any change in the intricate structure of a gene is likely to impair the delicate balance within an organism and between an organism and its environment.[15]

What causes mutations? Rates of mutation increase among organisms which are exposed to certain chemicals or to dosages of radiation such as X-rays. But the majority of mutations are thought to occur because of occasional mismating of the chemical bases that make up DNA.[16]

[15] Stebbins, *Processes of Organic Evolution*, p. 24.
[16] Ibid., p. 29.

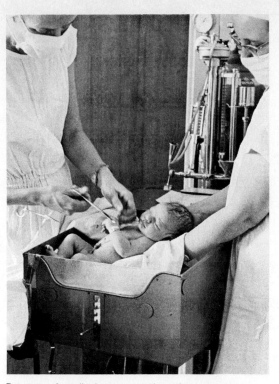

Because of medical care, mutations that were once lethal are not necessarily any longer. Human culture can alter biological evolution. (Eve Arnold, Magnum Photos.)

Just as a typist will make errors in copying a manuscript, so will DNA, in duplicating itself, occasionally change its code.[17] A mutation will result from such an error.

Not only are mutations usually harmful, they are sometimes lethal. Tay-Sachs disease, for example, is caused by two recessive mutant genes. Its effects are blindness, severe retardation, and death by the age of three or four. An organism with both recessive mutant genes for a given harmful trait probably will die before it can reproduce—and often before it is born. But the trait can be passed on by individuals who are heterozygous for the recessive gene.

We can discuss the relative merits or disadvantages of a mutant gene *only* in terms of the physical, cultural, and genetic environment of

[17] George and Muriel Beadle, *The Language of Life*, p. 123.

that gene.[18] Galactosemia, for example, is caused by a recessive mutant gene and usually results in mental retardation and blindness. It can be prevented, however, by dietary restrictions begun at an early age. In this instance, the intervention of human culture counteracts the mutant gene and allows the afflicted individual to lead a normal life. Thus, some cultural factors can modify the effect of natural selection by helping to perpetuate a harmful mutant gene. People with the galactosemia trait who are enabled to function normally reproduce and pass on one of the recessive genes to their children. Without cultural interference, natural selection would prevent such reproduction. In most cases, however, natural selection works to retain only those mutations which aid survival.

Even though mutations are infrequently adaptive, those that are adaptive will multiply in a population relatively quickly, by natural selection. As Dobzhansky has suggested, "Consistently useful mutants are like needles in a haystack of harmful ones. A needle in a haystack is hard to find, even though one may be sure it is there. But if the needle is valuable, the task of finding it is facilitated by setting the haystack on fire and looking for the needle among the ashes. The role of the fire in this parable is played in biological evolution by natural selection."[19]

The Origin of Species

One of the most controversial aspects of Darwin's theory was the suggestion that one species could, over time, evolve into another species. *Speciation,* or the development of a new species, does not happen suddenly. Nor is it the result of one or two mutations in the history of a single family.

Speciation may occur if one subgroup of a species finds itself in a radically different environment. In the subgroup's adaptation to the new environment, enough genetic changes may occur to result in a new variety or race. Races, however, are not separate species. They are simply slight variants of a single species that can interbreed. As Dobzhansky explains, "Perhaps there is no recorded instance of intermarriage between some races, say of Eskimos with Papuans, but Eskimos as well as Papuans do interbreed with other races; channels, however tortuous, for gene exchange exist between all human races."[20]

But a species cannot breed successfully with a different species. Generally, the genetic makeup of separate species is so different that reproduction is impossible. If members of different species did mate, it is unlikely that the egg would be fertilized or, if it were, that the embryo would survive. If birth did occur, the offspring would either die or be infertile. What is the explanation for this differentiation? How does one group of organisms become so unlike another group having the same ancestry that it forms a totally new species?

Speciation may occur if the populations become so separated from each other geographically that gene exchanges are no longer possible. In adapting to their separate environments, the two populations may undergo enough genetic changes to prevent them from interbreeding. Numerous factors can prevent the exchange of genes. Two species living in the same area may breed at different times of the year, or their behavior during breeding, e.g., courtship rituals, may be distinct. The difference in body structure of closely related forms may in itself bar interbreeding. Geographic barriers may also prevent interbreeding.

Once species differentiation does occur, the evolutionary process cannot be reversed—the new species can no longer mate with other species related to its parent population. Humans and gorillas, for example, had the same distant ancestors, but their evolutionary paths have irreversibly diverged.

[18]Theodosius Dobzhansky, *Mankind Evolving: The Evolution of the Human Species* (New Haven: Yale University Press, 1962), pp. 138–40.
[19]Ibid., p. 139.

[20]Ibid., p. 193.

"I say, eat, drink, and be merry, for tomorrow we will be listed under 'extinct' in the Encyclopaedia Britannica." (Ed Fisher, ROTHCO, courtesy of *Saturday Review*.)

Cultural and Biological Evolution

Until now in this chapter, we have discussed only biological evolution. But humans have also evolved culturally. We became hunters and gatherers, using tools to augment our muscles and teeth. We began to grow plants and animals for our food. We built cities and complex political systems. How is cultural variation like or unlike biological evolution?

The major difference between the two is that the mechanism for transmitting traits is different in the two kinds of evolution. Biologically, traits are transmitted by the replication of DNA; culturally, they are transmitted by learning and imitation. Accordingly, the sources of variability differ in that cultural evolution proceeds from recombination of learned behaviors rather than from genetic recombination, and from invention rather than mutation.[21] Also, cultures are not closed or reproductively iso-

lated, as species are. A culture can borrow new things and behaviors from other cultures, but a species cannot borrow genetic traits from another species. The custom of growing corn, which has spread from the New World to many other areas, is an example of this phenomenon. Finally, cultural evolution is more subject to conscious human control. Human beings can plan their futures and change their behavior.

All of these differences, however, do not alter the fact that traits—whether genetic or cultural—are subject to natural selection. According to Nissen, "Behavioral incompetence leads to extinction as surely as does morphological disproportion or deficiency in any vital organ. Behavior is subject to selection as much as bodily size or resistance to disease."[22]

Biological and cultural evolution in humans may not be completely separate processes. As we shall see later, some of the most important biological features of humans—such as two-legged walking and relatively large brains—may have been favored by natural selection because our ancestors made tools (a cultural trait). Con-

[21]Donald T. Campbell, "Variation and Selective Retention in Socio-Cultural Evolution," in *Social Change in Developing Areas: A Re-Interpretation of Evolutionary Theory*, ed. Herbert Barringer, George Blankstein, and Raymond Mack (Cambridge, Mass: Schenkman, 1965), pp. 19–49.

[22]Henry W. Nissen, "Axes of Behavioral Comparison," in *Behavior and Evolution*, ed. Anne Roe and George Gaylord Simpson (New Haven: Yale University Press, 1958), pp. 183–205.

versely, the biological feature of prolonged human immaturity after birth may require the human cultural feature of prolonged parental care.

There is no reason to suppose that natural selection, either biological or cultural, will cease. However, we have no way of knowing in which direction the process will take us.

Summary

1. If we think of the history of the universe in terms of twelve months, the history of humans would take up only about one and one-half hours of this period. Although the universe is some 15 billion years old, modern humans have existed for only about 40,000 years.

2. Carl Linnaeus, the Comte de Buffon, Jean Baptiste Lamarck, and Erasmus Darwin produced studies that took issue with the biblical view of the creation of humans and other life forms. They paved the way for the ideas of Charles Darwin and others.

3. Darwin and Wallace theorized that species evolved gradually, over long periods of time, through natural selection. Those organisms which were best adapted to a particular environment lived longest and produced the most offspring.

4. In the process of natural selection, changes in species can be expected to occur as the environment changes or as some members of a species move into a new environment. Natural selection can also operate on the behavioral or social characteristics of populations.

5. Mendel's and subsequent research in genetics and our understanding of the structure and function of DNA, the "language of life," help us to understand the mechanisms by which traits may be passed from one generation to the next.

6. Natural selection depends upon variation within a population. The two sources of bio-

logical variation are genetic recombination and mutation.

7. Speciation—the development of a new species—occurs if one subgroup of a species finds itself in a radically different environment. In adapting to a separate environment, a subgroup may undergo enough genetic changes to prevent its interbreeding with the rest of the species. Once species differentiation occurs, the evolutionary process cannot be reversed.

8. Humans are a product of the interaction of biological and cultural evolution. Culturally, traits are transmitted by learning and imitation. Cultural evolution is more subject to conscious human control and change than is biological evolution. Still, both types of evolution are subject to natural selection.

Suggested Readings

Dobzhansky, T. *Mankind Evolving: The Evolution of the Human Species.* New Haven: Yale University Press, 1962.

Demonstrates that the mechanisms of evolution, primarily natural selection, are still active.

Eiseley, L. C. *Darwin's Century: Evolution and the Men Who Discovered It.* Garden City, N.Y.: Doubleday, 1958.

An historical treatment of evolutionary theory.

Irvine, W. *Apes, Angels and Victorians! Darwin, Huxley and Evolution.* New York: Meridian Books, 1971.

The personalities, domestic lives, and friends of Darwin and Huxley are revealed through descriptions of gossipy details, including letters. This information is closely related to the scientific pursuits of both great men, whose friendship forms the core of the book.

Mayr, E. *Animal Species and Evolution.* Cambridge: Harvard University Press, 1963.

A definitive work on systematics, taxonomy, and evolutionary theory.

Stebbins, G. L. *Processes of Organic Evolution.* 2d ed. Englewood Cliffs, N.J.: Prentice-Hall, 1971.

This book emphasizes the processes at work in evolution, rather than the specific sequences or outcomes of evolution. The last chapter deals with the processes of evolution in humans.

Young, L. B., ed. *Evolution of Man.* New York: Oxford University Press, 1970.

A comprehensive set of reprinted articles on evolutionary theory, its development, and the issues it raises about human control of evolution.

The Surviving Primates

3

In the days when newsreels were part of every movie showing, the comic antics of trained chimpanzees used to be reported as an antidote to news of human disasters. Since then, the news has grown no less sobering, but monkey and ape watching has come a long way. Serious observers have learned to go far beyond the circus to laboratory studies and observations of nonhuman primates in their natural settings. They attempt to understand how different primates have adapted anatomically and behaviorally to their environments. Such studies may help us understand the behavior and evolution of the human primate.

How can living primates such as chimpanzees tell us anything about the anatomical and behavioral adaptations of humans or of the primates that were our ancestors? After all, each surviving primate has its own history of evolutionary divergence from the earliest primate forms. And contrary to what some believe, the monkeys and apes that we see in the zoos today are not our ancestors—all living primates, including humans, evolved from early primates which are now extinct. Nonetheless, we can still learn much about humans and our own probable evolution from the comparative study of living primates.

In conjunction with fossil evidence, anatomical and behavioral comparisons of the living primates may help us reconstruct what the early primates were like. For example, those traits that are characteristic of most of the living primates (such as living, or sleeping, in trees) are likely to have been characteristic of our primate ancestors. Such an inference can be checked against the fossil record. Anatomical and behavioral differences may also point by analogy to the life-style of extinct primates. For example, if we know that modern primates which swing through the trees have a particular kind of shoulder bone structure, we can infer that similar fossil bones probably belonged to an animal that also swung through the trees. Differing adaptations of the living primates may also suggest why certain divergences occurred in primate evolution. Thus, if we know what

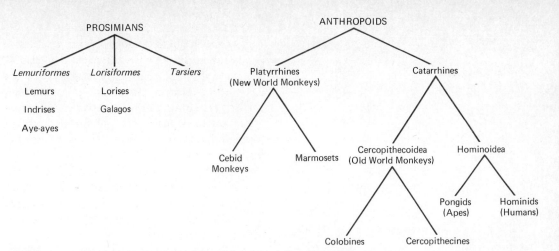

FIGURE 1 A Simplified Classification of the Surviving Primates

traits belong to humans, and humans alone, this knowledge may suggest why the line of primates which led to humans branched away from the line leading to chimpanzees and gorillas.

In this chapter, we shall look at both the similarities and differences among living primates. After an introduction to the animals in the order Primates, we shall examine their common features. Then we shall study the variety of adaptations exhibited by the different primates. We shall close with a look at the traits which make humans different from all other primates. The purpose of this chapter is to help us understand more about humans. Therefore, we shall emphasize the features of primate anatomy and behavior which have the greatest bearing on human evolution.

The Living Primates

The order Primates is divided into two suborders: the *prosimians* (literally, premonkeys) and the *anthropoids.* The prosimians include lemurs, lorises, and tarsiers. Some anthropologists also consider tree shrews to be prosimians; but most believe this classification is somewhat questionable and so we have omitted tree

shrews from our discussion.[1] The suborder anthropoids includes monkeys, apes (gorillas, chimpanzees, orangutans, and gibbons) and humans. Figure 1 shows a simplified classification of the surviving primates.

PROSIMIANS

The prosimians resemble other mammals more than the anthropoid primates. The prosimians depend much more on smell for information than do anthropoids. They have specialized tactile hairs (like whiskers). And, in contrast to the anthropoids, they have more mobile ears, longer snouts, and relatively fixed facial expressions. However, the prosimians also exhibit many traits shared by all the primates, including grasping hands, stereoscopic vision, and enlarged visual centers in the brain—traits that were apparently favored by their life in trees.

Lemuriformes Lemurs and their relatives, the indris and the aye-aye, are found only on two island areas off the southeastern coast of Africa: Madagascar and the Comoro Islands. This

[1]C. B. G. Campbell, "On the Phyletic Relationships of the Tree Shrews," *Mammal Review* 4, no. 4 (1974): 125–43; also J. R. Napier and P. H. Napier, *A Handbook of Living Primates* (New York: Academic Press, 1967), pp. vi–vii.

group of primates ranges in size from the rat-sized mouse lemur to the 4-foot-long indris, by far the most monkeylike of the group in behavior as well as appearance. All members of the lemur group produce single offspring, although twins and even triplets are common among many species. Most of the primates in this group are quadrupeds which walk on four feet (hands) in the trees. The indrises are an exception: they use their hindlimbs alone to push off from one vertical position to another, in a highly specialized mode of locomotion called *vertical clinging and leaping.* Lemurs are mostly vegetarians, eating fruit, leaves, bark, and flowers. Some lemurs are very social, living in groups ranging from four or five members to as many as sixty. Others, particularly the nocturnal lemurs, seem to be more solitary. Those living in groups also seem to be territorial—making warning and threatening gestures when other lemur troops appear.[2]

Lorisiformes Representatives of this group are found in both Southeast Asia and sub-Saharan Africa. All are nocturnal and live in trees, and some eat insects as well as vegetation. They usually give birth to single infants.

There are two major subfamilies, the lorises and the galagos (bushbabies), and they show wide behavioral differences. The bushbabies are quick, active animals, hopping between branches and tree trunks in the vertical clinging and leaping pattern. On the ground they often resort to a kangaroolike hop. Lorises are much slower, walking sedately along branches hand over hand in the quadrupedal fashion. Little is known of the social life of any of the lorisiformes. Because they are nocturnal, they are difficult to observe in their natural habitats.[3]

Tarsiers The tree-living tarsiers, found on the islands of Southeast Asia, are nocturnal insect-eaters. They are well equipped for night vision, possessing enormous eyes, extraordinary eye-

A tarsier's disk-like fingertips help it grasp tree trunks after long-distance leaps. Large eyes are adaptations for the tarsier's nocturnal way of life. (UPI photo.)

sight, and enlarged visual centers in the brain. The tarsier gets its name from elongated tarsal bones (the bones of the arch of the foot) which give it tremendous leverage for long jumps. Tarsiers are very skilled at vertical clinging and leaping. Little is known about their social patterns, except that they seem not to congregate in groups larger than pairs.[4]

The tarsier has a number of traits that have caused a few physical anthropologists to classify it as an anthropoid instead of a prosimian. Its brain is larger and more highly developed than other prosimian brains; its snout is shorter; its eyes are closer together and are protected by bony orbits. But the anthropoids have many traits which the tarsier does not share. For this reason, we consider the tarsier to be a prosimian, but one with some highly developed specializations.

ANTHROPOIDS

The anthropoid suborder includes monkeys and apes as well as humans. Most anthropoids share several traits in varying degree. They have rounded brain cases; shrunken, nonmobile outer ears; and relatively small, flat faces instead

[2] John Buettner-Janusch, *Physical Anthropology: A Perspective* (New York: John Wiley & Sons, 1973), pp. 124–46.
[3] Ibid., pp. 113–24.

[4] Ibid., p. 112.

New World monkeys are completely arboreal, and their tails are an asset in balancing; many Old World species spend at least some of their time on the ground.) New World and Old World monkeys have different dental formations: the New World species have three premolars, whereas other anthropoids have two.

There are two main families of New World monkeys: cebid monkeys and marmosets. The marmosets are quite small, have claws instead of fingernails, and give birth to multiple young. The various cebid monkeys differ widely in shape, size, activity patterns (one species is nocturnal), and habitat. While all the New World monkeys are completely arboreal, different species occupy different levels within the trees: in this way they differ in both diet and locomotor patterns. Most species of New World monkey are omnivorous, although a few eat only plant food. All New World monkeys live in flocks or troops. Spider monkeys live in large communities which break into small foraging groups. But even when they cannot see each other, groups keep in touch by calling out to one another in a range of vocalizations.[6]

Old World Monkeys The Old World monkeys, or cercopithecoids, are biologically closer to humans than to New World monkeys. They have catarrhine (sharp) noses and the same number of teeth as apes and humans. However, unlike most apes and humans, and unlike New World monkeys as well, the females in Old World monkey species commonly have sexual skin which becomes red and swollen during ovulation or *estrus*. Another unusual characteristic of Old World monkeys is the callouses, or *ischial callosities*, on their bottoms—an adaptation which enables them to sit in trees or on the ground in comfort for long periods of time. (Some monkeys in Uganda sit upright almost 90 percent of the time, even while sleeping![7])

A juvenile New World spider monkey uses an arm, legs, and a prehensile tail to secure his grip completely. (Robert Hermes, National Audubon Society Collection/Photo Researchers.)

of muzzles. They have highly efficient reproductive systems, with a placenta which is more fully formed than in any prosimian except the tarsier.[5] They have highly dextrous hands. We will discuss three major groups of anthropoids: New World monkeys; Old World monkeys; and apes and humans.

New World Monkeys The New World monkeys are called *platyrrhines* (flat-nosed) to distinguish them from the *catarrhines* (sharp-nosed)—the group which includes Old World monkeys, apes, and humans. Besides the shape of the nose and nostrils, a number of other anatomical features distinguish New World from Old World monkeys. Some New World monkeys have a prehensile or grasping tail; no Old World monkeys do. All New World monkeys have tails; not all Old World monkeys do. (This difference is the result of a difference in life-style. The

[5]Napier and Napier, *A Handbook of Living Primates*, pp. 32–33.

[6]Personal communication of Klein in David Pilbeam, *The Ascent of Man* (New York: Macmillan, 1972), pp. 19–20; also Buettner-Janusch, *Physical Anthropology*, p. 159.

[7]Observation by M. Rose cited in Alison Jolly, *The Evolution of Primate Behavior* (New York: Macmillan, 1972), pp. 34–36.

The Old World monkeys are strikingly versatile as compared to their American cousins, and they are able to adapt to a wide variety of different habitats. Old World monkeys live both in trees and on the ground. Some species, like the gelada baboon, are completely terrestrial. Macaque monkeys are so adaptable that they are found both in tropical jungles and on snow-covered mountains, and they range from Africa to the Rock of Gibraltar and even to Japan. There are only two major subfamilies of Old World monkeys and they are distinguished on the basis of habitat and diet.

Colobine Monkeys This group includes Asian langurs, the African colobus monkeys, and several other species. These monkeys live mostly in trees and their diet consists principally of leaves. Their digestive tracts are equipped to obtain maximum nutrition from a high-cellulose diet—they have pouched stomachs, which provide a large surface area for breaking down food, and very large intestinal tracts. These monkeys are quadrupeds, leaping and walking on four feet, but some occasionally brachiate.[8]

All colobine monkeys live in social groupings, although we know few details about the kinds of relationships within these groups. Many observations have been made of the langurs of northern India. These monkeys form many different types of social groups, from all-male clubs to one-male "harems" to mixed-sex groups. The kind of group they live in seems to depend upon their environment: one-male groups and stray males are commonest in harsh or crowded conditions.[9] We shall learn more about the relationship of primate group behavior to environment later in this chapter.

Cercopithecine Monkeys Monkeys in this subfamily are more terrestrial than arboreal, but their habitats vary widely. Guenons live completely in the trees; macaques are comfortable

both on the ground and above it; and some baboons are completely terrestrial. A better way to define this group is by diet. They are omnivorous, eating insects and some small animals as well as fruits and leaves. Many of these monkeys, particularly the terrestrial ones, are characterized by a great deal of sexual dimorphism. The males are larger, have longer canines, and are more aggressive than the females. Although the monkeys in this group are quadrupeds, many, like the patas monkey which lives on open ground, run on their two hindlimbs for short distances.

Many studies have been made of the social behavior of different kinds of monkey troops, particularly terrestrial monkeys. Much of the earlier research on terrestrial monkeys focused on relationships between males of the group. Perhaps for this reason, investigators thought of male dominance hierarchies as a major component of social behavior. As we shall see later, the importance of male dominance hierarchies may depend largely upon habitat differences. More recent studies, which have focused on females, indicate that the mother-child bond may be an important basis of social organization among some Old World monkeys. In some cases, the mother tie seems to form the basis for social grouping over many generations.[10]

The Hominoidea: Apes and Humans This group includes two separate families: the apes, including gibbons, orangutans, gorillas, and chimpanzees; and humans. Several characteristics distinguish them from the other primates. Their brains are relatively large, especially the areas of the cerebral cortex which are associated with the ability to integrate data. The hominoids have several skeletal and muscular traits which point toward their common ancestry. All have fairly long arms, short trunks, and no tails. Their blood proteins show many similarities, too. This blood likeness is especially noticeable among chimpanzees, gorillas, and

[8] To brachiate is to move forward by swinging arm over arm along a horizontal support.
[9] S. I. Rosen, *Introduction to the Primates* (Englewood Cliffs, N.J.: Prentice-Hall, 1974), pp. 88–92.

[10] Jane B. Lancaster, *Primate Behavior and the Emergence of Human Culture* (New York: Holt, Rinehart and Winston, 1975), pp. 12–23.

"Maybe *you're* descended from a lemur, but *I'm* not descended from any lemur." (Drawing by W. Miller; © 1972 The New Yorker Magazine, Inc.)

humans. For this reason we think that chimpanzees and gorillas are evolutionarily closer to humans than are the gibbons, who probably branched off at some earlier point.

Gibbons Found in the jungles of Southeast Asia, the agile gibbons and their close relatives, the siamangs, stand about 3 feet tall and weigh under 25 pounds. They are mostly fruit-eaters, although they also eat small birds and insects. They are spectacular brachiators, with long arms and fingers which let them swing hand over hand through the trees. A gibbon can move more than 30 feet in a single forward swing.

C. R. Carpenter's pioneering studies of gibbons have told us a great deal about the animals' social behavior.[11] Gibbons live in small

family groups consisting of an adult pair and one or two immature offspring. The pair bonding of gibbons is quite unusual among primates. When the young reach adulthood, they are driven from home by the adults. There is little sexual dimorphism in gibbons, nor is there any clear pattern of dominance of either sex. In contrast to the other apes, but like many arboreal primates, gibbons are highly territorial. Males frequently fight over territorial boundaries.

Orangutans Unlike gibbons, orangutans are clearly recognizable as male or female. Found only on the islands of Borneo and Sumatra, the males are 4 feet tall and the females usually half that size. Male orangutans have large vocal sacs connected to their larynxes which can be blown up to an enormous size. Both sexes have very expressive faces; their agile lips twist many

[11]C. R. Carpenter, "A Field Study in Siam of the Behavior and Social Relations of the Gibbon (*Hylobates lar*)," *Comparative Psychology Monographs* 16, no. 5 (1940): 1–212.

ways in what is probably a form of communication. Because of human encroachment on the wilderness, the orangutans are rapidly becoming extinct. Therefore, they are hard to find in their natural habitat, and much of their behavior remains a mystery. We do know that there is at least a three-year spacing between births, which is one reason for their small population. The males are solitary, forming no long-term family ties and staying close to the females only around mating time.

Gorillas Much of what we know about the largest of the apes, the gorilla, has been summed up in two books by George Schaller, *The Mountain Gorilla* and *The Year of the Gorilla*,[12] written from observations he made in the dense tropical forests of western Uganda and eastern Zaire. Gorillas are large animals. In their natural habitat, the adult male weighs up to 450 pounds and the female up to 250 pounds. (Captive gorillas in zoos are generally fatter because of their sedentary life.) They travel mostly on the ground on all fours, in a form of locomotion known as *knuckle walking.* To support the weight of their heavy, well-developed chests, gorillas walk on the thickly padded knuckles of their forefingers. They sleep on the ground in nests they prepare with great care each time they bed down. Gorillas' arms and legs are well suited for brachiation, and the animals are excellent brachiators when young. But their size as adults makes this form of locomotion precarious at best. Gorillas vary in their social and individual behavior, so it is difficult to generalize about their ways. They seem to lead quiet, peaceful lives, mostly within loose, mixed-sex groups of varying size. They use their enormous strength mainly to tear apart vegetation which they eat.

Chimpanzees Because they are more sociable and are easier to find and "adopt," chimpanzees have been studied far more than gorillas. In their natural state, chimpanzees behave in a way

that is radically different from their behavior in captivity; but even in the wild they show similarities to humans. Recent studies have noted that they exhibit many gestures and postures similar to ours in behavioral situations common to both species. A good part of our information about chimpanzees in the wild comes from recent studies made by Jane van Lawick-Goodall at Gombe National Park in Tanzania.[13]

Chimpanzees also show many similarities to their close relatives, the gorillas. They are both arboreal and terrestrial. Like gorillas, they are good brachiators, especially when they are young, and they spend many hours in the trees. But they move best on the ground, and when they want to cover long distances they come down from the trees and move around by knuckle walking. Occasionally, they stand and walk upright, usually when they are traveling through tall grass or are trying to see long distances. Like gorillas, chimpanzees sleep in nests which they carefully prepare anew—complete with a bunch of leaves as a pillow—each time they bed down.

Chimpanzees are somewhat sexually dimorphic. A large male may stand 5 feet tall and weigh 100 pounds. In their food habits, chimpanzees are omnivores. For quite some time, it was thought that they ate only plant food. However, studies at Gombe Park have shown that not only do they eat insects and small lizards, but they actively hunt and kill larger animals.[14] They have been observed hunting and eating a range of animals that includes monkeys, young baboons, and bushbucks in addition to smaller prey like lizards and birds. Of course, this diet reflects the prey available at the Gombe reservation where the chimpanzees live and so it may not be the most accurate representation of their diet. Prey is

[12] George Schaller, *The Mountain Gorilla: Ecology and Behavior* (Chicago: University of Chicago Press, 1963); and *The Year of the Gorilla* (Chicago: University of Chicago Press, 1964).

[13] Jane Goodall, "My Life among Wild Chimpanzees," *National Geographic*, August 1963, pp. 272–308; idem, *In the Shadow of Man* (Boston: Houghton Mifflin, 1971).

[14] Chimpanzees are not the only primates to eat some meat, for a number of both Old and New World monkeys eat small animals. Only baboons, though, are predators like the chimpanzees. See Geza Teleki, "The Omnivorous Chimpanzee," *Scientific American*, January 1973, pp. 32–42.

caught by the males, which hunt either alone or in small groups. It is then shared with as many as fifteen other chimpanzees in friendly social gatherings which may last up to nine hours.[15]

The social activities of chimpanzees go far beyond sharing meat. They usually live in large communities which split into smaller, flexible groups. There are long-term ties, usually between mothers and children. Hugging, kissing, and patting are all common gestures among friends. Studies have been made of chimpanzees' ability to communicate by human-taught sign language, and we shall look at these findings about chimpanzees later in this chapter.

Hominids The second grouping of the hominoids—the *hominids*—consists of humans and their direct ancestors. Humans are anthropoids and they share the traits possessed by other families in this group. Of course, humans also have many distinctive characteristics which set them apart from other anthropoids and other hominoids. These traits will be discussed later in this chapter and also throughout much of the rest of this book.

General Primate Traits

We have briefly surveyed the various primates which live in the world today, focusing our attention on the ways they differ from one another. But all of these animals are members of the order Primates. Therefore, they share a complex of common traits which make them primates. It is to these traits that we now turn.

PRIMATES AS MAMMALS

All primates belong to the class Mammalia, and they share all the common features of mammals. Except for humans, their bodies are covered with hair or fur which provides insulation. And even humans have some hair in various places, though perhaps not for insulation!

[15]Ibid., pp. 35–41.

Mammals are warm-blooded or *homiothermic:* their body temperature is maintained at a constant level.

Mammals give birth to live young which have developed to a considerable size within the mother and which are nourished by suckling from the mother's mammary glands. The young have a relatively long period of dependency on adults after birth. This period is also a time of learning, for a great deal of adult mammal behavior is learned rather than instinctive. Play is a learning technique which is common to mammal young, and it is especially important to primates, as we shall see later in this chapter.

PHYSICAL FEATURES OF PRIMATES

Primates also share many traits which set them apart from other mammals.[16] None of these traits alone is unique to primates. Animals from other orders can be found which share one or more of the characteristics listed below. But the complex of all these physical traits *is* unique to primates.

Many skeletal features in the primates reflect an arboreal or tree-living existence. All primate hindlimbs are structured principally to provide support, although they are flexible enough to allow some primates—orangutans, for instance—to suspend themselves from their hindlimbs. The forelimbs are especially flexible, built to withstand both pushing and pulling forces. Each of the hindlimbs and forelimbs has one bone in the upper portion and two bones in the lower portion (with the exception of the tarsier). This feature is little changed since our earliest primate ancestors. It has remained in modern primates (although many other mammals have lost it) because the double bones give primates great mobility for rotating their arms and legs. Another characteristic structure of primates is the clavicle, or collarbone. The clav-

[16]Our discussion of general primate traits is largely based on J. R. Napier and P. H. Napier, *A Handbook of Living Primates* (New York: Academic Press, 1967), and S. I. Rosen, *Introduction to the Primates* (Englewood Cliffs, N.J.: Prentice-Hall, 1974).

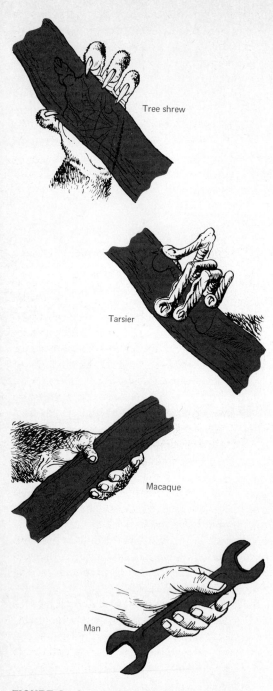

Tree shrew

Tarsier

Macaque

Man

FIGURE 2 Comparison of Primate Grasps
The greater precision of the grip of the macaque (an Old World monkey) and man is due to the presence of nails instead of claws and of a well-developed opposable thumb.

icle also gives primates great freedom of movement, allowing them to move the shoulders both up and down and back and forth. Although humans obviously do not use the flexibility for arboreal activity, these rotational abilities are used by humans for other activities. Without a clavicle we could not throw a spear or a ball; no fine tools could be made, no doorknobs could be turned, if we were without rotatable forearms.

Primate teeth reflect the omnivorous diet which generally characterizes the group. The chewing teeth (molars and premolars) are very unspecialized, particularly in comparison to those of other groups of animals, such as the grazers. The front teeth—incisors and canines—are often quite specialized, principally in the lower primates. For example, in many prosimians the slender, tightly packed lower incisors and canines form a "dental comb" which the animals use for grooming and perhaps feeding.

Primate hands are extremely flexible. All primates have *prehensile* hands which can be wrapped around an object, allowing them to grasp with one hand. Primates have five digits on both hands and feet (in some cases, one digit may be reduced to a stub) and their nails, with few exceptions, are broad and flat, not clawlike. This structure allows them to grip objects; so do the hairless, sensitive pads on fingers, toes, heels, and palms. Many primates have opposable thumbs—a feature which allows an even more precise and powerful grip.

Also extremely important to arboreal life is vision. Compared to other mammals, primates have a relatively larger portion of the brain devoted to vision rather than smell. Primates are characterized by stereoscopic or depth vision. Their eyes are directed forward, rather than sideways as in other animals—a trait which allows them to focus on an object with both eyes at once. Most primates also have color vision. By and large, these tendencies are more developed in anthropoids than in prosimians.

Finally, the primate reproductive system sets this order of animals apart from other

This female orangutan is a member of the primate sub-order of anthropoid apes, which contains our closest living relatives. Note the flattened nose and eyes in the front of the head, adaptations that reflect the relative importance of vision over smell among the primates. (Courtesy of David Agee Horr/Anthro-Photo.)

could a tree-living mother keep safe at one time? The young primates, except for humans, are relatively well developed at birth (prosimians, monkeys, and apes generally can cling to their mothers from birth), but they all (including humans) have a long maturation period. The rhesus monkey, for example, is not sexually mature until three years of age or the chimpanzee until about age nine. The period of dependency on adults is a time when many kinds of behavior patterns are learned, passed on from old to young.

PRIMATES AS SOCIAL ANIMALS

For the most part, primates are social animals. And just as physical traits like grasping hands or stereoscopic vision have developed as adaptations to the environment, so have many patterns of primate social behavior. For most primates, group life is crucial to survival, and so primates have evolved to be social creatures.

We can see how this is so by looking at two main areas of primate existence: food getting and self-defense. Recent studies of both birds and mammals by researchers J. H. Crook and J. F. Eisenberg suggest that the nature of most primates' food supply has influenced the extent to which they live and feed in groups.[18] For instance, animals which must use individual skills to catch food are likely to live and feed alone. This is true of most birds of prey, insectivores, and many small omnivores. The opposite seems to hold true when food supplies are abundant and distributed over large areas, like the grazing areas in open grassland or the abundant fruit supplies in forest regions. Among animals which eat the latter kinds of food, the common feeding pattern is cooperation, or noncompetitive eating.[19] The abundant-food, noncompetitive feeding pattern is typical of most primates. The result is that pri-

mammals. Primate males have a pendulous penis which is not attached to the abdomen by skin (a trait which is shared by a few other animals, including bats and bears). In most cases, primates do not have a "mating season." The females are fertile off and on throughout the year and most ovulate about once every four weeks. Most primate females have two mammary glands, or breasts, on the chest (a few prosimians have multiple nipples). The uterus is usually constructed to hold a single fetus, not a litter as with most other animals. This reproductive system can be seen as emphasizing quality over quantity—an adaptation which is probably related to the selective pressures of life in the trees.[17] After all, how many babies

[17]R. D. Martin, "Strategies of Reproduction," *Natural History,* November 1975, p. 50.

[18]Referred to in Jolly, *The Evolution of Primate Behavior,* pp. 85–90.

[19]This does not mean *sharing* food, a rare practice among primates. With the exception of the occasional meat-eating "dinner parties" of chimpanzees, primate groups other than human groups almost never socially share food.

FIGURE 3

The baboon troop organizes for defense when moving through the open savanna. Dominant males protect the mothers and infants in the center, while other adult males guard front and rear. (Courtesy of Irven DeVore/Anthro-Photo.)

mates often move in groups and feed side by side.

There is another reason for primates to live in groups. Groups are important for self-defense. Primates, especially those which live on open ground, are quite vulnerable when alone. They have no means of natural camouflage, nor can many of them flee to inaccessible places. But there is safety in numbers. Living in a group means that there are more animals on the lookout to spot predators. If an enemy is seen, the group can protect its individual members. Primates often cooperate to distract the enemy, allowing individual members to escape. The males of many species (especially terrestrial ones, like baboons) are larger and stronger than the females, and they have long, fierce-looking canines which they bare at potential predators. These may well be adaptations for protecting the group.

The needs of some primates for both food getting and self-defense seem to favor group life. However, not all primates live in groups, and the reason for this may be linked to the factors we have just discussed. Some lemurs, for instance, are nocturnal, and the darkness gives them natural protection from predators. Most of these lemurs spend their waking hours in solitude, not in a group. This is but one example of the way that specific ecological needs may influence species behavior and cause one primate to look, live, and act differently from other primates.

Dependency and Social Learning Experiments and observation show that youth is a time for learning and the way most primates learn reflects their highly social nature. The young learn from all the members of the group, not just from their mothers. According to Hans Kummer, primates live in "a type of society which through constant association of young and old and through a long life duration, exploits their large brains to produce adults of great experience."[20]

Just as human babies, primate infants are the center of attention. In many primate societies, childrearing is a group activity, not just the mother's job. Among baboons, the birth and subsequent rearing of a new baby is a central event which absorbs the attention of all the members of the troop. In other primate groups,

[20]Hans Kummer, *Primate Societies, Group Techniques of Ecological Adaptation* (Chicago: Aldine-Atherton, 1971), p. 38.

too, it is often not just the mother but the father or other female members of the group which devote special attention to raising the young. Infant monkeys and apes are dependent upon adults for a long period of time. Prolonged dependency offers an evolutionary advantage in that it allows infants more time to observe, note, and learn the complex behaviors essential to survival, while enjoying the care and protection of a mature teacher. Young primates learn manipulative and motor skills as well as social patterns. During infancy, chimpanzees learn how to move through the trees and on the ground, and they awkwardly attempt the intricacies of nest preparation, taking their first shaky steps toward mastering their physical environment. The ability to manipulate objects as tools is probably innate to chimpanzees, but the actual tool-using patterns are learned, often from the mother. Goodall cites an occasion when a female with diarrhea picked up a handful of leaves to wipe her bottom. Her two-year-old infant watched closely, and then twice picked up leaves to wipe its own clean behind.

Primate mother and child are bound together by the slow maturation of the young, but for the first few months they are literally inseparable. The infant is either nursing or being groomed, or it is clinging to the hair of its mother's belly. The offspring's instinct and ability to cling to the mother, coupled with the mother's knowledge of infant care (not instinctive, but learned from watching other mothers), ensure the closeness of the relationship. Under normal conditions, the mother offers psychological security as well as physical protection to the infant.

A number of experiments dealing with the processes occurring during the dependency period have shed light on all primate behavior, including that of humans. Dr. Harry Harlow of the University of Wisconsin has experimented with rhesus monkeys to determine the effect of maternal neglect and isolation on offspring.[21] He found that, as a result of either inadequate

Patty Cake, a baby gorilla, is cuddled by her foster mother after her arm was broken. Her foster mother cared for her for several months to encourage Patty Cake's normal social development. (Neal Boenzi, *The New York Times.*)

mothering or isolation from other infants, monkeys may suffer from an inability to lead normal social lives. They develop aberrant sexual activities and may even become juvenile delinquents. Harlow mated the socially deprived female monkeys with well-adjusted males. When these females gave birth, their behavior was not at all motherly, and they often rejected their babies entirely. Their abnormal behavior was offered as proof that mothering is more than instinctive. These experiments underline the importance of maternal care and attention for monkeys and, as a corollary, for humans. From this, we might conclude that indulging, or caring for, an infant is a socializing process that has developed as an adaptation among animals whose survival depends on a considerable amount of learned behavior.

Primates at Play Harlow's investigations have provided other information about social learning in young primates. The experiments which

[21]H. F. Harlow et al., "Maternal Behavior of Rhesus Monkeys Deprived of Mothering and Peer Association in Infancy," *Proceedings of the American Philosophical Society* 110 (1966): 58–66.

showed the importance of maternal care to baby rhesus monkeys also revealed that play is another crucial ingredient during the dependency period. Just as monkeys which were raised without mothers showed abnormal behavior as adults, so did monkeys raised with mothers but no peers to play with. In fact, when some of the monkeys which were raised without mothers were exposed to peers for regular playtimes, many of them behaved more normally. Of course, these experiments do not mean that normal behavior is always directly linked to either mother-love or play, for we cannot measure the effects of laboratory conditions on young monkeys. But Harlow's findings do indicate that both of these factors are important during the dependency period.

Scientists have just begun to study play as an important learning ground in two areas.[22] Play provides practice for physical skills which are necessary or useful in adulthood. For example, young monkeys racing through the trees at top speed are gaining coordination which may save their lives if they are chased by predators later on. Play is also a way of learning social skills and social relationships. The experience gained in play seems very important in developing the ability to interact and communicate with other members of the group. Also, some dominance relationships seem to be partly established through the rough-and-tumble kind of games older juveniles play, where winning depends upon such factors as size, strength, and agility. These qualities, or the lack of them, may influence the individual's status throughout his or her adult life. (Other factors also help to determine an individual's status. For instance, the mother's status has been shown to be very important.)[23] Sexual behavior is also practiced in play, although we cannot say that it is learned. Young baboons, langurs, and rhesus monkeys have been observed playing at mounting and presenting, although this form of play is tied as much to dominance relationships as it is to sex at this age.[24]

Variable Primate Adaptations

Thus far we have discussed common primate traits, most of which probably resulted from the primates' evolutionary adaptation to arboreal life. But there also are differences among the various primates. These differences may have developed because the various primates live in, and are adapted to, somewhat different environments.

ECOLOGY

Both diet and habitat seem to influence the kinds of social groups primates form.[25] We saw earlier that gibbons and many leaf-eating monkeys are highly territorial. They live in small groups which forage within a small range of forest, and they have highly ritualized spacing calls to fix their positions within their territory. While leaf-eating monkeys generally are territorial and form small groups, the opposite is true for primates which spend a great deal of time on the ground. These terrestrial monkeys and apes are usually omnivores. They tend to live in large groups, a pattern probably related to self-defense. They usually are not territorial; they range over a large area and the groups rarely battle with each other. As we mentioned in our discussion of chimpanzees, these primates often have a social life which is similar to that of humans, especially humans who live in small foraging bands. Within a large community of about forty to eighty animals, individual members are very flexible in forming and reforming small groups and in going off on their own. Such similarities to human behavior have

[22] Phyllis Jay Dohlinow and Naomi Bishop, "The Development of Motor Skills and Social Relationships among Primates through Play," in *Primate Patterns*, ed. P. Dohlinow (New York: Holt, Rinehart and Winston, 1972), pp. 321–25.

[23] D. S. Sade, "Some Aspects of Parent-offspring and Sibling Relationships in a Group of Rhesus Monkeys, with a Discussion of Grooming," *American Journal of Physical Anthropology* 23 (1965): 1–17.

[24] Dohlinow and Bishop, "The Development of Motor Skills and Social Relationships." pp. 323–24.

[25] Jolly, *The Evolution of Primate Behavior*, pp. 113–32.

led many anthropologists to think that we can discover much about the social life of our hominid ancestors by observing semi- or fully terrestrial primates like chimpanzees and the gelada baboons.

STATUS AND HIERARCHY

Just as primates have wide variations in the sizes of their social groups, they also show differences in the ways the groups are organized. The social systems of primates vary from groupings of individuals with more or less equal status to groupings with strict dominance hierarchies. In these hierarchies, each individual has a rank, relative to the other group members, which governs access to such things as food and sex. Although it used to be thought that dominance hierarchies were characteristic of particular kinds of primates, like baboons, recent field studies have questioned just how "natural" such hierarchies are. Earlier studies of baboons and rhesus monkeys living in open country gave the impression that strict dominance hierarchies were the rule in both these primate groups. These hierarchies, when they existed, seemed to reduce aggression somewhat by regulating which member ate first, or which male mated first with a female. Although dominance hierarchies changed over time, at any one time the hierarchy was topped by an "alpha male." After him, all other males were ranked differentially. A separate, lower hierarchy ranked females in similar fashion. Each member knew his or her rank in relation to every other member.

In recent years, the idea that hierarchies are a totally natural pattern for baboons has been challenged.[26] It has been suggested that dominance hierarchies occur in baboons living in unnatural or artificial territories like game preserves or parks. Such environments may be more stressful and competitive, leading to more aggressive behavior and thus perhaps favoring the emergence of dominance hierarchies. When Thelma Rowell observed baboons living in Ugandan forests, she found they acted very differently. They lived in flexible, peaceful groups with almost no evidence of dominance behavior. Therefore, dominance hierarchies may be largely a result of artificial, stressful environments.

AGGRESSION

Just as with dominance behavior, there is a wide variation in the amount of aggressive behavior shown by different primates. Some, like baboons, have been observed to be quite aggressive within the troop: many troop members carry scars as reminders of past battles within the group. At the other extreme, most arboreal monkeys, and some terrestrial monkeys like the patas monkeys, are very peaceful, with almost no battles within the group.

There have been some attempts to explain the variation in degree of in-group aggressive behavior among different primates. One suggestion is that more aggressive behavior may be exhibited in open country. Macaques and baboons are perhaps the best adapted to open country life and they show the most aggressive behavior. But Alison Jolly points out that this conclusion is by no means certain, since few species have been studied extensively.[27] And other animals in open country environments exhibit little or no aggression; for example, a terrestrial group of patas monkeys had no visible scars or injuries.[28]

Perhaps a more important factor determining degree of aggressive behavior is the amount of stress in the environment. Greater aggression may characterize those troops that live in unnatural game park environments. As previously noted, forest baboons, as compared to game park baboons, exhibited little aggressive behavior in the wild. But when Rowell removed some

---

[26] Thelma E. Rowell, "Forest-living Baboons in Uganda," *Journal of Zoology* 149 (1966): 344–64.

[27] Jolly, *The Evolution of Primate Behavior*, p. 178.

[28] K. R. L. Hall, "Aggression in Monkey and Ape Societies," in *Primates*, ed. P. C. Day (New York: Holt, Rinehart and Winston, 1968), pp. 149–62.

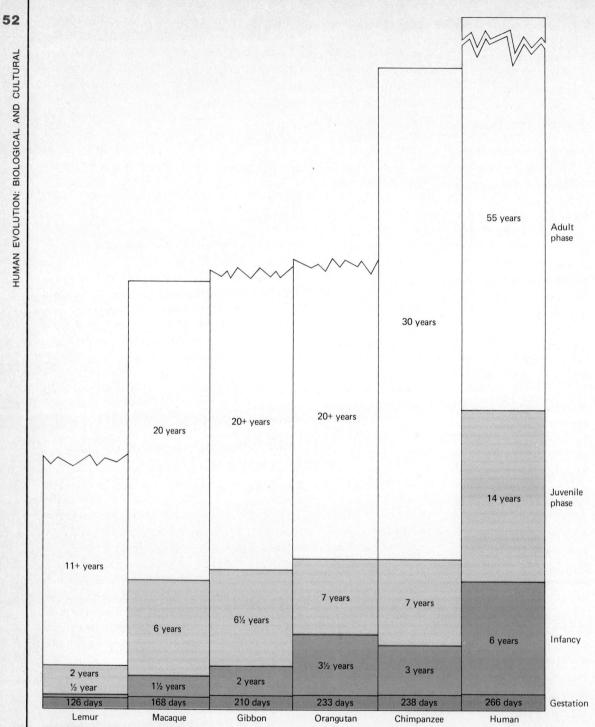

FIGURE 4 Primate Age Spans

(Adapted and reprinted with permission of Macmillan Publishing Co., Inc. from *The Evolution of Primate Behavior* by Alison Jolly. Copyright © 1972 by Alison Jolly.)

forest baboons to cages where food was given in "competition-inducing clumps," the frequency of aggression increased.[29] That more crowded or extremely limited environments may affect the expression of aggression is illustrated by a comparison between "rural" and "town-living" rhesus monkeys: Singh found the urban monkeys to be much more aggressive than their rural counterparts.[30]

Aggressive behavior between groups (which is usually referred to as territorial behavior) perhaps paradoxically is not predicted by a high frequency of in-group aggression. Arboreal monkeys and apes, which have the least in-group aggression, have the most fiercely defended territories. On the other hand, open country monkeys, some of which have high in-group aggression, generally manage to avoid intertroop confrontations. Perhaps this is because open country allows one troop to see another at a distance and therefore avoid it. This avoidance behavior is illustrated by Southwick's study of rhesus monkeys which inhabit temples in India. Usually, different groups of the monkeys coexist in peace. But once in a while, two groups will surprise each other coming around the corner of a temple. Only then, when there is no possible visual avoidance of conflict, do intergroup battles occur.[31]

DEVELOPMENT

As Figure 4 shows, there is a substantial difference between the life expectancies of lemurs and humans, but even the prosimians live relatively long lives. The life span increases progressively from the prosimians on up to humans. So do the length of pregnancy, the period of dependency when infants need adult care, and the juvenile phase before sexual maturity.

Although all newborn primates are relatively helpless, there is a wide variation in their capabilities and the kinds of care they receive from adults. A few prosimians, such as bush-

[29] Rowell, "Forest-living Baboons in Uganda," pp. 344–64.
[30] Referred to in Jolly, *The Evolution of Primate Behavior*, p. 182.
[31] Ibid., pp. 102–32.

babies, build nests for their helpless young. Many monkeys and prosimian babies are born with the ability to grasp, and they cling to their mothers' (sometimes their fathers') fur as the mothers make their rounds. A chimpanzee or gorilla baby cannot hold onto its mother, and she does not leave the infant in a nest. She carries her child in one arm for the first few months. The mother usually has the primary role in raising an infant but, especially in one-male groups, the father sometimes cares for the young.

Distinctive Human Traits

We have just looked at some of the differences among primates, and we have seen that within the order there are many social, physical, and behavioral patterns. We shall now turn to some of the features that distinguish us—humans—from the other primates. Although we like to think of ourselves as unique, many of the traits we shall discuss here are at the extreme of the continuum that can be traced from the prosimians through the apes.

PHYSICAL TRAITS

Of all the primates, only humans consistently walk erect on two feet. Gibbons, chimpanzees, and gorillas may stand or walk on two feet some of the time, but only for very short periods. All other primates require thick, heavy musculature to hold their heads erect; this structure is missing in humans, for our heads are better balanced on top of our spinal columns. A dish-shaped pelvis, peculiar to humans; straight lower limbs; arched, nonprehensile feet—all are related to human bipedalism. Because we humans are fully bipedal, we can carry objects without impairing our locomotor efficiency. (In a later chapter we shall consider the effects bipedalism may have had on such diverse traits as toolmaking, prolonged infant dependency, and the division of labor by sex.) Although many primates have opposable thumbs which enable

"I'm walking *upright!* By God, this calls for a drink or something!" (Ross, ROTHCO, Courtesy of *Saturday Review.*)

them to grasp and examine objects, the greater length and flexibility of the human thumb allows us to handle objects with more firmness and precision.

The human brain is very large and complex, particularly the cerebral cortex area. The brain of the average adult human measures about 1,370 cubic centimeters as compared to 525 cubic centimeters for the gorilla, the primate with the next largest brain. The frontal areas of the human brain are also large as compared to those of other primates, so that humans have more prominent foreheads than monkeys or gorillas. Human teeth reflect our completely omnivorous diet and they are not very specialized. Many other primates have long lower canines which are accommodated by a space in the upper jaw; in humans, the canines both look and act very much like incisors, and there are no spaces between the teeth. The human jaw is shaped like a parabolic arch, rather than a U-shape as in the apes, and it is composed of relatively thin bones and light muscles. Humans have chins; other primates do not.

There are a few other distinctively human physical traits which are as yet poorly understood. One is our relative hairlessness. A second is the sexual receptiveness of human females, who are sexually responsive more or less continuously, unlike most other primate females which are receptive only in their estrus periods. The disappearance of estrus in human evolution has probably contributed to the growth of more emotional, individual sexual relationships, a tendency which has likely been furthered by the development of face-to-face intercourse, another distinctively human trait.

BEHAVIORAL ABILITIES

In comparison with other primates, a much greater proportion of human behavior is learned and culturally patterned. As with many physical traits, we can trace a continuum in the learning abilities of all primates. The great apes, including orangutans, gorillas, and chimpanzees, are probably about equal in learning ability.[32] Old

[32] Duane M. Rumbaugh, "Learning Skills of Anthropoids," in *Primate Behavior*, ed. L. A. Rosenblum (New York: Academic Press, 1970), vol. 1, pp. 52–58.

and New World monkeys do much less well in learning tests and, surprisingly, gibbons perform more poorly than most monkeys.

Toolmaking The same kind of continuum is evident in inventiveness and toolmaking. There is no evidence that any nonhuman primates except great apes use tools, although several species of monkeys use "weapons," dropping branches, stones, or fruit onto predators below them on the ground. Chimpanzees both fashion and use tools in the wild. They strip leaves from sticks and then use the sticks to "fish" termites from their mound-shaped nests. They use leaves to mop up termites, to sponge up water, or to wipe themselves clean. In captivity, chimpanzees have been observed to be very inventive toolmakers. One mother chimpanzee was seen examining and cleaning her son's teeth, using tools she had fashioned from twigs to aid her. She even extracted a baby tooth he was about to lose.[33]

Humans have usually been considered the only toolmaking animal, but observations like these call for modification of the definition of toolmaking. If we define toolmaking as modifying a natural object to make it suitable for a specific purpose, then at least some of the great apes are toolmakers. As far as we know, though, humans are still unique in their ability to use one tool to make another. In the words of van Lawick-Goodall, "The point at which tool-using and tool-making, as such, acquire evolutionary significance is surely when an animal can adapt its ability to manipulate objects to a wide variety of purposes, and when it can use an object spontaneously to solve a brand-new problem that without the use of a tool would prove insoluble."[34]

Language Only humans have spoken, symbolic language. But, as with toolmaking abilities, the line between human language and the communications of other primates is not as sharp as we once thought. In the wild, prosimians, monkeys, and apes use sounds to communicate territorial information. Chimpanzees are especially communicative, using gestures and many vocalizations in the wild. Researchers have used this "natural talent" to teach chimpanzees symbolic language in experimental settings.

Beatrice and R. Allen Gardner raised a female chimpanzee named Washoe and trained her to communicate with startling effectiveness by means of some 175 of the American Sign Language hand gestures.[35] After a year of training, she was able to associate gestures with specific activities. For example, if thirsty, Washoe would make the signal for "give me" followed by the one for "drink." As she learned, the instructions grew more detailed. If all she wanted was water, she would merely signal for "drink." But if she craved soda pop, as she did more and more, she prefaced the drink signal with the sweet signal—a quick touching of the tongue with her fingers. More recently, the Gardners have been very successful in training a younger chimpanzee named Lucy to talk by the same method.

Other chimpanzees have had similar success in learning symbolic language. One named Sarah has been taught to read and write with plastic symbols; her written vocabulary is 130 "words."[36] She can perform complex tasks like simultaneously putting an apple in a pail and a banana in a dish on written command—a feat which requires an understanding of sentence structure as well as words. A 2½-year-old chimpanzee named Lana became so proficient in a symbolic language called "Yerkish" that she scored 95 on some tests in comprehension and sentence completion that she was given after 6 months of training.[37]

Other Human Traits Although many, if not most, primates are omnivores, eating insects

[33]"The First Dentist," *Newsweek*, March 5, 1973, p. 73.
[34]Goodall, *In the Shadow of Man*, p. 240.

[35]R. Allen Gardner and Beatrice T. Gardner, "Teaching Sign Language to a Chimpanzee," *Science*, August 1969, pp. 664–72.
[36]Ann James Premack and David Premack, "Teaching Language to an Ape," *Scientific American*, October 1972, pp. 92–99.
[37]Duane M. Rumbaugh, Timothy V. Gill, and E. C. von Glaserfeld, "Reading and Sentence Completion by a Chimpanzee (Pan)," *Science*, November 1973, pp. 731–33.

and small reptiles in addition to plants, with some even hunting small mammals, humans eat proportionately more meat than any other primates. We are also the only primate that is completely terrestrial. We do not even sleep in trees, as many other ground-living primates do. Perhaps our ancestors lost their perches when the forests receded; or cultural advances like weapons or fire may have eliminated the need to seek nightly shelter in the trees. In addition, we have the longest dependency period of any of the primates, requiring extensive parental care for at least six years and usually requiring partial care until we reach sexual maturity in the early teens.

Finally, humans are unlike other primates in having a division of labor by sex. Among nonhuman primates, both males and females forage for themselves after infancy. In humans, there is more role specialization, perhaps as a result of adaptations made by our hunting ancestors. Women, who cared for the children, probably remained near home base to gather vegatation and small game. Men, unencumbered by infants and small children, were freer to hunt and chase large animals. We shall consider the consequences of human sex roles in a later chapter.

Having examined our so-called "unique" traits and the traits we share with other primates, we need to ask what selective forces may have favored the emergence of primates, and then, what forces may have favored the line of divergence leading to humans. These questions are the subject of our next chapter.

Summary

1. Although no living primate can be a direct ancestor of humans, we do share a common evolutionary history with the other surviving primates. Study of the behavioral and anatomical features of our closest living relatives may help us make inferences about primate evolution. Studying distinctive human traits may help us to understand why the line of primates that led to humans branched away from the line leading to chimpanzees and gorillas.

2. The prosimians—lemurs, lorises, and tarsiers—are in some respects closer to other mammals than are the anthropoid primates—monkeys, apes, and man. Prosimians, however, have typical primate traits: grasping hands, stereoscopic vision, and small litter size with an extended period of infant dependency.

3. The anthropoids are subdivided into the New World monkeys, Old World monkeys, and the Hominoids (apes and humans). All the anthropoids have hands well adapted for grasping; stereoscopic and color vision; single births; rounded skulls; small, nonmobile outer ears; and relatively small, flat faces. New World monkeys are totally arboreal, unlike Old World monkeys, some of which are also adapted for ground living.

4. Among Old World monkeys, which have adapted to a variety of environments, there is a great diversity of behavior. The range of behavior patterns of these monkeys, including aggressiveness and the presence or absence of dominance hierarchies, seems to be closely tied to environmental factors like the threat of predators and the abundance and type of food supply.

5. The anthropoid apes are the gorilla, chimpanzee, orangutan, and gibbon.

6. Along with the gorilla, the chimpanzee has blood chemistry and molecular genetics remarkably similar to those of humans, as well as anatomical and behavioral similarities to humans. Wild chimpanzees have been seen to create and use tools, modifying a natural object to fulfill a specific purpose. High conceptual ability is also demonstrated by the chimpanzee's facility in learning sign language. Washoe, a chimpanzee raised in isolation, has been taught to use 175 hand gestures of the American Sign Language to communicate with her human teachers.

7. Primates share many social behavioral traits such as group living. The group is an adaptation for defense and learning. Immature primates can learn about their environment while still being protected by adult group members.

8. The differences between humans and the other anthropoids show us what makes humans distinctive as a species. Humans are totally bipedal, walking on two legs with the arms unneeded for locomotion. The human brain is the largest and most complex, particularly in the cerebral cortex area. Human females have no estrus period. The offspring have a proportionately longer dependency stage; and in comparison with other primates, more human behavior is learned and culturally patterned. The following behavioral traits are unique to humans: a division of labor by sex; spoken, symbolic language; and the use of tools to make other tools.

Suggested Readings

DeVore, I., and Eimerl, S. *The Primates*. New York: Time-Life Books, 1966.

An introduction to the primates at an elementary level. Colorful pictures.

Dolhinow, P., ed. *Primate Patterns*. New York: Holt, Rinehart and Winston, 1972.

An introduction to what we have learned from recent field studies of various primates.

Jolly, A. *The Evolution of Primate Behavior*. New York: Macmillan, 1972.

Discussion of research and theory relating to variable primate adaptations.

Kummer, H. *Primate Societies*. Chicago: Aldine-Atherton, 1971.

An examination of the social behavior of hamadryas baboons as an evolutionary adaptation for species survival. Readable and interesting, with comments on the analogies that can be drawn between human and primate social organization.

Lancaster, J. *Primate Behavior and the Emergence of Human Culture*. New York: Holt, Rinehart and Winston, 1975.

An introduction to human behavior as the product of a long evolutionary history, concentrating on the results of recent primate studies that are most relevant to understanding human behavior.

Napier, J. R., and Napier, P. H. *A Handbook of Living Primates*. New York: Academic Press, 1967.

A systematic presentation, genus by genus, of the whole Primate order, with comments on general primate traits.

Rosen, S. I. *Introduction to the Primates: Living and Fossil*. Englewood Cliffs, N.J.: Prentice-Hall, 1974.

An introduction to the primates at an intermediate level.

Primate Evolution: From Early Primates to Hominids

4

The story of primate evolution is still fragmentary and tentative. And it will probably always be so, because all of our information about it has been learned indirectly. Paleontologists have to make inferences or educated guesses about what happened in evolutionary history, where and when events occurred, and why they happened the way (we think) they did. These inferences make use of a number of kinds of information—fossilized bones and teeth from extinct biological forms; indicators of ancient environments and climates discovered by geologists; and comparisons of the anatomical, physiological, and behavioral characteristics of living animals. But despite the possibility that paleontological inferences may always be tentative, some inferences are more strongly supported by the available evidence than others. A particular inference based on one kind of evidence can be checked against other kinds of evidence. In this way, some inferences come to be discarded and others tentatively accepted. This chapter describes the main features of current theory and evidence about primate evolution, from the appearance of the earliest primates possibly 90 million years ago to the emergence about 15 million years ago of the first hominids.

Interpreting the Fossil Record

How can paleontologists speak about what may have happened millions of years ago? Needless to say, there is no written record from that period from which they can draw inferences. But we do have another kind of evidence for primate evolution: fossils. And we have ways of "reading" the records left by fossils and of telling how old fossils are.

WHAT ARE FOSSILS?

A fossil may be an impression of an insect or leaf on sediment now turned to stone. Or it may consist of the actual mineralized remains of an animal's skeletal structure. It is this second type

The primates probably evolved from a creature like this tree shrew who has claws rather than nailed fingers, a long snout, and eyes on the side of the head. (A. W. Ambler, National Audubon Society Collection/Photo Researchers.)

of fossil—bone turned to stone[1]—which has given paleontologists the most information about primate evolution.

Nobody completely understands why and how animal remains turn to fossils, but we do have a sketchy understanding of the process. When an animal dies, all the organic matter which made up its body quickly begins to deteriorate. The teeth and skeletal structure are composed largely of inorganic mineral salts, and soon they are all that remains. Under most conditions, these parts eventually deteriorate too. But once in a great while conditions are favorable—for instance, when volcanic ash, limestone, or highly mineralized groundwater is present to form a high-mineral environment. Under such circumstances, the minerals in the ground become bound into the structure of the teeth or bone and produce a fossil.

What Can We Infer from Fossils? Paleontologists can tell a great deal about an extinct animal from its fossilized bones or teeth, but reading

fossil records is not always easy to do. For one thing, the very formation of a fossil depends a good deal on luck; so does the discovery of that fossil by the right person eons later. In addition, fossils are often fragmented or distorted, and similar fossils may come from widely distant geographical areas. Although we can tell the age of a fossil with some accuracy, methods of dating are not always exact enough for the paleontologist to determine whether a fossil is older than, contemporaneous with, or more recent than, other fossils. For this reason, evolutionary lines are difficult to trace.

A further complication is a man-made one: the problem of taxonomy. Over the period of time that paleontologists have been discovering primate remains, different assumptions have guided scientists in making judgments about the taxonomic status of fossils. Even when paleontologists agree in theory, they often have honest differences of opinion about the status of a fossil. Some paleontologists believe the first hominids evolved about 15 million years ago from Miocene apes; others think the hominids branched away at an earlier stage; still others think this split occurred in far more recent times.

[1] S. I. Rosen, *Introduction to the Primates: Living and Fossil* (Englewood Cliffs, N.J.: Prentice-Hall, 1974), p. 155.

TABLE 1 An Overview of Human Evolution: Biological and Cultural

Time (years ago)	Geologic Epoch	Fossil Record (first appearance)	Archaeological Periods (Old World)	Major Cultural Developments (first appearance)
5,500 (3,500 B.C.)			Bronze Age	Cities and states; social inequality; full-time craft specialists
10,000 (8,000 B.C.)			Neolithic	Domesticated plants and animals permanent villages
14,000 (12,000 B.C.)			Mesolithic	Broad spectrum food collecting; increasingly sedentary communities; many kinds of microliths
40,000		Earliest Humans in New World / Modern Humans *Homo sapiens sapiens*	Upper Paleolithic	Cave paintings; female figurines; many kinds of blade tools
	Pleistocene		Middle Paleolithic	Religious beliefs (?); burials; Mousterian tools
100,000		Neandertal *Homo sapiens*		
250,000		Earliest *Homo sapiens* (?) Fontéchevade Swanscombe Steinheim		
700,000		*Homo erectus*	Lower Paleolithic	Use of fire; big game hunting; Acheulean tools
1,800,000		*Homo erectus* (?)		Hunting and/or scavenging; seasonal campsites; division of labor by sex (?); Oldowan tools
5,000,000	Pliocene	Earliest Definite Hominids *Homo* (?) *Australopithecus*		Earliest stone tools
22,500,000	Miocene	Earliest Hominids (?) *Ramapithecus* *Dryopithecus*		
38,000,000	Oligocene	Earliest Apes and Monkeys *Aegyptopithecus* *Propliopithecus* / *Parapithecus* *Apidium*		
53,500,000	Eocene	*Plesiadapis* *Tetonius*		
65,000,000	Paleocene			
90,000,000	Cretaceous	Earliest primates (?) *Purgatorius*		

Geological dates from W. A. Berggren and J. A. Couvering, "The Late Neogene: Biostratigraphy, Geochronology and Paleoclimatology of the Last 15 Million Years in Marine and Continental Sequences," *Palaeogeography, Palaeoclimatology, Palaeoecology* 16 (1974):13–16, 165.

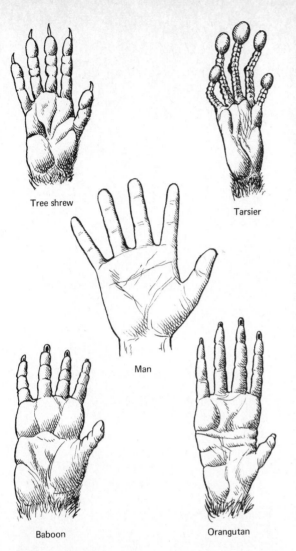

Tree shrew

Tarsier

Man

Baboon

Orangutan

FIGURE 1

The evolution of primate hands included a shift from claws (retained by the modern tree shrew) to nails. The thumb became increasingly opposable and the fingers more flexible. Lengthened fingers and palm are adaptations of the brachiating orangutan; a short thumb stays out of the way as the ape swings from branch to branch.

Finally, there has been a tendency to overclassify primates from the more recent epochs, simply because more fossil finds date from more recent epochs. Almost every major find from the Pleistocene epoch (which began about 2 million years ago) has been given a separate

scientific name, even though some of the finds might more properly be classified as belonging to the same species.[2] In contrast, fewer finds have been made from earlier epochs. The result is an overall picture of hominid evolution which shows very slow development in the early stages, then rapid evolution in the later stages—a picture which may reflect the ideas of the paleontologists who drew it as much as it does the actual evolutionary path it is meant to portray.

Despite all these problems, fossils do provide an enormous wealth of information. In the study of primate evolution, paleontologists ask two important questions as they examine an animal fossil. What was the animal's means of food getting? And what was its means of locomotion? Often the answers to both of these questions can be determined from a few fragments of bone or teeth.

Much of the evidence for primate evolution comes from teeth, which, along with jaws, are the most common animal parts to be preserved as fossils. Dentition provides clues to evolutionary relationships because animals with close evolutionary histories often have similar teeth. Dentition also suggests the relative size of an animal and often offers clues about its diet. From the structure of the teeth and our knowledge of living animals, we can infer whether an early animal was primarily a meat-eater or a herbivore.

Paleontologists can tell much about an animal's posture and locomotion from fragments of the skeleton.[3] They can often judge whether the animal was a brachiator and whether it walked on all fours (a quadruped) or upright (a biped). The bone structure also tells much about soft tissues. The form and size of muscles can be estimated by marks found on the bones to which the muscles were attached. Tunnels or grooves in the bones made by arteries may indicate the arteries' relative size, and with this

[2] Elwyn L. Simons, *Primate Evolution: An Introduction to Man's Place in Nature* (New York: Macmillan, 1972), pp. 25–26.
[3] Bernard G. Campbell, *Human Evolution: An Introduction to Man's Adaptations*, rev. ed. (Chicago: Aldine, 1974), p. 2.

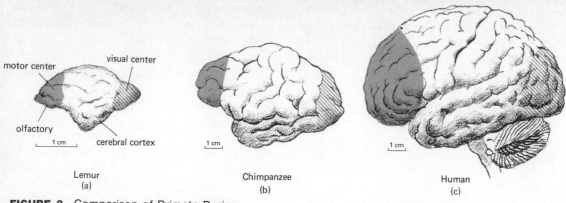

FIGURE 2 Comparison of Primate Brains

The visual center is relatively large in all primates. The motor area increases in the higher primates, and the olfactory lobe (which receives impulses concerned with the sense of smell) decreases in relative size. The cerebral cortex became increasingly complex, as indicated by convoluted folds. (Adapted from *Physical Anthropology: A Perspective* and from *Origins of Man*, by John Buettner-Janusch. Copyright © 1973 by John Buettner-Janusch. Reprinted by permission of John Wiley & Sons, Inc.)

information the paleontologist may be able to judge the functional importance of different parts of the body. Finally, fragments of the skull or vertebrae provide clues about the proportions and structure of the brain and spinal cord. From such evidence, scientists can tell whether areas of the brain associated with vision, or smell, or memory were enlarged.

Dating Fossils

Scientists use different methods to estimate the age of a fossil, depending upon the conditions present in the deposit where the fossil was found or in the fossil itself. There are two main approaches to dating fossils.[4] The first, *relative dating*, is used to determine the age of a specimen or deposit relative to another known specimen or deposit. The second type, *chronometric* or *absolute dating*, is used to measure the actual age of a specimen or deposit.

RELATIVE DATING METHODS

Bones or teeth found in a deposit are not always the same age as other remains and objects

found in the site. Sometimes remains from different periods are washed or blown together by water or wind. Sometimes human remains are buried for ceremonial or religious reasons and thus are misplaced in a far older stratum than they would naturally occupy. Relative dating makes it possible to arrange all the objects found in a site in chronological order even though the exact age of a specimen may be unknown.

A major part of relative dating involves determining the age of teeth or bones in order to establish their contemporaneity with other fossil material in the same deposit, or with the deposit itself. Three major methods for relatively dating fossil bones are the fluorine, nitrogen, and uranium tests (sometimes known as the F-U-N trio).[5] All are based upon the same general principle: bones and teeth undergo a slow transformation in chemical composition when they remain buried for long periods of time, and this transformation reflects the mineral content of the groundwater in the area in which they are buried. Fluorine is one mineral which is present in groundwater; therefore, the older a fossil is, the higher will be its fluorine content. Proportions are reversed for nitrogen:

[4] Kenneth P. Oakley, "Analytical Methods of Dating Bones," in *Science in Archaeology*, ed. Don Brothwell and Eric Higgs (New York: Basic Books, 1963), pp. 24–34.

[5] Ibid., p. 26.

the higher the fluorine content of a fossil, the smaller is the amount of nitrogen present. Uranium, like fluorine, is present in groundwater, and so the longer that bones or teeth remain in the ground, the greater will be their uranium content. Thus, older bones have relatively higher concentrations of uranium than recent bones. But a possible problem arises with these F-U-N tests because the mineral content of bones reflects the mineral content of the groundwater in the area. A 30-million-year-old fossil from a high-mineral area may have the same fluorine content as a 50-million-year-old fossil from a low-mineral site; hence, relative dating methods usually cannot be used to find the relative ages of specimens from different sites. Instead, these tests are restricted to specimens from the same site or from closely neighboring sites.

Each of the relative dating methods, used alone, can give only tentative evidence. But when the three methods are combined and confirm—that is, cross-date—each other, they are very effective. Of the three methods we have discussed, the uranium test is by far the most reliable when used alone. It is not strictly a relative dating method. There seems to be some consistency in the increase in radioactivity with age, even in bones from different deposits. The uranium test has another distinct advantage over the other tests: because uranium is radioactive, measuring the radioactivity does not require the destruction of any part of the sample in testing.

CHRONOMETRIC OR ABSOLUTE DATING METHODS

The radiocarbon or C^{14} method of dating is perhaps the most popularly known method of determining the absolute age of a specimen. But it is not used as often as some other methods to study primate evolution for one important reason: the half-life, or rate of deterioration, of C^{14} is relatively short. This means that radiocarbon dating is not reliable beyond about 70,000 years ago—and the primate paleontologist is interested in fossils as early as the Cretaceous pe-

riod, over 65 million years ago! *Potassium-argon* and *fission-track* methods are much more useful for studying the time-depth of primate evolution.

Potassium-Argon Dating A radioactive form of potassium (K^{40}) decays at an established rate and forms argon (Ar^{40}). Since the rate of disintegration is known, it is possible to determine the age of the deposit by gauging the ratio of potassium to argon. The half-life of K^{40} is a known quantity to scientists. This means that the age of a material containing potassium can be measured by the ratio of K^{40}/Ar^{40} it contains.[6] Radioactive potassium's (K^{40}'s) half-life is very long—1,330 million years. This means that K-Ar dating may be used to date samples from 5,000 years old up to 3 billion years old. In fact, it was the method used to determine the age of the earth.

The K-Ar method is used to date minerals and rocks in a deposit, not the fossil specimens themselves. Potassium is especially common in igneous minerals and volcanic glass, and it is also found in some sedimentary rocks.[7] Because volcanic deposits are quite likely to have been formed at the same time as fossils found in the deposits, the K-Ar method is especially well suited to dating these kinds of finds. Potassium-argon dating has some limitations, too. Not all fossil deposits include volcanic material, nor do all sedimentary deposits contain potassium-containing minerals. This means that other methods must be used to date many fossil deposits.

Fission-Track Dating The fission-track method is the newest means of determining absolute age. It has been used only since the 1960s to date fossil deposits.[8] Like the K-Ar method, it dates minerals contemporaneous with the deposit in which fossils are found. But the kinds of samples it can be used to date—such as crystal, glass, and many uranium-rich minerals—

[6] W. Gentner and H. J. Lippolt, "The Potassium-Argon Dating of Upper Tertiary and Pleistocene Deposits," in *Science in Archaeology*, ed. Don Brothwell and Eric Higgs, pp. 72–84.
[7] Ibid., p. 75.
[8] Robert L. Fleischer et al., "Fission Track Dating of Bed I, Olduvai Gorge," *Science*, 2 April 1965, pp. 72–74.

include a much wider variety than those that can be dated by the K-Ar method. The age range of fission-track dating, like that of K-Ar dating, is quite extensive: 20 years to 5 billion years.[9]

How does it work? This method is basically the simplest of all the methods discussed here. It entails counting the number of paths, or tracks, etched in the sample by the fission (explosive division) of uranium atoms as they disintegrate. Scientists know that U–238, the most common uranium isotope, decays at a slow, steady rate. This decay takes the form of spontaneous fission, and each separate fission leaves a scar or track on the sample which can be seen through a microscope when chemically treated. To find out how old a sample is, one simply counts the tracks, then measures their ratio to the uranium content of the sample.

The fission-track method has been used to date Bed I at Olduvai Gorge in Tanzania, East Africa (where some early hominids were found).[10] It was able to corroborate earlier K-Ar estimates that the site dated back close to 2 million years. The fact that K-Ar and fission-track methods use different techniques and have different sources of error makes them very effective as checks on each other. When the two methods support each other, they provide very reliable evidence.

The Emergence of Primates

With a rudimentary understanding of the kinds of information which fossils provide and of the methods of dating which allow scientists to tell the age of fossils, we can look at, and suggest answers to, some major questions about primate evolution. When did the earliest primates appear? What were they like, and what kind of animal did they evolve from? Where did they live? What was their environment like? And which of their traits seem to have been favored by that environment?

THE EARLIEST PRIMATES

Finds made by two paleontologists in eastern Montana in 1964 suggest that some very early primates may have existed as far back as the late Cretaceous period—some 90 million years ago. Molars from two species (one from the Cretaceous period, the other from the Paleocene) of this ancestral primate called *Purgatorius* show some definite primate characteristics.[11] The earlier of these species is very old indeed: it was contemporaneous with at least six species of dinosaurs. In fact, this specimen was recovered from the same site that also contained the *Triceratops* skeleton now mounted in the American Museum of Natural History in New York City.

Both of these earliest primate finds illustrate how much of the paleontologist's work often depends upon inference. We think *Purgatorius* was a primate, but it is impossible to tell for sure. The Cretaceous specimen consists of only one tooth found with fauna dating from that period. Because the tooth has some characteristics like those found in the teeth of some later Paleocene primates, we think that it represents a very early primate form. Fossil finds from the middle Paleocene epoch (about 60 million years ago) are much more abundant; several genera have been identified. While the earliest *Purgatorius* remains consist only of teeth, we have some skeletal parts of these later primates.

THE PALEOCENE ENVIRONMENT

Paleocene and early Eocene archaic primates have been found in both Europe and North America. The similarities between some European and North American finds are often quite striking. For example, a cat-sized primate called

[9]Robert L. Fleischer and Howard R. Hart, Jr., "Fission-Track Dating: Techniques and Problems," in *Calibration of Hominid Evolution*, ed. W. A. Bishop and J. A. Miller (Toronto: University of Toronto Press, 1972), p. 474.

[10]Fleischer et al., "Fission Track Dating of Bed I, Olduvai Gorge."

[11]L. Van Valen and R. E. Sloan, "The Earliest Primates," *Science*, 5 November 1967, pp. 743–45; Frederick S. Szalay, "The Beginnings of Primates," *Evolution* 22 (1968): 19–36.

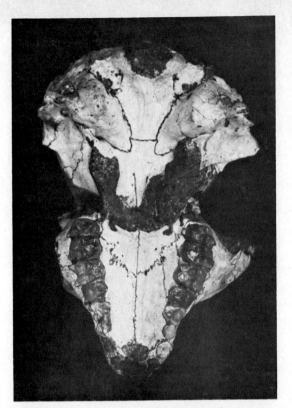

Unlike the archaic primate *Plesiadapis*, late Eocene tarsiiforms like *Rooneyia* are totally modern in their anatomy. This specimen of a jaw and part of a skull was found in Texas. (Dr. Frederick S. Szalay.)

Plesiadapis was first discovered in northern France. Later finds of a somewhat earlier-dated species of the same animal have been made in Wyoming and Colorado. These forms differ very little from the French specimens, except in their smaller size. It seems likely that *Plesiadapis* originated in North America, then may have spread to Europe at a later period—by which time it had evolved into a larger form.[12]

How could a North American primate spread to Europe? The answer to this question is provided by the *theory of continental drift*.[13] At one time, the major continents were not separated as they are today. Instead, they were so close together that they almost formed a single supercontinent, and the rest of the earth was covered by sea. *Plesiadapis* and a few other early primates probably ranged from North America to Europe, sharing a single genetic pool. Only in relatively recent times (geologically speaking) have the continents moved far enough apart so that the intervening seas could block gene flow between related populations.

During the late Cretaceous and early Paleocene, many new mammal forms began to appear—so many that this time is known as the beginning of the "age of mammals." Larger reptiles like dinosaurs were dying out, and at the same time many new and different mammal forms were branching out from the more primitive Cretaceous ones. We think that primates evolved from one of these radiations or extensive diversifications, probably from insectivores which made a move to the trees.

These changes in the earth's population may have been favored by the environmental changes which marked the end of the Cretaceous period and the beginning of the Paleocene. Shifts in climate, vegetation, and fauna signal the beginning of every major epoch, and many important changes were taking place at this time.

Throughout the Mesozoic era, which ended with the Cretaceous period, the continents were bunched together. About the time of the late Cretaceous, the continents were beginning to take their shapes as we recognize them today. North America and Europe were still very close and probably touched one another. But the gradual elevation of the land and a drying-up of the extensive inland seas were all part of a gradual shift, or drift, which continued in later epochs. The climate of the Cretaceous period was almost uniformly damp and mild. Around the beginning of the Paleocene epoch, both seasonal and geographic fluctuations in temperature began to develop. At this time the climate became much drier in many areas, as vast swamplands disappeared. With changes

[12] D. E. Russel, "Les Mammifères Paléocènes," *Mémoires du Muséum d'Histoire Naturelle* 13 (1964): 1–324, as cited in Simons, *Primate Evolution*, pp. 110–12.

[13] A. Hallam, "Alfred Wegener and the Hypothesis of Continental Drift," *Scientific American*, February 1975, pp. 88–97.

in climate came changes in vegetation. During the late Cretaceous period, the first deciduous trees, flowering plants, and grasses were evolving.

The Move to the Trees The new kinds of plant life opened up sources of food and protection for new animal forms. They created new ecological niches or *econiches:* small, specialized parts of the whole habitat which provided both resources and opportunities for adaptation. The econiche which was important to primate evolution was the late Cretaceous forest. The new deciduous plant life provided an abundant food supply for insects. The result was that insects proliferated in both number and variety, and this led, in turn, to an increase in the mammals that ate the insects, the insectivores. The insectivores were very adaptable, for they took advantage of many different econiches—underground, in the water, and in the trees.

It is this last adaptation which we think was most important to primate evolution. The forest econiche had been only partially exploited in earlier periods. But sometime during the late Cretaceous period, several different kinds, or taxa, of small animals, one of which was the archaic primate, began to take advantage of this niche.

Adapting to Life in the Trees One important adaptation early primates made to living in the trees was a change of diet, from one of insects to a mainly herbivorous diet of seeds, fruit, and leaves.[14] Following this change in diet, natural selection favored many other behavioral and physiological modifications. One was a change in dentition which would allow these early primates to chew tough husks and fruits. Relatively lower-cusped, bulbous teeth are one identifying feature of many of the earliest primates (indeed, the *only* identifying feature in some cases where no skull or bones exist). It should be noted that while we think this transition to an arboreal life and away from a pre-

dominantly insectivorous diet was basic to the original radiation of primates, we cannot document the actual branching-off with any fossil records. We think that primates evolved from the basically insectivorous animals that took to the trees. But to date, our only supporting fossil evidence, at least from the Cretaceous period, is the one *Purgatorius* tooth.

In any case, primates had moved to the trees by the Eocene epoch (some 54 to 38 million years ago) and this transition favored many other adaptations besides changes in dentition. Animals which live, and move around, in trees need a sharp sense of vision in order to keep from falling. Three-dimensional binocular vision has the great advantage of letting an animal judge distances from branch to branch. As a result, once primates moved to the trees, strong selective forces were at work to move the eyes closer together at the front of the face. Another sensory adaptation favored by a treetop life was a sharpened sense of hearing. Both of these sensory changes took place at a relatively early stage: they were already incorporated into the brain structure of some early Eocene prosimians. This is shown by a 50-million-year-old brain endocast of the Eocene primate *Tetonius* which has been described by Radinsky.[15] The brain has large occipital and temporal lobes, which are the regions associated with perception, integration, and memory of visual and auditory messages.

As vision and hearing became keener, the importance of the sense of smell was gradually reduced. Vision and hearing were crucial to survival in the treetops, but the sense of smell was relatively unimportant. This adaptation, like the increase in hearing and vision, was reflected in some structural changes. Primates gradually began to have shorter and shorter snouts (a modification which also was more suitable for eating a diet of fruits, seeds, and leaves).[16] We can see all of these modifications continued into later epochs.

---

[14] Szalay, "The Beginnings of Primates," pp. 32–33.

[15] Leonard Radinsky, "The Oldest Primate Endocast," *American Journal of Physical Anthropology* 27, no. 3 (November 1967): 385–88.
[16] Szalay, "The Beginnings of Primates," pp. 33–34.

Primates also made skeletal and muscular adaptations to life in the trees. These had to do with the development of a more specialized means of locomotion. Instead of walking on all fours as their ancestors had done on the ground, primates gradually shifted to a more efficient system of vertical clinging and leaping.[17] This means of locomotion is the same as that used by living prosimians such as tarsiers. Powerful, elongated hindlimbs are used to propel the animal as it leaps from one spot, and the feet are used to grasp the branch or trunk as it lands at another spot. The hands are used mostly to cling to treetrunks and hold the animal in a vertical position while it rests. The skeletal remains of some Eocene primates show that their means of locomotion might have been quite similar to the vertical clinging and leaping used by modern prosimians. Both the forelimbs and hindlimbs show other related adaptations: elongated digits, and a mobile thumb and big toe which allowed the animals to grasp branches more firmly.

THE EARLY PRIMATES: WHAT THEY LOOKED LIKE

From all the clues provided by fossils, comparative anatomy, physiology, behavior, and our knowledge of the Paleocene and Eocene environments, we can put together a composite sketch of what early primates must have been like.

The primates of the Paleocene epoch seem to have been very similar to the shrew-like insectivores we think they evolved from—so close, in fact, that it is often difficult to distinguish one from the other. Most of these primates were quite small; the cat-sized *Plesiadapis* found in late Paleocene deposits in France is among the largest early primates we know of.[18] Its mode of locomotion is believed to have been similar to a squirrel's: it probably got around by

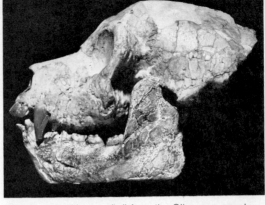

This *Aegyptopithecus* skull from the Oligocene epoch has teeth that are similar to the Dryopithecine apes of the Miocene epoch. Many anthropologists think that *Aegyptopithecus* may be the ancestor of Dryopithecine apes and hence an early common ancestor of both modern apes and humans. (Courtesy of the Peabody Museum of Natural History, Yale University.)

springing and jumping, instead of walking on all fours.

By the later Eocene epoch, primates were more specialized to living in the trees. Vertical clinging and leaping was a common method of locomotion. Eocene prosimians not only moved around the way modern prosimians do; some also looked quite a bit like living prosimians. Through the evolutionary process of natural selection, their eyes became located closer together and their faces became shorter. Digits became longer and were specialized for grasping.

All primates did not adapt in the same way to life in the trees. There was a great deal of diversification among all mammals during the Paleocene and Eocene epochs, and the primates were no exception. Evolution seems to have proceeded very rapidly during these years.

The Emergence of Early Monkeys and Apes

Sometime during the late Eocene or early Oligocene epochs (between about 38 and 32 million years ago), the ancestors of both monkeys and apes began to evolve separately from

---

[17]J. R. Napier and A. C. Walker, "Vertical Clinging and Leaping—A Newly-Recognized Category of Locomotor Behaviour of Primates," *Folia Primatologica* 16, no. 3–4 (1976): 204–19.

[18]Simons, *Primate Evolution*, p. 112.

prosimian stocks. Our knowledge of this branching-out is still sketchy. It is based almost entirely upon a number of fossils unearthed by Elwyn Simons and others in an area of Egyptian desert southwest of Cairo which is known as the Fayum.

THE FAYUM

The Fayum today is an uninviting area of desert badlands, but during the Oligocene epoch it was a tropical rainforest, quite close to the shores of the Mediterranean Sea. The area had a warm climate, and it contained many rivers and lakes. The Fayum, in fact, was far more inviting than the northern continents were at this time, for the climates of both North America and Eurasia were beginning to cool during the Oligocene epoch. The general cooling seems to have resulted in the virtual disappearance of primates from the northern areas, at least for a time.

Fayum Apes and Monkeys   Another interesting change that had taken place by the Oligocene epoch was the probable disappearance of the archaic prosimian forms. We know that these early primates were very common during the Eocene time, but no evidence has yet been found of Oligocene prosimians living in the Fayum. Instead, two taxa of anthropoidea now inhabited the area: *pongids* and *parapithecids*. Paleontologists think the early pongids were the ancestors of modern apes. Two genera of Oligocene apes (pongids) have been distinguished. The older is called *Propliopithecus* and dates from about 32 million years ago.[19] This form may have been the ancestor of another Fayum ape, *Aegyptopithecus,* which is about 29 million years old. The teeth of this later genus are very similar to those of a Miocene ape called *Dryopithecus* (which we shall meet later in this chapter). For this reason, many anthropologists think that *Aegyptopithecus* may be the ancestor of modern apes and perhaps of humans too.[20]

[19] Ian Tattersall, *Man's Ancestors* (London: John Murray, 1970), pp. 27–31.
[20] Elwyn L. Simons, "The Earliest Apes," *Scientific American,* December 1967, pp. 28–35.

Old World monkey molar   Ape molar

FIGURE 3
Molars can distinguish fossil monkeys from apes. The Old World monkey molar (*left*) has four cusps, one at each corner, joined by ridges. The ape molar (*right*) has five cusps, separated by grooves which resemble the letter Y. *Dryopithecus*'s lower molars had the ape-like Y–5 pattern. (Adapted from "The Early Relatives of Man" by Elwyn L. Simons. Copyright © 1964 by Scientific American, Inc. All rights reserved.)

Both of the Fayum apes were small animals. Both probably lived in trees, and they looked quite a bit like monkeys. Why, then, do we identify them as apes instead of monkeys? The reason is that even as far back as the Oligocene epoch, different taxa of primates can be identified by different dental patterns. Humans, apes, and Old World monkeys have a total of 32 teeth: 2 incisors, 1 canine, 2 premolars, and 3 molars on each side of each jaw (this "dental formula" is expressed as 2:1:2:3). New World monkeys have a total of 36 teeth, for they have 3 premolars instead of 2 on each side of each jaw (2:1:3:3). As we go back further in time, we find that some early forms had even more teeth: most Mesozoic mammals had 44 teeth. It is interesting to note that this evolutionary trend toward fewer teeth is still going on. Many humans have no third molars or "wisdom teeth" at all. If this trend continues in the future, humans may characteristically have a total of 28 teeth instead of 32.

Propliopithecus and *Aegyptopithecus* are classified as apes instead of monkeys because, as Elwyn Simon says, they have the skulls of monkeys but the teeth of apes.[21] Besides the dental formula, structural characteristics of the teeth identify these forms as apes. In later Miocene

[21] Ibid., p. 35.

apes and in *Aegyptopithecus,* lower molars become progressively longer toward the back of the jaw, while *Propliopithecus* has uniformly sized molars. Other dental characteristics, such as the cusp pattern on each molar, the size of the canines, and the shape of the mandible or lower jaw, help to identify different taxa of early primates, and they also identify these two Fayum forms as apes.

Most of the Fayum primate fossils were not those of apes. There are far more specimens of the family *Parapithecidae:* small, monkeylike animals. Two genera are most common in the Fayum finds. One of these, a short-faced monkey called *Apidium,* has teeth which some anthropologists believe resemble those of certain modern New World monkeys. The other, *Parapithecus,* is much closer dentally to Old World monkeys (cercopithecids). It is possible that *Parapithecus* is the ancestor of modern Old World monkeys.

SELECTIVE FORCES IN OLIGOCENE EVOLUTION

Evidence of teeth and skeletons from the Fayum suggests that during the Oligocene epoch primates still lived in trees. Natural selection favored a number of traits in the treetop existence of Oligocene primates, and we can see evidence of these traits in the Fayum fossils.

Selective pressures toward keen vision over smell were probably at work as early as the Paleocene epoch, and this trend continued during the Oligocene epoch. In most cases, the result seems to have been a progression toward shorter snouts and flatter faces (one modern exception is the baboon).[22] As the sense of vision improved, bony walls developed to enclose the orbits and protect the eyes. Selection continued to work toward closer-set eyes which provided vision with greater depth perception.

Another characteristic favored by the arboreal environment of the Fayum was greater brain size. Intelligence, including an increased ability to integrate and store visual and auditory messages, was important for survival in the trees.

We saw earlier that some Eocene primates probably moved about in the trees by vertical clinging and leaping. This method of locomotion is still used by some prosimians today. But most modern monkeys and apes use a quadrupedal means of locomotion, walking on four feet in the trees and on the ground. Skeletal parts of *Aegyptopithecus* suggest that it still lived in the trees, but it probably walked on all fours like modern monkeys. It may even have been a brachiator.

MIOCENE ANTHROPOIDS

During the Miocene epoch (which began about 22 million years ago), the split between monkeys and apes became wider in terms of their dentition, skeletal anatomy, and, by inference, behavioral adaptations. The Miocene, which along with the later Pliocene is sometimes called the "age of apes," saw the development and diversification of the dryopithecines. These early apes lived from about 23 to 12.5 million years ago and were probably ancestral to modern chimpanzees, gorillas, and possibly even the hominids. Paleontologists think the dryopithecine apes are descended from *Aegyptopithecus,* for the teeth of some specimens of these two apes are very similar.[23] (Gibbons may have branched away from this line at an earlier point, perhaps from the Oligocene ape *Propliopithecus.*)

Apes spread to nearly their present geographical distribution in the Old World during the Miocene epoch. There are records of *Dryopithecus* all the way from Spain to China, and in India and Africa as well.

The few skeletal parts we have suggest that by the Miocene epoch apes were no longer completely arboreal. To be sure, they probably spent much of their time in the trees. But their increased body size suggests that they would have been more successful foraging for at least some of their food on the ground, as compared

[22] Ibid., pp. 28–35.

[23] David Pilbeam, *The Ascent of Man* (New York: Macmillan, 1972), p. 44.

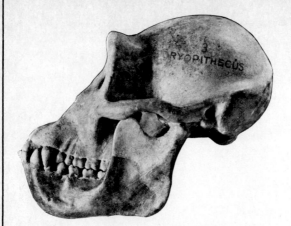

Skull of *Dryopithecus*, an extinct early ape. Note the heavy brow ridges, protruding face, and large canines. (Courtesy of the American Museum of Natural History.)

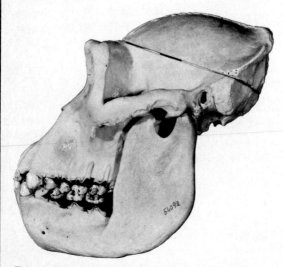

This skull of a modern female gorilla is similar to the skull of *Dryopithecus*. (Courtesy of the American Museum of Natural History.)

with depending entirely upon fruits and leaves that often could only be located in the thinner, hard-to-reach parts of the trees.

Several species and subspecies of *Dryopithecus* are known, and they show a wide range in both size and means of locomotion.[24] The largest form probably looked quite a bit like

[24] Ibid., pp. 44–48.

a modern gorilla, although it had a more monkeylike, long-nosed face. It was somewhat larger than the smaller species (and smaller than the larger species) of living African gorillas, and paleontologists think it could be their ancestor. A smaller *Dryopithecus* species resembled modern chimpanzees more closely, and that *Dryopithecus* may be their ancestor. Both of these forms of *Dryopithecus* walked on all fours, perhaps on the knuckles of their hands and "feet" as the modern gorillas and other apes do.

In general, dryopithecine apes were far more advanced, in terms of brain size and general appearance, than the Fayum apes from which they probably evolved. The fact that the Miocene apes spent at least some of their time out of the trees is especially important from an evolutionary standpoint, for some of the traits favored by natural selection on the ground probably led to the emergence of hominids.

The Emergence of Hominids

Who or what are hominids, and how do they differ from other primates? The family *Hominidae* comprises humans and their direct ancestors. It includes at least two genera and probably three: *Homo* (including modern humans); *Australopithecus* (a hominid of the Pliocene and Pleistocene epochs); and *Ramapithecus,* which was roughly contemporary with the later dryopithecine apes but which shows a number of characteristics that lead most scientists to classify it as a hominid. In general, hominids are characterized by a number of identifying traits. They are bipeds, walking on two feet. They have an enlarged brain. Their faces are relatively small and relatively nonprotruding. And their teeth are small and are arranged on the jaws in a continuous parabolic curve. Hominoids are not the same as hominids; hominoids are the superfamily of primates which contains both pongids (apes) and hominids.

There is some controversy over when the hominids began to branch away from the other hominoids. Paleontologists think that it was at

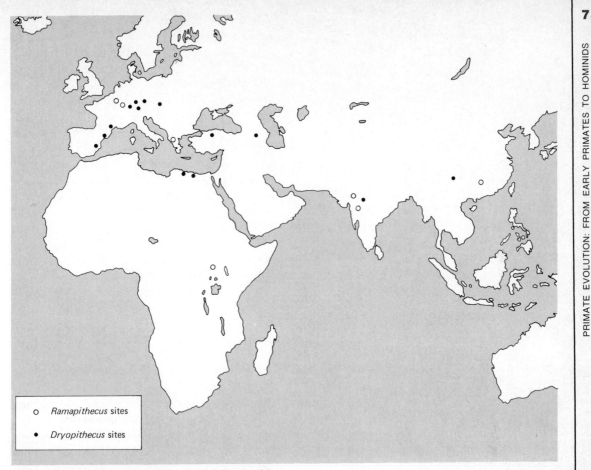

| o | *Ramapithecus* sites |
| • | *Dryopithecus* sites |

Site Distribution of *Dryopithecus* and *Ramapithecus*

some point closely after, or during, the time that *Dryopithecus* inhabited Africa and Eurasia. Estimates range anywhere from 20 million years to 15 million years ago. In contrast to the paleontologists, Sarich and Wilson estimate this split to be as recent as 3.5 million years ago.[25] This estimate is not based on fossil records but on comparative biochemical analyses of the blood proteins of living primates. It works on the assumption that the closer different forms (for instance, apes and humans) are in the chemical

makeup of their blood, the closer they are in "evolutionary distance." Since Sarich and Wilson's estimate does not seem to be supported by the fossil record, most paleontologists do not accept such a recent date for the split between hominids and other hominoids.

It is not clear yet whether hominids are the descendants of some form of *Dryopithecus* or whether our ancestors evolved from a different group of primates. The first finds of *Ramapithecus* were initially thought to be a species of *Dryopithecus;* not until recent years have they been recognized as a separate grouping or taxon. It is likely that the ancestors of later hominids were some dryopithecine apes which began to move out of the trees and onto the

[25] Vincent M. Sarich and Allan C. Wilson, "Quantitative Immunochemistry and The Evolution of the Primate Albumins," *Science,* 23 December 1966, pp. 1563–1566. See also Vincent M. Sarich, "The Origin of Hominids: An Immunological Approach," in *Perspectives on Human Evolution,* ed. S. L. Washburn and Phyllis C. Jay (New York: Holt, Rinehart and Winston, 1968), vol. 1, pp. 99–121.

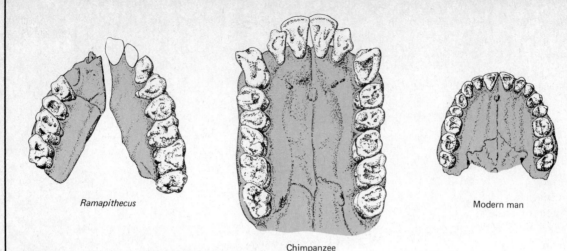

Ramapithecus

Chimpanzee

Modern man

FIGURE 4

Ramapithecus's jaw, which curves out toward the back of the mouth, resembles the human jaw more closely than an ape's jaw. In both *Ramapithecus* and modern man, the tooth rows are not parallel, as they are in apes. A small canine tooth also distinguishes *Ramapithecus* from the apes and helped to identify this fossil as hominid. (Adapted from Elwyn L. Simons, ''On the Mandible of *Ramapithecus*,'' Proceedings of the National Academy of Sciences, United States.)

ground during the Miocene epoch—but we are not sure.[26]

RAMAPITHECUS

The oldest suspected hominid is *Ramapithecus,* specimens of which are about 14 to 12 million years old and have been found in Europe, Asia, and Africa. There is some controversy as to whether *Ramapithecus* is truly a hominid or not. Since we have no fossil remains other than jaws and teeth, no final classification can yet be made. But even on the basis of the available fossil evidence, a number of features place *Ramapithecus* close to, and probably in, the hominid line.

Most important are similarities between the teeth of *Ramapithecus* and later hominids. While apes have long canines which look very different from incisors, hominids and ramapithecines have small canines which are similar in both appearance and function to the incisor teeth. The molars and premolars of *Ramapithecus* also suggest a hominid kind of dentition, since they

are relatively flat, with broad chewing surfaces. A final, tentative inference suggested by *Ramapithecus's* teeth is that he may have had a relatively long infancy and adolescence, as compared to apes. This is suggested by the differential wear of the first to second to third molars, which appear to have erupted at different times, just as in modern humans, and which therefore suggest a longer infancy and adolescence than occur in the apes.[27]

The shape of *Ramapithecus's* jaw is also more reminiscent of later hominids like the Pleistocene australopithecines than it is of apes. The lower jaw is relatively broad and shallow, curving out in a parabolic arch (see Figure 4). This suggests that this early form had a face more humanlike than apelike in both shape and function.

WHAT WAS RAMAPITHECUS LIKE? PUTTING TOGETHER THE PIECES

With no more fossil evidence than teeth and jaws, it is still impossible for us to be sure what

[26]Pilbeam, *The Ascent of Man,* p. 46.

[27]Ibid., pp. 94–96.

Ramapithecus was like. But the way that paleon-tologists have drawn inferences from these few fossils is a good illustration of the process of educated guessing that plays such a large part in piecing together the history of primate and hominid evolution.

What can we infer from the teeth and jaws of *Ramapithecus?* The differences between the dentition of *Ramapithecus* and that of the Mio-cene apes suggest that there were changes in *Ramapithecus's* diet. What the actual diet was is subject to some controversy, but there is agree-ment that the change in diet was probably an adaptation to a somewhat different econiche than that of the apes. During the Miocene epoch, there was a gradual drying trend, which appears to have resulted in a reduction in the tropical rain forests and an increase in open woodlands and grasslands (savannas). As a re-sult of the changing environment, some of the Miocene apes may have begun to exploit more open country for food. As many paleontologists now believe, ramapithecines may have evolved in adaptation to this more open country niche. Clifford Jolly has suggested that many of the hominid adaptations, including adaptations of the teeth and jaws, may have been favored by an increasing dependence upon seed-eating in the open country.[28] He suggests that the forag-ing habits of *Ramapithecus* may have been quite similar to those of the present-day gelada ba-boon, because he sees a number of parallels in the structure of the teeth and jaws of the two primates. The present-day gelada baboon lives in open grassy areas and feeds mostly on seeds which it picks off the ground. Jolly argues that the reduction in canines and incisors in *Ramapithecus* may have been favored by a de-pendence upon seed-eating, since large canines and incisors would have blocked the side-to-side grinding required for seed-eating.

Frederick Szalay disagrees with Jolly about the diet of early hominids.[29] He argues that the

This baboon attempts to extract seeds while sitting up-right, a posture which leaves his forelimbs free to ma-nipulate the seeds. One theory suggests that a shift from a fruit-based to a seed-based diet may have fa-vored a similar adaptation among our early ancestors. (Courtesy of Irven DeVore/Anthro-Photo.)

dentition of the hominids is *not* consistent with a heavy dependence upon seed-eating. He notes that most animals which are grass- and seed-eaters have progressively larger molars toward the back of the jaw (the third being the largest), whereas hominids have a smaller third molar. He suggests that early hominid dentition is more appropriate for meat tearing and bone crushing—adaptations which would have been necessary if the early hominids had become dependent upon hunting and scavenging in their open country habitat.

At one time, it was thought that the smaller hominid canines may have resulted from an increasing dependence upon tools.[30] If tools

[28]Clifford J. Jolly, "The Seed-Eaters: A New Model of Hominid Differentiation Based on Baboon Analogy," *Man* 5 (1970): 5–24.

[29]Frederick S. Szalay, "Hunting-Scavenging Protohominids: A Model for Hominid Origins," *Man*, n.s. 10 (1975): 420–29.

[30]For references and a summary of this earlier theory, see Jolly, "The Seed-Eaters," pp. 5–7.

were used, instead of teeth, to tear meat or vegetation apart, or for defense against predators, then selection in favor of large canines might have been relaxed. But as both Jolly and Szalay point out, this theory does not suggest any positive advantage for canine reduction, only that tool use might have made it possible. But dietary changes—either a switch to seed-eating or a switch to meat-eating—might have positively selected for reduced canines and other alterations in dentition.

Much of what we think about *Ramapithecus* is still subject to controversy. The reasons for *Ramapithecus's* more hominidlike teeth and jaws are open to debate. Whether or not *Ramapithecus* walked erect is still unknown, and therefore its classification as a hominid is uncertain. But we do know that *Ramapithecus's* jaws and teeth show many hominidlike features. And we also know that ramapithecines were quite successful evolutionarily, at least for a period, judging from their wide distribution. We know from fossils that ramapithecines lived in what is now Germany, India, Greece, the Hunan province of China, and Africa. This evidence of success suggests that a form as adaptable as *Ramapithecus* probably did leave some survivors, some of which very likely evolved into a later form that we are more certain was a hominid. One thing is sure: bipedal primates which are clearly hominids did emerge at least several million years ago. What conditions may have favored the emergence of a bipedal adaptation, and what consequences that adaptation may have had for the emergence of human culture, is the subject of the next chapter.

Summary

1. We cannot be sure about how primates evolved. But fossils, a knowledge of ancient environments, and an understanding of comparative anatomy and behavior give us enough clues so that we have a tentative idea of how, when, and why primates and hominids first appeared.

2. There are two main approaches to dating fossils. Relative dating methods using fluorine, nitrogen, and uranium tests tell whether a fossil is about the same age as the deposit in which it is found. Absolute tests like potassium-argon and fission-track dating give the approximate age of a ossil or deposit.

3. We believe that living primates—prosimians, New World monkeys, Old World monkeys, apes, and humans—are descendants of small, originally terrestrial insectivores which resembled modern tree shrews.

4. Changes in climate favored the extensive development of forests. The early primates began to exploit these forests, which provided a largely untapped econiche with many new food resources.

5. Life in the trees favored the development of many primate adaptations, including improved hearing and vision, reduced importance of the sense of smell, a herbivorous diet, and vertical clinging and leaping as a means of locomotion. These changes were reflected in structural modifications over millions of years.

6. All our fossil remains of Oligocene primates come from the Egyptian Fayum, where both apes and monkeys were very common and lived in trees.

7. During the Miocene epoch, an ape known as *Dryopithecus* was common in Europe, Asia, and Africa. It was probably ancestral to modern chimpanzees and gorillas. It may be the strain from which *Ramapithecus* evolved in the Miocene epoch. *Ramapithecus* is thought to be the oldest hominid.

Suggested Readings

Campbell, B. *Human Evolution: An Introduction to Man's Adaptations.* 2d ed. Chicago: Aldine, 1974.
A good general introduction to physical anthropology.

Hill, W. C. O. *Evolutionary Biology of the Primates.* New York: Academic Press, 1972.
Examines the evolution of the order Pri-

mates from archaic prosimians to modern humans, with special emphasis on selected body systems: brain and nervous system, cranial and dental anatomy, digestive and respiratory tracts, and reproductive system anatomy and physiology. Advanced level.

Simons, E. L. *Primate Evolution.* New York: Macmillan, 1972.

A clear, complete discussion of primate evolution from the early Paleocene prosimians through the emergence of *Ramapithecus.*

Tattersall, I. *Man's Ancestors.* London: John Murray, 1970.

An up-to-date, concise treatment of fossil primates. Excellent photographs accompany the clearly written text.

Early Hominids and Their Cultures

5

The ramapithecines from the middle Miocene epoch probably were hominids, but there is no definite fossil evidence that they walked erect. Definite bipedalism *is* indicated for hominids who lived in East Africa more than 3 million years ago. Most of these definitely bipedal hominids have been classified as australopithecines. Whether or not some of them were directly ancestral to modern humans is currently a subject of some debate, since recent finds indicate that forms possibly belonging to our own genus *Homo* may date back as far as some of the australopithecines. If paleontologists come to agree that the *Homo* lineage is as old as the australopithecine, it is not likely that the australopithecines were ancestral to us. In this chapter we shall discuss the emergence of the definitely bipedal hominids—those classified as australopithecines, those possibly belonging to the genus *Homo*, and those definitely belonging to the genus *Homo*. We shall also discuss what is known or suspected about the life-styles or cultures of these various hominids.

Adapting to a Changing Environment

Throughout our discussion of evolution, we have noted the enormous influence of the changing environment upon anatomical and behavioral adaptations. What environmental changes may have been responsible, at least in part, for the emergence of bipedal hominids?

The answer, according to John Napier and others, lies in the environmental changes in Africa, the apparent birthplace of the human lineage.[1] The hominoid apes flourished at the very beginning of the Miocene epoch, when lush tropical rain forests were the predominant econiche. Somewhat later in the Miocene, about 16–11 million years ago, a drying trend set in which continued into the Pliocene. Gradually the African rain forests, deprived of intense humidity and rainfall, dwindled and gave way

[1]John Napier, "The Antiquity of Human Walking," *Scientific American*, April 1967, pp. 56–66.

mostly to grasslands—or *savannas*—and scattered deciduous woodlands. The tree-dwelling primates did not completely lose their customary habitats since some forest areas remained, and natural selection continued to favor the better adapted tree dwellers in those forest areas. But in the new, more open econiches, those characteristics that facilitated adaptation to ground living began to be favored in primates and other animals. In the evolutionary line leading to humans, these adaptations included bipedalism, improved vision, a more sophisticated brain and nervous system, and forms of social organization that may have been appropriate for life in open country.

The Development of Bipedalism

Perhaps the most crucial change in early hominid evolution was the development of bipedalism, or walking on two legs. There are several possible explanations for this development. While all have a degree of merit, some are more plausible than others. In the opinion of many anthropologists, bipedalism was adaptive for life amid the tall grasses of the savannas. True, an upright animal is more conspicuous. But stereoscopic (depth) vision, orginally an adaptation to tree life, combined with an erect posture, may have made it easier to spot ground predators as well as potential prey. It has been suggested that ancestral primates "were sometimes forced to move through the grass between forest areas and that, since this necessitated raising their level of vision, bipedal abilities would have had selective advantages.[2] This theory does not adequately account for the development of bipedalism, however. Baboons and some other Old World monkeys live in savanna-type environments; yet although they can, and do occasionally, stand erect, they have not evolved fully bipedal locomotion.

Other theories stress the importance of freeing the hands. If some hand activity is critical while an animal is moving, selection may favor bipedalism because it fully frees the hands for other activities at the same time. What hand activities might have been so critical?

One suggestion is that carrying food in the hands may have been increasingly important in the new econiche on the ground, particularly if the prehominids were scavenging or hunting meat. Because of the danger of predators, it may have been advantageous to take meat from the kill site to a safer place. Thus, if it was necessary to carry food from one locale to another, moving about only on the hindlimbs would have been adaptive.[3] Similarly, food carrying may be related to the development of partial bipedalism in nonhuman primates. Jane Goodall has seen chimpanzees "loading their arms with choice wild fruits, then walking erect for several yards to a spot of shade before sitting down to eat."[4] The fact that chimpanzees do occasionally carry food for short distances, but are not bipedal, raises the question of why occasional food carrying among prehominids should have favored full-time bipedalism. Perhaps something more important than food carrying was also being done with the hands.

The most likely possibility is that those early terrestrial (ground-living) prehominids were using, and perhaps even making, tools which they needed as they moved about. Consider how advantageous such tool use may have been. Washburn has noted that some contemporary ground-living primates dig for roots to eat, "and if they could use a stone or a stick they might easily double their food supply."[5] Pilbeam also suggests why tool use by the early savanna dwellers may have appreciably increased the number and amount of plant foods that they could eat: in order to be eaten, many of the plant foods in the savanna probably had

[2]Kenneth Oakley, "On Man's Use of Fire, with Comments on Tool-Making and Hunting," in *Social Life of Early Man*, ed. S. L. Washburn (Chicago: Aldine, 1964), p. 186.

[3]Gordon W. Hewes, "Food Transport and the Origin of Hominid Bipedalism," *American Anthropologist* 63 (1961): 687–710.
[4]Jane Goodall, "My Life among Wild Chimpanzees," *National Geographic*, August 1963, p. 293.
[5]Sherwood Washburn, "Tools and Human Evolution," *Scientific American*, September 1960, p. 63.

TABLE 1 An Overview of Human Evolution: Biological and Cultural

Time (years ago)	Geologic Epoch	Fossil Record (first appearance)	Archaeological Periods (Old World)	Major Cultural Developments (first appearance)
			Bronze Age	Cities and states; social inequality; full-time craft specialists
5,500 (3,500 B.C.)				
			Neolithic	Domesticated plants and animals permanent villages
10,000 (8,000 B.C.)				
			Mesolithic	Broad spectrum food collecting; increasingly sedentary communities; many kinds of microliths
14,000 (12,000 B.C.)				
		Earliest Humans in New World	Upper Paleolithic	Cave paintings; female figurines; many kinds of blade tools
40,000		Modern Humans *Homo sapiens sapiens*		
	Pleistocene		Middle Paleolithic	Religious beliefs (?); burials; Mousterian tools
100,000		Neandertal *Homo sapiens*		
		Earliest *Homo sapiens* (?) Fontéchevade		
250,000		Swanscombe Steinheim		
700,000		*Homo erectus*	Lower Paleolithic	Use of fire; big game hunting; Acheulean tools
		Homo erectus (?)		
1,800,000				Hunting and/or scavenging; seasonal campsites; division of labor by sex (?); Oldowan tools
	Pliocene	Earliest Definite Hominids		Earliest stone tools
5,000,000		*Homo* (?) *Australopithecus*		
	Miocene	Earliest Hominids (?) *Ramapithecus*		
22,500,000		*Dryopithecus*		
		Earliest Apes and Monkeys *Aegyptopithecus* *Propliopithecus*		
	Oligocene			
		Parapithecus		
38,000,000		*Apidium*		
	Eocene			
53,500,000		*Plesiadapis* *Tetonius*		
	Paleocene			
65,000,000				
90,000,000	Cretaceous	Earliest primates (?) *Purgatorius*		

Geological dates from W. A. Berggren and J. A. Van Couvering, "The Late Neogene: Biostratigraphy, Geochronology and Paleoclimatology of the Last 15 Million Years in Marine and Continental Sequences," *Palaeogeography, Palaeoclimatology, Palaeoecology* 16 (1974): 13–16, 165.

to be chopped, crushed, or otherwise prepared with the aid of tools.[6] In the new open country niche, tools may have been used also to kill and butcher animals for food. Without tools, primates in general are not well equipped physically for regular hunting. Their teeth and jaws are not sharp and strong enough, and their speed afoot is not fast enough. So the use of tools to kill and butcher game might have even further enlarged the potential supply of food available in the savanna environment. Finally, tools may have been used as weapons against predators, which would have been a great threat to relatively defenseless ground-dwelling prehominids. As Wolpoff has noted: "Faced with a predator, a hominid who knew how to use a club for defense but did not have one available was just as dead as one to whom the notion never occurred."[7] In Wolpoff's opinion, it was the advantage of carrying weapons *continuously* that was responsible for transforming occasional bipedalism to completely bipedal locomotion. Any or all of the manual activities mentioned above may have been the critical factor(s) favoring the development of bipedalism.

The Impact of Bipedalism on Human Evolution

Although the circumstances that favored the development of bipedalism are still controversial, the immensity of its impact on human evolution, and on the emergence of culture in particular, is undisputed. Not only did bipedalism influence the development of toolmaking and the expansion of the brain, but it also had profound effects on human social behavior as well. For example, the long period of dependency of the human infant and the early definition of male and female roles may be traced, in part, to the influence of bipedalism.

[6]David Pilbeam, *The Ascent of Man* (New York: Macmillan, 1972), p. 153.
[7]Milford H. Wolpoff, "Competitive Exclusion among Lower Pleistocene Hominids: The Single Species Hypothesis," *Man* 6 (1971): 602.

BIPEDALISM, TOOLMAKING, AND THE EXPANSION OF THE BRAIN

Although the origin of toolmaking is still not completely understood, two characteristics of our primate ancestors—grasping hands and stereoscopic vision—preadapted the terrestrial primates for the use of tools. The ability to grasp objects and to perceive them in three dimensions facilitates the use and making of tools. But since nonhuman primates also have these same two characteristics, the abilities alone cannot account for the origin of human toolmaking. Clearly, some other factor or factors must have been involved.

Traditionally, the development of bipedalism in hominids was thought to be crucial for the origin of tool use and toolmaking, since bipedalism would have freed the hands for such activities. As we noted above, recently some anthropologists have argued that the sequence was reversed—that tool use and toolmaking came first. According to this theory, the advantages of tool use and toolmaking were so great that natural selection would have favored a more complete bipedalism in a sometimes terrestrial primate. Thus, those terrestrial primates that were more efficient tool users would have been better able to survive in the grassland environment. It may be, however, that both of these theories are partially correct: bipedalism may have interacted with tool use and toolmaking, each one favoring an increase in the other. The benefits derived from efficient tool use would favor a more complete bipedalism, which in turn would free the hands even further for improved tool use and toolmaking.

From australopithecines to the later hominid *Homo erectus*, the volume of the brain expanded, probably in conjunction with the selective forces that adapted the hominids to open-country life. The australopithecine cranial capacity ranged from about 450 to 580 cubic centimeters (cc). *Homo erectus*'s cranial capacity ranged from 900 to 1,200 cc. However, it should be noted that the australopithecine cranial capacity was already relatively large, especially in

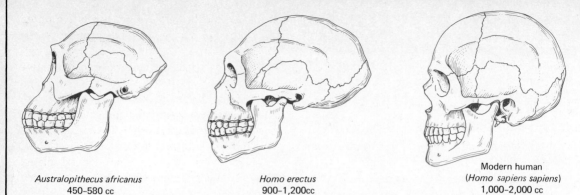

Australopithecus africanus
450–580 cc

Homo erectus
900–1,200cc

Modern human
(Homo sapiens sapiens)
1,000–2,000 cc

FIGURE 1 Comparison of the Range of Cranial Capacities in *Australopithecus africanus, Homo erectus*, and Modern Humans, Demonstrating the Increased Brain Size in Hominid Evolution

the *africanus* form, considering that most of these australopithecines probably weighed only 50–70 pounds. (*Homo erectus* was about the size of a modern human.) Since at least some of the early hominids were toolmakers, the emergence of toolmaking may have favored the expansion of the brain. If we assume that toolmaking was crucial to the survival of our ancestors in the grassland environment, then natural selection may have favored improved motor and conceptual skills, perhaps made possible by an enlarged brain. The larger brain size may, in turn, have favored the evolution of more sophisticated toolmaking.

OTHER CONSEQUENCES OF BIPEDALISM AND TOOLMAKING

In addition to toolmaking and the enlargement of the brain, several other human characteristics may be related to bipedalism. A prolonged period of infant dependency, division of labor between men and women, and food sharing may be traceable, in part, to two-legged walking.

The human pelvis is primarily adapted for upright, two-legged walking and running. As natural selection favored increasing brain size, it also favored the widening of the female pelvis to allow larger-brained babies to be born. But there was probably a limit to how far the pelvis could widen and still be adapted to bipedalism.

Something had to give, and that something was the degree of physical development of the human infant at birth: the human infant is born with cranial bones so plastic that they can overlap. Because birth takes place before the cranial bones have hardened, the human infant with its relatively large brain can pass through the opening in the mother's pelvis.

Another effect of bipedalism, perhaps a consequence of lessened maturity at birth, is the extended period of infant and child dependency that is so distinctively human. Compared to other animals, we spend not only a longer proportion of our life span but also the longest absolute period of time in a dependent state. Prolonged infant dependency has probably been of great significance in human cultural evolution. According to Dobzhansky:

it is this helplessness and prolonged dependence on the ministrations of the parents and other persons that favors in man the socialization and learning process on which the transmission of culture wholly depends. This may have been an overwhelming advantage of the human growth pattern in the process of evolution.[8]

Although some use of tools for hunting may have influenced the development of bipedalism, full bipedalism may have made it possible for more efficient toolmaking and con-

[8] Theodosius Dobzhansky, *Mankind Evolving* (New Haven: Yale University Press, 1962), p. 196.

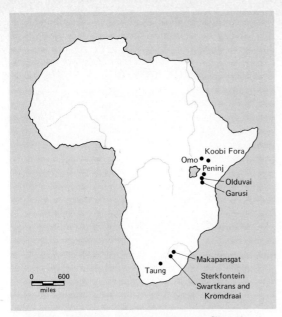

Location of Major *Australopithecus* Sites in East and South Africa.

(Adapted from L. S. Leakey and P. V. Tobias, *Olduvai Gorge*, Vol. 2, Cambridge University Press, 1965.)

sequently more efficient hunting to develop. As we shall see, there are definite archaeological signs that early hominids were hunting or scavenging animals at least as far back as Lower Pleistocene times.

The development of hunting, combined with longer infant and child dependency, may have fostered a division of labor by sex, with men doing the hunting while women tended the children and did other work closer to home. The demands of nursing might have made it difficult for women to hunt. Certainly, it would be awkward, if not impossible, for a mother carrying a nursing child to chase animals. Alternatively, if she left the child at home, she would not be able to travel very far to hunt. Since the men would have been freer to roam farther from home, they probably became the hunters early in human evolution. While the men were away hunting, the women may have gathered wild plants within an area that could be covered in a few hours.

The division of labor by sex may have given rise to another distinctively human characteris-

tic: the sharing of food. If men primarily hunted and women primarily gathered plant foods, the only way each sex could obtain a complete diet would be to share the results of their respective labors.

What is the evidence that the physical and cultural changes we have been discussing occurred during the evolution of the hominids? We shall now trace the sequence of known hominid fossils and how they are associated with the development of bipedalism, brain expansion, toolmaking, and other aspects of cultural development.

Early Hominid Fossils

THE CONTROVERSY OVER THEIR CLASSIFICATION

Undisputed hominids dating back to the Pliocene epoch (about 3.5 million years ago) have been found in East Africa.[9] Still unclassified hominid remains may date back more than 5 million years.[10] Most anthropologists agree that some of these early hominids were ancestral to modern humans, but there is much debate about how to classify the fossils. Some scholars include all these early hominid fossils in one variable species of *Australopithecus*, while others divide them into the gracile and robust species known respectively as *Australopithecus africanus* and *Australopithecus robustus*. Still others see the australopithecines as even more variable, consisting of two separate genera or groups of species—*Australopithecus* and *Paranthropus*. (Those fossils that are classified as *Paranthropus* by some physical anthropologists are the same ones classified as *Australopithecus robustus* by others.) A fourth school of thought divides the early hominids into three groups—two groups of *Australopithecus* plus one group of early *Homo*.

[9] Glynn Isaac, "The Diet of Early Man: Aspects of Archaeological Evidence from Lower and Middle Pleistocene Sites in Africa," *World Archeology* 2 (1971): 287. See also "Man Traced 3.75 Million Years by Fossils Found in Tanzania," *New York Times*, 31 October 1975, pp. 1, 43.

[10] Mark L. Weiss and Alan E. Mann, *Human Biology and Behavior* (Boston: Little, Brown, 1975), p. 172.

These different classification schemes are directly related to the issue of which fossil forms are thought to be ancestral to modern humans.[11] Those who separate the robust and gracile forms think that the robust form died out, while the gracile form continued to evolve toward modern humans. Those who recognize the two genera *Australopithecus* and *Paranthropus* contend that the former was a carnivorous toolmaker who later developed into *Homo*, while the vegetarian *Paranthropus* became extinct. Those who believe that there were three groups of early hominids think that both *Australopithecus* and *Paranthropus* died out, while their contemporary, the early *Homo*, went on to become *Homo habilis*, *Homo erectus*, and eventually, modern humans.

Australopithecines

RAYMOND DART'S TAUNG CHILD

In 1925, Raymond Dart, professor of anatomy at the University of Witwatersrand in Johannesburg, South Africa, presented the first evidence suggesting that an erect bipedal hominid existed in the Pliocene epoch. As he separated the bones from the matrix of material found in Taung, South Africa, Dart realized that he was looking at more than the remains of an ape. He described the experience.

On December 23, the rock parted. I could view the face from the front, although the right side was still embedded. The creature that had contained this massive brain was no giant anthropoid such as a gorilla. What emerged was a baby's face, an infant with a full set of milk teeth and its permanent molars just in the process of erupting.[12]

By the teeth Dart identified the fossil as the remains of a five- to seven-year-old child. He named the specimen *Australopithecus africanus*,

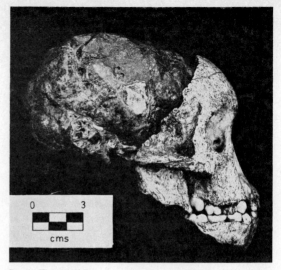

Dart's Taung child, *Australopithecus africanus*. The full set of deciduous (milk) teeth and the erupting permanent molars enabled Dart to identify this specimen as a child. (Courtesy of F. S. Szalay.)

which means "southern ape of Africa." Dart was certain that the skull was that of a bipedal animal. He based his conclusion upon the fact that the *foramen magnum*, the hole in the base of the skull through which the spinal cord passes enroute to the brain, faced downward, indicating that the head was carried directly over the spine. (In monkeys and apes, this passageway is near the back of the skull, in a position more appropriate to a less erect head posture.) Furthermore, the Taung child's incisors and canine teeth were short, definitely more human than apelike.

Dart's conclusion met with widespread skepticism among his colleagues for at least three reasons. First, he had based his conclusion upon only a single fossil. Second, no other hominid fossils had yet been found in Africa. And last, some anthropologists thought that the Taung fossil might be the remains of an exceptionally large-brained chimpanzee.

After years of controversy, Dart's conclusion that this fossil was a hominid was finally accepted. More recent fossils found in both East and South Africa confirm that the australo-

[11] Frank E. Poirier, *Fossil Man: An Evolutionary Journey* (St. Louis: C. V. Mosby, 1973), p. 122.
[12] Raymond Dart, "*Australopithecus africanus:* The Man-Ape of South Africa," *Nature* 115 (1925): 195.

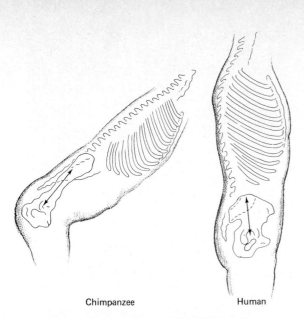

FIGURE 2 Comparison of the Pelvis of a
Chimpanzee and a Human
The human's pelvis curves back, carrying the spine and
trunk erect. The S-shaped spinal column is found only
in hominids. The chimpanzee's pelvis does not curve
back but carries the spine and trunk forward. (Adapted
from William Howells, *Evolution of the Genus Homo*
[Reading, Mass.: Addison-Wesley, 1973], p. 30.)

pithecines were definitely bipedal. Various dating techniques indicate that some of these fossils are as old as 3.5 million years.[13]

AUSTRALOPITHECUS AFRICANUS

Since the Taung child's discovery a half-century
ago, the remains of more than 100 other
australopithecines have been unearthed. From
this abundant evidence a fairly complete picture
of *A. africanus* can be drawn. "The brain case is
rounded with a relatively well-developed forehead. Moderate brow ridges surmount a rather
projecting face."[14] The estimated cranial capacity for the various finds from Taung and Sterk-
fontein is between 428 and 485 cc. In contrast,

modern humans have a cranial capacity of between 1,000 and 2,000 cc., with the majority
falling between 1,350 and 1,450 cc. Although
seemingly small in absolute size, the brain of
A. africanus is relatively large considering that
the hominid's probable body weight has been
estimated at 50–70 pounds.[15]

Australopithecines retained the large chin-
less jaw of the ape, but their dental features
were similar to those of modern humans, with
broad incisors, short canines, and a parabolic
dental arch. Though the premolars and molars
were larger than in modern humans, their form
was quite similar. Presumably, function and use
were also similar. There is evidence from an
analysis of the jaws of young australopithecine
individuals that the eruption of permanent teeth
followed the delayed pattern characteristic of
modern children. This implies that the australopithecines had about as long a period of childhood as modern humans.[16]

The broad, bowl-shaped pelvis, which is
very similar to the human pelvis in form and in
areas for muscle attachments, provides additional evidence for bipedalism. In both
A. africanus and modern humans, the pelvis
curves back, carrying the spine and trunk erect.
In contrast, the ape's pelvis does not curve back;
hence, the spine and trunk of the ape are carried
forward.

The shape of the curve of the australopithecine spine also suggests that these
hominids walked erect. The bottom part of the
vertebral column forms a curve, causing the
spinal column to be S-shaped. This *lumbar curve*
and the S-shaped spinal column are found only
in hominids. Recent analyses of hip joint and
femoral bone fossils also indicate that the
australopithecines walked fully upright, with
the same direct, striding gait observed in modern humans.[17]

[13]F. Clark Howell, "Remains of Hominidae from Pliocene/
Pleistocene Formation in the Lower Omo Basin, Ethiopia," *Nature*
223 (1969): 1234–39.
        [14]Pilbeam, *The Ascent of Man*, p. 107.

[15]Ralph Holloway, "The Casts of Fossil Hominid Brains,"
Scientific American, July 1974, pp. 106–15.
        [16]Alan Mann, "Hominid and Cultural Origins," *Man* 7 (1972):
382.
        [17]Owen Lovejoy, Kingsbury Heiple, and Albert Bernstein,
"The Gait of *Australopithecus*," *American Journal of Physical Anthropology* 38, no. 3 (1973): 757–79.

AUSTRALOPITHECUS ROBUSTUS

A note of confusion was introduced into the study of australopithecines when Broom made new hominid fossil discoveries at Kromdrai and Swartkrans in South Africa. The larger, more robust australopithecines which he found exhibited a number of characteristics that led Broom and others to conclude that they were part of a separate species, distinguishable from *A. africanus*. These *Australopithecus robustus* specimens, as they were called, had larger molars and premolars, smaller incisors and canines, and well developed cranial crests and ridges. While *A. africanus* is estimated to have weighed 50–70 pounds, *A. robustus* probably weighed 100–150 pounds.

As we have already mentioned, anthropologists are not in agreement as to whether these *robustus* fossils are, in fact, the representatives of a separate species or a separate genus. The most prominent supporter of two separate australopithecine groupings is J. T. Robinson.[18] His "dietary hypothesis" that *Australopithecus* (*A. africanus*) was a carnivore and *Paranthropus* (*A. robustus*) was a vegetarian is based partly upon the dental and jaw evidence. In addition, he points to ecological data supposedly suggesting that *A. africanus* lived in a relatively dry period or in dry areas, while the plant-eating *robustus* form lived in a wetter period or in an environment favoring lush vegetable growth. Robinson's theory has been attacked on a number of grounds. Butzer reexamined some of the sites where the two types of australopithecines were found, and he does not think the evidence supports Robinson's suggestion that the two forms lived in different environments.[19] Milford Wolpoff points out that it is unlikely that two separate species would develop in a single econiche.[20] C. Loring Brace has suggested that

the differences in the two sets of fossils may be attributable to male/female differences in size within the same species.[21] Alternatively, David Pilbeam and Stephen J. Gould suggest that the apparent differences may simply be proportional variations in body size. They note that a wide range of individual differences is commonly found in an animal species.[22]

Satisfactory resolution of these and other issues concerning the australopithecines awaits new fossil finds and new theories to assimilate those finds.

MEGANTHROPUS

No traces of an australopithecine have yet been found in Europe, but Asian digs have yielded fragments of a lower jaw of a hominid. The large size of the jaw led its discoverer to name the specimen "Meganthropus." However, the teeth are so similar to those of *A. robustus* that Meganthropus may be a representative of *A. robustus*. Of special interest here is the possibility that australopithecinelike creatures might have inhabited Southeast Asia and Africa at approximately the same time.

HABILIS: HOMO OR AUSTRALOPITHECUS?

Homo habilus is the designation for the skeletal remains of several hominids, found at Olduvai Gorge in Tanzania, which date from about 1.8 million years ago. The *habilis* skull has a cranial capacity of about 650 cc, which is slightly higher than the upper limit observed in *A. africanus*.[23] There is some controversy as to how *habilis* should be classified. Because of its similarities to *A. africanus*, some classify this hominid as a variant of *A. africanus*.[24] Some classify *habilis* as an advanced australopithecine (*Australopithecus*

[18]J. T. Robinson, "Adaptive Radiation in the Australopithecines and the Origin of Man," in *African Ecology and Human Evolution*, ed. F. C. Howell and F. Boulière (Chicago: Aldine, 1963), pp. 385–416.

[19]Karl W. Butzer, "Another Look at the Australopithecine Cave Breccias of the Transvaal," *American Anthropologist* 73 (1971): 1197–1201.

[20]Wolpoff, "Competitive Exclusion among Lower Pleistocene Hominids," pp. 601–13.

[21]C. Loring Brace, "Sexual Dimorphism in Human Evolution," in *Man in Evolutionary Perspective*, ed. C. Loring Brace and James Metress (New York: John Wiley and Sons, 1972), pp. 251–52.

[22]David Pilbeam and Stephen Jay Gould, "Size and Scaling in Human Evolution," *Science*, 6 December 1974, p. 900.

[23]Ian Tattersall, *Man's Ancestors* (London: John Murray, 1970), p. 49.

[24]Ibid.

habilis), intermediate between *A. africanus* and *Homo erectus*.[25] Other physical anthropologists believe that since it has several traits which australopithecines lack, it should be placed in the genus *Homo* (*Homo habilis*). But even though *habilis*'s cranial capacity is larger than *A. africanus*'s, it is still closer to that of *A. africanus* than to the capacity of *Homo erectus*.

Tools found at Olduvai may have been made by *habilis*. Mary Leakey concedes that "although the australopithecine may well have made simple 'tools' to meet his requirements, I am of the opinion that the larger brained *Homo habilis* whose hand bones also indicate a degree of manual dexterity was most likely to have been responsible for the Oldowan [tool assemblage]."[26]

Early Homo Finds

At a news conference on October 31, 1975, Mary Leakey announced the finding of teeth and jaws in Tanzania, twenty-five miles south of Olduvai, which date back 3.75 million years. In her opinion, the fossils belong to our own genus *Homo*.[27] If other researchers concur that the fossils are *Homo* rather than australopithecine, we will have the first proof that early *Homo* forms were contemporaneous with australopithecines. This, in turn, will support the Leakeys' hypothesis that the australopithecines were a side branch of the hominid line and were not ancestral to modern humans.

These recent discoveries lend further credence to a discovery made by Richard Leakey in 1972. At Lake Rudolf in Kenya, he found a fossil (labeled the "1470" skull) which he thought was 2.6 million years old and a representative of the genus *Homo*.[28] The "1470" cranium has a brain capacity of over 800 cc, almost twice the average of *A. africanus*.[29] According to Pilbeam and Gould,[30] this fossil shows cranial, postcranial and dental differences from the australopithecines. In particular, they suggest that the "1470" skull's cranial capacity is relatively larger, given its likely body size, than the australopithecines' cranial capacity. Hence Pilbeam and Gould argue that the "1470" fossil should be classified in the genus *Homo*.

Although the "1470" skull has recently been redated as 1.6 million years old,[31] both this find and the apparently earlier Mary Leakey find, discussed above, suggest that representatives of our genus lived at the same time as some australopithecines. Since these specimens have been discovered so recently, few paleontologists have had a chance to view and classify them. Future analysis of these most recent finds may resolve the question of whether or not some of the australopithecines were ancestral to later humans.

Early Hominid Cultures

TOOL TRADITIONS

The earliest patterned stone tools (and the first indication of hominid culture)[32] have been dated back almost 3 million years.[33] These tools seem to have been made by striking a stone with another stone to remove a flake, a technique known as *percussion flaking*. A number of blows were struck to create a *unifacial* tool, or a tool worked on one side. Further blows struck at a right angle to the facets left by the original blows produced a *bifacial* tool (i.e., a tool worked

---

[25] Pilbeam, *The Ascent of Man*, p. 143.

[26] Mary D. Leakey, "A Review of the Oldowan Culture from Olduvai Gorge, Tanzania," *Nature* 210 (1966): 466.

[27] "Man Traced 3.75 Million Years by Fossils Found in Tanzania," *New York Times*, 31 October 1975, pp. 1, 43.

[28] Richard E. F. Leakey, "Evidence for an Advanced Plio-Pleistocene Hominid from East Rudolf, Kenya," *Nature* 242 (1973): 447–50.

[29] Philip Tobias, "New Developments in Hominid Paleontology in South and East Africa," *Annual Review of Anthropology* 2 (1973): 312.

[30] Pilbeam and Gould, "Size and Scaling in Human Evolution," p. 900.

[31] G. H. Curtis et al., "Age of KBS Tuff in Koobi Fora Formation, East Rudolf, Kenya," *Nature* 258 (1975): 395–98.

[32] Regularly patterned tools are archaeological signs of culture. This is because *culture* is conventionally defined as learned and shared patterns of behavior, thought, and feeling. Therefore, tools made according to a standard pattern and found in different places presuppose some culture.

[33] Glynn Ll. Isaac, Richard E. F. Leakey, and Anna K. Behrensmeyer, "Archeological Traces of Early Hominid Activities, East of Lake Rudolf, Kenya," *Science*, 17 September 1971, pp. 1129–33.

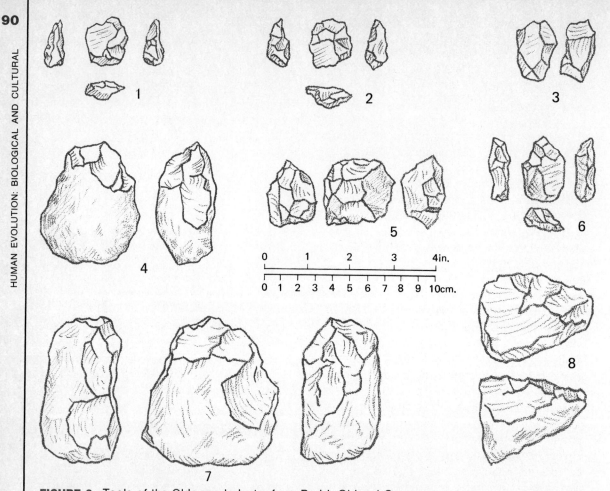

FIGURE 3 Tools of the Oldowan Industry from Bed I, Olduvai Gorge

Numbers 1, 2, minimally retouched flakes; 3, modified chunks with utilized notches; 4, 5, bifacially worked choppers; 6, flake scrapers; 7, protohandaxes; 8, unifacial choppers. (From *The Prehistory of Africa* by J. Desmond Clark. © 1970 in London, England, by J. Desmond Clark. Reprinted by Praeger Publishers, New York.)

on two sides) which could be used for chopping. The flakes struck from the pebble core could also be used. When it became dull, the pebble tool could be discarded and a new one quickly fashioned with a few careful blows from a hammerstone or other pebble tool.

Tools more than 2.6 million years old have been found in a campsite east of Lake Rudolf in Kenya by Richard Leakey and his colleagues. Most of the tools were flakes or flake fragments, although a few choppers and light-duty tools were found as well.[34] What were the tools used for? What do they tell us about early hominid culture? Unfortunately, little can be inferred about life-styles from the tool sites because little else is found associated with these tools.

In contrast, finds of later tool assemblages at Olduvai Gorge have yielded a rich harvest of cultural information. The Olduvai site was uncovered accidentally in 1911 when a German entomologist, chasing a butterfly, followed it into the gorge and found a number of fossil remains. Beginning in the 1930s, Louis and Mary Leakey patiently searched the gorge for clues to the evolution of early humans. Of the Olduvai site Louis Leakey wrote:

[34] Ibid., p. 1131.

Olduvai is a fossil hunter's dream, for it shears 300 feet through stratum after stratum of earth's history as through a gigantic layer cake. Here, within reach, lie countless fossils and artifacts which but for the faulting and erosion would have remained sealed under thick layers of consolidated rock.[35]

The oldest cultural materials from Olduvai (Bed I) date from Lower Pleistocene times. Artifacts found in Bed I include collections of natural stones (called *manuports*) and chipped stone tools, with bashers, choppers, and flaked knives predominating. While they are simple in form, these tools are evidence that whoever made them had systematic knowledge of stoneworking technology.[36] The kind of tool assemblage found in Bed I, and to some extent in later layers, is referred to as *Oldowan*. Clark speculates that some of these tools were used to break down tough plant fibers and nuts and to crack animal bones. Experiments with some of these tools suggest that they could have been used to sharpen sticks for digging out plants or small animals from the ground. Some of the flakes appear to have been useful for skinning and cutting.[37] These tools and associated fragments of animal bones seem to indicate that the toolmakers subsisted on a partly carnivorous diet based upon hunting or scavenging and brought meat back to a home base. Bringing meat back home suggests that the early hominids in Olduvai were practicing a characteristic human custom—food sharing.[38]

LIFE-STYLES

The data from Bed I and the lower part of Bed II (the next oldest layer) suggest a few other things about the social organization and economic practices of the early hominids in the area of Olduvai. First, it seems that campsites may have been shifted seasonally; most of the sites in

[35] L. S. B. Leakey, "Finding the World's Earliest Man," *National Geographic*, September 1960, p. 424.

[36] J. Desmond Clark, *The Prehistory of Africa* (New York: Praeger, 1970), p. 68.

[37] Ibid., pp. 69–70.

[38] Isaac, "The Diet of Early Man," p. 288.

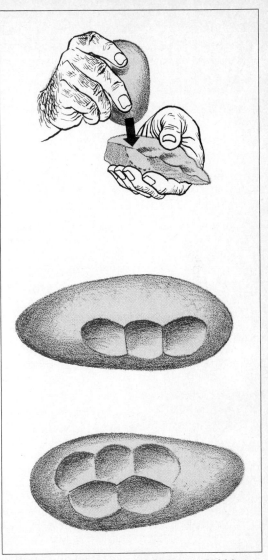

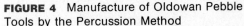

FIGURE 4 Manufacture of Oldowan Pebble Tools by the Percussion Method

Using a hammerstone, the toolmaker strikes a blow near the edge of the pebble to break off flakes (*top*). A pebble from which three flakes have been removed by blows from a hammerstone (*center*). The pebble is turned over, and two more flakes are removed adjacent to the ridges created by the three previous flake scars. The result is a crooked working edge where the ridges of the flake scars meet (*bottom*). Tools also were made from flakes. (Adapted from F. Clark Howell, *Early Man*, a Time-Life Books publication; and from *Tools of the Old and New Stone Age* by Jacques Bordaz. Copyright © 1970 by Jacques Bordaz. Copyright © 1958, 1959 by The American Museum of Natural History. Reproduced by permission of Doubleday & Company, Inc.)

what is now the Olduvai Gorge appear to have been dry season sites, judging by a recent analysis of the kinds of animal bones found there.[39] Second, the size of some site areas and the amounts of cultural and bone material in them suggest that some of the bands of early hominids were larger than family groups.[40] Third, whether the early Olduvai hominids were hunters or scavengers, they apparently exploited a wide range of animals. Although most of the bones are from medium-size antelopes and wild pigs, even large animals, such as elephants and giraffes, seem to have been eaten.[41]

Finally, and most tentatively, the early Olduvai hominids may have had a division of labor by sex—the males doing the hunting or scavenging, the females doing the nearby gathering and child tending. Although such a division of labor is by no means obvious in the archaeological record, there are some facts which are consistent with it. In recent hunter-gatherer societies, it is mostly the men who hunt and bring back meat to be shared with members of the band. Since the early Olduvai hominids show evidence of prolonged infant dependency in their delayed eruption of permanent teeth,[42] the problem of how to hunt *and* care for nursing children may already have emerged. Thus, a division of labor by sex may well have been a part of the early hominid life-style.

In summary, it now appears that a number of physical and cultural features were associated with bipedalism in the early hominids: a relatively enlarged brain, prolonged infant and child dependency, patterned stone tools, and some dependence upon hunting or scavenging. Probably the early hominids also lived in multi-family bands, had a division of labor by sex, and shared food. Whether or not some of the early hominids are to be classified as belonging to the genus *Homo*, there is no question that

hominids from later in the Pleistocene epoch can be so classified. Conventionally, these hominids are now referred to as *Homo erectus*.

Homo erectus

DISCOVERY OF HOMO ERECTUS IN JAVA

In 1891, Eugene Dubois, a Dutch anatomist digging in Java, found what he called *Pithecanthropus erectus*, meaning "erect ape man." (We now refer to this hominid as *Homo erectus*.) Since the discovery was the first humanlike fossil (*Australopithecus* was not discovered until the 1920s), no one was certain, not even Dubois himself, whether the animal was an ape or a human.

The actual find consisted of a cranium and a thighbone. For many years it was thought that the fragments were not even from the same animal. The skull was too large to be that of a modern ape and was smaller than that of an average human, with a cranial capacity between the average ape's 500 cc and the average modern human's 1,400 cc. The thighbone, however, matched that of a modern human. Did the two fragments, in fact, belong together? The question was resolved by fluorine analysis. The amount of fluorine which accumulates in bones increases as the bones lie in the earth. If fossils from the same deposit contain the same amount of fluorine, they are of the same age; if they contain different amounts, fluorine analysis can establish their relative ages. The skull fragment and thighbone found by Dubois were tested for their fluorine content and were found to be of the same age.

A later discovery made by G. H. R. von Koenigswald in the mid-1930s, also in Java, not only confirmed Dubois's earlier speculations and extended our knowledge of *Homo erectus*'s physical characteristics but also gave us a better understanding of this early human's place in time. The Java finds date back 700,000 years ago. As we shall see below, *Homo erectus* may be even older.

[39]John D. Speth and Dave D. Davis, "Seasonal Variability in Early Hominid Predation," *Science*, 30 April 1976, pp. 441–45.
[40]Glynn Ll. Isaac, "Studies of Early Culture in East Africa," *World Archeology* 1 (1969): 11.
[41]Isaac, "The Diet of Early Man." p. 289.
[42]Mann, "Hominid and Cultural Origins," p. 382.

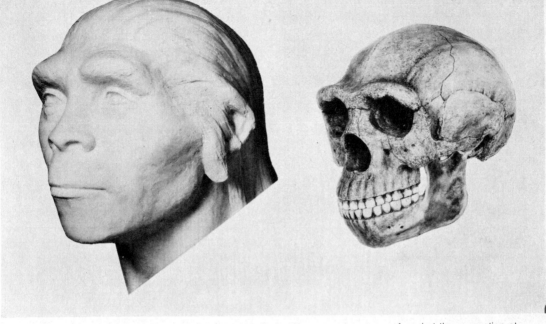

Franz Weidenreich's reconstruction of the head and skull of a *Homo erectus* woman found at the excavation at Choukoutien, China. Note the small teeth as in modern humans, but brow ridges are still present. (Courtesy of the American Museum of Natural History.)

HOMO ERECTUS OUTSIDE OF JAVA

Between the times of Dubois's and von Koenigswald's discoveries, Davidson Black, a Canadian anatomy professor teaching in Peking, China, found a single molar in a large cave at nearby Choukoutien. Confident that the tooth was from a hitherto unknown hominid genus, he set out to excavate the area extensively. After digging carefully for two years, he found a skull in limestone which he dubbed "Peking man." Black died in 1934, and his work was carried on by Franz Weidenreich. The original finds at Choukoutien were lost during the Japanese invasion of China in December 1941, but Weidenreich had sent casts of the fossils to the United States. Other *Homo erectus* fossils have been located in Germany, Hungary, Czechoslovakia, Morocco, Algeria, Israel, and South and East Africa, indicating a widespread

distribution of the genus.[43] Until very recently it was not thought that *Homo erectus* was older than about 700,000 years.

On March 8, 1976, Richard Leakey and Donald Johanson held a news conference to report a find in Kenya indicating that *Homo erectus* may be much older than previously believed. The Kenya find, a skull, has been tentatively dated as 1.5 million years old. Since the skull was found in the same area where australopithecine fossils of the same age have been found, Leakey suggests this is further evidence that the ancestors of modern humans did not include australopithecines.

PHYSICAL CHARACTERISTICS OF HOMO ERECTUS

The *Homo erectus* skull was long, low, thickly walled, with a flat frontal area and prominent

[43]Poirier, *Fossil Man*, pp. 134–37.

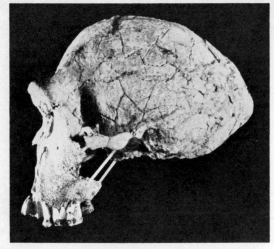

On March 8, 1976, Richard Leakey and Donald Johanson reported finding a *Homo erectus* skull from Kenya dated tentatively as 1.5 million years old. If others agree that this find is *Homo erectus*, this will indicate that *Homo erectus* is much older than previously believed. (National Geographic Society photograph.)

brow ridges. The teeth of *Homo erectus* were relatively small and arranged as in modern humans. The brain was larger than that found in any of the australopithecines but smaller than the average brain of a modern human.[44] The rear part of the brain, the visual center, was as fully developed as in modern humans. The center and sides of the brain—the speech, sensory, memory, and motor areas—were larger than the australopithecines' but smaller than those of modern humans. The comparative underdevelopment of the forebrain, that part of the brain that controls conceptual thought, also suggests that *Homo erectus*'s capacity for language and culture was probably not as well developed as in modern humans. From the neck down, *Homo erectus* was practically indistinguishable from *Homo sapiens*. The size of the long bones indicates that a *Homo erectus* male was about 5 feet 6 inches tall, the same height as the average European man.

There are some differences between the Java and Peking specimens with respect to cranial capacity and dental features. The Peking

[44] Tattersall, *Man's Ancestors*, pp. 51–54.

specimens had higher and less sloping foreheads, and their cranial capacity was about 1,000 cc as compared with the 900 cc average for the Java specimens. *Homo erectus* from Peking had a shorter, rounder palate than the Java forms. Thus, the Peking *erectus* face more closely resembled the modern human face, but the jaw did not have a chin. The teeth in the Peking jaw were smaller than those of the australopithecines and the Java *erectus* specimens. The smaller teeth in the Peking specimens, especially the smaller canines, may be related to the use of fire, perhaps for cooking. (We shall discuss the use of fire below.)

Homo erectus Cultures

TOOL TRADITIONS

A toolmaking tradition known as the *Acheulean*, after the site at St. Acheul, France, where the first examples were found, is generally associated with *Homo erectus*. But this tradition may precede *Homo erectus* in time, and it persists into later times when *Homo sapiens* was on the scene. An Acheulean type of tool assemblage is characterized by large cutting implements, such as the so-called handaxes and cleavers, made from large flakes. Tens of thousands of such tools have been found, indicating their widespread and varied use. Early Acheulean tools are cruder and more haphazard in design than the specialized creations of the later Acheulean.

During the Acheulean period, a technique was developed which enabled the toolmaker to produce flake tools of a predetermined size, instead of simply chipping the flakes away from the core at random. In the *Levalloisian* method, the toolmaker first shaped the core and prepared a "striking platform" at one end. Flakes of predetermined size could then be chiseled off.

THE USE OF FIRE

For the first time in the archaeological record, some of the *Homo erectus* sites show evidence of the deliberate use of fire. Thousands of splin-

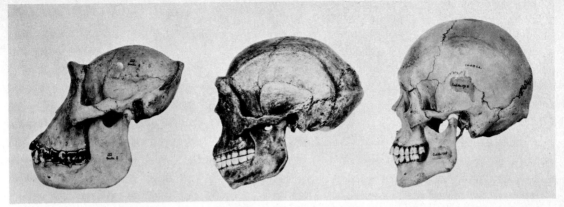

Note the large canines in the gorilla and their reduction in the *Homo erectus* and modern human (left, center, and right, respectively). The brow ridges are reduced in *Homo erectus* and absent in the modern human. Note, too, the reduction of the flaring upper and lower jaws, the emergence of the chin, and the more rounded cranium in the modern human. (Courtesy of the American Museum of Natural History.)

Acheulean hand ax, found at St. Acheul, France, in 1871. (Courtesy of the American Museum of Natural History.)

tered and charred animal bones found in the Choukoutien caves may have been the remains of the Peking population's meals. Evidently, these hominids were hunters who had learned how to use fire. Traces of deliberate use of fire have also been observed at the Escale Cave in southern France's Durance Valley and in Torralba, Spain. Although these three *Homo*

erectus sites differ culturally from each other in several respects, all are notable for their early control over this immeasurably significant force. Where or when the use of fire began is not known. The most reasonable guess is that naturally occurring fires, produced by volcanoes and lightning, may have been used by *Homo erectus* to sustain and start other fires.

Of tremendous importance to human cultural development, the making of fires was a major step in increasing the energy under human control. Cooking with fire made animal meat, including human flesh, more digestible. The charred and split human bones found among the remains of sheep, mammoths, and ostriches in the Choukoutien caves suggest that cannibalism was practiced; from the discovery of many split long bones, we can infer that the *Homo erectus* population there ate the marrow. Brains, too, were probably part of the diet at Choukoutien. In several skulls there, the foramen magnum, the opening at the base of the skull, had been enlarged, presumably to remove the brain within.

BIG-GAME HUNTING

Some of the *Homo erectus* sites have produced highly persuasive evidence of cooperative big-game hunting. Although *Homo erectus* was still

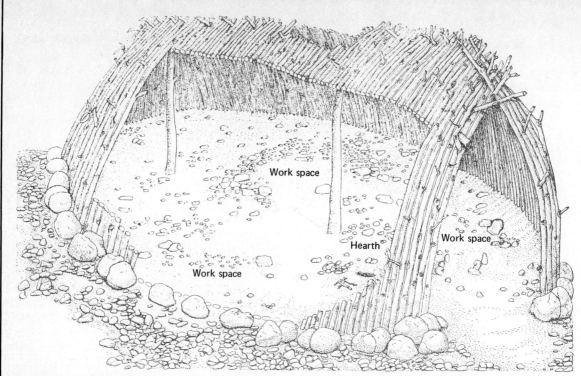

FIGURE 5 A Reconstruction of the Oval Huts Built at Terra Amata by Visiting Hunters
These huts were approximately 30 by 15 feet in size. (From "A Paleolithic Camp at Nice," by Henry de Lumley. Copyright © 1969 by Scientific American, Inc. All rights reserved.)

heavily dependent upon plant food, numerous finds of bones of medium- and large-size animals indicate the use of more efficient hunting methods, employing spears, stone-throwing, and fire. F. Clark Howell, who excavated the sites at Torralba and Ambrona, Spain, found a substantial number of elephant remains and the unmistakable signs of human presence in the evidence of fire and tools. Howell suggests that *Homo erectus* used fire to frighten elephants into muddy bogs, where they would be unable to escape.[45] To hunt elephants in this way, these hominids probably had to plan and work cooperatively in fairly large groups. Game was undoubtedly plentiful then, as it still is in some parts of Africa. A 1959 census of 230 square miles of Africa counted 7,400 buffaloes and 1,026 elephants—in all, about 130,000 pounds of big game per square mile.[46]

Some anthropologists theorize that organized group hunting (as well as more sophisticated stoneworking) could only have been achieved through the hominids' ability to speak and effectively communicate the new techniques. Increased cranial capacity and muscular modifications of the jaw support the contention that *Homo erectus* had at least some speech ability.[47]

CAMPSITES

Homo erectus living sites were usually located close to water sources, lush vegetation, and large stocks of herbivorous animals. Some camps have been found in caves, but most were

[45] F. Clark Howell, "Observations on the Earlier Phases of the European Lower Paleolithic (Torralba-Ambrona)," in *Recent Studies in Paleoanthropology, American Anthropologist*, Special Publication, April 1966, pp. 111–40.

[46] John E. Pfeiffer, *The Emergence of Man* (New York: Harper & Row, 1969), p. 113.
[47] Clark, *The Prehistory of Africa*, pp. 100–102.

in open areas surrounded by some rudimentary fortifications or windbreaks. Several African sites are marked by stony rubble clearly brought there by *Homo erectus,* possibly for the dual purpose of securing the windbreaks and providing ammunition in a sudden attack.[48]

All the base campsites display a wide variety of tools, indicating that the camp was the center of many group functions. More specialized sites away from camp have also been found, marked by the predominance of a particular type of tool. For example, a butchering site in Tanzania contained dismembered hippopotamus carcasses and rare heavy-duty smashing and cutting tools. Workshops are another kind of specialized site encountered with some regularity. Workshops are characterized by tool debris and are located close to a source of natural stone suitable for toolmaking.[49]

One of the most complete examples of a *Homo erectus* camp is the Terra Amata site near Nice, on the French Riviera. The camp appears to have been seasonally occupied by visiting hunters in the late spring or early summer. (The time has been fixed by analysis of pollen found in fossilized human feces.) A series of stakeholes driven into sand and paralleled by lines of stones marks the spots where the hunters constructed huts roughly 30 by 15 feet in size. A basic feature of each hut was a central hearth which seems to have been protected from drafts by a small wall built just outside the northeast corner of the hearth. The evidence indicates that the Terra Amata visitors gathered seafood such as oysters and mussels, did some fishing, and hunted in the surrounding area. Judging by the animal remains, they hunted both small and large animals but preferred the young of larger animals such as stags, elephants, boars, rhinoceroses, and wild oxen. Some of the huts contain recognizable toolmakers' areas, scattered with tool debris; occasionally, the impression of an animal skin shows where the toolmaker actually sat.[50]

[48] Ibid., pp. 94–95.
[49] Ibid., pp. 96–97.
[50] Henry de Lumley, "A Paleolithic Camp at Nice," *Scientific American,* May 1969, pp. 42–50.

The cultures of the early hominids and *Homo erectus* are known collectively as the Lower Paleolithic. In the next chapter, we shall discuss the emergence of *Homo sapiens* and some of the cultural developments in the Middle and Upper Paleolithic periods.

Summary

1. The drying climate which occurred about 16–11 million years ago diminished the African rain forests and gave rise to grasslands. This change reduced the econiches for tree dwellers and created selective pressures for terrestrial adaptation—pressures which favored bipedalism, improved stereoscopic vision, and a complex brain and nervous system in the line leading to humans.

2. One of the most crucial changes in early hominid evolution was the development of bipedalism. There are several theories to explain its development: it may have increased the emerging hominid's ability to see predators and potential prey while moving through the tall grasses of the savanna; by freeing the hands for carrying it may have facilitated transferring food from one place to another; and finally, tool use, which required free hands, may have favored two-legged walking.

3. In addition to toolmaking and the enlargement of the brain, several other human characteristics may be related to bipedalism. A prolonged period of infant dependency, division of labor between men and women, and food sharing may be traceable, in part, to two-legged walking.

4. The dimensions of the female pelvis and the birth canal are primarily adapted to bipedalism. Because of increased brain size, the infant must be born while still immature in order to pass through the birth canal. The hominid infant therefore remained dependent upon its mother for a long time. Females carrying children were probably able to forage for vegetation but may have been de-

pendent upon males for meat. Sexual division of labor, then, as well as the distinctively human habit of food sharing, seems to have been influenced by bipedalism.

5. Undisputed hominids dating back to the Pliocene (about 3.5 million years ago) have been found in East Africa. Unclassified hominid remains may date back more than 5 million years, but there is much debate about how to classify them. We do not know whether some of these fossils belong to our own genus *Homo* or to the genus of *Australopithecus*.

6. The earliest patterned stone tools (and the first indication of hominid culture) have been dated back almost 3 million years. At least some of the early hominids probably hunted or scavenged for meat and lived in multi-family bands.

7. Later hominids (*Homo erectus*) from later in the Pleistocene period can be definitely classified as belonging to the genus *Homo*. *Homo erectus*, perhaps older than 700,000 years, had teeth arranged as in modern humans but a brain smaller than the average brain of modern humans. *Homo erectus* sites show that these hominids had mastered the use of fire and probably hunted big-game cooperatively. The *Acheulean* tool tradition—characterized by large cutting tools, such as hand-axes and cleavers, made from large flakes—is generally associated with *Homo erectus*.

Suggested Readings

Clark, J. D. *The Prehistory of Africa*. New York: Praeger, 1970.
An overview of the fossil and archaeological records in Africa.

Coles, J. M., and Higgs, E. S. *The Archeology of Early Man*. London: Faber and Faber, 1970.
In this introduction to Paleolithic archaeology, the authors present an encyclopedic inventory of major sites, organized according to geographical region: Africa, Europe, Asia, the New World. Each section is preceded by a chronology of the area and a short summary of environmental factors during the Pleistocene epoch.

Howells, W. *Evolution of the Genus Homo*. Reading, Mass: Addison-Wesley, 1973.
A discussion of the processes and problems of the study of early human fossils, tracing human evolution from australopithecines to Neandertals.

Leakey, M. D. *Olduvai Gorge*. Cambridge: Cambridge University Press, 1971.
This is an updated version of Leakey's monumental report of Olduvai. Photographs, maps, and diagrams form an exhaustive catalog of the site and the fossils that were unearthed there. This is the most complete primary source on Oldowan cultures.

Pfeiffer, J. E. *The Emergence of Man*, revised and enlarged ed. New York: Harper & Row, 1972.
A well-written survey of human evolution which incorporates results from modern-day hunter-gatherers. Particularly relevant here are chapters 1–7.

Pilbeam, D. *The Ascent of Man*. New York: Macmillan, 1972.
A concisely written review of major evolutionary trends leading to the development of *Homo sapiens*. The author outlines the major evolutionary stages according to the various geographical areas in which specimens have been discovered.

The Emergence of Homo sapiens and Middle and Upper Paleolithic Cultures

6

The last *Homo erectus* fossils date from about 300,000 years ago. Fossil evidence for what happened during the following 200,000 or so years is almost totally lacking. What we do have from that period (300,000–100,000 years ago) can almost be held in two hands. Those scanty remains suggest that early forms of our species, *Homo sapiens,* may have emerged about 250,000 years ago. Undisputed remains of *Homo sapiens* become plentiful after about 75,000 years ago. Many of these fossils are called Neandertals, after the valley in Germany where some of them were found. Finally, about 35,000 years ago, we see the first undisputed examples of modern humans. In this chapter we shall discuss the fossil evidence for the transition from *Homo erectus* to modern humans. In addition to reviewing the fossil evidence bearing on that transition, we shall also discuss how cultures varied in the Middle and Upper Paleolithic periods, from about 80,000 to about 14,000 years ago.

Early Homo sapiens

A few fragmentary fossil remains from the Mindel-Riss interglacial period in Europe (perhaps 300,000 to about 200,000 years ago) suggest to some anthropologists that *Homo sapiens* may have emerged by that time. Whether these fossils belong to our own species or not, they show signs of being closer evolutionarily to modern humans than to *Homo erectus.*

THE STEINHEIM SKULL

Discovered in Steinheim, Germany, in 1935, this find consisted of an almost complete skull, lacking only part of the face and the lower jaw. The cranial capacity of the skull is about 1,150 cc, which is in the upper part of the range for *Homo erectus.* But a number of the skull's characteristics are similar to those found in later, more modern humans. For example, the back of the Steinheim skull is rounded, like the modern human head, and there is little projection of the face beyond the brow ridges.[1]

THE SWANSCOMBE SKULL

Three skull fragments discovered at different times over a period of twenty years at Swanscombe, England (not far from London) apparently come from the same individual. The back of the Swanscombe skull seems very similar to the Steinheim skull, but it has been estimated that the Swanscombe skull has a somewhat greater cranial capacity (around 1,300 cc).[2] Taken together, the Swanscombe and Steinheim finds suggest that a post-*Homo erectus* hominid having some modern features existed by about 200,000 years ago.

THE FONTÉCHEVADE FOSSILS

Discovered in 1947 in France, the Fontéchevade find consists of skull fragments from two different individuals who lived between 200,000 and 145,000 years ago.[3] Thus, the Fontéchevade hominids lived somewhat later than the ones found at Steinheim and Swanscombe. The Fontéchevade specimens show some more modern features than either Steinheim and Swanscombe: there appear to be no brow ridges and the forehead seems to be fairly steep. But the bone structure is fairly thick, which is not a particularly modern feature.[4] Whether the Fontéchevade specimens should be grouped taxonomically with the earlier possible *Homo sapiens* found at Steinheim and Swanscombe, or with the later so-called Neandertal varieties of *Homo sapiens*, is a matter of some dispute among physical anthropologists. Trinkaus has recently suggested that the Fontéchevade fossils may lack brow ridges because they could be from

[1] Ian Tattersall, *Man's Ancestors* (London: John Murray, 1970), p. 55.

[2] Ibid., pp. 55–56.

[3] This recently revised absolute date is given in R. Saban, "Les Restes Humains de Rabat (Kébibat)," *Annales de Paléontologie* (*Vertébrés*) 61 (1975): 196–97.

[4] Tattersall, *Man's Ancestors*, p. 56.

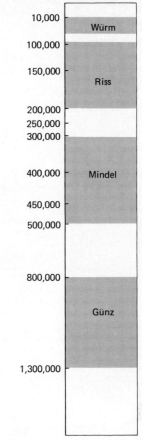

FIGURE 1

The accompanying diagram illustrates the chronology of the four major Pleistocene glaciations in Alpine Europe (Günz, Mindel, Riss, and Würm) when ice sheets advanced in that area. These were separated by three interglacials (Günz-Mindel, Mindel-Riss, and Riss-Würm), when the ice sheets retreated and the climate became warmer. A more recent picture of the glaciations suggests that each major glaciation consisted of many advances and retreats of the ice sheet, rather than one huge advance or glacial period and one large retreat and interglacial. (Adapted from R. Saban, "Les Restes Humains de Rabat (Kébibat)," *Annales de Paléontologie* (*Vertébrés*) 61 [1975]:196–97.)

immature individuals. Hence, they might have developed brow ridges if they had lived longer; and if so, they might be classifiable as Neandertal. In any case, he points out that the

TABLE 1 An Overview of Human Evolution: Biological and Cultural

Time (years ago)	Geologic Epoch	Fossil Record (first appearance)	Archaeological Periods (Old World)	Major Cultural Developments (first appearance)
5,500 (3,500 B.C.)			Bronze Age	Cities and states; social inequality; full-time craft specialists
			Neolithic	Domesticated plants and animals permanent villages
10,000 (8,000 B.C.)				
			Mesolithic	Broad spectrum food collecting; increasingly sedentary communities; many kinds of microliths
14,000 (12,000 B.C.)				
40,000		Earliest Humans in New World Modern Humans *Homo sapiens sapiens*	Upper Paleolithic	Cave paintings; female figurines; many kinds of blade tools
	Pleistocene		Middle Paleolithic	Religious beliefs (?); burials; Mousterian tools
100,000		Neandertal *Homo sapiens*		
250,000		Earliest *Homo sapiens* (?) Fontéchevade Swanscombe Steinheim		
700,000		*Homo erectus*	Lower Paleolithic	Use of fire; big game hunting; Acheulean tools
1,800,000	————	*Homo erectus* (?)		Hunting and/or scavenging; seasonal campsites; division of labor by sex (?); Oldowan tools
5,000,000	Pliocene ————	Earliest Definite Hominids *Homo* (?) *Australopithecus*	————	Earliest stone tools
22,500,000	Miocene ————	Earliest Hominids (?) *Ramapithecus* *Dryopithecus*		
38,000,000	Oligocene ————	Earliest Apes and Monkeys *Aegyptopithecus* *Propliopithecus* *Parapithecus* *Apidium*		
53,500,000	Eocene ————	*Plesiadapis* *Tetonius*		
65,000,000	Paleocene ————			
90,000,000	Cretaceous	Earliest primates (?) *Purgatorius*		

Geological dates from W. A. Berggren and J. A. Couvering, "The Late Neogene: Biostratigraphy, Geochronology and Paleoclimatology of the Last 15 Million Years in Marine and Continental Sequences," *Palaeogeography, Palaeoclimatology, Palaeoecology* 16 (1974):13–16, 165.

evidence is so scanty as to preclude a definite conclusion about the taxonomic status of the Fontéchevade fossils.[5]

The Neandertals

Somehow, through the years, the Neandertals have become the victims of their cartoon image. Usually portrayed as burly and more ape than human, they are misrepresented. Actually, they might go unnoticed in a cross-section of the world's population.

In 1856, three years prior to Darwin's publication of *On the Origin of Species,* a fossil was discovered in a cave in the Neander Valley (*Tal* is the German word for valley) near Dusseldorf, Germany. After Darwin's revolutionary work was published, the Neandertal fossil was acclaimed as a premodern human by evolutionists and dismissed as an oddity by doubters. The controversy centered around whether Neandertal was an early human or a modern pathological freak. "A prominent anatomist reported that the fossils were those of an idiot who had suffered rickets and other bone diseases and had a violent disposition. The flat forehead and heavy brows, he explained, had been caused by blows on the head."[6]

Neandertal's position continued to be controversial until the discovery of two more skulls in Belgium in 1887 and then the finding of numerous other remains throughout the world (in Europe, Morocco, Israel, Iraq, China, Indonesia, North and South Africa) after the turn of the century. These fossils were also referred to as Neandertal because they resembled the fossil in the Neander Valley. However, all these finds could not be dismissed as oddities, as aberrations with no relation to humans. Now it was clear that they represented a widely distributed population of humans.

Part of the reason for the previous relega-

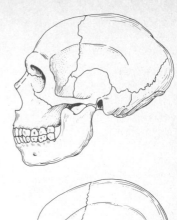

A Classic or Western European Neandertal

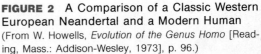

A Modern Human

FIGURE 2 A Comparison of a Classic Western European Neandertal and a Modern Human (From W. Howells, *Evolution of the Genus Homo* [Reading, Mass.: Addison-Wesley, 1973], p. 96.)

tion of Neandertal to less than *Homo sapiens* status was based upon a highly respected, but erroneous, study of a skeleton uncovered in 1908 in southern France, near the village of La Chapelle-aux-Saints. The curvature of the spine and feet of the skeleton was said to suggest ape-like qualities. The specimen was therefore classified as the remains of an ape-like creature.

This misleading study was regarded as a credible and valuable source of information about Neandertals until 1957, when William Straus and Alec Cave examined the skeleton.[7] They concluded that the specimen was probably an elderly Neandertal male between forty and fifty years of age who suffered from arthritis of the jaws, spine, and possibly the lower limbs. Neandertal likenesses to modern hu-

[5] Erik Trinkaus, "A Reconsideration of the Fontéchevade Fossils," *American Journal of Physical Anthropology* 39 (1973): 25–35.

[6] John E. Pfeiffer, *The Emergence of Man* (New York: Harper & Row, 1969), p. 160.

[7] W. L. Straus and A. J. E. Cave, "Pathology and Posture of Neandertal Man," *Quarterly Review of Biology* 32 (1957): 348–63.

mans, long overlooked because of the emphasis on the differences, could no longer be ignored. As a result, Neandertals are now classified as *Homo sapiens.*

Physical anthropologists have traditionally distinguished two kinds of Neandertals—a western European, or "classic," form (classic because it was found first), and other forms referred to as "progressive" or "generalized." The terms "classic" and "progressive" or "generalized" are unfortunate, because the classic form seems to have appeared later in time than some of the other Neandertals. The classic Neandertals, which are found only in western Europe, are no more than about 70,000 years old; but other Neandertals (which are found in Asia, Africa, and Europe) may be as much as 100,000 years old.[8]

THE CLASSIC FORM

The various specimens of classic Neandertal are very similar to each other in appearance. Their cranial capacity averages 1,470 cc, which is about 100 cc more than the average capacity in modern humans. They had thick skulls, heavy brow ridges, large eye sockets, broad noses, long jaws, low foreheads, forward projection of the face (*prognathism*), and no chins. It has been estimated from the skeletons that classic Neandertal males averaged just over 5 feet in height and about 160 pounds in weight. The body build appears to have been stocky and muscular.[9]

F. Clark Howell and Carleton Coon have suggested that the distinctive classic Neandertal features may be adaptations to the glacial environment of western Europe at that time. During the period in which the Neandertals lived, glaciers extended southward over northern Europe; the climate was very cold and dry. Most of the region was covered with ice and snow, and reindeer and cave bear roamed the area. Classic Neandertal's large nose (indicated by the size of

the nasal bones and aperture) may have been an adaptation to the cold temperature.

Because of its size and construction, arteries near the nasal passages were protected from the cold. There was, therefore, no chilling of blood that went to the brain—a critical factor, since the brain cannot tolerate much variation in temperature. Another function of the large nose was to warm and moisten cold, dry air before it went to the lungs.[10]

Other features of the classic Neandertals, such as the long projecting face and the sloping forehead, may also have been adaptations to the cold and dry environment near the glaciers. Steegman compared some modern human populations and found that those with longer, more projecting faces seemed to have more tolerance for cold. And those with more sloping foreheads seemed to maintain a more even skin temperature under cold conditions.[11] As we shall see in the next chapter, a short, stocky build like that of the classic Neandertals may also be an adaptation to a cold environment.

OTHER NEANDERTALS

Before, during, and perhaps after the period when the classic Neandertals lived in western Europe, other hominids resembling them in some respects were living in eastern Europe, the Near East, various parts of Africa, central Asia, Southeast Asia, and China. It is not so easy to describe the general features of these other Neandertal-like hominids, because they vary more than the classic specimens from western Europe. But it seems that these other Neandertals were generally not so short and stocky. Their foreheads were higher and less sloping, and the backs of their skulls were more smoothly rounded, as compared with the classic or western European specimens.[12]

[8] Saban, "Les Restes Humains," pp. 196–97.
[9] Kenneth A. R. Kennedy, *Neanderthal Man* (Minneapolis: Burgess, 1975), pp. 39–42.

[10] Carleton Coon, quoted in Fred T. Adams, *The Way to Modern Man* (New York: Columbia University Press, 1968), p. 250.
[11] A. T. Steegman, Jr., "Cold Response, Body Form and Craniofacial Shape in Two Racial Groups in Hawaii," *American Journal of Physical Anthropology* 37 (1972): 193–221, as referred to in Kennedy, *Neanderthal Man,* p. 43.
[12] Kennedy, *Neanderthal Man,* p. 53.

THE PLACE OF NEANDERTALS IN RECENT HUMAN EVOLUTION

The position of the Neandertals in the evolutionary lineage leading to modern humans is still debated. In particular, experts disagree as to whether or not the western European or classic variety of Neandertal is in the direct line of descent to modern humans. The controversy arose primarily because from the time of the initial find in 1848 until the 1930s there was no clear, discernible fossil record of change from a burly, barrel-chested creature whose face resembled *Homo erectus* to the chinned, high-domed features of modern men and women. It was not until the 1930s that the first so-called generalized Neandertals were found.

Several theories attempt to explain what happened to the Neandertals. One explanation is based upon the acceptance of a distinction between classic Neandertals and generalized Neandertals, with the latter more closely approximating the appearance of modern humans. As we noted earlier, classic Neandertals may have been a specialized form—adapted to, and entirely enclosed within, the western European glacial environment—who subsequently became extinct. According to this theory, modern humans have descended from the generalized Neandertals.

Another view is that all of the Neandertals and modern-type humans are variants of the same species, and that they interbred.

The archaeological and geological evidence suggests that populations from the Middle East and the Mediterranean regions moved into Europe at various times during the late middle and upper Pleistocene. There was probably considerable mixture of genes as the result of migrations. The morphological variability of the late middle and upper Pleistocene hominids of Europe reflects such movements. The Neandertals may have been absorbed and dominated culturally much as the American Indians were, beginning in the sixteenth century, by European settlers and conquerors.[13]

One theory gaining acceptance is that variety should be expected in fossil hominids. "Just as we have racial variations in our present world, so must there have existed racial varieties of prehistoric peoples."[14] The distinction between classic and other Neandertals may be misleading. "Brace and other modern anthropologists believe that . . . his differences fall well within the range of variation common to modern man. And, if this is true, it is possible that we can trace our development through him."[15]

To summarize then, it appears most probable that Neandertals were derived from a generalized *Homo sapiens* gene pool (e.g., the Steinheim variety of *Homo sapiens*). Because the generalized Neandertals are so widespread, it is probable that *Homo sapiens sapiens* (modern humans) gradually evolved from them—the result of natural selection and adaptation to the environment. The western European Neandertals, living under extreme glacial conditions and thus demonstrating adaptations to an arctic climate, were probably more isolated than other Neandertals. Physical isolation implies genetic isolation as well; this may account for less physical variation among the classic Neandertals than is found in the generalized Neandertals.

THE CULTURES OF THE NEANDERTALS

The period of cultural history associated with the Neandertals is called the Middle Paleolithic and dates from about 80,000 to about 40,000 years ago. Tool assemblages from this period are generally referred to as *Mousterian*.

The Mousterian Toolmaking Tradition The Mousterian tool complex is named after the tool assemblage found in a rock shelter at Le Moustier in the Dordogne region of France. A Mousterian type of tool assemblage differs from an Acheulean assemblage in that the Mousterian has a higher proportion of flake

[13]John Buettner-Janusch, *Origins of Man* (New York: John Wiley and Sons, 1966), p. 151.

[14]Sharon S. McKern and Thomas W. McKern, *Tracking Fossil Man* (New York: Praeger, 1970), p. 104.
[15]Ibid., p. 110.

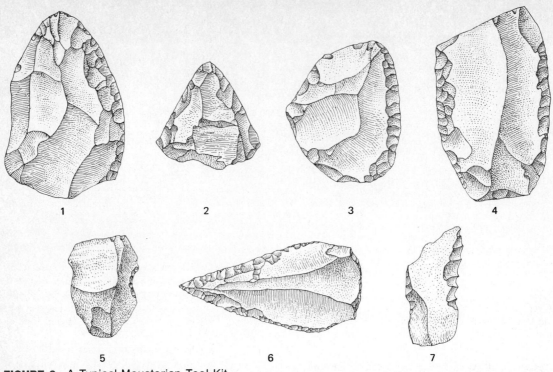

FIGURE 3 A Typical Mousterian Tool Kit

A Mousterian tool kit emphasized sidescrapers, 1–4; notches, 5; points, 6; and denticulates, 7. How these stone arti-facts were actually used is not known, but the points may have been hafted to wood shafts, and denticulates could have been used to work wood. The tools illustrated here are from Mousterian sites in western Europe. (From "Ice-Age Hunters of the Ukraine," by Richard G. Klein. Copyright © 1974 by Scientific American, Inc. All rights reserved.)

tools. Neandertals seem to have improved the Levalloisian flake technique of *Homo erectus*. In the Levalloisian technique, the core is carefully shaped by percussion flaking (i.e., it is a "pre-pared core") before the flake is struck off. In this way, the toolmaker can control the size and shape of the flake desired, thus producing different types of tools. The Mousterian tech-nique of producing flakes is basically the same as the Levalloisian technique; a prepared core and percussion flaking are used. But with the Mousterian technique, instead of obtaining only two or three long, large Levalloisian flakes, the toolmaker flaked until the core was almost completely used up. The flakes were then re-touched to make specialized tools.[16] Not only did this conserve the flint but, since most of the core was used, it also resulted in more cutting or working edge of tool per pound of flint.

Size and Permanence of Communities The communities or local groups of the Neandertal hunter-gatherers seem to have been somewhat smaller in size than the bands of recent hunter-gatherers. Burials in some sites suggest that the Neandertal bands included between ten and thirty individuals. In many areas it appears that the bands moved seasonally, apparently in pursuit of the available game. However, some Neandertal groups were probably not so no-madic. For example, in the Dordogne Valley in France, the inhabitants seem to have been rela-tively sedentary, probably because game and other food resources were continously available in the vicinity.[17]

[16]Jacques Bordaz, *Tools of the Old and New Stone Age* (Garden City, N.Y.: Natural History Press, 1970), p. 39.

[17]Kennedy, *Neanderthal Man*, p. 88.

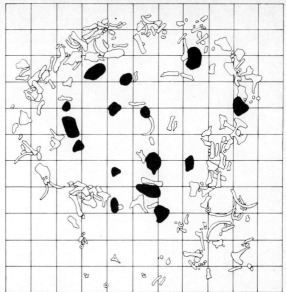

FIGURE 4

A reconstruction of a house at Moldova, western Russia, is shown at the left. At the right is a bird's-eye view depicting the distribution of artifacts actually found at the site. (From ''Ice-Age Hunters of the Ukraine,'' by Richard G. Klein. Copyright © 1974 by Scientific American, Inc. All rights reserved.)

Housing Caves, earlier inhabited by *Homo erectus,* also provided shelter for Neandertals. Ralph S. Solecki's discovery of Neandertal fossils in Shanidar Cave, Iraq, enables us to make some inferences about Neandertal life there. This cave, apparently a good choice of housing since it has a warm southern exposure and is well protected from winter winds, moved Solecki to speculate about its past inhabitants.

We still know comparatively little about the Big Cave of Shanidar. But standing before the deep cut that we have sliced into its floor, we can see the general outlines of that history. We see Neanderthal man crouching over a fire nearly 100,000 years ago, and looking out from a cave mouth at a valley landscape not too different from the one today. He goes forth to hunt tortoises, wild goats and wild pigs. . . . Apparently he does not try to tackle the swift deer or tackle the dangerous bear, wolf or leopard (at least their bones are practically absent in the deposits of Shanidar Cave). The splintered bones of his game show that he cracked open the bones to suck out every bit of marrow.[18]

Most of the homesites which have been uncovered are caves such as the site of Shanidar. However, some Neandertals lived in the open, as at a site in Moldova, western Russia, where they lived in river-valley houses framed with wood and covered with animal skins. Mammoth bones, which have been found distributed in patterned arrangements around the remains of hearths, were apparently used to help hold the animal skins in place on top of the houses. Even though the winter climate was cold near the edge of the glacier at that time, there would still have been animals to hunt in the vicinity because the plant food for the game was not buried under deep snow. The hunters probably moved away in the summer to higher land between the river valleys. In all likelihood, the higher ground was grazing land for the large herds of animals that the Moldova hunters depended upon for meat. On the winter river-valley sites archaeologists have found skeletons of wolf, arctic fox, and hare, with their paws missing. These animals probably were skinned for pelts that were made into clothing.[19]

[18]Ralph S. Solecki, "Shanidar Cave," *Scientific American,* November 1957, pp. 63–64.

[19]Richard G. Klein, "Ice-Age Hunters of the Ukraine," *Scientific American,* June 1974, pp. 96–105.

HUMAN EVOLUTION: BIOLOGICAL AND CULTURAL

Evidence of Religious Beliefs   Enough evidence exists to raise a strong possibility that some Neandertals believed in an afterlife. At Le Moustier, the skeleton of a boy fifteen or sixteen years old was found, laid out with a beautifully fashioned stone ax near his hand. With the body were charred wild cattle bones, perhaps the remnants of a funeral feast or possibly buried to provide food for the youth in another world. Near Le Moustier, graves of three other children and two adults, apparently interred together in a family plot, were also discovered.

The degree of elaboration that could go into a Neandertal burial, and what may be the prehistoric precedents of some of our contemporary customs, are illustrated in Shanidar Cave.

At least one of the individuals, a man with a badly crushed skull, was buried deep in the cave with special ceremony. One spring day about 60,000 years ago members of his family went out into the hills, picked masses of wild flowers, and made a bed of them on the ground, a resting place for the deceased. Other flowers were probably laid on top of his grave; still others seem to have been woven together with the branches of a pinelike shrub to form a wreath.[20]

How can we possibly know this? We know from experience how fragile flowers are, but one part of the flower—the pollen—may be preserved. Through pollen analysis, archaeologists have been able to infer that flowers—including ancestral forms of modern grape hyacinths, bachelor's buttons, hollyhocks, and yellow flowering groundsels—were buried with the bodies at Shanidar Cave. Pollen analysis entails microscopic identification of pollen from modern plants.

When these have been identified, it is possible to take a standard number of grains from samples in a vertical stratigraphic section and count the number from each species of plant. By plotting the relative frequencies of various species through time, one can make a pollen diagram describing the changing vegetation for the area involved.[21]

[20] Pfeiffer, *The Emergence of Man*, p. 171.
[21] Frank Hole and Robert F. Heizer, *An Introduction to Prehistoric Archeology*, 2d ed. (New York: Holt, Rinehart and Winston, 1969), p. 247.

Excavation of Neandertal burial site, Shanidar, Iraq, by Ralph Solecki. The skeleton is an adult male. Flower pollen was found around and on top of the body. (Courtesy of Ralph S. Solecki.)

The significance of the pollen in the Shanidar burial site is still controversial, but it may indicate how long ago humans began to associate flowers with the rituals of death.

Funerals were probably not the only religious rituals. There may have been other ceremonies involving bears, which seem to have been objects of worship as well as part of the Neandertal diet. The bear cult is inferred from the circumstantial evidence of seven bear skulls, placed in a line and facing the entrance of a cave in eastern Austria. The skulls were in a rectangular vault. Another site in southern France contained a nearly complete bear skeleton and the remains of almost twenty others, in a spot marked by a unique structure as something special. The structure consisted of a rectangular pit covered by a flat stone slab weighing almost a ton. The careful placement of the bear skeletons and skulls suggests that bears were thought of as more than a source of meat. They evidently symbolized something special to the human cave dwellers who were willing to reserve a prominent place for them in the prehistoric household.

The Emergence of Modern Humans and Upper Paleolithic Cultures

HOMO SAPIENS SAPIENS

Cro-Magnon humans, who lived in western Europe 30,000–35,000 years ago, were once thought to be the earliest known specimens of modern humans, or *Homo sapiens sapiens.* However, some paleontologists say that equally old, or even older, fossils found elsewhere are also indistinguishable from modern humans.[22] The Cro-Magnons and those other specimens of *Homo sapiens sapiens* differed from Neandertals in that they had higher, more bulging foreheads, thinner and lighter bones, smaller faces and jaws, chins (the bony protuberances that remain after projecting faces recede), and slight bone ridges (or no ridges at all) over the eyes and at the back of the head.

DATING UPPER PALEOLITHIC REMAINS

Radiocarbon Dating Radiocarbon dating is a widely used method for dating remains up to 50,000–60,000 years old. Thus, it can be used for dating remains from the Upper Paleolithic. Radiocarbon dating stems from the principle that all living matter possesses a certain amount of a radioactive form of carbon (carbon 14, or C^{14}). Radioactive carbon, which is produced when nitrogen 14 is bombarded by cosmic rays, is absorbed from the air by plants and is then ingested by animals which eat the plants. After an organism dies, it no longer takes in any of the radioactive carbon. Carbon 14 decays at a slow but steady pace and reverts to nitrogen 14.

By "decays" we mean that the C^{14} gives off a number of beta radiations per minute. The rate at which the carbon decays is known: C^{14} has a half-life of 5,730 years. In other words, half of the original amount of C^{14} in organic matter will have disintegrated 5,730 years after the organism's death; half of the remaining C^{14} will have disintegrated after another 5,730 years; and so on. After about 50,000–60,000 years, the amount of C^{14} remaining in the organic matter is too small to permit accurate dating.

To discover how long the organism containing the C^{14} has been dead (i.e., to determine how much C^{14} is left and therefore how old the organism is) we count the number of beta radiations given off per minute per gram of material. Modern C^{14} emits about 15 beta radiations per minute per gram of material, while C^{14} which is 5,730 years old emits only half this amount (indicating the half-life of C^{14}) per minute per gram of material. Thus, the amount of beta radiations given off per minute per gram will tell us how much C^{14} is left and therefore how old the material is. For example, if the material emits 15 radiations per gram each minute, the organism is only recently dead and we can date it to the present. If the material gives off 7.5 radiations a minute per gram, which is only half the amount given off by modern C^{14}, this means only half of the C^{14} is left. Since the half-life of C^{14} is 5,730 years, the organism must be 5,730 years old.[23]

To test the accuracy of the radioactive carbon dating method, it was used to judge the age of parts of the Dead Sea Scrolls and some wood from an Egyptian tomb, the dates of which were already known from historical records. The results based on C^{14} analysis agreed very well with the historical information.

Varve Analysis Varve analysis is one of the oldest methods used to date archaeological remains. The method is based upon the observation that varves—which are annually deposited layers of silt—remain in lake basins from the run-off of melting glacial ice.

---

[22] David Pilbeam, *The Ascent of Man* (New York: Macmillan, 1972), p. 183.

[23] Hole and Heizer, *An Introduction to Prehistoric Archeology*, p. 218.

Varves are composed of a double layer with coarse sediments at the bottom and fine sediments at the top; the finer sediments settle during the winter while the lake is frozen over, and the coarser material is deposited in the summer when it is warmer and melting is increased. Varves may range in thickness from a few millimeters to more than 15 inches, though these maximum and minimum values are seldom reached.[24]

To date a site, the varves are counted, with each varve indicating one year of deposition. The number of varves indicates the number of years spanned. However, the method is restricted in its application because varves only accumulate near ice, and many places frozen during Pleistocene times were no longer supplied with silt once the ice retreated. Futhermore, the longest known sequence of varves goes back only 17,000 years.

UPPER PALEOLITHIC CULTURES

Strictly speaking, the term "Upper Paleolithic" refers only to cultures in Europe, Africa, and Asia. The Upper Paleolithic cultures of *Homo sapiens sapiens* date from 40,000–35,000 B.C. to a period prior to the emergence of agriculture (12,000–8,000 B.C., depending upon the area). The earliest known sites, dating from 35,000 B.C., have been excavated in southwestern Asia and in Europe. Upper Paleolithic peoples were mainly hunters and gatherers who probably lived in nomadic bands. However, studies of some sites show clusters of neighboring shelters with thick, layered walls, implying that their inhabitants planned to stay for a while.

Excavations also suggest that population was increasing; this inference is drawn from the size of the settlements. For the first time, we see evidence of art in the form of clay figurines and the famous cave paintings in France and Spain. The great variety of tool types suggests increasingly varied productive activities and more efficient exploitation of the environment.

As was the case in the known Middle Paleolithic sites, most of the Upper Paleolithic remains that have been excavated were situated in caves and rock shelters. However, a few open sites have also been excavated, and evidence of dwellings has been found in these. At two southern Russian sites (Gagarino and the upper level of Kostienki IV) and at the Czechoslovakian dig of Dolní Věstonice, some round to oval house plans with diameters of 15 to 20 feet have been uncovered.[25] Their size indicates that each hut was probably inhabited by a single family.

At other Russian sites (Puskari and the lower level of Kostienki IV), dwellings were composed of rows of two or three individual family units joined together end-to-end, each unit with its own hearth.[26] In Kostienki IV, two such multiple-unit structures have been excavated. One structure is about 100 feet long and 16 feet wide; the second is about 70 feet long and 16 feet wide.[27] Each rectangular structure contains a row of hearths along its central axis and pits which were used for storage. A few pits contain hare bones and red ochre, which may have been used for the coloring and tanning of hare skins.[28] One of the structures has two low earthen ridges about 25 inches high extending across the floor and dividing the area into three parts; each part is believed to be a separate unit, or room. Because the hearths are located along the central axis and very few artifacts have been found along the edges of the structures, it is believed that the dwellings had gabled roofs, with eaves which almost touched the floors.[29]

Tools: The Blade Technique Upper Paleolithic toolmaking appears to have its roots in the Mousterian tradition, since Mousterian flake tools are found in many Upper Paleolithic assemblages. Numerous blade tools have also been uncovered. Blades were found in Middle

---

[24] Ibid., p. 236.

[25] Grahame Clark and Stuart Piggott, *Prehistoric Societies* (New York: Alfred A. Knopf, 1965), pp. 75–76.

[26] Ibid., p. 76.

[27] Richard G. Klein, *Man and Culture in the Late Pleistocene* (San Francisco: Chandler, 1969), pp. 170, 174.

[28] Ibid., pp. 170–75.

[29] Ibid., pp. 171, 174.

FIGURE 5 Reconstruction of an Upper Paleolithic Settlement at Moravia, Czechoslovakia
Huts made of skins, held in place by mammoth tusks and bones, provided shelter against the cold climate. (Adapted from Grahame Clark and Stuart Piggot, *Prehistoric Societies.* © 1965, Alfred A. Knopf, Inc.)

Paleolithic assemblages as well, but they were not widely used until the Upper Paleolithic.

In the blade technique of toolmaking, a core is prepared by shaping it with a hammerstone into a pyramidal or cylindrical form. Then a series of blades, twice as long as they are wide, are struck off until the core is used up. The blade technique used on flint in this period was more economical than previous toolmaking methods. Professor Leroi-Gourhan of the Musée de l'Homme in Paris has calculated that with the old Acheulean core technique, a 2-pound lump of flint yielded 16 inches of working edge and produced only two handaxes. If the more advanced Mousterian technique were used, a lump of equal size would yield 2 yards of working edge. The Upper Paleolithic blade technique, however, greatly surpassed the earlier methods by yielding 25 yards of working edge.[30] With the same amount of material, a significantly greater number of tools could be produced with the blade technique. Getting the most out of the valuable resource was particularly important in those areas lacking large flint deposits.

Bordaz believes that the evolution of tool-making techniques, which continually increased the amount of usable edge that could be gotten out of a lump of flint, was significant since people could then spend more time in regions where flint was unavailable.

Hunters and gatherers can only carry a limited amount of material with them during their seasonal migrations and hunting expeditions. With more efficient methods of knapping flint, their range could be extended farther and for longer periods of time into areas where flint was locally unavailable, of poorer quality, or difficult in access.[31]

The Upper Paleolithic period is also noted for the production of large numbers of bone and antler tools. The manufacture of these implements may have been made easier by the development of many varieties of burins. *Burins* are chisel-like stone tools used for carving, and bone and antler needles, awls, and projectile points could be produced with them.[32] Burins sometimes were found in Middle and Lower Paleolithic sites, but a great number and variety of burins were present only in the Upper Paleo-

[30] Bordaz, *Tools of the Old and New Stone Age,* p. 68.

[31] Ibid., p. 57.
[32] Ibid., p. 68.

Solutrean laurel leaf blade. (Courtesy of the American Museum of Natural History.)

lithic. Pressure flaking also appeared during the Upper Paleolithic. In the traditional percussion method, used since Oldowan choppers were first made at least 2 million years before, the core was struck with a hammerstone to knock off the flake. In pressure flaking, small flakes were struck off by pressing against the core with a bone, wood, or antler tool. Pressure flaking gave the toolmaker greater control in the shaping of the tool, as is evidenced by the beautiful Solutrean laurel leaf blades made during this period.

Ideally, the study of tools should reveal not only how the implements were made but also how they were used. One way of suggesting what a particular tool was used for in the past is to observe the manner in which that tool is used by members of contemporary societies, preferably societies with subsistence activities and environments similar to those of the ancient toolmakers. This method of study is called *ethnographic analogy*. The problem with reasoning from ethnographic analogy, however, is readily apparent: we cannot be sure that the original use of a tool has not changed. For example, just because we use an implement called a toothbrush on our teeth does not mean that a much later society will also use it on their teeth. When selecting contemporary cultures that may provide the most informative and accurate comparisons, we should try to choose those that derive from the archaeological culture we are interested in. If the recent and archaeological cultures being compared are historically related—such as prehistoric and contemporary Pueblo cultures in the southwestern United States, for example—there is a greater likelihood that both groups used a particular kind of tool in similar ways and for similar purposes.

The use to which a particular tool was put can sometimes be inferred from its wear marks—scratches and nicks on the tool resulting from its use. For example, S. A. Semenov has inferred that blades from a site in Siberia were used as meat knives. Only one of the edges of each blade was sharp and polished on both sides, indicating that only one edge of the blade was used. The polish, occurring on both sides of the sharp edge, indicated to Semenov that both sides of this edge of the blade had been used as a knife "to cut into a soft material into which it had been sunk, probably meat."[33] The inference that meat was the material which was cut is based upon the observation that used tools tend to show scratches or marks which suggest in what direction the tool was moved, the tool's position on the object worked, and the kind of object worked.

The validity of this method can be tested by comparing the wear marks on the prehistoric tools with those on similar tools used by con-

---

[33] S. A. Semenov, *Prehistoric Technology*, trans. M. W. Thompson (Bath, England: Adams and Dart, 1970), p. 103.

temporary people. Bordaz has described the flintworking process among present-day Australian aborigines.[34] By studying the use marks on the aborigines' blades and noting the use to which the blades are put, we can find out if use marks correctly indicate the blades' functions. For example, if the Australians use their blades as both knives and spear points, do the use marks on the knives differ from those on the spear points, and do all of the knives have the same type of use marks? When these questions have been answered, the use marks on the prehistoric tools can be compared with the marks on the contemporary implements. Similar marks suggest similar functions.

Another way to draw inferences about the use of ancient tools is to make the tools and then use them as prehistoric people may have done. One of the masters of prehistoric stoneworking techniques is Don Crabtree. His efforts to recreate the handiwork of prehistoric cultures have increased our appreciation of our ancestors' abilities. By duplicating their work, Crabtree hopes to learn the "extinct skills" of the early craftsmen. His experiments with flaking different materials have indicated that prehistoric Indians in America may have heat-treated flints in order to pressure flake them more easily. Crabtree and Butler have reported:

If I attempt to pressure flake an untreated piece of flint collected at a quarry site, the largest flake that I can detach by pressure will usually measure no more than half an inch in length. But if the same material is heated, I can easily press off flakes of more than two inches in length with a hand held flaker. In addition to improving the working qualities of silica minerals, heat treatment also produces a distinct change in the texture and lustre of these minerals, and often a change in color as well.[35]

Inventions   During the Upper Paleolithic, probably for the first time, spears were shot

[34] Bordaz, *Tools of the Old and New Stone Age*, pp. 65, 108.
[35] Don E. Crabtree and B. Robert Butler, "Notes on Experiment in Flint Knapping: 1 Heat Treatment of Silica Materials," *Tebiwa* 7, no. 1, (January 1964): 1.

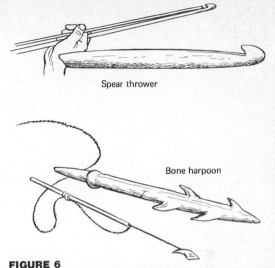

Spear thrower

Bone harpoon

FIGURE 6
During the Upper Paleolithic, the spear thrower and bone harpoon were invented. (Adapted from R. J. Braidwood, *Prehistoric Men*.)

from a spear thrower rather than manually thrown. We know this because bone and antler *atlatls* (the Aztec word for "spear thrower") have been found at some sites. A spear which was propelled off a grooved board could be sent through the air with increased force, causing it to travel farther and hit harder, and with less effort by the thrower. The bow and arrow, in essence a variation or miniaturization of the spear thrower, was used in Egypt and presumably elsewhere during the Upper Paleolithic. Harpoons, which were used for fishing and perhaps for reindeer hunting, were also invented at this time.

Art   The earliest discovered traces of art are from Upper Paleolithic sites. We might expect that early artistic efforts would be crude, but the cave paintings of Spain and southern France show a marked degree of skill.

Peter J. Ucko and Andrée Rosenfeld, whose work forms the basis of our discussion in this section, have identified three principal locations of art in caves: (1) in obviously inhabited rock shelters and cave entrances, the art probably being conceived as decoration or as "art for art's sake"; (2) in "galleries" immediately off the inhabited areas of caves; and (3) in the inner reaches of caves, where the difficulty of access has been interpreted by some as a sign that magical-religious activities were performed there.[36]

The subjects of the paintings are mostly animals, with only a few humans. Perhaps, like many contemporary peoples, Upper Paleolithic men and women believed that the drawing of a human image could cause death or injury. If that were indeed the ancient people's belief, it might explain why human figures are rarely depicted in cave art. The animal paintings rest on the bare walls, with no backdrops or incidental environmental trappings. The preponderance of animal paintings suggests that the people sought to gain an advantage in the hunt. This theory is supported by evidence of chips in the painted figures, perhaps made by spears thrown at the drawings. But if hunting magic was the chief motivation for the paintings, it is difficult to explain why only a few paintings show signs of being speared. If the purpose of the artwork was not only to gain dominance over the game, perhaps the paintings were inspired by the people's need to increase the supply of animals. Cave art seems to have reached a peak toward the end of the Upper Paleolithic period, when the herds of game were decreasing.

Another interpretation of Upper Paleolithic cave art has been suggested by André Leroi-Gourhan. He conducted a statistical analysis of the types of paintings and their locations within each of sixty-six caves. Leroi-Gourhan concluded that the choice of subject and placement of the paintings were not haphazard or arbitrary but probably had some symbolic significance. For example, female animals were usually located in the central chambers of the caves and were associated with what may be considered to be female signs—enclosed circles. Male animals, located at the entrances and back portions of the caves, were associated with presumably male signs—dots and barbed symbols.[37] The work of Leroi-Gourhan suggests, then, that the symbolism of the Upper Paleolithic cave painters may have been quite modern.

Upper Paleolithic art was not confined to cave paintings. Many shafts of spears and similar objects were decorated with figures of animals. Figurines representing the human female in exaggerated form have also been found at Upper Paleolithic sites. Called "Venuses," these women are portrayed with broad hips and large breasts and abdomens. It has been suggested that the figurines may have been an ideal type, or an expression of a desire for fertility, but there is no evidence to support these assumptions.

DIVERSITY OF UPPER PALEOLITHIC CULTURES

Although we have generalized about the characteristics of the people living in the Upper Paleolithic period, we must remember that there were many diverse groups of hunting and gathering peoples whose sites date from about 40,000 to 10,000 years ago. Our knowledge of the social organization and cultural differences among these different peoples is scanty. One reason for this may be that until recently, many Old World archaeologists have not been interested in drawing inferences about social organization from material remains. Rather, they have concentrated on establishing chronologies and classifications of tools. On the basis of the kinds of tools found and the nature of the sites in which those implements were discovered, archaeologists have distinguished a number of Upper Paleolithic cultures in the Old World.

Upper Paleolithic Cultures in Europe The European Upper Paleolithic period includes the Aurignacian and Gravettian traditions, which

---

[36] Peter J. Ucko and Andrée Rosenfeld, *Paleolithic Cave Art* (New York: McGraw-Hill, 1967).

[37] André Leroi-Gourhan, "The Evolution of Paleolithic Art," *Scientific American*, February 1968, pp. 58–70.

A cave painting from Lascaux, France. The chips in the rock's surface may indicate that spears were thrown at them in an attempt to ensure successful hunting. (René Burri, Magnum Photos.)

constitute the early Upper Paleolithic; the briefer Solutrean culture during the middle Upper Paleolithic, and the Magdalenian tradition of the late Upper Paleolithic.

Aurignacian One of the oldest and most widespread Upper Paleolithic cultures is the Aurignacian. Thought to have originated in southwestern Asia, radiocarbon dating has placed its earliest appearance at 35,000 B.C. Its subsequent spread throughout western Europe, probably through the Balkans, is suggested by the distribution of Aurignacian tools in that area. A popular tool of the period was the burin, or graver, used primarily for carving wood, bone, ivory, and similar materials. The Aurignacian peoples lived in caves or rock shelters. They are credited with producing the earliest cave paintings in western Europe, including the older ones among the spectacular works at Lascaux, France.

The Aurignacian economy centered on animals moving in herds—horses, mammoths, and

The meaning of the "Venus" figurine, an exaggerated female figure, is not known. (Courtesy of the American Museum of Natural History.)

reindeer—which provided the people with food, skins, sinews, bones, and antlers. Hunting these animals must have been a group effort, and the hunters may have followed the herds in seasonal migrations.[38]

Gravettian Spanning the period from 22,000 to 18,000 B.C., the Gravettian culture was centered primarily in eastern and central Europe. Because they lived during a brief recession of the ice sheet during the fourth glaciation, the Gravettians were able to reside in skin-covered tents or oval huts. Fossils indicate that mammoths were widely hunted by the Gravettians, who used the animal's bones and ivory for tools and fuel.

Gravettian artists created "Venus" figurines and pins, beads, and pendants decorated with minute geometric patterns. Evidently, the Gravettians buried their dead wearing clothing and ornaments; specimens have been found with parts of their clothing still preserved.

Solutrean The Solutrean culture, with sites in France and Spain, dates between 18,000 and 15,000 B.C. Unlike the Gravettians before them, the Solutreans lived during a very cold period in the fourth glaciation.

Solutrean flintworkers created a distinctive set of Upper Paleolithic stone tools—the laurel leaf blades. The blades appear to have been made by the pressure flaking process, which gave the toolmaker greater control in the shaping of the tool. Bordaz suggests several possible functions: the smaller, thicker laurel leaves may have been attached to wooden shafts and used as projectile points. Some of the larger and more finely made blades may have served a ritual function or may have been aesthetic examples of the flintworker's skill.[39] The lustrous surface and slightly greasy feel of the laurel leaf blades support the conclusion that the tools were treated with heat before flaking.[40] In the

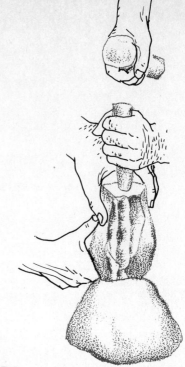

FIGURE 7
One way to remove blades from a core is to hit them with a punch. The object being struck is the punch, which is made of bone or horn. (From Brian M. Fagan, *In The Beginning* [Boston: Little, Brown and Company, 1972], p. 195.)

last part of the Solutrean period, bone tools were made more frequently, and needles with "eyes" made their first appearance.[41]

Magdalenian The last tradition of the Upper Paleolithic in Europe is the Magdalenian culture, dating from 15,000 to 8000 B.C. Magdalenians used blade tools and developed ways of conserving their stone resources by making many very small blades (microliths) from one stone. During Magdalenian times the number of microliths increased. These small, razorlike blade fragments, 1 inch long or less, were probably attached to wooden or bone handles to form a cutting edge. The microlithic trend extended into, and gained importance in, the

[38] Chester S. Chard, *Man in Prehistory* (New York: McGraw-Hill, 1969), p. 151.
[39] Bordaz, *Tools of the Old and New Stone Age*, p. 76.
[40] Crabtree and Butler, "Notes on Experiment in Flint Knapping: 1 Heat Treatment of Silica Materials," pp. 1–6.

[41] F. H. Bordes, *The Old Stone Age*, trans. J. E. Anderson (Toronto: World University Library, 1968), p. 159.

Mesolithic period which followed. Barbed harpoons made of bone and antler have been found at Magdalenian sites; they were probably used to hunt reindeer. During the Magdalenian period, the *atlatl*, or spear thrower, was invented.

With the Magdalenians, the high point of Upper Paleolithic cave art and tool decoration seems to have been reached. In addition to beautifully drawn figures, for the first time we see the use of more than one color in a painting. As we noted earlier, Magdalenians may have sought to gain success in the hunt through their art.

Upper Paleolithic Cultures in Asia and Africa
Except for some sites in the Near East and Asiatic Russia, few Upper Paleolithic sites have been excavated in Asia. Sites in Syria and Israel show an increasing use of blade tools and the invention of new tool types. In the earlier stages of the Upper Paleolithic, the blades are associated with Mousterian materials. The later stages have a number of new tools and new varieties of old tools—for example, many kinds of scrapers and burins.[42]

In North Africa, sites of the Upper Paleolithic Aterian culture, dated from 37,000 years ago, have been found.[43] Its flaking technique evidently was derived from the Mousterian tradition. Contemporary with the Aterian was a blade industry known as the Dabban, which appears to have been confined to the Mediterranean coast of North Africa. Many of these African sites were located in caves, and they were always near either permanent or intermittent waterholes—usually the former. As in Europe, the trend was toward smaller and lighter tools.[44]

In Africa south of the Sahara, the Middle Paleolithic populations had carried on the Acheulean handax tradition of *Homo erectus*. Between 44,000 and 38,600 B.C. this tradition probably evolved into the Upper Paleolithic Sangoan-Lupemban complexes adapted to forest conditions.[45] Sangoan culture and its later form, Lupemban, are characterized by core tools—handaxes and picks necessary for exploiting the resources of the forest environment. Also in South Africa, Upper Paleolithic sites dated between 35,000 and 20,000 years ago contain a blade industry and the remains of structures. These are semicircular arrangements of stones which may have been used to make the foundations of windbreaks.

Caves and rock shelters, as well as open sites, were used by Upper Paleolithic people in Africa. Clark notes that the size of the Upper Paleolithic sites indicates increasing populations. In addition, faunal remains from sites in Africa south of the Sahara suggest that Upper Paleolithic peoples were specializing in hunting certain animal species. At a site in South Africa, hunters concentrated on antelope, goats, bison, cattle, and deer, while in Zambia warthog and zebra were hunted. The range of species hunted by Upper Paleolithic peoples (from twelve to forty-nine species per site) was much greater than the range for Middle Paleolithic peoples (between eight and nineteen species per site).[46] "This certainly suggests that a greater significance now [during the Upper Paleolithic] attached to hunting and that more efficient and selected methods were used."[47]

Like the European and Asian Upper Paleolithic peoples, the African counterparts were hunting and gathering groups, with their hunting focused upon herd animals. They, too, seem to have migrated seasonally, living in caves, rock shelters, and open sites. The size of the camps indicates that small bands of people lived in them.

The Earliest Humans and Their Cultures in the New World

No earlier forms of humans than *Homo sapiens sapiens* have been found in North and South America. Therefore, migrations of humans to

[42] Ibid., pp. 198–200.
[43] J. D. Clark, *The Prehistory of Africa* (New York: Praeger, 1970), pp. 126–28.
[44] Ibid., p. 155.
[45] Ibid., pp. 110–13.
[46] Ibid., pp. 132–38.
[47] Ibid., p. 141.

the New World had to take place sometime after the emergence of *Homo sapiens sapiens*. Migrations to the New World had been in progress long before the final retreat of the last North American glaciers. During certain periods in late Pleistocene times the Bering Strait, which now separates Siberia and North America, was a grassy plain over 1,000 miles wide. Asian hunters following herds of big game probably crossed into the New World and moved down through a glacier-free corridor alongside the Rocky Mountains. Archaeologists differ on the time during which people could have entered North America. Some maintain that the corridor was open for 3,000 years—from 26,000 to 23,000 B.C. For the next 13,000 years, until 10,000 B.C., the corridor was presumably closed. Thereafter, new bands of migrants could once again have entered North America.[48] In any event, modern humans had moved down as far as South America at least by 16,000 B.C.[49]

Little is known about these early immigrants because only a few sites have been explored. Some of the earliest New World peoples did use pressure flaking and produced bone tools, burins, blade or flake endscrapers, and leaf-shaped knives, just as their earlier European counterparts did. The tool assemblages from the few earliest, scattered sites are quite similar to each other and to somewhat earlier traditions in northeast Asia.[50] This is not surprising, considering that the earliest Americans had come from northeast Asia by way of the Bering Strait region.

We are more certain about the traditions in the New World dating from about 12,000 years ago. Beginning at that time, we see growing diversification of toolmaking traditions, most of which are associated with evidence of big-game hunting. Three such traditions in what is now the United States are the Llano, Folsom, and Plano traditions. Almost all of the sites are kill-sites, where game had been slaughtered and

These two bison ribs and an arrowhead were found in the position shown here in Folsom, New Mexico. They probably date from 9000–7000 B.C. (Courtesy of the American Museum of Natural History.)

then butchered. Most of the sites occur along ancient lakes or creeks, where the animals probably came to drink, or at the bases of cliffs, over which the herds were probably stampeded.

THE LLANO CULTURE

Dating from 9500 to 7000 B.C., this tradition is named after the "Llano Estacado," or Staked Plains of the southwestern United States. This region, below the range of the ice sheets, had a cool, moist climate and extensive stretches of grassland. Evidently, herds of large animals were abundant at this time. Llano tool kits are associated mainly with mammoths and mastodons, but also with bison, wild camels, and wild horses.[51] In the eastern United States, fluted points were associated with deer remains at Bull Brook in Massachusetts.[52] These are lancelike points which had a flake removed at the center of the base, probably to facilitate attaching the points to wooden shafts. The Llano tool kit is best known for its Clovis fluted points, but it also includes blades and flakes, choppers, scrapers, knives, hammerstones, and bone tools.

[48] Chard, *Man in Prehistory*, pp. 141–42.

[49] Thomas C. Patterson, *America's Past* (Glenview, Ill.: Scott, Foresman, 1973), p. 30.

[50] Ibid., p. 32.

[51] J. D. Jennings, *Prehistory of North America* (New York: McGraw-Hill, 1968), pp. 71–72.

[52] D. S. Byers, "Comments on R. Mason's *The Paleo Indian Tradition in Eastern North America*," *Current Anthropology* 3, no. 2 (1962): 247–48.

THE FOLSOM CULTURE

Most of the sites for this culture, dating from 9000 to 7000 B.C., are kill-sites in the Southwest and West, where herds of now extinct bison were driven over cliffs or were trapped in box canyons and killed. At Folsom, New Mexico, the remains of twenty-three bison were found in association with Folsom fluted points. The Folsom tool kit consists of Folsom fluted points, blades, flakes, choppers, knives, gravers, scrapers, hammerstones, and implements made of bone. The tools have been associated with wolf, turtle, rabbit, horse, fox, deer, and camel, but principally with bison.[53]

THE PLANO CULTURE

Dating from 7000 to 6500 B.C., the Plano culture spanned a period when the climate in the Southwest was becoming drier and more temperate. The abundant lakes and marshes of the Llano tradition were diminishing. Game, too, was changing, as the modern bison and antelope replaced the mammoth and the giant longhorn bison. The hunting way of life continued, with local variations.

The Plano tool kit consists of unfluted lancelike knives and points. In addition to blades, flakes, choppers, drills, gravers, hammerstones, scrapers, and bone tools, milling stones have been found. These stones were probably used to grind vegetation.[54]

Summary

1. Early forms of our species, *Homo sapiens*, may have emerged about 250,000 years ago. The remains found at Swanscombe, England, and Steinheim, Germany, suggest that a post-*Homo erectus* hominid with some modern skull features existed by about 200,000 years ago. The Fontéchevade fossils found in France which date somewhat later (between 200,000 and 145,000 years ago) show even more modern features.

2. Undisputed *Homo sapiens* fossils became plentiful after 75,000 years ago. Most of these fossils are called Neandertals. There are two kinds of Neandertals—classic, and progressive or generalized. Classic or western European Neandertals average 1,470 cc in cranial capacity (100 cc more than the average capacity in modern humans). They had thick skulls, heavy brow ridges, large eye sockets, broad noses, long jaws, low foreheads, prognathism, and no chins. Their body build appears to have been stocky and muscular. Many of the classic Neandertal's features may have been adaptations to the glacial environment of western Europe. Generalized or progressive Neandertals vary in appearance more than the classic forms. But compared to classic Neandertals, they probably were not so short and stocky; their foreheads were higher and less sloping; and their skulls were more smoothly rounded in the back.

3. The position of Neandertals in the evolutionary lineage leading to modern humans is still debated. Some anthropologists believe that the classic Neandertals eventually became extinct, while the generalized form led to modern humans. Others feel that the differences in Neandertals were similar to modern-day variation in humans.

4. Neandertals are associated with the Mousterian technique of toolmaking, which yielded more working edge per pound of flint than did the earlier Acheulean and Levalloisian techniques. Evidence for supernatural beliefs is also found in the Neandertal culture.

5. Cro-Magnon humans (*Homo sapiens sapiens*) emerged about 30,000–35,000 years ago. The differences between Cro-Magnon and Neandertal specimens are found mainly in the skull. Other fossils equally as old as, or older than, Cro-Magnon humans may also

[53]Jennings, *Prehistory of North America*, pp. 72–88.
[54]Ibid., p. 73.

be indistinguishable from modern humans.

6. The Upper Paleolithic cultures of *Homo sapiens sapiens* in the Old World date roughly from 40,000–35,000 B.C. to 12,000–8,000 B.C. Hunting and gathering were the primary methods of food getting. Excavations suggest that the population was increasing; this inference is based upon the size of settlements. The first evidence of art appears during this time.

7. The blade technique used during the Upper Paleolithic period yielded even more working edge per pound of flint than did the Mousterian method of toolmaking. Pressure flaking gave the toolmaker greater control over the shape of the tool. Investigators attempt to determine the functions of ancient tools by observing modern cultures having similar technologies and by making and using the tools themselves.

8. The function of the art found in Upper Paleolithic caves is generally thought to be magical or religious, an attempt to ensure successful hunting. Upper Paleolithic peoples also began to decorate their tools. Small "Venus" figurines, depicting women with exaggerated breasts, hips, and abdomens, have also been found.

9. Using artifacts found at various sites, archaeologists have identified several cultural traditions dated to the Upper Paleolithic in Europe: the Aurignacian and Gravettian traditions of the early Upper Paleolithic, the Solutrean of the middle Upper Paleolithic, and the Magdalenian of the late Upper Paleolithic.

10. Similar cultural diversity has been found in Africa, the Near East, and Asia. Relatively fewer sites have been excavated in these areas and the patterns of variation are not yet as well established as the cultural developments in Europe. Still, the same trends toward lighter tools, conservation of flint, increased populations, and increased emphasis on hunting can be seen.

11. Modern humans probably arrived in the New World via a land bridge across the Bering Strait at least by about 20,000 years ago. Some of the early New World cultures resemble the Upper Paleolithic cultures of Europe, Africa, and Asia in the use of blade tools, burins, bone tools, pressure flaking, and leaf-shaped knives. The early migrants to the New World were probably also big-game hunters, but unique to this part of the world is the use of fluted points.

Suggested Readings

Bordes, F. H. *The Old Stone Age.* Translated by J. E. Anderson. Toronto: World University Library, 1968.
Chapters 12–19 summarize world-wide findings of the Upper Paleolithic, with Chapters 12–14 presenting the European evidence. Artifactual materials are described and illustrated extensively.

Butzer, K. W. *Environment and Archeology: An Ecological Approach to Prehistory.* 2d ed. New York and Chicago: Aldine-Atherton, 1971.
An introduction to the ecological perspective in archaeology. Butzer discusses material dealing with all aspects of the Pleistocene. His unifying principle is an ecological approach to the study of prehistory. The second half of the book is particularly valuable, since it deals with Pleistocene environments in major world areas and the human cultural responses to those environments.

Kennedy, K. A. R. *Neanderthal Man.* Minneapolis: Burgess, 1975.
A book devoted exclusively to the physical and cultural features of the Neandertals and to their place in human evolution.

Oakley, K. P. *Man the Tool-Maker.* Chicago: University of Chicago Press, 1967.
Chapters 7–8 discuss refinements in Paleolithic tool assemblages and certain general correlations which can be made between anatomical developments and tool types. Chapter 9 discusses the remains of Paleo-

lithic dwellings and the cave art of the
Upper Paleolithic period.

Pfeiffer, J. E. *The Emergence of Man.* 2d ed. New
York: Harper & Row, 1972.
Chapters 8–11 deal with the emergence of
the Neandertals and other *Homo sapiens*
specimens, and with the cultural developments of the Middle and Upper Paleolithic
periods, including cave art and burial practices.

Human Variation

7

In the preceding chapter, we discussed the emergence of people like ourselves, *Homo sapiens sapiens,* some 40,000 years ago. Just as the cultures of those human beings differed in some respects, so do the cultures of peoples in recent times. But anthropologists are also concerned with how recent human populations vary physically—how they resemble, or differ from, each other.

Human populations vary in their frequencies of biological traits, both visible and invisible. External or visible characteristics (such as skin color, height, and body build) are, of course, the most obvious biological variations. Populations also vary in internal, invisible biological traits such as susceptibility to disease. How can we explain all of these variations? It appears that many, if not most, of them may represent *adaptations* to different environments.

General Factors Producing Human Variation

Human variation is the result of one or more of the following general factors: mutation and natural selection, genetic drift, and gene flow.

MUTATION AND NATURAL SELECTION

Mutations, or changes in the chemistry of a gene, are the ultimate source of all biological variations. Mutations can be lethal or sublethal, reducing the reproductive rates of their carriers. They can also be beneficial, enhancing the potential for survival in a particular environment. Although most mutations are harmful, mutations that are beneficial occur occasionally. Because natural selection favors them, the traits produced by the beneficial mutations become characteristics of the population. For example, in an earlier chapter we discussed the advantage dark moths had over light moths when areas of England became industrialized. Predators could not easily see the darker moths against the soot-covered trees, and these moths soon outnumbered the lighter variety.

7

But certain traits that are found among human populations, such as red (versus blond or black) hair color or thick (versus thin) lips, may not make any difference in survival, no matter where the carriers of these traits live. Hence, so far as we know, they are neutral traits. Yet, these traits are unevenly distributed among the world's populations. Natural selection did not seem to account for their distribution, as neutral traits do not seem to confer any advantages on their carriers. The differing frequencies of neutral traits in human populations may result from genetic drift or from gene flow.

GENETIC DRIFT

The term *genetic drift* is now used to refer to various random processes that affect gene frequencies in small, relatively isolated populations. Genetic drift is also known as the *Sewall Wright effect*, named for the geneticist who first directed attention to this kind of evolutionary process.[1]

One variety of genetic drift occurs when a small population derived recently from a larger one expands in relative isolation.[2] Referred to as the *founder effect*, this process might occur, for example, if a family with ten children—all of whom exhibit a particular rare, but neutral, trait—moved to a tiny country hamlet. If all members of the family remained in the hamlet, married, and produced children who also stayed there and produced more children, and if the hamlet remained isolated from the outside world, the trait might become relatively common among residents of the area in a few generations.[3]

GENE FLOW

A *gene pool* consists of all the genes possessed by the members of a given population. *Gene flow* is the process whereby genes pass from the gene pool of one population to the gene pool of another population through mating and reproduction. Unlike the other three evolutionary processes (mutation, natural selection, and genetic drift), which act generally to differentiate populations, gene flow tends to work in the opposite direction, making differing populations more similar over time as genes are exchanged between them. For example, if a group of blue-eyed Scandinavians interbreeds with a population of dark-eyed Italians, the proportion of genes for blue eyes in the Italian population will increase. Hence, gene flow partially accounts for human variation by making some populations look similar even though originally they were different.

Although gene flow is often made possible by the migration of populations, it does not necessarily follow from the migration. For example, a religious group may move to a new place but refuse to interbreed with the natives of that area. In the United States, the Amish of Pennsylvania have tried to remain isolated. Nevertheless, some marriages have occurred between Amish and non-Amish people, and reproduction has introduced new genes into the Amish population's gene pool.[4]

Kinds of Human Variation

The most noticeable biological variations among human populations are those which are on the surface—skin color, body build, stature, and shape of facial features. There are also many biological variations which we do not see, such as variation in susceptibility to different diseases. Certain of these variations may be explainable as adaptations to differing physical or social environments or as consequences of other physical or cultural changes. However, there are many biological variations among human populations for which we do not yet have any explanations.

[1] Laura Newell Morris, *Human Populations, Genetic Variation, and Evolution* (San Francisco: Chandler, 1971), p. 302.

[2] Ibid., p. 309.

[3] H. Bentley Glass, "The Genetics of the Dunkers," *Scientific American*, August 1953, pp. 76–81.

[4] Morris, *Human Populations, Genetic Variation, and Evolution*, pp. 409–10.

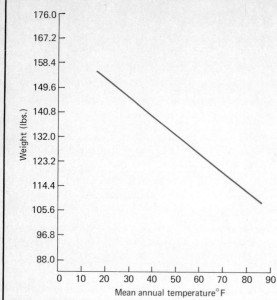

FIGURE 1

Graph demonstrating the relationship of mean body weight in a population to the mean annual temperature of the area in which the population is located. The graph supports the application of Bergmann's rule to human populations, suggesting that the lower the mean annual temperature, the higher the mean body weight of the population. (After Stanley M. Garn, *Human Races*, 3rd ed., 1971. Courtesy of Charles C Thomas, Publisher, Springfield, Illinois.)

BODY BUILD AND FACIAL CONSTRUCTION

Scientists have suggested that the body build of many birds and mammals may vary according to the temperature of the environment in which they live. For example, Julian Huxley, in a series of studies on the puffin (a short-necked sea bird), found that the puffins in cold northern regions were considerably larger than those living in warmer southern areas.[5] *Bergmann's rule* describes what seems to be a general relationship: the smaller-sized populations of a species inhabit the warmer parts of its geographical range, and the larger-sized populations inhabit the cooler areas.

[5]Julian Huxley, *Evolution in Action* (New York: Mentor Books, 1957), pp. 43–44.

The studies by D. F. Roberts of variations in the mean body weights of people living in regions with widely differing temperatures have provided evidence in support of Bergmann's rule.[6] Roberts discovered that the lowest body weights were found among residents of areas with the highest mean annual temperatures, and vice versa. For example, where the mean annual temperatures are 70°–82° F., people weigh, on the average, only 96 to 100 pounds. Populations with average weights over 160 pounds live where the temperature averages 40° F.

Allen's rule describes another probable kind of variation in body build. This rule states that protruding body parts (particularly arms and legs) are relatively shorter in the cooler areas of a species's range than in the warmer areas.

The rationale behind these theories is that the long-limbed, lean body type that is often found in tropical regions provides more surface area in relation to body mass and thus facilitates the dissipation of body heat. In contrast, the chunkier, shorter-limbed body type found among the residents of cold regions helps to retain body heat by reducing the amount of surface area relative to body mass. The build of the Eskimos appears to exemplify Bergmann's and Allen's rules. Their relatively large bodies and short legs may be adapted to the cold temperatures in which they live.

It is not clear, however, whether differences in body build between populations are due solely to natural selection of different genes under different conditions of cold or heat. Some of the variation may be induced during the life span of individuals.[7]

Riesenfeld has recently provided some experimental evidence suggesting that extreme cold affects body proportions. Rats raised under conditions of extreme cold generally show changes that resemble characteristics of humans

[6]D. F. Roberts, "Body Weight, Race, and Climate," *American Journal of Physical Anthropology*, n.s. II (1953): 533–58, cited in Stanley M. Garn, *Human Races*, 3rd ed. (Springfield, Ill.: Charles C Thomas, 1971), p. 73.

[7]Marshall T. Newman, "The Application of Ecological Rules to the Racial Anthropology of the Aboriginal New World," *American Anthropologist* 55, no. 3 (August 1953): 311–27.

The long-limbed, lean body type that is often found in tropical regions, such as that of this man from Kenya, provides more surface area in relation to body mass and thus may facilitate the dissipation of body heat. (Ken Heyman.)

rower noses than persons in warmer regions. This difference may be due to the low absolute humidity associated with cold air rather than with cold by itself. A relatively narrow nose may be a more efficient humidifier and heater of cold air than a broad nose.[10]

HEIGHT

Although adaptation to heat and cold may have some effect on the varying height of human populations, as stated in Allen's rule, discussed above, such variation may also be produced by other conditions. Physical or psychological stress, nutrition, medical care, and other factors unrelated to temperature may affect human stature.

For example, Thomas K. Landauer and John W. M. Whiting examined the relationship between certain infant care practices judged to be stressful and the stature of adult males in eighty societies.[11] The impetus for this study came from previous research suggesting that rats which were stressed in infancy (that is, subjected to apparently stressful treatment such as handling, electric shock, vibration, and temperature extremes) developed longer skeletons, longer tails, and were also somewhat heavier than nonstressed rats.

Landauer and Whiting examined, collected, and correlated data about infant care procedures and adult male stature in humans. In some societies, children are subjected to stressful practices from birth to age two years. These practices include circumcision; branding of the skin with sharp objects; the piercing of the nose, ears, or lips for the insertion of ornaments; and the molding and stretching of the head and limbs for cosmetic purposes. In these societies, the male adults average more than 2 inches taller than males raised in societies which do not practice such customs.

in cold environments. These cold-related changes include long-bone shortening consistent with Allen's rule.[8]

Like body build, facial structure may be affected by the environment. Riesenfeld found that the facial width of rats increased in cold temperatures. Nasal openings also grew smaller in rats exposed to cold temperatures.[9]

Temperature-related effects are also evident in the structure of human faces. For example, people living in cold climates have higher, nar-

[8] Alphonse Riesenfeld, "The Effect of Extreme Temperatures and Starvation on the Body Proportions of the Rat," *American Journal of Physical Anthropology* 39, no. 3 (November 1973): 427–59.

[9] Ibid., pp. 452–53.

[10] A. T. Steegman, Jr., "Human Adaptation to Cold," in *Physiological Anthropology*, ed. Albert Damon (New York: Oxford University Press, 1975), pp. 130–66.

[11] Thomas K. Landauer and John W. M. Whiting, "Infantile Stimulation and Adult Stature of Human Males," *American Anthropologist* 66 (1964): 1008.

Landauer and Whiting found it impossible to introduce controls for all the possible variables that might account for their results. Yet their analysis suggested that certain variables known, or thought, to be related to height could not account for their results. For example, genetic differences alone do not seem to account for the results linking stress to greater height. When the sample was divided into the five major geographical regions of the world (Africa, Eurasia, Insular Pacific, North and South America), the investigators found that, although the average height in one region might be greater than that in another, within each region those societies with stress before the age of two years produced adult males who were more than 2 inches taller, on the average, than the males in other societies in the region who had not been stressed.

Another cultural factor which may influence adult stature is early mother-infant separation, which may also be a stress experience. In a cross-cultural study of sixty-nine societies, Gunders and Whiting found that males are taller in societies that practice early mother-infant separation than they are where such customs are lacking or are minimally practiced.[12]

In most areas of the world people are getting taller, and some have suggested that this trend is a result of better nutrition and medical care. For example, between the first and second World Wars, the average height of males in the United States increased by 2 inches.[13] Comparisons made in the eighteenth and nineteenth centuries in England, France, and Germany also seem consistent with this hypothesis. Those from affluent upper-class families were shown to be significantly taller than those from poorer families. And stature decreased during times of famine in those countries.[14]

The trend toward greater stature might also be explained by *heterosis* or *hybrid vigor*. These terms refer to the possibility that matings between individuals with different genetic characteristics produce healthier and more numerous offspring. As a result of our increased social and geographic mobility, matings between different kinds of people are fairly common nowadays across cultures and continents. Increased height in the offspring of these matings may be partially a consequence of the "hybrid vigor" so produced.[15]

Any or all of the genetic or environmental factors discussed above may affect human size. Further research will probably help determine which of these factors are the most important.

SKIN COLOR

Human populations obviously differ in average skin color. Many people consider skin color the most important indicator of racial distinction and sometimes treat others differently solely on this basis. But anthropologists, in addition to being critical of racial discrimination (for reasons we shall discuss later in this chapter), also note that skin color is not a good indicator of race. For example, extremely dark skin is found most commonly in Africa. However, there are natives of southern India whose skin is as dark as, or darker than, that of many Africans. Yet, these people are not closely related to Africans, either genetically or historically.

Nevertheless, the very fact that there are people in the world with markedly different skin colors leads us to the interesting question, How can we explain this wide range of hues? The answer appears to be extremely complex. Scientists do not yet fully understand why some people have very light skin whereas others have either very dark, "reddish," or "yellowish" skin. But we do have some theories that may partially account for variation in skin color.

We know that skin color is influenced by *melanin*. The more melanin there is in the skin, the darker the skin will be. Furthermore, the

[12] S. Gunders and J. W. M. Whiting, "Mother-Infant Separation and Physical Growth," *Ethnology* 7, no. 2 (April 1968): 196–206.

[13] William A. Stini, *Ecology and Human Adaptation* (Dubuque, Iowa: Wm. C. Brown, 1975), p. 3.

[14] Ibid., pp. 3–4.

[15] Albert Damon, "Stature Increase among Italian-Americans: Environmental, Genetic, or Both?" *American Journal of Physical Anthropology* 23, no. 4 (December 1965): 401–08.

amount of melanin in the skin seems to be related to the climate in which a person lives. *Gloger's rule* states that populations of birds and mammals living in warm, humid climates have more melanin (and therefore darker skin, fur, or feathers) than do populations of the same species living in cooler, drier areas. On the whole, this association with climate holds true for people as well as for birds and other mammals. Darker-skinned human populations do live mostly in warm climates (although all residents of warm climates do not have dark skins). Dark pigmentation seems to have at least one specific advantage in tropical climates: melanin protects the sensitive inner layers of the skin from the sun's damaging ultraviolet rays. Therefore, dark-skinned people living in sunny areas are safer from sunburn and skin cancers than light-skinned people.

What, then, might be the advantages of a light-colored skin? Presumably, there must be some benefits; otherwise, through the process of natural selection, human populations would all tend to have relatively dark skin color. Although light-skinned people are more susceptible to sunburn and skin cancers than are darker people, the ultraviolet radiation that light skin absorbs also facilitates the body's production of vitamin D. Vitamin D is necessary for the proper growth and maintenance of bones. Too much vitamin D, however, can cause illness. Thus, the light-colored skin of people in temperate latitudes maximizes ultraviolet penetration, perhaps insuring production of sufficient amounts of vitamin D for good health, whereas the darker skin of people in tropical latitudes minimizes it, thereby preventing illness from too much vitamin D.[16]

ADAPTATION TO HIGH ALTITUDE

Oxygen constitutes 21 percent of the air we breathe at sea level. At high altitudes, the percentage of oxygen in the air is the same, but because the barometric pressure is lower, we take in less oxygen with each breath.[17] This leads to discomfort and a condition known as *hypoxia*, or oxygen deficiency. We breathe more rapidly, our hearts beat faster, and all activity is more difficult. During the 1968 Olympic Games in Mexico City, it was thought that the high altitude might have had an adverse effect on those athletes who were unaccustomed to it.[18] Certainly, performing athletic feats at 7,500 feet must have been difficult for those who were accustomed to life at sea level.

Since high altitudes present such difficulties for human beings, how is it that populations numbering in the millions can live out their lives, healthy and productive, at altitudes of 6,000, 12,000, or even 17,000 feet? Populations in the Himalayas and the Andes Mountains seem to have adapted to their environments. Not only have they survived the stress of hypoxia, but they have also come to terms, physiologically, with extreme cold, deficient nutrition, strong winds, rough countryside, and intense solar radiation.[19]

As compared with sea-level populations, high-altitude dwellers have a higher than normal number of red blood cells in their circulatory systems so that the potential for carrying oxygen is greater. Their blood is "thicker" and their hearts appear to be larger, perhaps in order to pump the heavier liquid. Also, the respiration rate of mountain people is slower than that of sea-level populations. For this reason, their demand for oxygen is reduced—in a process similar to that of hibernating animals.[20]

In physical appearance, the Himalayan and Andean peoples are also similar. They have very large chests (a result of their increased lung size and capacity) and relatively short legs (a reaction to the stress of extreme cold and poor nutrition). In childhood, the trunks of their bodies grow rapidly while their legs grow quite

---

[16]W. Farnsworth Loomis, "Skin-Pigment Regulation of Vitamin-D Biosynthesis in Man," *Science*, 4 August 1967, pp. 501–6.

[17]Stini, *Ecology and Human Adaptation*, p. 53.

[18]Raymond J. Hock, "The Physiology of High Altitude," *Scientific American*, February 1970, pp. 52–62.

[19]Richard B. Mazess, "Human Adaptation to High Altitude," in *Physiological Anthropology*, ed. Albert Damon, p. 168.

[20]Stini, *Ecology and Human Adaptation*, p. 59.

slowly. There is no spurt of growth at preadolescence, as is found in sea-level populations.

Because these populations are not isolated (many mountain inhabitants choose mates from among sea-level groups), these traits are thought to develop in people as a result of their living in the highlands. They are not thought to be present in the people's genes at birth.[21]

SUSCEPTIBILITY TO INFECTIOUS DISEASES

Certain populations seem to have developed inherited resistances to some infectious diseases. That is, populations that were repeatedly decimated by these diseases in the past now have a high frequency of genetic characteristics which minimize the effects of these diseases. As Arno Motulsky has pointed out, if there are genes that protect a person from dying when he or she is infected by one of the diseases prevalent in the area, these genes will tend to become more common in succeeding generations.[22]

A field study of the infectious disease myxomatosis in rabbits lends support to this theory. When the virus responsible for the disease was first introduced into the Australian rabbit population, more than 95 percent of the infected animals died. But, among the offspring of animals exposed to successive epidemics of the disease, the percentage of animals which died from myxomatosis decreased from year to year. The more epidemics the animals' ancestors had lived through, the smaller the percentage of current animals that died of the disease. Thus, the data suggested that the rabbits had developed a genetic resistance to myxomatosis.[23]

Infectious diseases seem to follow a similar pattern among human populations. When tuberculosis first strikes a population which has had no previous contact with it, the disease is commonly fatal. But some populations seem to

have inherited a resistance to death from tuberculosis. For example, the Ashkenazi Jews in America (those whose ancestors came from central and eastern Europe) are one of several populations whose ancestors survived many years of exposure to tuberculosis in the crowded European ghettos where they previously lived. Although the rate of tuberculosis infection is identical among American Jews and non-Jews, the rate of tuberculosis mortality is significantly lower among Jews than among non-Jews in this country.[24] After reviewing other data on this subject, Motulsky concludes it is likely "that the present relatively high resistance of Western populations to tuberculosis is genetically conditioned through natural selection during long contact with the disease."[25]

We tend to think of measles as a childhood disease that kills virtually no one. Indeed, it is rapidly becoming a childhood disease that almost no one gets anymore, because we now have a vaccine against it. But when first introduced into populations, the measles virus can kill large numbers of people. In 1949, the Tupari Indians of Brazil numbered about 200 people. By 1955, two-thirds of the Tupari had died of measles introduced into the tribe by rubber gatherers in the area.[26] Large numbers of people died of measles in epidemics in the Faroe Islands in 1846, in Hawaii in 1848, in the Fiji Islands in 1874, and among the Canadian Eskimos quite recently. It is possible that where mortality rates from measles are low, populations have acquired a genetic resistance to death from this disease.[27]

SICKLE CELL ANEMIA

Another biological variation, the causes of which we are beginning to understand, is an abnormality of the red blood cells known as *sickle cell anemia*, or *sicklemia*. This is a condition in which the red blood cells assume a crescent

---

[21] Hock, "The Physiology of High Altitude."

[22] Arno Motulsky, "Metabolic Polymorphisms and the Role of Infectious Diseases in Human Evolution," in *Human Populations, Genetic Variation, and Evolution,* ed. Laura Newell Morris (San Francisco: Chandler, 1971), p. 223.

[23] Ibid., p. 226.

[24] Ibid., p. 229.

[25] Ibid., p. 230.

[26] Ibid., p. 233.

[27] Ibid., p. 233.

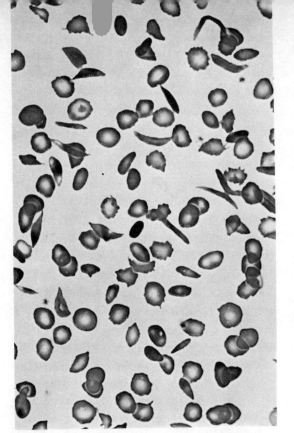

This photomicrograph illustrates the crescent-shaped red blood cells characteristic of sickle cell anemia. (Courtesy, C. Lockard Conley, M.D., Department of Medicine, The Johns Hopkins Hospital.)

parent only. Since it is a recessive gene, these children generally will not develop sicklemia. (In some cases, a heterozygous individual may have a mild case of anemia.) However, a heterozygous person is a "carrier"; that is, he or she can pass on the trait. And if a carrier mates with a person who is also heterozygous for sicklemia, the statistical probability is that 25 percent of their children will have the homozygous form of this condition.

Without medical care, individuals homozygous for sicklemia usually die before reaching maturity.[28] Since this would tend to decrease the number of sickle cell genes in a population's gene pool, and since the gene is recessive, why has sicklemia not disappeared? At the very least, we would expect the condition to have become extremely rare, assuming that natural selection should have continuously weeded out this potentially lethal trait.

And yet, sickle cell anemia is still very common—particularly in equatorial Africa, where up to 40 percent of the population carry the trait. Nine percent of American blacks also carry the sickle cell trait.[29] For this reason, the sickle cell trait was once thought to be a specifically "Negroid" characteristic. But research has shown that this is not quite the case. The sickle cell trait crosses "racial" lines. It is widespread in Greece, Turkey, and India. Why does the trait occur so frequently?

Recent studies indicate that the heterozygous carrier of the sickle cell trait may be protected against a kind of malaria which kills many people in the regions where sicklemia is most prevalent. (Malaria is carried principally by the *Anopheles gambiae* mosquito, common in tropical areas.) Motulsky points out that the sickling trait does not necessarily keep people from contracting malaria, but it greatly decreases the rate of mortality from malaria—and in evolutionary terms, the overall effect is the same.[30] Heterozygous carriers have also been

(sickle) shape when they are deprived of oxygen, instead of the normal (disk) shape. The sickle-shaped red blood cells tend to rupture, thereby causing severe anemia. The abnormally shaped cells also tend to form clumps which clog smaller blood vessels. This impairs circulation and causes pains in the abdomen, back, head, and extremities. The heart may become enlarged and brain cells may atrophy.

The sickle cell trait is an inherited condition for which people can be either homozygous or heterozygous. A person who is homozygous for the trait has received a sickling gene from each parent and will therefore have sickle cell anemia.

Offspring who are heterozygous for the trait have received the sickle cell gene from one

[28] Ibid., p. 237.
[29] Anthony C. Allison, "Sickle Cells and Evolution," *Scientific American*, August 1956, p. 87.
[30] Motulsky, "Metabolic Polymorphisms," p. 238.

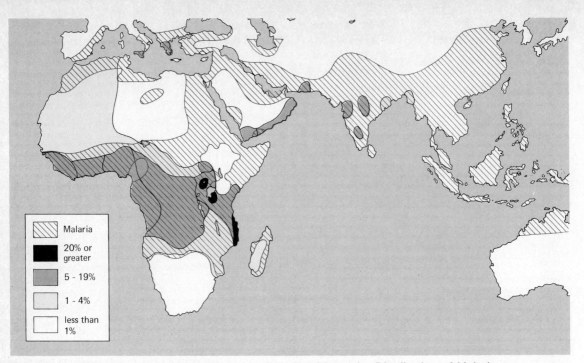

Geographical Distribution of Sicklemia and Its Relationship to the Distribution of Malaria
(Adapted from *Physical Anthropology: A Perspective,* by John Buettner-Janusch, © 1973 by John Wiley & Sons, Inc. Reprinted by permission of John Wiley & Sons, Inc.)

reported to have higher fertility in malarial areas.[31]

The point is that, since persons homozygous for sicklemia rarely reproduce, and since many "normal" persons (those completely lacking the sickle cell gene) die early or reproduce less because of malaria, individuals who are heterozygous for sicklemia may be favored by natural selection in malarial regions. Hence, the sickling trait is likely to persist among certain populations until the threat of malaria entirely disappears. When that happens, the sickle cell trait will no longer confer any advantage on its carriers.[32]

LACTASE DEFICIENCY

When educators discovered that black schoolchildren very often did not drink milk, they assumed that lack of money or of education (regarding the presumed necessity for young children to ingest a certain amount of dairy products daily) explained this behavior. These assumptions provided the impetus for establishing the school milk programs so prevalent around the country.

However, it now appears that many people lack an enzyme, lactase, which is necessary to break down lactose, the sugar in milk. Without lactase, a person cannot digest milk properly and drinking it will cause bloating, cramps, stomach gas, and diarrhea. A study conducted in Baltimore, among 312 black and 221 white children in grades 1 through 6 in two elementary schools, indicated that 85 percent of the black children *and* 17 percent of the white children were milk intolerant.[33]

More recent studies indicate that milk intolerance is frequently found in many parts of

[31]Research reported in Frank B. Livingston, "Malaria and Human Polymorphisms," *Annual Review of Genetics* 5 (1971): 33–64, esp. pp. 45–46.
[32]Allison, "Sickle Cells and Evolution," p. 87.

[33]Jane E. Brodey, "Effects of Milk on Blacks Noted," *New York Times,* 15 October 1971, p. 15.

the world.[34] The condition is common in adults among Orientals, Southern Europeans, Mediterranean peoples (Arabs and Jews), West Africans, North American blacks, Eskimos, and North and South American Indians.

What accounts for this widespread adult intolerance of milk? One hypothesis is that milk tolerance is a physiological adaptation resulting from continuous milk consumption over the life span. Another possible explanation is that a regulatory gene is involved—although the function of regulatory genes is not yet fully understood.[35] McCracken suggests that perhaps all human populations were once lactase deficient.[36] With the advent of dairy farming and the common use of milk as a basic food by some populations, natural selection might have favored those individuals with the genetic ability to produce lactase in adulthood.

The Concept of Race

Fortunately, internal variations such as lactase deficiency have never engendered tensions among peoples—perhaps because such differences are not immediately obvious. Unfortunately, the same cannot be said for some of the more obvious, external human differences.

WHAT IS RACE?

For as long as any of us can remember, countless numbers of aggressive actions—from fistfights to large-scale riots and country-wide civil wars—have stemmed from tension and misunderstandings among various "races." "The race problem" has become such a common phrase that most of us take the concept of race for granted, without bothering to consider what it does, and does not, really mean.

But do we really know what race is? What

do we mean when we refer to the "human race"? Obviously, that phrase is supposed to include all people and does not have anything to do with the concept of race. The very sloppiness of our language helps to confuse the issue of race. The "Aryan race" is best known as the group of blond-haired, blue-eyed, white-skinned persons whom Hitler wanted to dominate the world, to which end he attempted to destroy as many members of the "Jewish race" as he could. But is there an Aryan race? Technically, Aryans are any people who speak one of the Indo-European languages. However, the Indo-European languages include such disparate modern tongues as Greek, Hindi, Polish, Icelandic, German, Gaelic, and English, and many Aryans speaking these languages have neither blond hair nor blue eyes. Similarly, the Jewish race does not exist in anthropological terms, since all kinds of people may be Jews. There are light-skinned Danish Jews and swarthy Jewish Arabs. One of the most orthodox Jewish groups in the United States is based in New York City and is composed entirely of black people.

Nevertheless, most people in this country do identify themselves with a racial group, most often one of the three races most popularly recognized: the Caucasoid (white), Negroid (black), and Mongoloid (yellow and red). Many people think that certain biological traits are characteristic of each race. Another popular belief is that although the races have become "adulterated" through miscegenation (intermarriage and interbreeding between different races), some individuals still exist who typify the "pure" Caucasoid, Negroid, and Mongoloid types. The inaccuracy of such a classification should be obvious. Although many Caucasoids have straight hair and light skin, some have curly or quite frizzy hair and rather dark skin. Not all Negroids have wide noses or thick lips. And many people do not fit into any of the three major racial types at all.

But racial stereotypes persist—largely because of the ease with which such obvious traits as skin color can be recognized and used to classify people. In itself, this tendency to attri-

[34] Gail G. Harrison, "Primary Adult Lactase Deficiency: A Problem in Anthropological Genetics," *American Anthropologist* 77, no. 4 (December 1975): 812–35.

[35] Ibid., pp. 826, 829.

[36] Robert D. McCracken, "Lactase Deficiency: An Example of Dietary Evolution," *Current Anthropology* 12, no. 4–5 (October-December 1971): 479–500.

Map of the World Illustrating the Locations of Nine Geographical Races According to Garn
(After Stanley M. Garn, *Human Races*, 3rd ed., 1971. Courtesy of Charles C Thomas, Publisher, Springfield, Illinois.)

bute certain biological factors to all members of a supposed race, while inaccurate, is not disturbing. What is disturbing is the frequent association of the race concept with ethnocentrism and racism.

Race concepts have often been, and still are, used by certain groups to justify their exploitation of other groups. A blatant example of how present-day racism is linked to inaccurate concepts of race is the treatment accorded American blacks. Most of the people who still justify the virtual elimination of black persons' civil rights do so because of a belief in the blacks' inherent (i.e., genetic) inferiority to whites. In fact, no such inferiority has been demonstrated. This racist outlook is a remnant of slavery days, when the white slaveholders assumed that their servants were inferior—and tried to convince the slaves that they were—in order to perpetuate the system.

The major difficulty with the race concept is its arbitrariness. The number of races into which the world's population can be divided depends upon who is doing the classifying, because each classifier may use different traits as the basis for the classification. All variable traits—such as skin color; bloodtype; hair, nose, and lip shape—should be considered when developing a racial classification. But, unfortunately for the classifiers, many of these traits do not vary together. Even the supposedly distinguishing features of a Mongoloid person—the so-called *Mongoloid spot*, a dark patch of skin at the base of the spine which disappears as the person grows older; shovel-shaped incisor teeth; and an *epicanthic fold*, a bit of skin overlapping the eyelid—are not limited to peoples traditionally classified as Mongoloids. Southern Africa's Bushmen have epicanthic folds, for example, and Caucasoids can have Mongoloid spots.

Thus, since the number and types of races in each classification of peoples depends upon the traits used in the classification, and since many anthropologists base their classifications on different traits, there is no "right" or "wrong" number of races. Boyd says there are five races; Coon recognizes nine; and Birdsell counts thirty-two.[37]

Racial taxonomies in anthropology typically involve the identification of both geographical races and local races. A *geographical race* is a set of at least once-neighboring populations which has certain distinctive trait frequencies. Thus, the traditional trio of races (Negroid, Mongoloid, Caucasoid) would be considered geographical. Garn identifies a total of nine geographical races: European-Caucasoid and Western Asiatic; Northern Mongoloid and Eastern Asiatic; African-Negroid; Indian; Micronesian; Melanesian; Polynesian; American; and Australian.[38] A *local race* is like a *Mendelian population*—that is, it is a breeding population, or local group, whose members usually interbreed with each other. Garn identifies approximately thirty-two local races.[39]

Not only do anthropologists disagree on the number of races into which people can be classified. Some even argue that there is no such thing as race. Ashley Montagu has long held this opinion, and it has more recently been adopted by other physical anthropologists, including C. Loring Brace, Frank Livingstone, and Jean Hiernaux. They do not pretend that all people are the same physically. They merely point out that "race" is an artificial construct, developed to justify the different treatments accorded different peoples.

RACIAL AND CULTURAL VARIATION: IS THERE A RELATIONSHIP?

In the past, biological variation was believed to be related not only to the geographical location of a particular group of people but also to their cultural characteristics. Even today, many persons hold the racist viewpoint that the biological inferiority of certain races is reflected in the supposedly primitive quality of their cultures.

"We don't consider ours to be an underdeveloped country so much as we think of yours as an overdeveloped country." (Courtesy *Saturday Review*, January 10, 1970.)

Racists refuse to recognize that the facts of history very often contradict their theories.

Race and Civilization Many of today's so-called underdeveloped nations—primarily in Asia, Africa, and South America—had developed complex and sophisticated civilizations long before Europe had reached beyond a simple level of technology or tribal organization. The advanced societies of the Shang dynasty in China, the Mayans in Mesoamerica, and the African empires of Ghana, Mali, and Songhay were all founded and developed by nonwhites.

Between 1523 and 1028 B.C., China had a complex form of government, armies, metal tools and weapons, and production and storage facilities for large quantities of grain. The early Chinese civilization also had a form of writing and elaborate religious rituals.[40] During a span

---

[37]Theodosius Dobzhansky, *Mankind Evolving: The Evolution of the Human Species* (New Haven: Yale University Press, 1962), p. 266.
[38]Garn, *Human Races*, pp. 152–67.
[39]Ibid., pp. 169–79.

[40]L. Carrington Goodrich, *A Short History of the Chinese People* (New York: Harper & Row, 1959), pp. 7–15.

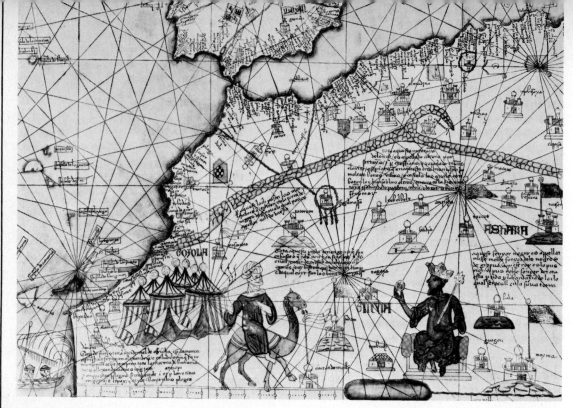

The West African kingdom of Mali flourished while Europe was in its Dark Ages. This map, drawn in 1375, shows an Arab trader coming to bargain with Mali's ruler. The writing says, "This Negro Lord is called Musa Mali, Lord of the Negroes of Guinea. So abundant is the gold which is found in his land that he is the richest and most noble king in all the land." (Photo Bibliotheque Nationale, Paris.)

of six centuries, from A.D. 300 to 900, the Mayans were a large population with a thriving economy. They built many large and impressively beautiful cities, centered around great pyramids and luxurious palaces.[41] According to legend, the West African civilization of Ghana was founded during the second century A.D. By A.D. 770 (the time of the Sonniki rulers), Ghana had developed two capital cities—one Moslem and the other non-Moslem—each with its own ruler and both supported largely by Ghana's lucrative gold market. Ghana's empire was destroyed largely by Berber tribesmen, who wanted to convert the unbelievers to Islam and to gain control of their gold.[42]

[41] Michael D. Coe, *The Maya* (New York: Praeger, 1966), pp. 74–76.
[42] Elizabeth Bartlett Thompson, *Africa, Past and Present* (Boston: Houghton Mifflin, 1966), p. 89.

Considering how long Europeans lagged behind other peoples in the development of a civilization, it seems odd that some whites should even dare to label Africans, South Americans, and other societies as "backward" in terms of historical achievement, or as "biologically inferior" in terms of capacity for civilization. But racists, both white and nonwhite, choose to ignore that all races have achieved remarkable advances in civilization. Most significantly, such people refuse to believe that they can acknowledge the achievements of another race without in any way downgrading the achievements of their own.

Race, Culture, and Infectious Disease Although biological variations cannot set fixed limits on the development of a particular culture, they may strongly influence it. Earlier, we discussed how continued exposure to epidemics of infectious diseases, such as tuberculosis and measles, can cause succeeding generations to acquire a genetic resistance to death from such diseases. But, on a short-term basis, differential susceptibility to disease may have affected the outcome of contact between different societies. An example of this is the rapid defeat of the Aztecs by Cortez and his conquistadores. In 1520, a member of Cortez's army unwittingly transmitted smallpox to the Indians. The disease spread rapidly through the population, killing at least one-half of the Indians, who were thus at a considerable disadvantage in their battle with the Spanish.[43]

Outbreaks of smallpox repeatedly decimated many American Indian populations in North America a century or so later. In the early nineteenth century, the Massachusetts and Narragansett Indians, with populations of 30,000 and 9,000, respectively, were reduced by smallpox to a few hundred members. Extremely high mortality rates were also noted among the Crow, the Blackfoot, and other Indian groups during the nineteenth century. The germ theory alone cannot explain these epidemics. Once the European settlers realized how susceptible the Indians were to smallpox, they purposely distributed infected blankets to them. Motulsky calls the spread of smallpox probably "one of the first examples of biological warfare."[44]

Race and Intelligence Perhaps the most controversial aspect of the racial distinctions made among people is the relationship, if any, between race and intelligence.

In the nineteenth century, European white supremacists attempted to find scientific justification for what they felt was the genetically inherited mental inferiority of blacks. They did this by measuring skulls. It was believed that the larger the skull, the greater the cranial capacity and the bigger (hence, also "better") the brain.

Interest in skull measurement was first aroused by a number of separate researchers in different parts of Europe who tried to determine the relative intelligence of round-headed versus narrow-headed individuals. Not surprisingly, their results were generally either inconclusive or contradictory. Paul Broca held that round-headed Frenchmen were superior in intelligence to narrow-headed Frenchmen, while Otto Ammon concluded that Baden's more intelligent residents had narrow heads. The Italian, Livi, concluded that southern Italians with round heads were of superior intelligence.

Although the skull-measuring mania of Broca, Ammon, and others quickly disappeared and is no longer upheld as evidence of racial superiority, the actions of these men paved the way for other attempts to justify racism. Other, more insidious, and often more powerful, "facts" are used today to demonstrate the presumed intellectual superiority of white people, namely, statistics from intelligence tests.

The first large-scale intelligence testing in this country began with our entry into World War I. Thousands of draftees were given the so-called Alpha and Beta IQ tests to determine their military assignments. Later, psychologists arranging the test results according to race found what they had expected—blacks consistently scored lower than whites. This was viewed as scientific proof of the innate intellectual inferiority of blacks and was used to justify further discrimination against blacks, both in and out of the army.[45]

However, Klineberg's subsequent statistical analyses of IQ test results demonstrated that blacks from northern states scored higher than blacks from the South. Although dedicated racists explained that this was due to the northward migration of innately intelligent blacks, most academics attributed the result to the influence of superior education and more stimulating environments in the North. When further studies showed that northern blacks scored

[43]Motulsky, "Metabolic Polymorphisms," p. 232.
[44]Ibid.

[45]Otto Klineberg, *Negro Intelligence and Selective Migration* (New York: Columbia University Press, 1935); idem, *Characteristics of the American Negro* (New York: Harper & Row, 1944).

higher than southern whites, the better-education-in-the-North theory gained support—but again racists insisted such results were due to northward migrations by all innately intelligent whites.

As a further test of his conclusions, Klineberg gave IQ tests to black schoolgirls, born and partly raised in the South, who had spent varying lengths of time in New York City. He found that the longer the girls had been in the North, the higher their average IQ.

In addition to providing support for the belief that blacks are not inherently inferior to whites, these findings suggested that cultural factors can and do influence IQ scores, and that IQ is not a fixed quantity but can be raised by contact with an improved environment. (It should have long been obvious that biological variations alone could not account for IQ differences between white and black people, because it is common knowledge that a large percentage of the blacks in America have some white ancestors, and many American whites have black ancestors. Thus, the distinctions between the two races are blurred.)

One of the most controversial viewpoints on the relationship of race to intelligence is held by a psychologist, Arthur Jensen. Jensen maintains that environment has an extremely limited influence on IQ. He asserts that, in general, most black people cannot reach the IQ level of most whites, whatever changes are made in their surroundings. Jensen bases his interpretation on statistical evidence that there is approximately a 15-point difference between the average IQ scores of American blacks and whites. He believes that as much as 80 percent of this gap is genetically determined and therefore cannot be modified through environmental changes.[46]

Recently, however, the rationale for all "heritability" studies has been questioned on statistical and logical grounds. Because performance on an IQ test is not simply a genetic

Hopefully, we will create a society where everyone is given the same opportunity to develop as he or she chooses, regardless of race. (Charles Gatewood.)

trait like eye color, it is not possible, as of now, to say how large a percentage of an IQ score is genetically, as opposed to environmentally, caused. Therefore, it has been suggested that using IQ test scores to determine inherited differences in intelligence is like trying to understand how a clock works by watching its hands move and listening to it tick.[47]

In any case, increasingly less importance is now being attached to IQ test results. Although it was once thought that the Binet test series could be of considerable value to educators, it is now widely recognized that IQ tests are hopelessly culture-bound. That is, an IQ test can measure how well a black child may compete with white children in a white school system—but nothing more. IQ tests cannot indicate the upper limits of a person's mental capacities, whatever his or her race or environment. And

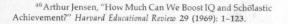

[46] Arthur Jensen, "How Much Can We Boost IQ and Scholastic Achievement?" *Harvard Educational Review* 29 (1969): 1–123.

[47] M. W. Feldman and R. C. Lewontin, "The Heritability Hang-Up," *Science*, 19 December 1975, pp. 1163–68.

studies have clearly shown that a deprived child, whether black or white, will generally have a lower IQ than an affluent child of either race. A child's IQ can increase with an improved environment; it can also decrease if environmental stimuli are decreased.

Thus, the primary objection to Jensen's findings is that IQ tests cannot give results that are equally valid for both black and white children. Also, since most poor black children experience more anxiety than white children in the test situation itself (a stressful examination, in a strange room, supervised by unknown and usually white people, for an unknown purpose), their test scores tend to be lower than those of white children more familiar with such procedures.

Dobzhansky emphasizes that no truly valid comparisons can be made of racially based IQs until both black and white people have equal opportunities to develop their potentials. He stresses the need for an open society existing under the democratic ideal—where every person is given an equal opportunity to develop whatever gifts or aptitudes he or she possesses and chooses to develop.[48]

The Future of Human Variation

Laboratory fertilization, subsequent transplantation of the embryo, and successful birth have been accomplished with nonhuman mammals. And *cloning*—the exact reproduction of an individual from cellular tissue—has been achieved with frogs.

What are the implications of such research for the genetic future of humans? Will it someday be possible to control the genetic makeup of our species? If so, will the effects be positive or negative?

It is interesting to speculate on the development of a "perfect human." Aside from the serious ethical question of who would decide

what the perfect human should be like, there is the serious biological question of whether such a development might, in the long run, be detrimental to the human species. For that which is perfectly suited to one physical or social environment may be totally unsuited to another. And the collection of physical, emotional, and intellectual attributes that might be "perfect" in the twentieth century could be inappropriate in the twenty-first.[49]

In the long run, the perpetuation of genetic variability is probably more advantageous than the creation of a "perfect" and invariable human being. In the event of dramatic changes in the world environment, absolute uniformity in the human species might be an evolutionary dead end. Such uniformity might lead to the extinction of the human species if the new environmental conditions favored genetic or cultural variations that were no longer present in the species. Perhaps our best hope for maximizing our chances of survival is to tolerate, and even encourage, the persistence of many aspects of human variation, both biological and cultural.[50]

Summary

1. Biological variation in humans, as well as in other species, is the result of one or more of the following processes: mutation and natural selection, genetic drift, and gene flow.

2. Human biological variations can be both external (such as skin color, body build, stature, and shape of facial features) and internal (such as susceptibility to disease). Certain of these variations may be explained as adaptations to differing physical or social environments or as consequences of other physical

---

[48]Dobzhansky, *Mankind Evolving*, p. 243.

[49]J. B. S. Haldane, "Human Evolution: Past and Future," in *Genetics, Paleontology, and Evolution,* ed. Glenn L. Jepsen, Ernst Mayr, and George Gaylord Simpson (New York: Atheneum, 1963), pp. 405–18.
[50]George Gaylord Simpson, *The Meaning of Evolution* (New York: Bantam Books, 1971), pp. 297–308.

or cultural changes. However, there are many biological variations among human populations for which we do not yet have any explanations.

3. The major problem with the concept of race is its arbitrariness. The number of races into which the world's population can be divided depends upon who is doing the classifying, because each classifier may use different traits as the basis for classification. Racial classifiers identify both geographical and local races. A geographical race is a set of at least once-neighboring populations which has certain distinctive trait frequencies. A local race is a breeding population—that is, a local group whose members usually interbreed with each other. Race concepts have often been, and still are, used by some groups to justify their exploitation of other groups.

4. Perhaps the most controversial aspect of racial discrimination is the relationship, if any, between race and intelligence. Attempts have been made to prove "scientifically," by IQ tests and other means, the innate intellectual superiority of one race over another. But there is no proof that IQ tests truly measure intelligence. Even if we should have culture-free measures of genetically determined intelligence, no truly valid IQ comparisons could be made until the people being compared had equal opportunities to develop their potentials.

Suggested Readings

Dobzhansky, T. *Mankind Evolving: The Evolution of the Human Species.* New Haven: Yale University Press, 1962.

A well-written introduction to the interaction between cultural and biological components in human evolution. Keeping the technical details and vocabulary of genetics to a minimum, Dobzhansky discusses natural selection and biological fitness in human populations by class, caste, and race.

Garn, S. M. *Human Races.* 3rd ed. Springfield, Ill.: Charles C Thomas, 1971.

A comprehensive introduction to racial studies, with emphasis on such current research areas as race mixture, natural selection, ecology and race, disease and race, and the relationship between race, behavior, and intelligence.

Harrison, G. A.; Weiner, J. S.; Tanner, J. M.; and Barnicot, W. A. *Human Biology: An Introduction to Human Evolution, Variation, and Growth.* New York: Oxford University Press, 1964.

A detailed and technical study of all aspects of human biology. Especially useful are sections 3, 4, and 5, which deal with biological variation in human populations, human ecology, human growth, and the effects of evolution on modern humans.

Laughlin, W. S., and Osborne, R. H., eds. *Human Variation and Origins: An Introduction to Human Biology and Evolution.* San Francisco: Freeman, 1967.

A collection of *Scientific American* offprints, which serves as a survey of topics in human biology. Written for the beginning student, each article is prefaced by a summary and is generously illustrated with photographs, tables, and figures.

Morris, L. N. *Human Populations, Genetic Variation, and Evolution.* San Francisco: Chandler, 1971.

This book is a collection of papers dealing with human evolution from a genetic point of view; each section contains a summarizing introduction by the editor.

Origins of Food Production and Settled Life

8

During the late Upper Paleolithic, which we know best archaeologically in Europe, people depended for their food upon hunting migratory herds of large animals such as wild cattle, antelope, bison, and mastodons. These hunters probably lived in nomadic bands, and followed the migrations of the animals. Beginning about 12,000 B.C., people in some regions began to be less dependent upon big-game hunting and relied more on relatively stationary food resources like fish, shellfish, small game, and wild plants. Marine and riverine food supplies may have become more abundant in many areas after the glaciers withdrew. As the ice melted, the level of the oceans rose and formed many inlets and bays where crabs, clams, and sea mammals could be found. In some areas, particularly Europe and the Near East, the exploitation of local and relatively permanent resources may account for an increasingly sedentary way of life. The cultural period in Europe and the Near East during which these developments took place is called the *Mesolithic,* or middle Stone Age.[1] Other areas of the world show a similar switch to what is called "broad spectrum" food collecting, but they do not always show an increasingly sedentary life style along with new kinds of food collecting.

We see the first evidence of a changeover to food production—the cultivation and domestication of plants and animals—in the Near East about 8000 B.C. This shift has been referred to as the *Neolithic revolution,* and it occurred, probably independently, in a number of other areas besides the Near East. There is evidence of cultivation sometime after 6800 B.C. in the lowland plains of Southeast Asia (what is now Malaya, Thailand, Cambodia, and Vietnam) and in sub-Saharan Africa by perhaps 4000 B.C. In the New World, there appear to have been a number of places of original cultivation and domestication. The highlands of Mesoamerica (after about 5000 B.C.) and the central Andes around Peru (by about 5600 B.C.) were probably the

---

[1] Lewis R. Binford, "Post-Pleistocene Adaptations," in *Prehistoric Agriculture,* ed. Stuart Struever (Garden City, N.Y.: Natural History Press, 1971), p. 27.

most important in terms of food plants still used today.

In this chapter, we discuss what is believed about the origins of food production and settled life (sedentarism): how and why people in different places may have come to cultivate and domesticate plants and animals, and to live in permanent villages. Agriculture and a sedentary life did not necessarily go together. In some regions of the world, people began to live in permanent villages before they cultivated and domesticated plants and animals, while in other places people planted crops without settling down permanently. It should also be noted that much of our theory about why people first began to raise their own food, and why they began to live in villages, is based on research in the Near East and Europe. Hence, much of our discussion focuses on those two areas. As much as we can, however, we try to indicate how data from other areas appear to suggest patterns different from, or similar to, those in Europe and the Near East.

Dating Recent Remains

How do archaeologists establish the dates when developments such as the cultivation and domestication of plants and animals first occurred? Like earlier cultural remains, Neolithic materials can be dated by both absolute and relative methods. In addition to the carbon-14 and varve analysis procedures discussed in the last chapter, the absolute age of sites and specimens can be estimated by two other methods: thermoluminescence and dendrochronology.

Thermoluminescence is a recently developed dating method. It is so new that it has not yet been totally worked out. But someday it may be accurate enough to date even small, isolated pieces of pottery.[2] The method takes advantage of two facts. First, some of the minerals used in making pottery have the property of storing

A scientist is measuring the thermoluminescence of a piece of ancient pottery to determine its age. (The Museum Applied Science Center for Archaeology, University Museum, University of Pennsylvania.)

energy in the form of trapped electrons. Second, the ceramic material in pottery contains some radioactive impurities which release particles at a known rate. These particles cause mineral atoms to ionize and release electrons, which are then stored in the pottery. When a pot is originally fired, the heating process releases the trapped electrons that are present. This release shows up as visible energy in the form of light rays, or thermoluminescence. This means that a brand-new fired pot will release virtually no light rays when heat-tested. But after time, radioactive impurities in the pottery cause electrons to be trapped again, at the same known rate. The older a piece of pottery, the more electrons will be trapped in it.

To date a piece of pottery, the scientist takes a small sample and heats it very quickly to release the trapped electrons. Then the light released is measured in relation to the radioactive material in the sample. A very old piece of pottery will normally release a great deal of thermoluminescence. One reason this dating method is especially promising is that pottery is such a common find in relatively recent archaeological sites.

Dendrochronology, or tree-ring dating, was first applied to archaeological remains in the southwestern United States in the early 1900s. It

[2]Brian Fagan, *In the Beginning* (Boston: Little Brown, 1972), p. 54.

is based upon the principle that each year a tree adds on a layer of growth. The number of rings in a cross-section of a tree indicates how old the tree was when it was cut. The concentric rings within the cross-section are not equal in width. During a year of little moisture, the tree expands with a thin layer; but during times of heavy moisture, the tree grows more, adding thick layers. The cross-section of a tree, then, is a pattern of thick and thin rings. All the trees in a certain area will have the same pattern, as they all are subject to the same climatic conditions. A master chart of the tree-ring patterns can be drawn up for a region, starting with the present and working backward in time. For example, we could cut down a live tree and chart its ring pattern from the day it was cut (the present) to the day it began to grow. Then we could find an older tree and match its ring pattern with the oldest ring pattern on our first tree. By using progressively older trees, matching their latest ring patterns with those of the younger trees, dendrochronology provides us with an absolute method of dating cultural remains in some areas to a particular year within the past few thousand years.

Using dendrochronology, we can date cultural remains such as house beams by matching up the ring pattern in the house beam with a section of the master chart ring patterns and counting how far back the last, or most central, ring on the house beam (the central ring represents the year the tree was cut down and used for the house) is from the first ring on the master chart (which indicates the present). We can then determine how old the beam is.[3] Not all trees can be used in dendrochronology, since many do not live long enough. Redwoods and bristlecone pine trees are used mainly in the southwestern United States, because their life spans are especially long. Certain environments, too, do not permit the use of dendrochronology. For example, in areas where there is very little variation in rainfall, there will be very little variation in ring width.

Pollen analysis is a relative dating method. This method is based on the fact that many living plants produce pollen which they release into the air. If the pollen is deposited in sites such as swampy bogs, clays, or even seabeds, it may be preserved for a very long period of time. Different pollens can be identified under a high-powered microscope. The kind of plant life varies within each geographical zone from one period to the next. Palynologists, or pollen analysts, have examined successive samples of stratified earth to compile a history of plant life for several different areas. Dating a site or specimen is a matter of obtaining a pollen-containing sample, then measuring the proportions of different types of pollen in the sample, and comparing the results with a master chart for the same geographical area. We can assume that a site dates from the period whose pollen profile it matches.[4]

With the help of dating methods like those discussed above, archaeologists have put together a rough profile of how, and when, people first began to live in settled villages and to produce their own food.

Pre-agricultural Developments

EUROPE

Late Upper Paleolithic Europeans lived in an environment of rolling grassy plains which were nourished by water from the melting glaciers and were stocked with a variety of animals. Immense herds of wild horses, bison, mammoths, and reindeer grazed in grasslands which became more extensive as the glaciers thawed in an ever more temperate climate. These Upper Paleolithic Europeans were largely nomadic. In those spacious, flat steppes the animal herds roamed far and wide, and the hunters were obliged to follow suit.

But this hunting way of life lasted for only a comparatively brief time in Europe. After about

[3] Frank Hole and Robert F. Heizer, *An Introduction to Prehistoric Archeology,* 2d ed. (New York: Holt, Rinehart and Winston, 1969), pp. 252–55.

[4] Fagan, *In the Beginning.*

10,000 years ago, the glaciers began to disappear, and with their disappearance came other environmental changes. As the ice receded, the oceans rose and the waters inundated some of the richest fodder-producing coastal plains. The tundras and grasslands eventually gave way to dense mixed forests, mostly birch, oak, and pine. The mammoths became extinct, and while the forested areas were still filled with wild cattle, elk, red deer, roe deer, and wild boar, it became harder to stalk and kill animals sheltered by the thick woods. During this time, too, the melting of the glaciers created islands, inlets, and bays and moved the sea inland; and the warming waterways began to abound with fish and other aquatic resources.[5]

In the scenario sketched for this period by archaeologists, environmental conditions in Europe were such that natural selection may have favored the development of new technology to adjust to the new environment. Hunting the deer and small game inhabiting the new, dense forests was probably very hard work. Even more important, the density of animals per square mile decreased. Traditional hunting efforts were probably no longer productive. Hunters could no longer obtain large quantities of meat simply by remaining close to the huge herds of mammoths and wild cattle that roamed the grassy plains and tundra, as they were able to do during Upper Paleolithic times. Thus, some archaeologists believe that the environmental changes induced Mesolithic Europeans to turn from big-game hunting to the intensive collecting of wild grains, mollusks, fish, and small game to fill the void created by the extinction of the mammoths and the northward migration of reindeer.

The Maglemosian Culture of Northern Europe
Some adaptations to the changing environment can be seen in the cultural remains of settlers in northern Europe who are referred to as Maglemosians. Their name derives from the peat bogs (*magle mose* in Danish means "great

bog") where their remains have been found.

To deal with the new, more forested environment, the Maglemosians made stone axes and adzes to chop down trees and form them into various objects. Large timbers appear to have been split for making houses; trees were hollowed out for canoes; and smaller pieces of wood were made into paddles. The canoes presumably were built for travel, and perhaps for fishing, on the numerous lakes and rivers that abounded in the post-glacial environment.

We know many other things about the Maglemosians' culture. Although fishing was fairly important, as suggested by the frequent occurrence of pike bones and fish hooks, the Maglemosians apparently depended mainly on hunting for food. The hunted game included elk, wild ox, deer, and wild pig. In addition to many fishing implements and the adzes and axes mentioned above, the Maglemosians' tool-kit included the bow and arrow. Some of their tools were ornamented with finely engraved designs. Ornamentation independent of tools also appears in amber and stone pendants and small figurines such as the head of an elk.[6]

Like the Maglemosian finds, many of the European Mesolithic sites are along lakes, rivers, and oceanfronts. Finds like *kitchen middens*, which are piles of shells that centuries of Mesolithic seafood-eaters had discarded, and remains of fishing equipment, canoes, and boats, indicate that Mesolithic people depended much more heavily upon fishing than had their ancestors in Upper Paleolithic times.

THE NEAR EAST

Cultural developments in the Near East seem to have paralleled those in Europe.[7] Here, too, there was a shift from nomadic big-game hunting to the utilization of a broad spectrum of natural resources. Before plants were cultivated in the Near East, there is evidence that people subsisted on a variety of resources which included fish, mollusks, and other water life; wild ungu-

---

[5] Chester S. Chard, *Man in Prehistory* (New York: McGraw-Hill, 1969), p. 171.

[6] Grahame Clark and Stuart Piggot, *Prehistoric Societies* (New York: Alfred A. Knopf, 1965), pp. 144–48.
[7] Binford, "Post-Pleistocene Adaptations," pp. 45–49.

Here, a Turkish field worker demonstrates harvesting techniques with a reconstruction of a Mesolithic stone sickle. (Jack R. Harlan.)

lates like deer, sheep and goats; and wild grains, nuts, and legumes.[8] The increased utilization of such stationary food sources as wild grain may partially explain why people in the Near East began to lead more sedentary lives during the Mesolithic.

Even today, a traveler passing through the Anatolian highlands of Turkey and other mountainous regions in the Near East may see thick stands of wild wheat and barley that grow as densely as if they had been cultivated. Wielding flint sickles, Mesolithic people could easily have harvested a bountiful crop from such wild stands. Just how productive this type of resource can be was demonstrated recently by researchers in a field experiment duplicating prehistoric conditions. Using the kind of flint-blade sickle a Mesolithic worker would have used, they were able to harvest a little over 2 pounds of wild grain in an hour. A Mesolithic

family of four, working only during the few weeks of the harvest season, probably could have reaped more wheat and barley than they needed for the entire year.[9]

The amount of wild wheat harvested in the experiment prompted Flannery to conclude, "Such a harvest would almost necessitate some degree of sedentism—after all, where could they go with an estimated metric ton of clean wheat?"[10] Moreover, the stone equipment used for grinding would be a clumsy burden for any nomadic group to carry. Part of the harvest would probably be set aside for immediate consumption, ground, and then cooked either by roasting or boiling. The rest of the harvest would be stored to supply food for the remainder of the year. A grain diet, then, could have been the impetus for the construction of roasters, grinders, and storage pits by the Mesolithic foragers, as well as for the erection of solid, fairly permanent housing. Once the village was built, the Mesolithic band may have been reluctant to abandon it. We can visualize the earliest preagricultural settlements clustered around such naturally rich regions, as archaeological evidence indeed suggests they were.

The Natufians of the Near East Eleven thousand years ago, the Natufians, a group of people living in the area which is now Israel and Jordan, inhabited caves and rock shelters and built villages on the slopes of Mount Carmel, Israel. At the front of their rock shelters, they hollowed out basin-shaped depressions in the rock, possibly for storage pits. Examples of Natufian villages are also found at the site of Eynan in Israel.

Eynan is a stratified site containing the remains of three villages in sequence, one atop the other. Each village consisted of about 50 circular "pit" houses. The floor of each house was sunk a few feet into the ground, so that the walls of

[8] Kent V. Flannery, "The Origins of Agriculture," *Annual Review of Anthropology* 2 (1973): 274.

[9] Jack R. Harlan, "A Wild Wheat Harvest in Turkey," *Archaeology* 20, no. 3 (June 1967): 197–201.

[10] Kent V. Flannery, "The Origins and Ecological Effects of Early Domestication in Iran and the Near East," in *Prehistoric Agriculture,* ed. Stuart Struever (Garden City, N.Y.: Natural History Press, 1971), p. 59.

the house consisted partly of earth, below ground level, and partly of stones, above ground level. Pit houses had the advantage of retaining heat longer than houses built solely above ground. The villages appear to have had stone-paved walks; circular stone pavements ringed what seem to be permanent hearths; and the dead were interred in village cemeteries. Their tools suggest that the Natufians harvested wild grain intensively. Sickles recovered from their villages have a specific sheen, which experiments have shown to be the effect of flint striking grass stems, as the sickles would have been used in the cutting of grain. The Natufians are the earliest Mesolithic peoples known to us to have stored surplus crops. Beneath the floors of their stone-walled houses, they constructed plastered storage pits. In addition to wild grains, the Natufians exploited a wide range of local resources.[11]

OTHER AREAS

People in other areas of the world also shifted from hunting big game to the collecting of many types of food before they began to practice agriculture. The still-sparse archaeological record suggests that such a change occurred in southeast Asia, which may have been one of the important centers of original plant and animal domestication. The faunal remains in inland sites indicate that many different sources of food were being exploited from the same base camps. For example, at base camps we find the remains of animals from high mountain ridges as well as lowland river valleys; birds and primates from nearby forests; bats from caves; and fish from streams. The few coastal sites indicate that many different kinds of fish and shellfish were collected, and animals such as deer, wild cattle, and rhinoceros were hunted.[12] As in Europe, the pre-agricultural developments in

southeast Asia probably were responses to changes in the climate and environment, including a warming trend, more moisture, and higher sea level.[13]

In Africa, too, the pre-agricultural period was marked by a warmer, wetter environment (between about 5500 B.C. and 2500 B.C.). The now numerous lakes, rivers, and other bodies of water provided fish, shellfish, and other resources that apparently allowed people to settle more permanently than they had before. For example, there were lakes in what is now the southern and central Sahara desert, where people hunted hippopotamus and crocodile and where they fished. This pattern of broad-spectrum food collecting seems also to have been characteristic of the areas both south and north of the Sahara.[14]

At about the same time, in the Americas, people were beginning to exploit a wide variety of wild food resources, just as they were in Europe, Asia, and Africa. For example, evidence from Alabama and Kentucky shows that by about 5000 B.C., people began to collect freshwater mussels as well as wild plants and small game. In the Great Basin of what is now the United States, people were beginning to spend longer and longer each year collecting the wild resources around and in the rivers and glacial lakes.[15]

PRE-AGRICULTURAL DEVELOPMENTS: A SUMMARY

It is apparent that the pre-agricultural switch to broad-spectrum collecting was fairly common throughout the world. The changes in climate that were occurring may have been partially responsible for the decline in the availability of big game, particularly the large herd animals. But it has been suggested that another possible

[11] J. Mellaart, "Roots in the Soil," in *The Dawn of Civilization*, ed. S. Piggott (London: Thames and Hudson, 1961), pp. 41–64.

[12] Chester Gorman, "The Hoabinhian and After: Subsistence Patterns in Southeast Asia During the Late Pleistocene and Early Recent Periods," *World Archaeology* 2 (1970): 315–16.

[13] Kwang-Chih Chang, "The Beginnings of Agriculture in the Far East," *Antiquity* 44, no. 175 (September 1970): 176. See also Gorman, "The Hoabinhian. . . ," pp. 300–319.

[14] J. Desmond Clark, *The Prehistory of Africa* (New York: Praeger, 1970), pp. 171–72.

[15] Thomas C. Patterson, *America's Past: A New World Archaeology* (Glenview, Ill.: Scott, Foresman & Co., 1973), p. 42.

cause of that decline was human action, specifically overkill of some of these animals. In the New World, it seems that the extinction of many of the large Pleistocene animals, such as the mammoth, may have coincided with the movement of humans from the Bering Strait region to the southern tip of South America.[16] The worldwide rise in sea level also may have favored more broad-spectrum collecting as fish and shellfish resources became more available.

Does the switch to broad-spectrum collecting explain the increasingly sedentary way of life we see in various parts of the world in pre-agricultural times? The answer seems to be yes, and no. In some areas of the world—some sites in Europe, the Near East, Africa, and Peru—settlements became more permanent. In other areas, such as the semi-arid highlands of Mesoamerica, the switch to broad-spectrum collecting was not associated with increasing sedentarism. Indeed, even after the highland Mesoamericans began to cultivate plants, they still did not live in permanent villages.[17] Why the difference? It would seem that it is not simply the switch to broad-spectrum collecting that accounts for increasing sedentarism in many areas. Rather, judging from a comparison of settlements on the Peruvian coast, the more permanent settlements seem to have been located nearer (within three-and-a-half miles) to most, if not all, of the diverse food resources exploited during the year. The community that did not have a year-round settlement seems to have depended upon more widely distributed resources. What accounts for sedentarism may thus be the *proximity* of the broad-spectrum resources,[18] rather than the broad spectrum itself.

MESOLITHIC TECHNOLOGY

Technologically, Mesolithic cultures did not differ radically from Upper Paleolithic cultures. (Mesolithic, like the term Upper Paleolithic, properly applies only to cultural developments in the Old World. However, we use the term "Mesolithic" here to denote some general pre-agricultural trends.) The trend toward smaller and lighter tools continued. Microliths, small blades $\frac{1}{2}$ inch to 2 inches long, which were made in late Upper Paleolithic times, were now used in quantities. In fact, some archaeologists have singled out this technique in tool manufacture as the defining feature of the Mesolithic.[19] In place of the one-piece flint implement, Mesolithic peoples in Europe, Asia, and Africa equipped themselves with composite tools—that is, tools made of more than one material. Microliths could be fitted into grooves in bone or wood to form ·arrows, harpoons, daggers, and sickles.

A sickle, for example, was made by inserting several microliths into a groove in a wooden or bone handle. The blades were held in place by resin. A broken microlith could be replaced like a blade in a razor. Besides being adaptable for many uses, microliths could be made from many varieties of available stone; Mesolithic people were no longer limited to flint. Since they did not need the large flint nodules to make large core and flake tools, they could use small pebbles of flint to make the small blades.[20]

Domestication of Plants and Animals

Neolithic means "new stone age," and the term originally signified the cultural stage in which

[16]Paul S. Martin, "The Discovery of America," *Science,* 9 March 1973, pp. 969–74.

[17]Kent V. Flannery, "The Origins of the Village as a Settlement Type in Mesoamerica and the Near East: A Comparative Study," in *Territoriality and Proxemics,* ed. Ruth Tringham (Andover, Mass.: Warner Modular Publications, 1973), R1, pp. 1–31.

[18]Thomas C. Patterson, "Central Peru: Its Population and Economy," *Archaeology* 24 (October 1971): 316–21; 318–19.

[19]V. Gordon Childe, "The New Stone Age," in *Man, Culture and Society,* ed. Harry L. Shapiro (New York: Oxford University Press, 1956), p. 96.

[20]S. A. Semenov, *Prehistoric Technology,* trans. M. W. Thompson (Bath, England: Adams and Dart, 1970), pp. 63, 203–4.

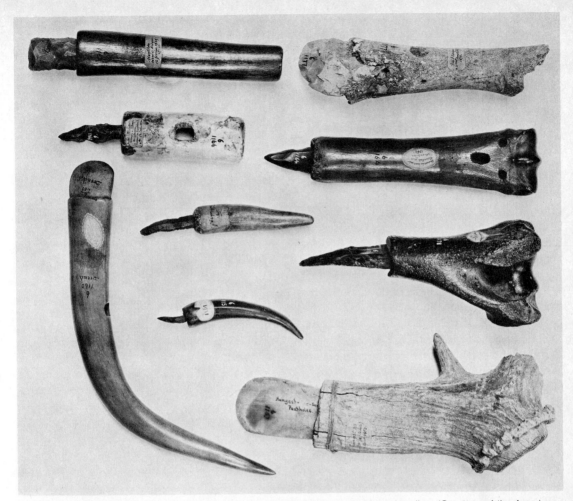

Tools made from microlith blades and chipped stone attached to bone and horn handles. (Courtesy of the American Museum of Natural History.)

humans invented ground stone tools and pottery. However, we now know that both of these characteristics were present in earlier times, so we cannot define the Neolithic stage of culture on the basis of these two criteria. At present, Western archaeologists define the Neolithic in terms of the presence of domesticated plants and animals. In the Neolithic stage of culture, people began to produce food, rather than merely collect it.

The line between food collecting and food producing occurs when people begin to plant crops and to keep and breed animals. How do we know when this transition occurred? In fact, archaeologically we do not see the beginning of food production. We can see only signs of it after plants and animals show differences from their wild varieties. When people plant crops we refer to it as "cultivation." It is only when the crops cultivated and the animals raised are different from wild varieties that we speak of plant and animal "domestication."

How do we know, in a particular site, that domestication had occurred? Domesticated plants have characteristics different from those of wild plants of the same types. For example, wild grains of barley and wheat have a fragile rachis (the seed-bearing part of the stem) which shatters easily, releasing the seeds. Domesticated grains have a tough rachis, which does not shatter easily.

How did the domesticated plants get to be different from the wild varieties? Artificial or human selection, deliberate or inadvertent, obviously was required. Consider why the rachis of wheat and barley may have changed. As we said, when wild grain ripens in the field, the seed-bearing part, or rachis, shatters easily, scattering the seed. This is selectively advantageous under wild conditions, since it is nature's method of propagating the species. Plants with a tough rachis, therefore, have only a slight chance of reproducing themselves under natural conditions but are more desirable for planting. When humans arrived with sickles and flails to collect the wild stands of grain, the seeds harvested probably contained a higher proportion of tough-rachis mutants, since these could best withstand the rough treatment of harvest processing. The harvested seeds would, if planted, be more likely to produce tough-rachis plants. If in each successive harvest, seeds from tough-rachis plants would be less likely lost, then tough-rachis plants would come to predominate.[21]

Domesticated species of animals also differ from the wild varieties. For example, the horns of wild goats in the Near East are shaped differently from those of domesticated goats.[22] But differences in physical characteristics may not be the only indicators of domestication. Some archaeologists believe that imbalances in the sex and age ratios of animal remains at sites suggest that domestication had occurred. For example, at Zawi Chemi Shanidar in Iraq, the proportion

of young to mature sheep remains was much higher than the ratio of young to mature sheep in wild herds. The inference to be drawn from this evidence is that the animals were domesticated, the adult sheep being saved for breeding purposes while the young were eaten. (If mostly young animals were eaten, and only a few animals were allowed to grow old, most of the bones found in a site would be from the young animals that were killed regularly for food.) At Jarmo, in northeastern Iraq, the proportion of male to female sheep remains was much higher than in normal wild herds of sheep. This evidence may indicate that the females were saved for breeding and the males were butchered for food.[23]

THE NEAR EAST

The Fertile Crescent, that arc stretching from the western slopes of the Zagros Mountains in Iran through southern Turkey and southward to Israel and the Jordan Valley, was one of the earliest centers of plant and animal domestication. We know that several varieties of domesticated wheat were being grown there after about 8000 B.C., as were barley, lentils, and peas. And there is evidence that goats, sheep, pigs, cattle, and dogs were being raised at about the same time. Let us turn to a few of the early Neolithic sites in the Near East to see what life there may have been like after people began to be dependent upon domesticated plants and animals for food.

Jarmo Sometime around 6000 B.C., the village of Jarmo, in northeastern Iraq, had about 25 houses—mud huts divided into rectangular rooms with matted floors—and a population estimated at 150. The settlement was occupied year-round. Although the villagers still apparently hunted and gathered snails, acorns, and pistachio nuts, there is evidence from charred

[21] Daniel Zohary, "The Progenitors of Wheat and Barley in Relation to Domestication and Agricultural Dispersal in the Old World," in *The Domestication and Exploitation of Plants and Animals,* ed. Peter J. Ucko and G. W. Dimbleby (Chicago: Aldine-Atherton, 1969), pp. 47–66, 60.

[22] Kent V. Flannery, "The Ecology of Early Food Production in Mesopotamia," *Science,* 12 March 1965, p. 1252.

[23] Ibid., p. 1253. For the view that a high proportion of immature animals does not necessarily indicate domestication, see Stephen Collier and J. Peter White, "Get Them Young? Age and Sex Inferences on Animal Domestication in Archaeology," *American Antiquity* 41 (1976): 96–102.

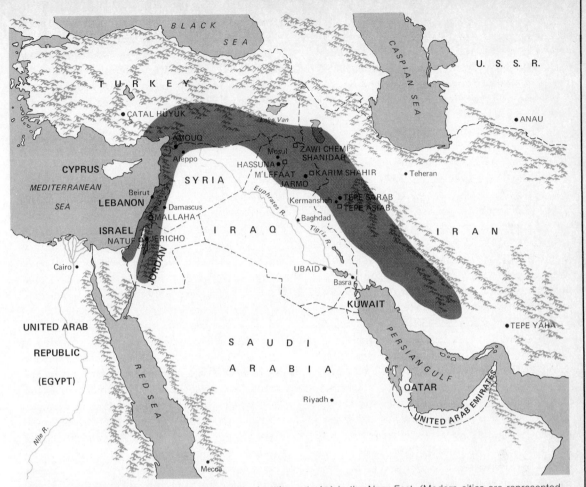

Some excavated villages (□) and early agricultural settlements (●) in the Near East. (Modern cities are represented by ●) The colored arc is the so-called "Fertile Crescent." (Adapted from R. J. Braidwood. "The Agricultural Revolution.")

grain kernels and the imprints of plant remains in clay that they were cultivating barley and wheat. The animal remains suggest that they had domesticated goats and probably dogs, too, judging from doglike figurines. Artifacts uncovered in Jarmo consisted of tools necessary for agriculture. There were microliths for sickles used to harvest grain, querns (large, rather flat stones upon which grain is ground), and mortars and pestles for pounding other plant food. The people at Jarmo evidently did some trading. Decorative seashells found at the site probably came from the nearest seacoast along the Persian Gulf, and the nearest source of the obsidian or volcanic glass used for tools was an area about 200 miles away.[24]

Çatal Hüyük On a wind-swept plateau in the rugged, mountainous region of southern Turkey stand the remains of a mud-brick town. It is known as Çatal Hüyük—*hüyük* being the Turkish word for a mound formed by a succession of settlements, one built on top of another.

[24]Robert J. Braidwood, "The Agricultural Revolution," *Scientific American*, September 1960, p. 130.

About 5600 B.C., a people occupied this adobe town. Some 200 houses have been excavated and they are interconnected in pueblo fashion. The inhabitants decorated walls of their houses with imaginative murals and their shrines with symbolic statuary. The murals depict what seem to be religious scenes and everyday events. Archaeologists peeling away frescoes found layer upon layer of murals, indicating that old murals were plastered over to make way for fresh paintings. Several rooms are believed to have been shrine rooms. They contain many large bull murals, and clay bull figurines, and have full-sized clay heads of cattle upon the walls. Other "shrine room" murals depict scenes of life and death, painted in red and black, respectively. Clay statuettes of a pregnant woman and of a bearded man seated on a bull have also been found in these rooms. Although the precise beliefs of these Neolithic people are unknown, their art and shrine rooms have given rise to considerable speculation about their religion and ritual.

Farming was well advanced at Çatal Hüyük. Lentils, wheat, barley, and peas were grown in quantities that produced a surplus. Archaeologists were astonished at the richly varied handicrafts, including beautifully carved wooden bowls and boxes, that the people of the town produced. They also had obsidian and flint daggers, spearheads, lanceheads, scrapers, awls, and sickle blades. Bowls, spatulas, knives, ladles, and spoons were made from bone. The houses contained belt hooks, toggles, and pins carved from bone. Evidence also suggests that men and women wore jewelry fashioned from bone, shell, and copper and that they used obsidian mirrors.[25]

Since Çatal Hüyük is located in a region with few raw materials, the town evidently depended upon its merchants and traders to secure the rich variety of materials needed for the products popular among the people. The traders had to procure shells from the Mediterranean,

[25]James Mellaart, "A Neolithic City in Turkey," *Scientific American*, April 1964, pp. 94–104.

timber from the hills, obsidian (volcanic glass which can be ground into sharp tools) from fifty miles away, and marble from western Turkey.

Jericho The site of Jericho is actually the town mentioned in the Bible, located in a fertile oasis north of the Dead Sea in Israel. As is true with many similar archaeological sites, Jericho marks the location of not one group but of several groups of people, who lived in the same area at different times. Remains of these earlier settlements—in the form of tools, bits of clothing or ornaments, houses, and so forth—are found in horizontal levels of earth. Artifacts from the first group to settle there are found in the bottom layer of soil; the original people may have moved or died out, or their settlement may have burned. Then, over the remains of their settlement, the next group built their village—and so on, with the remains of the area's most recent inhabitants closest to the top.

The earliest level is a Mesolithic village dated to 7800 B.C. Above this level are the remains of a Neolithic village dated to 6800 B.C. This village covered about 8 acres and contained round, semisubterranean houses with stone foundations, adobe brick walls, and wattle-and-daub roofs (twig frameworks plastered over with mud). The walls and floors were also plastered with mud, which probably cooled the rooms. Like the site at Jarmo, Jericho had no pottery in its lower levels.

In later levels, when the village spanned about 10 acres, the residents built a heavy wall around the settlement. It was 6 feet wide, with a massive stone tower 21 feet high which still stands today. The wall and tower indicate periodic conflict with enemies. It may be that the early Neolithic inhabitants were conquered by another group, as there is a distinct break in cultural continuity early in the prehistory of Jericho. That is, the cultural remains in one pre-ceramic level of occupation are markedly different from those found in the succeeding level. Also, in the succeeding level, the adobe bricks in the house walls have a different shape than before. The houses are now built around

Excavation at Çatal Hüyük, a Neolithic settlement in southern Turkey. (Courtesy of Ralph S. Solecki.)

courtyards, and the floors are covered with lime plaster.

Evidence suggests that people often were buried beneath the houses. Several of the skulls had faces molded onto them in plaster (probably a replica of the features of the deceased) with cowrie shells symbolizing the eyes. Trade is indicated, since obsidian from western Turkey, turquoise from the Sinai Peninsula, and marine shells from the seacoast all were found at the site.

Domesticated plants or animals have not yet been found at Jericho, but the available evidence suggests they were present. Jericho

was located in a fertile oasis where grains could be grown easily, and harvesting tools (sickles) and milling equipment were found at the site.

POSSIBLE EXPLANATIONS OF THE EMERGENCE OF FOOD PRODUCTION IN THE NEAR EAST

We know that an economic revolution had occurred in the Near East after about 8000 B.C., as people began to domesticate plants and animals. But why did domestication occur? Many theories have been suggested to answer this question. Gordon Childe's theory, which was popular in the 1950s, proposed that a drastic change in climate may have been the cause of domestication in the Near East.[26] According to Childe, who was relying on the climate reconstruction of others, the post-glacial period was marked by a decline in the summer rainfall in the Near East and North Africa. As the rains decreased, people were forced to retreat into shrinking pockets, or *oases*, of food resources surrounded by desert land. The lessened availability of wild resources provided an incentive for people to cultivate grains and domesticate animals, according to Childe.

Today, few anthropologists would support Childe's theory. Braidwood disputes Childe on two grounds. First, the climatic changes were nowhere near so dramatic as Childe had assumed, and therefore the "oasis incentive" probably never existed. And second, the climatic changes that occurred in the Near East after the retreat of the last glaciers had probably occurred at earlier interglacial periods too, but there had never been any similar food-producing revolution before. Hence, according to Braidwood, there must be more to the explanation of why people began to produce food than simply changes in climate.[27]

Braidwood's archaeological excavations in the Near East indicated to him that domestication began in regions where the local plants and animals were species that could be domesticated. Wild sheep, goats, and grains were found in areas with the oldest farming villages. In addition, Braidwood and Willey believed that people did not undertake domestication until they had learned a great deal about their environment and until culture had evolved far enough for them to handle such an undertaking. "Why did incipient food production not come earlier? Our only answer at the moment is that culture was not ready to achieve it."[28] As Braidwood wrote earlier:

In my opinion there is no need to complicate the story with extraneous "causes." . . . Around 8,000 B.C. the inhabitants of the hills around the fertile crescent had come to know their habitat so well that they were beginning to domesticate the plants and animals they had been collecting and hunting. . . . From these "nuclear" zones cultural diffusion spread the new way of life to the rest of the world.[29]

But many archaeologists now think that we should try to explain why people in the Near East were not "ready" earlier to achieve domestication. Both Binford and Flannery suggest that *some change* in external circumstances, not necessarily environmental, must have induced or favored the changeover to food production.[30] As Flannery points out, there is no evidence that there was a very great economic incentive for hunter-gatherers to become food producers. In fact, as we shall see later in Chapter 12, some contemporary hunter-gatherers may actually obtain adequate nutrition with far *less* work than many agriculturalists. Instead, both Binford and Flannery think that the incentive to domesticate animals and plants probably came from population pressure. As populations expanded in the most bountiful hunting-gathering areas, people spread to surrounding regions (marginal zones) which had fewer natural resources. The incentive to cultivate grains and domesticate animals may have come from an effort to reproduce the bounty available in the more endowed areas.

Flannery notes that the site of Tell Mureybat in Syria is located in a nuclear zone. Dating to about 8000 B.C., it had clay-walled houses, milling equipment, and roasting pits and was occupied by a fairly sedentary population of hunters and collectors of wild cereals. This evidence indicates that sedentarism is possible with a hunting-gathering economy if the area is rich enough in wild cereal resources. Given this possibility, selective pressures for domestication would not be as strong in the rich nuclear zones as in the less bountiful areas next

[26] As referred to in Gary A. Wright, "Origins of Food Production in Southwestern Asia: A Survey of Ideas," *Current Anthropology* 12 (October 1971): 447–78; 453–54.

[27] Braidwood, "The Agricultural Revolution," p. 130.

[28] Robert J. Braidwood and Gordon Willey, "Conclusions and Afterthoughts," in *Courses Toward Urban Life* (Chicago: Aldine-Atherton, 1962), p. 342.

[29] Braidwood, "The Agricultural Revolution," p. 74.

[30] Binford, "Post-Pleistocene Adaptations," pp. 22–49. Also Flannery, "The Origins and Ecological Effects of Early Domestication in Iran and the Near East," pp. 50–79.

to them. These less favored regions would have had less bountiful wild grain resources, and the people living in such locations might have wished to increase the amount of available grain. Hence, they might have been more likely to experiment with cultivation.

Of the three theories about why people in the Near East began to produce their own food, which is correct? At this point, nobody knows for sure why people began to raise their own food instead of collecting the resources provided by nature. Childe's theory has now been rejected because his assumed drastic change in climate did not occur. The Binford-Flannery model has received some support from archaeological evidence in the Near East. It seems that in at least one region, the Levant (the southwestern part of the Fertile Crescent), there was population increase followed by domestication in more marginal areas.[31] Whether this explanation of domestication will be supported for other areas in the Near East remains to be seen. As Flannery himself has recently suggested, this explanation may apply only to the Near East, not to other centers of domestication.[32]

POPULATION GROWTH DURING THE NEOLITHIC

About the time that people first began to change over from hunting and gathering to food production, the population in the Near East increased greatly. Indeed, the Fertile Crescent was perhaps where the first population explosion in human history occurred.

Traditionally, population expansion was thought to be a result of the domestication of plants and animals. It was assumed that hunting and gathering peoples had small populations because they could not obtain enough food to support larger ones, and that domestication increased these peoples' opportunity to obtain food, thereby facilitating an increase in population.[33]

Recently, as we have seen, the opposite view has been proposed—namely, that population growth itself stimulated the cultivation of fields and the domestication of wild animals.[34] But why did the population grow? It has been suggested that increased sedentarism may have been responsible for population expansion.[35] For nomadic peoples, the care of a number of young children can be especially burdensome and awkward. Very small children must be carried by someone, usually the mother; and if the same mother had several such children, they would be a liability when the band traveled from one campsite to another. Contemporary hunter and gatherer societies may widen the intervals between births of children, principally because of the heavy responsibilities that fall to the mother and the difficulty of carrying the young.

The !Kung Bushmen of the Kalahari Desert in Africa are hunting and gathering people whose women must carry their infants on their backs or shoulders when they gather plants or move from one camp to another. Not surprisingly, Bushmen children are generally spaced an average of four years apart. But once a group becomes more sedentary, a Bushman woman could shorten the intervals between births without greatly increasing her work load. Indeed, sedentary Bushmen groups have closer birth spacing than nomadic Bushmen groups.[36] Thus, sedentarism may have initiated the population explosion, which was perhaps later accelerated by the development of more advanced techniques of food production.

Population growth may also have increased because of the greater value of children, who in agricultural, sedentary situations may have been able to help their parents with chores and sub-

[31] Wright, "Origins of Food Production in Southwestern Asia," p. 470.

[32] Flannery, "The Origins of Agriculture," p. 307.

[33] V. Gordon Childe, *Man Makes Himself* (New York: Mentor Books, New American Library, 1951), p. 61.

[34] This view seems to have been stimulated by Ester Boserup, *The Condition of Agricultural Growth: The Economics of Agrarian Change under Population Pressures* (Chicago: Aldine-Atherton, 1965).

[35] Robert Sussman, "Child Transport, Family Size, and the Increase in Human Population Size During the Neolithic," *Current Anthropology* 13 (April 1972): 258–67; and Richard B. Lee, "Population Growth and the Beginnings of Sedentary Life among the !Kung Bushmen," in *Population Growth: Anthropological Implications*, ed. Brian Spooner (Cambridge, Mass.: M.I.T. Press, 1972), pp. 329–42.

[36] Lee, "Population Growth and the Beginnings of Sedentary Life," pp. 329–42.

The !Kung Bushmen of the Kalahari Desert on the move. Spacing births an average of four years apart helps to assure that a woman will not have to carry more than two children at a time. (Courtesy of Irven DeVore/Anthro-Photo.)

sistence activities (in contrast to nomadic, hunting-gathering lifestyles where there is often not as much work to be done and the work is harder for children to do). There is some evidence from recent population studies that where children contribute more to the economy, fertility rates are higher.[37]

DOMESTICATION OF PLANTS AND ANIMALS IN OTHER AREAS

A number of areas in the world other than the Near East appear to have been early centers of

plant and animal domestication. One such area, which may have been a center of domestication almost as early as the Near East, was mainland Southeast Asia. The dates of the earliest cultivation there are not clear. Some plants found in Spirit Cave in northwest Thailand date from about 6800 B.C., but these specimens are not clearly distinguishable from wild varieties. They may have been wild, or they may have been cultivated but not yet changed in appearance.

We can say that most of the early cultivation in mainland Southeast Asia seems to have occurred in the plains and low terraces around rivers, although the main subsistence foods of early cultivators were probably the fish and shellfish living in nearby waters. The first plants to be domesticated were probably not cereal grains, as in the Near East. Indeed, some early

[37] Benjamin White, "Demand for Labor and Population Growth in Colonial Java," *Human Ecology* 1, no. 3 (March 1973): 217–36. See also John D. Kasarda, "Economic Structure and Fertility: A Comparative Analysis," *Demography* 8, no. 3 (August 1971): 307–18.

cultivated crops may not have been used at all for food. Bamboo and bottle gourds, for example, were probably grown for use as containers. However, other plants were probably grown to be eaten: herbs, roots and tubers like taro and yams, fruits, beans, and water chestnuts.[38]

The first evidence of cereal cultivation outside of the Near East is some foxtail millet found in the Hwang-ho or Yellow River Valley in north China. It dates from the fifth millennium B.C., although it was probably first cultivated sometime earlier. Wheat and barley probably spread to China from western parts of Asia. Rice may be native to Southeast Asia, although there is still no real evidence as to where it was originally domesticated. It probably was domesticated sometime between 6800 and 4000 B.C.[39]

There is evidence that certain cereal grains, the African millets and sorghum, were first domesticated in Africa perhaps as early as 4000 B.C. The wild forms of those plants are believed to be native to the savanna belt which stretches from west to east, south of the Sahara. In addition to these grains, the ass, cat, and guinea fowl may also have been domesticated in Africa. The presence of the tsetse fly in most of west and equatorial Africa may have precluded attempts to domesticate larger animals. Tsetse flies carry a disease which even today makes it impossible to raise large animals such as cattle in many parts of Africa.[40]

In the New World, evidence of independent domestication of plants comes from at least four areas: the highlands of Mesoamerica, in areas like Tehuacán where possibly domesticated corn was being grown between 5000 and 3000 B.C.; the central Andes around Peru, where domesticated beans were being cultivated by about 5600 B.C. and cotton, chili peppers, manioc, peanuts, and potatoes were being grown somewhat later;[41] the Caribbean lowland areas of South America, where root crops such as

Corn evolved in the Tehuacán Valley of central Mexico from tiny wild corncobs, about 7,000 years ago, to modern corn, about 3,500 years ago. (Courtesy of Paul Mangelsdorf and R. S. MacNeish.)

manioc and sweet potatoes may have been domesticated;[42] and possibly the eastern United States where squash and sunflowers may have been cultivated after 1000 B.C.[43]

On the whole, domestic animals were far less important economically in the New World than they were in many parts of the Old World. The only animals domesticated in the New World were dogs, muscovy ducks, turkeys, guinea pigs, alpacas, and llamas. The Central Andes was the only area where animals were a significant part of the economy.[44] Guinea pigs, ducks, and turkeys were raised for food, alpacas mainly for their fur, and llamas for transporting goods. Animal domestication in the New World

---

[38] Chang, "The Beginnings of Agriculture in the Far East," pp. 175–85.

[39] Flannery, "The Origins of Agriculture," pp. 284–86.

[40] Clark, *The Prehistory of Africa*, pp. 202–6.

[41] Flannery, "Origins of Agriculture," pp. 288–89, 304–5.

[42] William T. Sanders and J. Marino, *New World Prehistory* (Englewood Cliffs, N.J.: Prentice-Hall, 1970), p. 48.

[43] Stuart Struever and Kent D. Vickery, "The Beginnings of Cultivation in the Midwest-Riverine Area of the United States," *American Anthropologist* 75 (1973):1197–1220.

[44] Patterson, *America's Past: A New World Archaeology*, pp. 44–45.

differed from that in the Old World because different wild species were found in the two hemispheres. The Old World plains and forests were the homes for the wild ancestors of the cattle, sheep, goats, pigs, and horses that we know today. In the New World, the Pleistocene herds of horses, mastodons, mammoths, and other large animals were long extinct, allowing few opportunities for large animal domestication.

Although evidence from Mexico and other parts of the Americas indicates that cultivation was underway between the fifth to third millennia B.C., permanent villages were probably not established in the Andes until about 2500 B.C. and in areas of Mesoamerica until about 1500 B.C.[45] Archaeologists once thought that settled village life followed as a matter of course, once people had learned to domesticate plants. But evidence from the arid highlands of Mesoamerica contradicts this, and the reason may be that in highland Mesoamerica resources were widely distributed and relatively scarce in the dry season. For example, MacNeish suggests the early cultivators depended mostly on hunting during the winter and on seed-collecting and pod-picking in the spring. In addition to their food-collecting activities, in the summer they planted and harvested crops such as squash, and in the fall collected fruit and harvested the avocados they had planted. These varied activities required the people to spend most of the year in small groups, aggregating into larger groups only in the summer and only in certain moister areas.[46]

Consequences of Food Production

Regardless of why, where, and when food production originated in different parts of the world, its development had profound effects upon many aspects of human life. As we have seen, populations increased in some places before and in all places after the changeover to food production. In all areas except apparently the Central Andes and highland Mesoamerica, the switch to food production was preceded or accompanied by the establishment of permanent villages, some quite large.

In the permanent villages, houses became more elaborate and comfortable and construction methods improved. The materials used in construction depended upon whether timber or stone were locally available or whether a strong sun could dry mud bricks. A modern architect might find to his or her surprise that bubble-shaped houses were known long ago in Neolithic Cyprus. Families in the island's town of Khirokitia made their homes in large, domed, circular dwellings shaped like beehives which had stone foundations and mud-brick walls. Often, to create more space, the interior was divided horizontally and the second floor was propped firmly on limestone pillars.

Sizable villages of solidly constructed, gabled, wood houses were built in Europe on the banks of the Danube and along the rims of Alpine lakes.[47] Many of the gabled wooden houses in the Danube region were "longhouses," long, rectangular structures that apparently sheltered several family units. In Neolithic times these longhouses had doors, beds, tables, and other furniture which bore close resemblance to those in our society. We know the Danubians had furniture because miniature clay models have been found at their sites. Several of the chairs and couches seem to be models of padded and upholstered furniture with wooden frames, indicating that the Neolithic European craftsmen were creating fairly sophisticated furnishings.[48] Such furnishings are the results of an advanced tool technology put to use by a people who, because they were staying in one area, could take time to make furniture.

For the first time, apparel made of woven

[45]Flannery, "The Origins of the Village . . . ," p. 1.

[46]Richard S. MacNeish, "The Evaluation of Community Patterns in the Tehuacán Valley of Mexico and Speculations about the Cultural Processes," in *Ecology and Agricultural Settlements,* ed. Ruth Tringham (Andover, Mass.: Warner Modular Publications, 1973), R2, pp. 1–27.

[47]Clark and Piggott, *Prehistoric Societies,* pp. 240–42.
[48]Ibid., p. 235.

textile appeared. This development was not simply the result of the domestication of flax (for linen), cotton, and wool-growing sheep. The sources of fiber alone could not produce cloth. It was the development by Neolithic society of the spindle and loom for spinning and weaving that made textiles possible. True, textiles can be woven by hand without a loom, but it is a slow and laborious process, impractical for producing garments.

At first, Neolithic ceramicists continued the older pottery tradition inherited from sedentary Mesolithic cultures, making plain earthenware. They produced large urns for grain storage, mugs, cooking pots, and dishes. To improve the retention of liquid, the Near East potters may have been the first to glaze the earthenware's porous surface. Later, Neolithic ceramics became more artistic. Designers shaped the clay into graceful forms and painted colorful patterns on the vessels.

It is probable that virtually none of these architectural and technological innovations could have occurred until humans became fully sedentary. Nomadic hunting and gathering cul-

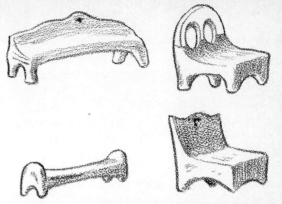

FIGURE 2 Clay Models of Furniture Found at a Neolithic Site in Bulgaria
These models indicate that Neolithic craftsmen were creating fairly sophisticated furnishings as a result of an advanced tool technology. (After Grahame Clark and Stuart Piggott, *Prehistoric Societies*, © 1965, Alfred A. Knopf, Inc.)

tures would have found it difficult to carry many material goods, especially fragile items such as pottery. Thus, many Neolithic goods would not have been advantageous to the nomad, and neither would Neolithic architecture. It was only when humans became fully sedentary that these goods would have provided advantages, by enabling villagers to cook and store food more effectively and to house themselves more comfortably.

There is also evidence of long-distance trade in the Neolithic, as we have already noted. Obsidian from southern Turkey was being exported to sites in the Zagros mountain range of Iran and to the Levant (e.g., Israel, Jordan, Syria). Great amounts of obsidian were exported to sites about 190 miles from the source of supply; more than 80 percent of the tools used by residents of those areas were made of obsidian.[49] Marble was being sent from western to eastern Turkey, and seashells from the coasts were traded to distant inland regions. Such trade suggests a considerable amount of contact between various Neolithic communities.

FIGURE 1 Plan and Reconstruction of a Neolithic Danubian House
This gabled structure probably sheltered several families. Three rows of postholes indicate where timbers were sunk into the soil. (After W. Buttler, "Pits and Pit Dwellings in Southeast Europe," *Antiquity* 10[1936]: 35.)

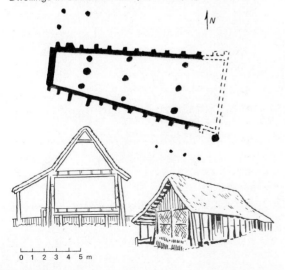

0 1 2 3 4 5 m

[49]Colin Renfrew, "Trade and Culture Process in European History," *Current Anthropology* 10 (April–June 1969): 156–57; 161–69.

About 3500 B.C. cities first appeared in the Near East. These cities had political assemblies, kings, scribes, and specialized workshops. The specialized production of goods and services was supported by surrounding farming villages which sent their produce to the urban centers. A dazzling transformation had taken place in a relatively short time. Not only had people settled down, but they had also become civilized or urbanized. (The word "civilized" refers to living in cities.) Urban societies seem to have developed first in the Near East, and somewhat later around the eastern Mediterranean, in the Indus Valley of northwest India, in northern China, and in Mexico and Peru. In the next chapter we turn our attention to the rise of the earliest civilizations.

Summary

1. In the period prior to the emergence of plant and animal domestication (called the *Mesolithic* in Europe and the Near East) there seems to have been a shift in many areas of the world to less dependence on big-game hunting and greater dependence on what is called broad-spectrum collecting. This broad spectrum of resources frequently included aquatic resources such as fish and shellfish; a variety of wild plants; and a wide variety of smaller game. Climatic changes may have been partially responsible for the change to broad-spectrum collecting as the retreating glaciers may have left more waterways, bays, and inlets where aquatic life could flourish.

2. In addition to carbon-14 and varve analysis, archaeologists can estimate the absolute age of Mesolithic and later sites and specimens from thermoluminescence and dendrochronology (tree-ring dating). Pollen analysis is a relative dating method.

3. In some sites in Europe, the Near East, Africa, and Peru, the switch to broad-spectrum collecting seems to be associated with the development of more permanent communities. In other areas, such as the semi-arid highlands of Mesoamerica, the switch to broad-spectrum collecting was not associated with the development of more permanent villages. In that area, fairly permanent settlements only emerged well after the domestication of plants and animals.

4. We see the first evidence of a changeover to food production—the cultivation and domestication of plants and animals—in the Near East after about 8000 B.C. This shift has been referred to as the *Neolithic Revolution,* and it occurred, probably independently, in a number of areas besides the Near East. There is evidence of cultivation sometime after 6800 B.C. in the lowland plains of Southeast Asia and in sub-Saharan Africa by perhaps 4000 B.C. In the New World domestication may have occurred independently in four areas: the Mesoamerican highlands (Mexico) between 5000 and 3000 B.C.; Peru by about 5600 B.C.; the Caribbean lowland areas of South America; and possibly the eastern United States.

5. Regardless of why food production originated, it ultimately seems to have had important consequences for human life. Populations increased in some places before and always after food production developed. In all areas except perhaps Mesoamerica, early agriculture is associated with more permanent villages. In the permanent villages, houses and their furnishings became more elaborate, textiles were made, and pottery was painted. There is evidence of long-distance trade in the Neolithic, suggesting a good deal of contact between communities.

Suggested Readings

Flannery, K. V. "The Origins of Agriculture." *Annual Review of Anthropology* 2 (1973): 271–310.
A recent review of the theories and evidence relating to the origins of agriculture in two areas of the Old World and two areas of the New World.

Leonard, J. N. *The First Farmers.* Boston, Mass.: Little, Brown, 1973.

A popularly written account of early food producers, with particular emphasis on the Near East. Colorful and informative pictures.

Struever, S. S., ed. *Prehistoric Agriculture.* Garden City, N.Y.: Natural History Press, 1971.

A large collection of articles on the development of agriculture in Mesoamerica, South America, the Near East, Europe, and North America.

Ucko, P. J., and G. W. Dimbleby, eds. *The Domestication and Exploitation of Plants and Animals.* Chicago: Aldine-Atherton, 1969.

A collection of papers from a conference of anthropologists and biologists. Topics include the environmental backgrounds of domestication, methods of inferring domestication of plants and animals worldwide, and variation in domesticated forms.

Wright, G. A. "The Origins of Food Production in Southwestern Asia: A Survey of Ideas." *Current Anthropology* 12 (1971): 447–77.

Theories about early food production in the Near East are reviewed, and the available data are examined for their bearing on those theories.

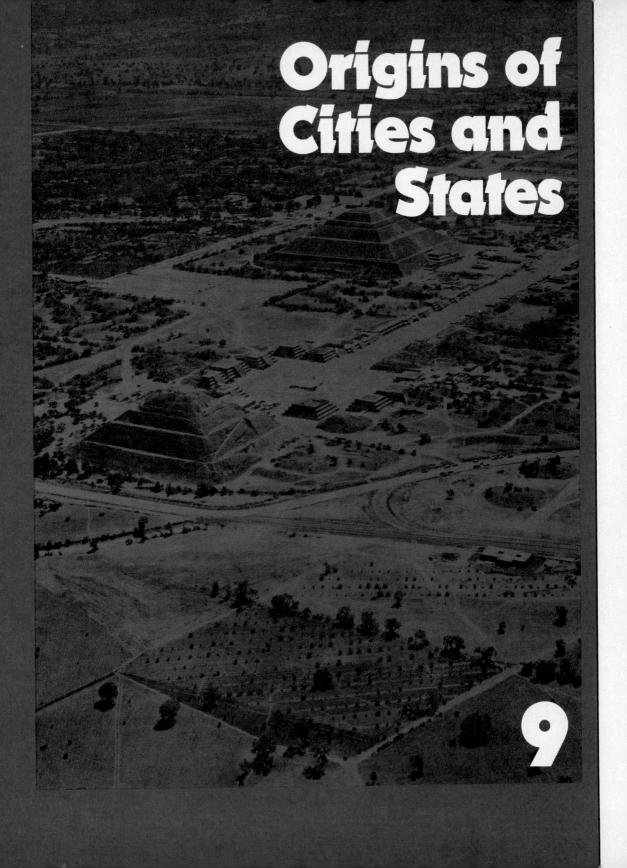

Origins of
Cities and
States

9

From the time agriculture first developed until about 5500 B.C., people in the Near East lived in fairly small villages. There were few differences in wealth and status from household to household; and there was apparently no governmental authority beyond the village. There is no evidence that these villages had any public buildings or craft specialists, or that one community was very different in size from its neighbors. In short, these settlements had none of the characteristics we commonly associate with "civilization."

But sometime around 5500 B.C. in the Near East—and at later times in other places—the archaeological record suggests that a great transformation began to take place in the quality and scale of human life. For the first time, we can see evidence of differences in wealth and status among households. Communities began to differ in size and began to specialize in certain crafts. There are signs that some political officials had acquired authority over several communities. By about 3500 B.C. in the Near East, we can see many, if not all, the conventional characteristics of civilization: large cities; many kinds of full-time craft specialists; monumental architecture; great differences in wealth and status; and the kind of strong centralized political system we call the "state."

This type of transformation has occurred many times and in many places in human history. The most ancient civilizations arose in the Near East around 3500 B.C., in northwestern India around 2500 B.C., in northern China around 1650 B.C., and in the New World (in Mexico and Peru) around the time of Christ.[1] At least some of these most ancient civilizations evolved independently of the others—for example, those in the New World and those in the Old World. Why did they do so? What conditions favored the emergence of centralized, state-type political systems? What conditions favored the establishment of cities? (We ask this last question separately because archaeologists are not yet certain that all the very ancient state

9

[1]Elman R. Service, *Origins of the State and Civilization: The Process of Cultural Evolution* (New York: W. W. Norton, 1975), p. 5.

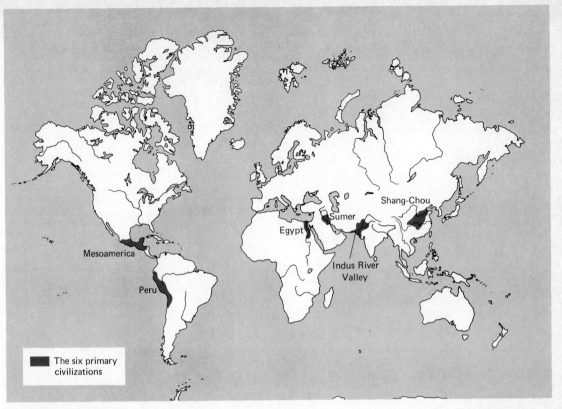

Six Early Civilizations
(Adapted from *Origins of the State and Civilization: The Process of Cultural Evolution*, by Elman R. Service. By permission of W. W. Norton & Company, Inc. Copyright © 1975 by W. W. Norton & Company, Inc.)

societies had cities when they first developed centralized government.) In this chapter, we shall discuss some of the things that archaeologists have learned or suspect about the growth of the most ancient civilizations. Our discussion is focused primarily on the Near East and Mexico because archaeologists know most about the sequences of cultural development in these two areas.

Archaeological Inferences about Civilization

The most ancient civilizations have been studied by archaeologists rather than historians because those civilizations evolved prehistorically—before the advent of writing. How do

archaeologists infer that a particular people in the preliterate past had social classes, cities, or centralized government?

As we noted above, it appears that the earliest Neolithic societies were egalitarian—that is, people did not differ much in wealth or prestige. Later, some societies became ranked—in other words, some people inherited greater status or prestige. Perhaps the clearest evidence of ranking in an ancient society is provided by burial finds. For example, we know from ancient Egyptian tombs and cemeteries that the nobility were buried with all the trappings of wealth and rank—jewelry, weapons, food, sumptuous furnishings, and religious objects—but commoners were not. (We know those buried with riches were nobles because we also have written records describing them.) Thus, we are fairly sure that a society has dif-

"I thought I'd bury a few things to show future generations how advanced we were: a spoon, a knife, a plate, a book, etc." (© *Punch*, ROTHCO.)

ferences in status if only some people are buried with certain objects. And, we can be fairly sure that rank is assigned at birth rather than achieved in later life if we find children's tombs with evidence of rank. Child burials from as early as 5500–5000 B.C. at Tell es-Sawwan in Iraq, and from about 800 B.C. at La Venta in Mexico, are filled with statues and ornaments which suggest that the deceased children were of noble birth.[2]

Archaeologists think that states first evolved sometime around 3500 B.C. in Greater Mesopotamia, the area now shared by southern Iraq and southwestern Iran. Archaeologists and historians do not always agree on how a state should be defined, but most seem to agree that centralized decision-making affecting a substantial population is the key criterion. There are other characteristics that are usually but not always found in the first states. Such states usually have cities with public buildings; full-time religious and craft specialists; and often an official art style. There is a hierarchical social structure topped by an elite class from which the leaders are drawn. The government tries to claim a monopoly on the use of force; our own state society says that citizens do not have the right "to take the law into their own hands." The state uses its force or threat of force to tax its population and to draft people for work or war.[3]

How can archaeologists tell, from the information provided by material remains, whether a society was a state or not? In part this depends upon what is used as a criterion of the state. For example, Wright and Johnson define the state as a centralized political hierarchy with at least three levels of administration.[4] But how might archaeologists infer that such a hierarchy existed in the past in some area? Wright and Johnson suggest that the way settlement sites differ in size is one indication of how many levels of administration there were in an area.[5]

During the early Uruk period (just before 3500 B.C.) in what is now southwestern Iran, there were some fifty settlements which seem to fall into three groups in terms of size. There were about 45 small villages; 3 or 4 "towns"; and one large center, Susa. These three types of settlements seem to have been involved in a three-level administrative hierarchy, since many small villages could not trade with Susa without passing through a settlement intermediate in size. And since a three-level hierarchy is Wright and Johnson's criterion of a state, they think that a state had emerged in the area by early Uruk times.

Evidence from the next period, middle Uruk, suggests that a state had already emerged. This evidence takes the form of clay seals which were apparently used in trading.[6] "Commodity sealings" were used to keep a shipment of goods tightly closed until it reached its destination, and "message sealings" were used to keep track of goods sent and received. The clay seals found in Susa include many message seals and "bullae" (clay containers which served as bills of lading for goods received). The villages, in contrast, had few message seals and "bullae." This finding suggests that Susa administered the regional movement of goods and that Susa was the "capital" of the state.

[2]Kent V. Flannery, "The Cultural Evolution of Civilizations," *Annual Review of Ecology and Systematics*, Vol. 3 (1972), pp. 399–425.
[3]Ibid.

[4]Henry T. Wright and Gregory A. Johnson, "Population, Exchange, and Early State Formation in Southwestern Iran," *American Anthropologist* 77 (1975), p. 267.
[5]The following discussion draws from ibid., pp. 269–74.
[6]Ibid., pp. 271–72.

Tigris River Valley—site of ancient civilizations. (Georg Gerster, Rapho/Photo Researchers.)

Let us turn now to the major features of the cultural sequences leading to the first states in southern Iraq.

Cities and States in Southern Iraq

Early farming communities have not been found in the arid lowland plains of southern Iraq—the area known as Sumer, where some of the earliest cities and states developed. Perhaps such communities have not been found in Sumer because silt from the Tigris and Euphrates rivers has covered them. Or, as has been suggested, Sumer may not have been settled by agriculturalists until people learned how to drain and irrigate the river-valley soils which were otherwise too wet or too dry for cultivation.

At any rate, small communities partially dependent on agriculture had emerged in the hilly areas north and east of Sumer early in the Neolithic. Later, by about 6000 B.C., a mixed herding-farming economy developed in those hilly areas.

THE FORMATIVE ERA

Elman Service calls the period from about 5000 to 3500 B.C. the formative era, for it saw the coming together of many changes which seem to have played a part in the development of cities and states. Service suggests that with the development of small-scale irrigation, lowland river-areas began to attract settlers. Not only did the rivers provide water for irrigation, but they also provided mollusks, fish, and water birds for food. And they provided routes by which to import needed raw materials such as hardwood and stone which were lacking in the region of Sumer.

During this period we see a number of changes which suggest an increasingly complex social and political life. We see differences in status reflected in child burials with statues and ornaments. We see different villages specializing in the production of different goods, pottery in some, copper and stone tools in others.[7] We see the building of temples in certain places that may have been centers of political as well as religious authority for several communities.[8] Some anthropologists think that chiefdoms, each with authority over a number of villages, had developed by this time.[9]

SUMERIAN CIVILIZATION

By about 3500 B.C., there were about a dozen city-states in the area of Sumer. Each consisted of a city, usually enclosed in a fortress wall, and a surrounding agricultural area. Shortly after

---

[7] Flannery, "The Cultural Evolution of Civilizations," pp. 399–425.
[8] Service, *Origins of the State and Civilization*, p. 207.
[9] Ibid., and Flannery, "The Cultural Evolution of Civilizations," pp. 399–425.

Reconstruction of the Sumerian city of Ur, as it looked in 2000 B.C. A temple can be seen in the background. (Courtesy of the American Museum of Natural History.)

the first forms of writing appeared—about 3000 B.C.—all of Sumer was unified under the domination of a single government. After that time, Sumer became a glittering area, culturally, intellectually, and technologically. It had great urban centers. Imposing temples, which were commonly set on artificial mounds (in the city of Warka the temple mound was 40 feet high), dominated the cities. The empire was very complex, with an elaborate system for the administration of justice; codified laws; specialized government officials; a professional standing army; and even, in the cities, functioning sewer systems. Sumerians were involved in business and trade, and the government regulated commerce. Among the many specialized crafts were brickmaking, pottery, carpentry, jewelrymaking, leatherworking, metallurgy, basketmaking, stonecutting, and sculpture. Sumerians learned to construct and use wheeled wagons, sailboats, horse-drawn chariots, and spears, swords, and armor of bronze.[10]

As economic specialization developed, social stratification became more elaborate. Sumerian documents describe a fully-developed system of social ranking: nobles, priests, merchants, craftsmen, bureaucrats, soldiers, farm-

[10] Our description of Sumerian civilization here is based upon Samuel Noel Kramer, *The Sumerians* (Chicago: University of Chicago Press, 1963).

ers, free citizens, and slaves all had their special place. Slaves were common in Sumer; they were often captives, brought back as the spoils of war. Metallurgists belonged to the working class aristocracy because they possessed closely guarded trade secrets. Like nuclear physicists in our society, metallurgists were respected both for their somewhat mysterious knowledge and because their profession was strategically important for the society.

Agricultural production was boosted by a new farming technology. Oxen were harnessed to plows and to carts that ran on wooden wheels. A Sumerian "Farmer's Almanac" indicates that a seeder plow was invented for the purpose of planting. Threshing was done by running an animal-drawn wagon, and then a special threshing sled, over the grain. The irrigation system, a complex network of canals which attests to the management and planning skills of the Sumerians, was perhaps the greatest technological advance of all.

A key invention was writing, of which we first see evidence around 3000 B.C. The earliest Sumerian writings were in the form of ledgers, containing inventories of items stored in the temples and records of livestock or other items owned or managed by the temples. Sumerian writing was wedged-shaped, or *cuneiform*, formed by pressing a stylus against a damp clay tablet. For contracts and other important documents, the tablet was fired to create a virtually permanent record. (Egyptian writing, or *hieroglyphics,* appeared about the same time. It was written on rolls woven from papyrus reeds, from which our word *paper* derives.)

Cities and States in Middle America

Cities and states emerged in Mesoamerica at a later date than they did in the Near East. The later appearance of civilization in Mesoamerica may be linked to the later emergence of agriculture in the New World, as we saw in the last chapter. We shall focus primarily on the developments that led to the rise of the central Mexican city-state of Teotihuacán, which reached its height shortly after the time of Christ.

THE FORMATIVE PERIOD

The formative period in the area around Teotihuacán (1000–300 B.C.) was characterized initially by small, scattered farming villages on the hilly slopes just south of the Teotihuacán Valley. There were probably a few hundred people in each hamlet, and each of these scattered groups was probably politically autonomous. After about 500 B.C., there seems to have been a population shift to settlements on the valley floor, probably in association with the use of irrigation. Between about 300 and 200 B.C. we see the emergence of small "elite" centers in the valley, each of which had an earth or stone raised platform. Residences or small temples of poles and thatch originally stood on these platforms. The fact that some individuals, particularly those in the elite centers, were buried in special tombs with ornaments, headdresses, carved bowls, and a good deal of food indicates the presence of some social inequality.[11] The elite centers may indicate the presence of a number of chiefdoms.

THE CITY AND STATE OF TEOTIHUACÁN

By about 200 B.C. we have evidence that a town stood in the center of the valley at a place where there were 80 permanent springs. The same site later grew into the city of Teotihuacán. By 100 A.D., half of the valley's population lived in the city, and by 700 A.D. about 100,000 people, about 90 percent of the valley population, lived there.[12]

At the height of its power (200–500 A.D.), much of Mesoamerica seems to have been influenced by Teotihuacán. Archaeologically, this is suggested by the extensive spread of Teotihuacán-style pottery and architectural elements. Undoubtedly there were large numbers of people in Teotihuacán who were engaged in production for and the conduct of long-distance trade. Perhaps 25 percent of the city's population worked at various specialized crafts, mostly the manufacture of projectile points and cutting-and-scraping tools made from volcanic obsidian. The Teotihuacán Valley had major deposits of obsidian, which was apparently in great demand over much of Mesoamerica. Judging by materials found in graves, there was an enormous flow of foreign goods into the city, including precious stones, feathers from colorful birds in the tropical lowlands, and cotton.[13]

The layout of the city of Teotihuacán shows a tremendous amount of planning. This suggests that, from its beginning, the Valley may have been politically unified under a centralized state. Mapping of the city has revealed that the streets and most of the buildings are laid out according to a grid pattern. The grid follows a basic modular unit of 57 meters. Residential structures are often squares of this size, and many streets are spaced according to multiples of the basic modular unit. Even the river that ran through the center of the city was channeled to conform to the grid pattern. Perhaps the most outstanding feature of the city was the colossal scale of its architecture. Two pyramids domi-

[11]Mary W. Helms, *Middle America* (Englewood Cliffs, N.J.: Prentice-Hall, 1975), pp. 34–36 and pp. 54–55.

[12]René Millon, "Teotihuacán," *Scientific American,* June 1967, pp. 38–48; and Helms, *Middle America,* pp. 51–84.
[13]Helms, *Middle America,* pp. 61–63.

The ancient city of Teotihuacán had two pyramids, the Pyramid of the Moon (*foreground*) and the Pyramid of the Sun (*background*). More than 4,000 buildings, most no longer visible, spread for miles beyond the center of the city. At the peak of the city-state's power, the population was probably about 100,000. (From Millon, Urbanization at Teotihuacán, Mexico, v. 1, pt. 1, Fig. 7, Austin, 1973. Copyright © 1973 by René Millon. All rights reserved.)

nate the metropolis, the so-called Pyramid of the Moon and the Pyramid of the Sun. At its base the latter is as big as the great Pyramid of Cheops in Egypt. At the height of its power, the metropolis of Teotihuacán had a larger area than imperial Rome.[14]

THE CITY OF MONTE ALBAN

At roughly the same time as Teotihuacán another early Middle American state arose in the Valley of Oaxaca in southern Mexico. In the formative period, from about 1300 B.C. to 300 A.D., great population growth took place in

the valley. Toward the end of this period, there were apparently a number of independent political units, each consisting of a center and dependent communities. (That these units were independent is suggested by their somewhat different art styles.) Not until 300 A.D. is there any evidence of political unification in the valley. The center of that new unity was the city of Monte Albán.[15]

Why the city of Monte Albán became the political center of the valley has been a puzzle. It was located on top of a mountain in the center of the valley, far from either good soil or permanent water supplies which could have been

---

[14]Millon, "Teotihuacán," pp. 38–44.

[15]Richard Blanton, "The Origins of Monte Albán," in *Cultural Continuity and Change*, ed. C. Cleland (New York: Academic Press, 1976), pp. 223–32.

used for irrigation. (Even finding drinking water must have been difficult.) No natural resources for trade were nearby, nor is there much evidence that Monte Albán was used as a ceremonial center. Because the city was at the top of a steep mountain, it is unlikely that it could have been a central marketplace for valley-wide trade. Why, then, did Monte Albán rise to become one of the early centers of Mesoamerican civilization? Blanton suggests that it may have originally been founded in the late formative period (500–400 B.C.) as a neutral place where representatives of the different political units in the valley could reside to coordinate activities affecting the whole valley. Thus Monte Albán may have been like the cities of Brasilia, Washington D.C., and Athens, all of which were originally founded in "neutral," nonproductive areas. Such centers without obvious resources would not, at least initially, threaten the various political units involved. Later, such a center might become the metropolis that dominated a more politically unified region, as Monte Albán came to do in the Valley of Oaxaca.

OTHER "CENTERS" OF MESOAMERICAN CIVILIZATION

In addition to Teotihuacán and Oaxaca, there apparently were other Mesoamerican state societies, which developed somewhat later. For example, there are a number of centers with monumental architecture, presumably built by speakers of Mayan languages, in the highlands and lowlands of modern-day Guatemala and the Yucatán peninsula of modern-day Mexico. From surface appearances the Mayan centers do not appear to be as densely populated or as urbanized as Teotihuacán or Monte Albán. Some anthropologists have attributed the apparently low density of population in the Mayan centers to the apparently small possibility of intensive agriculture in those areas, now mostly covered by dense tropical forest. But evidence recently presented suggests that the Mayan centers may have been more densely populated and more dependent on intensive

agriculture than was once surmised.[16] It may be that Mayan urbanization has not been so easy to discover because of the dense tropical forest that now covers much of the area of Mayan civilization.

The First Cities and States in Other Areas

So far we have discussed the emergence of cities and states in Southern Iraq and Mesoamerica whose development is best, if only imperfectly, known archaeologically. But other state societies probably arose more or less independently in many other areas of the world, as well. We say "independently" because such states seem to have emerged without colonization or conquest by other states.

Almost at the same time as the Sumerian empire, the great dynastic age was beginning in the Nile Valley in Egypt. The "Old Kingdom," or early dynastic period, began about 3100 B.C. There is evidence that the ancient Egyptians traded with Sumer at a very early date—an exchange which may have influenced the formation of the state in Egypt.[17]

In the Indus Valley of northwestern India, one or more state societies apparently developed by about 2500 B.C. As with Egypt, state formation in the Indus Valley may have been preceded by trade with the Sumerian empire. This external trade, coupled with the development of irrigation techniques, may partially explain the development of Indus civilization. That a state-level of political organization existed prior to the founding of the Indus Valley cities of Harappa and Mohenjo-daro is suggested by the fact that those cities were built according to a precise geometric plan.[18]

In China, we know that by 1650 B.C. the so-called Shang dynasty in northern China had

[16]B. L. Turner, "Population Density in the Classic Maya Lowlands: New Evidence for Old Approaches," *Geographical Review* 66, no. 1 (January 1970): 72–82.
[17]Service, *Origins of the State and Civilization,* pp. 225–37.
[18]Ibid., pp. 238–46.

A temple at the Mayan site of Tikal, dating between 300 and 900 A.D. (Courtesy of the American Museum of Natural History.)

all the earmarks of statehood: a very stratified, specialized society; religious, economic, and administrative unification; and a pronounced Shang art style.[19]

In South America state societies may have emerged by the time of Christ in the area of modern-day Peru.[20] In sub-Saharan Africa after about 800 A.D., the western Sudan had a succession of city-states. One of them was called Ghana, and it became a major source of gold for the Mediterranean world.[21] And in North America by 1050 A.D. there is some evidence suggestive of a state-level society in the area around St. Louis. Huge mounds of earth 100 feet high mark the site called Cahokia.[22]

Theories about the Origin of the State

We have seen that states developed in many parts of the world. Why did they evolve when, and where, they did? A number of theories have been proposed to explain the rise of the earliest states.

IRRIGATION THEORY

In many of the areas in which early state societies were formed, irrigation seems to have been associated with the development of civilization. Irrigation made the land habitable or very productive in parts of Mesoamerica, southern Iraq, the Nile Valley, and other areas. It has been suggested that the labor and management needed for the upkeep of an irrigation system leads to the formation of a political elite (the overseers of the system) who eventually become the governors of the society.[23] Proponents of this view believe that both the city and civilization were outgrowths of the administrative requirements of an irrigation system.

Critics note that this theory does not seem to apply to all areas where cities and states may have independently emerged. For example, in southern Iraq, the irrigation systems serving the early cities were generally small in scale and probably did not require extensive labor and management. Large-scale irrigation works were not constructed until after cities had been fully established.[24] Thus, irrigation could not have been the main stimulus for the development of cities and states in Sumer. Even in China, for which the irrigation theory was first formulated, there is no evidence of large-scale irrigation as early as Shang times.[25]

Although large-scale irrigation may not have always preceded the emergence of the first cities and states, even small-scale irrigation systems could have resulted in unequal access to productive land and so may have contributed to the development of a stratified society.[26] In addition, irrigation systems may have given rise to border and other disputes between adjacent groups, thereby prompting people to concentrate in cities for defense and stimulating the development of military and political controls. Finally, as Adams and Service both suggest, the main significance of irrigation—either large- or small-scale—may have been its intensification of production, a development which, in turn, may have indirectly stimulated craft specialization, trade, and administrative bureaucracy.[27]

POPULATION GROWTH, CIRCUMSCRIPTION, AND WAR

Another explanation of the origin of states suggests that population growth in an area of phys-

[19]Kwang-Chih Chang, *The Archaeology of Ancient China* (New Haven: Yale University Press, 1968), pp. 235–55.

[20]Thomas C. Paterson, *America's Past* (Glenview, Ill.: Scott, Foresman and Co., 1973), pp. 98–99.

[21]Service, pp. 129–30.

[22]Melvin L. Fowler, "A Pre-Columbian Urban Center on the Mississippi," *Scientific American*, August 1975, pp. 92–101.

[23]Karl Wittfogel, *Oriental Despotism: A Comparative Study of Total Power* (New Haven: Yale University Press, 1957).

[24]Robert M. Adams, "The Origin of Cities," *Scientific American*, September 1960, p. 153.

[25]Paul Wheatley, *The Pivot of the Four Quarters* (Chicago: Aldine, 1971), p. 291.

[26]Adams, "The Origin of Cities," p. 153.

[27]Ibid.; also Service, *Origins of the State and Civilization*, pp. 274–75.

Sophisticated irrigation techniques have been used in Peruvian river valleys since pre-Columbian times. Here, terracing is being used to obtain water for crops in the Andean valley. (Carl Frank, Photo Researchers.)

ical or social circumscription may be the "prime mover." Competition and warfare in such a situation may lead to the subordination of defeated groups who are obliged to pay tribute and to submit to the control of a more powerful group.[28] Carneiro illustrates this theory by describing how the state may have emerged on the northern coast of Peru.

After the people of that area first settled into an agricultural village life, population grew at a slow, steady rate. Initially, new villages were formed as population grew. But in the narrow coastal valleys, backed by high mountains, fronted by the sea, and surrounded by desert, this splintering-off process could not continue indefinitely. The result, Carneiro suggests, was increasing land shortage and warfare between villages as they competed for the land. Since the high mountains, the sea, and the desert blocked any escape for losers, the defeated villagers had no choice but to submit to political domination. In this way, chiefdoms may have become kingdoms as the most powerful villages grew to control entire valleys. As chiefs' power expanded over several valleys, states and empires may have been born. Carneiro notes that physical or environmental circumscription may not be the only kind of circumscription that gives rise to the state. Just as important may be social circumscription. People living at the center of a high-density area may find that their migration is blocked by surrounding settlements just as effectively as by mountains, sea, and desert.

Carneiro suggests that his theory applies to many areas besides the northern coast of Peru,

---

[28] Robert L. Carneiro, "A Theory of the Origin of the State," *Science,* 21 August 1970, pp. 733–38. Also see William T. Sanders and Barbara J. Price, *Mesoamerica* (New York: Random House, 1968), pp. 230–32.

including southern Iraq and the Indus and Nile valleys. While there were no geographical barriers in areas like northern China or the Mayan lowlands on the Yucatán peninsula, he suggests that the development of states in those areas may have been the result of social circumscription. Carneiro's theory seems to be supported for southern Iraq, where there is archaeological evidence of population growth, circumscription, and warfare.[29] And there is evidence of population growth prior to the emergence of the state in the Teotihuacán Valley[30] and in the Valley of Oaxaca.[31]

But the circumscription theory leaves some questions unanswered. For example, it is not clear why the victors in war would let the defeated populations remain and pay tribute. If the victors wanted the land so much in the first place, why wouldn't they drive the defeated out? Another problem with circumscription theory is that population growth is not always associated with state formation. Data from southwestern Iran indicate that there was population growth long before states emerged, but that just prior to their emergence, the population apparently declined.[32]

LOCAL AND LONG-DISTANCE TRADE

It has been suggested that trade may have been a factor in the emergence of the earliest states.[33] Wright and Johnson have theorized that the organizational requirements of producing items for export, redistributing the items imported, and defending trading parties would foster state formation.[34]

Does the archaeological evidence support the theory that trade played a crucial role in the formation of the earliest states? In southern Iraq and the Mayan lowlands, long-distance trade routes may indeed have been a factor stimulating bureaucratic growth. In the lowlands of southern Iraq, as we have already seen, the people needed wood and stone for building, and they traded with the highland people for these items. In the Mayan lowlands the development of civilization seems to have been preceded by long-distance trade, as farmers in the lowland regions traded with faraway places in order to obtain salt, obsidian for cutting blades, and hard stone for grinding tools.[35] On the Susiana Plain, long-distance trade did not become very important until after Susa became a city-state, but short-distance trade may have played the same kind of role in the formation of states. What the situation was like in other areas of early state formation is not yet known.

EVALUATING THE VARIOUS THEORIES

Why do states form? As of now, no one theory seems to fit all of the known sequences culminating in early state formation. The reason may be that different conditions in different places may have favored the emergence of centralized government. After all, the state, by definition, implies an ability to organize large populations for a collective purpose. In some areas, this purpose may have been the need to organize trade with local or far-off regions. In other cases, the state may have emerged as a way to control defeated populations in circumscribed areas. In still other instances, a combination of factors may have fostered the development of the

---

[29] T. Cuyler Young, Jr., "Population Densities and Early Mesopotamian Urbanism," in *Man, Settlement, and Urbanism*, ed. P. J. Ucko, R. Tringham, and G. W. Dimbleby (Cambridge, Mass.: Schenkman, 1972), pp. 827–42.

[30] Sanders and Price, *Mesoamerica*, p. 141.

[31] Blanton, "The Origins of Monte Albán," p. 225.

[32] Wright and Johnson, "Population, Exchange, and Early State Formation . . . ," p. 276.

[33] Karl Polanyi, Harry Pearson, and C. M. Arensberg, *Trade and Market in the Early Empires* (Glencoe, Ill.: Free Press, 1957), pp. 257–62; and William T. Sanders, "Hydraulic Agriculture, Economic Symbiosis, and the Evolution of States in Central Mexico," in *Anthropological Archeology in the Americas*, ed. Betty J. Meggers (Washington: Anthropological Society of Washington, 1968), p. 105; as referred to in Wright and Johnson, "Population, Exchange, and Early State Formation . . . ," p. 277.

[34] Wright and Johnson, "Population, Exchange, and Early State Formation . . . ," p. 277.

[35] William L. Rathje, "The Origin and Development of Lowland Classic Maya Civilization," *American Antiquity* 36, no. 3 (July 1971): 275–85.

state-type of political system. It is still not clear what the specific conditions were that led to the emergence of the state in each of the early centers. But since the question of why states formed is a lively and active focus of research today, more satisfactory answers may come out of ongoing and future research.

Summary

1. Archaeologists and historians do not always agree on how a state should be defined, but most seem to agree that centralized decision-making affecting a substantial population is the key criterion. Most states have cities with public buildings; full-time craft and religious specialists; an "official" art style; and a hierarchical social structure topped by an elite class from which the leaders are drawn. Most states maintain power with a monopoly on the use of force. Force or the threat of force is used by the state to tax its population and to draft people for work or war.

2. Early state societies arose within the Near East in what is now southern Iraq and southwestern Iran. Southern Iraq or Sumer was unified under a single government just after 3000 B.C. It had large urban centers, imposing temples, codified laws, a standing army, wide trade networks, a complex irrigation system, and a high degree of craft specialization.

3. One of the earliest city-states to rise in Mesoamerica was Teotihuacán in central Mexico. The city of Teotihuacán itself stood in the valley center at a place where many permanent springs provided water for irrigation. At the height of its power (200–500 A.D.), Teotihuacán appears to have influenced much of Mesoamerica. Another early Mesoamerican city-state was centered in the Valley of Oaxaca at Monte Albán.

4. City-states arose early in other parts of the New World: in Guatemala, the Yucatán peninsula of Mexico, Peru, and possibly near St. Louis. In the Old World, early states developed in Egypt, the Indus Valley of India, northern China, and West Africa.

5. Several theories try to explain why states arose. The irrigation theory suggests that the administrative needs of maintaining extensive irrigation systems may have been the impetus for state formation. The circumscription theory suggests that states emerge when competition and warfare in circumscribed areas leads to the subordination of defeated groups who are obliged to submit to the control of the more powerful group. Theories involving trade suggest that the organizational requirements of producing exportable items, redistributing imported items, and defending trading parties would foster state formation. Which theory is correct? At this point, no one theory is able to explain the formation of every state. Perhaps different organizational requirements in different areas favored centralized government.

Suggested Readings

Adams, R. McC. *The Evolution of Urban Society.* Chicago: Aldine, 1966.

A discussion of ecological, social, and historical factors possibly related to the rise of urban societies in Mesopotamia and pre-Hispanic Mexico.

Helms, Mary W. *Middle America: A Culture History of Heartland and Frontiers.* Englewood Cliffs, N.J.: Prentice-Hall, 1975.

A survey of cultural development from prehistoric to modern times in Mexico and central America. See Chapters 4–6 for material particularly relevant to this chapter.

Kramer, Samuel Noel. *The Sumerians: Their History, Culture and Character.* Chicago: University of Chicago Press, 1963.

A description of Sumerian culture, based largely on the earliest written records.

Sanders, William T., and Price, Barbara J. *Mesoamerica: The Evolution of a Civilization.* New York: Random House, 1968.

A descriptive and theoretical analysis of the factors and processes that may have shaped culture history in Mexico and Guatemala.

Service, Elman R. *Origins of the State and Civilization: The Process of Cultural Evolution.* New York: Norton, 1975.

A survey of prehistoric and some historic state societies. An attempt is made to evaluate some theories of the origin of the state.

Wheatley, Paul. *The Pivot of the Four Quarters.* Chicago: Aldine, 1971.

An extensive survey of the details of early urban life in different areas of the world.

Cultural Variation

III

The Concept of Culture

10

We all consider ourselves to be unique individuals, each with a set of personal opinions, preferences, habits, and quirks. Indeed, all of us *are* unique individuals, and yet most of us share a surprising number of feelings, beliefs, and habits with other members of our society. The characteristics that we share, many of which we take for granted and never think about, constitute what anthropologists refer to as our culture.

When we compare ourselves with people in other societies, we become especially aware of cultural differences and similarities. For example, most societies known to anthropologists think it is perfectly correct, and even desirable, for a man to have more than one wife at a time. In our society we do not allow this kind of marriage, but it is perfectly legal for a man or woman to marry a series of spouses, provided he or she is not married to more than one spouse at a time. We may have different opinions about whether we want to marry at all, or if we do choose to marry, about the kind of person we want to have as a marriage partner. But hardly anyone in our society would question why it is not possible here to be married to more than one spouse simultaneously. In addition, newly married couples in most societies live with, or next door to, one set of in-laws. In our society, most newly married couples do not live very near their in-laws and, in fact, prefer to avoid such an arrangement.

Cultural Relativity

In any society, people tend to feel strongly that their own customary behaviors and attitudes are the correct ones, that people who do not share those patterns are immoral or inferior. But our own customs and ideas may appear bizarre or barbaric to an observer from another culture. A Hindu in India, for example, would consider our custom of eating beef both primitive and disgusting. In his culture, the cow is a sacred animal and may not be slaughtered for food. Even our most mundane customs—the daily rituals we take for granted—might seem thoroughly absurd when viewed from the perspective of a

10

foreign culture. A visitor to our society might justifiably take strange notes on certain behaviors which seem quite ordinary to us, as the following extract shows:

The daily body ritual performed by everyone includes a mouth-rite. Despite the fact that these people are so punctilious about the care of the mouth, this rite involves a practice which strikes the uninitiated stranger as revolting. It was reported to me that the ritual consists of inserting a small bundle of hog hairs into the mouth, along with certain magical powders, and then moving the bundle in a highly formalized series of gestures.

In addition to the private mouth-rite, the people seek out a holy-mouth man once or twice a year. These practitioners have an impressive set of paraphernalia, consisting of a variety of augers, awls, probes, and prods. The use of these objects in the exorcism of the evils of the mouth involves almost unbelievable ritual torture of the client. The holy-mouth man opens the client's mouth and, using the above mentioned tools, enlarges any holes which decay may have created in the teeth. Magical materials are put into these holes. If there are no naturally occurring holes in the teeth, large sections of one or more teeth are gouged out so that the supernatural substance can be applied. In the client's view, the purpose of these ministrations is to arrest decay and to draw friends. The extremely sacred and traditional character of the rite is evident in the fact that the natives return to the holy-mouth man year after year, despite the fact that their teeth continue to decay.[1]

We are likely to protest that to understand and appreciate the behaviors of a particular society—in this case our own—an observer must be acquainted with that society's culture and the reasons for its customs. The observer must know, for example, that periodic visits to the "holy-mouth man" are for medical, not magical, purposes. Because strong, healthy teeth are valued highly in our society, we are willing to spend much time and money on dental care.

The anthropological attitude that a society's customs and ideas should be understood in the context of that society's problems and opportunities is called *cultural relativity*. Because this attitude fosters empathy and understanding, it is *humanistic*; because it requires impartial observation and involves an attempt to explain customs, the attitude is *scientific*.

In general, cultural relativity is impeded by two different, but commonly held, attitudes. The first attitude is the tendency toward negative evaluation, which usually results from ethnocentrism. The second attitude is the tendency toward a positive evaluation, which often takes the form of a naive yearning for the simple life of the "noble savage."

ETHNOCENTRISM

The person whose vision is strictly limited to his or her own needs and desires is generally ineffective in dealing with other people. We call such an individual egocentric, and we would be sorry to have such a person for a psychiatrist. The person who judges other cultures solely in terms of his or her own culture is ethnocentric. Not only are such people ill equipped to do anthropological work, but they may be unable to recognize and solve social problems in their own culture.

For example, an ethnocentric American would view as barbaric the ceremonies that initiate adolescent boys into manhood in many societies. These ceremonies often involve hazing, difficult tests of courage and endurance, and painful circumcision. The ethnocentric American would be unable to understand why anyone would willingly endure such hardships merely to be publicly accepted as an adult. However, the same type of ethnocentric thinking would make it difficult for such a person to question the American custom of confining the aged in institutions, which is a practice that observers from another culture might find indefensible. Ethnocentrism, then, hinders our understanding of the customs of other people and, at the same time, keeps us from having creative insight into our own customs.

[1] Horace Miner, "Body Rituals among the Nacirema," *American Anthropologist* 58 (1956): 504–5. Reproduced by permission of the American Anthropological Association from the *American Anthropologist* 58:504–5, 1956.

Because we are ethnocentric about many things, it is often difficult to criticize our own customs—some of which might be shocking to a member of another society. Here, pictured above, an aged Chinese woman, very much the center of her family, presents a sharp contrast to an elderly American couple who seem isolated and abandoned. (Photograph of Chinese family by Henri Cartier-Bresson, Magnum Photos; photograph of American couple by Jim Jowers for Nancy Palmer Photo Agency.)

THE "NOBLE SAVAGE"

Whenever we are weary of the complexities of civilization, we may long for a way of life that is "closer to nature" or "simpler" than our own. For instance, a young American whose father is holding two or three jobs just to provide his family with bare necessities might briefly be attracted to the life-style of the !Kung Bushmen of the Kalahari Desert. The Bushmen share their food and therefore are often free to engage in leisure activities during the greater part of the day. They obtain all of their food by hunting animals and gathering wild plants. Since they have no facilities for refrigeration, sharing a freshly killed animal is clearly more sensible than hoarding rotten meat. Moreover, the sharing, as it turns out, provides a kind of social security system for the Bushmen. If a hunter is unable to catch an animal on a certain day, he can obtain food for himself and his family from someone else in his band. Conversely, at some later date, the game he catches will provide food for the family of some other unsuccessful hunter. This system of sharing also insures that persons too young or too old to help with the collecting of food will still be fed.

However, the food-sharing system of the !Kung Bushmen is a solution to the problems posed by their special environment and is not necessarily a practical solution to problems in our own society. Moreover, there are other aspects of Bushmen life that would not appeal to many Americans. For example, when the nomadic Bushmen decide to move their camps, the women must carry all the family possessions, substantial amounts of food and water, and all young children below age four or five. This is a sizable burden to carry for any distance. And since the Bushmen travel about 1,500 miles in a single year,[2] it is unlikely that most American women would find the Bushman way of life enviable in all respects.

[2] Richard B. Lee, "Population Growth and the Beginnings of Sedentary Life among the !Kung Bushmen," in *Population Growth: Anthropological Implications,* ed. Brian Spooner (Cambridge, Mass.: MIT Press, 1972), pp. 329–42.

The point is not that we should avoid comparing our culture with others, but that we should not romanticize about other cultures. Their behaviors probably are, or were, appropriate to their environments, just as our behaviors probably are, or were, appropriate to our own environment. Cultural relativity asks that all customs of a society be viewed in terms of that society, rather than in terms of our own.

Toward a Definition of Culture

In everyday usage, the word *culture* refers to a desirable quality that we can acquire by attending a sufficient number of plays and concerts and trudging through several miles of art galleries. The anthropologist, however, has a different definition. In the following extract, Ralph Linton makes clear how the layman's definition of culture differs from the anthropologist's:

It (culture) refers to the total way of life of any society, not simply to those parts of this way which the society regards as higher or more desirable. Thus culture, when applied to our own way of life, has nothing to do with playing the piano or reading Browning. For the social scientist such activities are simply elements within the totality of our culture. This totality also includes such mundane activities as washing dishes or driving an automobile, and for the purposes of cultural studies these stand quite on a par with "the finer things of life." It follows that for the social scientist there are no uncultured societies or even individuals. Every society has a culture, no matter how simple this culture may be, and every human being is cultured, in the sense of participating in some culture or other.[3]

Culture, then, refers to innumerable aspects of life. To most anthropologists, culture encompasses the behaviors, beliefs, and attitudes, and also the products of human activity, that are characteristic of a particular society or population. Each of us is born into a complex culture

[3]Ralph Linton, *The Cultural Background of Personality* (New York: Appleton-Century-Crofts, 1945), p. 30.

that will strongly influence how we live and behave for the remainder of our lives.

CULTURE IS SHARED

If only one person thinks or does a certain thing, that thought or action represents a personal habit, not a pattern of culture. For something to be considered cultural, it must be generally shared by some population or group of individuals. For example, we share certain values, beliefs, and behaviors with our families and friends (although anthropologists are not particularly concerned with this type of cultural group). We share cultural characteristics with segments of our population whose ethnic or regional origins, religious affiliations, and occupations are the same as our own. We have certain practices in common with all Americans. We even share certain characteristics with people beyond our national borders who have similar interests (such as the members of the International Union of Anthropological and Ethnological Sciences) and with the inhabitants of other societies that share so-called Western culture.

When we talk about the shared customs of a society, which constitute the central concern of cultural anthropology, we are referring to a *culture*. When we talk about the shared customs of a subgroup within a society, which are a central concern of sociology, we are referring to a *subculture*. And when we study the shared customs of some group that transcends national boundaries, we are talking about a phenomenon for which we do not even have a name—a fact that reflects how relatively infrequent and recent this kind of sharing is. At the moment, we must refer to such a phenomenon by labeling it geographically—for example, we speak of "Eastern European culture."

CULTURE IS LEARNED

Not all things shared generally by a population are cultural. The typical hair color of a population is not cultural. Neither is sleeping or eating.

At an early age, children learn the customs of their society. Here a young boy imitates the limbering-up exercises of a soccer team, illustrating that even play involves learned behavior. (Elliott Erwitt, Magnum Photos.)

For something to be considered cultural, it must be learned as well as shared. A typical hair color (unless dyed) is not cultural because it is genetically determined. Sleeping and eating are not cultural actions in themselves because we do not have to learn to do them, but when and where to sleep and how and what to eat are learned activities. All people eat, but different cultures satisfy this instinctive or biological need in vastly different ways. Americans do not think that dogs are edible, and indeed the idea of eating dogs horrifies us. But in China, as in some other societies, the meat of the dog is considered delicious. In our society, many people consider a baked ham to be a holiday dish. However, in several societies of the Middle East, including those of Egypt and Israel, eating the meat of a pig is forbidden. Humans eat because they must; but what and when and how they eat is learned and varies from culture to culture.

To some extent, all animals exhibit learned behaviors, some of which may be shared by most individuals in a population and may therefore be considered cultural. However, different animal species vary in the degree to which their shared behaviors are learned or are instinctive. The sociable ants, for instance, despite all their patterned social behavior, do not appear to have much, if any, culture. They divide their labor, construct their nests, form their raiding columns, and carry off their dead, all without having been taught to do so and without imitating the behavior of other ants. In contrast, most of the behavior of humans appears to be culturally patterned. And we are increasingly discovering that our closest biological relatives—the monkeys and the apes—also exhibit a good deal of cultural behavior. For example, in 1953, scientists at the Japan Monkey Center were able to observe how a particular behavioral innovation spread from monkey to monkey and eventually became a part of a group's culture. The scientists left some sweet potatoes on a beach, near the place where a group of Japanese monkeys lived. Attracted by the food, a young female began to wash the sand off the potatoes by plunging them into a nearby brook. Previously, the monkeys had rubbed their food clean, but this washing behavior spread throughout the group and eventually replaced their former habit of rubbing off the sand. After a number of years, 80 to 90 percent of the monkeys were washing sweet potatoes. This learned habit had become a part of the monkeys' culture.[4]

Experimenters have shown that apes and monkeys learn a wide variety of behaviors. Some of their learned responses are as basic as those involved in maternal care and others are as frivolous as the taste for candy. The proportion of an animal's life span that is spent as childhood seems to reflect the degree to which the animal depends upon learned behavior for survival. Monkeys and apes have relatively long childhoods as compared to other animals. Hu-

[4]Jun'ichiro Itani, "The Society of Japanese Monkeys," *Japan Quarterly* 8 (1961): 421–30.

mans have by far the longest childhood of any animal, reflecting our great dependence on learned behavior. Although humans acquire some learned behavior by imitation, as do monkeys and apes, most human learned behavior is acquired with the aid of a unique mechanism—language.

Language All people known to anthropologists, regardless of their kind of society, have had a highly complex system of spoken, symbolic communication that we call language. Language is *symbolic* in that a word or phrase can represent what it stands for *whether or not that thing is present.*

This symbolic quality of language has tremendous implications for the transmission of culture. It means that a human parent can tell a child that a snake, for example, is dangerous and should be avoided. The parent can then describe the snake in great detail, giving particulars of its length, diameter, color, texture, shape, and means of locomotion. The parent also can predict the kinds of places where the child is likely to encounter snakes and explain how the child can avoid the reptiles. Should the child encounter a snake, then, he or she will probably recall the symbolic word for the animal, remember as well the related information, and so avoid danger.

If symbolic language did not exist, the human parents would have to wait until their baby actually saw a snake and then, through example, show the child that such a creature was to be avoided. Without language we could not transmit or receive information symbolically, and thus we would not be heir to so rich and varied a culture.

To sum up, we may say that something is cultural if it is a learned belief, value, or behavior that is generally shared by the members of a population. Anthropologists are usually concerned with the cultural characteristics of a "society," by which they mean a group of people who occupy a particular territory and speak a common language which is not generally un-

derstood by neighboring peoples.[5] Hence, when an anthropologist speaks about *a* culture, he or she is usually referring to that set of learned and shared beliefs, values, and behaviors generally characteristic of a particular society. But now that we have defined what is cultural, we must ask further, How does an anthropologist go about deciding which *particular* behaviors, values, and beliefs of individuals are cultural?

Describing a Culture

INDIVIDUAL VARIATION

Describing a particular culture might seem relatively uncomplicated at first: you simply observe what the people in that society do and then record their behavior. But consider the very real difficulties that might be encountered in doing this. How would you decide which people to observe? And what would you conclude if all twelve of the first dozen people you observed or talked to behaved quite differently in the same situation? Admittedly, you would be unlikely to encounter such extreme divergence of behaviors. Yet there would tend to be significant individual variations in the actual behavior patterns of your subjects, even when they were responding to the same generalized situation and conforming to cultural expectations.

To help us understand how an anthropologist might make sense of diverse behaviors, let us examine this diversity as it exists in a situation with which we are all familiar—the American football game.

When Americans attend a football game, various members of the crowd behave differ-

[5] A matter of convention usually determines where we say a particular society leaves off and another begins, since societies are not always clearly separate with respect to language. For example, some might say that Canadians and Americans form a single society because both groups generally speak English and also share many common beliefs, values, and practices. But because there are two political entities (nations) involved, others might prefer to speak of separate Canadian and American cultures. This overlapping of cultural limits is found in many areas of the world, since political boundaries do not always correspond to linguistic boundaries.

ently while a singer is performing the "Star-Spangled Banner." As they stand and listen, some men remove their hats; a child munches popcorn; a former soldier stands at attention; a cheerleader searches the lines of players for her favorite athlete; and the two head coaches take a final opportunity to intone secret chants and spells designed to sap the strength of the opposing team. Yet despite these individual variations, most of the people at the game respond in a basically similar manner: nearly everyone stands silently, facing the flag. Moreover, if you go to a number of football games, you will observe that many aspects of the event are notably similar. Although the plays used will vary from game to game, the rules of the game are never different; and although the colors of the uniforms vary for each team, the players never appear on the field dressed in swimsuits.

Although the variations in individual reactions to a given stimulus are theoretically limitless, in fact they tend to fall within easily recognizable limits. The child listening to the anthem may continue to eat his popcorn, but he probably will not do a rain dance. Similarly, it is unlikely that the coaches will react to that same stimulus by running onto the field and embracing the singer. Variations in behavior, then, are confined within socially acceptable limits, and it is part of the anthropologist's goal to find out what these limits are. He or she may note, for example, that some limitations on behavior have a practical purpose: a spectator who disrupts the game by wandering onto the field would be required to leave. Other limitations are purely traditional. In our society it is considered proper for a man to remove his overcoat if he becomes overheated; but other spectators would undoubtedly frown upon his removing his trousers even if the weather was quite warm. Using such observations, the anthropologist attempts to discover the customs and the ranges of acceptable behavior that characterize the society under study. By focusing on customary behavior, rather than on individual variation, the anthropologist is able to describe the culture of the group.

For example, an anthropologist interested in describing courtship procedures in the United States would initially encounter a variety of behaviors. The anthropologist may note that one couple prefers to go to a concert on a first date, while another couple chooses to go bowling; some couples have very long engagements and others never become engaged at all; some couples emphasize the religious rituals in the marriage ceremony while others are married by civil authorities, and so on. Despite this variability, the anthropologist, after further observation and interviewing, might begin to detect certain regularities in the courting practices. Although couples may do many different things on their first and subsequent "dates," they nearly always arrange the dates by themselves, they try to avoid their parents when on dates, they often manage to find themselves alone at the end of a date, they put their lips together frequently, and so forth. After a series of more and more closely spaced encounters, a man and woman may decide to declare themselves publicly as a couple, either by announcing that they are "engaged" or by revealing that they are living together or intend to do so. Finally, if the couple decides to marry, they must in some way have their union recorded by the civil authorities.

In our society a person who wishes to marry cannot completely disregard the customary patterns of courtship. If a man saw a woman on the street and decided that he wanted to marry her, he could conceivably choose a quicker and more direct form of action than the usual dating procedure. He could get on a horse, ride to the woman's home, snatch her up in his arms, and gallop away with her. In Sicily, until recently, such a couple would have been considered legally "married," even if the woman had never met the man before or had no intention of marrying. But, in the United States, any man who acted in such a fashion would be arrested and jailed for kidnapping and would probably have his sanity seriously challenged. Such behavior would not be acceptable in our society; therefore it could not be considered cultural.

Although life styles of these three American couples appear very different, their courtship patterns all have certain aspects in common. Romantic love, for example, seems to be an attitude shared by all of them. (Hiroji Kubota, Magnum Photos; Sepp Seitz, Magnum Photos; Horoji Kubota, Magnum Photos.)

Although individual behaviors may vary, most social behavior falls within culturally acceptable limits.

CULTURAL CONSTRAINTS

A primary factor limiting the range of individual behavior variations is the culture itself. The noted French sociologist, Emile Durkheim, stressed that culture is something outside of us, external to the individual on whom it exerts a strong coercive power. We do not always feel the constraints of our culture because we generally conform to the types of conduct and thought which it requires. Yet when we do try to oppose the cultural constraints, their strength becomes apparent.

Cultural constraints are of two basic types, direct and indirect. Naturally, the direct constraints are the more obvious. For example, if you wear clothing which is atypical of our culture, you will probably be subject to ridicule and a certain amount of social isolation. But if you choose to wear only a scanty loincloth, you will receive a stronger, more direct cultural constraint—arrest for indecent exposure.

Although indirect forms of cultural constraint are less obvious than direct ones, they are no less effective. Durkheim illustrated this point when he wrote: "I am not obliged to speak French with my fellow-countrymen, nor to use the legal currency, but I cannot possibly do otherwise. If I tried to escape this necessity, my attempt would fail miserably."[6] In other words, if Durkheim had decided he would rather speak Serbo-Croatian than French, nobody would have tried to stop him. But no one would have understood him either. And, although he would not have been put into prison for trying to buy groceries with Icelandic money, he would have had difficulty convincing the local merchants to sell him food.

In a series of experiments on conformity, Solomon Asch revealed how strong social con-

straints can be. Asch coached the majority of a group of college students to give deliberately incorrect answers to questions involving visual stimuli. A "critical subject," the one student in the room who was not so coached, had no idea that other participants would purposely misinterpret the evidence presented to them. Asch found that in one-third of the experiments, the critical subject *consistently* allowed his own correct perceptions to be distorted by the obviously incorrect statements of the others. And in another 40 percent of the experiments, the critical subjects yielded to the opinion of the group some of the time.[7]

The existence of social or cultural constraints, however, is not necessarily incompatible with individuality. Cultural constraints are usually exercised most forcefully around the limits of acceptable behavior. Thus, there is often a broad range of behavior within which individuals can exercise their uniqueness. And individuals do not always give in to the wishes of the majority. In the Asch experiments, many individuals (one-fourth of the critical subjects) consistently retained their independent opinions, even in the face of complete disagreement with the majority.

IDEAL VERSUS ACTUAL CULTURAL PATTERNS

Every society develops a series of *ideal cultural patterns* which tend to be reinforced through cultural constraints. The ideal cultural patterns are the behaviors that most members of the society consider to be correct and proper in particular situations. Such ideal patterns are often called *norms*. However, we all know that people do not always behave according to the standards that they express. If they did, there would be no need for direct or indirect constraints. Some of our ideal patterns differ from actual behavior because the ideal is outmoded, based on the way that society used to be. Other

[6] Emile Durkheim, *The Rules of Sociological Method*, trans. Sarah A. Soloway and John H. Mueller, ed. George E. E. Catlin, 8th ed. (New York: Free Press, 1936), p. 3.

[7] Solomon Asch, "Studies of Independence and Conformity: A Minority of One against a Unanimous Majority," *Psychological Monographs*, 70 (1956): 1–70.

ideal patterns may never have been actual patterns and may represent merely what people would like to see as the correct behavior. Deviations from ideal patterns, therefore, may be either harbingers of future culture or vestiges of old culture.

To illustrate the difference between ideal and actual culture, let us consider the idealized belief, long cherished in America, that doctors are selfless, friendly people who choose medicine as their profession because they feel themselves "called" to serve humanity, and who have little interest in either the money or prestige of their position. Of course, many physicians do not measure up to this ideal. Nevertheless, the continued success of television programs that portray the average American M.D. as a paragon of virtue indicates that the ideal of the noble physician is deeply rooted in our collective psyche.

PROCEDURES FOR DISCOVERING CULTURAL PATTERNS

There are two basic ways in which an anthropologist can discover cultural patterns. When dealing with those customs which are overt or highly visible within a society—for example, our custom of having a nationally elected public official known as a president—the investigator can determine the existence of such practices and study them with the aid of a few knowledgeable persons. On the other hand, when dealing with a particular sphere of behavior which encompasses many individual variations, or when the people studied are unaware of their pattern of behavior, the anthropologist must collect information from a sample of individuals and derive the *modal* response.

The mode is a statistical term that refers to the most frequently encountered response in a given series of responses; it is thus a way of expressing a general cultural pattern. Suppose that an anthropologist wants to describe the time of day when the members of a society eat dinner. The records of the behavior of fifty people show that some have dinner at 5:45 P.M.,

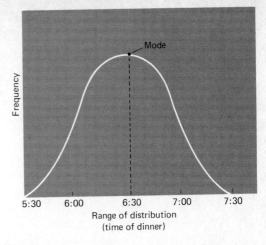

FIGURE 1   Frequency Distribution Curve

others at 6:00, and still others at 6:30 or 7:00, but that most people eat dinner around 6:30 P.M. The anthropologist will say that the members of that society generally eat dinner at 6:30 P.M., for this time represents the modal behavior of those people.

The mode is determined by measuring the variability of a given behavior pattern. When an anthropologist wants to describe a behavior in which there are many variations, he or she first records the behavior patterns of each of the persons being observed. Next, the investigator tabulates the number of times each class of behavior (in the example above, each dinnertime) occurs; this gives the *frequency distribution* of each class. To obtain a frequency distribution curve, the anthropologist transfers the figures to a graph which measures the range of distribution along the horizontal axis and the frequency along the vertical axis. The figures plotted on the graph are connected by a line that forms a curve. Usually, such a curve slopes upward to a high point and then downward; the highest point represents the mode. Because of its shape, this kind of curve is called a *bell curve* (see Figure 1).

Frequency distributions may be calculated on the basis of responses given by all the members of a particular population. However, to save time, the anthropologist usually relies upon data obtained from a representative sample of persons. Ideally, the members of this sample would be selected randomly from the society or community—that is, all types of individuals would have an equal chance to be chosen. If a sample is "random," it will probably include examples of all frequent variations of behavior exhibited within the society or community in roughly the proportions in which they occur. In theory, the random sample is a useful device; in fact, it has not yet been used extensively in anthropological fieldwork. Since it is relatively easy to make generalizations about *overt* or conscious aspects of a culture, such as dinner hours and courtship procedures, random sampling of these behaviors is often not necessary. But in dealing with *covert* or unconscious aspects of culture, such as a society's ideas about how far people should stand from one another when talking, random sampling may be needed to enable the investigator to generalize correctly about cultural patterns. The reason is that, by definition, most people are not aware of their covert or unconscious cultural patterns. (If persons were aware of them, the patterns would not be covert.) Furthermore, in identifying covert aspects of culture, the anthropologist must use considerable subjective judgment, and he or she is more likely to draw erroneous conclusions in the absence of random sampling.

Some Basic Assumptions about Culture

CULTURE IS GENERALLY ADAPTIVE

There are some cultural behaviors that, if carried to an extreme, would decrease the chances of survival of a particular society. For example, certain tribes in New Guinea view women as essentially unclean and dangerous individuals with whom physical contact should be as limited as possible. Suppose one such tribe decided to adopt homosexuality as its customary sexual pattern. Clearly, we would not expect such a society to survive for long. Although this example may appear extreme, it indicates that customs that diminish the survival chances of a society are not likely to persist. Either the people clinging to those customs will become extinct, taking the customs with them, or the customs will have to be replaced, thereby permitting the people to survive. By either process, *maladaptive* customs (those that diminish the survival chances of a society) are likely to disappear. Those customs of a society which enhance the survival chances of the society are *adaptive* and are likely to persist. Hence we assume that, if a society has survived to be described in the annals of anthropology, much if not most of its cultural repertoire is or was adaptive.

When we say that a custom is adaptive, however, we mean that it is adaptive only with respect to the particular conditions of a specific physical and social environment. What may be adaptive in one environment may not be adaptive in another. Therefore, when we ask ourselves why a society has a particular custom, we might ask if that custom makes sense as an adaptation to that society's particular environmental conditions.

Many cultural behaviors that would otherwise appear incomprehensible to us may be understandable as a society's response to its environment. For example, we might express surprise at the postpartum sex taboos in certain societies that prohibit women from engaging in sexual intercourse until their two-year-olds are ready to be weaned. But in the tropical areas where such taboos exist, they may represent a people's means of adjusting to their physical environment. If there were no such taboo and a mother quickly became pregnant again, she could no longer continue nursing her infant. Without its mother's milk, the child might succumb to *kwashiorkor*, a severe protein deficiency disease that is common in those tropical areas. The taboo, then, may serve to give the infant a better chance for survival.[8] Thus, a long post-

[8] John W. M. Whiting, "Effects of Climate on Certain Cultural Practices," in *Explorations in Cultural Anthropology*, ed. Ward Goodenough (New York: McGraw-Hill, 1964), pp. 511–44.

partum sex taboo may be an adaptive custom in certain tropical countries. In nontropical areas where kwashiorkor is not a problem, the same taboo may not be advantageous.

Just as culture represents an adjustment to the physical environment and to biological demands, it may also represent an adjustment to the social environment—that is, to neighboring peoples. For example, we do not know for sure why the Hopi Indians began building their settlements on the tops of mesas. They must have had strong reasons for doing so, because there were many difficulties in building on such sites—the problem of hauling water long distances to the settlements, for instance. It is possible that the Hopi chose to locate their villages on mesa tops for defensive reasons when the Athapaskan-speaking groups of Indians (the Navajo and Apache hunting tribes) moved into the Hopi area. In other words, the Hopi may have adjusted their living habits in accordance with social pressures.

A given custom represents one society's adaptation to its environment; it does not represent all possible adaptations. Different societies may choose different means of adjusting to the same situation. Thus, in areas of South America where people's diets are low in protein, there is no long postpartum sex taboo, but induced abortion is a common practice. This custom may serve the same function of spacing out live births and thereby preventing too-early weaning of children. The Hopi Indians, when suddenly confronted by the hostile, expansionist Navajo and Apache hunting tribes, clearly had to take some action to protect themselves. But instead of deciding to build their settlements on easily defended mesa tops, they could conceivably have developed a standing army. Why a society develops a particular response to a problem, rather than some other possible response, always requires explanation. The choice may depend largely on whether or not a particular response is possible, given the existing cultural repertoire. For example, in the Hopi case, a standing army would not have been a likely response to the problem of invaders because the Hopi economy probably could not

Near Walpi, Arizona, this Hopi Indian mesa settlement is believed to have been built by the Hopis in 1700 for defense, in this case against Spanish colonialism. (Hiroji Kubota, Magnum Photos.)

have supported any large group of full-time specialists such as soldiers. Full-time specialists have to be fed by the regular production of more food than the people involved in food-production generally need, and such a level of food-production was not present among the Hopi. The strategy of moving their villages to easily defended mesa tops may have been the easiest option, given the Hopi economy, and is the one they took.

Even though we assume that cultures that survive long enough to be described are generally adaptive, not *all* culture traits are necessarily adaptive. Some traits—such as clothing styles and rules of etiquette—may be "neutral" in terms of adaptation. That is, they may have no direct relationship to biological needs or environmental conditions at the present time. Consider, for example, the buttons and incompletely closed seam at the end of a man's suit jacket sleeve. This style does not appear to have any adaptive value now. In the past, when there was no central heating in buildings, the style may have been quite adaptive, enabling the wearer to close the sleeves tightly about the wrist. Neutral traits may once have had adaptive consequences.

We must remember that a society is not forced to adapt its culture to changing environmental circumstances. First, even in the face of changed circumstances, people may choose not to give up what they have. Second, although people may alter their behavior according to what they perceive will be helpful to them, what they perceive to be helpful may not prove to be adaptive. However, considering the large number of diverse cultures that have survived to be described, we can assume that cultures are generally adaptive and that people, at least sometimes, make the right moves.

CULTURE IS MOSTLY INTEGRATED

When we hear of an unfamiliar cultural pattern, our natural response is to try to imagine how that pattern would work in our own society. We might wonder, for example, what would happen if American women adopted a long postpartum sex taboo—say, three years of abstinence after the birth of a baby. Such a question is purely whimsical, for the customs of one culture cannot easily be grafted onto another culture. A long postpartum sex taboo presupposes a lack of effective birth control methods, but our society already has many such methods. Moreover, a long postpartum sex taboo could conceivably affect a number of important aspects of our culture, ranging from the tradition that marriage is romantic to the allowable number of wives per man. The point is that with such a taboo imposed on it, our culture would no longer be our culture. Too many other aspects of the culture would have to be changed to accommodate the one new behavior. This is so because our culture is mostly integrated.

In saying that a culture is mostly *integrated,* we mean that the elements or traits which make up that culture are not just a random assortment of customs but are mostly adjusted to or consistent with each other. One reason anthropologists believe that culture tends to be integrated is that culture is generally adaptive. If certain customs are more adaptive in particular settings, then those "bundles" of traits will generally be found associated under similar conditions. For example, the !Kung Bushmen, as we have mentioned, subsist by hunting wild animals and gathering wild plants. They also are nomadic, have very small communities, have low population densities, share food within their bands, and have few material possessions. These cultural traits usually occur together when people depend upon hunting and gathering for their food. Such associations imply that cultures tend to be integrated by virtue of their adaptational requirements.

Some aspects of culture may tend to be integrated for another reason. Research in social psychology has suggested that there is a tendency for people to modify beliefs or behaviors when those beliefs or behaviors are not cognitively consistent with other information.[9] If such a tendency toward cognitive consistency is generally found in humans, we might expect that some aspects of a culture would tend to be integrated for this reason. For example, if a society believes that its gods cure illness, and subsequently many of its people die from European-introduced diseases (which has happened in many parts of the world in the last 400 years), that society would be likely to alter its belief in the ability of its gods to cure illness. Cultural integration, then, may be cognitively, as well as adaptively, induced.

CULTURE IS ALWAYS CHANGING

The statements that culture is generally adaptive and that culture is mostly integrated both imply that culture is always changing. Cultural adaptation is cultural change in response to environmental changes. And granted that culture tends toward integration, if one aspect of culture changes in response to change in the environment, other aspects of culture will probably change accordingly. Individual variation or

[9]Roger Brown, *Social Psychology* (New York: Free Press, 1965), pp. 549–609.

deviation from cultural rules may provide the raw material of culture change. Something that starts out as unusual or peculiar behavior may be picked up by others as an appropriate response in the face of changing circumstances. When enough people adopt the new behavior, it becomes cultural by definition.

If we assume that cultures are more than random collections of behaviors, beliefs, and values—that cultures tend to be adaptive, integrated, and changing—then the similarities and differences between cultures should be understandable. That is, we can expect that similar circumstances within or outside the culture will give rise to, or favor, similar cultural responses. Although we may assume that cultural variation is understandable, the task of discovering which particular circumstances favor which particular cultural patterns is a large and difficult one. In the chapters that follow, we hope to convey the main points of what anthropologists think they know about aspects of cultural variation, and what they do not know.

Summary

1. Despite very strong individual differences, the members of a particular society are in close agreement in their responses to certain phenomena because they share common attitudes, values, and behaviors which constitute their culture.

2. The anthropological attitude that a society's customs and ideas should be viewed within the context of that society's culture is called cultural relativity. In general, cultural relativity is impeded by two different, but commonly held, attitudes: first, the tendency toward negative evaluation, or ethnocentrism; second, the tendency toward positive evaluation, which often takes the form of a naive yearning for the simple life of the "noble savage."

3. A culture may be defined as the set of learned beliefs, values, and behaviors generally shared by the members of a society or population.

4. Culture is shared by the members of a particular population. The size of the group within which cultural traits are shared can vary from a particular society or a segment of that society to a group that transcends national boundaries.

5. Another defining feature of culture is that it is learned. Humans are unique in the number and complexity of the learned behavior patterns that they transmit to their young. And they have a unique way of transmitting their culture: through language.

6. Anthropologists seek to discover the customs and ranges of acceptable behavior that comprise the culture of a society under study. In doing so, they focus on general or shared patterns of behavior rather than on individual variations. One way of generalizing about cultural patterns is to collect information from a sample of individuals and derive the *modal,* or most frequent, response.

7. Every society develops a series of ideal cultural patterns which represent what most members of the society believe to be the correct behavior in particular situations. Such ideal patterns are often called *norms.* A society's norms, however, do not always agree with actual behavior.

8. In studying any cultural trait, anthropologists generally have little difficulty identifying the modal behavior because the range of variation is seldom wide. One important factor that limits the range of individual variation is the culture itself, which acts directly or indirectly as a constraint on behavior. The existence of cultural constraints, however, is not necessarily incompatible with individuality.

9. Several assumptions are frequently made about culture. First, culture is generally adaptive to the particular conditions of the physical and social environment. What may be adaptive in one environment may not be adaptive in another. Some cultural traits may

be neutral in terms of adaptation, some may merely have been adaptive in the past, and still others may be maladaptive. Second, culture is mostly integrated in that the elements or traits which make up the culture are mostly adjusted to or consistent with each other. Third, culture is always changing.

Suggested Readings

Casagrande, J. B., ed. *In the Company of Man: Twenty Portraits by Anthropologists.* New York: Harper & Row, 1960.

A collection of papers in which anthropologists discuss their experiences with field informants. The papers cover a wide geographical range and deal with societies ranging in complexity from hunting and gathering groups to pastoralists and peasants.

Freilich, M., ed. *The Meaning of Culture.* Lexington, Mass.: Xerox, 1972.

Several different views of culture are presented. See chapters 7–21.

Golde, P., ed. *Women in the Field: Anthropological Experiences.* Chicago: Aldine, 1970.

This group of papers deals in general with women's experiences as anthropologists in the field and in particular with their unique problems as women in a male-dominated field. The editor has attempted to focus on three main points of view in each paper: the personal and subjective, the ethnographic, and the methodological and theoretical.

Kroeber, A. L. *The Nature of Culture.* Chicago: University of Chicago Press, 1952.

A collection of papers on the nature of culture by a distinguished pioneer in American anthropology.

Spindler, G. D., ed. *Being an Anthropologist: Fieldwork in Eleven Cultures.* New York: Holt, Rinehart and Winston, 1970.

A series of reports by thirteen anthropologists describing how they and their families adapted to life in eleven different cultural situations. The papers are case studies in which both subjective problems of field study and methodological problems and techniques are discussed. For the benefit of students in anthropology, the papers were selected on the basis of differences in theoretical and methodological positions, as well as variation in location and type of fieldwork.

Williams, T. R. *Field Methods in the Study of Culture.* New York: Holt, Rinehart and Winston, 1967.

A discussion of the ways in which anthropologists study and describe cultures.

Language and Culture

Few of us can remember the moment when we first became aware that words signify something. Yet that moment was a milestone for us, not just in the acquisition of language but in becoming acquainted with all the complex, elaborate behavior that constitutes our culture. Without language, the transmission of complex traditions would be virtually impossible, and each person would be trapped within his or her own world of private sensations.

To recapture that instant when language became meaningful, we must rely on those like Helen Keller, who came to language late. Miss Keller, left deaf and blind by illness at the age of nineteen months, gives a moving personal account of the afternoon on which she first established contact with another human being through words.

She [my teacher] brought me my hat, and I knew I was going out into the warm sunshine. This thought, if a wordless sensation may be called a thought, made me hop and skip with pleasure.

We walked down the path to the well house, attracted by the fragrance of the honeysuckle with which it was covered. Someone was drawing water and my teacher placed my hand under the spout. As the cool stream gushed over one hand she spelled into the other the word *water,* first slowly, then rapidly. Suddenly I felt a misty consciousness as of something forgotten—a thrill of returning thought; and somehow the mystery of language was revealed to me. I knew then that *w-a-t-e-r* meant the wonderful cool something that was flowing over my hand. That living word awakened my soul, gave it light, hope, joy, set it free! There were barriers still, it is true, barriers that could in time be swept away.

I left the well house eager to learn. Everything had a name, and each name gave birth to a new thought. As we returned to the house every object which I touched seemed to quiver with life. That was because I saw everything with the strange, new sight that had come to me.[1]

[1]Helen Keller, *The Story of My Life* (New York: Dell, 1974), p. 34. Originally published in 1902.

11

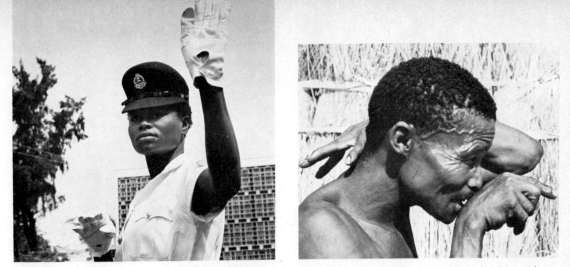

Human communication is not limited to spoken language; in all societies, humans also communicate in signs and gestures. Here a Nigerian policewoman signals oncoming traffic to stop and a Bushman hunter uses sign language to silently indicate the presence of a secretary bird. (Photo of policewoman by Marc and Evelyne Bernheim, Woodfin Camp Associates. Photo of Bushman courtesy of Irven DeVore/Anthro-Photo.)

Communication

Against all odds, Helen Keller had come to understand the essential function which language plays in all societies, namely, that of communication. The word *communicate* comes from the Latin verb *communicare,* to share, to impart that which is *common.* We communicate by agreeing, consciously or unconsciously, to call an object, a movement, or an abstract concept by a common name. For example, all speakers of English have agreed to call the color of grass green, even though we have no way of comparing precisely how two people actually experience this color. What we share is the agreement to call this sensation *green.* Any system of language consists of publicly accepted symbols by which individuals try to share private experiences.

Our communication obviously is not limited to spoken language. We communicate directly through body stance, gesture, and tone of voice; indirectly through systems of signs and symbols, such as algebraic equations, musical scores, painting, code flags, and road signs. But despite all the competing systems of communication available to us, we must recognize the overriding importance of language. It is the primary transmitter of culture from generation to generation; it is the vehicle we employ to share and to transmit our complex configuration of attitudes, beliefs, and patterns of behavior.

ANIMAL COMMUNICATION

Systems of communication are not unique to human beings. Other animal species communicate in a variety of ways. One way is by sound: a bird may communicate by a call that a territory is his and should not be encroached upon; a squirrel may utter a cry which leads other squirrels to flee from danger. Another means of animal communication is by odor. An ant releases a chemical when it dies, and its fellows then carry it away to the compost heap. Apparently the communication is highly effective: a healthy ant painted with the death chemical will be dragged to the funeral heap again and again.

Another means of communication, body movement, is used by bees to convey the location of food sources. Von Frisch discovered that the black Austrian honeybee—through a choice of round dance, wagging dance, or a short, straight run—could communicate not only the

"The thing to bear in mind, gentlemen, is not just that Daisy has mastered a rudimentary sign language but that she can link these signs together to express meaningful abstract concepts." (Drawing by Lorenz; © 1974 *The New Yorker* Magazine, Inc.)

precise direction of the source of food but also its distance from the hive.[2]

Although primates use all three methods of communication—sound, odor, and body movement—sound is the method that most concerns us here. The great apes exhibit a variety of call systems in their natural habitats, from the relatively limited system of the gibbon to the more comprehensive one of the chimpanzee. But no matter how many calls a species of ape may have in its repertoire, each call is mutually exclusive. One call might be a request for female companionship, another, a warning of danger. The ape cannot combine parts of two calls to obtain a third call which will combine two messages. The ape's system of communication, in other words, is *closed*.

Several people have attempted to teach chimpanzees human speech. One couple, who adopted a baby chimpanzee to raise with their own newborn son, abandoned the project a year later when it became obvious that the human child was imitating the ape, not the ape the child. Keith and Cathy Hayes recorded that they were able to elicit only four recognizable words from an ape after years of effort.[3]

Perhaps the most complex system of communication the chimpanzee is able to learn is a system of signs. In 1967, Adriaan Kortlandt reported that chimpanzees had learned hand gestures which signify "Come with me," "May I pass?" "You are welcome," "Stop!" and "Be off!" among others.[4] Using this insight, Allen and Beatrice Gardner succeeded in teaching the American Sign Language (ASL) to their chimpanzee Washoe. The amazing extent of Washoe's ability to use the 150 signs she had learned was recorded when she was with other chimpanzees on an island and noticed that the humans across the water were drinking iced tea.

[2]K. von Frisch, "Dialects in the Language of the Bees," *Scientific American,* August 1962, pp. 78–87.

[3]Emily Hahn, "Chimpanzees and Language," *New Yorker,* 24 April 1971, p. 54.
[4]Ibid., p. 54.

"She kept signing, 'Roger ride come gimme sweet eat please hurry hurry you come please gimme sweet you hurry you come ride Roger come give Washoe fruit drink hurry hurry fruit drink please.' . . . A plane flew over just then, and Washoe mentioned that, too. She signed, 'You me ride in plane.'"[5]

Subsequent work with other chimpanzees, named Sarah and Lana, suggests that chimpanzees can use other kinds of nonverbal symbols besides ASL gestures to form sentences and to communicate their needs. Sarah was taught to use differently shaped and colored pieces of plastic, each representing a word (and she had a vocabulary of about 130 "words").[6] Lana was taught to use computer-controlled equipment, pressing keys on a console to make sentences, and even showing when those sentences were ended by pressing a key which meant "period."[7]

THE ORIGINS OF LANGUAGE

There has been much speculation about how early humans may have developed language. Special attention has been directed to the question of how selection may have favored an *open* language. An open language is like all known human languages in that utterances can be combined to produce new meanings. Hockett and Ascher have suggested a possible chain of events.[8] As a starting point in their theory, they cite the major climatic changes in East Africa, in the Miocene epoch, which led to a drastic reduction in the number of trees. The ensuing competition for space and food forced some primate species onto open ground. Those that survived in the new, more open environment were the ancestors of humans. Hominid bipedalism probably developed around this time,

with consequences for carrying and ultimately for speech. The forearms could now be used to transport food and weapons over long distances, while the mouth was freed for chatter.

Hockett and Ascher suggest that the final stage in the development of an open language must have come about through a blending of two calls to produce a new call. Precisely how this blending procedure occurred is subject to speculation. What is certain is that a call system of communication was eventually changed to a system based upon small units of sound which could be put together in many different ways to form meaningful utterances. For example, an American can combine "care" and "full" ("careful") to mean one thing, then use each of the two elements in other combinations to mean different things. "Care" can be used to make "carefree," "careless," or "caretaker"; "full" can be used to make "powerful" or "wonderful."

The movement from calls to language, which may have taken millennia in the evolution of humans, takes but a few years for children. Nonetheless, the acquisition of language by children may offer some insights into the origins of speech. Although a specific language, like other cultural patterns, is learned and shared, the process by which a child acquires the structure, or grammar, of language seems to be inborn and therefore precultural. Apparently a child is equipped from birth with the capacity to reproduce all of the sounds used by the world's languages and to learn any system of grammar. The language the child learns is the one that is spoken by his or her parents. Since this language is a system of shared patterns, it can be re-formed into an infinite variety of expressions and be understood by all who share these patterns. In this way, for example, T. S. Eliot could form a sentence never before formed, "In the room the women come and go talking of Michelangelo,"[9] and the sense of his sentence, though not necessarily his private meaning, could be understood by fellow speakers of English.

[5] Ibid., p. 98.

[6] Ann James Premack and David Premack, "Teaching Language to an Ape," *Scientific American*, October 1972, pp. 92–99.

[7] Duane M. Rumbaugh, Timothy V. Gill, and E. C. von Glasersfeld, "Reading and Sentence Completion by a Chimpanzee (Pan)," *Science*, 16 November 1973, pp. 731–33.

[8] C. F. Hockett and R. Ascher, "The Human Revolution," *Current Anthropology* 5 (1964): 135–68.

[9] T. S. Eliot, "The Love Song of J. Alfred Prufrock," in *Collected Poems 1909–1962* (New York: Harcourt Brace Jovanovich, 1963).

The child's acquisition of the structure and meaning of language has been called the most difficult intellectual achievement in life. If that is so, it is pleasing to note that he or she accomplishes it with relative ease and vast enjoyment. What has been called a "difficult intellectual achievement" may in reality be a natural response to the capacity for language which is one of humans' genetic characteristics. All over the world children begin to learn language at about the same age—in no culture do children wait until they are seven or ten years old to learn language. By twelve or thirteen months children are able to name a few objects and actions. In addition, they seem able to grasp the underlying grammar. They are able to make one key word stand for a whole sentence: "out!" for "take me out for a walk right now"; "bottle!" for "I want my bottle now."

The child's progression to two-word sentences at about eighteen months of age clearly indicates the possession of a basic sense of grammar. Of all the possible two-word combinations, he or she chooses grammatical sentences structured around a key word such as "see" ("see daddy," "see horse," "see water") or "bye-bye" ("bye-bye moon," "bye-bye car"). The child seems to acquire the grammar with little or no direct teaching from the parents. Grammar, in fact, appears to be of first importance, as evidenced by the five-year-old who, confronted with the unfamiliar "Gloria in Excelsis," sang quite happily, "Gloria eats eggshells." To make the words fit the structure of English grammar was more important than to make the words fit the meaning of the Christmas pageant.

Psycholinguists have become aware of the inadequacy of the usual learning methods—imitation, practice, reinforcement—to explain the child's early acquisition and creative use of grammatical structure. One set of theoreticians of grammar suggests that there may be a "language acquisition device" in the brain, as innate to humans as are the call systems of the other animals. As the forebrain evolved, this language acquisition device may have become part of our biological inheritance. Whether this device in fact exists is not yet clear. But we do know that the actual development of individual languages is not biologically determined, for all human beings would speak the same brain-generated language if language were simply a biological attribute. Instead, about 6,000 mutually unintelligible languages have been identified. More than 2,000 of them still are spoken today, most of them by peoples who do not have a native system of writing.

"PRIMITIVE" LANGUAGES

Intuitively, we might suppose that languages of nonliterate peoples or peoples without writing would be much less developed than languages spoken by technologically advanced, literate societies. But this is in no sense true. The sound systems, vocabularies, and grammars of technologically simpler peoples are in no way inferior to those of more complex societies.[10]

Of course, Australian aborigines will not be able to name the sophisticated machines used in our society; their language, however, has the potential for doing so. All languages possess the amount of vocabulary that their speakers need, and they expand in response to modernization or other cultural changes. Moreover, the language of a technologically simple people, while lacking terminology for some of our conveniences, may have a rich vocabulary to deal with events or natural phenomena that are of particular importance to that society.

Contrary to common notions, the grammars of those languages spoken by technologically simple peoples are also equal in complexity to our own. Some of these languages, as we shall see, recognize distinctions that cannot easily be expressed in English.

Descriptive Linguistics

People expect to be disoriented in a foreign country if they do not know the language. Even

---

[10]Franklin C. Southworth and Chandler J. Daswani, *Foundations of Linguistics* (New York: Free Press, 1974), p. 312.

anthropologists who are trained in linguistics are a little confused when they arrive to do fieldwork among a people who speak a language unknown to them. But within a short time, the anthropologist's training in linguistics will facilitate discovering the rules of that language. Every language has rules or principles that determine what sounds are to be used, and in what combinations or sequences, to convey meaning.

In order to study the diversities of human languages, linguists have had to develop ways of describing languages that would enable them to compare languages systematically. In everyday communication we may talk about verbs and nouns and parts of speech; but the linguist cannot compare languages in those terms because many languages do not convey verbal or other meanings as English does. Therefore, linguists have had to invent special descriptive concepts, such as phoneme and morpheme, to permit them to describe all languages in the same systematic and comparable terms.

PHONEMES

From the exceedingly wide variety of possible human sounds, each language has selected some sounds, or *phones,* and ignored others. The linguist studying a language will notice which speech sounds occur and which are used most frequently. Once a linguist has identified the phones, he or she will identify how these sounds are grouped by the speakers of the language into *phonemes.* A phoneme is a set of varying sounds which do not make any difference in meaning to the speaker of the language. In other words, if one phone of a phoneme class is substituted for another phone of the same class, the speaker will not say that the meaning of the utterance is different.

The way in which sounds, or phones, are grouped into phonemes varies from language to language. In English the sound of the *l* in *lake* is considered quite different from the sound of *r* in *rake*; the two phones belong to different phonemes. In Chinese, however, *l* and *r* could be used interchangeably in the initial position in a word without making a difference in meaning; in Chinese, then, these two phones belong to the same phoneme. Thus, when sounds in a particular position in a word make a difference in meaning, they are said to belong to different phonemes.

As the anthropologist begins to analyze the phonemes of a language, he or she will attempt to write them down. Undeniably, this would be a very troublesome undertaking were linguists restricted to using their own alphabets, To surmount this difficulty, linguists have developed the International Phonetic Alphabet (IPA), which provides a symbol for every sound that occurs in every known language. Using this alphabet, linguists are able to record the utterances which they must analyze to arrive at a list of phones and phonemes used in a language.

Estimates of the number of phonemes used in the world's languages vary from around 15 (some Polynesian languages) to just under 100 (some languages of the Caucasus). English has 46 phonemes. Languages differ, then, not only in the number and kinds of sounds they use, but also in the ways those sounds are grouped into phonemes.

MORPHEMES

A structural description of a language includes an analysis of sounds or sequences of sounds that convey meaning to the speakers of that language. The smallest unit of language that has a meaning is a *morph.* One or more morphs with the same meaning make up a *morpheme.* For example, the prefix *in-* as in "indefinite," and the prefix *un-* as in "unclear," are morphs that belong to the morpheme meaning "not." A morph or morpheme should not be confused with a word. Although some words are single morphs or morphemes (for example, *for* and *giraffe* in English), many words are built upon a combination of morphs, generally prefixes, roots, and suffixes. Thus *cow* is one word, but the word *cows* contains two meaningful units: a root (*cow*) and a suffix (pronounced like *z*) meaning more than one.

It seems likely that the intuitive grasp

which children have of the structure of their language includes a recognition of morphology. Once they learn that the morph /-z/ added to a noun-type word indicates more than one, they plow ahead with *mans, childs;* once they grasp that the morpheme class /-t/ or /-d/ added to the end of a verb indicates that the action took place in the past, they apply this concept generally and invent *runned, drinked, costed.* They see a ball roll near*er* and near*er,* and they transfer this to a kite which goes upp*er* and upp*er.* From their mistakes as well as their successes, we can see that they understand the regular uses of morphemes. By the age of seven, they have mastered many of the irregular forms as well—that is, they learn which morphs of a morpheme are used when.

The child's intuitive grasp of the dependence of some morphemes upon others corresponds to the linguist's recognition of *free* morphemes and *bound* morphemes. A free morpheme has meaning standing alone—that is, it can be a separate word. A bound morpheme displays its meaning only when attached to another morpheme. The phrase "attached to" is rather loosely applied. The morph /-t/ of the bound morpheme meaning "past tense" is actually attached to the root *walk* to produce *walked,* but how should we consider the morpheme *the* in relation to *man* in *The man walked?* *The* has no meaning by itself, but it is grammatically significant. *The* must precede a noun. In the sentence "The man walked," *The* and *-ed* are bound; *man* and *walk* are free morphemes.

GRAMMAR

The grammar of a language consists of *morphology* (the ways in which morphemes are combined to form words) and *syntax* (the ways in which words are arranged to form phrases and sentences). English relies heavily upon syntax to convey meaning, whereas some other languages rely more heavily upon morphology.

Syntax In many languages, there are rules that govern the ways in which words may be ar-

ranged to form meaningful utterances. As we have seen, children seem to grasp these rules intuitively. English-speaking children will say, "I want my green dog," not, "Want dog my green I." Except for their use of pronouns ("Me want my green dog" is a common error), they really do not think to structure their sentences in any way other than according to the rules of syntax in English. In languages, such as English, which have many free morphemes, the order of words is crucial for meaning. "The dog bit the child" has a different meaning from "The child bit the dog." In such languages, one order may be correct whereas the opposite order is incorrect. Thus, the American says "white house" but not "house white," while the Frenchman says "house white" or *maison blanche.* An analysis of one of Lewis Carroll's nonsense sentences in *Through the Looking-Glass* points up the extent to which syntax alone is meaningful in English:

'Twas brillig, and the slithy toves
Did gyre and gimble in the wabe

Simply from the ordering of words in the sentence, we can surmise which part of speech a word is, as well as its function in the sentence. "Brillig" is an adjective; "slithy" an adjective; "toves" a noun and subject of the sentence; "gyre" and "gimble" verbs; and "wabe" a noun and the object of a prepositional phrase. Of course, an understanding of morphology helps too. The *-y* ending on "slithy" is an indication that it is an adjective, and the *-s* ending on "toves" tells us that we most probably have more than one of these creatures.

The way in which English words are put together seems so natural to the native speaker that he or she is usually surprised to discover how differently speakers of other languages form their sentences. For example, English-speakers would translate "I would like" into French as *je voudrais.* Yet the English phrase contains three words, three morphemes; the French contains two words, four morphemes. *Je voudrais* translates literally as "I like would I"; the four morphs are *je/ voudr/ ai/ s.*

Morphology In many languages, the meaning of an utterance does not depend much, if at all, on the order of the words. Rather, meaning may be determined by how the morphs in a word are ordered. For example, in Luo (a language of East Africa) the same bound morpheme may mean the subject or object of an action. If the morpheme is the prefix to a verb, it means the subject; if it is the suffix to a verb, it means the object. Another way that meaning may be changed is to alter or add to a root morph. For example, in German there are so-called case endings, or declensions, that indicate parts of speech. Hence the verb, and even the subject and object, may appear at different places in the sentence; but the meaning of the sentence will be clear because the verb, noun, and object are indicated by different suffixes.

The main point about grammatical variation among languages is that meaning is not always—or even usually—conveyed, as in English, by the way words are ordered. If order of words is not significant, then something has to be done to the morphs to indicate what the utterance means. In some languages, for instance, what is considered a sentence in English is a single word, made up of bound morphs which are altered in various ways (either internally, or by prefixes and suffixes) to indicate the meaning of the sentence-word (see Table 1).

Transformational Grammar For much of its history, linguistics has concerned itself with descriptive and prescriptive grammars, both of which concentrate on the sound and structure of given sentences. However, the approach of transformational grammar, originated by Noam Chomsky, attempts to examine both *surface structure*, or the appearance of a sentence, and *deep structure*, the underlying relationship which presumably determines how the sentence was formulated. In other words, transformational grammar presents a model that explains the various ways in which elements in the language system may be structured. Because Chomsky's system uses complex representations of symbolic logic and because it is still the subject of

TABLE 1

Compare the following English words with the equivalent French, Wishram, and Takelma expressions.*

English:	He will give it to you.
French:	Il vous (*or* te) le (*or* la) donnera.
	he-you (*or* thee)-him (*or* her)-to give will he
Wishram:	ačimlúda
	will-he-him-thee-to-give-will
Takelma:	?òspink
	will give-to-thee-he or they in the future

* Wishram is a Chinookan dialect of the Columbia River region; Takelma is an all-but-extinct Indian language of southwestern Oregon.

much controversy among linguists, we will not present his method in any detail. What is important to understand is that transformational grammar tries to see all the elements of a language, semantic as well as structural, as a total system with characteristic ways of operation. It does not take for granted that what *looks* similar must *be* similar, and it shows that elements which look different may have underlying structures in common.

The deep-structure approach of transformational grammar may provide a means of finding corresponding processes in all the disparate languages of humans. If similar processes are found when the deep structures of historically unrelated languages are compared, we shall be able to conclude that there are some universals underlying the great diversities of human language. Chomsky would attribute these universals to a language faculty which is part of "the structure of the mind." In other words, Chomsky suggests that universals would point to a physical basis of linguistic patterning that is expressed in a myriad of forms.

Historical Linguistics

The field of historical linguistics is interested in discovering how languages change over time. Naturally, written works provide the best data for establishing such changes. For example, the following passage from Chaucer's *Canterbury Tales*, written in the English of the fourteenth century, has recognizable elements but is different enough from modern English to require a translation.

A Frere ther was, a wantowne and a merye,
A lymytour, a ful solempne man.
In alle the ordres foure is noon that kan
So muchel of daliaunce and fair langage.
He hadde maad ful many a mariage
Of yonge wommen at his owene cost.
Unto his ordre he was a noble post.

Ful wel biloved and famulier was he
With frankeleyns over al in his contree,
And eek with worthy wommen of the toun;
For he hadde power of confessioun,
As seyde hymself, moore than a curat,
For of his ordre he was licenciat.[11]

A Friar there was, wanton and merry,
A limiter, a full solemn [very important] man.
In all the orders four there is none that knows
So much of dalliance [flirting] and fair [engaging]
    language.
He had made [arranged] many a marriage
Of young women at his own cost.
Unto his order he was a noble post [pillar].
Full well beloved and familiar was he
With franklins [wealthy landowners] all over his
    country,
And also with worthy women of the town;
For he had power of confession,
As he said himself, more than a curate,
For of his order, he was a licentiate [licensed by
    the Pope].

From this comparison we can recognize a number of changes. Some words, such as *eek* have passed out of our vocabulary; and, of course, a great many words are spelled differently today. In some cases, meaning has changed: full, for example, would be translated today as "very." What is less evident is that changes in pronunciation, or *phonology*, have occurred. For example, the *g* in *mariage* (marriage) was pronounced *zh*, as in the French

---

[11]Geoffrey Chaucer, *The Canterbury Tales*, General Prologue.

from which it was borrowed, whereas now it is pronounced like the *g* in *George*, which is more in accordance with standard English phonemics.

THE COMPARATIVE METHOD

Some changes in language follow discernible patterns which enable linguists to hypothesize relationships between divergent tongues. By comparative analysis of cognates (words of similar sound and meaning) and grammar, historical linguists can test the notion that certain languages are related—that is, that they derive from a common ancestral language, or protolanguage. The goals are to reconstruct the features of the protolanguage, to hypothesize how the daughter languages separated from the protolanguage or from each other, and to establish the approximate dates of such separations.

It is through the comparison of languages that the probable derivation of many modern languages, including English, has been hypothesized. As early as 1786, Sir William Jones, an Englishman serving as a judge in Calcutta, noticed similarities between Sanskrit, Greek, and Latin and suggested that they must be derived from a single source. In 1822, Jacob Grimm, one of the brothers Grimm, formulated rules to describe the sequences of phonetic change from Sanskrit (which he believed to be closest to the original Indo-European tongue) to later languages such as Greek, Latin, German, and English. Using cognates, he observed changes like the one from *p* to *f* (Sanskrit *pitar*, English "father"; Sanskrit *pat*, English *foot*). From these he derived laws of phonetic change for this language family.

Close examination of cognates denoting certain plants and animals also has suggested that the ancestral home of Proto-Indo-European was somewhere in northern Europe. Paul Thieme notes that cognate names for certain trees of northern Europe, such as the oak and birch, are found in most of the modern Indo-European languages, whereas cognates for the more southern trees, such as the olive, fig, and cypress, are not found as frequently. Moreover, the modern Indo-European languages contain no cognates for tiger, elephant, or any of the animals characteristic of Asia or India. However, they do contain cognate words for creatures distributed throughout northern and central Europe, including the wolf, salmon, and bear. From such evidence, Thieme has placed the center of dispersion for Indo-European languages in the area south of the Baltic Sea, encompassing the Vistula, the Oder, and the Elbe rivers. Migration to the east produced the Baltic and Slavic languages; to the west, Germanic and Romance languages; to the south, the Indic and Iranian languages. This theory is by no means confirmed, and other linguists have argued for other centers of dispersion, including southern Russia, Scandinavia, and southwestern Asia.[12]

Once linguists identify the common parent of several languages, they are usually interested in dating the times of divergence between the daughter languages. Through such research, they may be able to shed some light on the origin and movements of a given people. This information may then be pieced together with relevant findings from archaeology, physical anthropology, and historical documents to reconstruct some of the details of the history of particular peoples and cultures.

GLOTTOCHRONOLOGY

One method of establishing a date for the divergence between two languages is *glottochronology*. This method is based upon the assumption that a language replaces its basic vocabulary at a constant rate. By examining changes in languages for which we have written records going back several thousand years, some linguists have estimated that 19 percent of the basic vocabulary is lost after 1,000 years (81 percent is retained). The basic vocabulary of a language consists of a list of words for things, such as parts of the human body, that are universal in

[12] Paul Thieme, "The Comparative Method for Reconstruction in Linguistics," in *Language in Culture and Society,* ed. Dell Hymes (New York: Harper & Row, 1964), pp. 585–98.

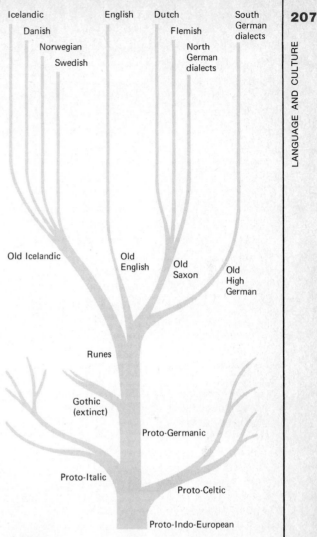

FIGURE 1
The Germanic languages developed from a common ancestral Proto-Germanic language, which had previously derived from Proto-Indo-European.

human experience and consequently are not likely to be replaced in response to changes in geographical location or culture. If we assume that the rate of change holds true for languages for which we have no written records, then we can estimate the date of divergence of two languages which appear to be related, by calculating the percentage of basic vocabulary shared between them. Both languages should retain about 81 percent of their parent language per 1,000 years; but if their respective speakers are not in contact, they will probably not retain the same 81 percent. Statistically, then, the percentage of words shared between related languages should be closer to 81 percent of the 81 percent, or 66 percent, after 1,000 years of divergence. In other words, should we discover that two languages share 66 percent of their basic word lists, we could say that their ancestral speech communities probably separated about 1,000 years ago. If they share less than 66 percent of basic vocabulary, we would say that the two languages probably separated earlier.

Applying the glottochronological method to basic word lists in modern languages, we can estimate, for example, that the split between the Germanic and Romance branches of Indo-European must have occurred about 1000 B.C. Of course, not all linguists are in agreement with all of the assumptions of glottochronology. Nevertheless, the technique has enlarged the possibilities of research into cultural history.

PROCESSES OF LINGUISTIC DIVERGENCE

The historical or comparative linguist hopes to do more than record and date linguistic divergence. Just as the physical anthropologist may attempt to develop explanations for human variation, so may the linguist investigate the possible causes of linguistic variation. When groups of people speaking the same language lose communication with one another because they become either physically or socially separated, they begin to accumulate small changes in phonology, morphology, and grammar (which occur continuously in any language). Eventually, if the separation continues, the two former dialects of the same language will become separate languages—that is, they will be mutually unintelligible.

Even when geographic isolation is not complete, there may still be a great deal of dialect differentiation because of social barriers to communication between neighboring areas. Northern India provides an excellent example.

Three thousand years ago, invaders speaking an Indo-European language conquered northern India and their language became dominant. In succeeding years, the language began to diversify into regional dialects. Variations in topography and climate played a part in the partial isolation of the incipient dialect groups, but the most powerful influence was the emergence of largely self-supporting and semi-isolated villages and regions. Thus, one language was transformed, in the course of time, into hundreds of local dialects. Today, the inhabitants of each village understand the dialects of the surrounding villages and, with a little more difficulty, the dialects of the next farther circles of villages. But slight dialect shifts accumulate village by village, and over the space of 1,000 miles it seems as if different languages are being spoken at opposite ends of a region. Yet at no boundary is there such an abrupt change of language that neighboring villagers cannot converse easily.[13]

Whereas isolation brings about divergence between speech communities, contact results in greater resemblance. This is particularly evident when contact between mutually unintelligible languages introduces "borrowed" words, usually naming some new item borrowed from the other culture—tomato, canoe, sputnik, and so on. Bilingual groups within a culture may also introduce foreign words, especially when the mainstream language has no real equivalent. Thus, "siesta" has come into English, and "le weekend" into French.

Conquest and colonization often result in extensive borrowing. For example, the Norman conquest of England introduced French as the language of the new aristocracy. It was 300 years before the educated classes began to write in English. During this time the English borrowed words from French and Latin, and the two languages—English and French—became more alike than they would otherwise have been. About 50 percent of the English general vocabulary has been borrowed from French.

[13]John J. Gumperz, "Speech Variation and the Study of Indian Civilization," *American Anthropologist* 63 (1961): 976–88.

An example of an English word that has been "borrowed" by the French. "The Drugstore" chain operates in Paris. (S. Duroy, Rapho/Photo Researchers.)

In those 300 years of extensive borrowing, the grammar of English remained relatively stable. It lost most of its inflections or case endings, but it adopted none of the French grammar. In fact, borrowing of grammar is extremely rare. Sapir, a pioneer in American linguistics, believed it to be nearly impossible, although there may be cases of grammatical borrowing in India, where three language families have come to exist side by side. Interestingly enough, borrowing by one language from another can make the borrowing language more different from its sister languages (those derived from a common ancestral language) than it would otherwise be. As a result of the French influence, the English vocabulary looks quite different from its sister languages—German, Dutch, and Scandinavian—to which it is actually most similar in terms of phonology and grammar.

Relationship Between Language and Culture

Some attempts to explain the diversity of languages have focused on the possible interactions between language and other aspects of culture. On the one hand, if it can be shown that a culture may affect the structure and content of its language, then it would follow that linguistic diversity derives at least in part from cultural diversity. On the other hand, the direction of influence between culture and language might work in reverse; the linguistic structures might affect other aspects of the culture.

CULTURAL INFLUENCES ON LANGUAGE

One way a society's language may reflect its corresponding culture is in lexical content, or vocabulary. Which experiences, events, or objects are singled out and given simple or single-morph names may be a result of cultural characteristics. For example, Brent Berlin and Paul Kay have investigated why different societies vary in the number of simple color terms their languages have. Based upon their study of first 20, and later over 100, different languages, Berlin and Kay found that some languages have only two simple words to denote, roughly, dark and light. These languages express other colors by combining terms, such as "fresh leaf" for green, or "cut orchid fibers" for yellow. Berlin and Kay suggest that there is a fixed sequence by which color categories are added to a language and that the evolution of color terminology parallels the evolution of the culture in its economic and technological aspects.[14] This finding may indicate that cultural complexity influences lexical content, although recent research suggests that variation in eye pigmentation may mostly be responsible for variation in color terminology.[15]

The vocabulary of a language may also reflect everyday distinctions that are important in the society. It appears that those aspects of the environment or culture which are of special importance to people will receive greater attention in their language. Even within a single society speaking the same language there may be lexical variation from one region to another or between different subcultures. An adult farmer in the American Midwest may know three simple words for boat—boat, ship, canoe—and a few compound variations such as rowboat, sailboat, motorboat, steamship. Yet a six-year-old child who lives on Long Island Sound where sailing is a major pastime may be able to distinguish many kinds of sailboat, such as catboat, ketch, yawl, sloop, schooner, as well as subclasses of each, such as bluejay, sunfish, weekender.

As the domains that we choose to name may vary even for two speakers of the same language, the differences in how and what we name appear even more startlingly between languages. For instance, English has three common words—*bring, take,* and *carry*—to express how an object, either animate or inanimate, may be moved from one place to another. The Garo language of northeast India has, instead, one term *ra* for inanimate objects and one term *rim* for animate objects. Affixes *ang* and *ba* can be added to either root to indicate direction away from, or toward, the speaker. Garo has no general term for *carry* but instead has words for

different kinds of carrying: *ol-* means specifically "to carry something in a basket that is held in a strap over the forehead"; *itchil-* means "to carry on the head"; *ripe-* means "to carry on the shoulder," as one might carry a log; *ke-* means "to carry in a bag that hangs from a strap over the shoulder"; *detom-* means "to carry in the arms." It seems that the Garo language focuses on particular categories or actions that are important in Garo culture.[16]

There are many interesting examples of "focal areas" in different cultures being reflected in their respective vocabularies. In a study of the Kwakiutl, a coastal Indian tribe of the Pacific Northwest, Franz Boas showed that Kwakiutl geographical terms reflect their awareness of the importance of hunting, fishing, and other food-gathering activities essential to their survival. Locations on land are given names such as "having-blueberries" and "having-hunter's-lodge"; areas of coastal waters are described as "having-difficult-currents," "having-spring-salmon."[17] One might compare the importance of river crossings to the early English, who designated Ox-ford and Cambridge—names which in modern times have lost their original meanings.

Most of the examples we could accumulate would show the influence of the culture in naming things visible in the environment. Evidence for cultural influence on the grammatical structure of a language is less extensive and convincing. Harry Hoijer draws attention to the verb categories in the language of the Navajo, a traditionally nomadic people. These categories center largely on the reporting of events, or "eventings," as he calls them. Hoijer notes that "in the reporting of actions and events, and the framing of substantive concepts, Navajo emphasizes movement and specifies the nature, direction, and status of such movement in considerable detail." For example, Navajo has one category for eventings that are in motion and

---

[14] Brent Berlin and Paul Kay, *Basic Color Terms: Their Universality and Evolution* (Berkeley: University of California Press, 1969).
[15] Marc H. Bornstein, "The Psychophysiological Component of Cultural Difference in Color Naming and Illusion Susceptibility," *Behavior Science Notes* 8 (1973): 41–101.

[16] R. Burling, *Man's Many Voices* (New York: Holt, Rinehart and Winston, 1970), pp. 10–13.
[17] Franz Boas, *Geographical Names of the Kwakiutl Indians* (New York: Columbia University Press, 1934).

another for eventings that have ceased moving. Hoijer concludes that the emphasis on events incessantly in the process of occurring reflects the Navajo's own nomadic experience over the centuries, an experience reflected in their myths and folklore.[18]

We would probably be mistaken, however, to overemphasize the possibility of culture as a determinant of linguistic structures. Some evidence to the contrary exists. Goodenough has found, in his study of property relationships on Truk, an atoll in the Caroline Islands of the central Pacific, that grammatical distinctions in forming the possessive do not parallel Trukese concepts of ownership. Although there are several very important concepts of ownership, leasehold, or gift in Trukese culture, the language offers only a single affix to the noun, denoting "my."[19] Thus, it appears on the basis of present knowledge that culture may often influence vocabulary, but seldom grammar.

LINGUISTIC INFLUENCES ON CULTURE

Sapir-Whorf Hypothesis   There is no general agreement among ethnolinguists—those anthropologists who are interested in the relationship between language and culture—that linguistic elements by themselves may influence other aspects of culture. The Sapir-Whorf hypothesis is the classic formulation of the basic issue. Edward Sapir asserted that language is not merely a symbolic inventory of our environment and experience but is a force in its own right. It "actually defines experience for us by reason of its formal completeness and because of our unconscious projection of its implicit expectations into the field of experience."[20] Sapir went so far as to suggest that language, in some ways, possesses despotic powers. In a discussion of conceptual categories in different

Culture seems to influence language, particularly in terms of vocabulary. The Garo language of northeastern India, for example, has different words to indicate the various kinds of carrying that are important in that culture. (Photograph by Marilyn Silverstone, © 1965 Magnum Photos.)

languages, he made the point that categories such as number, gender, tense, mode, and a host of others "are not so much discovered in experience as imposed upon it because of the tyrannical hold that linguistic form has upon our orientation in the world."[21]

[18] Harry Hoijer, "Cultural Implications of Some Navaho Linguistic Categories," *Language* 27 (1951): 111–20.

[19] Ward H. Goodenough, *Property, Kin and Community on Truk* (New Haven: Yale University Press, 1951), pp. 61–64.

[20] Edward Sapir, "Conceptual Categories in Primitive Languages," *Science* 74 (1931): 578.

[21] Ibid.

The concept of *forced observation* concerns itself with a similar hypothesis. Forced observation is often used to describe certain features of grammar which seem to compel a person to express reality in a particular way. English provides an example. The English language has tenses; Chinese does not. An English speaker is accustomed, one might even say *forced*, to specify whether an event occurred in the past, is occurring now, or will occur in the future. Not so the Chinese. It might follow, therefore, that an English speaker is being "programmed" by his or her language structure toward a different time perspective than the Chinese.

The possible effect of language on culture has been investigated by Benjamin Lee Whorf, first Sapir's student and subsequently his colleague. Whorf was particularly interested in the ways a language might structure a people's conceptions of space and time, and he set out to compare Hopi with Standard Average European (SAE) usage. In essence, he discovered that SAE usage objectified time, made it finite, and spoke about it in spatial terms (as in "three hours long," or "a stretch of time"). The Hopi language does not include such spatial terminology. For the Hopi, time is not a motion or a quantity but simply a "getting later of everything that has ever been done." Whorf thought that the SAE structure facilitates our thinking of "summer" or "September" or "morning" as actually containing specific quantities of time. But this is not the case in the Hopi linguistic structure. A Hopi says "when it is morning" (not "in the morning") and "summer is only when conditions are hot" (not "summer is hot").[22]

The implications of Whorf's findings are intriguing. On the one hand, SAE objectification of time may favor materialistic thought patterns. Its conception of time as extending into the past and into the future in equal, space-like units facilitates thinking of time in pro rata quantities (as in wage calculations) and may be partially responsible for the high value we place on speed and other quantifiable experiences. On the other hand, for the Hopi, who see time as "a getting later of everything that has ever been done," the language seems to favor an emphasis on repetition or the accumulation of experience (in contrast to the SAE usage in which time is "spent" or "saved" or "borrowed").

Despite such suggestive examples, the influence of language on other aspects of culture is far from demonstrated.

The Ethnography of Speaking

Linguists have traditionally concentrated on studying language as a system of rules governing what is considered acceptable speech in a particular society. Recently, however, some linguists have begun to study predictable variations in the ways people actually use their language when speaking. On the one hand, we may deal with language as a socially shared system of symbols, generated by a similarly shared system of rules; and on the other hand, we may consider how people customarily speak differently in different social contexts. This second type of linguistic study, called sociolinguistics, is concerned with the ethnography of speaking—that is, with cultural and subcultural patterns of speaking in different social contexts.

The sociolinguist may ask, for example, what kinds of things does one talk about in casual conversation with a stranger. A foreigner may know English vocabulary and grammar well but may not know that one typically chats to a stranger about the weather, or where one comes from, and not about what one ate that day or how much money one earns. A foreigner may be familiar with much of the culture of an American city, but if that person divulges the real state of his or her health and feelings to the first person who says "How are you?" he or she has much to learn about American small talk.

---

[22] John B. Carroll, ed., *Language, Thought, and Reality: Selected Writings of Benjamin Lee Whorf* (New York: John Wiley and Sons, 1956), pp. 65–86.

The way in which people address one another is also of interest to sociolinguists. In English, the forms of address are relatively simple. One is called either by a first name or by a title (such as Mrs., Dr., or Professor) followed by a last name. A study by Roger Brown and Marguerite Ford indicates that terms of address vary with the nature of the relationships between the speakers.[23] The reciprocal use of first names generally signifies an informal or intimate relationship between two people. When the title and last name are used reciprocally, there is usually a more formal or business-like relationship between people who are roughly equal in status. Nonreciprocal use of first names and titles in English is reserved for speakers who recognize marked difference in status between themselves. This difference can be a function of age (as when a child refers to her mother's friend as Mrs. Miller and is in turn addressed as "Sally"), or it can be drawn along occupational lines (as when a person refers to his boss by title and last name and is in turn addressed as "John"). In some cases, generally between boys and between men, the use of the last name alone represents a middle ground between the intimate and the formal usages.

Forms of address in some cultures reveal much about the status of the person addressed. Among the Nuer of the Sudan, a person's sex, relative age, and family group can be expressed by choosing among a variety of names. For example, soon after birth each boy is given a personal name which is used by his paternal relatives and by close friends in the paternal village. His maternal grandparents give him another name which is used by his mother's family and close friends. At his initiation, a boy is given an ox and acquires an ox-name (the name of the ox) which members of his peer group may then use instead of his personal name. A girl may choose an ox-name from the bull calf of a cow she milks; the name is used only by her age-group friends, often at dances

where boys and girls call out their friends' ox-names with other titles suggesting friendship. On formal occasions, a man may be greeted by his father's relatives with the paternal clan name, or by his mother's relatives with the maternal clan name. A man may be addressed as "son of" followed by his father's personal name, or as "father of" followed by his eldest child's name. A young person may address any elderly man as *gwa*, father, and an older man may call a young man *gatda*, my son. A woman may choose a cow-name from a cow she milks, or she may be called "mother of" followed by her eldest child's name.[24] Although much of the same information can be expressed through the English system of given names, nicknames, surnames, hyphenated names, and generic terms such as sonny, Miss, sir, and ma'am, the Nuer system of address is more structured and considerably more informative than the English. Why this may be so is presumably related to how Nuer and English speakers differ in their social organization.

In most languages, a person's choice of vocabulary seems to indicate the social status of the user. Clifford Geertz, in his study of Javanese, has shown that the vocabularies of the three rather sharply divided social groups—peasants, townsmen, and aristocrats—reflect their separate positions. For example, the word *now* will be expressed by a peasant as *saiki* (considered the lowest and roughest form of speech), by a townsman as *saniki* (considered somewhat more elegant), and by an aristocrat as *samenika* (the most elegant form).[25] Some languages possess variations in speech style or vocabulary based upon sex. For example, sex differences in language use have been noted for some American Indian societies in Canada, California, and South America and in some societies in Thailand and Siberia. Mary Haas has analyzed the speech of men and women in Koasati, a Muskogean language of southwestern

[23] Roger Brown and Marguerite Ford, "Address in American English," *Journal of Abnormal and Social Psychology* 62 (1961): 375–85.

[24] E. E. Evans-Pritchard, "Nuer Modes of Address," *Uganda Journal* 12 (1948): 166–71.

[25] Clifford Geertz, *The Religion of Java* (Glencoe, Ill.: Free Press, 1960), pp. 248–60.

Louisiana. She found, for example, that differences appear in certain indicative and imperative verb forms. One of her male informants characterized the speech of the women as "easy, slow, and soft. It sounds pretty." As the men of the tribe do not use women's speech, it seems we may assume that they associate it with women's role in society.[26]

Variations in language use based upon age appear more frequently in the world's languages than do variations based upon sex. For instance, a special vocabulary, "baby talk," is often used for communicating with children. In certain languages (English, for instance), use of baby talk varies with parental choice and ingenuity. Some parents or elders use words such as *choo-choo, woof-woof,* or *ta-ta* when speaking to infants; other do not. The Comanche Indians, on the other hand, have developed a special baby talk which forms a uniform and distinct part of their language. About forty words and phrases have been supplied by Casagrande; these words cover general topics of communication. For instance, *"koko:* stands for 'fruit, candy, cookies; any snack between meals; give me . . .'; *nana:* stands for 'it might hurt, get away; blood; sore, hurt.'"[27] These words and phrases have three points in common with those for baby talk in most languages: they represent whole sentences; they use simple sounds; and they depend upon repetition of those sounds.

Baby talk is initiated by adults to help children begin to learn the language. Looked at from another point of view, it is one instance of the way one person changes his or her speech as the social context changes. John Fischer's study of children in a semirural New England village indicates another instance of changing the mode of speech to fit the social context. Although we might expect that children below the age of eleven would not have acquired an awareness of

proper formality in conversation, Fischer found that the children responded to the degree of formality of a situation by changing their speech. Their varying use of the *-ing* and *-in* verb suffixes showed that the children consistently preferred the *-ing* ending in more formal contexts. For example, the *-ing* suffix would be used with formal verbs such as *correcting, visiting,* or *criticizing,* whereas *-in* would be used with informal verbs such as *hittin, swimmin,* or *chewin.*[28]

The field of sociolinguistics has only recently emerged. At the present time, sociolinguists seem to be interested primarily in describing variation in the use of language. Eventually, however, sociolinguistic research may enable us to understand why such variation in language use exists. Why, for example, do some societies use many different status terms in address? Why do other societies use modes of speaking that vary with the sex of the speakers? If we can understand why language varies in different contexts, this might also suggest why structural aspects of language change over time. For as social contexts in a society change, so might the structure of the language tend to change.

Summary

1. The essential function which language plays in all societies is that of communication. Although our communication is not limited to spoken language, language is of overriding importance because it is the primary vehicle through which human culture is shared and transmitted.

2. Systems of communication are not unique to humans. Other animal species communicate in a variety of ways—by sound, odor, body movement, and so forth. Primates also communicate, but their system of communication is closed. Human language is dis-

[26]Mary R. Haas, "Men's and Women's Speech in Koasati," *Language* 20 (1944): 142–49.
[27]Joseph B. Casagrande, "Comanche Baby Talk," *International Journal of American Linguistics* 14 (1948): 11–14.

[28]John L. Fischer, "Social Influences on the Choice of a Linguistic Variant," *Word* 14 (1958): 47–56.

tinctive as a communication system in that it permits an infinite number of combinations and recombinations of meaning.

3. A structural description of a language usually begins with an analysis of sounds and of the way they are grouped. From the wide variety of possible human sounds, each language has selected some sounds, or phones, and ignored others. How sounds are grouped into phonemes also differs from language to language. The phoneme is a set of varying sounds which do not make any difference in meaning to the speakers of the language.

4. A structural description of a language also includes an analysis of sounds or sequences of sounds that convey meaning. The smallest unit of meaning is a morph. One or more morphs with the same meaning make up a morpheme.

5. The grammar of a language may consist of morphology (the ways in which morphemes are combined to form words) and syntax (the ways in which words are arranged to form phrases and sentences). English relies heavily on syntax to convey meaning, whereas some other languages rely more heavily on morphology.

6. By comparative analysis of cognates and grammar, historical linguists test the notion that certain languages derive from a common ancestral language, or protolanguage. The goals are to reconstruct the features of the protolanguage, to hypothesize how the daughter languages separated from the protolanguage or from each other, and to establish the approximate dates of such separations.

7. When groups of people speaking the same language lose communication with one another because they become either physically or socially separated, they begin to accumulate small changes in phonology, morphology, and grammar. Eventually, if the separation continues, the two former dialects of the same language will become separate languages—that is, they will become mutually unintelligible.

8. Whereas isolation brings about divergence between speech communities, contact results in greater resemblance. This is particularly evident when contact between mutually unintelligible languages introduces "borrowed" words, usually naming some new item borrowed from the other culture.

9. Some attempts to explain the diversity of languages have focused on the possible interaction between language and other aspects of culture. On the one hand, if it can be shown that a culture may affect the structure and content of its language, then it would follow that linguistic diversity derives at least in part from cultural diversity. On the other hand, the direction of influence between culture and language might work in reverse: the linguistic structures might affect other aspects of the culture.

10. Recently, some linguists have begun to study variations in how people actually use their language when speaking. This type of linguistic study, called sociolinguistics, is concerned with the ethnography of speaking—that is, with cultural and subcultural patterns of speaking in different social contexts.

Suggested Readings

Burling, R. *Man's Many Voices: Language in Its Cultural Context.* New York: Holt, Rinehart and Winston, 1970.

A clearly written introduction to issues of current interest in anthropological linguistics. The book provides coverage of such topics as componential analysis, semantics, the effect of social setting on language, Black English, verse and linguistic games, and nonhuman versus human communication.

Giglioni, P. P. *Language and Social Context.* London: Nicholls, 1972.

An anthology of articles on sociolinguistics. Topics include the sociology of language; language and class; socialization and social structure; language conflicts and change.

Greenberg, J. H. *Anthropological Linguistics: An Introduction.* New York: Random House, 1968.

A nontechnical treatment of the fundamental nature and goals of anthropological linguistics.

Hoijer, H., ed. *Language History,* from *Language,* by Leonard Bloomfield. New York: Holt, Rinehart and Winston, 1965.

A reprint of Chapters 17–27 of Bloomfield's *Language* (1933), the classic, authoritative, and still relevant introduction to the fundamental theory and methodology of historical linguistic research.

Hymes, D., ed. *Language in Culture and Society: A Reader in Linguistics and Anthropology.* New York: Harper & Row, 1964.

A collection of sixty-nine articles discussing the wide range of anthropological interests in language.

Southworth, F. C., and Daswani, C. J. *Foundations of Linguistics.* New York: Free Press, 1974.

An introduction to the basic concerns and methods of linguistics in all its aspects.

Food Getting

12

Although it may be true that "man does not live by bread alone," without bread or the equivalent we cannot live at all. Therefore, throughout history, humans have spent much of their time getting food. During the 2 to 5 million years that humans have been on earth, 99 percent of the time they have obtained food by gathering wild plants, hunting wild animals, and fishing. Agriculture is a relatively recent phenomenon, dating back only about 10,000 years. And industrial or mechanized agriculture is less than a century old! Richard B. Lee and Irven DeVore have noted that of the 80 billion people who have ever lived, 90 percent have been hunter-gatherers and 6 percent have been agriculturalists. As members of an industrial society, we are among the remaining 4 percent.[1]

Food-getting activities take precedence over other activities important to survival. Reproduction, social control (the maintenance of peace and order within a group), defense against external threat, and the transmission of knowledge and skills to future generations—none could take place without food-derived energy. And the way a society gets its food may also have profound effects upon other aspects of its culture.

Food Collection

Food collection may be generally defined as all forms of *subsistence technology* in which food getting is dependent upon naturally occurring resources—that is, wild plants and animals. There are still some societies that live mostly by collecting wild foods. As of 1966, it was estimated that hunter-gatherer societies included some 30,000 people in a world population of 3.3 billion.[2] These 30,000 hunter-gatherers generally live in what have been called the "marginal" areas of the earth—deserts, the Arctic, and dense tropical forests—which are habitats that

[1]Richard B. Lee and Irven DeVore, eds., *Man the Hunter* (Chicago: Aldine, 1968), p. 3.
[2]John E. Pfeiffer, *The Emergence of Man*, rev. and enl. ed. (New York: Harper & Row, 1972), p. 350.

do not allow easy exploitation by modern agricultural technologies.

Anthropologists are very interested in studying the relatively few hunter-gatherer societies that are still available for observation. These groups may help us understand some aspects of human life in the past, when all people were hunter-gathers. But we must be cautious in drawing inferences about the past from our observations of contemporary hunter-gatherers, for two reasons. First, earlier hunter-gatherers lived in almost all types of environments, including some very bountiful ones. Therefore, what we observe among contemporary hunter-gatherers, who generally live in marginal environments, may not be comparable to what would have been observable in more favorable environments in the past. Second, contemporary hunter-gatherers are not "relics" of the past; they, like all contemporary societies, have evolved and are still evolving. This means that the adaptations we observe in contemporary hunter-gatherers may be different from the adaptations made by hunter-gatherers years ago. Let us examine two examples of food-collecting societies, each of which is situated in a different environment.

THE AUSTRALIAN ABORIGINES

The Ngatatjara aborigines of western Australia have been studied extensively as one of the few remaining examples of a society that still makes, and depends upon the use of, stone tools.[3] These people live on the edge of the Gibson Desert, a terrain so inhospitable that white settlers have avoided it. Rainfall in the area is usually less than 8 inches per year and temperatures rise to about 120° F. in summer. The few permanent water holes that exist are separated by hundreds of square miles of sand, scrub, and rock.

On a typical day, just before dawn, each person eats breakfast from a separate supply of food prepared the night before. Then, in the search for the new day's food, the men and the women go their separate ways. The women are more productive as food collectors, providing about 70 percent of the total quantity. They go out in the cool hours of the morning and again in the late afternoon, balancing wooden bowls filled with drinking water on their heads and carrying their babies strapped to their shoulders or hips, while their older children walk alongside. The women return with their bowls full of berries or roots which they have turned up with their digging sticks. Meanwhile, the men hunt, usually in pairs or small groups. The whole band or local group spends the midday period resting, gossiping, and making tools.

Ambush is the men's preferred method of hunting in the heat of the summer (though big game might be stalked over long distances, should a good opportunity arise). Ordinarily, the men build a blind in scrub near a water hole. Or they may dig out a fresh soak hole in a dried creek bed and place the blind on a bank overlooking the hole. The men then lie patiently in the blind, hoping for a chance to hurl a spear at an emu or a kangaroo. However, they often have to settle for much smaller game, such as rabbits, lizards, and snakes.

The Ngatatjara aborigines are a nomadic people—that is, they move their campsites frequently in search of food. Their campsites may be isolated and inhabited by only a small number of people, or they may be clustered in groups, with the total camp complex including as many as eighty persons. The aborigines never establish a campsite next to a water hole. If they should be too close, their presence would frighten game away and might cause tension with neighboring bands, who also wait for game to come to the scarce watering spots.

THE COPPER ESKIMOS

The Copper Eskimos, so called because they fashion tools by cold hammering copper nuggets, numbered between 700 and 800 people in the years 1913–1916. This was before they had

---

[3] The discussion of the Australian aborigines is based upon Richard A. Gould, *Yiwara: Foragers of the Australian Desert* (New York: Charles Scribner's Sons, 1969).

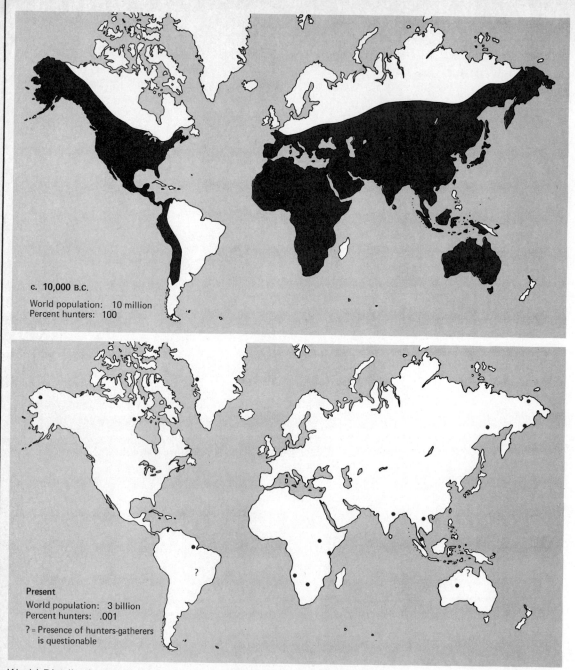

c. **10,000** B.C.

World population: 10 million
Percent hunters: 100

Present

World population: 3 billion
Percent hunters: .001

? = Presence of hunters-gatherers
is questionable

World Distribution of Hunter-Gatherers: Past (top) and Present (bottom)

About 10,000 B.C. people depended upon food collection. Today, hunter-gatherers comprise only a small fraction of the world population, and they inhabit marginal areas of the earth. (Adapted from map "Known Living Sites of Contemporary Hunter-Gatherers" in *The Emergence of Man,* Revised and Enlarged Edition by John E. Pfeiffer [Harper & Row, 1972].)

been significantly affected by contact with Westerners.[4] Today, they live in groups, each numbering about fifty persons, in the vicinity of Coronation Gulf in the Canadian Arctic, a difficult habitat by any standards. Winter lasts nearly nine months, and the sun is not visible for weeks at a time. Only during a brief summer interval do mean daily temperatures rise above the freezing point. The land surface is treacherous in winter; in summer, it is often boggy and difficult to cross because of the heavy thaw.

The Copper Eskimos are governed by the seasons much more than the Australian aborigines are. In winter, the Eskimos depend upon seals and an occasional polar bear for their food supply. Accordingly, the hunters establish themselves and their families on the pack ice offshore, or next to it, in groups of related families. The method of hunting is called *maupok,* meaning "he waits," and each hunter does just that, beside a seal's breathing hole. He stands or sits in absolute quiet and at peak attentiveness, sometimes for hours at a time, until the seal surfaces to breathe. Then he thrusts a harpoon into the animal and waits until his catch is exhausted. Finally, the hunter enlarges the hole in the ice and hauls the animal out.

Seals are indispensable to the Eskimos in winter. For many months, especially in the last half of the season, seal meat forms the staple, if not the only, food. Seal blubber provides clear-burning cooking and lighting oil, and sealskin is used to make ice boots, kayaks, oil storage bags, buckets, and a variety of items.

With the coming of spring, the Copper Eskimos split up into smaller groups and move onto the shore. Then fish becomes an important source of food. Also, lean caribou are hunted, not only for their meat but for the largely undigested vegetables in their stomachs, which are pulled out and eaten raw, on the spot, by the hunters. By summer, the groups have moved on again and have redivided. Small

[4]Diamond Jenness, *The People of the Twilight* (Chicago: University of Chicago Press, 1959). Describes fieldwork done as part of the Thule (Danish) expedition between 1913 and 1918.

The Ngatatjara aborigines of western Australia and the Copper Eskimos of the Arctic exploit very different environments. Yet they both depend upon hunting and gathering for food. (Top photograph by Richard A. Gould. Both photographs courtesy of the American Museum of Natural History.)

bands of men head inland to hunt full-grown caribou. Some of the meat is dried in strips and preserved. The women soften the hides by chewing them and then use them to make tents and clothing. Older men and most of the women and children pass the summer at fishing camps, catching and drying salmon, lake trout, and other fish.

In the fall, after the southward-bound caribou have been hunted, the Copper Eskimos settle down to await the formation of the pack ice. Usually they have ample supplies of meat and dried fish, so most of their time is utilized in preparing winter clothing and in repairing or making dogsleds, harpoons, lances, and similar articles. The skill, ingenuity, and craftsmanship of the Eskimos is particularly evident in their snow houses or *igloos*. These are built with snow blocks which are cut from firm drifts with copper (or bone) knives. The blocks are shaped with the inside edges beveled so that the igloo will taper inward and upward to a dome, with the whole building being consolidated by a key block.

POSSIBLE CONSEQUENCES OF FOOD COLLECTING

Despite the differences in terrain and climate under which they live and the different food-collecting technologies they use, Australian aborigines, Eskimos, and most other hunter-gatherers seem to have certain cultural patterns in common. Most live in small communities, in sparsely populated territories, and follow a nomadic life-style, forming no permanent settlements. They do not recognize individual land rights as a rule. Their communities do not generally have different classes of people and tend to have no specialized or full-time political officials. Division of labor is based principally on age and sex. Men generally do most of the hunting, women do most of the gathering.[5]

Although it may seem that the hunting-gathering way of life is difficult, there is evidence that it is not necessarily grueling or insecure. Making a living seems to be relatively easy for two Australian aborigine groups[6] and for the !Kung Bushmen of the Kalahari Desert of southern Africa. For example, since the Bushmen can collect an adequate amount of food with only a few hours' work a day, they have much leisure time.[7] In general, the hunting-gathering way of life may simply be less productive than the agricultural way of life, not less secure. The lower level of productivity among food collectors means that fewer people can be supported in a given territory.

Food Production

Beginning about 10,000 years ago certain peoples, in widely separated geographical locations, made the revolutionary changeover to *food production;* that is, they began to cultivate and then domesticate plants and animals. With domestication of these food sources, people acquired control over certain natural processes, such as animal breeding and seeding. Today, most peoples in the world depend for their food upon some combination of domesticated plants and animals.

HORTICULTURE

Horticulture is farming carried out with relatively simple tools and methods. Only small amounts of land are worked at one time, mostly with hand tools, and without the benefit of draft animals, plows, and systems of irrigation. There are two kinds of horticulture. Extensive or shifting cultivation is a method in which land is

[5] Data from Robert B. Textor, comp., *A Cross-Cultural Summary* (New Haven: HRAF Press, 1967) and Elman R. Service, *The Hunters* (Englewood Cliffs, N.J.: Prentice-Hall, 1966).

[6] Frederick D. McCarthy and Margaret McArthur, "The Food Quest and the Time Factor in Aboriginal Economic Life," in *Records of the Australian-American Scientific Expedition to Arnhem Land,* ed. C. P. Mountford, vol. 2, *Anthropology and Nutrition* (Melbourne: Melbourne University Press, 1960).

[7] Richard B. Lee, "What Hunters Do for a Living, or, How to Make Out on Scarce Resources," in *Man the Hunter,* ed. Lee and DeVore, p. 39.

worked for short periods, then is left idle to regenerate for some years before being used again. Generally, the slash-and-burn system of clearing fields for cultivation (described below) is employed. The other method of horticulture is more or less continuous cultivation of root and tree crops.

The Jivaro The Jivaro have long attracted world attention with their practice of shrinking and preserving human heads. They number perhaps 8,000 and live in small village groups along the eastern slopes of the Andes, in a tropical rain forest region difficult for outsiders to penetrate.[8]

The Jivaro depend for subsistence on garden produce, particularly manioc roots. These large, starchy tubers, rather like parsnips in color and texture, are made into flour or into beer, which is an important item in the Jivaro's diet. The men are responsible for the initial clearing of a "garden" or vegetable plot in the jungle; the women then take care of its cultivation. Clearing is done by the slash-and-burn method. First, the undergrowth is cut away from a given area. Then rings are cut in the bark of the smaller trees so that they will weaken and topple. Only the larger trees are cut down by hand—a formidable undertaking because of the exceptional hardness of the wood. Finally, after the cut trees and brush have lain on the ground for several months in the dry season, they are set afire. The cleared ground is cultivated with digging sticks and is used for a short time by the community, until the soil is exhausted. Then the group must move to a new site and prepare a new garden plot in the same manner.

Hunting and fishing also play a useful role in the economy of the Jivaro. The men spend considerable time hunting monkeys and birds with blowguns and poisoned darts. Lances may be used for larger animals. Fish are usually poisoned in man-made lagoons in the rivers. The economy of the Jivaro is essentially

The Amahuaca Indians of Peru practice slash-and-burn agriculture. Men and boys cooperate in clearing the forest for cultivation. Even a giant kapok tree is felled. (Cornell Capa, Magnum Photos.)

self-sufficient, but the tribe obtains machetes, steel axes, and shotguns from the outside world by means of neighborhood-to-neighborhood trading partnerships. This relative self-sufficiency is reflected in the society as a whole. The Jivaro are proud, independent people who are still as determined to avoid, and if need be to fight off, cultural incursions as they were long ago when the Incas and the Spaniards attempted to penetrate their territory.

The Kpelle Another horticultural society, the Kpelle, numbers about 86,000 persons.[9] They live in the central and western provinces of Liberia, a tropical forest habitat characterized by a relatively small area of virgin forest and a proportionately larger area of secondary bush. The region has two distinct seasons: a rainy season, lasting from May to October, and a dry season.

Rice is the principal subsistence and cash crop, with manioc root taking second place. Like

[8]This discussion is based upon Michael J. Harner, *The Jivaro* (Garden City, N.Y.: Anchor Books, 1973).

[9]James L. Gibbs, Jr., *Peoples of Africa* (New York: Holt, Rinehart and Winston, 1965), pp. 197–240.

the Jivaro, the Kpelle use the slash-and-burn method of farming.

Men and women together clear the jungle growth. The collected brush is set afire just before the rainy season begins so that the ashes can be beaten into the earth as a fertilizer. In July, during the rainy season, the women plant the rice seeds. Then, for a period of about two weeks, practically the whole population of a town sleeps near the newly planted land to keep birds from plundering the germinating seeds. The women weed the rice beds while the men build granaries to store the grain which will be harvested from October to December. After the crop has been painstakingly cut stalk by stalk, it is left to dry in the sun for some weeks to prevent dampness and spoilage.

The Kpelle seem to have reached so high a level of productivity and general sophistication in their horticultural technology that further advance could only come from a change to intensive agriculture. Food surpluses are traded for cash, which is then used to buy new clothes and equipment.

Possible Consequences of Horticulture The cultures of horticultural peoples tend to vary appreciably according to the relative richness of their environments and their opportunities for cultural borrowing. In most horticultural societies, however, simple farming techniques have tended to yield more food from a given area than is generally available to hunting and gathering peoples. Consequently, horticulture is generally able to support larger, more densely populated communities. The way of life of horticulturalists is generally more sedentary than that of hunter-gatherers, although communities may move after a number of years to farm a new series of plots. In contrast to most hunter-gatherer groups, some horticultural societies exhibit the beginnings of social differentiation. For example, some persons may be part-time craftsmen or part-time political officials; and certain members of a kin group may have more status than other individuals in the society.

INTENSIVE AGRICULTURE

Intensive agriculture is characterized chiefly by technological aspects that are missing in horticulture. These include using plows and other improved farming implements, using draft animals (and, in later stages of development, machines), applying fertilizers to the land, and developing irrigation and other water storage techniques.

Rural Greece The village of Vasilika is situated at the foot of Mount Parnassus on the Boeotian plain. In recent times, its population has numbered some 220 inhabitants.[10]

Grapevines and wheat are cultivated for domestic use. The agricultural year begins in March with pruning of the vines and hoeing of the fields, which are regarded as men's work. Winemaking commences in September, after the grain harvest, and involves the whole family. Everyone goes to the fields to gather the grapes into large baskets. After the leaves and stems are removed, the fruit is trampled by the men, and the newly pressed grape juice, or *must*, is transferred to barrels.

The villagers use horses to plow their wheat fields in October, and in November they sow the seed by hand. The wheat crop is harvested the following summer, generally by machine. Wheat constitutes the staple village food and is eaten as bread, as a cereal (called *trakhana*), or as noodles. It is also commonly bartered for other food items, such as fish, olive oil, and coffee.

Cotton and tobacco are raised for cash income. In this dry plains country, the success of the cotton crop depends upon irrigation, and the villagers use efficient diesel pumps to distribute water from the local water table. The real work in the cotton fields begins after the spring plowing and seeding have been completed. Then the young plants must be hoed and mulched, a task done mostly by women.

[10] The discussion of rural Greece is based upon Ernestine Friedl, *Vasilika: A Village in Modern Greece* (New York: Holt, Rinehart and Winston, 1962).

Irrigation, which begins in July is men's work. It is usually done three times a season and involves the clearing of shallow ditches, the mounting of pumps, and the channelling of the water. Cotton picking, which starts in October, is considered women's work. For picking, as well as for the hoeing and harvesting, a farmer owning more than five acres usually calls in hired laborers from neighboring villages and pays them cash wages. The cotton ginning is carried out by centrally located contractors, who are paid on the spot with 6 percent of each farmer's crop. Most of the seed reclaimed in the ginning is used for the next year's planting. The remainder is pressed into cakes to serve as supplementary fodder for the ewes at lambing time. Tobacco yields a larger cash income than does cotton, and the tobacco crop fits well into what otherwise would be slack periods in cultivation.

Animal husbandry plays a relatively minor role in the villagers' economic life. Each farmer has a horse or two for the heavy draft work, a mule or donkey, about two dozen sheep, and some fowl.

Farmers at Vasilika are responsive to modern developments; they are prepared to experiment to a certain extent, especially with mechanization. Where the amount of acreage under cultivation warrants the expense, tractors are hired for plowing. Specialists are regularly called upon to handle harvesting, cotton ginning, and similar tasks. Indeed, the Greek farmer is content to be a farmer and to rely totally on the skills of others to repair his roof, maintain his water pump, or provide the mechanical know-how for his production.

Rural Vietnam: The Mekong Delta The village of Khanh Hau, situated along the flat Mekong Delta, comprised about 600 families in the late 1950s.[11] (After this period, village life may have been disturbed by the Vietnam War.) The delta area has a tropical climate with a rainy season that lasts from May to November. As a whole, the delta has been rendered habitable only by extensive drainage operations.

In the Mekong Delta, wet rice cultivation is practiced, using irrigation. Here, two women cultivate a paddy with hand-driven rotary hoes. (Courtesy of the United Nations.)

Wet rice cultivation is the principal agricultural activity of Khanh Hau. It is part of a complex, specialized arrangement that involves three interacting components: (1) an extensive system of irrigation and water control; (2) a variety of specialized equipment, including plows, waterwheels, threshing sledges, and winnowing machines; (3) a clearly defined set of socioeconomic roles—from those of landlord, tenant, and laborer to those of rice miller and rice merchant.

In the dry season, the farmer decides what sort of rice crop he will plant—whether of long (120 days) or short (90 days) maturation. His choice depends upon the capital at his disposal, the current cost of fertilizer, and the anticipated demand for rice. The seedbeds are prepared as soon as the rains have softened the ground in

---

[11] This discussion is based upon Gerald Cannon Hickey, *Village in Vietnam* (New Haven: Yale University Press, 1964), pp. 135–65.

May. The soil is turned over and broken up as many as six separate times, with two-day intervals for "airing" between each operation. While the soil is being plowed and harrowed in this fashion, the rice seeds are soaked in water for two days to stimulate sprouting. Before the seedlings are planted, the paddy is plowed once more and harrowed twice in two directions at right angles.

Planting is a delicate, specialized operation which usually must be done quickly and it is performed by hired male labor. But efficient planting is not enough to guarantee a fair crop. Proper fertilization and irrigation are equally important. In the irrigating, steps must be taken to ensure that the water level remains at exactly the proper depth over the entire paddy. Water is distributed by means of scoops, wheels, and mechanical pumps. The rice crop is harvested, threshed, winnowed, and dried when it ripens during the period from late September to May. Normally, the rice is sorted into three portions: one is set aside for use by the household in the following year; one is for payment of hired labor and other services (such as loans from agricultural banks); and one is for cash sale on the market.

The villagers also cultivate garden produce; raise pigs, chickens, and the like; and frequently engage in fishing. The village economy usually supports three or four implement makers and a much larger number of carpenters.

Possible Consequences of Intensive Agriculture In contrast to horticultural groups, societies with intensive agriculture are more likely to have towns and cities, a high degree of craft specialization, and to have more complex political organization. Women in intensive agricultural societies generally contribute less to subsistence than do women in horticultural societies. Intensive agricultural societies are also more likely to face food shortages, even though intensive agriculture is generally more productive than horticulture.[12] The reason may be that

[12] Data from Textor, *A Cross-Cultural Summary.*

An industrialized society such as our own usually derives its food supply from both intensive agriculture and herding. In many parts of the United States, for example, cattle raising is a large-scale industry. (Erich Hartmann, Magnum Photos.)

intensive agriculture—which is practiced mainly in nontropical areas where rainfall can be unreliable—is more vulnerable to severe drought which can hurt, and even destroy, the entire food supply. Or perhaps intensive agriculturalists are more likely to face food shortages because they are often producing crops for a market. If the market demand drops, they may not have enough cash to buy all the other food they need.

PASTORALISM

Pastoralism is a relatively rare form of subsistence technology practiced by nomadic people in which food getting is based largely upon the maintenance of large herds of animals. Most agriculturalists raise some animals, but only a relatively small number of peoples depend principally upon domesticated herds of animals for their livelihood. Pastoralism is usually associated with terrain such as steppes, rolling hills, and grasslands. These are areas of low rainfall where cultivation is difficult without (or even with) irrigation, but where grasses are plentiful enough to support herds of animals.

The Basseri The Basseri are a tribe of about 16,000 tent-dwelling, pastoral nomads who live in southern Iran.[13] Their herds consist principally of sheep and goats, though donkeys and camels are raised for draft work and the more wealthy men have horses for riding. Theirs is a dry, arid habitat, with rainfall averaging no more than 10 inches a year.

The Basseri's pastoral way of life is based upon a regular, migratory exploitation of the grazing lands within their territory, which measures about 15,000 square miles in all. In winter, when the mountains to the north are covered with snow, the plains and foothills to the south offer extensive pasturage. During the spring, the grazing is excellent on a plateau near the center of the territory. By summer, when most of the lower-lying pastures have dried up, sufficient food for the herds may be found in the mountains at an altitude nearly 6,000 feet above sea level.

Annual migrations are so important to the economy of the Basseri—as well as to other groups of pastoral nomads in southern Iran—that there has developed the concept of *il-rah*, or "tribal road." A major pastoral tribe, such as the Basseri, will have its traditional route and schedule. The route refers to the localities in the order in which each is visited and follows the existing passes and lines of communication. The schedule regulates the length of time each location will be occupied and depends upon the maturation of different pastures and the movements of other tribes. The *il-rah* is regarded, in effect, as the property of the tribe. Local populations and authorities recognize the tribe's right to pass along roads and cultivated lands, to

draw water from the public wells, and to pasture its flocks on public land.

The Basseri generally herd sheep and goats together, with one shepherd responsible for a flock of 300 to 400 animals. Milk and its by-products are the most important commodities, but wool, hides, and meat are also important to the economy of the Basseri. Both wool and hides are traded, but they are of even greater use within the tribe. The Basseri are skilled spinners and weavers, especially the women, much of whose time is spent at these activities. Saddle bags and pack bags are woven on horizontal looms from homespun wool and hair, as are carpets, sleeping rugs, and the characteristic black tents made of panels of woven goat hair. Woven goat hair provides an exceptionally versatile cloth. For winter use, it retains heat and repels water; in summer, it insulates against heat and permits free circulation of air. Lambskin hides also serve many purposes. When plucked and turned inside-out, the hides are made into storage bags to hold water, buttermilk, sour milk, and other liquids.

Most of the Basseri must obtain through trade the necessities and luxury items that they do not produce within the community. The staple items they sell are butter, wool, lambskins, rope, and, occasionally, livestock.

The Lapps The Lapps live and move with their reindeer herds in northwestern Scandinavia where Finland, Sweden, and Norway share common frontiers. It is a typical Arctic habitat: cold, windswept, with long, dark days for half the year. Though the Lapps gradually have come under modern cultural influences in the twentieth century, theirs is still very largely a pastoral form of life.[14]

The Lapps herd their reindeer either intensively or extensively, using the latter method most often today. In the intensive system, the herd is constantly under observation within a

---

[13] The discussion of the Basseri is based upon Fredrik Barth, *Nomads of South Persia* (Oslo: Universitetsforlaget, 1964; Boston: Little, Brown, 1968).

[14] The discussion of the Lapps is based upon Ian Whitaker, *Social Relations in a Nomadic Lappish Community* (Oslo: Utgitt av Norsk Folkemuseum, 1955) and also T. I. Itkonen, "The Lapps of Finland," *Southwestern Journal of Anthropology* 7 (1951): 32–68.

TABLE 1 Consequences of Variation in Food Getting

	Food Collectors		Food Producers	
	Hunter-Gatherers	Horticulturalists	Pastoralists	Intensive Agriculturalists
Population density	Lowest	Low-moderate	Low	Highest
Maximum community size	Small	Small-moderate	Small	Large towns and cities
Nomadism/permanence of settlements	Generally nomadic or seminomadic	More sedentary—houses may be moved after several years	Generally nomadic or seminomadic	Permanent communities
Food shortages	Rare	Infrequent	Frequent	Frequent
Trade	Minimal	Minimal	Very important	Very important
Full-time craft specialists	None	None or rare	Some craft specialists	High degree of craft specialization
Individual differences in wealth	Generally none	Generally minimal	Yes	Yes, in land, animals, and money
Political leadership	Informal	Some part-time political officials	Part- and full-time political officials	Many full-time political officials

general, fenced area for the whole year. The Lapps live with their animals at all times and always know the number of animals in their charge. Intensively herded reindeer and other animals are accustomed to human contact. Hence, the summer corralling of the females for milking and the breaking-in of the ox-reindeer for use as draft animals are not difficult tasks.

The extensive system involves allowing the animals to migrate over a large area. It requires less surveillance and encompasses larger herds. Under this system, the reindeer are allowed to move through their seasonal feeding cycles watched by only one or two "scouts." The other Lapps stay with the herd only when it has settled in its summer or winter habitat. But milking, breaking-in, and corralling in general are more arduous in the extensive system because the animals are less accustomed to humans.

Even under the extensive system, which theoretically permits Lapps to engage in subsidiary economic activities such as hunting and fishing, the reindeer herd is the essential, if not the only, source of income. A family may possess as many as 1,000 reindeer, but usually the figure is half that number. Studies show 200 to be the minimum number of reindeer needed to provide for a family of four or five adults.

The Lapps eat the meat of the bull reindeer; the females are kept for breeding purposes. Bulls are slaughtered in the fall, after the mating season. Meat and hides are frequently sold or bartered for other food and necessities.

Possible Consequences of Pastoralism Pastoralism is a highly specialized form of food production involving the care of large animal herds. It is practiced today mostly in habitats which cannot support cultivation but can provide sufficient pasture for a herd on the move.

Even though they are nomadic, pastoral societies tend to have more individual differences in wealth and more craft specialization than societies which are dependent upon food collection. Individuals or families may own property, particularly animals, but herding is often organized by groups of families. Especially to be noted is the interdependence between pastoral groups and agricultural groups. That is, trade is usually necessary for pastoral groups; in fact, a large proportion of their food may actually come from trade with agricultural groups.[15] Possibly because of their dependence upon intensive agriculturalists, who are themselves often short of food, the pastoralists are also vulnerable to food shortages.[16]

Causes of Food-Getting Diversity

Of great interest to anthropologists is the question of why different societies have different methods of food getting. Archaeological evidence suggests that major changes in food getting—such as the domestication of plants and animals—have been independently invented in at least several areas of the world. Yet, despite these comparable inventions and their subsequent diffusion or spread by migration, there still is wide diversity in the means by which people obtain food. How is this to be explained?

ENVIRONMENTAL INFLUENCES

In looking for the possible effects of the physical environment on practices of food getting, we are first faced with a problem of definition: there is no one indisputable way of defining a physical habitat. Some anthropologists favor the kind of geographical focus exemplified by Preston James's classification of the world's land surface into eight principal types.[17] Using the

twin criteria of natural vegetation and surface features, James distinguishes between dry lands (deserts), tropical forests, "Mediterranean" scrub forests, mid-latitude mixed forests, grasslands, boreal forests, polar lands, and mountain lands.

Dry Lands Dry lands are the desert regions of the world. They comprise 18 percent of the total land surface but are occupied by only 6 percent of the earth's population. Contrary to popular belief, few parts of these areas are entirely barren or rainless. The typical landscape includes a cover of low shrubs and grasses.

James groups dry lands into five principal locations: North African and Asian, of which the Sahara, Arabian, Turkestan, and Gobi deserts are examples; North American, including northern Mexico, Arizona, New Mexico, southern California, and the Great and Wyoming basins; South American coastal deserts of Peru and western Argentina; South African, including the Namib and Kalahari deserts; and Australian, such as the Great Sandy, Gibson, and Great Victoria deserts.

Shortage of water has hampered the agricultural development of dry lands, except where there are either *oases*—small, fertile areas where crops can be grown with a simple technology—or rivers that could be tapped by irrigation. In dry land regions without oases, the existing technology has determined the living pattern. When the technology is simple, food getting may take the basic hunting-gathering form, as exemplified by the Australian aborigines or the Kalahari Bushmen. Or, with irrigation, it can take the intensive agricultural form, as exemplified by cultivation in Israel. Horticulture is apparently not possible in dry land areas, although pastoralism may be.

Tropical Forest Lands Tropical forests occupy 10 percent of the earth's land surface and are inhabited by 28 percent of the world's population. These are areas with abundant rainfall. But despite the attractiveness of lush vegetation and brilliant colorings, tropical forest lands do not

[15]Susan H. Lees and Daniel G. Bates, "The Origins of Specialized Nomadic Pastoralism: A Systemic Model," *American Antiquity* 39 (1974): 187–93.
[16]Data from Textor, *A Cross-Cultural Summary.*
[17]Preston E. James, *A Geography of Man,* 3rd ed. (Waltham, Mass.: Blaisdell, 1966).

usually offer favorable environments for intensive agriculture. This may be because heavy rainfall quickly washes away certain minerals from cleared land. Also, greater difficulty in controlling insect pests and weeds[18] may make intensive agriculture less profitable in tropical forest areas. Horticulture, with shifting cultivation and slash-and-burn preparation, as exemplified by the Jivaro, is generally practiced in such environments. In the past, however, hunting and gathering economies were found frequently in tropical forest areas. And today, there are a few areas (for example, the Mekong Delta of Vietnam) whose tropical forests were cleared and prevented from growing up again by the use to which the cleared land was put—rice cultivation in paddies. Tropical forest lands cover the Amazon Basin and parts of the Guianas, extending to southern Brazil; they form much of the Congo Basin, with fingers reaching into Liberia and Sierra Leone; they stretch from northeastern India along the Malay Peninsula to Indonesia, Melanesia, and northern Australia, and are also in parts of Burma, Thailand, and Vietnam.

"Mediterranean" Scrub Forests "Mediterranean" scrub forests comprise 1 percent of the earth's land mass and are occupied by 5 percent of the world's population. These areas are usually located between mountains and coasts and are characterized by mild, rainy winters and hot, dry summers. Besides occurring along the Mediterranean itself, such areas are found primarily in middle Chile, between Coquimbo and Concepcion, and in North America, between Los Angeles and Oregon. They provide an excellent habitat for human beings at any level of technology. California was populated by hunting-gathering peoples long ago, as were parts of Greece and Italy long before the emergence of Athens and Rome.

Mixed Forest Lands Although only 7 percent of the earth's land surface is classified as mixed forest, 42 percent of the world's population lives

[18]Daniel H. Janzen, "Tropical Agroecosystems," *Science,* 21 December 1973, pp. 1212–18.

in this type of region. Mixed forest areas contain varied surface features: mixed coniferous (cone-bearing evergreens) and broadleaf forests, rolling hills and low mountain ranges, large fertile plains and river valleys. This land type is found principally in North America, Europe north of the Mediterranean zone, most of China north of the tropics, Korea, and Japan. In prehistoric times, this kind of habitat supported only a small population, largely because peoples having stone technologies were unable to clear the forests of thick-trunked hardwoods. When bronze and iron tools were developed, however, people were able to clear the mixed forest lands. The areas then became so productive that they have been able to support large populations even to the present time.

Grasslands Grasslands occupy 19 percent of the earth's land surface and are inhabited by 10 percent of the world's population. These regions may be *steppes* (having dry, low grass cover), *prairies* (with taller, better-watered grass), or *savannas* (tropical grasslands). They are found extensively in North Africa, Mongolia, Manchuria, Russia, and North America, and in smaller areas elsewhere. The grassland habitat favors large game and hence supports both hunting and pastoral technologies, except where a machine technology makes intensive agriculture possible, as in parts of the United States and the Soviet Union today.

Boreal Forest Lands Only 1 percent of the world's population lives in boreal forest lands, which occupy 10 percent of the global land surface. Mainly coniferous, and not so dense as the forests of the tropics, these heavily wooded areas are found throughout the Northern Hemisphere in large sections of Canada, Alaska, Siberia, and Scandinavia. This type of region is generally unfavorable for food growing, perhaps because the growing season is relatively short.

Polar Lands Although polar lands comprise 16 percent of the earth's surface, only 1 percent of the total world population lives in these inhospitable regions. The type of land surrounding the North and South Poles varies from *tundras,* which have brief summer seasons (about six weeks), to heavily glaciated or iced areas. The food resources of this habitat include few plants; thus, as we have seen, the Eskimos subsist largely by fishing and hunting.

Mountain Lands Mountains occupy 12 percent of the earth's land surface and are inhabited by 7 percent of the world's population. James indicates that the world is "tied together" by more or less continuous chains of high mountains. From a core in Southeast Asia, these mountain chains extend on three axes: one through southern Asia and southern Europe to North Africa and the Atlantic coast of Africa; another via Tibet, across western China, Siberia, and down the west coasts of North and South America; and the third, partially submerged, across the Pacific Basin. Mountain lands vary in climate and terrain (and thus in habitat) according to their elevation. Although today no mountain regions are inhabited by food collectors, it is not clear whether this was also true in the past, particularly before the domestication of plants and animals. In any case, mountain lands are currently occupied by pastoralists and intensive agriculturalists.

The level of technological development has a significant effect on the type of food-getting practices in a particular environment. With the use of complex systems of irrigation, the Imperial Valley in California, a dry land area, has become one of the most productive regions in the world. (Burk Uzzle, Magnum Photos.)

Given this classification of habitats, what conclusion can we draw about the influence of environmental factors on food getting? Cross-cultural evidence indicates that neither food collection nor food production is significantly associated with any particular type of habitat.[19] Certain very general patterns are suggested, however, in comparisons between specific means of food production and specific types of habitat. Approximately 80 percent of all societies that practice horticulture or simple agriculture are in the tropics, whereas 75 percent of all societies that practice intensive agriculture are *not* in tropical forest environments.[20] The reason for the predominance of simple agriculture in

tropical regions may be that either the soil-depleting effects of high rainfall in these areas or the difficulties of weeding where vegetation grows so quickly—or both together—hinder the development of intensive agriculture.[21] There is also a problem of pest control in the tropics, as we have mentioned previously. Pastoralism is not usually found in tropical forest regions.[22] This is not surprising, since a dense jungle is hardly a likely spot to herd animals.

From the information available, anthropologists have generally concluded that the physical environment by itself has a limiting, rather than

[19]Data from Textor, *A Cross-Cultural Summary.*
[20]Ibid.

[21]For an argument supporting the "weeding" explanation, see Robert L. Carneiro, "Slash-and-Burn Cultivation among the Kuikuru and its Implications for Cultural Devleopment in the Amazon Basin," *Antropologica,* Supplement no. 2 (September 1961).
[22]Data from Textor, *A Cross-Cultural Summary.*

a strictly determining, effect on the major types of subsistence. In other words, some environments may not permit certain types of food getting, although allowing a number of others. The type of food getting that can be practiced in a particular kind of environment depends upon the inhabitants' level of technological development, as dramatically illustrated by the history of the Imperial Valley, a dry land region in California. The complex systems of irrigation now used in that area have made it one of the most productive regions in the world. Yet about 400 years ago, this same valley could support only hunting and gathering groups who subsisted on wild plants and animals.

THE ORIGIN AND SPREAD OF FOOD PRODUCTION

Although we recognize that the physical environment may limit the major types of food getting, we still need to ask why certain food-getting techniques are practiced in areas where other techniques are also possible. For example, in some environments, both hunting/gathering and agriculture/herding are possible, yet food production has generally supplanted food collection throughout the world. Because the changeover to food production is important for our understanding of contemporary variations in methods of food getting, we shall briefly review some of the current theories about why food production developed.

The idea that the changeover to food production would result "naturally" when people learned how to produce food has come under much criticism recently. The major criticism is that food collectors probably were not living poorly (judging by some of the data we have for contemporary hunter-gatherers) and probably did not have to work very hard to obtain adequate food. Why, then, should they choose to adopt techniques of food production, which usually require more work and may involve more threat of food shortage? Although anthropologists are still a long way from a definitive answer, one current view is that people would

not necessarily make the changeover to food production unless they *had* to.[23]

Why did they have to? Why did people in widely separated geographical locations—the Near East, Southeast Asia, Mexico, West Africa, and probably other areas—domesticate various plants and animals, perhaps independently? Binford, Flannery, Harner, and others think that the spur to domestication may have been the pressure of increasing population on available wild resources. Binford[24] suggests that population spillover from centers of wild plenty to more marginal areas would have favored domestication as a way of regaining the levels of production to which the people were accustomed in the optimum areas. Building on Binford's suggestion, Flannery argues that because they generally do not have to work very hard for sufficient food, hunter-gatherers have little incentive to seek the greater productivity per given area that is generally associated with agriculture. Only when hunter-gatherers do not have enough food might they be interested in cultivation. In the Near East, for example, Flannery believes that "cultivation began as an attempt to produce artificially, around the *margins* of the 'optimum' zone, stands of cereals as dense as those in the *heart* of the 'optimum' zone."[25]

Michael Harner also proposes that increasing population may have brought about domestication.[26] In his view, the key moment comes when a food-collecting community has utilized the food resources of its habitat to the point

[23] Some who espouse this view are: Lewis R. Binford, "Post-Pleistocene Adaptations," in *New Perspectives in Archaeology*, ed. L. R. Binford and S. R. Binford (Chicago: Aldine, 1968), pp. 313–41; Kent V. Flannery, "The Origins of Agriculture," in *Annual Review of Anthropology*, ed. Bernard J. Siegel, Alan R. Beals, and Stephen A. Tyler (Palo Alto, Calif.: Annual Reviews, 1973), vol. 2, pp. 271–310; Michael J. Harner, "Population Pressure and the Social Evolution of Agriculturalists," *Southwestern Journal of Anthropology* 26 (1970): 67–86.

[24] Binford, "Post-Pleistocene Adaptations."

[25] Kent V. Flannery, "Origins and Ecological Effects of Early Domestication in Iran and the Near East," in *Prehistoric Agriculture*, ed. Stuart Struever (Garden City, N.Y.: Natural History Press, 1971), p. 60. Originally published in *The Domestication and Exploitation of Plants and Animals*, ed. Peter J. Ucko and G. W. Dimbleby (Chicago: Aldine, 1969), pp. 73–97.

[26] Harner, "Population Pressure and the Social Evolution of Agriculturalists."

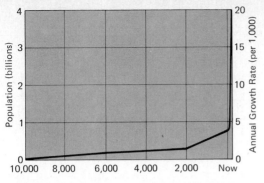

FIGURE 1 Population Growth Since 10,000 Years Ago

Note: The black line indicates the size of the population. (Adapted from "The History of the Human Population" by Ansley J. Coale. Copyright © 1974 by Scientific American, Inc. All rights reserved.)

where it has reached "the limit of population density." It is then obliged to supplement its usual sources of food supply with new, domesticated ones.

This view that the pressures of population increase may have *caused* the changeover to food production has only recently gained attention from anthropologists. Previously, the emphasis was on the reverse: population increase was regarded as the *product* of agriculture and herding. However, the archaeological evidence is not complete enough as yet to suggest which generally came first—population increase or food production—in the various areas of earliest animal and plant domestication. In any case, there *has* been considerable population growth since the development of food production, as can be seen in Figure 1.

Even if we understood why domestication developed in different parts of the world, we would still need to explain why it has generally supplanted food collection as the primary mode of subsistence. We cannot assume that food collectors would automatically adopt food production as a superior way of life once they understood the process of domestication. After all, domestication may entail more work and provide less food security than the food-collecting way of life.

The spread of agriculture may perhaps be linked to the need for territorial expansion. As a sedentary, food-producing population grew, it may have been forced to expand into new territory. Some of this territory may have been vacant, but much of it was probably already occupied by food collectors. Although food production is not necessarily easier than food collection, it is generally more productive per given unit of land. Greater productivity means that more people can be supported in a given territory. In the competition for land between the faster-expanding food producers and the food collectors, the food producers may have had a significant advantage: they had more people in a given area. Thus, the hunter-gatherer groups may have been more likely to lose out in the competition for land. Some groups may have adopted cultivation, abandoning the hunter-gatherer way of life in order to survive. Other groups, which remained food collectors, may have been forced to retreat into areas not desired by the cultivators. Today, the small number of remaining hunter-gatherers inhabit areas which are not particularly suitable for cultivation—dry lands, dense tropical forests, and polar regions.

Just as prior population growth might account for the origins of domestication, so at later periods further population growth and ensuing pressure on resources might at least partially explain the transformation of horticultural into intensive agricultural systems. Ester Boserup[27] has suggested that intensification of agriculture, with a consequent increase in yield per acre, is not likely to develop naturally out of horticulture because intensification requires much more work. She argues that people will only be willing to intensify their labor if they have to. Where emigration is not feasible, the prime mover behind intensification may generally be prior population growth.

Intensive agriculture has not yet spread into every part of the world. Horticulture continues

[27] Ester Boserup, *The Conditions of Agricultural Growth* (Chicago: Aldine, 1965).

to be practiced in certain tropical regions, and there are still some pastoralists and hunter-gatherers. As we noted earlier, some environments may make it difficult to adopt certain subsistence practices. For example, intensive agriculture cannot supplant horticulture in some tropical envronments without tremendous investments in chemical fertilizers and pesticides, not to mention the additional labor required.[28] And enormous amounts of water may be required to make agriculturalists out of hunter-gatherers and pastoralists who now exploit semiarid environments. Hence, the different kinds of food-getting practices we can observe today throughout the world are likely to be with us for some time to come.

Summary

1. Food collection, or hunting and gathering—which is dependent upon naturally occurring plants and animals—is the oldest human food-getting technology. Today, however, only a small number of societies practice it and they tend to inhabit marginal environments.

2. Hunting and gathering societies can be found in a number of different physical habitats. They are generally nomadic, and their populations are relatively small in number and low in density. The division of labor is usually along age and sex lines only. Personal possessions are limited, most resources being communally held, and economic relations are based on sharing. The community is generally a band of related families, with vaguely defined leadership; different classes of people are generally unknown.

3. Beginning about 10,000 years ago certain peoples, in widely separated geographical locations, began to make the revolutionary changeover to food production. Over the centuries, food production began to supplant food collection as the predominant mode of subsistence.

4. Horticulturalists practice cultivation with simple handtools. The slash-and-burn technique is frequently used to clear areas for cultivation. The food supply of horticulturalists is generally sufficient to support larger, more densely populated communities than can be fed by food collection. Their way of life is generally sedentary, although communities may move after a number of years to farm a new series of plots. In contrast to most hunter-gatherers, some horticulturalists exhibit the beginnings of social differentiation.

5. Intensive agriculture is characterized chiefly by technological aspects that are missing in horticulture. These include the use of plows and other improved farming implements; the use of draft animals (and, in later stages of development, machines); the application of fertilizers; and the development of irrigation and other water storage techniques. In contrast to horticultural societies, societies with intensive agriculture are more likely to have towns and cities, to have a high degree of craft specialization, and to have more complex political organization.

6. Pastoralism is a subsistence technology based on the care of large herds of animals. It is a highly specialized adaptation to low rainfall areas. The essential features of pastoralism are: a nomadic way of life; clearly defined seasonal areas of pasturage and access routes; and somewhat more complex sociopolitical systems than are found among hunter-gatherer groups.

7. Anthropologists generally agree that physical environment exercises a limiting, rather than determining, influence on the major types of food-getting technology. Food producers can generally support more people in a given territory than food collectors can. Therefore, the food producers generally may have had a competitive advantage in their confrontations with food collectors.

[28] Janzen, "Tropical Agroecosystems."

Suggested Readings

Boserup, E. *The Conditions of Agricultural Growth.* Chicago: Aldine, 1965.

A presentation of the theory that prior population growth is the major causal factor in agricultural development, at least in recent times.

Lee, R. B., and DeVore, I., eds. *Man the Hunter.* Chicago: Aldine, 1968.

The product of a 1966 symposium of the same name, this volume includes papers on the social organization, demography, and ecology of hunter-gatherers. Prehistoric hunter-gatherers and the role of hunting and gathering in the evolution of human culture are also discussed.

Leeds, A., and Vayda, A. P., eds. *Man, Culture and Animals: The Role of Animals in Human Ecological Adjustments.* Publication No. 78 of the American Association for the Advancement of Science. Washington, D.C.: American Association for the Advancement of Science, 1965.

A collection of papers dealing with the complex feedback relationship between environment and culture. The papers cover a wide range of subsistence patterns, from hunting and gathering to modern cattle ranching. All the authors share the attitude that culture is related to its surrounding natural environment.

Service, E. *The Hunters.* Englewood Cliffs, N.J.: Prentice-Hall, 1966.

An introduction to the basic features of the hunting-gathering way of life. The book includes an ethnographic appendix with descriptions of many hunting and gathering societies, as well as selected readings on the subject.

Struever, S., ed. *Prehistoric Agriculture.* Garden City, N.Y.: Natural History Press, 1971.

An up-to-date sourcebook which focuses on the problems involved in explaining the rise of agriculture. Part II is of particular interest, because it presents hypotheses to explain the beginnings of agriculture and its consequences in various parts of the world. The book also includes an extensive bibliography.

Ucko, P. J., and Dimbleby, G. W., *The Domestication and Exploitation of Plants and Animals.* Chicago: Aldine, 1969.

A collection of papers on the determinants of the transition to food production.

Economic Systems

13

When we think of economics, we think of things and activities involving money. We think of the costs of goods and services such as food, rent, haircuts, and movie tickets. We may also think of factories, farms, and other business enterprises that produce the goods and services we need or think we need. However, many societies (indeed, most that are known to anthropology) do not have money or the equivalent of the factory worker. In our society, the worker may stand before a moving belt for eight hours, tightening identical bolts that glide by. For this task the worker is given bits of paper which may be exchanged for food, shelter, and other goods or services.

All societies have economic systems, however, whether or not the systems involve the use of money. All societies have customs regulating the access to natural resources; customs for transforming those resources, through labor, into necessities and other desired items; and customs for distributing (and perhaps exchanging) goods and services.

The Allocation of Productive Resources

NATURAL RESOURCES

Every society has access to surrounding natural resources—land, water, plants, animals, minerals. Where a particular resource is concerned, every society has cultural rules for determining who has access to that resource and what can be done with it. In societies like our own, where land and many other things may be bought and sold, land is divided into precisely measurable units, the borders of which are sometimes invisible. Relatively small plots of land and the resources on them are usually "owned" by individuals. Large plots of land are generally owned collectively. The owner may be a government agency, such as the National Parks Service that owns land on behalf of the entire population of the United States. Or the owner may be what we call a corporation, which is a private collective of shareholders. In the United States, property ownership entails a more or

13

less exclusive right to use land resources in whatever way the owner wishes, including the right to sell, give away, or destroy those resources.

Our system of land allocation is alien to the thinking of most hunter-gatherers and most horticulturalists, for two reasons. First, in their societies, individual ownership of land, or ownership by a group of unrelated shareholders, is generally absent. If there is collective ownership, it is always by groups of related people (kinship groups) or by territorial groups (bands or villages). Second, even if there is collective ownership, such ownership has a different meaning from ours because land generally is not bought and sold.

Thus, it is society, and not the individual, which specifies what is considered "property" and what are the rights and duties associated with that property.[1] These specifications are social in nature, for they may be changed over time. For example, France has recently declared all its beaches to be public, thereby stating, in effect, that the ocean shore is not a resource which can be owned by an individual. As a result, all the hotels and individuals who had fenced off portions of the best beaches for their exclusive use have had to remove the fences. In our country, people are beginning to ask whether abuse of the rights of ownership is a factor in the growing pollution of our air and water. Hence, federal, state, and local governments are becoming more active in regulating exactly what people can do with the land they own. This particular type of regulation may be new, but our society has always limited the rights of ownership. For example, our land may be taken by the government for use in the construction of a highway; we may be paid compensation, but usually we cannot prevent confiscation. Similarly, we are not allowed to burn our houses, nor can we use them as brothels or munitions arsenals. In short, even under our highly individualistic system of ownership, property is not entirely private.

Societies differ in their rules as to how individuals have access to land and other natural resources and what can be done with those resources. These differences generally seem to be related to how the society gets its food. Let us now examine how hunter-gatherers, horticulturalists, pastoralists, and intensive agriculturalists structure rights to land in different ways.

As we noted above, members of hunter-gatherer societies generally do not own land individually. The reason probably is that for hunter-gatherers, land itself has no intrinsic value; what is of value is the presence of game and wild plant life on the land. If game moves away or food resources become less plentiful, the land is correspondingly less valuable. Therefore, the greater the possibility that the wild food supply in a particular locale will fluctuate, the less desirable it is to parcel out small areas of land to individuals and the more advantageous it is to make land ownership communal.

The Hadza of Tanzania, for example, do not consider that they have exclusive rights over the land on which they hunt. Any member of the group can hunt, gather, or draw water where he or she likes. The Hadza do not even restrict use of their land to members of their own society. Even though outsiders have steadily intruded on Hadza territory recently, such encroachment has not been protested.[2]

The allocation of natural resources that most closely approaches "ownership" among hunter-gatherers occurs in some societies in which the harvest of one fruit or nut tree, or of several trees, is allocated to one family by tradition. This was the custom among the people of the Andaman Islands in the Indian Ocean.[3] However, rather than being true ownership of a tree, this assignment of trees was probably only an extension of a division of labor by families. It would be a waste of time and effort (and proba-

[1] E. Adamson Hoebel, *The Law of Primitive Man* (New York: Atheneum, 1968), pp. 46–63. Originally published 1954.

[2] James Woodburn, "An Introduction to Hadza Ecology," in *Man the Hunter*, ed. Richard B. Lee and Irven DeVore, (Chicago: Aldine, 1968), pp. 49–55.

[3] A. R. Radcliffe-Brown, *The Andaman Islanders* (Cambridge: Cambridge University Press, 1922), p. 41.

bly not productive enough per capita) if the whole band gathered from a single tree. Therefore, the traditional right to harvest awarded to a family or an individual may have been favored for reasons of efficient work organization. The family was still obligated to share the fruits or nuts so acquired with families who collected little or nothing.

The territory of one hunter-gatherer band is typically surrounded by territories of other bands. In most hunter-gatherer societies, the communal ownership of land is extended to provide some degree of access to members of neighboring bands. Among the !Kung Bushmen, the right of "hot pursuit" is honored, and one band is allowed to follow its game into the territory of its neighbors. The sharing of water is perhaps most characteristic of the Bushmen's attitude toward the allocation of natural resources. Members of one band, as a matter of courtesy, must ask permission of a neighboring band to use a water hole in the other's territory. As a matter of tradition, the headman of a Bushmen band cannot refuse. The reasoning is quite sound: if one band helps it neighbors when they most need help, then that band can ask for help when it most needs assistance.

Among the Anbara, an Australian aborigine community of about 135 persons, groups of kinsmen or clans had nonexclusive claims on particular sections of land. Six clans, each with its own land area, formed the community. For example, one of the clans, the Mararagidf, felt a close tie to a certain land area, often claiming that its members had been born there and wished to die there. The Mararagidf hunted and built traps on their clan territory, but they could hunt in the whole Anbara area as well. And the other clans could enter Mararagidf territory when they wished. In other words, the six clans camped together and roamed the entire territory at will, but each clan had an emotional tie to its own land.[4]

Like hunter-gatherers, most horticulturalists seem to require a flexible system for allocating land resources. This may be because rapid depletion of the soil necessitates either letting some of the land lie fallow for several seasons or abandoning old garden plots completely and moving on to new areas after a few years. Therefore, horticulturalists generally require more land than they can actually use at any one time. There is no point in their claiming permanent access to land that, given the level of their technology, is not permanently usable.

In horticultural societies, individuals may be allocated land to use, but they do not generally own the land in our sense of "ownership." For instance, a man on Truk, a group of islands in the Pacific, may plant a breadfruit tree, which matures in 15 years and produces for 150 years. The tree is considered to be his, yet he cannot sell it. He may assign the use of it to his children, but if he does not, the tree reverts to other members of his kin group upon his death. Similarly, if he clears a plot of land for his own use, he maintains the right to use that garden as long as he works it. But the plot is under the same kind of agreement as the tree. If he stops working the land, someone else in his kin group may ask to take it over.[5]

The Siane of New Guinea have a system of clan ownership of farming land. The climate allows the land to be farmed all year, but the method of farming exhausts the land after about three harvests. The plot is then allowed to lie fallow for fifteen years, so that a village needs at least ten times as much land as it uses each year. Every male clan member has a right to use plots of land, and he has the assurance that he cannot be driven from the land. The clan, on the other hand, is assured that, since each man is a clan member, no one person has the power to dispose of the jointly held wealth of the kin group.

The territory of pastoral nomads far exceeds that of most horticultural societies. Since their wealth depends upon two elements—

[4]L. R. Hiatt, "Ownership and Use of Land among the Australian Aborigines," in *Man the Hunter,* ed. Richard B. Lee and Irven DeVore, pp. 99–102.

[5]Ward H. Goodenough, *Property, Kin, and Community on Truk* (New Haven: Yale University Publications in Anthropology, 1951).

mobile herds and fixed pasturage and water—pastoralists must combine the adaptive potential of both the hunter-gatherers and the horticulturalists. Like the hunter-gatherers they must know the potential of their territory, which can extend as much as 1,000 miles, so that they are assured a constant supply of grass and water. And like the horticulturalists, after their herds graze an area clean they must move on and let that land lie fallow until the grass renews itself. Also like the horticulturalists, they depend for their subsistence upon human manipulation of a natural resource—animals, as opposed to the horticulturalists' land.

Grazing lands are communally held among many pastoral nomads. Although the chief may be designated "owner" of the land, his title is merely a symbolic statement that the territory is the domain of the nomadic community. Such a community may have to make two types of agreements with outside groups concerning the allocation of natural resources. One type is an agreement with another nomadic group about the order in which the land they both graze is to be used. The other is an agreement with settled agriculturalists about rights to graze unused fields or even to clear a harvested field of leftover stubble.

Although grazing land tends to be communally held, it is customary among pastoralists for animals to be owned by individuals.[6] Barth has argued that if animals were not so owned, the whole pastoral group might be in trouble because the members might be tempted to eat up their productive capital—their animals—in bad times. With individual ownership of animals, a family whose herd drops below the minimum number of animals necessary for the family's survival must drop out of nomadic life, at least temporarily, to work for wages in sedentary agricultural communities. But in so doing, such a family does not jeopardize other pastoral families. On the other hand, if the fortunate were to share their herds with the

Pastoral nomads, like these Turkish herdsmen, travel over large areas of land that generally are considered the communal territory of the group. Individual families, however, usually own their animals. (Courtesy of the American Museum of Natural History.)

unfortunate, all would be apt to approach the edge of bankruptcy. Thus, Barth argues that individual ownership is adaptive for a pastoral way of life.[7] However, Dowling has questioned this interpretation. As he points out, pastoral nomads are not the only ones who have to save some of their "crop" for future production. Horticulturalists, too, must save their crop (in the form of seeds or tubers) for future planting. But horticulturalists generally lack private ownership of productive resources, and so the necessity to save for future production cannot explain private ownership of animals in many pastoral societies. Dowling suggests that private ownership of animals will develop only in those pastoral societies that are very dependent upon selling their products to nonpastoralists.[8] Thus, it may be the opportunity to sell their labor as well as their products that explains both the

[6]John H. Dowling, "Property Relations and Productive Strategies in Pastoral Societies," *American Ethnologist* 2 (1975): 422.

[7]Fredrik Barth, *Nomads of South Persia* (Boston: Little, Brown, 1968), p. 124.
[8]Dowling, "Property Relations and Productive Strategies in Pastoral Societies," pp. 419–26.

possibility of dropping out of nomadic life and the private ownership of animals among some pastoralists.

The continuing use of one area of land season after season is one of the factors upon which permanent possession of land is based. Under the Homestead Act of 1862, if a man cleared a 160-acre piece of land and farmed it for five years, the federal government would consider him the owner of the land. This practice was clearly similar to the custom in some societies by which the chief was obligated to assign a parcel of land to anyone who wished to farm it for his own needs. The difference is that once the American homesteader had become the owner of his land, he could dispose of it as he wished, by selling or giving it away.

This concept of private ownership of land resources—including the right to use the resources and the right to sell or otherwise dispose of them—is common among intensive agriculturalists, for whom land is relatively scarce. Once private ownership of land has become established, then the property owners use their economic, and hence political, power to pass laws which favor property owners. Thus, in the early years of the United States, only property owners could vote.

The nearly absolute control which a property owner apparently has over the use and disposal of property is offset by the real absoluteness with which the owner can lose his or her property. This happens, generally, through government action as the penalty for the owner's inability to pay taxes or to satisfy a debt. Or it could occur because the government decides to take the property for some public purpose (usually with some compensation to the owner) under the right of eminent domain. Thus, a family which has farmed its land for 100 years can lose it irrevocably in one year. This often happens as a result of events over which the family has no control—a national economic depression, a drought which causes a bad crop year, a change in climate such as the one which created the Oklahoma dust bowl, or a period of economic stagnation such as followed the Civil War.

TOOLS AND TECHNOLOGY

Humans are not the only tool users; some of the apes also devise and use tools. But all human societies have methods of toolmaking and traditions of tool use which are allocated within the society and are passed on to the next generation. A society is restricted in its tool use by its way of living. Hunter-gatherers and pastoralists must limit their tools and artifacts to what they can comfortably carry with them.

The tools most needed by hunter-gatherers are weapons for the hunt, digging sticks, and receptacles for gathering and carrying. Most hunters know the bow and arrow; Andaman Islanders used them exclusively for hunting game and large fish. Australian aborigines developed two types of boomerangs: a heavy one for a straight throw in killing game; and a light, returning one for playing games or for scaring birds into nets which had been strung between trees. The Semang of Malaya used poisoned darts and blowguns. The Congo Pygmies still trap elephants and buffalo in deadfalls and nets. Of all hunter-gatherers, the Eskimos probably have the most sophisticated weapons, including harpoons, compound bows, and ivory fishhooks. Yet the Eskimos also have relatively fixed settlements with more available storage space and use dog teams and sledges for transportation.[9]

Among hunter-gatherers, tools are generally considered to belong to the person who made them. But there is no way of gaining superiority over others through possession of tools, because whatever resources for toolmaking are available to one are available to all. In addition, the custom of sharing applies to tools as well as to food. If a member of the band asks to borrow a spear that another person is not using, that person is obligated to lend it. However, the spear is considered the personal property of the man who made it, and the man who kills an animal with it may be obligated to share the kill with the owner of the spear.

[9] Elman R. Service, *The Hunters* (Englewood Cliffs, N.J.: Prentice-Hall, 1966), pp. 10–11.

Among the Andaman Islanders, whatever a person made was individual personal property. Even if others had helped in making the object, it was still considered the individual's property. However, gift giving was so common among the islanders that possessions changed hands frequently.[10]

The !Kung Bushmen have few possessions—only bows and arrows, spears, digging sticks, receptacles for carrying, and so on. According to Elizabeth M. Thomas:

A Bushman will go to any lengths to avoid making other Bushmen jealous of him, and for this reason the few possessions that Bushmen have are constantly circling among the members of their groups. No one cares to keep a particularly good knife too long, even though he may want it desperately, because he will become the object of envy.[11]

Pastoralists, like hunter-gatherers, are somewhat limited in their possessions, for they too are nomadic. But unlike most hunter-gatherers, pastoralists can use their animals to carry some possessions. Each family owns its own tools, clothes, and perhaps a tent, as well as its own livestock. The livestock are the source of other needed articles, for the pastoralists often trade their herd products for the products of the townspeople. "Of the totality of objects contained in a nomad's home—be he a Kurd of West Iran or a Gujar in North Pakistan—only a small fraction have been produced by himself or his fellow nomads; and of the food such a family consumes in a year only a small fraction is pastoral products."[12]

Horticulturalists, on the other hand, are generally more self-sufficient than pastoralists. The knife for slashing and the hoe or stick for digging are their principal farming tools. What a person makes is considered his or her own; yet everyone is often obligated to lend tools to others. In Truk society, a man has first use of

his canoe and of his farming implements. Yet if a close kinsman needs the canoe and finds it unused, he may take it without permission. A distant kinsman or neighbor must ask permission if he wishes to borrow any tools, but the owner may not refuse him. If he were to refuse, the owner would risk being scorned and being refused if he were to need tools later.

The more complicated the construction of a tool, the more likely that tool is to be made by a specialist—which means that it must be acquired by trade or by money purchase. If horticulturalists wish to acquire metal hoes, they generally must produce a cash crop with which to purchase them. Any kinsman who helps in the production of the cash crop will be considered part owner of the tool that is purchased and will have a right to its use, as well as a say in its disposal.

However, in industrialized societies, when the tool in question is a diesel-powered combine which requires a large amount of capital for its purchase and upkeep, the person who has supplied the capital is likely to regard the machine as individual private property and to regulate its use and its disposal as he or she desires. A farmer may not have the capital to purchase the machine he needs, so he may have to borrow from a bank. He must then use the machine to produce enough surplus to pay for its cost and upkeep, as well as, ideally, for its replacement. He will therefore use the machine himself or allow family members or hired farmhands to use it on his crops; or he may rent it to neighboring farmers during slack periods to obtain a maximum return on his investment. He may even allow his tenants to use the machine for their own crops, but only in return for a part of their harvest.

In some intensive agricultural societies, several small farmers may form a machine cooperative in order to purchase together what they could not afford singly. In that case, each has the right to use the machine on his own land, but he may not rent, sell, or loan it without the permission of the others.

Some capital equipment is too expensive for even a cooperative to afford. A government

[10] Radcliffe-Brown, *The Andaman Islanders,* p. 41.
[11] Elizabeth Marshall Thomas, *The Harmless People* (New York: Alfred A. Knopf, 1959), p. 22.
[12] Fredrik Barth, "Nomadism in the Mountain and Plateau Areas of South West Asia," in *The Problems of the Arid Zone* (Paris: UNESCO, 1960), p. 345.

may then allocate tax money collected from all to build facilities to benefit some productive group: airports to benefit airlines, roads to benefit trucking firms, dams to benefit power companies. Such resources are collectively owned by the whole society, but they are subject to strict rules for their use, including additional payment. Other man-made productive resources in industrial societies, such as factories, may be jointly owned by shareholders who purchase a portion of a corporation's assets in return for a proportionate share of its earnings.

The Organization of Work

The organization of work varies from society to society. The type of society and its methods of food getting are so interrelated that separating the two is difficult. Yet, work organization can be seen to depend upon two distinct factors: the type of tools available and the type of work to be done.

The tools available obviously affect the way work is organized: a 10-acre field can be plowed by one person on a tractor, or by several people with oxen and plows, or by many people with hoes. The type of work is equally important: one lone Eskimo may wait for hours on the ice beside a seal's breathing hole to catch the seal, but the cooperation of many men is needed to catch a whale. One person may build some kitchen steps, but it takes many people to build a skyscraper.

THE DIVISION OF LABOR

Division of labor by sex is a universal economic characteristic. Early in life, children learn the tasks that will later be assigned to them as adults. This is true even in our own society, where children generally do few chores. There are certain tasks which in almost all societies are assigned to men, and others which are assigned to women. In most societies hunting is men's work, as are herding large animals, clearing fields, stonework, and metalworking. In addition to child care (which in almost all societies involves breast-feeding), women usually are responsible for fetching water, cooking, laundering, and gathering wild plants.[13]

These differences in division of labor by sex may be partially due to physical differences between men and women. For example, it has been argued that the assignment of tasks like hunting to men may be based upon their greater physical strength and their superior capacity to mobilize such strength in brief bursts of energy.[14] However, since women have sometimes been observed to engage in very heavy physical labor, there is some question as to whether the usually greater physical strength of males is not acquired through training for different roles, rather than the other way around.

Perhaps more important than differences in strength is the effect of reproductive and child-care activities on the division of labor. It has been suggested that women's tasks tend to be those which are more compatible with child care. These are tasks that do not take women far away from home for long periods of time, which do not place children in potential danger if they are taken along, and which can be stopped and resumed if child-care duties interrupt.[15] Tasks such as hunting and herding do not meet these requirements. Men, on the other hand, because they are not generally responsible for child care, can undertake more dangerous work that takes them farther afield. If this interpretation is correct, division of labor by sex should begin to lessen when women can be freed of the duties of child care by institutions such as day-care centers, which are beginning to appear in industrial societies like our own.

Age is also a universal basis for division of labor. Clearly, children cannot perform as much work as adults; usually, however, they are required to assist in the tasks assigned to adults. In many societies, boys and girls contribute a great deal more in labor than do children in our own society. For example, they help in such

---

[13] George Peter Murdock and Caterina Provost, "Factors in the Division of Labor by Sex: A Cross-Cultural Analysis," *Ethnology* 12 (1973): 207.

[14] Ibid., p. 211.

[15] Judith K. Brown, "A Note on the Division of Labor by Sex," *American Anthropologist* 72 (1970): 1074.

Kinship ties are an important basis for work organization in nonindustrial societies. Here, a Somali kin group draws water at its well for its herd. (Courtesy of United Nations.)

chores as child care, weeding, and harvesting.

In some societies, work groups are formally organized on the basis of age. Among the Nyakyusa of southeastern Africa, for example, cattle are the principal form of wealth; boys age six to eleven herd the cattle for their parents' village. The boys join together in herding groups to tend the cattle of their fathers and of any neighboring families which do not have a son of herding age.[16]

Kinship ties are an important basis for work organization, particularly in nonindustrial societies. For example, among the horticultural Kapauku of western New Guinea, the male members of a village are a kin group, and all work together to build drainage ditches, large fences, and bridges.[17] Among the pastoral Somali of eastern Africa, a herding group may consist of brothers, their sons, and all wives, unmarried daughters, and small children. Those members of the tribe who decided to settle on farmland apportioned within the British Protectorate did so as larger kin groups, not as individuals. As a result, the former cooperating pastoral kin groups became equally cooperative farming villages, depending upon kin affiliation for land and other forms of economic help.[18]

[16]Monica Wilson, *Good Company: A Study of Nyakyusa Age Villages* (Boston: Beacon Press, 1963). Originally published 1951.
[17]Leopold Pospisil, *The Kapauku Papuans of West New Guinea* (New York: Holt, Rinehart and Winston, 1963), p. 43.
[18]I. M. Lewis, *A Pastoral Democracy* (New York: Oxford University Press, 1961), pp. 107–9.

In industrial societies, work groups are not usually kin groups. This is because industrial work usually requires large groups of people to perform the necessary tasks. And so the large work parties required in factories, businesses, government, construction, and other areas of employment are not likely to be composed of people related to each other.

SPECIALIZATION OF LABOR

In societies with relatively simple technologies, there is little specialization of labor. But as its technology becomes more complex and a society is able to produce large quantities of food, more and more of its people are freed from subsistence work to specialize in some other tasks, as canoe builders, weavers, priests, potters, artists, and the like.

A day in the life of a hunter-gatherer, for instance, would be quite varied, involving a large number of skills. A man must know how to make his own traps and weapons as well as how to use them to catch a variety of animals. A woman must be an amateur biologist, able to identify and gather edible food. Both know how to cook, dance, and sing.

In contrast to hunter-gatherers, horticultural societies may have some part-time specialists. Some people may devote special effort to perfecting a particular skill or craft—pottery making, weaving, house building, doctoring—

With the development of intensive agriculture, full-time specialists, such as potters and weavers, begin to appear. Specialization reaches a peak in industrial societies. Here, a woman specializes in making coffee pots in a Japanese ceramics factory. (Henri Cartier-Bresson, Magnum Photos.)

and in return for their products or services are given food or other gifts. Among some horticultural groups, the entire village may partially specialize in making a particular product which can then be traded to neighboring people.

With the development of intensive agriculture, full-time specialists—potters, weavers, blacksmiths—begin to appear. The trend toward greater specialization reaches its peak in industrialized societies, where workers develop skills in one small area of the economic system. The meaninglessness of much of industrialized work was depicted by Charlie Chaplin in the film *Modern Times:* when he left the factory after repeatedly tightening the same kind of bolt all day long, he could not stop his arms from moving as if they were still tightening bolts.

We might expect that specialization of labor would produce more leisure time. After all, presumably specialists are more efficient at their work and can accomplish it more quickly. But somewhat surprisingly, people with simple technologies and less specialization seem to have more leisure.[19] Why might this be so?

[19] Service, *The Hunters*, pp. 12–13.

Perhaps it is because peoples with simpler technologies are more limited by the potentialities of the natural environment, whereas people with complex technologies are less limited. For example, it would not be beneficial for hunter-gatherers to kill more animals or collect more wild plants than they could consume within a given time. First of all, they could not keep or preserve them; and second, they might reduce the next season's supply of food by overhunting or overgathering this season. With complex technology, however, we can apparently produce more and more (although we are now beginning to realize that there are limits to production even in industrialized societies). The possibility of improving their economic position by producing more and storing the surplus (in freezers or as money in the bank) may encourage people to work harder. Or the desire to maintain their economic position in the face of inflation or other pressures may require people to work harder. Consequently, leisure time probably decreases with the development of advanced technology.

FORCED LABOR

The work we have discussed thus far has all been voluntary labor—voluntary in the sense that no formal organization exists within the society to compel people to work and to punish them for not working. Social training and social pressure are generally powerful enough to persuade an individual to perform some useful task. In both hunter-gatherer and horticultural societies, those individuals who can stand being the butt of jokes about laziness still will be fed. At most, they will be ignored by the other members of the group. There is no reason to punish them and no way to coerce them to do the work that is expected of them.

More complex societies have ways of forcing people to work for the authorities—whether those authorities be kings or presidents. An indirect form of forced labor is taxation. If a person's tax is 37 percent of his or her income (the average percentage of total earnings which is taken by the various levels of government in the United States) then that person is working about 4 months out of a year for the government. If a person decides not to pay the tax, the money will be forcibly taken or the person can be put in prison.

Money is the customary form of tax payment in a commercial society. In a politically complex but nonmonetary society, persons may pay their taxes in other ways—either by performing a certain number of hours of labor or by giving a certain percentage of what they produce. The *corvée*, a system of required labor, existed in the Inca empire in the central Andes prior to the Spanish conquest. Each commoner was assigned three plots of land to work: a temple plot, a state plot, and his own plot. The enormous stores of food that went into the state warehouses were used to supply the nobles, the army, the artisans, and all other state employees. If labor became overabundant, the people were still kept occupied; it is said that one ruler had a hill moved to keep some laborers busy. In addition to subsistence work for the state, each Inca commoner was liable to taxation by man-hours under a draft system. Men were subject to military service, to duty as personal servants for the nobility, and to all public service work.[20]

Another example of forced labor is tenant farming. In return for a house or shack and some acreage to farm, the tenant farmer owes a portion of his harvest to the owner. By manipulating the price for the tenant's crop, by making cash loans to the tenant at high interest rates, and by providing a store at which the tenant must buy his staple goods at exorbitant prices, the owner generally manages to keep the tenant working his farm as economically forced labor. If the tenant farmer tries to leave without paying these debts engineered by the owner, the owner can use the power of the state to make him pay. On the other hand, if the tenant farmer becomes obsolete through the introduction of mechanized farming, the owner can use the power of the state to make him leave.

The draft is a form of corvée in that a cer-

tain period of service is required, and failure to serve can be punished by a prison term or voluntary exile. To defend their territory, emperors of China had the Great Wall built along the northern borders of the empire. The wall extends over 1,500 miles, and thousands of laborers were drafted to work on it.

Slavery is perhaps the most extreme form of forced work. Slavery is most likely to be found in societies where land is plentiful and labor is in short supply.[21]

Distribution of Goods and Services

Goods and service are distributed in all societies by systems which, however varied, can be classified under three general types: reciprocity, redistribution, and monetary or commercial exchange.[22] The three systems often coexist in one society. For instance, when our commercial exchange system became shaky during the depression of the 1930s, the Barter Theater in Virginia operated by exchanging an evening's entertainment for a bag of potatoes or a slice of ham. Within a single society, however, one system of distribution usually predominates. That type of system seems to be associated with the society's food-getting technology and, more specifically, its level of productivity.

RECIPROCITY

The term *reciprocity* refers to giving and taking without the use of money; it ranges from pure gift giving to equalized barter and to self-interested cheating. In other words, reciprocity may take three forms: generalized reciprocity, balanced reciprocity, and negative reciprocity.[23]

[20]Julian H. Steward and Louis C. Faron, *Native Peoples of South America* (New York: McGraw-Hill, 1959), pp. 122–25.

[21]Michael Harner, "Scarcity, the Factors of Production, and Social Evolution," in *Population, Ecology, and Social Evolution*, ed. Steven Polgar (The Hague: Mouton, 1975), pp. 123–38.

[22]Karl Polanyi, "The Economy of Instituted Process," in *Trade and Market in the Early Empires*, ed. Karl Polanyi, Harry W. Pearson, and Conrad M. Arensberg (New York: Free Press, 1957), pp. 243–70.

[23]Marshall D. Sahlins, "On the Sociology of Primitive Exchange," in *The Relevance of Models for Social Anthropology*, ed. Michael Banton (London: Tavistock, 1965), pp. 145–49.

Generalized reciprocity is gift giving without any immediate return or conscious thought of return. A distribution system built around generalized reciprocity is like the indirect interdependencies in the world of nature. Each thing in nature provides something without expecting an equal or immediate return. Berry bushes manufacture prized food for birds; birds help propagate more berry bushes by depositing undigested seeds throughout the area. In the end, all the giving evens out.

Generalized reciprocity sustains the family in all societies. Parents give food to children because they want to, not because the child may reciprocate years later. Of course, usually someone—often the child who has grown up—feeds the parents when they are too old to make their own living. In this sense, all societies have some kind of generalized reciprocity. But some societies depend almost entirely upon it to distribute goods and services.

The !Kung Bushmen call "far-hearted" anyone who does not give gifts or who does not eventually reciprocate when given gifts. The practice of giving is not evidence of altruism but it is entrenched in the Bushmen's awareness of social interdependence. The !Kung remember quite well the gift-giving activities of everyone else in their own and other bands, and they express their approval or disapproval openly. The necessity to reduce tensions, to avoid jealousy and anger, and to keep all social relations peaceful, not only within their own band but between all !Kung bands, creates continuing cross-currents of obligation to friendship. These are maintained, renewed, or established through the generalized reciprocity of gift giving. The following two examples suggest how generalized reciprocity evens things out among the !Kung.

Lorna Marshall recounts how the Bushmen divided an eland which was brought to a site where five bands and several visitors were camping together, over 100 people in all. The owner of the arrow which had first penetrated the eland was, by custom, the owner of the meat. He first distributed the forequarters to the

Reciprocity is the predominant mode of economic distribution in most hunter-gatherer societies. Here, a !Kung Bushman is drying strips of meat on a branch before distributing them to others in his band. (Courtesy of Irven DeVore/Anthro-Photo.)

other two hunters who had aided in the kill. After that, the distribution was dependent generally upon kinship, as each hunter shared with his wives' parents, his wives, children, parents, and siblings, and they in turn shared with their kinsmen. Sixty-three gifts of raw meat were recorded, after which further sharing of raw and cooked meat was begun. Since each large animal is distributed in the same way, the sharing of such food by generalized reciprocity over the years results in evening out what people receive. Kinship seems to determine who participates in the sharing of food; maintaining peaceful relations and friendship are the motivations behind other gift giving.

Among the !Kung, the possession of something valuable is undesirable for it may lead to jealousy or even conflict. For example, when Marshall left the band which had sponsored her in 1951, she gave each woman in the band a present of enough cowrie shells to make a necklace—one large shell and 20 small ones. When she returned in 1952, there were no cowrie-shell necklaces and hardly a single shell among the people in the band; but the individual cowrie shells appeared by ones and twos in the ornaments of the people of neighboring bands.[24]

Balanced reciprocity is more explicit and short-term in its expectations of return than generalized reciprocity. In fact, it involves a straightforward immediate or limited-time trade. In balanced reciprocity, the exchange is usually motivated by desire or need for certain objects.

The Bushmen, for instance, trade with the Tswana Bantu: a gemsbok hide for a pile of tobacco; five strings of beads made from ostrich eggshells for a spear; three small skins for a good-sized knife.[25] The Semang, jungle hunter-gatherers of the Malay Peninsula, engage in "silent trade" with the settled Malay agriculturalists. In the belief that it is better not to establish personal contact with foreigners, the Semang leave their surplus jungle products at an agreed-upon place near a village and return later to take whatever has been left by the villagers—usually salt, beads, or a metal tool.[26]

Through trade, a society can dispose of goods which it has in abundance and obtain goods which are scarce in its own territory. Since trade transactions between neighboring peoples may be crucial to their survival, it is important for them to maintain good relations. Various societies have developed methods of peaceful exchange without the use of money. The Trobriand Islanders have worked out an elaborate scheme for trading food and other items with the people of neighboring islands. Such trade is essential, for some of the islands are small and rocky and cannot produce enough food to sustain their inhabitants; instead, their people specialize in building canoes, making pottery, and other crafts. Other islands produce far more yams, taro, and pigs than they need, yet the trade of such necessary items is carefully hidden beneath the panoply of the *Kula* ring, a ceremonial exchange of valued shell ornaments.

Two kinds of ornaments are involved in the ceremony of exchanges: white shell armbands (*mwali*) which travel around the circle of islands in a counterclockwise direction, and red shell necklaces (*soulava*) which travel in a clockwise direction. The possession of one or more of these ornaments allows a man to organize an expedition to one of his trading partners on another island. The high point of an expedition is the ceremonial giving of the valued *Kula* ornaments. Each member of the expedition receives a shell ornament from his trading partner and then remains on the island for two or three days as the guest of his partner. During the visitation time the real trading goes on. Some of the exchange takes the form of gift giving between trading partners; there is also barter between expedition members and others on the island. By the time the visitors leave, they have accomplished a year's trading without seeming to do so. (A somewhat similar occurrence was the American and Chinese ceremonial exchange of musk oxen and pandas during the Nixon administration. These animals are valued because they are rare, yet they are practically useless. Immediately after the exchanging of the gifts, the real trading of goods began between the two countries.)

Trading within the *Kula* ring is based upon mutual trust. Trade partnerships are lifelong and ensure hospitality and mutual aid as well as trade. An old chief may have as many as 100 trading partners in each direction. Maintaining the *Kula* ring achieves several advantages for the Trobriand Islanders. First, goods are traded with ease and enjoyment; the expedition takes on the

[24] Lorna Marshall, "Sharing, Talking and Giving: Relief of Social Tensions among !Kung Bushmen," *Africa* 31 (1961): 239–41.
[25] Ibid., p. 242.
[26] Service, *The Hunters*, p. 107.

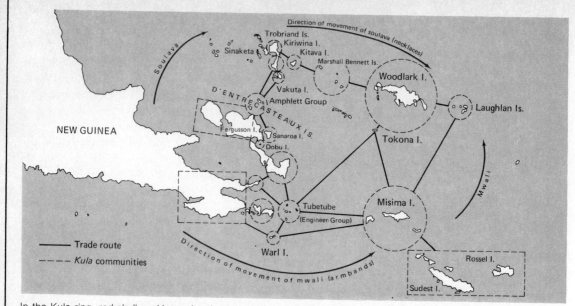

In the Kula ring, red shell necklaces (*soulava*) travel in a clockwise direction, while white shell armbands (*mwali*) travel in a counterclockwise direction. The solid lines show the overseas trade routes. The dotted circles identify the Kula communities, and the dotted squares show the areas indirectly affected by the Kula.

flavor of adventure rather than business. Second, the traditions of the islands remain alive. Much myth, romance, ritual, and history are linked to the circulating ornaments, especially the larger, finer pieces, which are well known and recognized as heirlooms. Third, the establishment of trade partnerships may have reduced social tensions and hostilities among the various island communities. Fourth, the *Kula* ring permits wide ownership of valuables. Instead of possessing one valued object permanently, a man is able, within his lifetime, to possess many valued things, each for a year or so. Each object, when it is received, arouses enthusiasm in a way that one lifelong possession could not do.[27]

Balanced reciprocity may involve labor as well as goods. The work parties of the Kpelle are an example of balanced reciprocity, since equal labor is expected in return and the date of the return work is generally fixed to coincide with the needs of the planting and harvest times. A cooperative work party, or *kuu*, may number anywhere from six to forty persons, all of whom generally are related somehow to the leader or are friends of one of the members. Each farmer rewards the work party's hard day's labor by providing a feast and sometimes rhythmic music to work by. Thus, in reality, two kinds of reciprocity coexist: one is the rather unequal return of food given for a day's work, which will even out eventually; the other is the work party's equalized labor on the farm of each of its members, which is balanced within a short term.[28]

Sometimes the line between generalized and balanced reciprocity is not so clear. Consider our gift giving at Christmastime. Although such gift giving appears to take the form of generalized reciprocity, there may be strong expectations of balance. Two friends or relatives may try to exchange presents of fairly equal

[27]Bronislaw Malinowski, "*Kula*: The Circulating Exchange of Valuables in the Archipelagoes of Eastern New Guinea," *Man* 51, no. 2 (1920): 97–105.

[28]James L. Gibbs, Jr., "The Kpelle of Liberia," in *Peoples of Africa*, ed. James L. Gibbs, Jr. (New York: Holt, Rinehart and Winston, 1965), p. 223.

value, based on calculations of what last year's gift cost. If a person receives a $1 present when he gave a $25 present, he will be hurt, perhaps angry. On the other hand, if he receives a $500 present when he gave a $25 present, he may well be dismayed.

Negative reciprocity is an attempt to take advantage of another for one's own self-interest. For instance, a !Kung Bushman told Lorna Marshall that he had been forced by someone from another tribe to trade the shirt and pants she had given him as a parting gift for a small enamel pan and a little cup.[29] Self-interest extends beyond uneven trade to raiding and other forms of theft.

Most hunting-gathering and horticultural societies depend upon some form of reciprocity for the distribution of their goods and labor. According to Sahlins, whether the reciprocity is generalized, balanced, or negative depends largely upon the kinship distance between persons. Generalized reciprocity is the rule for family members and close kinsmen. Balanced reciprocity is generally practiced among equals who are not closely related. A tribesman who would consider it demeaning to trade with his own family will trade with neighboring tribes. The desire to satisfy both parties represents the desire to maintain peaceful relations between two groups. Negative reciprocity is practiced against strangers and enemies.[30]

Reciprocal Exchange as a Leveling Device Reciprocal gift giving may do more than equalize the distribution of goods within a community, as in the Bushmen's sharing. It may also tend to equalize the distribution of goods between communities.

Many Melanesian societies have the custom of holding pig feasts in which 50, 100, or even 2,000 pigs are slaughtered. Vayda, Leeds, and Smith have suggested that these enormous pig feasts, though apparently wasteful, are just one of the outcomes of a complex of cultural prac-

tices that are highly advantageous. It is now generally agreed that a society cannot maintain its population at a level which can be supported by the food available during years of bumper crops, or even by the average expected production. It must limit its population to the number that can be supported by the food supply of its years of minimum production, even if those years occur only once in a generation. In addition, the society must overplant each year in anticipation of a drought which would sharply limit production. Yet this overplanting results in overproduction during average and exceptionally good years. The Melanesians provide for just that contingency by overplanting yams and taro for their three harvests each year. Since these root crops do not keep well over long periods, the surplus is fed to pigs, which become, in effect, food-storing repositories. Pigs are then available for needed food during lean years, as well as for the usual feasts held every year.

However, several years of good crops may cause the pig population to increase to menacing proportions—menacing, that is, to the yam and taro patches. When this happens, a village may hold a gigantic feast which results in sharp curtailment of the pig population and keeps the fields from being overrun by pigs. The pig feasts, then, serve to equalize the food consumption, and especially the protein consumption, of all the villages that participate in the feasts over the years. They also ensure an adequate supply of food for lean years as well as for good years.[31] Thus, the custom of pig feasts may be a way for villages to "bank" surplus food by storing up "social credit" with other villages, which will return that credit in subsequent feasts.

In some of the Melanesian societies, pig feasts fostered an element of competition among the men who gave them. "Big men"

---

[29]Marshall, "Sharing, Talking and Giving," p. 242.
[30]Sahlins, "On the Sociology of Primitive Exchange," pp. 149–58.

[31]Andrew P. Vayda, Anthony Leeds, and David B. Smith, "The Place of Pigs in Melanesian Subsistence," in *Proceedings of the 1961 Annual Spring Meeting of the American Ethnological Society, Patterns of Land Utilization and Other Papers,* ed. Viola E. Garfield, pp. 69–74.

Among the northwest Pacific coast Indians the potlatch served as a means of both disposing of surplus food and leveling wealth. Here, Indian women of British Columbia display the objects to be given away at a potlatch. (Courtesy of the American Museum of Natural History.)

might try to bolster their status and prestige by the size of their feasts. But competition was not enhanced by keeping wealth—it was enhanced by giving it away. A similar situation existed among many American Indian groups of the northwest Pacific coast, where a chief might attempt to enhance his status by holding a *potlatch*. At a potlatch, a chief and his group would give away blankets, pieces of copper, canoes, large quantities of food, and other items to their guests. The host chief and his group would later be invited to be guests at other potlatches. The competitive element in the potlatch appears to have intensified after contact with whites. Because of the fur trade, the number of trade goods increased and so more items could be given away. But a possibly more important factor was that as a result of population decline among the Indians caused by diseases (such as smallpox) introduced by European

traders, some chiefs had no direct heirs to inherit their titles. Distant relatives might compete for the vacant positions, with each competitor attempting to give away more than the others.[32] Chiefs may also have attempted to attract men to their half-empty villages by their spectacular giveaways.[33] Although the potlatch system seemed wasteful in the sense that goods were often destroyed in the competition, the system probably also served to equalize the distribution of goods among the competing groups.

The Pomo Indians of central California had another way to "bank" credit for previous generosity. A village that had an overabundance of

[32]Philip Drucker, "The Potlatch," in *Tribal and Peasant Economies*, ed. George Dalton (Garden City, N.Y.: Natural History Press, 1967), pp. 481–93.

[33]Marvin Harris, *Cows, Pigs, Wars and Witches* (New York: Vintage, 1975), p. 120.

fish or acorns might invite another village to a feast. In return for surplus fish or acorns, the guests would give the host village a certain number of beads. Before beginning the journey to the feast, the chief of the guest village would obtain from each family as many strings of beads as possible. Following a few days of feasting at the host village, the chief would trade the beads for the supply of surplus fish or acorns. Each member of the visiting village would be given an equal share of the food, regardless of how many beads had been contributed. But the members of a village would not be invited to a feast unless they brought beads to trade, and they could not obtain beads unless they had given food away themselves sometime in the past. Thus, giving away food and receiving beads in return served as a means of storing "social credit" for times of scarcity. At a later date, when food was scarce in the former host village, the villagers could use the beads they had acquired by giving in the past to obtain food from another village which had a surplus. The trade feasts, then, had the effect of equalizing the consumption of food, not only within a village but over a fairly widespread area.[34]

On one level of analysis, the Melanesian pig feasts, the northwest Pacific coast potlatches, and the Pomo trade feasts were all reciprocal exchanges between communities or villages. But these reciprocal exchanges were not just intercommunity versions of reciprocal gift giving between individuals. Because these feasts were organized by people who collected goods, they also involved another mode of distribution which anthropologists refer to as "redistribution."

REDISTRIBUTION

Redistribution is the accumulation of goods by a particular person, or in a particular place, for the purpose of subsequent distribution. Although redistribution is found in all societies, it becomes an important mechanism of distribution only in societies with political hierarchies—that is, with chiefs or other specialized officials and agencies. In all societies, there is some redistribution, at least within the family. Members of the family pool their labor or products or income for their common good. But beyond the family there is little or no redistribution in many societies. Particularly in hunter-gatherer and horticultural societies, which generally lack specialized political officials, the major mechanism of distribution is reciprocity, not redistribution. It seems, then, that redistribution on a territorial basis emerges when there is a political apparatus to coordinate centralized collection and distribution.

William Bartram has given an account of redistribution among eighteenth-century Creek Indians.

When all the grain is ripe, the whole town again assembles, and every man carries off the fruits of his labour, from the part of the town field first allotted to him, which he deposits in his own granary. . . . But previous to their carrying off their crops from the field, there is a large crib or granary, erected in the plantation, which is called the King's crib; and to this each family carries and deposits a certain quantity, according to his ability or inclination, or none at all if he so chooses, this in appearance seems a tribute or revenue to the mico (chief), but in fact is designed for another purpose, i.e., that of a public treasury, supplied by a few and voluntary contributions, and to which every citizen has the right of free and equal access, when his own private stores are consumed, to serve as a surplus to fly to for succour, to assist neighboring towns whose crops have failed, accommodate strangers, or travellers, afford provisions or supplies, when they go forth on hostile expeditions, and for all other exigencies of the state; and this treasure is at the disposal of the King or mico; which is surely a royal attribute to have an exclusive right and ability in a community to distribute comfort and blessings to the necessitous.[35]

[34] Andrew P. Vayda, "Pomo Trade Feasts," in *Tribal and Peasant Economies*, ed. George Dalton, pp. 494–500.

[35] William Bartram, *The Travels of William Bartram*, ed. Francis Harper (New Haven: Yale University Press, 1958), p. 326.

The account makes redistribution sound like an ideal arrangement in which the whole community benefits from its own efforts. But there are many other factors which influence the fairness with which the chief may redistribute the items. In many cases, it was the chief who apparently was the most "unfairly" treated. Identifying the chief in some American Indian villages became something of a joke among early ethnographers, who reported that they looked about for the poorest man. Apparently, the demands of redistribution were so great that the chief gave away everything he could accumulate and was left with prestige alone.

But in the African state of Bunyoro in western Uganda, for example, the king (called the *Mukama*) retained much of the wealth for himself and his close kinsmen. The Mukama had the authority to grant the use of land and all other natural resources to his subordinate chiefs, and they in turn granted it to the common people. In return, everyone was required to give to the Mukama large quantities of food, crafts, and even labor services. The Mukama then redistributed these goods and services, in theory at least, to all the people. The Mukama was praised with names that emphasized his generosity: *Agutamba* (he who relieves distress) and *Mwebingwa* (he to whom the people run for help). But it is clear that much of what the king redistributed did not find its way back to the common people who produced the bulk of the goods. Instead, the wealth was largely distributed according to rank within the state.[36]

Redistribution systems vary, then, from relative equality for all members of a community to gross inequality. At one extreme, illustrated by the Buin of Melanesia, "the chief is housed, dressed, and fed exactly like his bondsman."[37] Even though the chief owns most of the pigs, everyone shares equally in the consumption of the wealth. At the other extreme, a wealthy Indian landowner may live in luxury while the lower castes, dependent upon him for redistribution, live in poverty.

MONETARY OR COMMERCIAL EXCHANGE

The development of monetary or commercial exchange (commonly referred to as "market" exchange) probably occurs when food-getting technology becomes so efficient that supplies of food beyond the subsistence needs of the producers are regularly produced. Monetary exchange appears to be a more satisfactory means of distributing regular, large supplies of disposable food and other items than either feasts (usually generalized reciprocity) or barter (balanced reciprocity). With an increased food supply, more people are released from subsistence activities to specialize in various tasks—crafts, religion, warfare, and so on. No doubt the direct barter of food for services or of food for artifacts was employed fairly early (as it still is in relatively unproductive economies). But barter, as a personal transaction between two people or groups, succeeds most easily when the two parties know each other and have sufficient mutual trust to arrive at a fair exchange. Moreover, barter or balanced reciprocity can be relied upon as a method of distributing goods and services only if persons are always assured of finding someone who has an excess of what they want to obtain and a shortage of what they want to give away. Thus, it seems that monetary or commercial exchange (involving what we call "money"—for which nearly all goods and services can be exchanged) emerges when an economy develops to the point where (1) supplies of food regularly exceed the needs of those engaged in food production; (2) the population has become fairly dense (and includes many people who are strangers to one another); and (3) there are many craft and labor specialists who need (as do the food producers) what others have to offer.

Some anthropologists define money according to the functions and characteristics of

---

[36] John Beattie, *Bunyoro: An African Kingdom* (New York: Holt, Rinehart and Winston, 1960).

[37] R. C. Thurnwald, "Pigs and Currency in Buin: Observations about Primitive Standards of Value and Economics," *Oceania* 5 (1934): 125.

In societies with commercial exchange, goods and services are bought and sold in exchange for money. In this marketplace in Algeria, a wide range of products is traded. (Marc Riboud, Magnum Photos.)

the general-purpose money used in our own, and other, complex societies. According to this definition, money performs the basic functions of serving as a medium of exchange, a standard of value, and a store of wealth. Also, money is nonperishable, transportable, and divisible, so that transactions can be made when the goods being purchased differ in value. Other anthropologists, however, contend that an item used in exchange need not serve all the functions and have all the characteristics associated with money in an industrialized society in order to be considered "money."

In many societies, money is not an all-purpose medium of exchange. Many peoples, whose level of food production per capita is not sufficient to support a large population of nonproducers of food, often have what is called "special-purpose money." Special-purpose money

consists of objects of value for which only some goods and services can be exchanged on the spot or through a balanced reciprocity. In some parts of Melanesia, pigs are assigned value in terms of "shell money," which is lengths of shells strung together in units each roughly as long as the distance covered by a man's outstretched arms. According to its size, a pig will be assigned a value in tens of such units up to 100.[38] But the shell money cannot be exchanged for all the goods or services that a person might need. A northwest Pacific coast Indian could exchange food (but not most other goods and services) for a "gift of wealth," such as blankets. The gift was a "receipt" which entitled that person later to receive an equal amount of food (but little else).

[38] Ibid., p. 122.

George Dalton[39] has suggested that special- and general-purpose money can be distinguished in terms of the kind of preindustrial distribution system in which the money is used. There are marketless systems; systems with peripheral markets only; and those with money-dominated peasant markets.

In *marketless societies*, reciprocity (mostly generalized) and some redistribution are the major forms of distribution. Special-purpose money—goats, cattle, spears, shells—may sometimes be used, but only for particular purposes such as funeral or marriage gifts.

Peripheral market societies—the Trobriand Islands, for instance—generally follow the practices of marketless societies. But in addition, they have established marketplace sites at which some products are traded, either with special-purpose money or by barter (balanced reciprocity). These markets are called "peripheral" because they account for only a small part of a society's output of goods and because land and labor are never traded there. Two kinds of special-purpose shell money—Dap and Kö—are used by the Rossel Islanders. Dap shells are divided into 22 main values, Kö shells into 16 values. Generally, payments are made in some combination of Dap and Kö. Each value of Dap is designated for a special kind of purchase, such as a basket. The five most valued classes are used only on important occasions of generalized and balanced reciprocity. For instance, one shell is part of the bridewealth gift to the bride's kin; another is exchanged for pigs when a chief sponsors a pig feast. The special-purpose money is a symbol of the transaction, but the transaction is a socially determined one. For example, a man cannot "buy" a wife with the bridewealth Dap shell; the marriage is arranged by the two families, and the proper Dap shell merely formalizes the agreement.[40]

Societies with *money-dominated peasant markets* include land and labor among the goods and services which can be bought or sold. Peasants, however, although depending upon the markets to trade certain goods and services, usually produce by themselves most of what they need to live. In this sense, peasants differ from farmers in our own society and other industrialized societies who rely upon the marketplace to exchange their crops for almost all the goods and services they need.

Most people in peasant societies use general-purpose money as a means of assigning relative value to the goods and services they trade. General-purpose money is a universally accepted medium of exchange. It is used both for commercial transactions (buying and selling) and for noncommercial transactions (paying taxes or fines, personal gifts, contributions to religious and other charities). General-purpose money provides a way of "condensing" wealth. Paper money is easier to carry around than bushels of wheat; a checkbook is handier than a herd of sheep and goats. In addition, general-purpose money acts as a store of wealth.

The market town of Patzcuaro in Mexico illustrates the dependence of people on the market and the ability of the market to support large numbers of middlemen and other specialists. "Support," however, refers only to a minimum level, since the market area exists in an economy of what David Kaplan calls "shared poverty." The population of the market town is 12,000; that of the surrounding area is 14,000; and that of the lake district several miles around is 70,000. Most of the rural areas are agricultural, with growing populations but no increase in land. Some villages have concentrated on their own craft specialities, which reflect a traditional division of labor among several communities. The principal market is held once a week; smaller markets are held on three other days; and subsidiary markets are held in surrounding villages. About 75 percent of the market produce is food, about 20 percent is locally produced artifacts, and 5 percent is imported manufactured goods. The market is the only supplier of food for the townspeople and the only source of cash income for the rural inhab-

[39] George Dalton, "Primitive Money," *American Anthropologist* 67 (1965): 44–65.

[40] W. E. Armstrong, "Rossel Island Money: A Unique Monetary System," *Economic Journal* 34 (September 1924): 423–29.

itants. Prices are flexible and subject to bargaining. Labor is not included as a price factor, for all producers are households and labor is therefore "free." Since so many people are supported by the agricultural efforts of the rural inhabitants and there are few goods for export to bring new money into the area, the population is dependent upon the market as it is organized.[41]

Peasant communities often retain leveling mechanisms to limit the accumulation of wealth. One such mechanism in the regional market area of Amatenango in Guatemala is the honorary post of *alférez*. Four young men from rich families must take the post each year; their families must then spend large amounts in feasting local groups. The system serves to redistribute some wealth and also to support the market system by requiring purchases of food and local crafts.[42]

Of course, commercial exchange also occurs in the industrial societies of the modern world, as well as in societies with money-dominated peasant markets. In industrial societies, monetary exchange in markets and elsewhere dominates the economy, with prices and wages being regulated, or at least significantly affected, by the forces of supply and demand. A modern industrial economy may involve international as well as national "markets." In these, everything has a price, stated in the same money terms—natural resources, labor, goods, services, prestige items, religious and ceremonial items. Reciprocity is reserved for family members and friends or is hidden behind the scenes in business transactions. Redistribution, however, is an important mechanism of distribution. It is practiced in the form of taxation and the use of public revenue for transfer payments and other benefits to low-income families—welfare, social security, health care programs, and so on. But commercial exchange is the major way goods and services are distributed.

[41] David Kaplan, "The Mexican Marketplace Then and Now," in Proceedings of the 1965 Annual Spring Meeting of the American Ethnological Society, *Essays in Economic Anthropology*, ed. June Helm, pp. 86–92.
[42] Manning Nash, *Primitive and Peasant Economic Systems* (San Francisco: Chandler, 1966), p. 79.

Summary

1. All societies have economic systems, regardless of whether or not the systems involve the use of money. All societies have customs for regulating access to natural resources; for transforming those resources, through labor, into necessities and other desired items; and for distributing (and perhaps exchanging) goods and services.

2. Regulation of access to natural resources is a basic factor in all economic systems. The concept of private ownership of land—including the right to use resources and the right to sell or otherwise dispose of them—is common among intensive agriculturalists. In contrast, hunter-gatherers, horticulturalists, and pastoralists generally own land communally, in kin or territorial groups. Among pastoral nomads, however, animals are considered family property and are not usually shared.

3. The allocation of tools and technology is also part of any economic system. Tools are generally considered to belong to the person who made them. However, hunter-gatherers and horticulturalists tend to share tools such as weapons, knives, digging sticks, and hoes. Among intensive agriculturalists, toolmaking is a specialized activity. Owners of tools tend to regard them as private property, unless the capital required for their purchase is greater than any single person can afford.

4. Organization of labor varies from society to society according to different criteria. Division of labor by sex is universal. In many nonindustrial societies, large tasks often are accomplished through the cooperative efforts of a kinship group. In industrialized societies, cooperation of kin groups is not as prevalent as in simpler societies. Generally, the more technically advanced a society is, the more surplus food it produces, the more some members engage in specialized work. In some societies, work may be obligatory rather than voluntary. Taxation, the *corvée*,

tenant farming, the military draft, and slavery are all forms of forced labor.

5. Goods and services are distributed in all societies by systems which can be classified under three types: reciprocity, redistribution, and monetary exchange. Reciprocity refers to giving and taking without the use of money and may assume three forms: generalized reciprocity, balanced reciprocity, and negative reciprocity. Generalized reciprocity is gift giving without expectation of immediate return. In balanced reciprocity, individuals exchange goods and services whose values they calculate to be roughly equal. Negative reciprocity is generally practiced with strangers or enemies: one individual attempts to steal from another or to cheat in an uneven trade.

6. Redistribution refers to the accumulation of goods by a particular person, or in a particular place, for the purpose of subsequent redistribution. It becomes an important mechanism of distribution only in societies with political hierarchies.

7. Monetary or commercial exchange develops when food-getting technology becomes so efficient that surpluses of food are regularly produced. Also called market exchange, it is distinguished from reciprocity in that an all-purpose medium of exchange (money) is used to make transactions. Monetary or commercial exchange operates efficiently in areas of relatively dense population where people are not always personally acquainted and where there are many craft specialists. Market exchange is common among peasant communities and, on a much vaster scale, in our own and other industrialized societies.

Suggested Readings

Belshaw, C. S. *Traditional Exchange and Modern Markets.* Englewood Cliffs, N.J.: Prentice-Hall, 1965.
An attempt to explore the relationship of the economic system to social and political organization, with particular attention paid to problems of growth and modernization. The topics discussed include the economy and society, gift exchange and reciprocity, monetized peasant marketing, and conditions of modernization in a commercial economy.

Dalton, G., ed. *Tribal and Peasant Economies: Readings in Economic Anthropology.* Garden City, N.Y.: Natural History Press, 1967.
A collection of papers on tribal and peasant economies. The selection is intended to demonstrate the theoretical split between the "substantivists" and the "formalists"— between those who believe that economic theory cannot be applied to the study of noncommercial societies and those who believe it can.

LeClair, E. J., Jr., and Schneider, H. D., eds. *Economic Anthropology: Readings in Theory and Analysis.* New York: Holt, Rinehart and Winston, 1968.
A compilation focusing on both methodological and controversial issues. The underlying theme is that the economic system reflects diverse aspects of the society's culture.

Sahlins, M. D. *Tribesmen.* Englewood Cliffs, N.J.: Prentice-Hall, 1968.
Chapter 3, dealing with the ecology and subsistence economies of tribesmen, is of particular interest in the context of economic anthropology.

Service, E. R. *The Hunters.* Englewood Cliffs, N.J.: Prentice Hall, 1966.
A discussion of hunter-gatherer societies based upon data from the most extensively documented hunting and gathering groups.

Wolf, E. R. *Peasants.* Englewood Cliffs, N.J.: Prentice-Hall, 1966.
A theoretical basis for the study of peasant societies. Primary emphasis is on the definition of peasants in terms of economic factors and the continual effort required by such groups to balance limited resources against constantly competing demands.

Social Stratification

14

A long-enduring value in American society is the belief that "all men are created equal." These famous words from our Declaration of Independence do not mean that all people are equal in wealth or status, but rather that all are supposed to be equal before the law. In fact, modern industrial societies such as our own are socially stratified—that is, they are characterized by unequal access to advantages, whether those advantages be economic resources or social status.

Whether stratification exists in all societies is a matter of some dispute. The position taken by many sociologists has been stated by Kingsley Davis and Wilbert Moore: "Starting from the proposition that no society is 'classless,' or unstratified, an effort is made to explain, in functional terms, the universal necessity which calls forth stratification in any social system."[1] Sociologists who support this position have based their conclusions upon their observation of some inequality in all societies, for even the simplest societies exhibit differences in advantages based upon age or sex or ability. Some sociologists, then, equate all types of inequality with stratification.

However, unlike many sociologists, anthropologists contend that egalitarian societies do exist. These are societies in which access to economic resources, and to prestige or higher status, is available to all. In the anthropological view, most hunter-gatherer societies are egalitarian. Natural resources—food, water, materials for tools and shelter—are equally available to all. Moreover, in a society of hunter-gatherers, accumulation of food is unnecessary and is indeed futile since there are generally no storage or preservation techniques. Prestige or status is also equally available to all.

Anthropology has contributed to the study of social stratification by shifting the focus of study from the inequality inherent in human beings to the principles by which societies reg-

14

[1] Kingsley Davis and Wilbert Moore, "Some Principles of Stratification," in *Structured Social Inequality: A Reader in Social Stratification,* ed. Celia Heller (New York: Macmillan, 1969), p. 496.

TABLE 1 Stratification in Three Types of Societies

Type of Society	Socially Structured Unequal Access to:	
	Economic Resources	Prestige
Egalitarian	No	No
Rank	No	Yes
Class/caste	Yes	Yes

ulate access to status and economic rewards. A society in which economic resources are equally available to all, and every status position is open to every member of a particular age-sex group, is an egalitarian society, anthropologists conclude. Human inequality may be universal; social stratification is not.

Variation in Degree of Social Inequality

Some societies have customs or rules that give certain groups greater access to economic resources and prestige. If the rules specifying such differential access are not based on ability, age, or sex, we say that the society is socially stratified. Some societies may limit access only to prestige or status positions; others may limit access to both economic resources *and* status positions. Thus, three types of societies can be distinguished: egalitarian, rank, and class/caste societies. Egalitarian societies have no socially structured unequal access either to economic resources or to prestige; they are unstratified. Rank societies do not have socially structured unequal access to economic resources, but they do have socially structured unequal access to prestige. Rank societies, then, are partially stratified. Class/caste societies have structured unequal access to both economic resources and to prestige; they are more completely stratified. Table 1 summarizes these three types of societies.

EGALITARIAN SOCIETIES

Egalitarian societies can be found not only among hunter-gatherers but among horticulturalists and pastoralists as well. An important point to keep in mind is that *egalitarian* does not mean that all people within such societies are the *same*. There will always be differences among individuals in age and sex and in such abilities or traits as hunting skill, perception, health, creativity, physical prowess, attractiveness, and intelligence. Morton H. Fried has defined "egalitarian" as meaning that within a given society "there are as many positions of prestige in any given age-sex grade as there are persons capable of filling them."[2] For instance, if a person can achieve status in a society by fashioning fine spears and every person in the society fashions such spears, then every person acquires status as a spearmaker. If status is also acquired by carving bones into artifacts, and only three people are considered expert carvers of bones, then only those three achieve status as carvers. But the next generation might produce eight spearmakers and twenty carvers. In an egalitarian society, the number of prestigious positions is adjusted to fit the number of qualified candidates. We would say, therefore, that such a society is not socially stratified.

There are, of course, differences in status and prestige arising out of differences in ability. Hence, even in an egalitarian society differential prestige exists. However, although some persons may be better hunters or more skilled artists than others, there is still equal *access* to status positions for people of the same ability. Any prestige gained by achievement of status as a great hunter, for instance, is neither transferable nor inheritable. Because a man is a great hunter, it is not assumed that his sons are also great hunters. The egalitarian society keeps inequality at a minimal level.

In an egalitarian society, any differences in prestige that do exist are not related to eco-

[2]Morton H. Fried, *The Evolution of Political Society* (New York: Random House, 1967), p. 33.

In egalitarian societies all persons have equal access to both status positions and economic resources. Among the members of a !Kung Bushman band, for example, there is no visible difference in prestige or wealth. Although the second man from the right holds the position of headman, he has no power, nor does he enjoy any other advantages. (Courtesy of Irven DeVore / Anthro-Photo.)

nomic differences. Egalitarian groups depend heavily upon *sharing,* which insures equal access to economic resources despite differences in acquired prestige. For instance, in some egalitarian communities, members achieve status through hunting. But even before the hunt begins, how the animal will be divided and distributed among the members of the band has already been decided according to the norms of the culture. Thus, the culture works to separate the status achieved by members—recognition as great hunters—from actual possession of the wealth, which in this case would be the slain animal.

The Mbuti Pygmies of central Africa provide an example of a society almost totally equal: "Neither in ritual, hunting, kinship nor band relations do they exhibit any discernible inequalities of rank or advantage."[3] Their hunting bands have no leaders; recognition of the achievement of one person is not accompanied by privilege of any sort. Economic resources, such as food, are communally shared, and even tools and weapons are frequently passed from person to person. Only within the family are rights and privileges differentiated.

!Kung Bushman society is only slightly more complex, since each band has a headman. But the position of headman has no power or other advantage associated with it; the headman serves merely as a unifying symbol. A stranger must ask permission of the headman to take water from the band's water hole, a symbolic

[3] Michael G. Smith, "Pre-Industrial Stratification Systems," in *Social Structure and Mobility in Economic Development,* ed. Neil J. Smelser and Seymour Martin Lipset (Chicago: Aldine, 1966), p. 152.

gesture the headman cannot refuse. The headman is neither the leader of the hunt nor the chief decision maker. In fact, all the men hunt, and all share in decisions that affect the band.

Societies with age-sets—that is, groups of males differentiated by age—can also be classified as egalitarian. As each new age-set is established among the young, each older group moves up a notch, gaining more prestige and additional rights, such as the right to marry, the right to go on raids, the right to be councilmen or ritual leaders. The inequalities within the society at any one time are apparent, but each age-set is automatically promoted so that all rights, duties, and privileges are available equally to all men during their lifetimes. This procedure illustrates the basis on which a society is defined as egalitarian. Systems by which status can be achieved may vary, but all status positions in such a society are open to everyone within the qualifying age-sex group. This criterion does not apply to rank societies.

RANK SOCIETIES

Societies with social *ranking* generally practice agriculture or herding, but not all agricultural or pastoral societies are ranked. Ranking is characterized by socially structured unequal access to prestige or status, but *not* socially structured unequal access to economic resources. Unequal access to prestige is often reflected in the position of chief, a rank to which only some members of a specified group in the society can succeed. The chief retains the symbolic unifying role of headman, as among the Bushmen. But in addition, in the practical role of food distributor he has added prestige: he may receive a portion of the harvest and of the hunt, which he then redistributes to the rest of the group.

Redistribution of food by the chief symbolizes that the wealth is communally held. Although the chief may be designated "owner" of the land, the people always retain the right to use the land. In some Polynesian societies, for instance, the chief was designated "manager"

of the labor of others. He saw to it that the people did not neglect their fields or fail to give food to be redistributed to the community.[4] The chief of a rank society does not possess greater access to economic resources, nor is he generally excused from labor. In rank societies, the chief maintains his position and prestige by his generosity. According to our societal values, the chief may appear impoverished; but by the standards of his society, he has high status because he gives wealth away, rather than keeping it.

In rank societies, the position of chief is at least partially hereditary. The criterion of superior rank in some Polynesian societies, for example, was genealogical. Usually the eldest son succeeded to the position of chief, and different kinship groups were differentially ranked according to their genealogical distance from the chiefly line.

An example of a rank society is the Swazi of South Africa. Hilda Kuper reports that the Swazi are a horticultural people who invest their chief with "ownership" of the land.[5] The staples of their diet are maize and millet, produced cooperatively by men and women. Farming thus supplies the staple foods of the Swazi, although herding is a more prestigious occupation. Nevertheless, only 10 percent of Swazi land is given over to cultivation; cattle grazing claims 75 percent of the land.

Among the Swazi, the chief is recognized as the lineal descendant of the first ruler of the tribe. He is selected according to the rank of his mother. Both the chief and his mother are treated with great deference, are addressed with extravagant titles, and wear elaborate regalia. Members of the chief's lineage are called the "Children of the Sun," and collectively they comprise a distinct social elite. Other members of the society are ranked according to their relationship to the chief.

---

[4] Marshall Sahlins, *Social Stratification in Polynesia* (Seattle: University of Washington Press, 1958), pp. 6–8.
[5] Hilda Kuper, *A South African Kingdom: The Swazi* (New York: Holt, Rinehart and Winston, 1963).

In rank societies there is differentiated access to status positions but not to economic resources. Among the Dey of Liberia, the chief is clearly accorded greater prestige, but the house in which he lives (shown here) is no different from those of other villagers. (Courtesy of the American Museum of Natural History.)

All Swazis, however, regardless of their rank, do the same kinds of work, live in the same kinds of houses, and eat the same foods. The superior rank of the chief is evident by the many cows in his possession and by his right to organize work parties. Sharing is the principal way goods are distributed, and the chief shares (or redistributes) more than others. A man who accumulates too many cattle is in danger of public retaliation unless he shares them or lets others use them. If he does not, he may be accused of witchcraft and his cattle may be killed and eaten. This custom serves as a cultural means of preventing the accumulation of wealth. Labor, too, is shared; for example, a work party from a particular age-set might be called upon to help a family undertaking a construction job.

Although the Swazi have managed to retain much of the economic and social basis of their traditional rank society, the money economy of the white colonizers has altered their way of life. About 12,000 Swazi males are now employed as unskilled laborers; about 1,000 women work at farming or as domestics.

Unusual among rank societies are the nine-teenth-century northwest Pacific coast Indian tribes. They are unusual because their economy was based upon food collecting. But huge catches of salmon—which were preserved for year-round consumption—enabled them to support fairly large and permanent communities. In many ways, the northwest coast societies were similar to food-producing societies, even in their development of social ranking. Still, the principal means of proving one's status among the northwest coast Indians was by giving wealth away. The tribal chiefs celebrated solemn rites by grand feasts, called potlatches, at which they gave gifts to every guest.[6]

CLASS/CASTE SOCIETIES

In class/caste societies, as in rank societies, there is structured unequal access to prestige. But unlike rank societies, class/caste societies are also characterized by socially structured unequal access to economic resources. That is, not every type of person of the same sex or age

[6]Philip Drucker, *Cultures of the North Pacific Coast* (San Francisco: Chandler, 1965), pp. 56–64.

TABLE 2 American Social Classes in "Yankee City"

% of Income	% of Population	Social Classes and Characteristic Traits
45% for top 20% of the population	1.4	Upper Upper: "old family"; usually possessing wealth, but sometimes poor; active in charities, Episcopal or Congregational church, exclusive clubs; endogamous.
	1.6	Lower Upper: newly rich; imitate the U-U class and long to marry into that class.
	10.2	Upper Middle: professional men or store owners; active in civic affairs; respectable; long to be accepted by the groups above them, but almost never are.
	28.1	Lower Middle: white collar workers; respectable home owners, school teachers; looked down upon by all above them. Some members of recently integrated groups, such as Irish, Italians, French-Canadians, are in this group.
	32.6	Upper Lower: "poor but honest workers"; most of their income spent on food and rent.
5% for bottom 20% of the population	25.2	Lower Lower: thought by other classes to be lazy, shiftless, sexually proficient, and promiscuous. In reality, they are simply poor.

Summarized from W. Lloyd Warner and Paul S. Lunt, *The Social Life of a Modern Community* (New Haven: Yale University Press, 1941), p. 88.

has the same chance to obtain land, animals, money, or other economic benefits.

Whatever way economic stratification came into existence, which question we discuss later in the chapter, it has dominated the globe in the relatively short space of 10,000 years. Economically stratified societies range from somewhat open class systems to extremely rigid caste systems. We shall first examine the class system found in the United States.

Class Systems A class is a category of persons who have about the same opportunity to obtain economic resources and prestige. During the last fifty years, study after study has been made of classes in American towns. Sociologists have produced profiles of typical American communities known variously as "Yankee City," "Middletown," "Jonesville," and "Old City," all of which support the premise that the United States has distinguishable, though somewhat "open," social classes. Both the Warner and Lunt "Yankee City"[7] and the Lynds' "Middle-

town"[8] reached the conclusion that the social status or prestige of a family generally correlated with the occupation and wealth of the head of the family.

Towns in America have been described as having as few as two, and as many as eleven, social classes, but generally from four to six classes are recognized. In Warner and Lunt's "Yankee City," 99 percent of the city's 17,000 inhabitants were studied and classified over a period of several years. Warner and Lunt concluded that six groups emerged strongly enough to be called classes. They are summarized by characteristic traits in Table 2.

The way members of the highest and lowest classes perceive each other has also been observed and recorded. Table 3 summarizes such perceptions as they were revealed in a study of a town in the American South. The people at the top grouped the bottom two classes together and the people at the bottom grouped the top three classes together. This grouping suggests that the greater the social distance between

[7] W. Lloyd Warner and Paul S. Lunt, *The Social Life of a Modern Community* (New Haven: Yale University Press, 1941).

[8] Robert S. Lynd and Helen Merrell Lynd, *Middletown* (New York: Harcourt, Brace, 1929) and *Middletown in Transition* (New York: Harcourt, Brace, 1937).

CULTURAL VARIATION

TABLE 3 Perceptions of Social Classes

By Upper-Upper Class		By Lower-Lower Class
"Old aristocracy"	U-U	
"Aristocracy," but not "old"	L-U	"Society" or the "folks with money"
"Nice, respectable people"	U-M	
"Good people," but "nobody"	L-M	"Way-high-ups," but not "Society"
"Po' whites"	U-L	"Snobs trying to push up"
	L-L	"People just as good as anybody"

Allison Davis, Burleigh B. Gardner, and Mary R. Gardner, *Deep South: A Social-Anthropological Study of Caste and Class* (Chicago: University of Chicago Press, 1941), p. 65.

classes, the more likely it is that a group will lump together those other groups which are farthest away in the class hierarchy. Groups tend, however, to distinguish between other groups just above or just below themselves.

A person's identification with his or her social class is a process which begins quite early in life. The residence area chosen by our parents, our church, school, school curriculum, clubs, sports, college (or lack of college), marriage partner, and occupation are all influential in socializing us into a particular class group. On the whole, American society is a somewhat open society; that is, it is possible, through effort, to move from one class to another. A university education is the easiest means of moving upward. Lower-class persons may become "resocialized" at the university, which separates them from their parents and enables them gradually to learn the speech, attitudes, and manners characteristic of the higher class they wish to join. So successful is this process that students from a lower class who move into a higher class may find themselves ashamed to take their new friends to their parents' homes.

Although social class in America is not fully determined by birth, there is a high probability that most people will stay within the class into which they were born and to marry within that class. Identification with a particular group and the roles of that group begins in early childhood. The seven-year-old daughter of a poor farmer, for example, may be assigned the role of farm helper. She will have few privileges and her duties could include feeding the chickens, gathering the eggs, milking the cow, and harvesting certain crops. In contrast, the seven-year-old daughter of a wealthy businessman may be assigned the role of debutante-in-training. Her duties could include learning to ride, to play tennis, to play the piano, and to conduct herself properly at concerts and teas. Among her privileges would be respect from the servants of the house, a large variety of choice foods, a room or a suite of her own, private tutors. It is sometimes difficult to distinguish privileges from duties: she would have access to a variety of foods, but it might be more of a duty to learn to eat caviar, pâté de foie gras, and raw oysters.

By the time each of these girls is twenty years old she will have passed through many roles. At this point, the farmer's daughter and the debutante will have equal chances of achieving the role of wife, but highly unequal chances of achieving the role of wife of a millionaire. Each will be likely to marry someone from her own class at birth.

Class boundaries, though vague, have been established by custom and tradition; and sometimes they have been reinforced by the enactment of laws. Many of our laws deal with protection of property and thus tend to favor the upper and upper middle classes. The poor, in contrast, seem to be perennial losers in our legal system. The crimes that the poor are most likely to commit are dealt with quite harshly in our judicial system; and poor people rarely have the money to secure effective legal counsel.

Although some class societies have more open class systems than others, the greatest likelihood is that people will remain in the

Class societies are characterized by socially structured unequal access to both prestige and economic resources. Such occasions as the annual horse-racing meet at Ascot Heath in England provide glimpses of distinctions among social classes. (David Hurn, Magnum Photos.)

classes of their birth. For example, the Japanese class system has become more open in the last 100 years. A 1960 study of the upper-class business elite showed that 8 percent came from lower-class and 31 percent from middle-class backgrounds.[9] This social mobility was achieved chiefly by successful passage through the highly competitive university system. The Japanese class system is not completely open, however, for 61 percent of the business elite came from the relatively small upper class. The tendency to retain high class status even through changing times is clear.

Caste Systems In a caste system an individual's position in society is *completely* ascribed or determined at birth. Upward mobility is prohibited either by law or custom or both, and marriage is restricted to members of one's own caste. Thus, a caste is a *closed* class.

Questions basic to all stratified societies, and particularly to a caste society, were posed by John Ruskin: "Which of us . . . is to do the hard and dirty work for the rest—and for what pay? Who is to do the pleasant and clean work,

and for what pay?"[10] The questions have been answered in India by the maintenance of a rigidly constructed caste system—or hierarchy of statuses—whose underlying basis is economic; it involves an intricate procedure for the exchange of goods and services.[11]

Who is to do the hard and dirty work for the rest of society is clearly established: a large group of untouchables forms the bottom of the hierarchy. Among the untouchables are subcastes such as the Camars, or leatherworkers, and the Bhangis, who are sweepers. At the top of the hierarchy, performing the pleasant and clean work of priests, are the Brahmans. Between these two extremes are literally thousands of castes and subcastes. Each caste is traditionally associated with an occupation. For example, in a typical village the potter makes clay drinking cups and larger water vessels for the entire village population. In return, the principal landowner gives him a house site and supplies him twice yearly with grain. Some other castes owe the potter their services: the barber cuts his hair, the sweeper carries away

[9] Edward Norbeck, "Continuities in Japanese Social Stratification," in *Essays in Comparative Social Stratification,* ed. Leonard Plotnicov and Arthur Tuden (Pittsburgh: University of Pittsburgh Press, 1970).

[10] John Ruskin, "Of King's Treasuries," in *The Genius of John Ruskin: Selections from His Writings,* ed. John D. Rosenberg (New York: George Braziller, 1963), pp. 296–314.

[11] See Oscar Lewis with the assistance of Victor Barnouw, *Village Life in Northern India* (Urbana: University of Illinois Press, 1958).

his rubbish, the washer washes his clothes, the Brahman performs his children's weddings. The barber serves every caste in the village except the untouchables; he, in turn, is served by half of the others. He has inherited the families he works for, along with his father's occupation. He also receives a house site from the principal landowner and, at each harvest, all the grain he can lift. All castes help at harvest and at weddings for additional payment, which sometimes includes a money payment of one rupee.

This description is, in fact, an idealized picture of the caste system of India. In reality, the system operates to the advantage of the principal landowning caste—sometimes the Brahmans and sometimes other castes. Also, it is not carried on without some resentment and signs of hostility being shown toward the ruling caste by the untouchables and other lower castes. The resentment does not appear to be against the caste system as such; instead, the lower castes exhibit bitterness at their own low status and strive for greater equality. For instance, one of the Camars' traditional services is to remove dead cattle; in return, they can have the meat to eat and the hide to tan for their leatherworking. Since handling dead animals and eating beef are both regarded as unclean acts, the Camars of one village refused to continue this service. Thus, they lost a source of free hides and food in a vain attempt to escape their unclean status.

Since World War II, the economic basis of the caste system in India has been undermined somewhat by the growing practice of giving cash payment for services. For instance, the son of a barber may be a teacher during the week, earning a cash salary, and may confine his haircutting as an exchange service to weekends. However, he still remains in the barber caste (Nai) and must marry within that caste, thus reinforcing the social effects of the caste system.

Perpetuation of the caste system is ensured by the power of those in the upper castes, who derive three main advantages from their position: economic gain, gain in prestige, and sexual gain. The economic gain is most immediately

apparent. An ample supply of cheap labor and free services is maintained by the threat of sanctions. Lower caste members may have their use of a house site withdrawn; they may be refused access to the village well or to common grazing land for animals; or they may be expelled from their village. Prestige is also maintained by the threat of sanctions; the higher castes expect deference and servility from the lower castes. The sexual gain is less apparent but equally real. The high-caste male has access to two groups of females, those of his own caste and those of lower castes. High-caste females are kept free of the contaminating touch of low-caste males because low-caste males are allowed access only to low-caste women. Moreover, the constant reminders of ritual uncleanness serve to keep the lower castes "in their place." Higher castes do not accept water from untouchables, or sit next to them, or eat at the same table with them.

Although few areas of the world have developed a caste system like that of India, there are caste-like features in some other societies. For example, there is the caste-like status of blacks in the United States; their status is partially determined by the ascribed characteristic of skin color. Until recently, there were laws in some states prohibiting a black from marrying a white. Even when interracial marriage does occur, children of the union are often regarded as having lower status, even though they may have blonde hair and fair skin. In the South, where treatment of blacks as a caste was most apparent, whites traditionally refused to eat with blacks or, until recently, to sit next to them at lunch counters, on buses, and in schools. Separate drinking fountains and toilets for blacks and whites reinforced the idea of ritual uncleanness. The economic advantages and gains in prestige enjoyed by whites are well documented.

Another example of a caste group in class society is the Eta caste of Japan. Unlike the blacks in America, members of the Eta caste are physically indistinguishable from Japanese higher classes. They are an hereditary, endog-

In caste societies status and economic positions are ascribed at birth. This untouchable woman is assigned the task of cleaning bathrooms in a Bombay apartment building. The Brahman, in contrast, is a professor of metaphysics in Sanskrit. (Marilyn Silverstone, © 1964, Magnum Photos.)

amous group, comparable to India's untouchables. In the past, the Eta were a caste of about 400,000 segregated from other Japanese by place of residence, by denial of rights of citizenship, and by elaborate ritual. In recent years, the Eta have not only remained at the bottom of the hierarchy, but their ranks swelled to between 1 and 3 million as a result of the downward mobility that accompanied the decline in the farm population. Their occupations are traditionally those of farm laborer, leatherworker, basket weaver; their standard of living is very low.

In Rwanda, a country in east central Africa, a longtime caste system was overthrown, first by an election, then by a short revolution, in 1959–60. Three castes had existed, each distinguished from the others by physical appearance and occupation. The ruling caste, the Tutsi, were very tall and lean and comprised about 15 percent of the population. They were the landlords and practiced the prestigious occupation of herding. The agricultural caste, the Hutu, were shorter and stockier and comprised about 85 percent of the population. As tenants of the Tutsi, they produced most of the country's food. The Twa, comprising less than 1 percent of the population, were a pygmy group of hunter-gatherers who formed the lowest caste. It is believed that the three castes derived from three different language groups, who came together through migration and conquest. Later, however, they came to use a common language, although remaining endogamous and segregated by hereditary occupations. When the

Hutu united to demand more of the rewards of their labor, the king and many of the Tutsi ruling caste were driven out of the country. The Hutu then established a republican form of government, although the forest-dwelling Twa are still generally excluded from full citizenship.

Slavery Slaves are persons who do not own their own labor, and as such they represent a class. Slavery has existed in various forms in many times and places, regardless of race and culture. Sometimes it has been a closed class, or caste, system, sometimes a relatively open class system. In different slave-owning societies, slaves have had different rights.

In ancient Greece, slaves were often conquered enemies. Since city-states were constantly conquering one another or rebelling against former conquerors, slavery was a threat to everyone. Following the Trojan War, the transition of Hecuba from queen to slave was marked by her cry, "Count no mortal fortunate, no matter how favored, until he is dead."[12] Nevertheless, Greek slaves were considered human beings, and they could even acquire some status along with their freedom. For example, Andromache, the daughter-in-law of Hecuba, was taken as slave and concubine by one of the Greek heroes. When his legal wife produced no children, Andromache's slave son became heir to his father's throne. Although slaves had no rights under law, once they were freed either by the will of their master or by purchase, they and their descendants could become assimilated into the dominant group. In other words, slavery in Greece was not seen as the justified position of inferior people. It was regarded, rather, as an act of fate—"the luck of the draw"—that relegated a victim to the lowest class in society.

Among the Nupe, a society in central Nigeria, slavery was of quite another type.[13] The methods of obtaining slaves as part of the booty

of warfare, and later by purchase, were similar to those of Europeans; but the position of the slaves was very different. Mistreatment was rare. Male slaves were given the same opportunities to earn money as other dependent males in the household—younger brothers, sons, or other relatives. A slave might be given a garden plot of his own to cultivate, or he might be given a commission if his master were a craftsman or a tradesman. Slaves could acquire property, wealth, and even slaves of their own. However, all of a slave's belongings went to the master at the slave's death.

Manumission, the granting of freedom, was built into the system of slavery practiced by the Nupe. If a male slave could afford the marriage payment for a free woman, the children of the resulting marriage were free; the man himself, however, remained a slave. Marriage or concubinage were the easiest ways out of bondage for a slave woman. Once she had produced a child by her master, both she and the child had free status. The woman, however, was only figuratively free; if a concubine, she had to remain in that role. As might be expected, the family trees of the nobility and the wealthy were liberally grafted with branches descended from slave concubines.

The most fortunate slaves among the Nupe were the house slaves. They could rise to positions of power in the household as overseers and bailiffs, charged with law enforcement and judicial duties. (Recall the Old Testament story of Joseph, who was sold into slavery by his brothers. Joseph became a household slave of the pharaoh and rose to the position of second in the kingdom because he devised an ingenious system of taxation.) There was even a titled group of Nupe slaves—the Order of Court Slaves—who were trusted officers of the king and members of an elite. Slave status in general, though, was the bottom of the social ladder. In the Nupe system, few slaves, mainly princes from their own societies, ever achieved membership in the titled group of slaves.

In the United States, slavery originated as a means of obtaining cheap labor, but the slaves

---

[12] Euripides, *The Trojan Women.*

[13] S. F. Nadel, *A Black Byzantium: The Kingdom of Nupe in Nigeria* (London: Oxford University Press, 1942). The Nupe abolished slavery at the beginning of this century.

For many years after the Civil War, the "badges of slavery" remained in the United States. In public places in the South, for example, blacks were required to drink from separate water coolers and to use segregated rest rooms. (Russell Lee, Library of Congress, Prints and Photos Division, F.S.A. Collection.)

soon came to be regarded as deserving of their status because of their alleged inherent inferiority. Since the slaves were black, some whites justified slavery and belief in black people's inferiority by quoting fragments of religious writings ("they shall be hewers of wood and drawers of water"). The slaves could not marry or make any other contracts, nor could they own property. In addition, their children were also slaves, and the master had sexual rights over the female slaves. Because the status of slavery was determined by birth in the United States, slaves constituted a caste. Thus, during the days of slavery, the United States had both a caste system and a class system. And even after the abolition of slavery, as we have noted, some caste-like elements remained.

The Emergence of Class Society

Anthropologists are not certain why social stratification developed. Nevertheless, they are reasonably sure that higher levels of stratification emerged relatively recently in human history. Archaeological sites until about 7,500 years ago do not show any evidence of inequality. Houses do not appear to vary much in size and content. And burials seem to be more or less the same, suggesting that their occupants were treated more or less the same in life. That social stratification is a relatively recent development in human history is also suggested by the fact that certain cultural features associated with stratification also developed relatively recently. For example, most societies which are primarily dependent upon agriculture or herding have social classes.[14] Since agriculture and herding developed within the past 10,000 years, we may assume that most hunter-gatherers in the distant past lacked social classes. Other recently developed cultural features associated with class stratification include fixed settlements, political integration beyond the community level, the use of money as a medium of exchange, and the presence of at least some full-time specialization.[15]

Gerhard Lenski has suggested that the 10,000-year-old trend toward increasing inequality is currently being reversed. He argues that inequalities of power and privilege in industrial societies—measured in terms of the concentration of political power and the distribution of income—are less pronounced than inequalities in preindustrial, complex societies. Technology in industrialized societies is so complex, he argues, that those in power are compelled to delegate some authority to their subordinates if the system is to function effectively. In addition, a decline in the birth rate in industrialized societies, coupled with the need for skilled labor, has pushed the average wage of workers far above the subsistence level, resulting in greater equality in the distribution of income. Finally, Lenski suggests that the spread of democratic ideology, and particularly its acceptance by elites, has significantly broadened the political power of the lower classes.[16] Whether or not the trend toward greater inequality is, in fact, being reversed remains to be corroborated.

The kind of stratification system a particular society develops may be associated with certain factors. Caste systems, for example, seem to be characterized by intensive agriculture and the relatively undeveloped use of

money as a medium of exchange.[17] This is exemplified by the traditional situation in India, where castes exchange goods and services in a culturally prescribed way, without money entering into the transactions. In fact, compensation for services is typically delayed over time. The barber, for instance, must wait until harvest before he receives grain from the landowner in "payment" for his services. Slavery may develop in societies which have an abundance of resources, usually land, and a shortage of labor.[18] Obviously, warfare is a factor, too, since slaves are usually acquired by force.

But why did social stratification develop in the first place? On the basis of his study of Polynesian societies, Marshall Sahlins has suggested that an increase in agricultural productivity results in social stratification.[19] According to Sahlins, the degree of stratification is directly related to the production of a surplus, made possible by greater technological efficiency. The higher the level of productivity and the larger the agricultural surplus, the greater will be the scope and complexity of the distribution system. This, in turn, enhances the status of the chief who serves as redistributing agent. Sahlins argues that the differentiation between distributor and producer inevitably gives rise to differentiation in other aspects of life:

First, there would be a tendency for the regulator of distribution to exert some authority over production itself—especially over productive activities which necessitate subsidization, such as communal labor or specialist labor. A degree of control of production implies a degree of control over the utilization of resources, or, in other words, some pre-eminent property rights. In turn, regulation of these economic processes necessitates the exercise of authority in interpersonal affairs; differences in social power emerge.[20]

[14] Data from Robert B. Textor, comp., *A Cross-Cultural Summary* (New Haven: HRAF Press, 1967).

[15] Ibid.

[16] Gerhard Lenski, *Power and Privilege* (New York: McGraw-Hill, 1966), pp. 308–18.

[17] Data from Textor, *A Cross-Cultural Summary.*

[18] Michael J. Harner, "Scarcity, the Factors of Production, and Social Evolution," in *Population, Ecology, and Social Evolution,* ed. Steven Polgar (The Hague: Mouton, 1975), pp. 123–38.

[19] Sahlins, *Social Stratification in Polynesia.*

[20] Ibid., p. 4.

Gerhard Lenski's theory of the causes of stratification is similar to that of Sahlins. Lenski, too, argues that production of a surplus is the initial stimulus in the development of stratification, but he focuses primarily on the conflict that arises over control of that surplus. Lenski concludes that the distribution of the surplus will be determined on the basis of power. Thus, inequalities in power promote unequal access to economic resources and simultaneously give rise to inequalities in privilege and prestige.[21]

The theories of Sahlins and Lenski do not really address the question of why the redistributors will want or be able to acquire greater control over resources. After all, the redistributors in many rank societies do not have greater wealth than others.

It has been suggested that access to economic resources becomes unequal only when there is population pressure on resources in rank or chiefdom societies.[22] Such pressure may be the factor that induces redistributors to try to keep more land and other resources for themselves and their families.

C. K. Meek offers an example of how population pressure in northern Nigeria may have led to economic stratification. At one time, a tribal member could obtain the right to use land by asking permission of the chief and presenting him with a token gift in recognition of his status. But by 1921, the reduction in the amount of available land had led to a system under which applicants offered the chief large payments for scarce land. As a result of these payments, farms came to be regarded as private property and differential access to such property became institutionalized.[23]

Future research may provide more definite answers as to why social stratification emerges and why systems of stratification vary in different societies.

---

[21] Lenski, *Power and Privilege.*
[22] See Fried, *The Evolution of Political Society,* pp. 201–2, and Harner, "Scarcity, the Factors of Production, and Social Evolution," pp. 123–38.
[23] C. K. Meek, *Land Law and Custom in the Colonies* (London: Oxford University Press, 1940), pp. 149–50.

Summary

1. Whether social stratification exists in all societies is a matter of dispute. Some sociologists contend that stratification is universal because certain inequalities exist in all societies. However, anthropologists argue that egalitarian societies do exist—societies in which access to economic resources and to prestige and higher status is equally available to all.

2. The presence or absence of customs or rules that give certain groups unequal access to economic resources and prestige can be used to distinguish three types of societies. Egalitarian societies have no socially structured unequal access either to economic resources or to prestige. They are unstratified. Rank societies do not have socially structured unequal access to economic resources, but they do have socially structured unequal access to prestige. Rank societies, then, are partially stratified. Class/caste societies have socially structured unequal access to both economic resources and to prestige. They are more completely stratified.

3. Whatever way economic stratification came into existence, it has come to dominate the globe. Economically stratified societies range from somewhat open class systems to caste systems, which are extremely rigid, since caste membership is ascribed and fixed permanently at birth.

4. Slaves are persons who do not own their own labor; as such, they represent a class and sometimes even a caste. Slavery has existed in various forms in many times and places, regardless of race and culture. Sometimes slavery is a rigid and closed, or caste, system; sometimes it is a relatively open class system.

5. Social stratification appears to have emerged relatively recently in human history. This conclusion is based upon archaeological evidence and upon the fact that a number of

other cultural features associated with stratification developed relatively recently.

6. We still do not completely understand why social stratification developed. Some theories suggest that stratification developed as productivity increased and surpluses were produced. Others suggest that economic stratification emerges only when there is population pressure on resources in societies with rank.

Suggested Readings

Fried, M. H. *The Evolution of Political Society.* (New York: Random House, 1967.

Beginning with definitions of commonly used terms and drawing from several disciplines, the author attempts to develop a comprehensive theory of ranking, social stratification, and the state.

Genovese, E. D. *The Political Economy of Slavery.* New York: Pantheon, 1965.

A series of studies examining the political and economic reasons for the existence of slavery in the southern United States.

Heller, C., ed. *Structured Social Inequality.* New York: Macmillan, 1969.

This collection includes articles dealing with the theory of stratification, types of stratification, and social mobility. The editor provides a general introduction to the literature on social stratification, as well as an overview of the articles on each major topic covered.

Lenski, G. *Power and Privilege.* New York: McGraw-Hill, 1966.

A survey of the evolution of stratification theory. Basing his organization upon Hegel's suggestion that each idea generates an opposite one and that these eventually coalesce into a new theory, the author reviews the various theories proposed from ancient times to the present and seeks in this way to advance the development of stratification theory.

Plotnicov, L., and Tuden, A., eds. *Essays in Comparative Social Stratification.* Pittsburgh: University of Pittsburgh Press, 1970.

Eleven lectures by anthropologists, discussing various cultures in the light of different models of stratification systems.

Sex, Marriage, and the Family

15

Marriage and the family are virtually universal institutions in human societies and are intimately related to each other through sex. Although sex is generally involved in marriage and is certainly involved in the creation of families, we also know that it is even more pervasive than that.

Since sex is a biological drive, it is not surprising that it is found in all societies. Why marriage (and the resulting families which are produced) is nearly universal is a somewhat more perplexing problem—one that we shall attempt to deal with in this chapter. But the universality of sex does not mean that it is practiced in the same way everywhere. Nor does the near universality of marriage and the family require that marriage and family customs be the same in all societies. On the contrary, there is much variation from society to society in the degree of sexual activity permitted before marriage, outside of marriage, and even within marriage. There is also great variation in how one marries, whom one marries, and how many persons one marries. The only cultural universal about marriage regulations is that people are not permitted to marry (or to have sexual intercourse with) their parents, brothers, or sisters. Who belongs to the family varies too. The family often includes more individuals than just a man, a woman, and their immature offspring. A family may include two or more related married couples and their children.

Sex

A Hopi, speaking to an ethnographer, reported:

Next to the dance days with singing, feasting, and clown work, love-making with private wives was the greatest pleasure of my life. And for us who toil in the desert, these light affairs make life more pleasant. Even married men prefer a private wife now and then. At any rate there are times when a wife is not interested, and then a man must find someone else or live a worried and uncomfortable life.[1]

[1]Leo W. Simmons, *Sun Chief* (New Haven: Yale University Press, 1942), p. 281.

The president of the University of California, Clark Kerr, reported in *Time* magazine, "I find that the three major administrative problems on a campus are sex for the students, athletics for the alumni and parking for the faculty."[2]

These comments, made by very different people living in very different cultures, testify both to the intensity and to the ubiquity of the sex drive in human beings. The fact that Clark Kerr speaks of sex as a problem suggests something that anthropologists have long been aware of: no known human society has permitted its members to indulge in *unrestrained* sexual activity.

All societies regulate the sexual activity of their members, within and without marriage. As societies' cultures differ, so, naturally, do their approaches to sex. Some are permissive, others are restrictive. Some frown upon premarital sexual intercourse, others upon extramarital activity; still others allow both. Our own culture has traditionally been rather restrictive, insisting upon a blanket prohibition of all sexual relations outside marriage. Yet, recently, more permissive attitudes seem to be gaining acceptance.

SEXUALLY PERMISSIVE AND RESTRICTIVE CULTURES

A cross-cultural review of the range of attitudes toward childhood sexuality and toward premarital and extramarital sex reveals that societies vary from permissive to restrictive, but not necessarily with total consistency. For example, some societies are permissive with adolescents but not at all so with married people.[3]

Childhood Sexuality The sexual curiosity of children is met with a tolerant and open attitude in many societies. Among the Hopi Indians of the American Southwest, for example, parents often masturbate their children. When the children themselves masturbate, the parents pay no attention. All childhood sexual behavior is viewed permissively, although certain restrictions may be imposed at the onset of puberty.[4]

In contrast, in a Pacific island society (called East Bay to protect confidences), "great concern for sexual propriety" is demonstrated.[5] Children are discouraged from touching their genitalia in public, the boys through good-natured ridicule, the girls by scolding. From about their fifth year, children learn not to touch the other sex at all and are sensitive to lapses in modesty, which they frequently point out to one another. Boys must always remain a certain distance from a female.

Premarital Sex The degree to which sex before marriage is approved or disapproved varies greatly from society to society. The Trobriand Islanders, for example, approve of and encourage premarital sex, seeing it as an important preparation for later marriage roles. Both boys and girls are given complete instruction in all forms of sexual expression at the onset of puberty and are then allowed plenty of opportunity for intimacy. Some societies not only allow premarital sex on a casual basis but specifically encourage trial marriages between adolescents. Among the Ila-speaking peoples of Africa, girls are given houses of their own at harvest time where they may play at being man and wife with the boys of their choice. It is said that among these people virginity does not exist beyond the age of ten.[6]

On the other hand, there are many societies in which premarital sex is adamantly discouraged. For example, among the Tepoztlan Indians of Mexico, from the time of a girl's first menstruation her life becomes "crabbed, cribbed, confined." No boy is to be spoken to or encouraged in the least way. To do so would be to court disgrace, to show herself to be crazy or mad.

The responsibility of guarding the chastity and reputation of one or more daughters of

---

[2] "Evolution Before Life," *Time,* 17 November 1958, p. 64.
[3] Clellan S. Ford and Frank A. Beach, *Patterns of Sexual Behavior* (New York: Harper & Row, 1951), p. 83.
[4] Ibid., p. 188.
[5] William Davenport, "Sexual Patterns and Their Regulation in a Society of the Southwest Pacific," in *Sex and Behavior,* ed. Frank A. Beach (New York: John Wiley and Sons, 1965), pp. 164–74.
[6] Ford and Beach, *Patterns of Sexual Behavior,* p. 191.

marriageable age is often felt to be a burden by the mother. One mother said she wished her fifteen-year-old daughter would marry soon because it was inconvenient to "spy" on her all the time.[7]

In many Moslem societies, a girl's premarital chastity is tested after her marriage. Following the wedding night, blood-stained sheets are displayed as proof of the bride's virginity.

Extramarital Sex In their cross-cultural survey of sexual behavior, Ford and Beach found that among 139 societies, 61 percent forbade a married woman to engage in extramarital sex.[8] In many of these societies, men are punished for seducing married women, but concern is focused mainly on female marital fidelity. Sometimes the prohibition against such liaisons is a religious one. In Islamic countries, for example, the Koran prohibits all sexual activity outside wedlock. So does the Bible, wherever Christianity still exerts influence upon society.

In many of these restrictive societies, there is quite a difference between the restrictive code and actual practice. The Navajo forbid adultery, but the rule is loosely honored: "married men under 30 attain . . . 27 percent [of their sexual outlet] in other heterosexual contacts. . . . In men between 30 and 40 [this] drops to 19 percent, between 40 and 50 to 12 percent, over 50 to 4 percent."[9] And although American society prohibits extramarital sex in theory, Kinsey's studies showed that three-quarters of the married men interviewed admitted to wanting extramarital coitus, and over one-third experienced it.[10]

A substantial number of societies openly accept extramarital relationships. Among the Toda of India there is no censure of adultery; indeed, "immorality attaches to the man who begrudges his wife to another."[11] The Chuk-

Women in Moslem societies often are kept from public view. Here Moslem women in Afghanistan cover themselves when they appear in public places. (Marc Riboud, Magnum Photos.)

chee of Siberia, who often travel long distances, allow a married man to engage in sex with his host's wife, with the understanding that he will offer the same hospitality when the host visits him.[12]

Sex Within Marriage There is as much variety in the way coitus is performed as there is in sexual attitudes generally. Privacy is a nearly universal requirement; but whereas an American will usually find this in the bedroom, many other peoples are obliged to go out into the bush. The Siriono of Bolivia seem to have no option, for there may be as many as 50 hammocks 10 feet apart in their small huts.[13] In some cultures, coitus often occurs in the pres-

[7] Oscar Lewis, *Life in a Mexican Village: Tepoztlan Revisited* (Urbana: University of Illinois Press, 1951), p. 397.

[8] Ford and Beach, *Patterns of Sexual Behavior*, p. 115.

[9] Clyde Kluckhohn, "As an Anthropologist Views It," in *Sex Habits of American Men*, ed. A. Deutsch (Englewood Cliffs, N.J.: Prentice-Hall, 1948), p. 101.

[10] Ford and Beach, *Patterns of Sexual Behavior*, p. 117.

[11] Ibid., p. 113.

[12] Ibid., p. 114.

[13] Ibid., p. 69.

ence of others who may be sleeping or simply looking the other way.

Time and frequency of coitus are also variable. While night is generally preferred, some people such as the Rucuyen of Brazil and the Yapese of the Pacific Caroline Islands specifically opt for day. The Chenchu of India believe that a child conceived at night may be born blind. People in most societies abstain from intercourse during menstruation and during at least part of pregnancy. The Lesu, a people of New Ireland, an island off New Guinea, prohibit all members of the community from engaging in sex during the time between the death of any member and his burial.[14] Some societies prohibit sexual relations before various activities, such as hunting, fighting, planting, brewing, and iron smelting. Our own society is among the most lenient regarding restrictions on coitus within marriage, with rather loose restraints imposed only during mourning, menstruation, and pregnancy.

REASONS FOR SEXUAL RESTRICTIVENESS

Generally, societies which restrict sexuality in one area are also restrictive in other areas. Thus, most societies which frown upon sexual expression by young children punish premarital and extramarital sex.[15] Why are some societies less sexually permissive than others?

Although we do not as yet understand the reasons why, we do know that greater sexual restrictiveness tends to occur in more complex societies—that is, in those societies that have hierarchies of political officials, have part-time or full-time craft specialists, have cities and towns, and exhibit class stratification.[16] It may be that as social inequality increases and various groups of people have differential wealth, parents become more concerned with preventing their children from marrying "beneath them." Permissive premarital sexual relation-

"If I had my time over again, I'd do the same . . . except that I'd do it with Myrtle Higgins. . . ."
(© *Punch*/ROTHCO.)

ships might lead a person to become attached to someone who would not be considered a desirable marriage partner. Even worse (from the family's point of view), such "unsuitable" sexual liaisons might result in a pregnancy which could make it impossible for a girl to marry "well." Controlling mating, then, may be a way of trying to control property.

Marriage

Almost all societies we know of have had the custom of marriage. And if there is a universal rule-of-thumb regarding sexual practices, it is that all societies permit sexual activity within marriage.

WHAT IS MARRIAGE?

Marriage is a *socially approved sexual and economic union* between a man and a woman. It is presumed, both by the couple and by others, to be more or less permanent, and it subsumes reciprocal rights and obligations between spouses and between spouses and their future children.[17]

It is a socially approved sexual union in that

[14]Ibid., p. 76.
[15]Data from Robert B. Textor, comp., *A Cross-Cultural Summary* (New Haven: HRAF Press, 1967), p. 12.
[16]Ibid., p. 13.

[17]William N. Stephens, *The Family in Cross-Cultural Perspective* (New York: Holt, Rinehart and Winston, 1963), p. 5.

a married couple is not obliged to be discreet about the sexual nature of their relationship. A woman might say, "I want you to meet my husband," but she could not say, "I want you to meet my lover" without causing social feathers in most societies to ruffle. Although the union may ultimately be dissolved by divorce, couples in all societies begin marriage with permanence in mind. Implicit, too, in marriage are reciprocal rights and obligations. These may be more or less specific and formalized regarding matters of property, finances, and childrearing.

Marriage entails both a sexual and an economic relationship.

Sexual unions without economic co-operation are common, and there are relationships between men and women involving a division of labor without sexual gratification, e.g., between brother and sister, master and maidservant, or employer and secretary, but marriage exists only when the economic and the sexual are united into one relationship, and this combination occurs only in marriage.[18]

As we shall see later, the event which marks the commencement of marriage varies in different societies. In our society, a wedding ceremony of either a religious or civil nature is necessary before a relationship is recognized as a "marriage" (except in cases of common law marriages), but this is not the case in every culture. A Winnebago bride, for example, knows no such formal ritual. She goes with her groom to his parents' house, takes off her "wedding" clothes and finery, gives them to her mother-in-law, receives a plain set in exchange, and that is that.[19]

THE NAYAR EXCEPTION

There is one society in which marriage as we have defined it did not exist. Until late in the nineteenth century, the Nayar, a high-ranking caste group in southern India, seem to have treated sex and economic relations between men and women as things separate from marriage. About the time of puberty, Nayar girls took ritual husbands. The union was publicly established in a ceremony during which the husband tied a gold ornament around the neck of his bride. But from that time on he had no more responsibility for her. Usually, he never saw her again.

Customarily, the bride lived in a large household with her family, where she was visited over the subsequent years by a number of other "husbands." One might be a passing guest, another a more regular visitor; it did not matter, providing the "husband" met the caste restrictions. He came at night and left the following day. If a regular visitor, he was expected to make certain small gifts of cloth and betel nuts, hair and bath oil. If the father of her child, or one of a group who might be, he was expected to pay the cost of the midwife. But at no time was he responsible for the support of the woman or their child. Rather, her blood relatives retained such responsibilities.[20]

Whether or not the Nayar had marriage depends, of course, upon how we choose to define marriage. Certainly, Nayar marital unions involved no regular sexual component or economic cooperation; nor did they involve important reciprocal rights and obligations. According to our definition, then, the Nayar did not have marriage. However, rather than classify Nayar society as "marriageless," Kathleen Gough chooses to redefine marriage. "Marriage is a relationship established between a woman and one or more other persons, which provides that a child born to the woman (legitimately) is accorded full birth-status rights common to normal membership of his society or social stratum."[21] According to this definition, all societies we know of (including, now, the Nayar) have marriage.

[18] George P. Murdock, *Social Structure* (New York: Macmillan, 1949), p. 8.
[19] Stephens, *The Family in Cross-Cultural Perspective*, pp. 170–71.
[20] E. Kathleen Gough, "The Nayars and the Definition of Marriage," *Journal of the Royal Anthropological Institute* 89 (1959): 23–34.
[21] Ibid., p. 33.

WHY IS MARRIAGE NEARLY UNIVERSAL?

Since all, or almost all, societies practice marriage as we have defined it, we might assume that the custom is highly adaptive. Several interpretations suggest that marriage is so widespread because it solves certain problems found in all societies: how to share the work efforts of men and women; how to care for infant children; and how to minimize sexual competition.

Economic Benefits Most societies have a division of labor by sex, along the following lines:[22]

Males	Females
hunt and fish	gather food
herd	carry water
cut lumber	cook
quarry	make clothing
work with metal	make pottery

As long as a division of labor by sex exists, society has to have some mechanism by which men and women share the products of their labor. Marriage would be one way to solve this problem. However, we must ask whether marriage is the only possible solution. This seems unlikely, since the hunter-gatherer rule of sharing could be extended to include all the products brought in by both men and women. Or a small group of men and women might be pledged to cooperate economically. Thus, while marriage may solve the problem of sharing the fruits of division of labor, a sexual division of labor by itself does not seem to explain the universality of marriage.

Prolonged Infant Dependency Human infants have the longest period of infant dependency of any primate. The child's prolonged dependence generally places the greatest burden on the mother, who is the main child tender in most societies. Among hunter-gatherer groups, for

[22] Adapted from George P. Murdock and Caterina Provost, "Factors in the Division of Labor by Sex: A Cross-Cultural Analysis," *Ethnology* 12 (1973): 207.

example, this probably limited the woman's capacity to hunt or to work great distances from home. Occupied with child care, the female had to be supplied by men with food for both herself and her children. Although marriage is a solution to this problem, permanent mating is still not completely explained. After all, in hunter-gatherer societies the men may share their catch with the whole band—a group that usually includes many more people than their own families. There is no apparent reason why a group of men could not supply meat for a group of women and children.

Reduced Sexual Competition Unlike most other female primates, the human female is more or less continuously receptive to sexual activity. Some scholars have suggested that continuous female sexuality may have created a serious problem in that it may have fostered considerable sexual competition between males for females. It is argued that society had to prevent such competition in order to survive—that it had to develop some way of minimizing the rivalry between males for females in order to reduce the chance of lethal conflict. Again, permanent paired mating is *one* solution, but it is not clear why it is the only possible solution.

Could not sexual competition be regulated by cultural rules other than marriage? For instance, society might have adopted a rule whereby men and women circulated among all of the opposite-sex members of the group, with each person staying a specified length of time with each partner. Such a system presumably would solve the problem of sexual competition. However, if individuals normally came to prefer certain other individuals, a person might be reluctant to give up someone to whom he or she became particularly attached (even if only temporarily) and might be jealous of others' relations with that person. Because of such preferences and jealousies, competition might still be a problem. Perhaps more or less permanent mating may be the only practical solution to the

In Bulgaria, a Karakachan bride wears an elaborate veil as the members of her wedding party look on. (United Press International Photo.)

condition of continuous female sexuality; and at the same time, it may guarantee needed economic cooperation between men and women.

HOW DOES ONE MARRY?

The ways in which marriages are made can vary considerably. Some cultures have no ceremonies; some have relatively minor ones; and some have highly elaborate rituals, usually involving a succession of events phased over a number of days or months. In addition, in many societies marriages involve economic transactions of various types. The reasons why marriages are made in different ways in different societies are not yet fully understood.

Ceremonial Aspects of Marriage Among the Taramiut Eskimos, the betrothal is considered more important than the marriage and is ar-

ranged between the parents at, or before, the time their children reach puberty. Later, when the youth is ready, he moves in with his betrothed's family for a trial period. If all goes well—that is, if the girl gives birth to a baby within a year or so—the couple is considered married. At this time, the wife goes with her husband to his camp.[23]

In keeping with the general openness of their society's attitudes to sexual matters, a Trobriand couple, when they want to marry, advertise the fact "by sleeping together regularly, by showing themselves together in public, and by remaining with each other for long periods at a time."[24] When a girl accepts a small gift from a boy, she demonstrates that her par-

[23] Nelson H. Graburn, *Eskimos without Igloos* (Boston: Little, Brown, 1969), pp. 188–200.
[24] Bronislaw Malinowski, *The Sexual Life of Savages in North-Western Melanesia* (New York: Halcyon House, 1932), p. 77.

ents favor the match. Before long, she moves to the boy's house, takes her meals there, and accompanies her husband all day. Then, the word goes around that the couple is already married.[25]

The Kwoma of New Guinea practice a trial marriage followed by a ceremony which makes the couple husband and wife. The girl lives for a while in the boy's home. When the boy's mother is satisfied with the match and knows that her son is too, she waits for a day when he is away from the house. Until this time, the girl has been cooking only for herself, while the boy's food has been prepared by his womenfolk. Now the mother has the girl prepare his meal. The young man returns and begins to eat his soup. As the first bowl is nearly finished, his mother tells him that his betrothed cooked the meal, and his eating it means that he is now married. At this news, the boy customarily rushes out of the house, spits out the soup, and shouts, "Faugh! It tastes bad! It is cooked terribly!" A ceremony then makes the marriage official.[26]

Feasting is a common element of many elaborate wedding ceremonies. It expresses publicly the importance of the two families' being united by marriage. The Reindeer Tungus of Siberia set a wedding date after protracted negotiations between the two families and their larger kin groups. Go-betweens assume most of the responsibility for the negotiating. The wedding day opens with the two kin groups, probably numbering as many as 150 people, pitching their lodges in separate areas and offering a great feast. After the groom's gifts have been presented, the bride's dowry is loaded onto reindeer and is carried to the groom's lodge. There the climax of the ceremony takes place. The bride takes the wife's place, that is, at the right side of the entrance to the lodge, and members of both families sit around in a circle. The groom enters and follows the bride around the circle, greeting each guest, while the guests,

in their turn, kiss the bride on the mouth and hands. Finally, the go-betweens spit three times on the bride's hand, and the couple are formally man and wife. More feasting and reveling brings the day to a close.[27]

In many cultures, marriage includes ceremonial expressions of hostility. One form is the trading of insults between kin groups, such as occurs on the Polynesian atoll of Pukapuka. Mock fights are staged in many societies. On occasion, hostility can have really aggressive overtones, as among the Gusii of Kenya.

Five young clansmen of the groom come to take the bride and two immediately find the girl and post themselves at her side to prevent her escape, while the others receive the final permission of her parents. When it has been granted the bride holds onto the house posts and must be dragged outside by the young men. Finally she goes along with them, crying and with her hands on her head.[28]

But the battle is not yet over. Mutual antagonism continues right onto the marriage bed, even up to, and beyond, coitus. The groom is determined to display his virility, his bride equally determined to test it. "Brides," the LeVines remark, "are said to take pride in the length of time they can hold off their mates." Men can also win acclaim. If the bride is unable to walk the following day, the groom is considered a "real man."[29]

Two marriage practices almost guaranteed to engender hostility are capture and elopement. Wife capture and elopement are certainly expedient ways of acquiring a bride, but they entail the risk of alienating the "wronged" kinfolk. Both practices often destroy any possibility of achieving the economic and social cooperation which usually develops between families after a marriage. Moreover, the couple's children usually do not have the social status of children of more conventional marriages.

[25] Ibid., p. 88.

[26] J. W. M. Whiting, *Becoming a Kwoma* (New Haven: Yale University Press, 1941), p. 125.

[27] Elman R. Service, *Profiles in Ethnology* (New York: Harper & Row, 1963), p. 104.

[28] Robert A. LeVine and Barbara B. LeVine, "Nyansongo: A Gusii Community in Kenya," in *Six Cultures*, ed. Beatrice B. Whiting (New York: John Wiley and Sons, 1963), p. 65.

[29] Ibid.

Among the Arunta of Australia, for example, actual elopement, which occurs only when there is parental resistance to a marriage, leads to retaliation and may begin a feud. Captive marriage may be a by-product of a raid connected with such a feud.[30] North Alaskan Eskimos even promote capture. A girl, especially if she is considered unusually beautiful, is quite likely to be captured, often to become the second wife of a wealthy man. The fact that she may already be married is not a deterrent. Again, if a girl refuses to marry or for too long plays off one man against another, her family may encourage one of the men to abduct her, saying, "This is what she has been wanting."[31]

Economic Aspects of Marriage "It's not man that marries maid, but field marries field, vineyard marries vineyard, cattle marry cattle." In its down-to-earth way, this German peasant saying indicates that in many societies marriage involves economic considerations. In our culture, economic considerations may not be explicit; however, a person (and his or her family) may consider how the intended spouse will benefit economically. In many other societies, there are one or more explicit economic transactions that take place before or after the time of the marriage. The economic transaction may take several forms.

Bride Price Bride price (or bride wealth) is a gift of money or goods which is given to the bride's kin by the groom or his kin. The gift usually grants the groom the right to marry the girl and the right to her children. In 60 percent of the societies in Murdock's *World Ethnographic Sample,* the groom's kin customarily pay a bride price; in 50 percent of those societies, a "substantial" bride price is paid.[32] Payment can be made in a number of different currencies. Livestock and food are two of the more common. Among the Swazi of southern Africa:

The number of cattle varies with the girl's rank: twelve head is the current rate for commoners, princesses command fifteen or more. A boy's father should provide the animals for his son's first wife, and subjects contribute for their chief's main wife.[33]

The Gusii of Kenya, the Nyakyusa of Tanzania, and the Tiv of West Africa also pay in cattle; the Siane of New Guinea and the Ifugao of the Philippines provide pigs; the Navajo and Somali pay in horses. Food is used by the Hopi and Arapesh; the Kwakiutl pay in blankets.

The Subanun of the Philippines have an expensive bride price. They compute the sum as several times the annual income of the groom *plus* three to five years of bride service (described below).[34] Among the Manus of the Admiralty Islands off New Guinea, a groom requires an economic backer—usually an older brother or an uncle—if he is going to marry, but it will be years before he can pay off his debts. Depending upon the amount of the final bride price, payments may be concluded at the time of the marriage or may continue for years afterwards.[35]

Despite the connotations that the custom of paying a bride price may have for us, the practice does not reduce a woman to the position of a slave. Actually, she acquires prestige for herself and her family and perhaps compensates her kin for the loss of her services and those of her future children. Indeed, the fee paid can serve as a security. If the marriage fails through no fault of hers and the wife returns to her kin, the bride price might not be returned to the groom. On the other hand, the wife's kin may

[30] Baldwin Spencer and F. J. Gillen, *The Arunta: A Study of a Stone Age People* (London: Macmillan, 1927), vol. 1, p. 466.

[31] Robert F. Spencer, "Spouse-Exchange among the North Alaskan Eskimo," in *Marriage, Family, and Residence,* ed. P. Bohannan and J. Middleton (Garden City, N.Y.: Natural History Press, 1968), p. 187.

[32] Data tabulated in Allan D. Coult and Robert W. Habenstein, *Cross Tabulations of Murdock's World Ethnographic Sample* (Columbia: University of Missouri Press, 1965).

[33] Hilda Kuper, "The Swazi of Swaziland," in *Peoples of Africa,* ed. James L. Gibbs, Jr. (New York: Holt, Rinehart and Winston, 1966), p. 487.

[34] Charles O. Frake, "The Eastern Subanun of Mindanao," in *Social Structure in Southeast Asia,* ed. G. P. Murdock, Viking Fund Publications in Anthropology, no. 29 (Chicago: Quadrangle Books, 1960), pp. 51–64.

[35] Margaret Mead, *Growing Up in New Guinea* (London: Routledge & Kegan Paul, 1931), pp. 206–8.

pressure her to remain with her husband, even though she does not wish to, because they do not want to return the bride price or are unable to do so.

Bride Service   About 13 percent of the 565 societies in the *World Ethnographic Sample* have the custom of bride service. Generally, bride service requires the groom to work for his bride's family, sometimes before the marriage is finalized, sometimes afterward. Bride service varies in duration. In some societies it lasts for only a few months, in others it lasts as long as several years. Among the North Alaskan Eskimos, for example, the boy works for his in-laws after the marriage is arranged. To fulfill his obligation, he may simply catch a seal for them. The marriage may be consummated at any time while he is in service.[36] In some societies, bride service might sometimes substitute for bride price. An individual might give bride service to reduce or defray the amount of bride price required.

Exchange of Females   Only 16 societies (about 3 percent of those listed in the *World Ethnographic Sample*) have the custom whereby a sister or female relative of the groom is exchanged for the bride. For example, among the Tiv of West Africa, women are exchanged between the two families or kin groups involved in a marriage.

Gift Exchange   This marriage custom is reported for 15 societies (about 3 percent of Murdock's sample). In gift exchange, the two kin groups about to be linked by marriage exchange gifts of about equal value. For example, among the Andaman Islanders, as soon as a boy and girl indicate their intention to marry, their respective sets of parents cease all communication and begin sending gifts of food and other objects to each other through a third party. This arrangement continues until the marriage is completed and the two kin groups are united.[37]

Dowry   A *dowry* is a substantial transfer of goods or money from the bride's family to the married couple or to the groom's family. Payment of dowries was common in medieval and Renaissance Europe, where the size of the dowry often determined the desirability of the daughter. Only 4 percent of the societies in Murdock's sample offer dowries. Yet the custom is still practiced in parts of Eastern Europe and in sections of southern Italy and France, where land is often the major item provided by the bride's family.

Among the Rājpūts of India, the dowry includes money paid to the groom-to-be and, in lesser amounts, to members of his family and some of his servants. Expensive jewelry, kitchen utensils, clothing, and bedding are also included. The dowry is a major expense for the bride's parents, who often begin collecting the dowry items when the girl is an infant. After the marriage, the dowry is displayed for the benefit of the husband's female relatives, who inspect the bride as well.[38]

In only a small number of societies is compensation paid, even indirectly, to the groom's kin. If there are economic aspects to marriage, almost always it is the bride's kin who are compensated (by bride price, bride service, sister exchange). Why should this be? Murdock has shown that compensation to the bride's kin generally occurs when the bride moves away from home to live with, or near, the groom's kin. He suggests that the economic considerations transferred to the bride's kin are to compensate them for the loss of the bride's services, which now belong to the groom's kin.[39] And since it is much more usual for the bride to move away from home and to go to live with, or near, the groom's kin (than for the groom to move), it is not surprising that if marriage involves economic considerations at all, those considerations will generally be given to the bride's relatives.

---

[36] Spencer, "Spouse-Exchange among the North Alaskan Eskimo," p. 136.

[37] A. R. Radcliffe-Brown, *The Andaman Islanders* (London: Cambridge University Press, 1922), p. 73.

[38] Leigh Minturn and John T. Hitchcock, *The Rājpūts of Khalapur, India* (New York: John Wiley and Sons, 1966), pp. 57–59.

[39] Murdock, *Social Structure*, p. 20.

A TABLE OF
KINDRED AND AFFINITY,

WHEREIN WHOSOEVER ARE RELATED ARE FORBIDDEN
IN SCRIPTURE AND OUR LAWS TO MARRY TOGETHER.

A Man may not marry his	*A Woman may not marry with her*
1 GRANDMOTHER,	1 GRANDFATHER,
2 Grandfather's Wife,	2 Grandmother's Husband,
3 Wife's Grandmother.	3 Husband's Grandfather.
4 Father's Sister,	4 Father's Brother,
5 Mother's Sister,	5 Mother's Brother,
6 Father's Brother's Wife.	6 Father's Sister's Husband.
7 Mother's Brother's Wife,	7 Mother's Sister's Husband,
8 Wife's Father's Sister,	8 Husband's Father's Brother,
9 Wife's Mother's Sister.	9 Husband's Mother's Brother.
10 Mother,	10 Father,
11 Step-Mother,	11 Step-Father,
12 Wife's Mother.	12 Husband's Father.
13 Daughter,	13 Son,
14 Wife's Daughter,	14 Husband's Son,
15 Son's Wife.	15 Daughter's Husband.
16 Sister,	16 Brother,
17 Wife's Sister,	17 Husband's Brother,
18 Brother's Wife.	18 Sister's Husband.
19 Son's Daughter,	19 Son's Son,
20 Daughter's Daughter,	20 Daughter's Son,
21 Son's Son's Wife.	21 Son's Daughter's Husband.
22 Daughter's Son's Wife,	22 Daughter's Daughter's Husband,
23 Wife's Son's Daughter,	23 Husband's Son's Son,
24 Wife's Daughter's Daughter.	24 Husband's Daughter's Son.
25 Brother's Daughter,	25 Brother's Son,
26 Sister's Daughter,	26 Sister's Son, [band.
27 Brother's Son's Wife.	27 Brother's Daughter's Hus-
28 Sister's Son's Wife,	28 Sister's Daughter's Husband,
29 Wife's Brother's Daughter,	29 Husband's Brother's Son,
30 Wife's Sister's Daughter.	30 Husband's Sister's Son.

THE END.

PRINTED IN ENGLAND BY
EYRE AND SPOTTISWOODE, LTD., HIS MAJESTY'S PRINTERS, LONDON.

The incest taboo exists in all cultures, including twentieth-century England, as this page from an Anglican prayer book illustrates. (Courtesy of Ann Novotny.)

RESTRICTIONS ON MARRIAGE: THE UNIVERSAL INCEST TABOO

Hollywood and its press agents notwithstanding, marriage is not always based solely upon mutual love, independently discovered and expressed by the two life partners-to-be. Nor is it based upon sex alone. But even where love and sex are contributing factors, regulations specify whom one may or may not marry. Perhaps the most rigid regulation, found in *all* cultures, is the incest taboo.

The *incest taboo* refers to the prohibition of sexual intercourse or marriage between mother and son, father and daughter, and brother and sister. No society we know of has generally permitted sexual intercourse within the nuclear family (mother, father, and children). However, there have been societies in which incest was permitted within the royal family (though generally forbidden to the rest of the population). The Incan and Hawaiian royal families were two such exceptions to the universal incest taboo, but probably the most famous example was provided by Cleopatra of Egypt.

It seems clear that the Egyptian aristocracy and royalty indulged in father-daughter and brother-sister marriages. (Cleopatra was married to two of her younger brothers at different times.)[40] The reasons seem to have been partly religious—a member of the family of Pharaoh, who was a god, could not marry a commoner—and partly economic, for marriage within the family kept the royal property undivided.

Despite the practices of the ancient Egyptians, incestuous relationships have traditionally been felt to contravene primary human instincts. But if this is so, why would societies *forbid* incest, and why is this taboo applied universally? A number of explanations have been suggested.

Childhood Familiarity Theory This explanation, suggested by Westermarck, was given a wide hearing in the early 1920s. Westermarck argued that people who have been brought up together since earliest childhood, such as siblings, would not be sexually attracted to each other. This theory was subsequently rejected because there was evidence that some children *were* sexually interested in their parents and siblings. However, two recent studies have suggested that there may be something to Westermarck's theory.

[40] Russell Middleton, "Brother-Sister and Father-Daughter Marriage in Ancient Egypt," *American Sociological Review* 27 (1962): 606.

Yonina Talmon investigated marriage patterns among the second generation of three well-established collective communities in Israel (kibbutzim).[41] In these collectives, children live with many members of their peer group in quarters separate from their families; they are in constant interaction with their peers, from birth to maturity. The study reveals that, among 125 couples, there was "not one instance in which both mates were reared from birth in the same peer group,"[42] despite parental encouragement of marriage within the peer group. The same situation persisted with regard to nonmarital sexual relations among the members of the group, and the reasons given by the members of the same age group were quite specific. "They firmly believe that over-familiarity breeds sexual disinterest." One kibbutz member told Talmon, "we are like an open book to each other. We have read the story in the book over and over again and know all about it."[43] Talmon's evidence reveals not only the onset of disinterest and even sexual antipathy among children reared together, but a correspondingly heightened fascination with newcomers or outsiders, particularly for their "mystery."

Arthur Wolf's study of the Chinese in northern Taiwan also supports the theory that childhood familiarity produces sexual disinterest.[44] Wolf focused on a community still practicing the Chinese custom of t'ung-yang-hsi, or "daughter-in-law-raised-from-childhood."

When a girl is born in a poor family . . . she is often given away or sold when but a few weeks or months old, or one or two years old, to be the future wife of a son in the family of a friend or relative which has a little son not betrothed in marriage. . . . The girl is called a "little bride" and taken home and brought up in the family together with her future husband.[45]

[41]Yonina Talmon, "Mate Selection in Collective Settlements," *American Sociological Review* 29 (1964): 491–508.

[42]Ibid., p. 492.

[43]Ibid., p. 504.

[44]Arthur Wolf, "Adopt a Daughter-in-Law, Marry a Sister: A Chinese Solution to the Problem of the Incest Taboo," *American Anthropologist* 70 (1968): 864–74.

[45]Ibid., p. 864.

Wolf's evidence indicates that this arrangement is associated with sexual difficulties when the childhood "couple" later marries. Informants implied that familiarity results in disinterest and lack of stimulation. As an indication of their disinterest, these couples produce fewer offspring than spouses not raised together and they are more likely to seek extramarital sexual relationships.

Yet if all this is true, it still does not satisfactorily explain why incest is universally prohibited. Why is it necessary to have a *taboo* on incest? Why not simply rely on natural disinclinations?

Freud's Psychoanalytic Theory Freud's approach offers a possible explanation for the taboo. He proposed that the incest taboo is a reaction against unconscious incestuous desires. Freud suggested that the son is attracted to his mother (as the daughter is to her father) and, as a result, he feels jealousy and hostility toward his father. But the son knows these feelings cannot continue, for they might lead the father to retaliate against him; therefore, they must be renounced or repressed. Usually the feelings are repressed and retreat into the unconscious. But the desire to possess the mother continues to exist in the unconscious; and, according to Freud, the horror of incest is a reaction to, or a defense against, the forbidden unconscious impulse. Although Freud's theory may account for the aversion felt toward incest, it does not succeed in explaining the origin of the taboo. Indeed, the theory seems to assume at the outset that incest is already forbidden. If it were not, there would be no reason for the son or daughter to repress his or her incestuous desires.

Family Disruption Theory This theory, often associated with Malinowski, can best be summed up as follows: Sexual competition among family members would create so much rivalry and tension that the family could not function as an effective unit. Since the family must function effectively for society to survive, society has to curtail competition within the family. The incest taboo is thus imposed to keep the family intact.

But there are inconsistencies in this approach. Society could have shaped other rules about the sexual access of one member of the family to another which would also eliminate potentially disruptive competition. Also, why would brother-sister incest be so disruptive? As we noted, such marriages did exist in ancient Egypt. Brother-sister incest would not disrupt the authority of the parents, if the children were allowed to marry when mature. The family disruption theory, then, does not seem to explain adequately the origin of the incest taboo.

Cooperation Theory This theory was proposed by the early anthropologist Edward B. Tylor and was elaborated by Leslie A. White. It emphasizes the value of the incest taboo as a device to promote cooperation among family groups, thus helping communities to survive. As Tylor sees it, certain operations necessary for the welfare of the community can only be accomplished by large numbers of people working together. In order to break down suspicion and hostility between family groups, and make such cooperation possible, early humans developed the incest taboo to ensure that individuals would marry members of other families. The ties created by intermarriages would then serve to hold the community together. Thus Tylor explains the incest taboo as an answer to the choice "between marrying out and being killed out."[46] Although there may well be advantages to marriage outside the family, is the incest taboo necessary to promote cooperation with outside groups? Is it not possible, for example, that families could have required some of their members to marry with outside groups if they thought it necessary for survival, and could have permitted incestuous marriages when such alliances were not needed? Thus, although the incest taboo might enhance cooperation between families, the need for cooperation does not adequately explain the existence of the incest taboo in all societies, since other customs might also promote alliances between families.

Inbreeding Theory One of the oldest explanations for the incest taboo, this theory focuses on the potentially damaging consequences of inbreeding, or marrying within the family. People within the same family are likely to carry the same harmful recessive genes. Inbreeding, then, will tend to produce offspring who are more likely to die early of genetic disorders than the offspring of unrelated spouses. For many years, this theory was rejected because it was thought that inbreeding need not be harmful. After all, it works well with animals and it seems not to have produced defective offspring among the Hawaiian, Incan, and Egyptian royal lineages, if Cleopatra can be taken as an example. However, we now have a good deal of evidence, from humans as well as from other animals, that inbreeding is generally deleterious.[47] Genes that arise by mutation are usually harmful and recessive, and therefore the offspring of close relatives may inherit a double, and possibly lethal, dose of a recessive gene. Recently, a group of behavioral scientists suggested that for species with widely spaced births and few offspring, natural selection would favor some mechanism that prevents inbreeding. Inbreeding is probably particularly deleterious among animals (like humans) that produce few offspring at a time, since such species can ill afford many unnecessary deaths. (Animal breeders sometimes obtain beneficial effects with inbreeding, but they usually do not care about the death rate or high risk of defective offspring.) In humans, therefore, natural selection may have favored groups with the incest taboo—a cultural prohibition—since they would have had higher reproductive rates than groups without the taboo.[48] Whether or not people actually recog-

---

[46]As quoted in Leslie A. White, *The Science of Culture* (New York: Farrar, Straus and Giroux, 1949), p. 313.

[47]Curt Stern, *Principles of Human Genetics*, 3rd ed. (San Francisco: W. H. Freeman, 1973), pp. 494–95.

[48]David F. Aberle et al., "The Incest Taboo and Mating Patterns of Animals," *American Anthropologist* 65 (1963): 253–65.

nized the harmfulness of inbreeding, the demographic consequences of the incest taboo may account for its universality, since reproductive and hence competitive advantages probably accrued to groups practicing the taboo. Thus, although cultural solutions other than the incest taboo might provide the desired effect assumed by the family disruption theory and the cooperation theory, the incest taboo is the only possible solution to the problem of inbreeding.[49]

WHOM SHOULD ONE MARRY?

Probably every child in our society knows the story of Cinderella—how a poor, downtrodden, but lovely girl accidentally meets, falls in love with, and eventually marries, a prince. It is a charming tale, but as a guide to mate choice in our society it is quite misleading. The majority of marriages simply do not occur in so free and coincidental a way in any society, our own included. Aside from the familiar incest taboo, societies often have rules restricting marriage with other persons, as well as preferences about which other persons are the most desirable mates.

Even in a modern, urbanized society such as ours, where mate choice is, theoretically, free, people tend to marry within their own geographical area and class. For example, studies made in America over the last twenty years reveal that over one-half of all urban marriages occurred between people living less than a mile from one another.[50] Since neighborhoods are frequently made up of people from similar class backgrounds, it is unlikely that many of these alliances were Cinderella stories.

Arranged Marriages In an appreciable number of societies, marriages are completely arranged—negotiations being handled by the immediate families or by go-betweens. Sometimes betrothals are completed while the future partners are still children. This was formerly the custom in much of Hindu India, China, Japan, and eastern and southern Europe. Implicit in the arranged marriage is the conviction that the joining together of two kin groups to form new social and economic ties is too important to be threatened by free choice and romantic love.

An example of a marriage arranged for reasons of prestige comes from Clellan Ford's study of the Kwakiutl Indians of British Columbia. Ford's informant described his marriage as follows:

> When I was old enough to get a wife—I was about 25—my brothers looked for a girl in the same position that I and my brothers had. Without my consent, they picked a wife for me—Lagius' daughter. The one I wanted was prettier than the one they chose for me, but she was in a lower position than me, so they wouldn't let me marry her.[51]

Exogamy and Endogamy Marriage partners often must be chosen from *outside* one's own kin group or community; this is known as a rule of *exogamy*. Exogamy can take many forms. It may mean marrying outside a particular group of kinsmen or outside a particular village or group of villages. Often, then, spouses come from quite a distance away. For example, Rani Khera, a village in India, had 266 married women who had come from about 200 different villages averaging between 12 and 24 miles away; and 220 local women went to 200 neighboring villages to marry. As a result of these exogamous marriages, Rani Khera, a village of 150 households, was linked to 400 other nearby villages.[52]

A rule of *endogamy* obliges a person to marry *within* some group. The caste groups of India—legally abolished but still a social force—have traditionally been endogamous. The higher

---

[49] A mathematical model of early mating systems suggests that people may have noticed the harmful effects of inbreeding, once populations began to expand as a result of agriculture, and may have deliberately adopted the incest taboo. See Melvin Ember, "On the Origin and Extension of the Incest Taboo," *Behavior Science Research,* in press.

[50] William J. Goode, *The Family* (Englewood Cliffs, N.J.: Prentice-Hall, 1964), p. 30.

[51] Clellan S. Ford, *Smoke from Their Fires* (New Haven: Yale University Press, 1941), p. 149.

[52] W. J. Goode, *World Revolution and Family Patterns* (New York: Free Press, 1963), p. 210.

In many Hindu Indian families, marriages still are arranged. (Marilyn Silverstone, Magnum Photos.)

Cross-cousins are children of siblings of the opposite sex that is, a person's cross-cousins are father's sisters' children and mother's brothers' children. *Parallel-cousins* are children of siblings of the same sex. A person's parallel-cousins, then, are father's brothers' children and mother's sisters' children. The Chippewa Indians used to practice cross-cousin marriage as well as cross-cousin joking. With his female cross-cousins, the Chippewa brave was expected to exchange broad, risqué jokes; but he would not do so with his parallel-cousins, with whom a severe propriety was the rule. Generally, in any society in which cross-cousin marriage is allowed—but parallel-cousin union is not—there is a joking relationship between a man and his female cross-cousins. This attitude is in contrast to the formal and very respectful relationship the man maintains with his female parallel-cousins. Apparently, the joking relationship signifies the possibility of marriage, whereas the respectful relationship signifies the extension of the incest taboo to parallel-cousins.

What kinds of societies allow or prefer first cousin marriage? A recent cross-cultural study has presented evidence suggesting that cousin marriages are more apt to be permitted in relatively densely populated societies. Perhaps this is because the likelihood of such marriages, and therefore the risks of inbreeding, are minimal in those societies.[53]

Levirate and Sororate In many societies, the person whom an individual is obliged to marry after the death of his or her spouse may be determined by cultural rules. The *levirate* is the custom whereby a man is obliged to marry his brother's widow. In the *sororate,* a woman is obliged to marry her deceased sister's husband. Both of these customs are exceedingly common, being the obligatory form of secondary marriage in a majority of societies.[54]

Among the Chukchee of Siberia, the levir-

castes believed that marriage with lower castes would "pollute" them, and such unions were strictly forbidden. Caste endogamy is also found in some parts of Africa. In East Africa, a Masai warrior will never stoop to marry the daughter of an ironworker, nor will a ruling caste Tutsi (from Rwanda in East Central Africa) so much as think of joining himself to the family of a hunting caste Twa.

Cousin Marriages Our kinship terminology does not differentiate between types of cousins. In other societies such distinctions in terms are of great significance, particularly with regard to first cousins, because they define which cousins are suitable marriage partners (or, in some cases, which cousins are preferred mates) and which are not. A few societies allow, or even prefer, marriage with a cross-cousin but prohibit marriage with a parallel-cousin. Most societies, however, prohibit marriage with all types of first cousins.

[53]Ember, "On the Origin and Extension of the Incest Taboo," in press.
[54]Murdock, *Social Structure,* p. 29.

TABLE 1 Four Forms of Marriage

Form of Marriage		Males	Females
Monogamy		△	= ○
Polygyny	⎫ Polygamy	△	= ○ + ○ + ...
Polyandry	⎭	△ + △ + ...	= ○
Group Marriage		△ + △ + ...	= ○ + ○ + ...

△ represents male; ○, female; and =, marriage.

ate obliges the next oldest brother to become the successor husband. He cares for the widow and children, assumes the sexual privileges of the husband, and unites the deceased's reindeer herd with his own, keeping it in the name of his brother's children. If there are no brothers, the widow is married to a cousin of her first husband. Generally, the Chukchee regard the custom more as a duty than as a right. The nearest relative is obliged to care for a woman left with children and a herd.[55] Among the Murngin of Australia, the economic burden of a large household can be such that an elder brother might wish to foster a leviratic marriage even before his death.

If *wawa* (Elder Brother) has four or five wives, he may say to a single *yukiyoyo* (Younger Brother), "You see that one, you take her and feed her." *Yukiyoyo* says, if *wawa* is an old man, "No, you are an old man, I'll wait until you die, then I'll have them all." *Wawa* replies, "No, you take her now, *yukiyoyo*. I have many wives and you have none.[56]

HOW MANY DOES ONE MARRY?

We are accustomed to thinking of marriage as involving just one man and one woman at a time (*monogamy*), but most societies in the world allow a man to be married to more than one woman at the same time (*polygyny*). Polygyny's mirror image, one woman being married to more than one man at the same time (*polyandry*),

[55] Waldemar Bogoras, "The Chukchee," pt. 3, *Memoirs of the American Museum of Natural History*, vol. II, 1909, referred to in Stephens, *The Family in Cross-Cultural Perspective*, p. 195.

[56] W. Lloyd Warner, *A Black Civilization* (New York: Harper & Row, 1937), p. 62.

is practiced in very few societies. Polygyny and polyandry are the two variants of *polygamy*, or plural marriage. *Group marriage*, in which more than one man is married to more than one woman at the same time, sometimes occurs but is not generally customary in any known society. (See Table 1.)

Monogamy There was a time when Westerners seriously believed that monogamy was the end product of civilization. Polygyny was considered base and uncivilized. However, monogamy is not necessarily a hallmark of civilization, nor is polygyny a sign of barbarism.

Only about one-quarter of the 565 societies in Murdock's *World Ethnographic Sample* are "strictly monogamous." However, the majority of people living in societies permitting, or preferring, polygyny often practice monogamy, because no society habitually has twice as many marriageable women as men.

Polygyny Although it is not practiced in Western and other highly industrialized societies, polygyny is found in many societies throughout the world. Murdock's *World Ethnographic Sample* reports that over 70 percent of societies practice it, and there is ample evidence for its existence in our own cultural background. The Old Testament has many references to it. King David and King Solomon are just two examples of men polygynously married.

We have defined polygyny as the marriage of one man to more than one woman. Note that we only call marriage polygynous when the plural marriages are contemporaneous, not successive. Polygynous marriages are socially recognized marriages "involving residential cohabitation and economic cooperation as well as sexual association."[57]

In many societies polygyny is a mark of a man's great wealth or high status. In such societies, only the very wealthy can, and are expected to, support a number of wives. Some Moslem societies, especially Arabic-speaking ones, still

[57] Murdock, *Social Structure*, p. 26.

view polygyny in this light, However, in other groups, where women are important contributors to the economy, greater wealth may be obtained by having more than one wife.

Among the Siwai, a society in the South Pacific, status is achieved through feast giving. Since pork is the main dish at these feasts, the Siwai associate pig raising with prestige. Moreover, pigs are beloved pets to the Siwai.

When Siwai natives call their pigs by name, grin with pleasure as the beasts troop in squealing, carefully set out food for them in baskets and discuss their merit with noticeable pride, it becomes apparent to an observer that these people look upon their pigs as pets. . . . Even granted that a man must occasionally butcher a pig to celebrate an event, he rarely ever uses a pig which he, himself, has raised.[58]

This great interest in pigs sparks an interest in wives since, in Siwai society, women raise the food needed to raise pigs.

It is by no mere accident that polygynous households average more pigs than monogamous ones. Informants stated explicitly that some men married second and third wives in order to enlarge their gardens and increase their herds.[59]

Thus, while having many wives does not in itself confer status among the Siwai, the increase in pig herds that may result from polygyny is a source of prestige for the owner.

It is not necessary to be a marriage counselor to appreciate that a household with multiple wives is likely to be troublesome. Sinu, a Siwai, describes his plight.

There is never peace for a long time in a polygynous family. If the husband sleeps in the house of one wife, the other one sulks all the next day. If the man is so stupid as to sleep two consecutive nights in the house of one wife, the other one will refuse to cook for him, saying, "So-and-so is your wife; go to her for food. Since I am not good enough for you to sleep

with, then my food is not good enough for you to eat." Frequently the co-wives will quarrel and fight. My uncle formerly had five wives at one time and the youngest one was always raging and fighting the others. Once she knocked an older wife senseless and then ran away and had to be forcibly returned.[60]

Although jealousy among co-wives is generally a problem in polygynous societies, it seems to be lessened if one man is married to two or more sisters (*sororal polygyny*). It seems that sisters, having grown up together, are more likely to get along and cooperate as co-wives than are co-wives who are not also sisters (*nonsororal polygyny*). Polygynous societies often have the following customs or rules which presumably lessen jealousy among co-wives:[61]

1. Co-wives who are not sisters tend to have separate living quarters; sororal co-wives almost always live together. Among the Plateau Tonga in Africa, who practice nonsororal polygyny, the husband shares his personal goods and his favors among his wives, who live in separate dwellings, according to principles of strict equality. The Crow Indians practice sororal polygyny, and co-wives usually share the same tepee.

2. Co-wives have clearly defined equal rights in matters of sex, economics, and personal possessions. For example, the Tanala of Madagascar require the husband to spend a day with each co-wife in succession. Failure to do so constitutes adultery and entitles the slighted wife to sue for divorce and alimony of up to one-third of the husband's property. Furthermore, the land is shared equally among all the women, who expect the husband to help with its cultivation when he visits them.

3. Senior wives often have special privileges. The Tonga of Polynesia, for example, grant to the first wife the status of "chief wife."

<hr/>

[58] Douglas Oliver, *A Solomon Island Society* (Cambridge: Harvard University Press, 1955), pp. 352–53, as quoted in Stephens, *The Family in Cross-Cultural Perspective*, pp. 54–55.

[59] Ibid., p. 55.

[60] Oliver, *A Solomon Island Society*, pp. 223–24, as quoted in Stephens, *The Family in Cross-Cultural Perspective*, p. 58.

[61] This discussion is based on Stephens, *The Family in Cross-Cultural Perspective*, pp. 63–67.

Her house is to the right of her husband's and is called "the house of the father." The other wives are called "small wives" and their houses are to the left of the husband's. The chief wife has the right to be consulted first, and her husband is expected to sleep under her roof before and after a journey. Although this rule might seem to enhance the jealousy of the secondary wives, later wives are usually favored somewhat because they tend to be younger and more attractive. By this custom, then, the first wife may be compensated for her loss of physical attractiveness by increased prestige.

A potential for discord and jealousy exists not only among a man's wives, but among his children as well. Not surprisingly, the emotional ties between child and mother are deeper than those between child and father, and the resentment of a co-wife toward her younger counterpart may also be felt by her children. If the children of one wife seem to be receiving favored treatment from their father, rivalry may develop among the other siblings.

In view of the problems that seem to accompany polygyny, how can we account for the fact that it is so widespread? Linton[62] suggests that polygyny derives from the general primate urge to collect females. But if that were so, then why would not all societies practice polygyny?

Another explanation of polygyny is that it may occur most frequently in societies which have long postpartum sexual prohibitions.[63] In these societies, a couple must abstain from intercourse until their child is at least a year old. John Whiting suggests that couples may abstain from sexual intercourse for a long time after birth for health reasons. A Hausa woman reported:

A mother should not go to her husband while she has a child she is suckling. If she does, the child gets thin; he dries up, he won't be strong, he won't be healthy. If she goes after two years it is nothing, he is already strong before that, it does not matter if she conceives again after two years.[64]

The baby's illness seems to be kwashiorkor, a disease common in tropical areas which is probably caused by protein deficiency. By observing a long postpartum sex taboo, a woman has more widely spaced births. Therefore, each child is nursed longer and receives more protein from the mother's milk. The likelihood of a child's contracting kwashiorkor is thereby reduced. Consistent with Whiting's interpretation is the fact that societies with low-protein staples (those whose principal foods are root and tree crops such as taro, sweet potatoes, bananas, and breadfruit) tend to have a long postpartum sex taboo. Societies with long postpartum sex taboos also tend to be polygynous. Perhaps, then, a man's having more than one wife is a cultural adjustment to the taboo. As a Yoruba woman said:

When we abstain from having sexual intercourse with our husband for the 2 years we nurse our babies, we know he will seek some other woman. We would rather have her under our control as a co-wife so he is not spending money outside the family.[65]

Although we may agree that men might seek other sexual relationships during the period of a long postpartum sex taboo, it is not clear why polygyny is the only possible solution to the problem. After all, it is conceivable that all of a man's wives might be subject to the postpartum sex taboo at the same time. Furthermore, there are always sexual outlets outside marriage.

Another explanation of polygyny is that it may be a response to an imbalanced sex ratio, such that women outnumber men. Although no society we know of has twice as many women as men (so that all adults can be married polygynously), this does not mean that less than 2 to

[62] Ralph Linton, *The Study of Man* (New York: Appleton-Century-Crofts, 1936), p. 183.

[63] J. W. M. Whiting, "Effects of Climate on Certain Cultural Practices," in *Explorations in Cultural Anthropology,* ed. Ward H. Goodenough (New York: McGraw-Hill, 1964), pp. 511–44.

[64] Ibid., p. 518.
[65] Ibid., pp. 516–17.

A Yoruba king in western Nigeria is greeted by some of his 156 wives. The two older wives of the present king's father (at the right) are cared for by the young king. (Marc and Evelyne Bernheim, Woodfin Camp Associates.)

1 imbalances do not exist. An imbalanced sex ratio may occur because of the prevalence of warfare in such societies. Given that almost all adults are married in noncommercial societies, polygyny may be a way of providing spouses for surplus women. Indeed, there is some evidence that societies with imbalanced sex ratios in favor of women tend to have both polygyny and high male mortality in warfare. Conversely, societies with balanced sex ratios tend to have both monogamy and low male mortality in warfare.[66]

Polyandry Murdock's *World Ethnographic Sample* includes only four societies (less than 1 percent of the total) where polyandry, or the marriage of several men to one woman, is practiced. Polyandry can be *fraternal* (when the husbands are brothers) or *nonfraternal*.

Some Tibetans and the Toda of India practice fraternal polyandry. Marriage arrangements are quite unambiguous—the wife of one brother is accepted as the wife of all the brothers in a family, even of a brother who is born after the wedding itself. For the Toda, paternity does not reside with the biological father (whom anthropologists refer to by the Latin term *genitor*) but with the social father (Latin, *pater*) whose status is confirmed with a ceremony in the seventh month of the wife's pregnancy. Generally, the family lives in the same dwelling; but in Tibet, each husband had his own room if the household is sufficiently wealthy. The men decide when their wife will visit each of them.

One possible explanation for polyandry is female infanticide, which limits the number of women in a society. The Toda and Tibetans practice female infanticide,[67] and polyandry may therefore be a response to an imbalanced sex ratio in favor of men (though why female infanticide is practiced in the first place is not clear).

Another explanation, specific to Tibet, sug-

[66] Melvin Ember, "Warfare, Sex Ratio, and Polygyny," *Ethnology* 13 (1974): 197–206.

[67] Stephens, *The Family in Cross-Cultural Perspective*, p. 45.

gests that polyandry was a response to political and economic conditions among a certain class of serfs. These serfs were allocated a fixed amount of agricultural land by their lords, and the land could be passed on to their sons. It has been suggested that these serfs practiced polyandry as a way of preventing partition of a family's corporate lands. Rather than divide a small parcel of land between them, brothers married one woman and kept the land and household undivided. Those Tibetan groups with more land (the lords), or those with non-inheritable or no land, did not practice polyandry.[68]

The Family

The family is a social unit, consisting minimally of a married couple and the children that couple may have. Families, as we define them, are as nearly universal as marriage. The members of a family (particularly the parents and their young children) usually live in a common household and acknowledge certain reciprocal rights and obligations, especially with regard to economic activity. In a lifetime a person generally belongs to at least one family—*a family of orientation*—the one he or she is born into. Later, upon marrying, a person forms a new family—a *family of procreation.*

The family provides a learning environment for children. While no animal is able to care for itself at birth, a human is exceptional in that he or she is unable to do so for many years afterward. Since, biologically, humans mature late, they have few, if any, inborn or instinctive responses to simplify adjustment to their surroundings, and they have to learn a repertoire of beliefs and habits (which are mostly cultural) to become functioning adults in society. A family cares for and protects children while they acquire the cultural behavior, beliefs, and values necessary for their own, and their society's, survival.

THE EXTENDED FAMILY

Though we are accustomed to the family consisting of a married couple and their young children (called the *nuclear family*), this is not the most typical family arrangement. Societies that practice polygyny or polyandry will have somewhat larger family units. But most societies have families that go beyond the single monogamous, polygynous, or polyandrous family. The *extended family* is the prevailing form of family in more than half of the societies known to anthropology.[69] It consists of two or more monogamous, polygynous, or polyandrous families linked by a blood tie. Most commonly in the extended family, a married couple and one or more of their married children live in the same house or household. The constituent nuclear families are linked through the parent-child tie. However, an extended family is sometimes composed of families linked through a sibling tie. For example, such a family may consist of two married brothers, their wives, and their children. Extended families may be quite large, containing many nuclear families and including three generations.

Extended Family Life In a society composed of extended families, marriage does not bring as pronounced a change in life-style as it does in our nuclear family culture, where the couple moves to a new residence and forms a new, and basically independent, family unit. In extended families, the newlyweds are assimilated into an existing family unit. Margaret Mead describes such a situation in Samoa.

In most marriages there is no sense of setting up a new and separate establishment. The change is felt in the change of residence for either husband or wife and in the reciprocal relations which spring up between the two families. But the young couple live in the main household, simply receiving a bamboo pillow, a mosquito net and a pile of mats for their bed. . . . The wife works

[68] Melvyn C. Goldstein, "Stratification, Polyandry, and Family Structure in Central Tibet," *Southwestern Journal of Anthropology* 27, no. 1 (Spring 1971): 65–74.

[69] Coult and Habenstein, *Cross Tabulations of Murdock's World Ethnographic Sample.*

with all the women of the household and waits on all the men. The husband shares the enterprises of the other men and boys. Neither in personal service given or received are the two marked off as a unit.[70]

The young couple in Samoa, as in other societies with extended families, generally has little decision-making power over the governing of the household. Often, the responsibility of running the household rests with the senior male. Nor can the new family usually accumulate its own property and become independent; it is a part of the larger corporate structure.

So the young people bide their time. Eventually, when the old man dies or retires, *they* will own the homestead, they will run things. When their son grows up and marries, he will create a new subsidiary family, to live with them, work for the greater glory of *their* extended family homestead, and wait for them to die.[71]

The extended family is thus more likely to perpetuate itself as a social unit than the independent nuclear family. In contrast to the independent nuclear family, which by definition disintegrates with the death of the senior members (the parents), the extended family is always adding junior families (monogamous and/or polygamous) whose members eventually become the senior members when their elders die.

Possible Reasons for the Extended Family The extended family is the form of family found in the majority of the world's societies, but not all societies have extended families. How can we explain this variation? Since extended families are found more frequently in societies with sedentary agricultural economies, economic factors may play a role in determining family type. Nimkoff and Middleton have pointed out some features of agricultural life, as opposed to hunting-gathering life, that may help explain the

A Sikh extended family in Delhi, India. (Marilyn Silverstone, Magnum Photos.)

prevalence of extended families among agriculturalists. The perpetuating extended family may be a social mechanism that prevents economically ruinous subdivision of family property in societies where property is important. Property ownership is generally more important among food producers than among hunter-gatherers. Conversely, the need for mobility in hunter-gatherer societies may make extended families less likely in such economies. During certain seasons, the hunter-gatherers may be obliged to subdivide into nuclear families which scatter into other areas.[72]

However, it may not be agriculture alone that favors the development of extended family households. While agriculturalists *are* more likely to have extended family households than nonagricultural societies, the relationship between type of family and type of economy is very weak. Many agriculturalists lack extended family households, and many nonagricultural

[70] Margaret Mead, *Coming of Age in Samoa* (New York: William Morrow, 1928), as quoted in Stephens, *The Family in Cross-Cultural Perspective*, pp. 134–35.

[71] Mead, *Coming of Age in Samoa*, as quoted in Stephens, *The Family in Cross-Cultural Perspective*, p. 135.

[72] M. F. Nimkoff and Russell Middleton, "Types of Family and Types of Economy," *American Journal of Sociology* 66 (1960): 215–25.

societies have them. A different theory is that extended family households come to prevail in societies which have "incompatible" activity requirements that cannot be met by a mother or father in a one-family household. In other words, the suggestion is that extended family households are generally favored when the work a mother has to do outside the home (cultivating fields or gathering foods far away) makes it difficult for her also to care for her children and do other household tasks, or when the required outside activities of a father (warfare, trading trips, or wage labor far away) make it difficult for him to do his subsistence work. Cross-cultural evidence suggests that societies with such incompatible activity requirements are more likely to have extended family households than societies with compatible activity requirements, regardless of whether or not the society is agricultural. However, even though they have incompatible activity requirements, societies using commercial or monetary exchange may not have extended families. In these societies, a family can obtain the necessary help by "buying" the required services.[73]

Summary

1. Although all societies regulate sexual activity to some extent, some are much more permissive than others. Some societies allow both masturbation and sex play among children, while others forbid these acts. Some societies allow premarital sex, but others do not. Some allow extramarital sex in certain situations; others forbid it. While it is true that most societies are consistently either restrictive or permissive about sex, a few have different rules for different age groups. In general, it seems that as social inequality increases, so does sexual restrictiveness.

[73]Burton Pasternak, Carol R. Ember, and Melvin Ember, "On the Conditions Favoring Extended Family Households," *Journal of Anthropological Research,* in press.

2. Nearly all societies known today practice some form of marriage. Marriage is a socially approved sexual and economic union between a man and a woman which is presumed to be more or less permanent, and which subsumes reciprocal rights and obligations between spouses and between spouses and their children.

3. The way marriage is socially recognized varies greatly; it may involve a highly elaborate ceremony or none at all. Variations include childhood betrothals, trial marriage periods, feasting, elopement, and outright abduction.

4. Marriage arrangements often include an economic element. The most common form is bride price, in which the groom or his family gives an agreed-upon amount of money or goods to the bride's family. Bride service exists when the groom works for the bride's family for a specified period. In some societies, a female from the groom's family is exchanged for the bride; in others, gifts are exchanged between the two families. Dowry is a payment of goods or money by the bride's family to the married couple or to the groom's family.

5. No society generally allows marriage or sex between brothers and sisters, mothers and sons, or fathers and daughters.

6. Every society tells people whom they cannot marry, whom they can marry, and sometimes even whom they should marry. In quite a few societies, marriages are completely arranged by the couple's kin groups. Implicit in the arranged marriage is the conviction that the joining of two kin groups to form new social and economic ties is too important to be threatened by free choice and romantic love. Some societies have rules of exogamy which require marriage outside one's own kin group or community, while others have rules of endogamy requiring marriage within one's group. Although most societies prohibit all first-cousin marriages, some permit or prefer marriage with cross-cousins (children of siblings of the opposite sex) and

parallel-cousins (children of siblings of the same sex). Many societies have customs providing for the remarriage of widowed persons. The levirate is the custom whereby a man marries his brother's widow. The sororate is the practice of a woman marrying her deceased sister's husband.

7. We think of marriage as involving just one man and one woman at a time (monogamy), but most societies allow a man to be married to more than one woman at a time (polygyny). Polyandry—the marriage of one woman to several husbands—is very rare.

8. The nuclear family, consisting of a married couple and their children, is characteristic of our society. Yet, it is not the most typical family arrangement. Societies that practice polygamy will have somewhat larger family units. But most societies have the *extended family*. It consists of two or more monogamous, polygynous, or polyandrous families linked by blood ties.

Suggested Readings

Bohannan, P., and Middleton, J., eds. *Marriage, Family and Residence*. Garden City, N.Y.: Natural History Press, 1968.

A collection of papers on kinship, covering a wide range of ethnographic materials. The editors have divided the work into six sections: incest and exogamy; marriage; marriage forms; the family; residence and household; and special problems in the formulation of generalizations and theory in the study of kinship.

Fox, R. *Kinship and Marriage: An Anthropological Perspective*. Baltimore: Penguin Books, 1967.

An introduction to problems and theory in the study of kinship and marriage. Chapters 1 and 2 are of particular relevance to our discussion.

Goode, W. J. *World Revolution and Family Patterns*. New York: Free Press, 1963.

A review of the character of the family under conditions of social change, particularly under the influence of industrialization. Goode discusses factors of social organization which can encourage, or result from, industrialization: the rise of the nuclear family; the lessening of parental authority; decline of bride price or dowry; lessening of control of the husband over the wife; and greater equality in the distribution of inheritance.

Murdock, G. P. *Social Structure*. New York: Macmillan, 1949.

A classic cross-cultural analysis of variation in social organization. Chapters 1, 2, 9, and 10—on the nuclear family, composite forms of the family, the regulation of sex, and incest taboos and their extensions—are particularly relevant here.

Pasternak, B. *Introduction to Kinship and Social Organization*. Englewood Cliffs, N.J.: Prentice-Hall, 1976.

Chapters 3, 5, 6, and 7 present an up-to-date survey and critique of theories and evidence about variation in marriage and the family.

Stephens, W. N. *The Family in Cross-Cultural Perspective*. New York: Holt, Rinehart and Winston, 1963.

A descriptive and analytic survey of the family, marriage, sex restrictions, mate choice, and other topics.

Marital Residence and Kinship

16

In American society, and in many other industrial societies, a young man and woman usually establish a place of residence apart from their parents or other relatives when they marry, if they had not already moved away before. Our society is so oriented toward this pattern of marital residence—*neolocal* (new place) *residence*—that it seems to be the obvious and natural one to follow. Upper-income families in the United States, perhaps because they are financially able, begin earlier than other parents to train their children to live away from home by sending them to boarding schools at age thirteen or fourteen. In the army or at an out-of-town college, young adults learn to live away from home most of the year, yet may still return home for vacations. In any case, when a young person marries, he or she generally lives apart from family.

So familiar is neolocal residence to us that we tend to assume that all societies must practice the same pattern. On the contrary, of the 565 societies in Murdock's *World Ethnographic Sample,* only about 5 percent practice neolocal residence.[1] About 95 percent of the world's societies have some pattern of residence whereby a new couple settles within, or very close to, the household of the parents or some other close relative of either the groom or the bride.

Patterns of Marital Residence

In societies in which newly married couples customarily live with or close to their kin, there are several residence patterns that may be established. Since children in all societies are required to marry outside the nuclear family (because of the incest taboo), and since couples in almost all societies live together after they are

16

[1] Allan D. Coult and Robert W. Habenstein, *Cross Tabulations of Murdock's World Ethnographic Sample* (Columbia: University of Missouri Press, 1965).

married (with a few exceptions),[2] it is not possible for an entire society to practice a system in which all married offspring reside with their own parents. Some children, then, have to leave home when they marry. But which children remain at home and which reside elsewhere? Societies vary in the way they typically deal with the problem of which married children stay near their kin and which leave. Actually, there are only four societal patterns which occur with any sizable frequency. They are:

1. *Patrilocal residence:* the son stays and the daughter leaves, so that the married couple lives with or near the husband's parents (67 percent of all societies).[3]
2. *Matrilocal residence:* the daughter stays and the son leaves, so that the married couple lives with or near the wife's parents (15 percent of all societies).
3. *Bilocal residence:* either the son or the daughter leaves, so that the married couple lives with or near either the husband's parents or the wife's parents (7 percent of all societies).
4. *Avunculocal residence:* both son and daughter normally leave, but the son and his wife settle with or near his mother's brother (4 percent of all societies).

A fifth pattern of residence, of course, is neolocal, in which the newly married couple does not live with or near kin.

5. *Neolocal residence:* both son and daughter leave; married couples live apart from the relatives of either spouse (5 percent).

At first glance, it may seem irrelevant which pattern of residence a society has. But in fact, the pattern of residence often has profound effects upon other aspects of social organization and social life. Because the pattern of residence governs with whom or near whom individuals live, it largely determines the people those individuals interact with and the people they have to depend upon. If a married couple is surrounded by the kinsmen of the husband, for example, the chances are that those relatives will figure importantly in the couple's entire future. Whether the couple lives with or near the husband's or the wife's kin can also be expected to have important consequences for the status of the husband or wife. If married couples live patrilocally, as occurs in most societies, the wife may be far from her own kinsmen. In any case, she will be an "outsider" among a group of male relatives who have grown up together. The feeling of being an outsider is particularly strong when the wife has moved into a patrilocal extended family household.

Among the Tiv of central Nigeria,[4] the patrilocal extended family consists of the "great father" who is the head of the household, his younger brothers, his sons, and his younger brothers' sons. Also included are the in-marrying wives and all unmarried children. (The sisters and daughters of the household head who have married would no longer be living there, as they would have gone to live where their husbands lived.) Authority is strongly vested in the male line, particularly the eldest of the household, who has authority over bride price, disputes, punishment, and plans for new buildings.

A somewhat different situation exists if the husband comes to live with or near his wife's parents. Here, the wife and her kin take on somewhat greater importance, and the husband is the "outsider." As we shall see later, however, the matrilocal situation is not quite the mirror image of the patrilocal, since in matrilocal societies the husband's kinsmen are often not far away. Moreover, even though residence is matrilocal, the women often do not have as much to say about decisions in the household as their brothers do.

---

[2] In the very few societies in which married couples live apart, each with his or her own kin, we speak of a *duolocal* (two-place) pattern of residence. The Nayar of southern India, referred to in the last chapter, had such a pattern.

[3] Percentages calculated from Coult and Habenstein, *Cross Tabulations of Murdock's World Ethnographic Sample.*

[4] Laura Bohannan and Paul Bohannan, *The Tiv of Central Nigeria* (London: International African Institute, 1953).

If the married couple does not live with or near the parents or close kinsmen of either spouse, the situation is again quite different. Here, we would hardly be surprised to find that relatives and kinship connections do not figure very largely in everyday life.

Explanations of Variation in Marital Residence

A number of questions can be raised as to why different societies have different patterns of residence. First, since most societies have married couples living with or near kinsmen (as in patrilocal, matrilocal, bilocal, or avunculocal residence), why in some societies, such as our own, do couples typically live apart from kin (in neolocal residence)? And if societies do have couples living with or near kinsmen, why do most choose the husband's side (patrilocal residence) while others select the wife's side (matrilocal residence)? Why do some nonneolocal societies allow a married couple to go to either the wife's or the husband's kinsmen (bilocal residence), whereas most others do not generally allow an optional choice? (Because matrilocal, patrilocal, and avunculocal residence each specify just one pattern of residence, they are often referred to as nonoptional or *unilocal* patterns of residence.)

NEOLOCAL RESIDENCE

Why in some societies do couples live separately from kin, whereas in most societies couples live near, if not with, kin? Many anthropologists have suggested that neolocal residence is somehow related to the presence of a money or commercial economy. They argue that when people can sell their labor or their products for money, they can buy what they need to live, without having to depend upon kin. Since money is not perishable (unlike crops and other foods in a world largely lacking refrigeration), it can be stored for exchange at a later time. Thus, a money-earning family can resort to its own

savings during periods of unemployment or disability. This is impossible in nonmoney economies, where people must depend upon relatives for food and other necessities if, for some reason, they cannot provide their own food. There is some cross-cultural evidence to support this interpretation. Neolocal residence tends to occur in societies with monetary or commercial exchange, whereas societies without money tend to have patterns of residence that locate a couple near or with kin.[5] The presence of money, then, appears to be related to neolocal residence. Thus, money seems to *allow* a couple to live on their own. Still, this does not quite explain why they should choose to do so. Why couples, when given money, should *prefer* to live on their own is still not completely understood.

MATRILOCAL VERSUS PATRILOCAL RESIDENCE

As we have seen, most societies have patterns of marital residence that locate married couples with or near kin. But why, in some societies, does a married couple live with the husband's parents, and in others with the wife's parents? Traditionally, it has been assumed that, in those societies where married children live near or with kin, residence will tend to be patrilocal if males contribute most to the economy and to be matrilocal if women contribute most to the economy. However plausible this assumption may seem, the cross-cultural evidence does not support it. Where men do most of the subsistence work, residence is no more likely to be patrilocal than matrilocal. Conversely, where women do an equal amount or more of the subsistence work, residence is no more likely to be matrilocal than patrilocal.[6]

Another factor that more accurately pre-

[5] Melvin Ember, "The Emergence of Neolocal Residence," *Transactions of the New York Academy of Sciences* 30 (1967): 291–302.

[6] Melvin Ember and Carol R. Ember, "The Conditions Favoring Matrilocal versus Patrilocal Residence," *American Anthropologist* 73 (1971): 571–94. See also William T. Divale, "Migration, External Warfare, and Matrilocal Residence," *Behavior Science Research* 9 (1974): 75–133.

The most frequent pattern of marital residence is patrilocal, in which a son brings his bride to live in or near his father's household. Among the patrilocal Kassem of northern Ghana, a family compound has a sleeping hut for each wife (the cylindrical dwellings painted with abstract designs) and several granaries (the conical buildings covered by straw roofs). (Marc and Evelyne Bernheim, Woodfin Camp Associates.)

dicts whether residence will be matrilocal or patrilocal is the type of warfare practiced in a society. In most societies known to anthropology, neighboring communities or districts are often enemies. The type of warfare which breaks out occasionally between such groups may be called internal, since the fighting occurs between groups speaking the same language. In other societies, the warfare that occurs is never within the same society but only with other language groups. This pattern of warfare is referred to as purely external. Cross-cultural evidence suggests that in societies where warfare is at least sometimes internal, residence is almost always patrilocal rather than matrilocal. In contrast, residence is almost always matrilocal rather than patrilocal when warfare is purely external.[7]

How can we explain this relationship between type of warfare and matrilocal versus patrilocal residence? One theory is that patrilocal residence tends to occur with internal warfare because there may be concern in such societies over keeping sons close to home to help with defense. Since women do not usually comprise the fighting force in any society, having sons reside at home after marriage might be favored as a means of maintaining a loyal and quickly mobilized fighting force in case of surprise attack from nearby. On the other hand, matrilocal residence may tend to develop with purely external warfare. Under these circumstances, families need not fear attack from neighboring communities or districts, and it may not be so essential for sons to reside at home after marriage. If, in societies with purely external warfare, the women do most of the work, families might want their daughters to remain at home after marriage; and hence the

---

[7]Ember and Ember, "The Conditions Favoring Matrilocal versus Patrilocal Residence," pp. 583–85; Divale, "Migration, External Warfare, and Matrilocal Residence," p. 100.

pattern of residence might become matrilocal. The need to keep sons at home after marriage when there is internal warfare may take precedence over any considerations based upon division of labor. It is perhaps only when internal warfare is nonexistent that a female-dominant division of labor may give rise to matrilocal residence.[8]

BILOCAL RESIDENCE

In societies that practice bilocal residence, a married couple goes to live with or near either the husband's parents or the wife's parents. Elman Service has suggested that bilocal residence is likely to occur in societies which have recently suffered a severe and drastic loss of population, owing to the introduction of new infectious diseases.[9] Over the last 400 years, contact with Europeans in many parts of the world has resulted in severe population losses among many non-European societies which lacked resistance to the Europeans' diseases. Granted that couples need to live with some set of kinsmen in order to make a living in noncommercial societies, it seems likely that couples in depopulated, noncommercial societies might have to live with whichever spouse's parents (and other relatives) are still alive. This interpretation seems to be supported by the cross-cultural evidence: recently depopulated societies tend to have bilocal residence or frequent departures from unilocality, whereas societies that are not recently depopulated tend to have one or another pattern of unilocal residence.[10]

Avunculocal residence, in which a married couple lives with or near the husband's mother's brother, can perhaps be best understood in its relationship to matrilineal descent (which we shall discuss shortly).

The Structure of Kinship

In noncommercial societies, kinship connections structure many areas of social life—from the kind of access an individual has to productive resources, to the kind of political alliances which are formed between communities and larger territorial groups. In some societies, in fact, kinship connections have an important bearing on matters of life and death.

Recall the social system described in Shakespeare's *Romeo and Juliet.* The Capulets and the Montagues were groups of kin in lethal competition with one another, and the fatal outcome of Romeo and Juliet's romance was related to that competition. Although Romeo and Juliet's society had a commercial economy (but not, of course, an industrialized one), the political system of the city they lived in was a reflection of the way kinship was structured. Sets of kin of common descent lived together, and the various kin groups competed (and sometimes fought) for a prominent, or at least secure, place in the political hierarchy of the city-state. If a pre-industrial commercial society could be so structured by kinship, we can imagine how much more important kinship connections and kin groups are in many noncommercial societies that lack political mechanisms such as princes and councils of lords to keep the peace and initiate other activities on behalf of the community. It is no wonder, then, that anthropologists often speak of the web of kinship as providing the main structure of social action in noncommercial societies.

RULES OF DESCENT

If kinship is important in most societies, and particularly in noncommercial ones, there is still the question of which kin a person depends upon. After all, if every individual kept track of

---

[8]Ember and Ember, "The Conditions Favoring Matrilocal versus Patrilocal Residence." For a different theory, one which suggests that matrilocal residence precedes, rather than follows, the development of purely external warfare, see Divale, "Migration, External Warfare, and Matrilocal Residence," pp. 75–133.

[9]Elman R. Service, *Primitive Social Organization* (New York: Random House, 1962), p. 137.

[10]Carol R. Ember and Melvin Ember, "The Conditions Favoring Multilocal Residence," *Southwestern Journal of Anthropology* 28 (1972): 382–400.

Because the kindred is an ego-centered group in a bilateral system of descent, the kindreds are different for different people. Thus, although the relatives gathered here might represent the entire kindred for some members of this American family, other members will have somewhat different kindreds. (Photo by Jim Wells for *Life* magazine.)

all his or her relatives, distant as well as close, there would be an unmanageably large number of people in each person's network of kin. Consequently, in most societies where kinship connections are important, there is a rule that allocates each person to a particular and definable set of kin. Perhaps this is done because smaller sets of kin can have clearer and firmer ties than infinitely large sets of kin. The rules affiliating individuals with sets of kin are called *rules of descent*. By the particular rule of descent operating in their society, individuals can know more or less immediately to whom to turn for support and help in everyday matters and in life crises.

There are only a few known rules of de-

scent that affiliate individuals with different sets of kin:

1. *Bilateral* (two-sided) *descent* affiliates an individual more or less equally with his or her mother's and father's relatives.
2. *Patrilineal descent* (the most frequent rule) affiliates an individual with kinsmen of both sexes related to him or her *through men only*. In each generation, then, children belong to the kin group of their father.
3. *Matrilineal descent* affiliates an individual with kinsmen related to him or her *through women only*. In each generation, then, children belong to the kin group of their mother.

4. *Ambilineal descent* affiliates an individual with kinsmen related to him or her through men *or* women. In other words, some people in the society affiliate with a group of kinsmen through their fathers; and others, through their mothers. Consequently, the descent groups show both female and male genealogical links.

These rules are usually, but not always, mutually exclusive. Most societies can be characterized as having only one rule of descent; but sometimes two principles are utilized to affiliate individuals with different sets of kinsmen for different purposes. Some societies have what is called "double descent" (or double unilineal descent). In such cases, an individual affiliates for some purposes with a group of matrilineal kinsmen and for other purposes with a group of patrilineal kinsmen. Thus, two rules of descent, each traced through links of one sex only, are operative at the same time. Other combinations also occur. A society may have unilineal (matrilineal or patrilineal) and bilateral groups, or unilineal and ambilineal groups.

BILATERAL DESCENT

The bilateral rule of descent affiliates an individual with a group of kinsmen more or less equally on his father's and mother's sides. Consequently, this rule does not by itself exclude any relatives from membership in a person's set of kinsmen. In practice, however, a bilateral rule of descent affiliates a person only with close relatives on both his father's and mother's sides. This network of close relatives is called a *kindred*. In our own society, we can think of this group of kinsmen as including the people we might invite to weddings, funerals, or some other ceremonial occasion. The kindred, however, is not usually a very definite group. As anyone who has been involved in the planning of a wedding invitation list knows, a great deal of time may be spent deciding which relatives ought to be invited and which ones can legitimately be excluded. Societies with bilateral de-

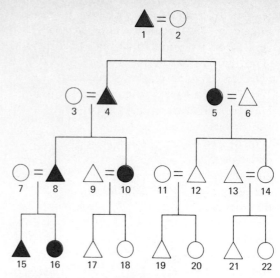

FIGURE 1 Patrilineal Descent

Individuals 4 and 5, who are the children of 1 and 2, affiliate with their father's patrilineal kin group, represented by the color. In the next generation, the children of 3 and 4 also belong to the color kin group, since they take their descent from their father who is a member of that group. However, the children of 5 and 6 do not belong to this patrilineal group, since they take their descent from their father who is a member of a different group. That is, although the mother of 12 and 14 belongs to the color patrilineal group, she cannot pass on her descent affiliation to her children; and since her husband (6) does not belong to her patrilineage, her children (12 and 14) belong to their father's group. In the fourth generation, only 15 and 16 belong to the color patrilineal group, since their father is the only male member of the preceding generation who belongs to the color patrilineal group. In this diagram, then, 1, 4, 5, 8, 10, 15, and 16 are affiliated by patrilineal descent; all the other individuals belong to other patrilineal groups.

scent differ in precisely how distant relatives have to be before they are lost track of or before they are not included in ceremonial activities. In societies like our own, in which kinship is relatively unimportant, fewer relatives are included in the kindred. In other bilateral societies, however, where kinship connections are somewhat more important, more relatives would be included in the kindred.

The distinctiveness of the bilateral system of descent is that, aside from brothers and sisters, no two people belong to exactly the same kin group. The kindred contains close relatives spreading out on both the father's and mother's sides, but the members of your kindred are affiliated only by way of their connection to you. Thus, the kindred is an *ego-centered* group of kin. Since different people (aside from brothers and sisters) have different mothers and fathers, your first cousins will have different kindreds, and even your own children will have a different kindred from yours. Because the kindreds are ego-centered and therefore are different for different people, one's kindred does not generally continue to get together after the death of the focal member. In our society, the kindred usually comes together only on certain occasions and then only temporarily.

UNILINEAL DESCENT

Both the matrilineal and patrilineal rules of descent are *unilineal* rules, in that a person is affiliated with a group of kinsmen through descent links of one sex only—either males only or females only. As Figure 1 indicates, in patrilineal systems the children in each generation belong to the kin group of their father; their father, in turn, belongs to the group of his father; and so on. An individual is affiliated, then, through descent links of the male sex only. Although a man's sons and daughters are all members of the same descent group, affiliation with that group is transmitted only by the sons to their children. In matrilineal systems, on the other hand (see Figure 2), children in each generation belong to the kin group of their mother. Although a woman's sons and daughters are all members of the same descent group, only her daughters can pass on their descent affiliation to their children.

Unilineal rules of descent affiliate an individual with a line of kinsmen extending back in time and into the future. By virtue of this line of descent (whether it extends through males or females), some very close relatives are excluded. For example, in a patrilineal system, your mother and your mother's parents do not be-

FIGURE 2 Matrilineal Descent

Individuals 4 and 5, who are the children of 1 and 2, affiliate with their mother's kin group, represented by the color. In the next generation, the children of 5 and 6 also belong to the color kin group since they take their descent from their mother who is a member of that group. However, the children of 3 and 4 do not belong to this matrilineal group since they take their descent from their mother who is a member of a different group; their father, although a member of the color matrilineal group, cannot pass his affiliation on to them under the rule of matrilineal descent. In the fourth generation, only 21 and 22 belong to the color matrilineal group, since their mother is the only female member of the preceding generation who belongs. Thus, individuals 2, 4, 5, 12, 14, 21, and 22 belong to the same matrilineal group. This rule of descent generates a group that is the mirror image of the group generated by a patrilineal rule.

long to your patrilineal group; but your father and his father (and their sisters) do. In your own generation in a matrilineal or patrilineal system, some cousins are excluded; and in your children's generation, some of your nieces and nephews are excluded. However, although unilineal rules of descent exclude certain types of relatives from membership in one's kin group (just as practical considerations restrict the effective size of kinship networks in our own society), the excluded relatives are not necessarily ignored or forgotten. Indeed, in many

The Chinese visually manifest the solidarity of descent groups. Descendants of common ancestors annually meet at the tomb of their ancestor to offer food sacrifices and incense. (Burton Pasternak.)

unilineal societies they may be entrusted with important responsibilities. For example, when a person dies in a patrilineal society, some members of his or her mother's patrilineal descent group may customarily be accorded the right to perform certain rituals at the funeral.

Unlike the bilateral rule of descent, unilineal rules of descent can form clear-cut, and hence unambiguous, groups of kinsmen, which can act as discrete units and continue to act as such even after the death of individual members. Referring again to Figures 1 and 2, we can see that the individuals shaded in color belong to the same patrilineal or matrilineal descent group without ambiguity—an individual in the fourth generation belongs to the respective group just as much as one in the first generation. If we imagine that the patrilineal group, for instance, has a name, say the Hawks, then an individual knows immediately whether or not he or she is a Hawk. If the individual is not a Hawk, then he or she belongs to some other group—for each person belongs to only one line. This fact is important if kin groups are to act as discrete or nonoverlapping units. It is difficult for people to act together unless they know exactly who should get together. And it is easier for individuals to act together as a group

if each one belongs to only one such group. In a bilateral system, in contrast, not only is it sometimes unclear where the boundary of the kindred is, but one person may belong to many different kindreds—his own and others' (his chldren's, his cousins', and so forth). Consequently, it is not surprising that the kindred only get together temporarily for ceremonial occasions.

Types of Unilineal Descent Groups In a society with unilineal descent, people usually refer to themselves as belonging to a particular unilineal group or set of groups because they believe that they share common descent in either the male line (patrilineal) or the female line (matrilineal). These people form what is called a *unilineal descent group.* Several types of unilineal descent groups are conventionally distinguished by anthropologists.

Lineages A *lineage* is a set of kin whose members trace descent from a common ancestor through known links. There may be patrilineages or matrilineages, depending, of course, upon whether the links are traced through males only or through females only. Lineages are often designated by the name of the common ancestor or ancestress. In some societies, people belong to a hierarchy of lineages. That is, they first trace their descent back to the ancestor of a minor lineage, then to the ancestor of a larger and more inclusive major lineage, and so on.

Clans A *clan* (also called a *sib*) is a set of kin whose members believe themselves to be descended from a common ancestor or ancestress but cannot specify the links back to that ancestor. In fact, the common ancestor may not even be known. Clans or sibs are often designated by an animal or plant name (called a *totem*) which may have some special significance for the group and at the very least provides a means of group identification. Thus, if someone says he or she belongs to the Bear, Wolf, or Turtle group, for example, others will know whether or not that person is a clansman.

Although it may seem strange to us that an animal or plant should be a symbol of a kin group, animals as symbols of groups are familiar in our own culture. Football and baseball teams, for example, are often named for animals (Detroit Tigers, Los Angeles Rams, Philadelphia Eagles, Atlanta Falcons). Voluntary associations, such as men's clubs, are sometimes called by the name of an animal (Elks, Moose, Lions). Entire nations may be represented by an animal, as the American Eagle, the British Lion, or the Russian Bear.[11]

The use of a totem to refer to one's clan or sib is common in societies with unilineal descent groups. The word *totem* itself comes from the Ojibwa American Indian word *ototeman* that means "a relative of mine." In some societies, people have to observe taboos relating to their clan totem. For example, clan members may be forbidden to kill or eat their totem.

The reasons for choosing animals and, very infrequently, plants to represent clans are problematic. Claude Lévi-Strauss suggests that particular qualities of animals may strike the human imagination, perhaps even the uncon-

Many northwest Pacific coast Indian societies constructed totem poles representing animals associated with their kin groups. Shown here are Beaver and Eagle totem poles of the Tlingit Indians. (National Museum of Canada, Ottawa, Canada.)

scious. These qualities are somehow representative of features important to the survival and even the behavior of clan ancestors—qualities such as vitality, aggressiveness, slyness, restlessness, or eternal unpredictability.[12]

Phratries A phratry is a unilineal descent group composed of a number of supposedly related clans or sibs. As with the clans, the descent links in phratries are unspecified.

Moieties When a whole society is divided into two unilineal descent groups, we call each group a moiety. (The word *moiety* comes from a

[11] George P. Murdock, *Social Structure* (New York: Macmillan, 1949), pp. 49–50.

[12] Claude Lévi-Strauss, *Totemism* (Boston: Beacon Press, 1962).

French word meaning "half.") The people in each moiety believe themselves to be descended from a common ancestor, although they cannot specify how.

Although we have distinguished several different types of unilineal descent groups, we do not wish to imply that all unilineal societies have only one type of descent group. Although some have just one type of group, many societies have two or more types in various combinations. For example, some societies have lineages and clans; others may have clans and phratries but no lineages; and still others may have clans and moieties but neither phratries nor lineages. Aside from the fact that a society which has phratries must also have clans (since phratries are combinations of clans), all combinations of descent groups are possible.

Patrilineal Organization Patrilineal organization is the most frequent type of descent system. The Kapauku Papuans, a people living in the central highlands of western New Guinea, are an example of a patrilineal society with many types of descent groups.[13] The hierarchy of groups to which a Kapauku is affiliated by virtue of the patrilineal descent system plays an extremely important part in life. Every Kapauku belongs to a patrilineage, to a patriclan which includes his or her lineage, and to a patriphratry which includes his or her clan.

The male members of a patrilineage—that is, all the living males who can trace their actual relationship through males to a common ancestor—constitute the male population of a single village or, more likely, a series of adjoining villages. In other words, the lineage is a territorial unit. The male members of the lineage live together by virtue of a patrilocal rule of residence and a fairly stable settlement pattern. A son stays near his parents and brings his wife to live in or near his father's house, while the daughters leave home and go to live with their husbands. If the group lives in one place over a

long period of time, the male descendants of one man will live in the same territory. If the lineage is large, it may be subdivided into sublineages composed of people who trace their descent from one of the sons of the lineage ancestor. The male members of a sublineage live in a contiguous block of territory within the larger lineage territory.

The members of the same patrilineage address each other affectionately, and within this group law and order is maintained by a headman. Killing within the lineage is considered a serious offense, and any fighting that takes place within the lineage is done with sticks, rather than with lethal weapons such as spears. The sublineage headman tries to settle any kind of grievance within the sublineage as quickly and as peacefully as possible. If a sublineage-mate commits a crime, all the members of the sublineage may be considered responsible and their property may be seized, or a member of the sublineage may be killed in revenge.

The Kapauku also belong to larger and more inclusive patrilineal descent groups—clans and phratries. All the people of the same clan believe that they are related to each other in the father's line, but they are unable to say how they are related. If a member of the patriclan eats the plant or animal totem, it is believed that the person will become deaf. A Kapauku is also forbidden to marry anyone from his or her clan; in other words, the clan is exogamous.

Unlike the members of the patrilineage, the male members of the patriclan do not all live together. Thus, the lineage is the largest group of patrilineal kinsmen that is localized. The lineage is also the largest group of kinsmen that acts together politically. Among clan members there is no mechanism for resolving disputes, and members of the same patriclan (who belong to different lineages) may even go to war with one another.

The most inclusive patrilineal descent group among the Kapauku is the phratry, each phratry being composed of two or more clans. The Kapauku believe that the phratry was originally one clan, but in a conflict between broth-

[13] Leopold Pospisil, *The Kapauku Papuans* (New York: Holt, Rinehart and Winston, 1963).

Members of a Kapauku patrilineage cooperate in constructing a dance house for a pig feast. The sponsor of the feast is the man in the foreground. (Courtesy Leopold Pospisil.)

ers of the founding family, the younger brother was expelled and formed a new clan. The two resulting clans are, of course, viewed as patrilineally related, since their founders are said to have been brothers. The members of a phratry observe all the totemic taboos of the clans which belong to that phratry. However, while intermarriage of members of the same clan is forbidden, members of the same phratry but of different clans may marry.

The Kapauku, then, are an example of a unilineal society with many types of descent groups. They have lineages with demonstrated kinship links and two kinds of descent groups with unknown descent links (clans and phratries).

Matrilineal Organization Although societies with matrilineal descent seem in many respects like mirror images of their patrilineal counterparts, there is one important way in which they differ. That difference has to do with who exercises authority in matrilineal systems. In patrilineal systems, descent affiliation is transmitted through males and it is also the males who exercise authority in the kin groups. Consequently, in the patrilineal system, the lines of descent and of authority converge. In a matri-

lineal system, however, while the line of descent passes through females, females rarely exercise authority in their kin groups—usually males do. Thus, unlike the patrilineal system, the lines of authority and descent do not converge in the matrilineal system.[14] Although anthropologists do not quite understand why this is so, it seems to be an ethnographic fact. In any case, since males exercise authority in the kin group, an individual's mother's brother becomes an important authority figure, because he is the individual's closest male matrilineal relative in the parental generation. The individual's father does not belong to the individual's own matrilineal kin group and thus has no say in kin group matters.

The divergence of authority and descent in a matrilineal system has some effect upon community organization and marriage within the community. Most matrilineal societies practice matrilocal residence. Daughters stay at home after marriage and bring their husbands to live with them; sons leave home to join their wives. But the sons who are required to leave will be

---

[14]David M. Schneider, "The Distinctive Features of Matrilineal Descent Groups," in *Matrilineal Kinship,* ed. David M. Schneider and Kathleen Gough (Berkeley: University of California Press, 1961), pp. 1–35.

Truk society has matrilineal descent groups. Here we see two great-aunts and two great-nieces who belong to one such group. Because residence is matrilocal, they live near each other in the same community. (Ward H. Goodenough, University of Pennsylvania.)

the ones who eventually exercise authority in their kin groups. This presents somewhat of a problem. The solution which seems to have been arrived at in most matrilineal societies is that, although the males move away to live with their wives, they usually do not move too far away; and indeed, they often marry women who live in the same village. Thus, matrilineal societies tend not to be locally exogamous—that is, members often marry people from inside the village—whereas patrilineal societies are often locally exogamous.[15]

The matrilineal organization on Truk, a group of small islands in the Pacific, illustrates the general pattern of authority in matrilineal systems.[16] The Trukese have both matrilineages and matriclans. The matrilineage is a property-owning group, whose members trace descent from a known common ancestor in the female line. The female lineage members and their husbands occupy a cluster of houses located on the matrilineage's land. The property of the

lineage group is administered by the oldest brother of the group. He allocates the productive property of his matrilineage and directs the work of the matrilineage members. The oldest brother of the lineage also represents the group in dealings with the district chief and all outsiders, and he must be consulted on any matter that affects the descent group. There is also a senior woman of the lineage who exercises some authority, but only insofar as the activities of the women are concerned. She may supervise the women's cooperative work (they usually work separately from the men) and may direct the management of the household.

Within the nuclear family, the father and mother have the primary responsibility for raising and disciplining their children. However, when a child reaches puberty, the father's right to discipline or exercise authority over the child ceases. The mother still continues to exercise her right of discipline, and her brother may interfere in this respect. A woman's brother rarely interferes with his sister's child before puberty, but after puberty he may exercise some authority, especially since he is an elder in the child's own matrilineage. On Truk, men

[15] Ember and Ember, "The Conditions Favoring Matrilocal versus Patrilocal Residence," p. 581.

[16] David M. Schneider, "Truk," in *Matrilineal Kinship*, ed. David M. Schneider and Kathleen Gough, pp. 202–33.

rarely move far from their natal homes. As Goodenough has pointed out, "Since matrilocal residence takes the men away from their home lineages, most of them marry women whose lineage houses are within a few minutes' walk of their own."[17]

Although there are some differences between the patrilineal and matrilineal systems, there are still many similarities. In both types of systems, there may be lineages, clans, phratries, moieties, and any combination of these. These kin groups, in either matrilineal or patrilineal societies, may perform any number of functions. They may regulate marriage; they may come to each other's mutual aid either economically or politically; and they may perform rituals together.

Now that we have learned something about matrilineal systems, the avunculocal pattern of residence, whereby married couples live with or near the husband's mother's brother, may become clearer. Although avunculocal residence is relatively rare, all avunculocal societies are matrilineal. As we have seen, the mother's brother plays an important role in decision making in most matrilineal societies. Aside from his brothers, who is a boy's closest male matrilineal relative? His mother's brother. Going to live with mother's brother, then, provides a way of localizing all male matrilineal relatives. But why should some matrilineal societies practice that form of residence, while most practice matrilocal residence (where female matrilineal relatives are localized)? The answer to this question may involve the prevailing type of warfare. Avunculocal societies, in contrast to matrilocal societies, all fight internally. Just as patrilocality may be a response to keep (patrilineally) related men home after marriage, so avunculocality may be a way of keeping related (in this case, matrilineally related) men together after marriage to provide for quick mobilization in case of surprise attack from nearby. Why the men so localized are matrilineally, rather than patri-

lineally, related may be a consequence of the prior existence and persistence of matrilineal descent groups.[18]

Functions of Unilineal Descent Groups Unilineal descent groups exist in societies at all levels of cultural complexity.[19] However, they are most common, apparently, in noncommercial food-producing (as opposed to food-collecting) societies.[20] Unilineal descent groups often have important functions in the social, economic, political, and religious realms of life.

Regulating Marriage In unilineal societies, individuals are not usually permitted to marry within their own unilineal descent groups. In some unilineal societies, however, marriage may be permitted within more inclusive kin groups while it is prohibited within smaller kin groups. In a few societies, marriage within the kin group is actually preferred. But in general, the incest taboo in unilineal societies is extended to all presumed unilineal relatives. For example, on Truk, which has matriclans and matrilineages, a person is forbidden by the rule of descent-group exogamy to marry anyone from his or her matriclan. Since the matrilineage is included within the matriclan, the rule of descent-group exogamy also applies to the matrilineage. Among the Kapauku, who have patriphratries, patriclans, and patrilineages, the largest descent group that is exogamous is the patriclan. The phratry may once have been exogamous, but the exogamy rule no longer applies to it. It is traditionally assumed in anthropology that rules of exogamy for descent groups may have developed because the alliances between descent groups that are generated by such rules may be selectively favored under the conditions of life faced by most unilineal societies.

Economic Functions Members of a man's lineage or clan are almost always required to side with

---

[17]Ward H. Goodenough, *Property, Kin and Community on Truk* (New Haven: Yale University Publications in Anthropology, 1951), p. 145.

[18]Melvin Ember, "The Conditions that May Favor Avunculocal Residence," *Behavior Science Research* 9 (1974): 203–9.

[19]Coult and Habenstein, *Cross Tabulations of Murdock's World Ethnographic Sample.*

[20]Data from Robert B. Textor, comp., *A Cross-Cultural Summary* (New Haven: HRAF Press, 1967).

him in any quarrel or lawsuit, to help him establish himself economically, to contribute to a bride price or fine, and to support him in life crises. The clans in China, for example, required that wealthier members insure that poor members were fed and that the higher education of bright students was financed. Where a clan is widely dispersed, the claim to mutual aid may be limited to the provision of hospitality to travelers.

Mutual aid often extends to economic cooperation on a regular basis. The unilineal descent group may act as a corporate unit in land ownership. For example, house sites and farmland are owned by a lineage among the Trukese and the Kapauku. Descent group members may also support each other in such enterprises as clearing virgin bush or forest for farmland, and in providing food and other things for feasts, potlatches, curing rites, and ceremonial occasions such as births, initiations, marriages, and funerals.

Money earned—either by harvesting a cash crop or by leaving the community for a period of time to work for cash wages—is sometimes viewed by the descent group as belonging to all. In recent times, however, young people in some places have shown an unwillingness to part with their money, viewing it as different from other kinds of economic assistance.

Political Functions The word *political,* as used by members of an industralized society, generally does not apply to the rather vague powers that may be entrusted to a headman or the elders of a lineage or clan. However, these persons may have the right to assign land for use by a lineage member or clansman, even if this right is purely symbolic and does not include the power to refuse land. Headmen or elders may also have the right to attempt to settle disputes between two members within a lineage, although they generally lack power to force a settlement. And they may act as intermediaries in disputes between a member of their own clan and a member of an opposing kin group.

Certainly one of the most important political functions of unilineal descent groups is their role in warfare—the attempt to resolve disputes within and without the society by violent action—for in middle-range societies the organization of such fighting is often in the hands of descent groups. The Tiv of central Nigeria, for instance, know quite well at any given moment which lineages they will fight with and which lineages they will fight against, which merit only a stick fight and which must be attacked with bows and arrows. If a man from an unfriendly lineage is caught taking food from a Tiv garden at night, the owner may kill him. The dead man's lineage retaliates by killing one person from the garden owner's lineage, which then retaliates in turn, and so on.

In no society is murder allowed within the smallest type of descent group. On the other hand, killing outside the lineage or the clan may be regrettable, but it is not viewed as a crime. It is interesting to note then that the murder of a brother, Cain's murder of Abel, because of favoritism, is the first crime mentioned in the Bible; it was punished by ostracism. Greek law viewed murder of a family member as an unforgivable, heinous crime. Yet, mythology recounts family murder after family murder: Agamemnon, his daughter; Medea, her brother; Heracles, his wife and children. Perhaps the underlying basis for the strong prohibition of murder within a family exists because that is where murder is most likely to occur, as present statistics continue to bear out.

Religious Functions A clan or lineage may have its own religious beliefs and practices, worshiping its own gods or goddesses and ancestral spirits.

The Tallensi of West Africa revere and try to pacify their ancestors. They view life as we know it as only a part of human existence; for them, life existed before birth and will continue to exist after death. The Tallensi believe that the ancestors of their descent groups have changed their form but have retained their interest in what goes on within the society. They can show their displeasure by bringing sudden disaster or minor mishap; and they can show their pleasure by bringing unexpected good fortune. But people can never tell what will please them— ancestral spirits are above all unpredictable. Thus, the Tallensi try to account for unexplainable happenings by attributing them to the ever-watchful ancestors. Belief in the presence of ancestors also provides security; if their ancestors have survived death, so will they. The Tallensi religion is thus a descent-group religion. The Tallensi are not concerned with other people's ancestors; they believe it is only one's own ancestors who plague one.[21]

The Hopi clans control their religion. The religion is one in which the unity of the people is evidenced by the interdependence of the clans, for each is considered a significant part of the whole. Each clan sponsors at least one of the religious festivals each year and is the guardian of the paraphernalia and the ritual. A festival is not exclusive to one clan, for all the Hopi clans participate. This clan responsibility for ceremonies is accepted as part of the will of the spirits or deities, and each clan is believed to have been assigned its ritual role before the emergence of Hopi people from the underworld.[22]

The Nayar castes of central Kerala in India derive from an ancient culture which was trading by sea as early as 800 B.C. Not only do various castes possess their own temples, but separate lineages within castes have their own shrines. Nayar temples are dedicated to Bhagavadi, the goddess of war, epidemic, land, and fertility, who is named differently by each lineage. This goddess is believed to control sickness and other misfortunes; and lineage members are expected to perform daily temple rites to her, as well as to sponsor annual festivals in her honor.[23]

Development of Unilineal Systems Unilineal kin groups often play very important roles in the organization of many societies. But not all societies have unilineal kin groups. In societies which have complex systems of political organization, political officials and agencies take over many of the functions that might be performed by kin groups, such as the organization of work, warfare, and the allocation of land. However, not all societies that lack complex political organization have unilineal descent systems. Why, then, do some societies have unilineal descent systems and others do not?

It is generally assumed that unilocal residence (patrilocal or matrilocal) is necessary for the development of unilineal descent. Patrilocal residence, if practiced for some time in a society, will generate a set of patrilineally related males who live in the same territory. Matrilocal residence over time will similarly generate a localized set of matrilineally related females. It is no wonder, then, that matrilocal and patrilocal residence are cross-culturally associated with matrilineal and patrilineal descent, respectively.[24]

But although unilocal residence might be necessary for the formation of unilineal descent groups, it is apparently not the only condition required. For one thing, many societies with unilocal residence lack unilineal descent groups. For another, merely because related males or related females live together by virtue of a patrilocal or matrilocal rule of residence, it does not necessarily follow that the related people will actually view themselves as a descent group and function as such. Thus, it appears that other conditions are needed to supply the impetus for the formation of unilineal descent groups.

There is some evidence that unilocal societies that engage in warfare are more apt to have unilineal descent groups than unilocal societies without warfare.[25] It may be, then, that the presence of fighting in societies lacking complex systems of political organization may provide an impetus to the formation of unilineal descent groups. This may be because unilineal descent groups provide individuals with unambiguous groups of persons that can fight or form alli-

[21] M. Fortes, *The Web of Kinship among the Tallensi* (New York: Oxford University Press, 1949).
[22] Fred Eggan, *The Social Organization of the Western Pueblos* (Chicago: University of Chicago Press, 1950).
[23] Kathleen Gough, "Nayar: Central Kerala," in *Matrilineal Kinship,* ed. David M. Schneider and Kathleen Gough, p. 330.

[24] Data from Textor, *A Cross-Cultural Summary.*
[25] Carol R. Ember, Melvin Ember, and Burton Pasternak, "On the Development of Unilineal Descent," *Journal of Anthropological Research* 30 (1974): 69–94.

ances as discrete units.[26] One distinguishing feature of unilineal descent groups is that there is no ambiguity about an individual's membership. It is perfectly clear whether someone belongs to a particular clan, phratry, or moiety. It is this feature of unilineal descent groups that enables them to act as discrete units, mostly, perhaps, in warfare.

Bilateral descent, in contrast, is ego-centered, and every person, other than siblings, has a slightly different set of kinsmen to rely upon. Consequently, in societies with bilateral descent, it is often ambiguous as to whom one can turn to and which person has responsibility for aiding another. Such ambiguity, however, might not be a liability in societies without warfare.

Whether the presence of warfare is, in fact, the major condition responsible for transforming a unilocal society into a society with unilineal descent groups is still not certain. However unilineal descent groups come into being, we know that they often are important in many spheres of activity, and it may be that some of these spheres other than warfare are responsible for their formation.

AMBILINEAL SYSTEMS

Ambilineal descent affiliates an individual with kinsmen related to him or her through men or women, as illustrated in Figure 3. In other words, some individuals affiliate with a group of kinsmen through their fathers, others through their mothers. Consequently, the descent groups show both male and female genealogical links. Societies with ambilineal descent groups are far less numerous than unilineal or even bilateral societies. However, ambilineal societies resemble unilineal ones in many ways. For instance, the members of an ambilineal descent group believe they are descended from a common ancestor, though frequently they cannot

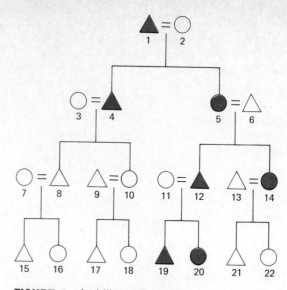

FIGURE 3 Ambilineal Descent
A hypothetical ambilineal group of kinsmen is indicated by the color. Members 4 and 5 belong to this group because of a male link, their father (1); members 12 and 14 belong because of a female link, their mother (5); and members 19 and 20 belong because of a male link, their father (12). This is a hypothetical example because any combination of lineal links is possible in an ambilineal descent group.

specify all of the genealogical links. The descent group is commonly named and may have an identifying emblem or even totem; land and other productive resources may be owned by the descent group; and myths and religious practices are often associated with the group. Marriage is often regulated by group membership, just as in unilineal systems, though kin group exogamy is not nearly so common in ambilineal as in unilineal systems. Moreover, ambilineal societies resemble unilineal ones in having various levels or types of descent groups. They may have lineages and higher orders of descent groups, distinguished (as in unilineal systems) by whether or not all the genealogical links to the supposed common ancestor are specified.[27]

[26] The importance of warfare and competition as factors in the formation of unilineal descent groups is also suggested by Service, *Primitive Social Organization*, and Marshall D. Sahlins, "The Segmentary Lineage: An Organization of Predatory Expansion," *American Anthropologist* 63 (1961): 332–45.

[27] William Davenport, "Nonunilineal Descent and Descent Groups," *American Anthropologist* 61 (1959): 557–72.

The Samoans of the South Pacific are an example of an ambilineal society.[28] There are two types of ambilineal descent groups in Samoa, corresponding to what would be called clans and subclans in a unilineal society. Both of these ambilineal groups are exogamous. Associated with each ambilineal clan are one or more chiefs. A group takes its name from the senior chief; subclans, of which there are always at least two, may take their names from junior chiefs.

The distinctiveness of the Samoan ambilineal descent system, as compared with unilineal descent systems, is that because an individual may be affiliated with an ambilineal group through his or her father or mother (and his or her parents, in turn, could be affiliated with any of their parents' groups), there are a number of ambilineal groups to which that individual could belong. Affiliation with a Samoan descent group is optional, and a person may theoretically affiliate with any or all of the ambilineal groups to which he or she is related. In practice, however, a person is primarily associated with one group—the ambilineal group whose land he or she actually lives on and cultivates—although he or she may participate in the activities (house building, for example) of several ambilineal groups. Since a person may belong to more than one ambilineal group in Samoa, the society is not divided into discrete kin groups, in contrast to unilineal societies where each person belongs to only one descent line. Consequently, the core members of each ambilineal group cannot all live together (as they could in unilineal societies), since each person belongs to more than one group and cannot live in several places at once.

Not all ambilineal societies have multiple descent group membership, as occurs in Samoa. In some ambilineal societies, a person may belong (at any one time) to only one group; and in such case, the society can be divided into discrete, nonoverlapping groups of kin.

Why do some societies have ambilineal descent groups? Although the evidence is not clear-cut on this point, it may be that societies with unilineal descent groups are transformed from ambilineal ones under special conditions—particularly in the presence of depopulation. We have already noted that depopulation may transform a previously unilocal society into a bilocal society. If that previously unilocal society also had unilineal descent groups, the descent groups may become transformed into ambilineal groups. If a society used to be patrilocal and patrilineal, for example, but some couples begin to live matrilocally, then their children may be associated with a previously patrilineal descent group (on whose land they may be living) through their mother. Once this happens regularly, the unilineal principle may become transformed into an ambilineal principle.[29]

Kinship Terminology

Our society, like all other societies, refers to a number of different kinsmen by the same *classificatory* term. Our kinship terminology is so much a part of our everyday usage that most people probably never stop to think about why we name relatives the way we do. For example, we call our "mother's brother" and "father's brother" (and often "mother's sister's husband" and "father's sister's husband") by the same term—"uncle." It is not that we are unable to distinguish between our mother's or father's brother or that we do not know the difference between *consanguineal kin* (blood kin) and *affinal kin* (kin by marriage). Instead, it seems that in our society we do not usually find it necessary to distinguish between our various types of "uncles."

However natural our system of kinship

[28] The description of the Samoan descent system is based upon M. Ember's 1955–56 fieldwork. See also Melvin Ember, "The Nonunilinear Descent Groups of Samoa," *American Anthropologist* 61 (1959): 573–77; Davenport, "Nonunilineal Descent and Descent Groups."

[29] Ember and Ember, "The Conditions Favoring Multilocal Residence," pp. 382–400.

classification may seem to us, countless field studies by anthropologists have revealed that societies differ markedly in how they group or distinguish relatives under the same or different terms. The kinship terminology may reflect the kind of family prevailing in a society, its rule of residence and its rule of descent, and other aspects of social organization. The kin terms may also give clues to prior features of the social system, if, as many anthropologists believe,[30] the kin terms of a society are very resistant to change. The major systems of kinship terminology are the Omaha system, the Crow system, the Iroquois system, the Hawaiian system, the Eskimo system, and the Sudanese system.

OMAHA SYSTEM

The Omaha system of kin terminology is named after the Omaha Indian tribe of North America, but this system of kin terminology is found in many societies around the world, usually those with patrilineal descent.[31]

Referring to Figure 4, we can see immediately which types of kin are lumped together in an Omaha system. First, father and father's brother (numbers 2 and 3) are both referred to by the same term. This contrasts markedly with our way of classifying relatives, in which no term that applies to a member of the nuclear family (father, mother, brother, sister) is applied to any other relative. What could account for the Omaha system of lumping? One interpretation is that father and father's brother are lumped in this system because most societies in which this system is found have patrilineal kin groups. Both father and father's brother are in the parental generation of my patrilineal kin group and may behave toward me similarly. My father's brother also probably lives near me, since patrilineal societies usually have patrilocal residence. The term for father and father's

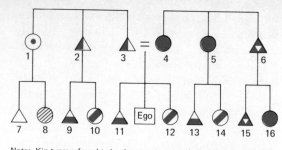

Note: Kin types referred to by the same term are marked in the same way.

FIGURE 4 Omaha Kinship Terminology System

brother, then, might be translated "male member of my patrilineal kin group in my father's generation."

A second lumping (which at first glance appears similar to the lumping of father and father's brother) is that of mother and mother's sister (numbers 4 and 5), both of whom are called by the same term. But more surprisingly, mother's brother's daughter (number 16) is also referred to by this same term. Why should this be? If we think of the term as meaning "female member of my mother's patrilineage of *any* generation," then the coverage of the term makes more sense. Consistent with this view, all the male members of my mother's patrilineage of any generation (mother's brother, number 6; mother's brother's son, number 15) are also referred to by the same term.

It is apparent, then, that relatives on the father's and the mother's sides are grouped differently in this system. For members of my mother's patrilineal kin group, I lump all male members together and all female members together regardless of their generation. Yet, for members of my father's patrilineal kin group, I have different terms for the male and female members of different generations. Murdock has suggested that a society lumps kin types, rather than separates them terminologically, when there are more similarities than differences among them.[32]

Using this principle, and recognizing that

[30] See, for example, Murdock, *Social Structure*, pp. 199–222.
[31] The association between the Omaha system and patrilineality is reported in Textor, *A Cross-Cultural Summary*.

[32] Murdock, *Social Structure*, p. 125.

societies with an Omaha system usually are patrilineal, I realize that my father's patrilineal kin group is the one to which I belong and in which I have a great many rights and obligations. Consequently, persons of my father's generation are likely to behave quite differently toward me than are persons of my own generation. Members of my patrilineal group in my father's generation are likely to exercise authority over me and I am required to show them respect. Members of my patrilineal group in my own generation are those I am likely to play with as a child and to be friends with. Thus, in a patrilineal system, persons on my father's side belonging to different generations are likely to be distinguished. On the other hand, my mother's patrilineage is relatively unimportant to me in a patrilineal society (since I take my descent from my father). And because my residence is probably patrilocal, my mother's relatives will probably not even live near me. Thus, inasmuch as my mother's patrilineal relatives are comparatively unimportant in such a system, they become similar enough to be lumped together.

Finally, in the Omaha system, I refer to my male parallel-cousins (my father's brother's son, number 9, and my mother's sister's son, number 13) in the same way I refer to my brother (number 11). I refer to my female parallel-cousins (my father's brother's daughter, number 10), and my mother's sister's daughter, number 14) in the same way I refer to my sister (number 12). Considering that my father's brother and mother's sister are referred to by the same terms I use for my father and mother, this lumping of parallel-cousins with siblings is not surprising. If I call my own mother's and father's children (other than myself) "brother" and "sister," then the children of anyone whom I also call "mother" and "father" ought to be called "brother" and "sister" as well.

CROW SYSTEM

The Crow system, named after another North American Indian tribe, has been called the mirror image of the Omaha system. The same

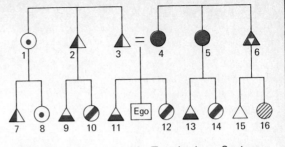

FIGURE 5 Crow Kinship Terminology System

principles of lumping kin types are employed, except that since the Crow system is associated with matrilineal descent,[33] the individuals in my mother's matrilineal group (which is my own) are not lumped across generations, whereas the individuals in my father's matrilineal group are lumped across generations. By comparing Figure 4 with Figure 5, we find that the lumping and separating of kin types is much the same in both, except that the lumping across generations in the Crow system appears on the father's side rather than on the mother's side. In other words, I call both my mother and my mother's sister by the same term (both female members of my matrilineal descent group in my mother's generation). I call my father, my father's brother, and my father's sister's son by the same term (all male members of my father's matrilineal group in any generation). I call my father's sister and my father's sister's daughter by the same term (both female members of my father's matrilineal group). And I refer to my parallel-cousins in the same ways I refer to my brother and sister.

IROQUOIS SYSTEM

The Iroquois system, named after the Iroquois Indian tribe of North America, is similar to both the Omaha and Crow systems in the way in which I refer to relatives in my parents' generation (see Figure 6). That is, my father and my

[33] The association between the Crow system and matrilineality is reported in Textor, *A Cross-Cultural Summary*.

father's brother are referred to by the same term (numbers 2 and 3), and my mother and mother's sister are referred to by the same term (numbers 4 and 5). However, the Iroquois system differs from the Omaha and Crow systems regarding my own generation. In the Omaha and Crow systems, one set of cross-cousins was lumped in the kinship terminology with the generation above. This is not true in the Iroquois system, where both sets of cross-cousins (mother's brother's children, numbers 15 and 16; and father's sister's children, numbers 7 and 8) are referred to by the same terms, distinguished by sex. That is, mother's brother's daughter and father's sister's daughter are both referred to by the same term. Also, mother's brother's son and father's sister's son are referred to by the same term. Parallel-cousins always have different terms from cross-cousins and are sometimes, but not always, referred to by the same terms as one's brother and sister.

Like the Omaha and Crow systems, the Iroquois system has different terms for relatives on the father's and mother's sides. Such differentiation tends to be associated with unilineal descent, which is not surprising since unilineal descent involves affiliation with either mother's or father's kin. Why Iroquois, rather than Omaha or Crow, terminology occurs in a unilineal society requires explanation. One possible explanation is that Omaha or Crow is likely to occur in a developed, as opposed to a de-

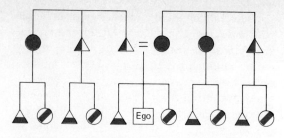

FIGURE 7 Hawaiian Kinship Terminology System

veloping or decaying, unilineal system.[34] Another possible explanation is that Iroquois terminology emerges in societies which prefer marriage with both cross-cousins,[35] who are differentiated from other relatives in an Iroquois system.

HAWAIIAN SYSTEM

The Hawaiian system of kinship terminology is the least complex in that it uses the smallest number of terms. In this system, all relatives of the same sex in the same generation are referred to by the same term. Thus, all my female cousins are referred to by the same term as my sister; all male cousins are referred to by the same term as my brother. Everyone known to be related to me in my parents' generation is referred to by one term if female (including my mother) and by another term if male (including my father). (See Figure 7.)

The Hawaiian system is associated with ambilineal descent.[36] In an ambilineal society, a person might be affiliated with an ambilineal group through his mother or his father at any given moment in time. If this is so, then any of my mother's or father's brothers or sisters might belong to my kin group. This creates similarity between all of my parents' siblings and might account for the lumping of persons in

[34] See Leslie A. White, "A Problem in Kinship Terminology," *American Anthropologist* 41 (1939): 569–70.

[35] Jack Goody, "Cousin Terms," *Southwestern Journal of Anthropology* 26 (1970): 125–42.

[36] This association is reported in Textor, *A Cross-Cultural Summary.*

FIGURE 6 Iroquois Kinship Terminology System

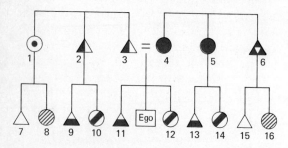

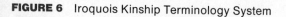

Note: Although not shown in this diagram, in the Iroquois system parallel cousins are sometimes referred to by different terms than one's own brother and sister.

the parental generation. Furthermore, if people related to me in my parents' generation are called by the same terms I use to refer to my mother and father, then all of their children would tend to be referred to by the same terms as my own brother and sister. And, since any of my cousins might also be in my ambilineal kin group, they also would tend to be referred to by the same terms as my brother and sister.

ESKIMO SYSTEM

Although the Eskimo system is so named because it is found in some Eskimo societies, it also is the terminological system which the United States and many other commercial societies use. (See Figure 8.)

The distinguishing features of the Eskimo system are that all cousins are lumped together under the same term but are distinguished from brothers and sisters, and all aunts and uncles are generally lumped under the same terms but are distinguished from mother and father. Unlike all the other systems we have discussed, in an Eskimo system no other relatives are generally referred to by the same terms used for members of the nuclear family—mother, father, brother, and sister. Perhaps this is because in societies with any of the other terminological systems, some kind of lineal descent group (either unilineal or ambilineal) is usually important. Also, such descent groups usually entail important roles for nonnuclear family members.

FIGURE 8 Eskimo Kinship Terminology System

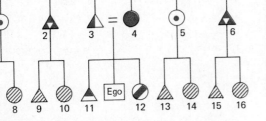

Note: In some Eskimo systems the cousin term may vary according to sex.

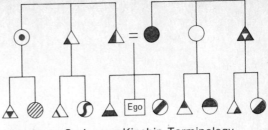

FIGURE 9 Sudanese Kinship Terminology System

Eskimo kinship terminology is not generally found where there are unilineal or ambilineal descent groups; the only kin group that may be present is the bilateral kindred.[37] The kindred in a bilateral descent system is an ego-centered group. Although relatives on both my mother's and my father's sides are equally important, my most important relatives are generally the closest. This is particularly true in our type of society where the nuclear family generally lives alone, separated from, and not particularly involved with, other relatives except on ceremonial occasions. Since the nuclear family is most important, we would expect to find that the kin types in the nuclear family are distinguished terminologically from all other relatives. And since the mother's and father's sides are equally important (or unimportant), it makes sense that we use the same terms (aunt, uncle, and cousin) for both sides of the family.

SUDANESE SYSTEM

Unlike the other terminological systems we have examined so far, a Sudanese system of kin terminology usually does not lump any relatives in the parents' and ego's generations. That is, a Sudanese system is usually a *descriptive* system in which a different term is used to refer to *each* of the relatives shown in Figure 9. What kinds of societies are likely to have such a system? Although societies with Sudanese terminology are likely to be patrilineal, they probably are

[37] Data from Textor, *A Cross-Cultural Summary.*

different from most patrilineal societies which have Omaha or Iroquois terms. Sudanese terminology is associated with relatively great political complexity, class stratification, and occupational specialization. It has been suggested that such a kinship system may reflect the need to make fine distinctions among members of descent groups who have different opportunities and privileges in the occupational or class system.[38]

Summary

1. In our society, and in many other industrial societies, a newly married couple usually establishes a place of residence apart from parents or relatives (neolocal residence). But about 95 percent of the world's societies have some pattern of residence whereby the new couple settles within, or very close to, the household of the parents or some other close relative of the groom or bride.

2. The four major patterns in which married couples live with or near kinsmen are:
   a. Patrilocal residence: the married couple lives with or near the husband's parents (67 percent of all societies).
   b. Matrilocal residence: the married couple lives with or near the wife's parents (15 percent of all societies).
   c. Bilocal residence: the married couple lives with or near either the husband's parents or the wife's parents (7 percent of all societies).
   d. Avunculocal residence: the son and his wife settle with or near his mother's brother (4 percent of all societies).

3. In most societies where kinship connections are important, there is a rule that allocates each person to a particular and definable set of kin. The rules affiliating individuals with sets of kin are called rules of descent.

4. There are only a few known rules of descent that affiliate individuals with different sets of kin:
   a. Bilateral descent affiliates an individual more or less equally with his or her mother's and father's relatives.
   b. Patrilineal descent affiliates an individual with kinsmen of both sexes related to him or her through men only. In each generation, then, children belong to the kin group of their father.
   c. Matrilineal descent affiliates an individual with kinsmen related to him or her through women only. In each generation, then, children belong to the kin group of their mother.
   d. Ambilineal descent affiliates an individual with kinsmen related to him or her through men or women. Consequently, the descent groups show both female and male genealogical links.

5. With unilineal descent (patrilineal or matrilineal), people usually refer to themselves as belonging to a particular unilineal group or set of groups because they believe that they share common descent in either the male line or the female line. These people form what is called a unilineal descent group. There are several types: lineages, or sets of kinsmen whose members trace descent from a common ancestor through known links; clans, or sets of kin who believe they are descended from a common ancestor but cannot specify the genealogical links; phratries, or groups of supposedly related clans; and moieties, unilineal descent groups without specified links to the supposed common ancestor when there are only two such groups in the entire society.

6. Unilineal descent groups are most common in societies in the middle range of cultural complexity—that is, in noncommercial food-producing (as opposed to food-collecting) societies. In such societies, unilineal descent groups often have important functions in the social, economic, political, and religious realms of life.

[38]Burton Pasternak, *Introduction to Kinship and Social Organization* (Englewood Cliffs, N.J.: Prentice-Hall, 1976), p. 142.

7. Societies differ markedly in how they group or distinguish relatives under the same or different kinship terms. The major systems of kinship terminology are the Omaha system, the Crow system, the Iroquois system, the Hawaiian system, the Eskimo system, and the Sudanese system.

Suggested Readings

Fox, R. *Kinship and Marriage: An Anthropological Perspective.* Baltimore: Penguin Books, 1967.

An introduction to social organization, focused on issues and principles in the study of various kinds of kinship groups.

Murdock, G. P. *Social Structure.* New York: Macmillan, 1949.

A pioneering cross-cultural analysis of variation in a number of aspects of social organization, including the family and marriage, kin groups, kinship terminology, the incest taboo and its extensions, and the regulation of sex.

Pasternak, B. *Introduction to Kinship and Social Organization.* Englewood Cliffs, N.J.: Prentice-Hall, 1976.

Chapters 4, 8, and 9 present an up-to-date survey and critique of theories and evidence about variation in residence and kinship.

Radcliffe-Brown, A. R., and Forde, D., eds. *African Systems of Kinship and Marriage.* New York: Oxford University Press, 1950.

A collection of essays describing the character and significance of kinship in some selected African societies.

Schneider, D. M., and Gough, K., eds. *Matrilineal Kinship.* Berkeley: University of California Press, 1961.

An extensive collection of theoretical and descriptive papers on matrilineal kinship. An introductory paper by Schneider discusses various theoretical issues. The ethnographic studies illustrate the various cultural expressions of matrilineal descent systems. In the final chapters, Gough and Aberle discuss how the ethnographic materials may relate to three main variables: subsistence methods, productivity of subsistence technology, and political development.

Schusky, E. L. *Manual for Kinship Analysis.* 2d ed. New York: Holt, Rinehart and Winston, 1971.

A brief manual explaining kin-type notation, genealogical tables, and types of kin terms. The author also presents the established concepts and terminology of patterns of descent and residence.

Associations and Interest Groups

17

Samuel Johnson, the eighteenth-century English author, was once asked to describe Boswell, his gregarious companion and biographer. "Boswell," he boomed, "is a very clubable man." Johnson did not mean that Boswell deserved to be attacked with bludgeons. He was alluding to Boswell's fondness for all sorts of clubs and associations, a fondness which he shared with many of his contemporaries. The tendency to form associations was not unique to eighteenth-century England. At all times and in all areas of the world, we find evidence of human beings' "clubability."

In this chapter, we shall examine the various kinds of nonkinship groups that are formed in different societies, how these groups function, and what general purposes they serve. The organizations that concern us here have the following characteristics in common: (1) some people are excluded from membership; (2) membership is based on commonly shared interests or purposes; (3) some kind of formal, institutional structure exists; and (4) there is a clearly discernible sense of mutual pride and belonging. Contemporary American society has an abundance of "interest groups"—to use the terminology of the political scientist—that exemplify these general characteristics. The membership of the American Pork Producers' Association is limited to farmers who raise hogs. The physicians who belong to the American Medical Association clearly share common interests and purposes. The United Auto Workers Union has its own constitution and bylaws. And the members of the Veterans of Foreign Wars can be said to feel mutual pride and a sense of belonging.

Associations or interest groups such as these vary in size and social significance. They also differ in two other important ways. One way is whether membership is voluntary or not. In Great Britain, for instance, as of 1972 a person could choose to join the military or stay out of it; in our country, joining the army was not completely voluntary until recently. The second way in which interest groups differ is in their prerequisites, or qualifications, for membership.

17

TABLE 1 Types of Nonkinship Organization

| Membership Criteria | Recruitment | |
	Voluntary	Nonvoluntary
Universally ascribed		Age-sets Unisex associations
Variably ascribed	Ethnic associations Regional associations	Conscripted army
Achieved	Examples: Occupational associations Political parties Special interest groups Secret societies Military clubs	

These "qualities" or criteria for membership fall into three general categories. One category is *universally ascribed qualities*, which are those an individual is born with and thus acquires automatically (such as age and sex). Another is *variably ascribed qualities*, which are those acquired at birth but which differ among persons of a given age-sex category (such as ethnicity, region of birth, or physical condition). A third category is *achieved qualities*, which are those the individual acquires by doing something.

Table 1 summarizes types of associations according to their criteria of recruitment and qualifications for membership. The specific conditions that favor the development of a particular type of organization may vary. However, nonvoluntary groups with universally ascribed membership—that is, age-sets and men's associations—tend to be found in relatively unstratified, or egalitarian, societies. In contrast, voluntary associations, with variably ascribed or achieved membership qualifications, appear to be found mostly in stratified societies. Presumably, this is because stratified societies are composed of people with different, and often competing, interests.

Nonvoluntary Associations

AGE-SETS

All societies utilize a vocabulary of *age terms* just as they utilize a vocabulary of kinship terms. For instance, as we distinguish between "brother," "uncle," and "cousin," so we also differentiate "infant," "adolescent," and "adult." Age terms refer to categories based upon age, or *age grades*. An age grade is simply a category of persons who happen to fall within a particular, culturally distinguished age range.

Age-set, on the other hand, is the term used to describe a group of persons of similar age and sex who move through some or all of life's stages together. For example, all the boys of a certain age range in a particular district might simultaneously become ceremonially initiated into "manhood." Later in life, the group as a whole might become "elders," and still later "retired elders." In societies with an age-set system, entry into the system is generally nonvoluntary and is based upon the universally ascribed characteristics of sex and age.

In most noncommercial societies, kinship forms the basis of the organization and administration of the society. However, there are some societies in which age-sets cross-cut kinship ties and form strong supplementary bonds. Three such societies are the Karimojong, the Nandi, and the Nyakyusa of Africa.

Karimojong Age-Sets The Karimojong number some 60,000 people. They are predominantly cattle herdsmen, and they occupy about 4,000 acres of semiarid country in northeastern Uganda. Their society is especially interesting because of its organization into combinations of age-sets and generation-sets. These groupings provide "both the source of political authority and the main field within which it is exercised."[1]

[1]Neville Dyson-Hudson, *Karimojong Politics* (Oxford: Clarendon Press, 1966), p. 155.

A Karimojong age-set comprises all men who have been initiated into manhood within a span of about five to six years. A generation-set consists of a combination of five such age-set units, covering twenty-five to thirty years. Each generation-set is seen as "begetting" the one which immediately follows it, and at any one time, two generation-sets are in corporate existence. The senior unit—whose members perform the administrative, the judicial, and the priestly functions—is closed; the junior unit whose members serve as warriors and policemen, is still recruiting. When all of the five age-sets in the junior generation-set are established, the junior generation-set will be ready (actually impatient) to assume the status of its senior predecessor. Eventually, grumbling but realistic, the elders will agree to a succession ceremony, moving those who were once in a position of obedience to a position of authority.

The Karimojong age system, then, comprises a cylical succession of four generation-sets in a predetermined continuing relationship. The *retired generation-set* consists of elders who have passed on the mantle of authority, since most of the five age-sets within the retired generation-set are depleted, if not defunct. The *senior generation-set* contains the five age-sets which actively exercise authority. The *junior generation-set* is still recruiting members and, although obedient to elders, has some administrative powers. The *noninitiates* are starting a generation-set.

The significance of the age- and generation-sets in Karimojong society gives particular importance to initiation into manhood. Initiation ceremonies are elaborate and fall into three parts, all supervised by the elders. The first part, called "spearing the ox," takes place in a ceremonial enclosure. Each initiate spears a beast from his family's herd and dismembers it according to a ritual pattern. The head and neck are carried away by the women for use in the later stages of the ceremony; the stomach sacs are carefully laid out unopened. The oldest tribal elder present and the local senior genera-

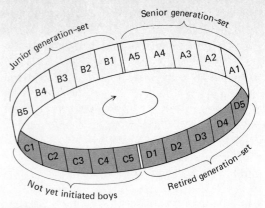

FIGURE 1

The Karimojong age system is composed of four distinct generation-sets (labeled A, B, C, and D in this diagram), which succeed each other cyclically. Each generation-set, in turn, is subdivided into five age-sets or potential age-sets. The senior generation-set (A) exercises authority. The junior age-set (B)—the warriors and policemen—is still recruiting. Generation-set D consists of retired age-sets. Non-initiated and not-yet-born boys constitute the potential age-sets C1–C5.

tion-set leader slit the sacs with a spear and anoint each initiate with the semidigested food which spills out. They then bless the initiate with the words, "Be well. Grow old. Become wealthy in stock. Become an elder."

In the second part of the ceremony, called "eating the tongue," the meat previously taken away by the women is boiled in clay pots and served to the men of the senior generation-set in the settlement, who bless the initiate and his family. The final part, called "cooking the stomach," takes place in the cattle corral, where a feast is held. The elders, the other adult men, and the initiates all sit and eat, each group in a separate circle. Before the initiation ceremony began, each boy was required to shave his head; after it, he is allowed to let his hair grow. Once his hair is sufficiently long, the initiate plasters it with mud and ties it back with a chain—the tangible symbol of his adult status.

Once initiated, a boy has become a man, with a clearly defined status and the ultimate certainty of exercising full authority together with his set partners. Indeed, a Karimojong is not expected to marry—and is certainly barred from starting a family—until he has been initiated. The initiation ceremony itself illustrates the essential political and social characteristics of the age-set system. Without the authority of the elders, the ceremony cannot be held; throughout the proceedings, their authority is explicit. The father-son relationship of adjacent generation-sets is emphasized, for fathers are initiating their sons.

Nandi Age-Sets The Nandi, a tribe of cattle herders and agriculturalists of western Kenya, provide another example of how age-sets may be organized.[2] As soon as he is born, the young Nandi male is a member of an age-set—that of the uninitiated. As he grows he will pass through initiation, symbolized by circumcision, to the warrior stage, and finally, if he lives long enough, through four more stages of "elderhood." The Nandi warrior-set theoretically holds the greatest authority in the system. It has the training, the means, and the power to carry out essential military operations—though in recent times, the occasion for demonstrating these qualities does not arise. There are altogether seven age-sets, which succeed each other in strict rotation. However, the focus is upon three of the seven: (1) the set composed of men about to become elders; (2) the set composed of men about to become warriors; and (3) the set composed of boys about to become initiated.

Initiation ceremonies take place about every fifteen years. Participation in the ceremony by initiates symbolizes their changed status—they move forward from boyhood to responsible adulthood. Boys are usually circumcised in their middle to late teens, although, if the family is wealthy enough, ten-year-old boys may participate in the ceremonies. The ritual of circumcision places much emphasis on the qualities of fortitude and physical toughness expected of a warrior. The ceremonies as a whole are carried out under the supervision of, and by the authority of, the warrior-set.

The initiates are separately housed, under the care of elderly men assigned to watch over them for the six-month initiation period. The initiation begins with a morning ceremony at which the boys' heads are anointed with a mixture of water, milk, and salt and are then shaved. The boys are given a strong purge and their clothes are taken away and replaced with girls' clothing. The next evening, after a dance ceremony, they hear the circumcision knife being sharpened outside of their huts, while warriors joke about the knife's eagerness to do its work. Later, during a procession, warriors beat the boys with nettles and drop hornets on them, as tests of endurance. Then each initiate has to confess his past misdeeds.

The circumcision itself is done in two steps. After a cut is made, each boy's face is scrutinized for signs of cowardice, and if he shows no fear, the rest of the operation is performed. To ease the pain which causes many initiates to faint, cold water is applied to the wound. Afterward, the initiates remain in seclusion for six months, wearing male apparel again, and during this time they are taught their duties as warriors. Finally, a feast celebrates their achievement of adult status.[3]

Nyakyusa Age-Villages The Nyakyusa, who live on the northwest shores of Lake Nyasa in the southeastern part of Africa, supply what might be termed the extreme example of age-set organization.[4] In this society, members of an age-set actually build a village together and settle down to live in it, later donating land to their sons so that the process may continue. Age-villages, such as those of the Nyakyusa, are quite rare today.

Between the ages of five and eleven, Nyakyusa boys sleep in their parents' homes and care for the family cattle. The cows of ten or

---

[2] See G. W. B. Huntingford, *The Nandi of Kenya: Tribal Control in a Pastoral Society* (London: Routledge and Kegan Paul, 1953).

[3] A. C. Hollis, *The Nandi: Their Language and Folklore* (Oxford: Clarendon Press, 1909), pp. 52–57.

[4] Monica Wilson, *Good Company: A Study of Nyakyusa Age-Villages* (Boston: Beacon Press, 1963).

Young boys of the Madingo tribe in Gambia undergo initiation into manhood. An adult male, dressed in a frightening costume, makes threatening gestures toward the boys with a knife. (Arthur Tress, Magnum Photos.)

so neighboring families are herded together; and the boys tending the animals begin to form close attachments, since they spend all their days together for about six years. At about twelve years of age, the boys begin hoeing in their fathers' fields and hand over the cattle-herding tasks to their younger brothers. The twelve-year-olds then leave their parental homes and live in a village of their own, returning to their own homesteads only for meals. Gradually, as the younger brothers mature and join the village, the community grows until at some point its members decide to close admittance.

The age-village is now complete, though its members still work their fathers' fields and eat their fathers' food. Upon reaching the age of twenty-five or so, the young men marry, bringing their wives to their village and setting up their own homes. Each young man now receives his own fields from his father and eats food prepared by his wife instead of by his mother. Eventually, the entire village assumes an autonomous life. After about a decade, when a number of such villages are established in the territory, the fathers ceremonially hand over full political authority to their sons and, as old men, step aside.

What is particularly interesting in the Nyakyusa system is its blending of family and age-set. When still quite young, the Nyakyusa male has already become accustomed to non-family social arrangements. Long before he becomes a father, with family obligations of his own, he is a fully involved participant in his own age-village, with specific communal and social responsibilities.

UNISEX ASSOCIATIONS

Unisex, as used here, has quite a different meaning from its current connotation in our own society, where it signifies something that is suitable for both sexes. Rather, we use the word *unisex* to describe a type of association that restricts its membership to one sex, most often male. Sex as a qualification is directly related to the purpose of the unisex association. For example, in many male unisex associations, this purpose is to strengthen the concept of male superiority and to offer men a refuge from females. In noncommercial societies, men's associations are similar to age-sets, except that there are only two sets, or stages: mature males, who are association members, and immature males, who are nonmembers.

In most noncommercial societies, women have few associations. Perhaps this is because in such societies the men are generally dominant in the kinship, property, and political spheres of life. (There is also the possibility that anthropologists, most of whom are men, have given women's associations less attention than men's associations.)

Unisex associations or clubs are also a feature of modern industrialized society. The Boy Scouts and the Kiwanis, the Girl Scouts and the League of Women Voters, are cases in point. Admission to these clubs, however, is voluntary and often is not based solely on ascribed criteria, as are the nonvoluntary unisex associations in noncommercial societies.

Mae Enga Bachelor Associations The Mae Enga are a group of about 30,000 sedentary horticulturalists living in the New Guinea highlands. Their society has received a great deal of attention from anthropologists for its practice of sexual segregation—indeed, for the strain of active hostility to women which runs through its culture.[5] It is the custom for Mae men to live in a separate, communal house. Up to the age of five, a young boy is permitted to live in his mother's house, although he is unconsciously aware of the "distance" between his father and mother. As he grows older, this awareness is made explicit by his father and elder clansmen. It is undesirable, he is told, to be so much in the company of women; it is better that he join the menfolk in their house and in their activities. As the boy grows up, the need to avoid contact with women is made abundantly clear to him. He is told that contact with menstrual blood or menstruating women, if not countered by magic rites, can "pollute" a man. It can "corrupt his vital juices so that his skin darkens and wrinkles and his flesh wastes, permanently dull his wits, and eventually lead to a slow decline and death."[6]

Since Mae culture regards a woman as potentially unclean, to say the least, it enforces strict codes of male-female behavior. These codes are designed to safeguard male integrity, strength, and possession of crops and other property. So strict are these regulations that many young men are reluctant to marry. However, the elders do try to impress upon the young men their duty to marry and reproduce. The men's association attempts to regulate the male's sexual relationships. The association is said to have several purposes: to cleanse and strengthen its members; to promote their growth; to make them comely to women; and, most important, to supervise contact between the sexes so that ultimately the "right" wives are procured for the men and the "right" children are born into the clan.

By the time he is fifteen or sixteen a Mae youth has joined the village bachelors' association. He agrees to take scrupulous care neither

---

[5] M. J. Meggitt, "Male-Female Relationships in the Highlands of Australian New Guinea," *American Anthropologist* 66 (Special Issue, 1964): 204–24.

[6] Ibid., p. 207.

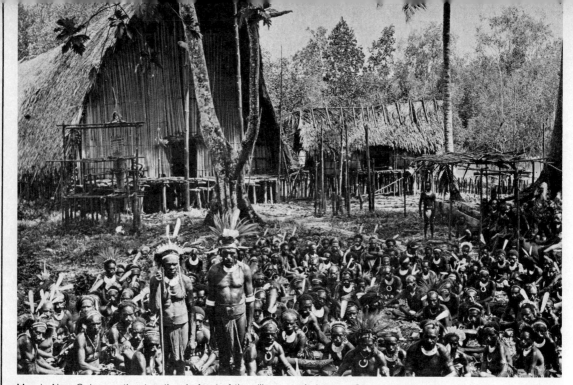

Men in New Guinea gather together in front of the village men's house. (Courtesy of the American Museum of Natural History.)

to copulate with a woman nor to accept food from her hands. As a club member, he will participate in the *sanggai* rituals. Bachelors, under the supervision of senior club members, go into seclusion, in a clubhouse deep in the forest, to undergo "purification." During four days of "exercises" (which are rather similar in purpose to those of a religious retreat), each youth observes additional prohibitions to protect himself from all forms of sexuality and impurity. For instance, pork is denied him, as women have cared for the pigs; and he may not look at the ground during excursions into the forest, lest he see feminine footprints or pig feces. His body will be scrubbed, his dreams discussed and interpreted. Finally, together with his club, now restored to purity and reprotected at least for a while against contamination, he will participate in organized dances and feasting with his chosen lady.

In Mae society, then, it would seem that the battle of the sexes has been won decisively by the men, though at the price, it might well be

argued, of some repression and internal tension. How does the Mae bachelor organization fit into the general social context? What sort of function does it fulfill? On an individual level, bachelor associations may strengthen, and attempt to reaffirm, a man's feeling of masculinity. On a community level, the association organizes the fighting strength of the village. The *sanggai* festivals afford the entire clan an opportunity to display its size, solidarity, and magnificence to its enemies, whom on other occasions it fights. Hostility toward women may not be surprising in view of the fact that a man's wife and mother come from neighboring clans (the Mae clan villages are exogamous) which are perpetually in conflict with his own. Male-female hostility, then, seems to reflect the broader, interclan hostility. The Mae have a succinct way of describing the situation: "We marry the people we fight."[7]

Men's houses, and occasionally women's,

[7] Ibid., p. 218.

are found among many peoples, especially in Melanesia, Polynesia, Africa, and South America. Men's associations generally involve bachelors, although older married men will often come by to instruct the youngsters and pass on the benefits of their experience. In more militant days, men's houses acted as fortresses and arsenals—even as sanctuaries to protect fugitives. By and large, they serve to strengthen—certainly to symbolize—male power and solidarity. As do age-sets, men's clubs often provide ties which cut across and supplement kinship bonds. Hence, they permit a given group of men in a given society to act together toward the realization of mutually agreed-upon objectives, irrespective of kin relationships.

Voluntary Associations

REGIONAL ASSOCIATIONS

Regional associations are clubs which bring together migrants from a common geographical background. Thus, they are often found in urban centers, which traditionally have attracted rural settlers. Membership is based upon the variably ascribed criterion of common regional origin. In the United States, for example, migrants from rural Appalachia have formed such associations in Chicago and Detroit. Many of these organizations have become vocal political forces in municipal government.

William Mangin has described the role of regional associations in helping rural migrants to adapt to urban life in Lima, Peru.[8] During the 1950s, Mangin closely studied a group of migrants from the rural mountains, the *serranos* from Ancash. Typically these *serranos*, about 120,000 in number, live in a slumlike urban settlement called a *barriada*. The *barriada* is not officially recognized by either the national government or the city authorities. Accordingly, it lacks all such normal city services as water

supply, garbage removal, and police protection. Its inhabitants have left their rural birthplaces for reasons generally typical of such population movements, whether they occur in South America or in West Africa. These reasons are generally social and economic, related to population and land pressure. However, the higher expectations associated with the big city—better education, social mobility, wage labor—are also compelling considerations.

Typically, also, the *serranos* from Ancash have formed a regional association, as have literally dozens of migrant groups, not only in Lima, but in the other coastal cities and in regional capitals. Club membership is open to both sexes. Men generally control the executive positions, and club leaders are often those men who have achieved political power in their hometowns. Women, who have relatively less economic and social freedom, nevertheless take an important part in club activities.

The *serrano* regional association performs a number of services for its members. First, it lobbies the central government on matters of community importance—for example, the supplying of sewers, clinics, and similar public services. This requires a club member to follow a piece of legislation carefully through the channels of government to make certain it is not forgotten or abandoned somewhere along the line. Second, the *serrano* association assists in acculturating newly arrived *serranos* to the conditions of urban life in Lima. The most noticeable rural traits—coca-chewing, and hairstyle and clothing peculiarities—are the first to disappear, with the men generally able to adapt faster than the women to the new conditions. The association also provides opportunities for fuller contact with the national culture. And finally, the group organizes social activities such as fiestas, acts as the clearing house for information transmitted to and from the home area, and supplies a range of other services to help migrants adapt to their new environment while still retaining ties to their birthplace.

In general, as Mangin's study reveals, regional clubs help to integrate their members into a more complex, urban environment. How-

[8]William P. Mangin, "The Role of Regional Associations in the Adaptation of Rural Migrants to Cities in Peru," in *Contemporary Cultures and Societies of Latin America*, ed. Dwight B. Heath and Richard N. Adams (New York: Random House, 1965), pp. 311–23.

ever, on occasion they may aggravate local rivalries—especially those related to individual interest groups in the hometown. But since club membership is voluntary, it is not uncommon for a dissatisfied group to break away to establish its own club.

ETHNIC ASSOCIATIONS

There are many types of ethnic interest groups, and generally they are found in cities. Membership in these associations is based upon the variably ascribed characteristic of ethnicity. Ethnic associations are particularly widespread in urban centers of West Africa. There, accelerated cultural change—reflected in altered economic arrangements, in technological advances, and in new urban living conditions—has weakened kinship relations and other traditional sources of support and solidarity.[9]

Tribal unions are frequently found in Nigeria and what is now Ghana. These are typical of most such associations in that they are extra-territorial (that is, they recruit members who have left their tribal locations), they have a formal constitution, and they have been formed to meet certain needs arising out of conditions of urban life. One such need is to keep members in touch with their traditional cultures. The Ibo State Union, for example, in addition to providing mutual aid and financial support in case of unemployment, sickness, or death, performs the service "of fostering and keeping alive an interest in tribal song, history, language and moral beliefs and thus maintaining a person's attachment to his native town or village."[10] Some tribal unions collect money to improve conditions in their ancestral homes; for example, education is an area of particular concern. Others publish newsletters that report

members' activities. Most unions have a young membership that exercises a powerful democratizing influence in tribal councils, and the organizations provide a springboard for those with national political aspirations.

"Friendly societies" differ from tribal unions in that their objectives are more limited, confined for the most part to mutual aid. Such a club has been formed by the wives of Kru migrants in Freetown, Sierra Leone. Kru men normally go to sea, still a hazardous occupation. The club is classified into three grades. An admission fee of one guinea (about $3 U.S. currency in 1972) permits entry into the lowest grade. Elevation to higher grades depends upon further donations. At the death of a member or her husband, the family receives a lump sum commensurate with her status in the club. The Yoruba Friendly Society in Nigeria uses another common approach to mutual aid. At regular intervals, all members contribute a fixed sum, and the total is given to one member at a time. In this way, significant amounts of capital are available, in rotation, for each member to buy trading stock, to purchase expensive new clothes (to keep up appearances in a government post, for example), or even to pay a bride price.

West African occupational clubs also fall into the ethnic category. They are African versions of trade unions, organized along tribal, as well as craft, lines. Their principal concern is the status and remuneration of their members as workers. The Motor Drivers' Union of Keta, in what is now Ghana, was formed to fund insurance and legal costs, to contribute to medical care in case of accident or illness, and to help pay for funeral expenses.

Finally, clubs that concentrate on entertainment and recreation are very common in West Africa. The dancing *compin* of Sierra Leone are typical. This is how Little describes them:

This is a group of young men and women concerned with the performance of "plays" of traditional music and dancing and with the raising of money for mutual benefit. . . . A "play"

---

[9] See Kenneth Little, *West African Urbanization* (New York: Cambridge University Press, 1965); Claude Meillassoux, *Urbanization of an African Community* (Seattle: University of Washington Press, 1968).

[10] Kenneth Little, "The Role of Voluntary Associations in West African Urbanization," *American Anthropologist* 59 (1957): 582.

Kikuyu tribeswomen, who have migrated to the city of Nairobi, Kenya, and formed a union of street sweepers, march in the Independence Day parade. (Marc and Evelyne Bernheim, Woodfin Camp and Associates.)

is generally given in connection with some important event . . . or as part of the ceremonies celebrating a wedding or a funeral. The general public as well as the persons honored by the performance are expected to donate money to the compin on these occasions. Money is also collected in the form of weekly subscriptions from the members.[11]

Some observers have suggested that the widespread incidence of ethnic associations in West Africa has virtually amounted to a resurgence of tribalism. The presence of such interest groups in urban areas has indeed seemed to slow the development of national identity and loyalty. On the other hand, the evidence indicates that these clubs serve important adaptive and integrative functions for both men and women, just as regional associations do in other areas of the world. To quote Little again, "Their combination of modern and traditional traits constitutes a cultural bridge which conveys, metaphorically speaking, the tribal individual from one kind of sociological universe to another."[12]

MILITARY ASSOCIATIONS

Military associations in noncommercial societies may be compared to our own American Legion or Veterans of Foreign War posts. They all seem to exist to unite the members through their common experiences as warriors, to glorify the activities of war, and to perform certain services for the community. Membership in

[11]Ibid., pp. 586–87.

[12]Ibid., p. 593.

such associations is usually voluntary and based upon the achieved criterion of participation in war. Among the American Plains Indians, military societies were common. The Cheyenne Indians, for example, were renowned for the courage of their warriors. Their military societies were not ranked by age, being open to any boy or man ready to go to war.[13]

Originally, the Cheyenne had five military associations: the Fox, the Dog, the Shield, the Elk (or Hoof Rattle), and the Bow-string (or Contrary). The last-named association was annihilated by the Pawnee in the middle of the nineteenth century. Later, two new associations were established, the Wolf and the Northern Crazy Dogs. While the various clubs may have had different costumes, songs, and dances, they were alike in their internal organization, each being headed by four leaders who were among the most important war chiefs.

Several of the Cheyenne military societies selected four virgin daughters of tribal leaders to serve as "maids of honor." The girls participated in the clubs' ceremonies and sat with the war chiefs during council meetings. Although women had no political authority, they were highly respected among the Cheyenne. The maids of honor of the military societies were looked upon as reflecting the ideals of female chastity and deportment. So important was the virtue of female chastity among the Cheyenne that a defiled maid of honor was believed to bring bad luck to the warriors of the association. As a result, the Dog and Contrary societies were unwilling to take the risk of having maids of honor affiliated with their clubs.

SECRET SOCIETIES

Secret societies are characterized principally by limited membership and by secret rituals which are generally believed to increase the supernatural powers of the members. As a rule, those who are not members, or who have attained only the lowest rank within such a society, are told only enough about the society to arouse fear and command respect. Those who advance through various degrees of initiation increase their social and political influence as they increase their supernatural expertise.

The *Poro* is a rather well-known secret society, with voluntary membership open to all males but contingent upon passing of a series of grueling physical tests.[14] It flourishes in Liberia, among the Kpelle, and in Sierra Leone, among such tribes as the Mende and the Temne. Since the Poro has features typical of most secret "clubs," it is worth examining in some detail.

The corporate identity of the Poro is personified by a figure named in various ways: the Grand Master, the Forest Thing, the *namu*. When *namu* makes a public appearance, usually to foretell a meeting of the society, he is always masked, wears a costume symbolic of his office, is accompanied by attendants, and speaks in a musical falsetto. His emergence from the forest causes great dread and anxiety. Noninitiates and women rush to seclude themselves within their homes. Should an uninitiated boy catch sight of *namu* he is taken away at once to undergo initiation; a woman is considered likely to die of poisoning.

The intense fear aroused by the Poro is a reflection of two basic attributes credited to the secret society. First, it is believed that the Poro is close to the spirits of its deceased members. These spirits are thought to exert enormous influence both in channelling supernatural powers and in acting as intermediaries between God and people. Second, the Poro is said to possess certain powerful medicines. These potions can be employed to further the interests of the group, but they can also be applied to the world at large, especially to bring disaster, should certain norms be disregarded or precepts disobeyed.

As a result, *namu* is held in great awe, and respect is always shown to the Poro. This defer-

---

[13] E. Adamson Hoebel, *The Cheyenne: Indians of the Great Plains* (New York: Holt, Rinehart and Winston, 1960).

[14] See Kenneth Little, "The Political Function of the Poro," *Africa* 35 (October 1965): 349–65; and 36 (January 1966): 62–71.

ence has direct sociopolitical consequences. It makes it easier for the Poro society to enforce obedience to certain social restrictions—for instance, the prohibition of incest and arson. In addition, fear of Poro strengthens the hands of political authority, since it is well known that chiefs occupy high positions within the Poro's hierarchy.

The Poro's initiation ceremonies employ procedures typical of those adopted by many secret societies. The aim is to turn an initiate, first, into a "good Poro man," and, second, into a useful member of the community. This means a period of attendance—it used to be between three and four years but has now been much shortened—at a "bush school" situated in a secluded part of the forest. There, each initiate must abandon his former status in favor of a new, Poro identity. He must undergo severe psychological "experiences" designed to etch deeply into his mind the sacredness and secrecy of Poro rituals. Also, he is required to learn the tribal history of his people as well as the skills he will need to attain a position in community life.

Secret societies undeniably have exerted great influence upon the political traditions of West Africa, though their very secrecy has made precise documentation hard to obtain. They bolster the authority of the chiefs and help maintain a code of social behavior. In recent years, secret societies have contributed effectively to opposition movements against colonial authority.

In industrialized societies, secret associations have had as prominent a role. Freemasonry, for example, exerted a powerful influence in much of Europe in the late eighteenth and nineteenth centuries, though in recent times its influence has greatly diminished. In our own society, the Ku Klux Klan is a well-known example of a secret organization. The Klan keeps its membership and its rituals secret. Klansmen wear hooded costumes and their insignia of office when appearing in public, and they have often used violence to try to impress the association's policies upon others. In some parts of

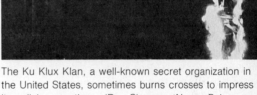

The Ku Klux Klan, a well-known secret organization in the United States, sometimes burns crosses to impress its policies on others. (Ron Sherman/Nancy Palmer Photo Agency.)

the South, particularly in the past, politicians and civic figures gained stature from their membership in the Klan.

Our examination of voluntary associations would not be complete without a passing mention of such organizations as trade unions, charitable organizations, political parties, bridge clubs, and various other associations, of which there are tens of thousands in our own and other complex societies. In all of these voluntary organizations, the qualities required for membership are "achieved" rather than ascribed or determined by birth. Generally, clubs of this category are more numerous where the society is larger and more diversified. They serve to bring together sets of people with common interests, aspirations, or qualifications. Opportunities to work for what are regarded as worthwhile social goals, or for self-improvement, or to satisfy a need for new and stimulating experiences are among the many motivations for joining clubs. Not the least is identification with a corporate body, and through it, the acquisition of status and influence.

Explaining Variation in Associations

Anthropologists are not content to provide descriptions of the structure and operation of human associations. They also seek to understand why different types of associations develop. For example, what may account for the development of age-set systems?

S. N. Eisenstadt's comparative study of African age-sets leads him to the hypothesis that when the kinship group fails to carry out functions important to the integration of society—such as political, educational, and economic functions—age-set systems arise to fill the void. Age-set systems may provide a workable solution to the society's need for functional divisions among its members. This is because age is a criterion that can be applied to all members of society in the allocation of roles.[15]

It is not at all clear why age-set systems arise to fill the void left by lack of a kinship organization. Many societies have kin structures that are limited in their scope; yet the majority of them have not adopted an age-set system.

B. Bernardi, in his critical evaluation of Nilo-Hamitic age-set systems,[16] also suggests that age-set systems arise to make up for a deficiency in social organization. But, in contrast to Eisenstadt, Bernardi specifically suggests why more social organization is necessary and what particular deficiencies in previous organization should favor development of age-sets. He hypothesizes that age-set systems arise in societies with a history of territorial rivalry which lack central authority and have only dispersed kin groups. When all three factors are present, he argues, the need for a mechanism of territorial integration is supplied by an age-set system.

A recent cross-cultural study suggests that territorial rivalry as indicated by warfare may be a factor favoring the development of age-set systems, but there is no evidence to support Bernardi's hypothesis that age-sets develop in societies which lack central authority and have only dispersed kin groups.[17] So it does not seem that age-set societies are generally more deficient in political or kinship organization. An alternative explanation, which is consistent with the cross-cultural evidence, is that age-set systems arise in societies that have both frequent warfare and local groups which change in size and composition through the year. In such situations, men may not always be able to rely on their kinsmen for cooperation in warfare because the kinsmen are not always nearby. Age-sets, however, can provide allies *wherever* one happens to be.[18] This interpretation suggests that age-set systems arise *in addition to*, rather than alternative to, kin-based and politically-based forms of integration.

In dealing with voluntary associations whose membership is of the "variably ascribed" type (that is, acquired at birth but not found in all persons of a given age-sex category), it is difficult to say exactly what causes them to arise. There is evidence to suggest that voluntary associations become more numerous (and more important) as the society harboring them advances in technology, complexity, and scale. No definitive explanation for this answer is yet available, but the following trends seem to be sufficiently established to merit consideration.

First, there is the factor of urbanization. Developing societies are becoming urban in character, and as their cities grow, so do the number of people separated from their tradi-

---

[15] S. N. Eisenstadt, "African Age Groups," *Africa* 24 (April 1954): 102.

[16] B. Bernardi, "The Age-System of the Nilo-Hamitic Peoples," *Africa* 22 (October 1952): 316–32.

[17] Madeline Lattman Ritter, "The Conditions Favoring Age-Set Organization" (M. A. thesis, Hunter College of the City University of New York, January 1974).

[18] Ibid.

tional kinship ties and local customs. It is not surprising, then, that the early voluntary associations should be mutual aid societies, established first to take over kin obligations in case of death, and later broadening their benefits in other directions. In this respect, the recent associations of the developing African societies in the "Third World" closely resemble the early English laboring class associations. These clubs also served to maintain the city migrant's contacts with his former traditions and culture. Similarly, the regional associations in Latin America resemble the regional associations of European immigrants to the United States. Such associations also seem to arise in response to the migrant's or immigrant's needs in the new home.

Second, there is an economic factor. Migrants and immigrants try to adapt to the new economic conditions, and group interests in the new situations have to be organized, promoted, and protected.

Why, then, do "variably ascribed" associations tend to be replaced by clubs of the "achieved" category in highly industrialized societies? Perhaps the strong focus on specialization in industrialized societies is reflected in the formation of specialized groups. Possibly the emphasis on achievement in industrialized societies is another contributing factor. Perhaps, too, the trend toward a standardized uniformity, encouraged by mass marketing and the mass media, is progressively weakening the importance of regional and ethnic distinctions. The result seems to be that the more broadly based organizations are being replaced by more narrowly based associations that are more responsive to particular needs which are not being met by the institutions of mass society.

Summary

1. Associations or interest groups have the following characteristics in common: (1) some people are excluded from membership; (2) membership is based on commonly shared interests or purposes; (3) some kind of formal, institutional structure exists; and (4) there is a clearly discernible sense of mutual pride and belonging. Membership varies according to whether it is voluntary or not, and according to whether the qualities of members are universally ascribed, variably ascribed, or achieved.

2. Age-set systems are examples of nonvoluntary, universally ascribed associations. They are composed of groups of persons of similar age and sex who move through life's stages together. Entry into the system is usually by an initiation ceremony. Transitions to new stages are usually marked by succession rituals. Unisex associations restrict membership to one sex. In noncommercial societies membership in such associations (usually male) is generally nonvoluntary.

3. Regional and ethnic organizations are voluntary, variably ascribed associations. Both usually occur in societies where technological advance is accelerating, bringing with it economic and social complexity. Despite a variety of types, regional and ethnic associations have in common an emphasis on (a) helping the members adapt to new conditions; (b) keeping members in touch with local traditions; and (c) promoting improved living conditions in local areas.

4. Variably ascribed associations tend to be replaced by clubs, whose membership is based on achieved qualities, in highly industrialized societies.

Suggested Readings

Bernardi, B. "The Age-System of the Nilo-Hamitic Peoples." *Africa* 22 (October 1952): 316–32.

A theoretical discussion of why age-set systems occur in some societies and not in others.

Eisenstadt, S. N. *From Generation to Generation:*

Age Groups and Social Structure. Glencoe, Ill.: Free Press, 1956.

A comparative and theoretical analysis of age groups in different societies. Chapters 2–5 give a detailed presentation of age groupings in a wide variety of societies, as well as classifications of types of societies and their functions.

Huntingford, G. W. B. *The Nandi of Kenya: Tribal Control in a Pastoral Society.* London: Routledge and Kegan Paul, 1953.

A general discussion of the political structure of this group. Particular attention is paid to the importance of age-sets as the basis for political organization.

Lowie, R. H. *Primitive Society.* New York: Boni and Liveright, 1920.

A classic, comparative work, discussing various elements of social organization. Chapter 10, "Associations," and Chapter 11, "Theory of Associations," contain comparative discussions of clubs and age groups in primitive societies.

Meillassoux, C. *Urbanization of an African Community.* Seattle: University of Washington Press, 1968.

A description of the changing structure of Mali society, particularly in terms of the decline of voluntary associations as important centers of power. Such associations continue to exist in Mali but are subordinate, and in opposition, to the new party system.

Wilson, M. *Good Company: A Study of Nyakyusa Age-Villages.* Boston: Beacon Press, 1963.

A monograph describing the social organization of the Nyakyusa, particularly the villages which are founded by members of a single age-set.

Political Organization: Social Order and Disorder

18

For most Americans, the term "political life" has many connotations. For example, it may call to mind the executive branch of government, from the president on a national level to the mayor on a local one; or legislative institutions from Congress to the city council; or administrative bureaus from federal government departments to local agencies. It may also evoke thoughts of political parties, interest groups, and such common political activities as lobbying, compaigning, and voting. In other words, when people living in the United States think of political life, they may think first of the complex process by which authoritative decisions (often called "public policies") are arrived at and implemented.

But "political life" has a still wider range of meaning in America, as in many other countries. It may also refer to ways of preventing or resolving trouble cases and disputes both within and without our society. Internally, a complex society such as ours may employ mediation or arbitration to resolve industrial disputes; a police force to prevent crimes or track down criminals; and courts and a penal system to deal with lawbreakers as well as with social conflicts in general. Externally, such a society may establish embassies in other nations and develop and utilize its armed forces both as a way of maintaining its security and as a means of supporting its domestic and foreign interests. All of these are political organizations and activities. They are mechanisms which complex societies have developed in order to establish social order and to minimize, or at least deal with, social disorder.

However, many societies do not have political officials or courts or armies. Nor do they have individuals or agencies which are formally responsible for making and implementing policy or for resolving disputes. Does this mean that they have no political life? If we mean political life as we know it in our own society, then the answer has to be that they do not. But if we look beyond our complex formal institutions and ask what functions these institutions perform, we find that all societies have customs

18

or procedures which result in policymaking and the resolution of disputes—ways and means of creating and maintaining social order and coping with social disorder.

A straightforward, working definition of the term "political"—one which may be applied to all societies—is not easy to frame, for the differences among forms of political organization are great. In general, we can say that the term "political" refers to customary behaviors—and to beliefs and attitudes—which pertain to policymaking and its execution (creating and maintaining social order) and to conflict resolution (minimizing social disorder). These customs are initiated by, or on behalf of, distinct territorial groups. The territorial groups involved may range from neighborhoods and hamlets to villages, towns, cities, regions, nations, and even groups of nations.

Variations in Political Organization

Elman Service has suggested that societies can be classified into four principal types of organization: bands, tribes, chiefdoms, and states.[1] We shall examine how political life is organized in each type of society, in order to obtain a general view of how societies vary in the ways they try to create and maintain social order and minimize social disorder.

BAND ORGANIZATION

Some societies are composed of a number of fairly small and usually nomadic groups of people. Each of these groups is called a "band" and is self-sufficient and autonomous. The band in such societies is the largest group that acts as a political unit. Since most contemporary food collectors have band organization, some anthropologists contend that band organization

characterized nearly all societies before the development of agriculture, or until about 10,000 years ago.

Societies with band organization have a number of features. First and foremost, such societies are generally at the hunter-gatherer (or collecting) level of food-getting technology. This means that they have to "find" food by prodding it out of the earth, taking it out of the water, or hunting it down, wherever nature has placed it. Consequently, bands are almost always nomadic. They move from place to place in a regular, seasonal pattern, following migratory game or exploiting seasonally varying plant or animal life, and carrying their few possessions with them.

Bands are typically small in size, and societies with bands typically have a low population density. Julian Steward has estimated that population density in band societies ranges from a maximum of about 1 person per 5 square miles to a minimum of 1 person per 50 or so square miles.[2] The primary factor determining the exact size of a band is probably its relative productivity and the sort of food-collecting technology it employs. The Guayaki of the Amazon Basin number about 20 individuals in their local bands; the Semang of the Malay Peninsula have 50; the Patagonian Tehuelche of South America number 400–500, perhaps the largest of all.[3] Band size often varies by season, the band breaking up or recombining according to the quantity of food resources available at a given time and place. Eskimo bands, for example, are smaller in the winter when food is hard to find and larger in the summer when there is sufficient food available to feed a larger group.

Societies with band organization are generally egalitarian; all individuals of a particular age-sex category have equal access to prestige and resources. Typically, the concept of private property is alien to band society. If there is any concept of resource ownership—ownership of

[1] Elman R. Service, *Primitive Social Organization: An Evolutionary Perspective* (New York: Random House, 1962).

[2] Julian Steward, *Theory of Culture Change* (Urbana: University of Illinois Press, 1955), p. 125.

[3] Morton H. Fried, *The Evolution of Political Society* (New York: Random House, 1967), p. 68.

Eskimo bands lack a permanent leader with formal authority. Decisions such as how a whale hunt is to be arranged and how the meat is to be divided are either agreed upon by the community as a whole or made by the "best qualified" member. (Courtesy of the American Museum of Natural History.)

land, for instance—that resource is thought to belong to the band as a whole. Thus, among hunting and gathering peoples, sharing of virtually all resources is the rule. All members of the band, for example, share in the distribution of game that is killed, even though all members were not directly involved in the hunt.

Political organization within the band is generally informal. The "modest informal authority"[4] that does exist within the band can be seen in the way that decisions affecting the entire group are made. Since the formal, permanent office of "leader" generally does not exist within a band, decisions such as when camp has to be moved or how a hunt is to be arranged are either agreed upon by the community as a whole or are made by the best qualified member. Leadership, when it is exercised by an individual, is not the consequence of "bossing" or of throwing one's weight about. Each band may have its informal headman, or its most proficient hunter, or its old man most accom-

plished in rituals. He may be one and the same person or he may be several persons, but he, or they, will have gained status through the community's recognition of his skill, good sense, and humility. Leadership, in other words, stems not from power but from influence, not from office but from admired personal qualities.

In Eskimo bands, each settlement may have its headman, who acquires his influence because the other members of the community recognize his good judgment and superior skills. The headman's advice concerning the movement of the band and other community matters is generally heeded; but the headman possesses no permanent authority and has no power to impose sanctions of any kind. Among the Iglulik Eskimos, for example, leadership exists only in a very restricted sense.

Within each settlement . . . there is as a rule an older man who enjoys the respect of the others and who decides when a move is to be made to another hunting center, when a hunt is to be started, how the spoils are to be divided, when the dogs are to be fed. . . . He is called

[4]Service, *Primitive Social Organization*, p. 109.

isumaitoq, "he who thinks." It is not always the oldest man, but as a rule an elderly man who is a clever hunter or, as head of a large family, exercises great authority. He cannot be called a chief; there is no obligation to follow his counsel; but they do so in most cases, partly because they rely on his experience, partly because it pays to be on good terms with this man.[5]

This lack of fixed authority is characteristic of political organization at the band level. A man will not acquire or maintain influence unless he has the abilities needed by the rest of the band.

Although the position of headman is often hereditary among the !Kung Bushmen, the authority of the headman is extremely limited; the position itself offers no apparent advantages and is not actively sought after. Like all Bushmen, the headman fashions tools and shelters, carries his possessions, and hunts for food. Indeed, the !Kung headman goes out of his way not to be envied for his possession of material goods.

However, while the authority of the !Kung headman is tenuous, he nevertheless has certain duties which are at least symbolic. He is generally held responsible for the way the band makes use of its food resources, although most of his decisions will be dictated by nature, long-standing custom, or consensus of band members. If there is theft by some person not affiliated with the band, he is expected to cope with the problem. And his consent is necessary for an outsider to be admitted to the band. Yet despite his customary duties, the !Kung headman is not necessarily the leader of the band. If he lacks the special abilities needed to lead in a given situation, the band turns to another person quite informally. No man of influence within the band, however, has formal authority or receives special privileges. At most, the headman is first among equals; at the least, as one headman was overheard to say, "All you get is the blame if things go wrong.[6]

[5] Therkel Mathiassen, *Material Culture of the Iglulik Eskimos* (Copenhagen: Gyldendalske, 1928).

[6] Lorna Marshall, "!Kung Bushmen Bands," in *Comparative Political Systems*, ed. Ronald Cohen and John Middleton (Garden City, N.Y.: Natural History Press, 1967), p. 41.

TRIBAL ORGANIZATION

Societies with tribal organization are similar to those with band organization in their egalitarian nature, lack of political hierarchies and classes, and informal leadership patterns. However, societies with tribal organization generally are food producers. Because cultivation and animal husbandry is generally more productive than hunting and gathering, population density of tribal societies is generally higher, local groups are generally larger, and the way of life is more sedentary than in the hunter-gatherer band.

What distinguishes tribal from band political organization is the presence of some pan-tribal associations (such as clans and age-sets) which can potentially integrate a number of local groups into a larger whole. Such multilocal political integration, however, is not permanent, and it is informal in the sense that it is not headed by political officials. Frequently, the integration is called into play only when an external threat arises; when the threat disappears, the local groups revert to self-sufficiency. In other words, a tribal society lacks a permanent multilocal political authority. Situations do arise which call for intergroup cooperation of some kind, but they are transitory, and a new situation may well require the coordination of quite different groups.[7] While tribal organization may seem fragile, the special associations which integrate local groups into larger political entities make for a substantial difference between societies with tribal and societies with band organization.

Kinship Bonds Frequently, pan-tribal associations are based upon kinship ties. Clans are the most common pan-tribal kinship groups. In some societies, clan elders have the right to try to settle disputes between clansmen or to attempt to punish wrongs committed against clansmen by members of different clans. In addition, kinship bonds often tend to unite members of the same descent group during

[7] Service, *Primitive Social Organization*, pp. 114–15.

periods of warfare; in many societies, the organization of warfare is the responsibility of the clan.[8]

The segmentary lineage system is another type of pan-tribal integration based upon kinship, although societies with segmentary lineage systems are less common than societies with clans. The whole society (tribe) is composed of like segments or parts, each similar to the others in structure and function. Every local segment belongs to a hierarchy of lineages, each one stretching farther and farther back genealogically. The hierarchy of lineages, then, unites the many segments into larger and larger genealogical groups. The closer two groups are genealogically, the greater their general closeness. In the event of a dispute between members of different segments, people more closely related to one contestant than to another take the side of their nearest kinsman.

The Tiv of northern Nigeria offer a classic example of a segmentary lineage system, one which links all of the Tiv into a single genealogical structure. The Tiv are a large tribe, numbering 800,000 in the 1950s. Figure 1 is a representation of the Tiv segmentary lineage structure. As Paul Bohannan explains:

The lineage whose apical ancestor is some three to six generations removed from living elders and who are associated with the smallest discrete territory (*tar*) I call the minimal segment; . . . it can vary in population from 200 people to well over a thousand. . . . The territory of a minimal segment adjoins the territory of its sibling minimal segment. Thus, the lineage comprising two minimal segments also has a discrete territory, and is in turn a segment of a more inclusive lineage, and of its more inclusive territory. In Figure 1, the whole system can be seen: the father or founder of segment *a* was a brother of the founder of segment *b*. Each is a minimal segment today, and each has its own territory. The two segments taken together are all descended from *1*, and are known by his name—the children of *1*. In the same way, the territory of lineage *1*, made up as it is of the

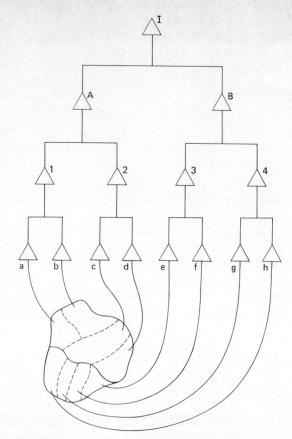

FIGURE 1   Tiv Lineage Segments and Their Territories

combined minimal territories *a* and *b*, combines with the territory of lineage 2, made up of the combined minimal territories of *c* and *d*, to form territory A, occupied by lineage segment A, all descended from a single ancestor "A." This process is extended indefinitely, right up to the apex of the genealogy, back in time to the founder who [is said to have] begot the entire people, and outwards in space to the edges of Tivland. The entire 800,000 Tiv form a single "lineage" (*nongo*) and a single land called *Tar Tiv*.[9]

Tiv lineage organization is the foundation of the political organization. A look at Figure 1

[8] Ibid., p. 126.

[9] Paul Bohannan, "The Migration and Expansion of the Tiv," *Africa* 24 (1954): 3.

helps to explain how. A dispute between lineages (and territories) *a* and *b* remains minor, since no more than "brother" segments are involved. But a dispute between *a* and *c* now involves lineages *1* and *2* as well, with the requirement that *b* assist *a* and *d* support *c*. This process of mutual support, often called *complementary opposition*, means that segments will unite only in a confrontation with some other group. Groups that will fight with each other in a minor dispute might coalesce at some later time against a larger group.

Externally, the system may be effective because it enables individual lineage segments to call on ever-increasing support when faced with border troubles. Conflicts within the society (between segments), especially in border areas, are often turned outward, "releasing internal pressure in an explosive blast against other peoples."[10]

However, Tiv segmentary lineage arrangements are not quite so massive or so powerful as they seem. The combinations we have described are temporary, forming and dissolving as the occasion demands. Sahlins sums up the limitations as follows:

> The segmentary lineage system is self-liquidating. It is advantageous in inter-tribal competition, but having emerged victorious it has no longer *raison d'être* [reason for being] and the divisive tendencies of tribal polity reassert themselves.[11]

Age-Set Systems Age-sets are pan-tribal groupings in which age, and not kinship, is the basis for political organization. We have already described age-set systems in a previous chapter; the discussion here will be restricted to political aspects of age-set systems.

Societies with age-set systems initiate their members either at birth or about the age of puberty. Anyone who refuses to become a member of an age-set will remain "disenfranchised" and be excluded from all significant

Age-sets are a pan-tribal grouping that may form the basis of political organization. Among the Karimojong, elders are respected for their ability to intercede with the deity on behalf of the tribe. Here a group of elders gathers at a public ritual. (N. & R. Dyson-Hudson.)

political decisions. One set (or group of sets) is usually in a position of authority, having replaced the set immediately preceding it; when it must retire in due course, it is replaced by the set immediately following it. Membership in the senior set bestows tribal-wide office insofar as each elder has authority because he belongs to the set which collectively holds authority. As is the case with segmentary lineages, different crises may bring members of an age-set together from different localities; but, as soon as the crisis is dealt with, the age-set will no longer operate as a unit.

The Karimojong, a society characterized by age-sets, are a people of northeastern Uganda who depend upon cattle herding and agriculture for their livelihood. Their political community includes elders who direct day-to-day affairs, large herd owners whose wealth enables them to have a say in certain activities, and initiated adult males whose responsibility it is to imple-

[10]Marshall D. Sahlins, "The Segmentary Lineage: An Organization of Predatory Expansion," *American Anthropologist* 63 (1961): 342.

[11]Ibid., p. 345.

ment policy once it has been decided. Initiation into an age-set, and public acceptance of tribal customs, means that a Karimojong will ultimately become an elder and perhaps a leader of his local community.

The Karimojong age-set system has an important bearing on the practical, day-to-day content of tribal life. As herdsmen, Karimojong adults are often widely separated from their usual settlements. Herders will meet, mingle for a while, then go their separate ways; but each man may call upon other members of his age-set wherever he goes. The age-set system is important among the Karimojong, because it immediately allocates to each individual a place in the universal ranking system and thereby establishes for him an appropriate pattern of response. A quarrel in camp will be settled by the representatives of the senior age-set who are present, regardless of which section of the tribe they may belong to.

Karimojong elders are respected for their practical knowledge and experience, but they are particularly credited with the gift of being able to intercede with the deity on behalf of the tribe—a gift which they demonstrate at regular public rituals. Age has granted them

experience of how and when the deity is best approached. Their impending death (relative to most members of the society) puts them in closer proximity to the boundaries of natural and supernatural. Most important, the deity is accessible to them, and generally amenable to their requests, more so than in the case of other men.[12]

The rituals serve political ends through prayers for economic security and betterment for each Karimojong. The elders can also use their supernatural power as punishment. The severe drought and the disease which swept through the tribe in the late nineteenth century are explained as being the consequences of the senior generation-set's displeasure with, and punishment of, its juniors.[13]

In theory, all Karimojong political leaders are equal in status; in fact, wealthy herd owners are usually able to exercise a telling influence over policy. Owners of large herds often have a number of wives and can count upon the support of numerous affinal groups. In addition, they are often owed a debt of gratitude in many communities for assistance they rendered during times of food scarcity.

Political leaders are not elected from among the elders, nor are they appointed; they obtain their positions informally. Usually a man's background, and the ability he has demonstrated in public debate over a period of time, will result in his being considered by the men of his neighborhood to be their spokesman. His function is to announce to the people what course of action seems required in a particular situation, to initiate that action, and then to coordinate it after it is begun. Although a spokesman may act as a decision maker in council, he does not necessarily take the lead in implementing decisions.

Most political leaders exercise their authority within the local sphere because the pastoral nature of the Karimojong economy, with its dispersed groups and movement from one feeding ground to another, offers no viable alternative. However, from time to time an elder may acquire the status of a prophet and be awarded respect and obedience on a tribal scale. He will be called upon to lead sacrifices (to avert communal misfortune), to undertake rainmaking (to bring prosperity), and so on. Yet even a prophet's prestige and authority do not mean that he assumes a position of overlord or chief.

CHIEFDOMS

Chiefdom organization differs from tribal organization in several important ways. Whereas tribes have associations that can informally integrate more than one community, chiefdoms have some formal authority structure integrating multicommunity political units. Compared with tribal societies, chiefdom societies generally are more densely populated, and their

[12]Neville Dyson-Hudson, *Karimojong Politics* (Oxford: Clarendon Press, 1966), p. 213.
[13]Ibid., p. 217.

Although tribal societies have no formal chief, informal leadership still exists. Here a Masai elder addresses the younger men of the tribe. (Marc and Evelyne Bernheim, Woodfin Camp and Associates.)

communities are more permanent, partly as a consequence of their generally higher economic productivity. Societies with chiefdoms may or may not be politically unified under one chief. Most chiefdom societies are composed of more than one multi-community political unit, each headed by a chief or, less commonly, by a council.

The position of chief, which is sometimes hereditary and generally permanent, bestows high status on its holder. Most chiefdoms have social ranking, with the chief and his family having greater access to prestige. An important responsibility of chiefs is to serve as redistrib-uting agents. The goods and services produced are often accumulated by the chief, who then reallocates them to the people. The chief may plan and direct the use of public labor, sometimes with significant economic consequences. He may supervise religious festivals, often acquiring religious status himself as a result. And he may have responsibility for directing military activities on behalf of the chiefdom.

In South Pacific chiefdoms, the chiefs carried out most of the duties we have just described. In Fijian chiefdoms, for example, the chief was responsible for the redistribution of goods and the coordination of labor.

[The chief] could summon the community's labor on his own behalf, or on behalf of someone else who requested it, or for general purposes. . . . Besides his right to summon labor he accumulated the greater proportion of the first fruits of the yam crop . . . and he benefited from other forms of food presentation, or by the acquisition of special shares in ordinary village distribution. . . . Thus, the paramount [chief] would collect a significant part of the surplus production of the community and redistribute it in the general welfare.[14]

The Tahitians had a history of large-scale warfare, with their chiefs coordinating land and naval forces in thrusts and counterthrusts. Tahitian society was clearly ranked—from the preeminence accorded to the families of the paramount chiefs, who were believed to have exceptional spiritual powers, down in various gradations to the lowest status of the general populace. Many of the early missionaries to Tahiti regarded the Tahitian chiefs as despots, because of the great deference and tribute paid to them by the common people. In fact, however, the chiefs did not really have tyrannical control over the daily lives of the islanders in their districts.

THE STATE

A state, according to one more or less standard definition, is "an autonomous political unit, encompassing many communities within its territory and having a centralized government with the power to collect taxes, draft men for work or war, and decree and enforce laws.[15] State societies, then, have a complex, centralized political structure, with a wide range of permanent institutions having legislative, executive, and judicial functions, and inevitably a large bureaucracy. Central to this definition of the state type of society is the concept of legitimate force to implement policies both internally and exter-

nally. In state societies, the government tries to maintain a monopoly on the use of physical force.[16] This monopoly of physical force can be seen in the development of formal and specialized instruments of social control: a police force, a militia, a standing army. Of course, the rulers of the state do not maintain the social order by force alone. The people must believe, at least to some extent, that those in power have a legitimate right to govern. If the people think otherwise about their rulers, history suggests that those in power may eventually lose their ability to maintain control.

In addition to their strictly political features, states are characterized by class stratification and hence by restricted access to basic economic resources. State societies are generally supported by a system of intensive agriculture. The high productivity of this system presumably allows for the emergence of cities, a high degree of economic and other kinds of specialization, commercial exchange (distribution of goods and services involving the use of money), and extensive foreign trade.

Ancient Rome was a complex state society that dominated the Mediterranean and Near East for hundreds of years. Roman society was clearly stratified, with the patricians, who controlled the bulk of the wealth and influence, sharply distinguished from the plebeians (common folk). The Romans made productive use of favorable agricultural conditions in Italy, and intensive agricultural methods were employed in the provinces, especially in Egypt, southern Gaul (France), and Spain. Roman commerce was world-wide (as the term was defined in those days), and Roman money was the principal medium of exchange around the entire Mediterranean area and within much of Europe.

Politically, Rome had a complex of institutions. During the imperial phase, which lasted for the first three centuries A.D., emperor and senate acted together in governing the Roman world, though the emperor tended to concen-

[14] Marshall Sahlins, *Moala: Culture and Nature on a Fijian Island* (Ann Arbor: University of Michigan Press, 1962), pp. 293–94.
[15] Robert L. Carneiro, "A Theory of the Origin of the State," *Science,* 21 August 1970, p. 733.

[16] See Max Weber, *The Theory of Social and Economic Organization,* trans. A. M. Henderson and Talcott Parsons (New York: Oxford University Press, 1947), p. 154.

In state societies, the government holds a monopoly on the legitimate use of physical force, as can be seen in the development of specialized instruments of social control—a police force, a militia, an army. Here Parisian police look on as student demonstrators participate in a sit-in. (United Press International Photo.)

trate on foreign and military affairs while the senate dealt with domestic matters. The Roman government employed a large bureaucracy, controlled the routes of communication, deployed substantial army and navy units throughout the empire, and made its power felt both internally and externally. The legitimacy and the sovereignty of the Roman state went more or less unquestioned for half a millennium.

Another example of a state society was the kingdom of Nupe in West Africa, now part of the nation-state of Nigeria. As is characteristic of state societies generally, Nupe society was quite rigidly stratified. At the top of the social

system was the king, or *Etsu*. Beneath the king, members of the royal family formed the highest aristocratic class. Next in rank were two other classes of nobility—the local chiefs and the military leaders. At the bottom of the social hierarchy were the commoners, who had neither rank nor power, nor any share in political authority.

The Nupe state was composed of two types of territorial units. One consisted of those towns and villages which were part of the royal domain and therefore were under direct rule of the king. The other consisted of communities which were designated as fiefs and were under the control of local lords. The state, however, had supreme authority over all local magistrates and lords. Although the people of the villages may have selected their own chiefs, the king had the right to confirm all such appointments, as well as the power to depose all local rulers, including the lords.

The Nupe king possessed ultimate authority in many judicial matters. Minor disputes and civil cases were handled by the local village councils, but serious criminal cases were the prerogative of the king. Such cases, referred to as "crimes for the king," were brought before the royal court by the king's local representatives. It was the king and his councillors who judged the cases and determined suitable punishments.

The most powerful influence of the state over the Nupe people was in the area of taxation. The king was given the power to impose and collect taxes from every household. Payment was made either in money (cowrie shells originally, and later British currency) or certain gifts, such as cloth, mats, and sometimes slaves. Much of the revenue collected was kept by the king, the remainder being shared with his local representatives and lords. In return for the taxes they paid, the people received security—protection against invasion and domestic disorder.[17]

FACTORS ASSOCIATED WITH VARIATION IN POLITICAL ORGANIZATION

The classification of types of political organization into band, tribe, chiefdom, and state implies an evolutionary trend from simpler to more complex forms, and from small-scale local autonomy to large-scale regional unification. It also implies a trend from a few temporary and informal political leaders to large numbers of permanent, specialized political officials and from the absence of political power to a monopoly of public force by a central authority. It has been suggested that this evolutionary trend

in political institutions may be associated with similar trends in other social realms. These are:

1. *Technology:* from food collection (hunting and gathering) to intensive food production (agriculture and animal husbandry)
2. *Population:* from small, local groups to large communities, and from low to greater population density
3. *Social status:* from egalitarian society to rank society, and finally to class-differentiated society
4. *Economic distribution:* from major emphasis on reciprocity in the distribution of goods and services, to redistribution, and finally to market or commercial exchange, using money as the principal medium of exchange

These suggested associations (summarized in Table 1) seem to be confirmed by the available cross-cultural evidence. With regard to the relation between the level of subsistence technology and political complexity, a cross-cultural study employing a small random sample of societies found that the greater the importance of agriculture in a society, the larger the population which is politically unified and the greater the number and types of political officials.[18] A massive cross-cultural survey reports a similar trend: the more intensive the agriculture, the greater the likelihood of state organization; and conversely, societies with no more than local political institutions are likely to depend upon hunting, gathering, and fishing.[19] With regard to community size, M. Ember's study also suggests that the larger the leading community, the wider the range of political officials in the society.[20] Textor presents a similar finding. He notes that societies with state organization tend to have cities and towns, whereas those with only local political organization are more likely to have communities with an average popula-

[17] S. F. Nadel, "Nupe State and Community," *Africa* 8 (1935): 257–303.

[18] M. Ember, "The Relationship between Economic and Political Development in Nonindustrialized Societies," *Ethnology* 2 (April 1963): 228–48.

[19] Data from Robert B. Textor, comp., *A Cross-Cultural Summary* (New Haven: HRAF Press, 1967).

[20] Ember, "The Relationship between Economic and Political Development in Nonindustrialized Societies."

TABLE 1 Suggested Trends in Political Organization and Other Social Characteristics

	Highest Level of Political Integration	Specialization of Political Officials	Predominant Mode of Subsistence	Community Size and Population Density	Social Differentiation	Major Form of Distribution
Band	Local group or band	Little or none, informal leadership	Hunting and gathering	Very small communities, very low density	Egalitarian	Reciprocity
Tribe	Sometimes multilocal	Little or none, informal leadership	Extensive (shifting) agriculture and/or herding	Small communities, low density	Egalitarian	Reciprocity
Chiefdom	Multilocal	Some specialized political officials	Extensive or intensive agriculture and/or herding	Large communities, medium density	Rank	Redistribution
State	Multilocal, often entire language group	Many specialized political officials	Intensive agriculture and herding	Cities and towns, high density	Class and caste	Market exchange

tion of less than 200 persons.[21] Cross-cultural research also tends to confirm that societies with higher levels of political integration are more likely to exhibit social differentiation, especially in the form of class distinctions.[22]

Does this evidence provide us with an explanation as to why political organization varies? Clearly, the data indicate that several factors are associated with political development, but exactly why changes in political organization occur is not yet satisfactorily understood. Theory and research, particularly in archaeology, have focused on the origins of state societies.

Resolution of Conflict

Political organization implies more than the making of policy, its administration, and enforcement. It also generally refers to the resolu-

---

[21] Data from Textor, *A Cross-Cultural Summary.*
[22] Raoul Naroll, "Two Solutions to Galton's Problem," *Philosophy of Science* 28 (January 1961): 15–39.

tion of conflict, which may be accomplished peacefully by the adjudication of disputes, by the negotiation of compromises, or by the threat of social sanctions. But if such procedures fail or are not possible because of the absence of mediating procedures, then disputes may erupt into violent conflict. When violence occurs within a political unit in which disputes are usually settled peacefully, we conventionally refer to such violence as crime. When the violence occurs between groups of people from separate political units—groups between which there is no effective procedure for settling disputes—we usually call such violence warfare.

PEACEFUL RESOLUTION OF CONFLICT

Most modern industrialized states have formal institutions and offices such as police, district attorneys, courts, and penal systems to deal with minor disputes and more serious conflicts that may arise in society. All of these institutions generally operate according to codified laws—that is, a set of written (and therefore explicit) rules stipulating what is permissible and what is not. Transgression of the law by individuals gives the state the right to take actions against them. The state has a monopoly on the legitimate use of force in the society, for it alone has the right to coerce its subjects into agreement with its regulations, customs, political edicts, and procedures.

However, many societies lack such specialized offices and institutions for dealing with conflict. Yet, since all societies have peaceful, regularized ways of handling at least certain disputes, some anthropologists speak in terms of the universality of law. E. Adamson Hoebel, for example, states the principle as follows:

Each people has its system of social control. And all but a few of the poorest of them have as a part of the control system a complex of behavior patterns and institutional mechanisms that we may properly treat as law. For, "anthropologically considered, law is merely one aspect of our culture—the aspect which employs the force of organized society to regulate individual and group conduct and to prevent redress or punish deviations from prescribed social norms."[23]

Law, then, whether informal as in simpler societies, or formal as in more complex societies, provides a means of dealing peacefully with whatever conflicts develop.

Peaceful Resolution of Conflict: Community Action Societies have found various ways of peacefully resolving disputes. One such way involves action on the part of the community as a whole. Eskimo societies, for example, frequently resolve disputes through community action. Within local groups, kinship ties are not particularly emphasized, and the family is regarded as autonomous in most matters. Eskimos believe that spirits—particularly if displeased—can determine much of a person's fate. Consequently, the Eskimos carry out their

daily tasks within a complex system of taboos. This system of taboos is so extensive that some have suggested that the Eskimos have no need for a formal set of laws.

Nevertheless, conflicts do take place and have to be resolved. Accordingly, there are "principles" which act as guides to the community in settling trouble cases. An individual's failure to heed a taboo or to follow the suggestions of a shaman leads to expulsion from the group, since the community cannot accept a risk to its livelihood. A person who fails to share goods voluntarily will find them confiscated and distributed to the community, and he or she may be executed in the process. A single case of murder, as an act of vengeance (usually because of the abduction of a wife, or as part of a blood feud), does not concern the community, but repeated murders do. Boas gives a typical example.

There was a native of Padli by the name Padlu. He had induced the wife of a native of Cumberland Sound to desert her husband and follow him. The deserted husband, meditating revenge . . . visited his friends in Padli, but before he could accomplish his intention of killing Padlu, the latter shot him. . . . A brother of the murdered man went to Padli to avenge the death . . . but he also was killed by Padlu. A third native of Cumberland Sound, who wished to avenge the death of his relatives, was also murdered by him.

On account of these outrages the natives wanted to get rid of Padlu, but yet they did not dare to attack him. When the *pimain* (headman) of the Akudmurmuit learned of these events he started southward and *asked every man in Padli whether Padlu should be killed. All agreed;* so he went with the latter deer hunting . . . and . . . shot Padlu in the back.[24]

Informal Adjudication Without Power Community action is not the only way that societies without codified laws peacefully resolve disputes. Some societies have informal adjudicators who resolve trouble cases, although such

[23]E. Adamson Hoebel, *The Law of Primitive Man* (New York: Atheneum, 1968; originally published 1954), p. 4, quoting S. P. Simpson and Ruth Field, "Law and the Social Sciences," *Virginia Law Review* 32 (1946): 858.

[24]Franz Boas, *Central Eskimos*, Bureau of American Ethnology, Annual Report no. 6 (Washington, D.C., 1888), p. 668.

Societies have found various ways of peacefully resolving disputes. A council of men among the Bakhtiari nomads of Iran meets to decide the fate of a man who stole an animal. (Tony Howarth, Woodfin Camp and Associates.)

adjudicators do not have the formal power needed to enforce their decisions. One such society is the Nuer of East Africa.

The Nuer are a pastoral and horticultural people, who live in villages grouped into districts. Each district is an informal political unit, with its own machinery for settling disputes. However, if a district has a large population residing over a wide area, it may be a long time before certain disputes are cleared up. On the higher, interdistrict level there is little chance of bringing feuding districts to a quick settlement, and there are few means of apportioning blame or of assessing damages other than by war.

Within a single community, however, disputes are more easily settled by the use of an informal adjudicator called the "leopard-skin chief." This man is not a political chief but a specialist mediator. His position is hereditary, has religious overtones, and makes its holder responsible for the social well-being of the district.

Matters such as cattle stealing rarely come to the attention of the leopard-skin chief; the parties involved usually prefer to settle in their own private way. But if, for example, a murder has been committed, the culprit will go at once to the house of the leopard-skin chief. Immediately the chief cuts the culprit's arm so that the blood flows; until the cut has been made the murderer may not eat or drink. If the murderer is afraid of vengeance by the slain man's family, he will remain at the house of the leopard-skin chief, which is considered sanctuary. Then, within the next few months, the chief attempts to mediate between the parties to the crime.

The chief elicits from the slayer's kin that they are prepared to pay compensation to avoid a feud and he persuades the dead man's kin that they ought to accept compensation. During this period neither party may eat or drink from the same vessels as the other, and they may not, therefore, eat in the house of the same third person. The chief then collects the cattle—till recently some forty to fifty beasts—and takes them to the dead man's home, where he performs various sacrifices of cleansing and atonement.[25]

[25] E. E. Evans-Pritchard, "The Nuer of the Southern Sudan," in *African Political Systems,* ed. M. Fortes and E. E. Evans-Pritchard (New York: Oxford University Press, 1940), p. 291.

The chief acts throughout as a go-between. He has no authority to force either of the parties to negotiate, and he has no power to enforce a solution once it has been arrived at. However, he is able to take advantage of the fact that, because both parties to the dispute belong to the same community and are anxious to avoid a blood feud, they are usually willing to come to terms.

Oaths and Ordeals Still another way of peacefully resolving disputes is through oaths and ordeals. Both oaths and ordeals involve appeals to supernatural power. An oath is the act of calling upon a deity to bear witness to the truth of what one says. An ordeal is a means used to determine guilt or innocence by submitting the accused to dangerous or painful tests believed to be under supernatural control.[26]

Oaths, as one would expect, vary widely in content according to the culture in which they are found. The Rwala Bedouin, for example, do the following:

In serious disputes the judge requires the *msabba* oath, so called from the seven lines drawn with a saber on the ground. The judge first draws a circle with a saber, then its diameter; then he intersects with five vertical lines, inviting the witness to step inside and, facing south, to swear: "A false oath is the ruin of the descendants, for he who [swears falsely] is insatiable in his desire [of gain] and does not fear for his Lord."

Scarcely is the oath finished when the witness jumps out of the circle and, full of rage, runs at his opponent, who has made him swear. The people present at the trial have to surround and hold him until he calms down.[27]

Ordeals fall into several types. A common one, found in almost every part of the world, is the scalding ordeal. Among the Tanala of Madagascar, the accused person, having first had his hand carefully examined for protective cover-

ing, has to reach his hand into a cauldron of boiling water and grasp, from underneath, a rock which is suspended there. He then plunges his hand into cold water, has it bandaged, and is led off to spend the night under guard. In the morning his hand is unbandaged and examined. If there are blisters, he is guilty. Another common type of ordeal involves the taking of poison; obviously, to survive is to establish one's innocence.

Oaths and ordeals have also been practiced in Western societies. Both were common in medieval Europe. Even today, in our own society, vestiges of oaths can be found: children can be heard to say, "Cross my heart and hope to die," and witnesses in courts of law are expected to swear on the Bible.

Why do some societies use oaths and ordeals? It has been argued that ordeals may render more than a mere chance verdict. Concerning the scalding ordeal, for example, Roberts suggests that there may be some relationship between the anxiety raised in a guilty person and severe blistering on the hand. But whether or not oaths or ordeals can establish guilt or innocence, we have to ask why some societies use them, while others do not. Roberts suggests that oaths and ordeals are found in fairly complex societies where there are relatively well-developed political institutions, yet the political officials lack sufficient power to make and enforce judicial decisions or would make themselves unnecessarily vulnerable were they to attempt to do so. In many parts of Africa, and also in medieval Europe, ruling groups had problems with succession and with maintaining continuous social control. To put their prestige and influence on the line behind every important judicial verdict was dangerous and impracticable. Hence, perhaps, they resorted to an appeal to the gods, which may have been "an important device allowing weak authority to maintain control at a reasonably low cost."[28] In contrast, smaller and less complex societies have probably no need for elaborate mechanisms to ascertain guilt. In such societies,

---

[26]John M. Roberts, "Oaths, Autonomic Ordeals, and Power," in *Cross-Cultural Approaches: Readings in Comparative Research*, ed. Clellan S. Ford (New Haven: HRAF Press, 1978), p. 169.

[27]Alois Musil, *The Manners and Customs of Rwala Bedouins*, American Geographical Society, Oriental Exploration Studies no. 6 (New York, 1928), p. 430.

[28]Roberts, "Oaths, Autonomic Ordeals, and Power," p. 192.

everyone is aware of what crimes have been committed and who the guilty parties probably are.

Codified Law and the Courts Codified laws and courts as a means of peacefully resolving disputes are used in our own society. But such mechanisms are not limited to modern industrialized states. From the late seventeenth to the early twentieth century, for example, the Ashanti of West Africa had a complex political system with elaborate legal arrangements. The Ashanti state was a military-based empire possessing legal codes that resembled those of many ancient civilizations.[29]

The most effective sanction underpinning Ashanti law and its enforcement was the intense respect—almost religious deference—accorded to the wishes of the ancestors and also to the elders as custodians of the ancestral tradition. Ashanti law was based upon a concept of natural law. This is a belief that there is an order of the universe whose principles lawmakers should follow in the decisions they make and in the regulations they design. Criminal and religious law were merged by the Ashanti in that crimes—especially acts of homicide, cursing a chief, cowardice, and sorcery—were regarded as sins against the ancestral spirits. In Ashanti court procedure, elders examined and cross-examined witnesses as well as parties to the dispute. There were also quasi-professional advocates and appeals against a verdict could be made directly to a chief. Particularly noteworthy was the emphasis placed upon intent when assessing guilt. Drunkenness constituted a valid defense for all crimes except murder and cursing a chief; and a plea of insanity, if proved, was upheld for all offenses. Ashanti punishments could be severe. Physical mutilation such as slicing off the nose or an ear—even castration in sexual offenses—was often employed. However, fines were more frequently imposed; and often those sentenced to death were allowed to commute their punishment to banishment and confiscation of goods.

Why do some societies have codified systems of law and others do not? One explanation advanced by E. Adamson Hoebel, A. R. Radcliffe-Brown, and others is that in small, closely knit communities there is little need for formal legal guidelines because competing interests are minimal. Simple societies need little codified law; there are relatively few matters to quarrel about, and the general will of the group is sufficiently well known and is demonstrated frequently enough to deter transgressors.

This point of view is corroborated in Richard Schwartz's study of two Israeli settlements. In one communal kibbutz, a young man aroused a good deal of community resentment because he had accepted an electric teakettle as a gift. It was the general opinion that he had overstepped the code about not having personal possessions, and he was so informed. Accordingly, he gave the kettle to the communal infirmary. Schwartz comments, "No organized enforcement of the decision was threatened, but had he disregarded the expressed will of the community, his life . . . would have been made intolerable by the antagonism of public opinion."[30] In this community, where people worked and ate together, not only did everyone know about transgressions, but a wrong-doer could not escape public censure. Thus, in such a community, public opinion was an effective sanction. In another Israeli community, however, where individuals lived in widely separated houses and worked and ate separately, public opinion did not work as well in resolving conflicts. Not only were community members less aware of problems, but they had no quick way of making their feelings known. As a result, they established a judicial body to handle trouble cases.

Unlike societies with small, closely knit communities, larger, more heterogeneous and stratified societies are likely to have more frequent disputes which at the same time are less visible to the public. Individuals in stratified

---

[29]Hoebel, *The Law of Primitive Man*, ch. 9.

[30]Richard D. Schwartz, "Social Factors in the Development of Legal Control: A Case Study of Two Israeli Settlements," *Yale Law Journal* 63 (February 1954): 475.

societies are generally not so dependent upon community members for their well-being and hence are less likely to know of, or care about, others' opinions. It is in such societies that codified laws and formal authorities for resolving disputes develop—in order, perhaps, that disputes may be settled impersonally enough so that the parties can accept the judicial decision and social order can be restored.

A good example of how more formal systems of law develop is the experience of towns in the American West during the gold rush period. The communities were literally swamped by large numbers of total strangers. The local townsfolk, having no control (authority) over these intruders because the strangers had no local ties, looked for ways to deal with the troublesome cases that were continually flaring up. A first attempt at a solution was to hire gunslingers—who were also strangers—to act as peace officers or sheriffs, but this usually failed. Eventually, towns succeeded in having federal authorities send in marshals backed by federal power.

Is there some evidence to support the theory that codified law is necessary only in larger, more complex societies? Data from a large, world-wide sample of societies suggest that codified law is generally associated with political integration beyond the local level. With particular reference to the way murder cases are handled, such cases are dealt with informally in societies with only local political organization. In societies with multilocal political units, murder cases tend to be adjudicated by specialized political authorities.[31]

VIOLENT RESOLUTION OF CONFLICT

People are likely to resort to violence when regular, effective alternative means of resolving a conflict are not available. When violence occurs between political entities such as communities, districts, or nations, some form of warfare is the result. The aim of the antagonists in each instance is to control the situation in order to obtain a particular objective for themselves—revenge for a killing, access to food, animals, raw materials, land, or markets—or to prevent the opponents from gaining that objective. The type of warfare, of course, varies in scope and in complexity from society to society. Sometimes a distinction is made between feuding, raiding, and large-scale confrontations.

Feuding Feuding is a state of recurring hostilities between families or groups of kinsmen, usually motivated by a desire to avenge an offense—whether insult, injury, deprivation, or death—against a member of the group. The most characteristic feature of the feud is that responsibility to avenge is carried by all members of the kin group. The killing of any member of the offender's group is considered appropriate revenge, since the kin group as a whole is regarded as responsible. Nicholas Gubser tells of a feud within a Nunamiut Eskimo community, caused by a husband's killing of his wife's lover, which lasted for decades. The Nunamiut take feuds seriously, as do many societies, especially when murder has been committed. Gubser describes what happens when a man is killed.

The closely related members of his kindred do not rest until complete revenge has been achieved. The immediate relatives of the deceased . . . recruit as much support from other relatives as they can. Their first action, if possible, is to kill the murderer, or maybe one of his closest kin. Then, of course, the members of the murderer's kindred are brought into the feud. These two kindreds may snipe at each other for years.[32]

Sometimes a full-scale battle takes place, as when the inland Nunamiut are drawn into a feud with coastal Eskimos over the abduction of a woman, after her kinfolk learn that she has been mutilated or possibly killed.

---

[31] Textor, *A Cross-Cultural Summary.*

[32] Nicholas J. Gubser, *The Nunamiut Eskimos: Hunters of Caribou* (New Haven: Yale University Press, 1965), p. 151.

Among the Dani of central New Guinea, warfare is characterized by formal battles. The two sides meet at an agreed-upon battle site to set up their lines and commence fighting with spears, sticks, and bows and arrows. (Photo by Karl Heider, © 1968 by the Film Study Center, Harvard University.)

Raiding Raiding is a short-term use of force, generally carefully preplanned and organized, to realize a limited objective. This objective is usually the acquisition of goods, animals, or other forms of wealth belonging to another (often a neighboring) community. Raiding is especially prevalent in pastoral societies in which cattle, horses, camels, or other animals are prized and an individual's own herd can be augmented by theft. Raids are often organized by temporary leaders or coordinators whose

authority may not endure beyond the planning and execution of the venture. Raiding differs from feuding in that it can more readily be terminated, temporarily or permanently, by recognized methods, such as truce or negotiated settlement.

Large-scale Confrontations Both feuding and raiding usually involve relatively small numbers of persons and almost always an element of surprise. Because they are generally attacked without warning, the victims are often unable to muster an immediate defense. Large-scale confrontations, in contrast, involve a large number of people, with both sides planning strategies of attack and defense.

Large-scale warfare is usually practiced among societies with intensive agriculture or industrialization. Only these societies possess a sufficiently advanced technology to support specialized armies, military leaders, strategists, and so on. However, large-scale confrontations are not limited to state societies alone. For example, they occur among the horticultural Dugum Dani of central New Guinea.

The military history of the Dani, with shifting alliances and confederations, is reminiscent of that of Europe, although Dani battles involve far fewer fighters and less sophisticated weaponry. Among the Dani, long periods of ritual warfare are characterized by formal battles which are announced through a challenge sent by one side to the opposing side. If the challenge is accepted, the protagonists meet at the agreed-upon battle site to set up their lines. Fighting with spears, sticks, and bows and arrows begins at mid-morning and continues until either nightfall or rain intervenes. There may also be a rest period during the midday heat during which both sides shout insults to one another or talk and rest among themselves. The front line of battle is composed of about a dozen active warriors and a few leaders. Behind them is a second line, still within arrow range, which is composed of those who have just left the forward line or are preparing to join it. The third line, outside arrow range, is composed of noncombatants—males too old or too young to participate and those recovering from wounds. This third line merely watches the battle taking place on the grassy plain. On the hillsides far back from the front line, some of the old men help to direct ancestral ghosts to the battle by gouging a line in the ground that points in the direction of the battlefield.[33]

Yet, as "total" as large-scale confrontations

may be, even warfare has cultural rules governing its conduct. Among the Dani, for instance, no fighting occurs at night, and weapons are limited to simple spears and bows and arrows. Similarly, in state societies, governments will sign "self-denying" pacts, restricting the use of poison gas, germ warfare, and so forth. Unofficially, private arrangements are common. One has only to glance through the memoirs of national leaders of the two World Wars to become aware of locally arranged truces, visits to one another's front positions, exchanges of prisoners of war, and so on.

In recent years, anthropologists have become interested in examining the relationships between types of warfare and types of political organization. Keith Otterbein, for example, in a cross-cultural study of some forty-six societies, found that the higher the level of political centralization, the more advanced the degree of military sophistication. In other words, chiefdoms and states are more apt to have complex military establishments, with a professional army and a hierarchy of military authority, than are bands and tribes. In addition, societies with complex political organizations are liable to have higher casualty rates and to wage war in order to gain political control over other groups. However, although military sophistication appears to increase with political development, the frequency of warfare seems to be no greater in complex states than in simple band societies.[34] Why most societies, on all levels of political complexity, have warfare is not yet understood.

Summary

1. All societies have customs or procedures which result in policymaking and the resolution of disputes—ways of creating and maintaining social order and coping with social disorder—although such customs vary from society to society.

---

[33]Karl Heider, *The Dugum Dani* (Chicago: Aldine, 1970), pp. 105–11.

[34]Keith Otterbein, *The Evolution of War* (New Haven: HRAF Press, 1970).

2. Societies with a band-type of political organization are composed of a number of fairly small, usually nomadic groups of people (bands). Each band is self-sufficient and autonomous, the band usually being the largest group that acts as a political unit. Societies with band organization generally are hunter-gatherers and egalitarian. In terms of political leadership, authority within the band is informal.

3. Societies with tribal organization are similar to those with band organization in their egalitarian nature, lack of political hierarchies and classes, and informal leadership patterns. In contrast to band societies, those with tribal organization generally are food producers, have a higher population density, and are more sedentary. Tribal organization is defined by the presence of some associations (such as clans and age-sets) which can potentially integrate more than one local group into a larger whole.

4. Chiefdom organization differs from tribal organization in that chiefdoms have formal authority structures integrating multi-community political units. Compared with tribal societies, chiefdom societies generally are more densely populated, and their communities are more permanent. The position of chief, which is sometimes hereditary and generally permanent, bestows high status on its holder. Most chiefdom societies have social ranking. An important responsibility of most chiefs is that of redistributing agent.

5. A state has been defined as a political unit composed of many communities and having a centralized government with the authority to make and enforce laws, collect taxes, and draft men for military service. In state societies, the government tries to maintain a monopoly on the use of physical force. In addition, states are generally characterized by class stratification, intensive agriculture (the high productivity of which presumably allows for the emergence of cities), commercial exchange, a high degree of economic and other kinds of specialization, and extensive foreign trade.

6. Societies have found various ways of peacefully resolving disputes. One such way involves action on the part of the community as a whole. Another is through the use of informal adjudicators, although such adjudicators do not have power to enforce their decisions. Still a third way is through oaths and ordeals. And finally, in societies such as our own, disputes are peacefully resolved generally through the use of codified laws and courts.

7. People are likely to resort to violence when regular, effective, alternative means of resolving a conflict are not available. When violence occurs between political entities such as communities, districts, or nations, we generally speak of warfare. The type of warfare varies in scope and in complexity from society to society.

Suggested Readings

Balandier, G. *Political Anthropology.* Translated from the French by A. M. S. Smith. New York: Random House, Pantheon Books, 1970.

A review of anthropological studies of political organizations, both theoretical and field studies. Topics discussed include the role of social stratification in political organization, links between the political and the sacred, and the development of the state.

Fried, M. H. *The Evolution of Political Society: An Essay in Political Anthropology.* New York: Random House, 1967.

In this theoretical work, the author begins with general remarks on the anthropology of political organization and goes on to describe differences between kinds of societies in terms of their political structures.

Harrison, R. *Warfare.* Minneapolis: Burgess Publishing Co., 1973.

A discussion of various explanations of warfare and how it relates to other aspects of culture.

Hoebel, E. A. *The Law of Primitive Man.* New York: Atheneum, 1968; originally published in 1954.

This book is divided into three parts: the theoretical and methodological background for the study of primitive law; discussion of legal systems among the Eskimo, Plains Indians, Trobrianders, and Ashanti; law and society—the relationship of law to religion and magic, its social functions, and development through time.

Service, E. R. *Primitive Social Organization: An Evolutionary Perspective.* New York: Random House, 1962.

A classification of primitive social organization into band society, tribal society, and chiefdoms, presenting the criteria by which these levels are defined and suggesting possible reasons for their development.

Swartz, M. J.; Turner, V. W.; and Tuden, A., eds. *Political Anthropology.* Chicago: Aldine, 1966.

A collection of essays on political systems around the world. Of particular interest is the introductory essay by the editors which gives a definition of the "political" in society and analyzes some key issues in political anthropology.

Culture and Personality

19

Customs and traditions vary widely from society to society. The Nupe of central Nigeria, for instance, developed centralized institutions of government and law. The Eskimos managed to get along without either. Some societies have a money economy in which goods and services are bought and sold. In other societies, goods and services are distributed only by reciprocal gift giving. Such differences, and others we have dealt with so far, are by definition cultural. Now we shall deal with another aspect of cultural variation—differences between societies with regard to common personality characteristics.

Our personality, which is the result of a complex interplay of forces, can be seen as the distinctive way we think, feel, and behave. Each of us is born unique, with certain inherited tendencies that influence our individual personality. However, the society in which we live may exert an even more powerful influence on our personality. The process of sharing and learning that produces other distinctive aspects of a society's culture also produces distinctive personality traits. If such personality traits are, in fact, commonly learned, then they are, by definition, cultural.

What accounts for personality differences in the world's societies? In this chapter, we shall discuss how personality traits are assessed by the trained observer, how a particular personality trait may become prominent in a particular society, and how typical personality traits themselves might influence other aspects of culture.

How Personality Is Formed

It is generally agreed that our personalities are the result of an interaction between our genetic inheritance and our life experiences, although not much is known yet about what specific factors give rise to which specific personality traits. To the extent, then, that all individuals have a unique combination of genetic traits and life experiences, we can say that in some ways no person is like any other person. But a considerable portion of one's life experiences (as well as of one's genes) are shared with others. Many life experiences occur within the context of family life—so much so that we often say a child's personality is largely shaped by his or her parents. For this reason, the personalities of members of the same family may resemble each other. But we have to consider why a particular family raises children the way it does. To some extent, all families are unique. Yet much of the way parents rear children is influenced by their culture—by the typical patterns of family life and by shared conceptions of the "right" way to bring up children.

It is not easy to determine to how great an extent members of our society share conceptions of the "right" way to bring up children, because as we look around at various families we observe differences in upbringing. It is only when we examine other societies and their patterns of childrearing that our cultural conceptions begin to become apparent. For example, the Marquesans of the South Pacific believe that nursing makes a child difficult to raise. Consequently, their pattern of feeding their children is irregular and is dependent upon the feelings of the adults rather than the convenience of the children. In contrast, the Chenchu of India do not wean children until they are five or six years old.[1] In most societies, toilet training becomes intensive after a child's second year, but there are marked differences in the techniques used to reach the same goal. The natives of Dahomey, in West Africa, punish bedsoiling by pouring a mixture of ashes and water over the head of the offender or by attaching "a live frog . . . to the child's waist, which so frightens [it] that a cure is usually effected."[2] Attitudes toward masturbation in children also vary. The Alorese of Indonesia regularly masturbate their children to pacify them; the Manus of New

Societies differ in their encouragement of dependency. Young Nepalese children are usually under the care of their older brothers and sisters since their parents are busy with other duties. (Frederick Ayer, Photo Researchers.)

Guinea, however, tend to believe masturbation shameful. Our own American culture generally attempts to prevent or restrict the habit in children. Attitudes toward sex play differ, from the more restrictive approaches of the Chiricahua Apache of the American Southwest, who separate sexes by the seventh year, to the Baiga of southern Asia, who encourage young children to engage in erotic play. The Hopi fill their young with dire warnings of the consequences of too early sexual experience. They tell boys to abstain lest they become dwarfs; and they warn small girls that they will become pregnant, thereby causing all people to die and the world to come to an end.[3]

---

[1] John W. M. Whiting and Irvin L. Child, *Child Training and Personality* (New Haven: Yale University Press, 1953), pp. 69–71.

[2] M. J. Herskovits, *Dahomey: An Ancient West African Kingdom* (New York: Augustin, 1938), pp. 272–73, quoted in Whiting and Child, *Child Training and Personality*, p. 75.

[3] Whiting and Child, *Child Training and Personality*, pp. 80–83.

Societies also differ in their encouragement of dependency. Kwoma mothers of New Guinea keep their infants nearby at all times and respond to their every whim. The Ainu mother of northern Japan, on the other hand, places her child in a hanging cradle during the day and lets it fend for itself, which usually means "a good deal of kicking and screaming until tired of it, followed by exhaustion, repose, and resignation."[4]

As these examples suggest, societies vary in how they customarily bring up children. We can assume that the way children are reared in part determines the types of personalities they will have. Also, different societies, with differing customs of childrearing, will tend to produce different kinds of people. This is not to suggest that personalities are not unique, even though many people in a society may share certain personality traits. As we have said, an individual's uniqueness is derived from his or her distinctive genetic endowment and personal life experiences—and thus one personality will always be different from another.

Cultural anthropologists are interested in shared patterns of behavior, belief, and feeling. They are therefore interested in those aspects of personality which are typically shared with others, with other members of the society or with other members of some subcultural group.

Modal Personality

The typical personality in a particular society is often referred to in terms of *modal personality* characteristics, those characteristics that occur with the highest frequency in the society. A personality characteristic can be thought of as more or less of a particular attribute. For example, aggressiveness is not present or absent in a person but is found to a greater or lesser degree in some people as compared with others. Similarly, we may say that the exhibition of a great deal of physical or verbal aggression is a modal

personality trait in some societies. Such a judgment is always relative, contrasting one society with others. When we speak of a modal personality characteristic such as aggressiveness, we mean that most people in the society display more aggressiveness than most people in some other society. For example, the Yanomamö Indians of the Brazil-Venezuela border area are described by Napoleon Chagnon, who did fieldwork among them, as showing a great deal of aggression in their interpersonal relationships. Threats and shouting frequently accompany demands, and a man's potential violence is often demonstrated.[5] As compared with other societies, the Yanomamö would rank high on aggressiveness as a modal personality trait.

Just as culture is never fixed or static, so modal personality is never static. Individuals often alter their behavior in adapting to changing circumstances. When enough individuals in a society have altered their own behavior or the way they bring up their children, modal personality characteristics presumably will also have changed.

METHODS OF ASSESSING MODAL PERSONALITY

A number of methods are available to the anthropologist to determine the modal personality traits in a particular society or subcultural group. Generally, these methods are similar to, and in fact are frequently derived from, the procedures used by psychologists to assess individual personality characteristics. They include *observation*, the *collection of life histories, projective tests,* and the *analysis of cultural materials.* Whatever the method selected, the assessment of personality must be made so as to be representative of the population studied. This can be done by measuring personality traits, in a representative sample of individuals from a community or a society, and determining those that occur with the highest frequency. Or personality assessments may also be made from certain

---

[4] B. D. Howard, *Life with Trans-Siberian Savages* (London: Longmans, Green, 1893), p. 67, as quoted in Whiting and Child, *Child Training and Personality*, p. 93.

[5] Napoleon A. Chagnon, *Yanomamö, The Fierce People* (New York: Holt, Rinehart and Winston, 1968).

cultural materials which presumably reflect the modal or typical personality.

Observation of Behavior Investigators may obtain their information by closely studying the way people behave, what they say, how they perform tasks, even the postures they take and the emotions they do or do not show in their activities.

In psychological research, behavior observations typically take place in controlled settings such as a laboratory. The anthropological use of behavior observation, on the other hand, requires some alteration in strategy and technique, since observation more typically takes place in natural settings. In the natural setting, the observer must cope with the problem of interfering with natural reactions and routines. Not only is the observer a stranger, but he or she is often engaged in the fairly unusual practice of recording behavior. Being visible, the researcher has to make the choice of interacting with the persons being observed or attempting to remain uninvolved and ignored.

Since behavior observation is a time-consuming and difficult process, the anthropologist has to decide whether the information may not be more easily obtained in some other way. Observation may be necessary when persons are unable to report accurately upon a particular type of behavior themselves. This may occur because the behavior patterns are unconscious and cannot be verbalized, or because behavior patterns conflict with the ideals of the society. If the researcher decides that observation is the only way to assess a domain of behavior, he or she must then carefully map out a plan of exactly what to observe, how to observe, and whom to observe. Observers cannot possibly record everything seen. They must focus on particular types of behaviors taking place between particular persons or in particular situations.[6] Even if modern equipment such as a movie or videotape camera is used, the observer must still decide who and what are to be focused on.

Life Histories These may take the form of biographies or "autobiographies" of individuals in a particular society. Life histories can be especially useful in disclosing an individual's values and attitudes and can produce significant information about childhood experiences. The effectiveness of this method greatly depends upon how the anthropologist is regarded by the group and upon his or her skills in interviewing. First, trust and respect must be established. Sensitivity to the personality of the subject and patience are other requisites for obtaining reliable data. Themes that recur are to be noted, as are the underlying attitudes and values of the subject. The content of dreams, visions, and fantasies also offers clues to personality factors. Life histories representing a cross-section of the society, however, are often extremely difficult for the anthropologist to obtain. Successful members of the community are either too busy or too uninterested to cooperate. In fact, it has been suggested that life history informants may be some of the more maladjusted individuals of the society. After all, what is the motivation to spend a great deal of time talking to the anthropologist?[7] Another problem in collecting biographical materials is that anthropologists are often unable to attain proficiency in the native language. Cora Du Bois made conscientious efforts to acquire fluency, yet she found it necessary to continue employing an interpreter and to cross-check all her translations even after a year of studying the people of Alor.[8]

Projective Tests These tests utilize stimuli that are ambiguous. In order to respond to those stimuli, the test subject is obliged to structure them according to his or her own preoccupations, needs, and conflicts, which are largely

---

[6]Beatrice Whiting and John Whiting, "Methods for Observing and Recording Behavior," in *A Handbook of Method in Cultural Anthropology,* ed. Raoul Naroll and Ronald Cohen (Garden City, N.Y.: Natural History Press, 1970), pp. 282–315.

[7]Victor Barnouw, *Culture and Personality* (Homewood, Ill.: Dorsey Press, 1963), pp. 198–99.

[8]Cora Du Bois, *The People of Alor: A Social-Psychological Study of an East Indian Island* (Minneapolis: University of Minnesota Press, 1944).

unconscious. Hence a person's personality is presumably "projected" into the ambiguous situation. Projective analysis takes various forms, including the interpretation of word associations and drawings. Two widely used tests are the Rorschach and the Thematic Apperception Test (TAT).

The Rorschach, invented by Hermann Rorschach, a Swiss psychiatrist, and published in 1922, consists of ten cards, each carrying an ink blot. Subjects are asked to describe what they see in the various shapes. From the kinds of images or ideas reported, inferences can be made about the subject's personality. Tendencies to see the blots a certain way have been noted in several societies. Samoans, Algerians, and Tuscarora Indians tend to see the blots whole, for example, while Zuni children tend to see each blot in many details.

The TAT uses a series of drawings, each of which is somewhat ambiguous. Subjects are asked what they think is going on in each scene (which usually portrays some life situation), what happened before, and how they think things will turn out. The narratives are then studied for insights into the subject's needs and conflicts. In an early TAT study, Henry tested 102 Hopi children using illustrations that had been redrawn by an Indian artist. The individuals depicted in the drawings looked like Indians and the settings looked like Hopi settings. The children's responses suggested to Henry that individual strivings were suppressed in deference to the group, and that these suppressions gave rise to anxiety. The children's TAT stories also suggested that the Hopi may instead alleviate their anxiety with such release mechanisms as malicious gossip, sibling jealousy, and acts of stealing and destruction.[9]

One of the difficulties in the cross-cultural use of such tests as the Rorschach and the TAT is that interpretations are often culture-bound. They may be based upon Western psychiatric concepts which do not necessarily pertain to individuals functioning in a very different kind of society.

Analysis of Cultural Materials Folktales, myths, and legends are a rich source of information about modal personality, as well as other cultural features of a society. Such cultural materials can be viewed as similar to projective materials, like the responses to the Rorschach or the TAT. Thus, it has been argued that popular folktales in a society may be projections of the needs and conflicts that are generally shared by the members of that society. For example, McClelland measured the strength of the need to achieve in nonliterate societies through an analysis of the content of popular folktales. He assumes that "since these stories are told and retold orally by many different people in the culture, the way in which they are told will come to reflect a kind of 'average level' of motivation among people of the tribe." McClelland draws a parallel between his method and the TAT.[10]

The assumption that folktales are projective of modal personality traits is supported by studies linking child-training practices in a society to measures of modal personality based on folktales. For example, Child, Storm, and Veroff found that societies with high reward for achievement in child training have a good deal of achievement motivation expressed in folktales.[11] Wright found that societies which severely punish children for aggression tend to express anxiety about aggression in their folktales.[12]

The comparative study of posture and gesture may also involve a kind of projective analysis. In one such study, Gregory Bateson and

[9] William E. Henry, *The Thematic Apperception Technique in the Study of Culture-Personality Relations*, Genetic Psychology Monograph no. 35 (1947), p. 91.

[10] David C. McClelland, *The Achieving Society* (New York: D. Van Nostrand, 1961), p. 64.

[11] I. L. Child, T. Storm, and J. Veroff, "Achievement Themes in Folktales Related to Socialization Practice," in *Motives in Fantasy, Action and Society*, ed. J. W. Atkinson (Princeton, N.J.: Van Nostrand, 1958), pp. 479–92.

[12] George O. Wright, "Projection and Displacement: A Cross-Cultural Study of Folk-Tale Aggression," *Journal of Abnormal and Social Psychology* 49 (1954): 523–28.

Margaret Mead analyzed Balinese postures and rhythms, especially as observed in dance movements, for clues to Balinese personality. They suggest that the slowness and deliberateness of many Balinese movements indicates passivity.[13] Some cultural anthropologists have extended this type of analysis to painting, music, sculpture, and other art forms. For example, Anthony Wallace has made a detailed examination of lowland Mayan art, on the basis of which he has suggested that the Maya were introspective and "polite and formal" in their social relationships.[14]

To understand why there is cultural variation in modal personality, we may pose two questions. What customs of childrearing may account for the observed differences in modal personality? And, what accounts for differences in childrearing?

Explaining Variation in Modal Personality

CHILDREARING AND MODAL PERSONALITY: FIELD STUDIES

Socialization and *enculturation* are terms used by both anthropologists and psychologists to describe the development, through the influence of parents and others, of patterns of behavior in children that conform to the standards deemed appropriate by the culture. We can make the general assumption that differences in childrearing account in part for personality differences. Still, we need to understand exactly which differences in child training make for which differences in personality.

To determine cause and effect in personality, the pioneer anthropologists in the field, such as Margaret Mead, Ruth Benedict, and Cora Du Bois, often concentrated on a single society or, at most, compared a few societies, seeking links between childrearing customs and adult personality traits.

The People of Alor Du Bois spent almost eighteen months on the island of Alor, in eastern Indonesia, studying the native Alorese. To understand Alorese modal personality, she did three things. She collected information on childrearing. She collected eight biographies, each with dream material. And she administered a broad range of projective tests—the Rorschach test to thirty-seven subjects, a word-association test to thirty-six subjects, and a drawing test to fifty-five children.[15]

Du Bois broke new ground when she asked specialists in various fields to assess and interpret her projective materials independently. These authorities were given no background briefing on Alorese culture or attitudes; neither were they permitted to see Du Bois's general ethnographic notes or interpretations. Abram Kardiner was given the life histories, Emil Oberholzer the Rorschachs, and Trude Schmidl-Waehner the children's drawings. Working with only these materials, each prepared an evaluation. The effectiveness of the test procedures employed by Du Bois, and her success in eliminating her own emotional or cultural biases, were confirmed by the work of these independent authorities. To a remarkable degree, their findings concurred with hers.

A rather unfavorable modal personality for the Alorese emerges from this many-sided investigation. Alorese of both sexes are described by Du Bois and her colleagues as suspicious and antagonistic, prone to violent and emotional outbursts often of a jealous nature. They tend to be uninterested in the world around them, slovenly in workmanship, and lacking an interest in goals. Kardiner drew attention to the absence of idealized parental figures in the life stories. Oberholzer noted the lack of capacity for sustained creative effort, indicated by his reading

[13] Gregory Bateson and Margaret Mead, *Balinese Character, A Photographic Analysis,* Special Publication of New York Academy of Sciences (New York: 1942), p. 15.

[14] Anthony F. C. Wallace, "A Possible Technique for Recognizing Psychological Characteristics of the Ancient Maya from an Analysis of Their Art," *American Imago* 7 (1950): 245.

[15] Du Bois, *The People of Alor.*

An Alor child throwing a temper tantrum expressing his hunger and frustration. Alorese children are not fed on demand, but when it is convenient for their parents. (Courtesy of Cora Du Bois, *The People of Alor*/University of Minnesota Press.)

of the Rorschach scores. Schmidl-Waehner identified a lack of imagination and a strong sense of loneliness manifested in the children's drawings.

Turning to the possible causative influences, Du Bois and her fellow researchers focused on the experiences of the Alorese during infancy and early childhood, up to the age of six or so. At the root of much of Alorese personality development, they suggested, is the division of labor in that society. Women are the major food suppliers, working daily in the family gardens, while men occupy themselves with commercial affairs, usually the trading of pigs, gongs, and kettledrums. Within about two weeks after giving birth, the mother returns to her outdoor work, leaving the infant with the father, a grandparent, or an older sibling. She deprives the newborn child of the comfort of a maternal presence and of breast-feeding for most of the day. In Freudian terms, the infant experiences oral frustration and resultant anxiety. At the same time, the baby suffers bewildering switches in attention, from loving and petting to neglect and bad-tempered rejection. Thus, maternal neglect is viewed as being largely responsible for Alorese personality.

But how do we know that maternal neglect is really responsible for the seeming suspiciousness and jealous outbursts of the Alorese? Perhaps maternal neglect is responsible, but it

could also be any number of other conditions of Alorese life. For example, some critics have suggested that the high prevalence of debilitating diseases in Alor may be responsible for much of their behavior.[16] For us to be more certain that a particular aspect of childrearing produces certain effects on modal personality, we must compare the people of Alor with people in other societies. Do other societies with this kind of maternal neglect show the same pattern of personality traits? If they do, then the presumed association becomes more plausible. If they do not, then the interpretation becomes questionable.

Many explanations of modal personality traits have been based on the analysis of single societies. Gorer and Rickman's "swaddling hypothesis" is another case in point.[17] They suggest that the custom of child swaddling is the key to an understanding of the great Russian character. From the day of birth,

the baby is tightly swaddled in long strips of material, holding its legs straight and its arms down by its sides. . . . When swaddled the baby is completely rigid; one informant said the infants were like sticks, another likened them to sausages, a third to parcels. The baby can be held in any position or by any part of it without bending.[18]

The authors maintain that this physical restraint against a child's natural desire for movement induces manic-depressive variations of mood characteristic of the "great Russian personality." Thus, Russians are presumed to be fond of huge feasts and drinking bouts because the release of the bindings in their infancy was always accompanied by food and love. They are supposedly ready to confess even uncommitted sins, because of unconscious guilt feelings arising from rage induced by the bindings.

This hypothesis was almost immediately attacked because of the inadequacy of its sam-

[16] Victor Barnouw, *Culture and Personality*, p. 115.
[17] Geoffrey Gorer and John Rickman, *The People of Great Russia* (New York: Chanticleer Press, 1950), p. 14.
[18] Ibid., pp. 97–99.

ple base and because it overlooked the fact that child-training practices had undergone radical changes with the accession to power of the Bolsheviks in 1917. Today, critics would also point out that the study failed to test its central hypothesis against data from other societies. If other societies that practice swaddling or its equivalent were found to exhibit manic-depressive tendencies, the Gorer-Rickman hypothesis might receive greater acceptance.

The analysis of a single society, then, even if the descriptions are correct, is not sufficient to justify the conclusion that specific childrearing customs are related to specific adult personality characteristics. Nevertheless, studies of a single society have a value in that they suggest possible connections for testing by comparative, or cross-cultural, studies. Also, if several single-society studies show the same relationship between a childrearing custom and a personality trait, we can be more confident that the hypothesis linking them may be correct.

Comparative studies of the type we are talking about are relatively rare. In part, the reason for this is that assessing modal personality in even one society is a time-consuming and expensive proposition. Making this assessment in many societies is obviously much more difficult.

An example of a study that was designed to compare children's behavior across several societies is the Six Cultures study. In addition to collecting ethnographic data and information on parental attitudes about bringing up children, the research teams observed children's social behavior in six different societies. Since six societies were being compared, it was possible to discover how differences in children's social behaviors across those societies might be related to differences in childrearing. One of the findings of the study, for example, was that where children were assigned many chores, including baby-tending, they were generally more likely to offer help to others. Where children were assigned few chores, they showed somewhat different behaviors: they were more likely to seek help and attention from others

and they were also more likely to boss others around.[19]

INFLUENCES ON CHILDREARING AND PERSONALITY

The cultural anthropologist seeks not only to establish connections between childrearing customs and personality traits, but to learn why those childrearing customs differ in the first place. Some anthropologists believe that childrearing practices are largely adaptive—that a society generally produces the kinds of personalities that are best suited to perform the activities necessary for the survival of the society. As Whiting and Child express it, "the economic, political and social organs of a society—the basic customs surrounding the nourishment, sheltering and protection of its members . . . seem a likely source of influence on child training practices."[20] The belief that childrearing practices are generally adaptive does not mean that societies always produce the kinds of persons they need. Just as in the biological realm, where we see poor adaptations and extinctions of species and subspecies, so we may expect that societies sometimes produce modal personalities that are maladapted to the requirements of living in that society. However, we expect that most societies that survived to be recorded have produced generally adaptive modal personalities.

Barry, Child, and Bacon have theorized that child-training practices may be adapted to the economic requirements of a society. They suggest that such requirements may explain why some societies strive to develop compliant children while others aim for self-reliance and individual initiative.[21] In a cross-cultural study, they found that agricultural and herding societies are

[19] Beatrice B. Whiting and John W. M. Whiting in collaboration with Richard Longabaugh, *Children of Six Cultures: A Psycho-Cultural Analysis* (Cambridge: Harvard University Press, 1975), pp. 82–103.
[20] Whiting and Child, *Child Training and Personality*, p. 310.
[21] Herbert Barry, III, Irvin L. Child, and Margaret K. Bacon, "Relation of Child Training to Subsistence Economy," *American Anthropologist* 61, no. 1 (February 1959): 51–63.

more likely to stress compliance, while hunting and gathering societies tend to stress individual assertion. Their theory is that agricultural and herding societies cannot afford departures from established routine, since such departures might jeopardize the food supply for long periods of time. Such societies are likely, therefore, to emphasize compliance with tradition. On the other hand, departures from routine in a hunter-gatherer society cannot cause much damage to a food supply that has to be collected anew almost every day. So, hunter-gatherers can afford to emphasize individual initiative.

Melvin Kohn has offered a parallel interpretation for the differences between working-class and middle-class values about childrearing in our own society.[22] Working-class parents, Kohn writes,

value obedience, neatness and cleanliness more highly than do middle class parents, and middle class parents in turn value curiosity, happiness, consideration, and—most importantly—self-control more highly than do working class parents; . . . working class parental values center on conformity to external proscriptions, middle class . . . on *self*-direction. To working class parents it is the overt act that matters: the child should not transgress externally imposed rules; to middle class parents it is the child's motives and feelings that matter: the child should govern himself.[23]

Kohn believes that these differences in outlook derive from contrasts in the working conditions of the two classes. Work done by members of the middle class generally requires initiative and self-direction, whereas those in the working class are generally expected to follow rules handed down by someone in authority. The parents' own occupational experiences, Kohn notes, "have significantly affected [their] conceptions of what is desirable behavior, on or off the job, for adults or for children."[24]

Economic factors may also partly explain why boys and girls are brought up differently in our society. But our society is by no means unusual in this regard. In a cross-cultural study, Barry, Bacon, and Child found some general differences in the way boys and girls are brought up.[25] In most societies there is more pressure on boys than on girls to be self-reliant, independent, and to strive for achievement, whereas there is usually more pressure on girls to be responsible and obedient. Barry, Bacon, and Child suggest that these near-universal sex differences in socialization may be largely attributable to traditional differences in the division of labor by sex. In most societies men usually perform more strenuous work which takes them further afield, and women, perhaps because of requirements of tending young infants, usually perform work that is closer to home.

Although most societies socialize boys and girls differently, some societies differentiate between boys and girls more than others. What accounts for extreme differentiation? Barry, Bacon, and Child suggest that certain cultural conditions make this differentiation more likely. If a society has tasks which require a great deal of physical strength, interchangeability of tasks is less likely. Thus, societies which hunt large animals or which keep large domesticated animals are more likely to have greater sex differentiation. Less differentiation between the sexes appears to be found in societies with independent nuclear families rather than extended families. With independent families, husbands and wives might have to interchange roles more, and thus boys and girls might have to be socialized more similarly.[26]

Childrearing practices for both sexes may also be affected by family form and household composition. Minturn and Lambert report, on the basis of data from the Six Cultures study, that children tend to be more strongly punished

[22] Melvin L. Kohn, "Social Class and Parent-Child Relationships: An Interpretation," *American Journal of Sociology* 68 (1963): 471–80.

[23] Ibid., p. 475.

[24] Ibid., p. 476.

[25] Herbert Barry, III, Margaret K. Bacon, and Irvin L. Child, "A Cross-Cultural Survey of Some Sex Differences in Socialization," *Journal of Abnormal and Social Psychology* 55 (November 1957): 327–32.

[26] Ibid.

for fighting with others when the family lives in cramped quarters. The more people living in a house, the less apt a mother is to permit disobedience.[27] This observation is consistent with the findings of a cross-cultural study, conducted by John Whiting, that societies with extended-family households are more likely to punish aggression in children severely than are societies composed of nuclear families.[28]

Personality as Integrating Culture

Some anthropologists, as well as other students of human variation, have suggested that personality or psychological processes may account for connections between two or more aspects of culture. Whiting and Child refer to this sort of connection as *personality integration of culture.* Thus, if certain aspects of culture, such as childrearing customs, influence the formation of certain personality traits, and these personality traits in turn give rise to other customs, then a knowledge of personality processes can help us to understand the link between these two aspects of culture.[29]

Kardiner, too, has suggested that cultural aspects influence personality through childrearing and that the resulting personality in turn influences the culture. He believes that *primary institutions*, such as family organization and subsistence techniques, are the source of early experiences that help form the basic personality (what we have called the modal personality). Personality, in turn, influences the growth of such *secondary institutions* as religion, folktales, and ways of thinking.[30] Presumably, these secondary institutions have little relation to the adaptive requirements of society. But some of these aspects of culture like art, music, and folklore may reflect and express the motives, conflicts, and anxieties of typical members of the society. If so, then we may perhaps best understand these aspects of culture by investigating the intervening psychological processes which may produce them. As an example of how personality may integrate culture, we turn to some suggested explanations for cultural preferences for games and for the custom of male initiation ceremonies.

In a cross-cultural study conducted by Roberts and Sutton-Smith, cultural preferences for particular types of games were found to be related to certain aspects of childrearing.[31] The researchers suggest that these associations may be a consequence of conflicts generated in many people in a society by particular types of child-rearing pressures. Games of strategy, for example, are associated with child training that emphasizes obedience. Roberts and Sutton-Smith propose that severe obedience training can create a conflict between the need to obey and the desire not to obey, thereby arousing anxiety. Such anxiety may or may not manifest itself against the person who instigates the anxiety. In any event, the conflict and the aggression itself can be played out on the miniature battlefields of games of strategy such as chess, or the Japanese game of Go. Similarly, games of chance may represent defiance of societal expectations of docility and responsibility. The general interpretation suggested by Roberts and Sutton-Smith is that players (and societies) initially become curious about games, learn them, and ultimately develop high involvement in them because of the particular kinds of psychological conflicts that are handled or expressed, but not necessarily finally resolved, by the games.[32]

The possible role of psychological processes in connecting different aspects of culture is also illustrated in cross-cultural work on male initia-

[27] Leigh Minturn and William W. Lambert, *Mothers of Six Cultures: Antecedents of Child Rearing* (New York: John Wiley and Sons, 1964), p. 289.

[28] J. W. M. Whiting, "Cultural and Sociological Influences on Development," in *Growth and Development of the Child in His Setting* (Maryland Child Growth and Development Institute, 1959), pp. 5–9.

[29] Whiting and Child, *Child Training and Personality*, pp. 32–38.

[30] Abram Kardiner, *The Individual and His Society* (New York: Golden Press, 1946), p. 471.

[31] John M. Roberts and Brian Sutton-Smith, "Child Training and Game Involvement," *Ethnology* 1, no. 2 (April 1962): 166–85.

[32] Ibid., p. 178.

tion ceremonies for boys at adolescence. In the ceremonies, boys are subjected to painful tests of manhood, usually including genital operations, which indicate the boys' transition to adulthood. Burton and Whiting found that initiation ceremonies tend to occur in patrilocal societies in which infant boys initially sleep exclusively with their mothers. They suggest that initiation rites in such societies are intended to break a conflict in sex identity. The conflict is believed to exist because boys in these societies would initially identify with their mothers, who exercise almost complete control over them in infancy. Later, when the boys discover that men dominate the society, they would identify secondarily with their fathers. This sex-role conflict is assumed to be resolved by the initiation ceremony which demonstrates a boy's manhood, thus strengthening the secondary identification.[33]

Italian boys are playing LaMorra, a game of chance. (David Seymour, Magnum Photos.)

Culture and Mental Illness

Throughout this chapter, we have been discussing the interaction between culture and personality, with an emphasis on modal personality traits. But cultures may also influence the development of *abnormal personalities.* It was once generally held that only the more complex Euro-American cultures produced serious mental disorders. Members of "primitive" societies were regarded as uncomplicated and free of neuroses. This view has recently been greatly modified. Many non-Western societies offer evidence of aberrant behavior, apparently as a result of mental illness. Among the questions raised by anthropologists have been: Is the rate of mental illness lower in technologically simple, nonliterate societies than in complex ones? Is it more difficult for individuals to adjust to some cultures than to others? What, in fact, constitutes mental "abnormality"?

This last point is crucial to the discussion,

for it points to differing standards of normal behavior among the world's cultures. Many German officials, for instance, were regarded in every way as normal by their neighbors and fellow workers during the period of Nazi control. Yet these officials committed acts of inhumanity which were so vicious that to many observers in other Western societies they appeared criminally insane. The Saora of Orissa (India) provide an example of behavior normal to one society which would be abnormal to another society. The Saora take for granted that certain of their womenfolk regularly are courted by lovers from the supernatural world, marry them, and have children (who are never seen, yet allegedly are suckled at night).[34] Behavior that is so alien to our own makes it no easy task for researchers to identify mental illness in other societies, let alone compare more complex and less complex societies for rates of mental disorder.

[33] Roger V. Burton and John W. M. Whiting, "The Absent Father and Cross-Sex Identity," *Merrill Palmer Quarterly of Behavior and Development* 7, no. 2 (1961): 85–95.

[34] Verrier Elwin, *The Religion of an Indian Tribe* (London: Oxford University Press, 1955), as cited in Victor Barnouw, *Culture and Personality,* p. 364.

Japanese students playing Go, a game of strategy. (Hiroshi Hamaya, Magnum Photos.)

Whether we use absolute or culturally relative standards to define mental illness, it seems that certain forms of mental illness appear in some societies and not in others. Great interest has been shown, for example, in the *Wiitiko* psychosis, a form of mental disorder found mostly among the males of some North American Indian tribes, including the Ojibwa and Cree. The afflicted individual has the delusion that he is possessed by the spirit of a Wiitiko, a cannibal giant, and he has hallucinations and cannibalistic impulses. One theory attributes the disorder to famine,[35] but critics have pointed out that not all of those afflicted with the psychosis are starving. A psychological reason has also been suggested: the subject sees the Wiitiko monster as a symbol of his mother who frustrated his dependency needs in childhood. He attempts to fight back by behaving like the monster, trying to destroy imagined persecutors by eating them.[36]

A mental disorder called *pibloktoq* occurs among some Eskimo adults of Greenland, usually women, who become oblivious to their surroundings and act in agitated, eccentric ways. They may strip themselves naked and wander across the ice and over hills until they collapse of exhaustion. Another disorder, *amok*, occurs in Malaya, Indonesia, and New Guinea. It is characterized by Honigmann as a "destructive maddened excitement . . . beginning with depression and followed by a period of brooding and withdrawal . . . [culminating in] the final mobilization of tremendous energy during which the 'wild man' runs destructively beserk."[37]

[35] Ruth Landes, "The Abnormal among the Ojibwa," *Journal of Abnormal and Social Psychology* 33 (1938): 14–33.

[36] Seymour Parker, "The Wiitiko Psychosis in the Context of Ojibwa Personality and Culture," *American Anthropologist* 62 (1960): 620.

[37] John J. Honigmann, *Personality in Culture* (New York: Harper & Row, 1967), pp. 398–406.

Mental disorders such as these used to be attributed to a combination of physical and psychological factors. The cold, dark, depressing aspects of Arctic winters have become almost a cliché of anthropological description, as has the depicting of tropical regions as enervating. There is reason to suspect that such classifications stem more from the inconvenience of the stranger who makes the investigation than from the attitudes of the inhabitants, who generally have experienced no other environment. Similarly, theories that associated lack of satisfaction in childhood with later manifestations of hysteria are weakened by the fact that comparable conditions in other societies do not always produce the disorder.

It has been suggested that certain mental illnesses, such as amok and pibloktoq, are not really different mental illnesses—they may merely be examples of the same illness which is expressed differently in different societies. Honigmann thinks that this may be true with regard to pibloktoq. The hysteria associated with that illness ultimately subsides under the ministrations of friends and relatives. This type of disorder "fits a social system like the Eskimo, where people are able freely to indulge their dependence; in a crisis it enables a distressed person dramatically to summon help and support."[38] A similar explanation has been offered for amok. "[It] discharges the individual from onerous social responsibilities without costing him social support." Amok usually occurs when a man has reached his early thirties and has acquired heavy financial and social obligations which reflect his rise in power and social prestige. Once he has "run amok," an individual will be a marked man, but not in the way our society uses the term. Honigmann sees amok as an "hysterial pattern of communication" and interprets its presence in the Gururumba of New Guinea in this way:

His behavior has given evidence that he is less capable than others of withstanding pressures of

social life. Hence neighbours reduce their expectations towards him, not pressing him to pay his debts promptly and not extracting from him prior commitments to provide food for feasts. He doesn't become an outcast, and he realizes he can't withdraw altogether from economic affairs, but he also knows he must limit his participation.[39]

More recently, Wallace has offered a theory that biological factors such as calcium deficiency may cause hysteria, and that dietary improvement may account for the decline of this illness in the Western world since the nineteenth century.[40] By the early twentieth century, the discovery of the value of good nutrition, coupled with changes in social conditions, led many people to drink milk, eat vitamin-enriched foods, and spend time in the sun. These changes in diet and activity increased their intake of vitamin D and helped them to maintain a proper calcium level. Concurrently, the number of cases of hysteria declined. Regarding pibloktoq, Wallace suggests that a complex set of related variables may cause the disease. The Eskimos live in an environment which supplies only a minimum amount of calcium. A diet low in calcium could result in two different conditions. One condition, rickets, would produce physical deformities potentially fatal in the Eskimos' hunting economy. Persons whose genetic makeup made them prone to rickets would be eliminated from the population through natural selection. A low level of calcium in the blood could also cause muscular spasms known as tetany. Tetany, in turn, may cause emotional and mental disorientation similar to the symptoms of pibloktoq. Since such attacks last for only a relatively short time and are not fatal, people who develop pibloktoq would have a far greater chance of survival with a calcium-deficient diet than those who had rickets in the arctic environment.

[39] Ibid., p. 406.
[40] Anthony F. Wallace, "Mental Illness, Biology and Culture," in *Psychological Anthropology*, ed. F. L. K. Hsu, 2d ed. (Cambridge, Mass.: Schenkman, 1972), pp. 363–402.

Universality of Psychological Development

So far, this chapter has dealt with possible causes and consequences of cultural differences in modal personality and in abnormal personality. Investigators in the field of psychological anthropology are also concerned with the question of human similarities. To what extent do all human beings develop psychologically in the same ways, and to what extent is psychological development affected by cultural differences? This concern focuses primarily on features of human development presumed to be *pan-human,* or universal, and attempts to determine how these features may be affected by cultural differences.

Most research on psychological development is done by psychologists in our own society or in other complex cultures. At the present time, it is still problematical whether or not the results of such research are generally valid for all societies, simple or complex. It is only by duplicating studies of psychological development or processes in a wide range of societies that we can be sure that psychological principles presumed to be universal are, in fact, universal.

For example, Freud assumed that young boys universally are sexual rivals of their fathers for possession of their mothers (the Oedipus complex). Thus, he suggested that all boys before the age of seven or so would show hostility toward their fathers. However, Freud's suggestion might be applicable only to his own and similar societies.

Malinowski, who worked in a matrilineal society, suggested that young boys in non-matrilineal societies may feel hostility to the father not as a sexual rival, but rather because of his role as the disciplinarian. He proposed this theory because he thought that the Oedipus complex works differently in matrilineal societies. Boys feel more hostile toward the mother's brother—who is the main authority figure in the matrilineal kin group—than toward their father.

This finding casts doubt on the validity of the Oedipal theory, at least as stated by Freud, as a universal principle of psychological development.

The Trobriand Islanders, Malinowski notes, trace their descent in the female line, so that the child is born into the mother's clan. The father is not seen as the sexual progenitor of children (instead, the people believe the mother is impregnated by one of her deceased female relatives). The father is neither the stern, authoritarian figure often found in European society nor the breadwinner for the family, since he is required to support his sisters and their families with his labor, while his wife's brother and her other male relatives support her and her children.[41] Regarding the Oedipus complex, Malinowski finds no evidence of repressed sexual longings for the mother in the few dreams he was able to cull from his informants (recollection of dreaming was uncommon). However, he did find occasional repressed longings for siblings. There are no Oedipus legends woven into the fabric of Trobriand folktales. Not a single case of mother-son incest seems to have been remembered, though a few incestuous relationships between siblings were remembered. Generally, hostility is not directed to the father but rather to the maternal uncle.

On the basis of this evidence, Malinowski reached several conclusions:

1. that the Oedipus complex is not universal;
2. that every type of culture produces its own psychological complexes;
3. that fathers in many patrilineal societies may be disliked more for their authoritarianism than for their sexual power.

Clearly, then, Malinowski's critique of Freud's theory of the Oedipus complex means that it is still an open question whether or not some Oedipal rivalry (directed at a boy's father or perhaps at his mother's brother) is a crucial

[41]Bronislaw Malinowski, *Sex and Repression in Savage Society* (Cleveland: World, 1968). First published in 1927.

and universal factor in psychological development.

The controversy over the universal existence of Oedipal conflict reflects the need for a great deal of research on just how applicable much of our knowledge of psychological principles is. After all, much of the research is confined to fairly complex and, in many ways, similar societies. How well do these principles work in very different societies? Are they modified by different cultures or environments? If we are to attempt to arrive at universal principles of human behavior, then we must attempt to test them more universally.

Summary

1. The individual's personality—the distinctive way a person thinks, feels, and behaves—is the result of an interaction between his or her genetic inheritance and life experiences. Different societies, with different methods of childrearing and different life experiences, will tend to produce different kinds of personalities.

2. The typical personality in a particular society is often referred to in terms of modal personality characteristics, those characteristics that occur with the highest frequency in the society. Anthropologists determine modal traits by various means: observation, life histories, projective tests, and the analysis of cultural materials.

3. Socialization and enculturation are terms used to describe the development, through the influence of parents and others, of behavior patterns in children that conform to the standards deemed appropriate by the culture.

4. The anthropologist seeks not only to establish connections between childrearing customs and personality traits, but to learn why these customs originated. Some anthropologists believe societies try to produce the kinds of personality that are best suited to perform the activities necessary for the survival of the society.

5. Some anthropologists have hypothesized that psychological processes may form a link between certain aspects of culture. This connection has been called personality integration of culture. Psychological processes may help us particularly to understand "expressive" or "projective" aspects of culture, such as art, music, folklore, and games, or other facets of culture not tied to the adaptive requirements of the society.

6. Anthropologists are also interested in the incidence of mental disorders in societies. Different kinds of mental illness observed in different societies have been attributed to variations in childrearing and other aspects of culture. Some mental illnesses may also have biological causes.

7. Anthropologists are concerned with variations in modal personality traits. They are also interested in features and principles of human development which are presumed to be universal but which may, or may not, be affected by cultural differences. For example, some doubt has been cast on the theory of the formation of the Oedipus complex (at least in the form stated by Freud) on the basis of studies of matrilineal societies. It is only by duplicating studies of psychological development or processes in a wide range of societies that we can be more sure that psychological principles presumed to be universal are in fact universal.

Suggested Readings

Hsu, F. L. K., ed. *Psychological Anthropology.* 2d ed. Cambridge, Mass.: Schenkman, 1972.
A collection of papers written especially for this book, focusing on the kinds of research conducted in different geographical regions and the different methods and techniques that have been used.

LeVine, R. A., ed. *Culture and Personality: Con-*

temporary Readings. Chicago: Aldine, 1974.

A collection of articles focusing on psycho-social universals, cultural variation in life cycles, and cultural views of abnormality.

Mead, M. *Coming of Age in Samoa.* 3rd ed. New York: William Morrow, 1961. Originally published in 1928.

A classic field study of socialization. The author describes daily activities in a Samoan village and the process of growing up there that apparently is without any sharp break or turmoil at the time of adolescence.

Munroe, R. L., and Munroe, R. H. *Cross-Cultural Human Development.* Monterey, Calif.: Brooks/Cole, 1975.

An up-to-date survey of cross-cultural studies of child development.

Whiting, B. B., and Whiting, J. W. M., in collaboration with Richard Longabaugh. *Children of Six Cultures: A Psycho-Cultural Analysis.* Cambridge: Harvard University Press, 1975.

Based on data collected in six different parts of the world, the authors analyze the effects of culture, age, and sex on children's social behavior.

Religion and
Magic

20

As far as we know, all societies have possessed beliefs which can be grouped under the term "religion." These beliefs vary from culture to culture and from year to year. Yet, whatever the variety of beliefs in things supernatural, we shall define *religion* as any set of attitudes, beliefs, and practices pertaining to *supernatural power*, whether that power be forces, gods, spirits, ghosts, or demons.

In our society, we divide phenomena into the natural and the supernatural, but not all languages or cultures make such a neat distinction. Moreover, what is considered supernatural—powers that are believed to be not human or subject to the laws of nature—varies from society to society. Some of the variations are determined by what a society regards as natural law. For example, some illnesses commonly found in our society are believed to result from the natural action of germs and viruses. In other societies (and even for some people in our own society) illness is thought to result from supernatural forces, and thus it forms a part of religious belief. Beliefs about what is, or is not, a supernatural occurrence also vary within a society at a given time or over time. For example, floods, earthquakes, volcanic eruptions, comets, and epidemics were once considered in Judaeo-Christian traditions to be evidence of supernatural powers intervening in human affairs. It is now generally agreed that they are simply natural occurrences. Yet as recently as 1833, a particularly vivid meteor display caused thousands of intelligent Americans to climb available hills to wait for the imminent end of the world at the hands of the supernatural. Thus, the line between the natural and the supernatural appears to vary in a society according to the current state of belief about the causes of things and events in the observable world.

In many cultures, what we would consider religious is embedded in other aspects of everyday life. It is often difficult to separate the religious (or economic or political) from other aspects of culture. That is, simpler cultures have little or no specialization. Hence, the various aspects of culture we distinguish (for example, in the chapter headings of this book) are not as separated and as easily recognized in simple societies as in complex ones like our own. However, it is sometimes difficult even for us to agree whether a particular custom of ours is religious or not. After all, the categorizing of beliefs as religious, or political, or social, is a relatively new custom. The ancient Greeks, for instance, did not have a word for religion; but they did have many concepts concerning the behavior of their gods and concerning their own expected duty to the gods. When a people's duties to their gods are linked with duty to their princes, it is difficult to separate religious ideas from political ideas. As an example of our own difficulty in labeling a particular class of actions or beliefs as "religious" or "social," consider our attitudes about wearing clothes. Is our belief that it is necessary to wear clothing, at least in the company of nonlovers, a religious principle, or is it something else? Recall that in Genesis, the wearing of clothes, or fig leaves, is distinctly associated with the loss of innocence: Adam and Eve, after eating the apple, covered their nakedness. Accordingly, when American missionaries first visited islands in the Pacific in the nineteenth century, they forced the native women to wear more clothes, particularly to cover their sexual parts. Were the missionaries' ideas about sex "religious" or "political," or perhaps both?

The Universality of Religion

Religious beliefs are evident in all known contemporary cultures and they can be inferred from artifacts found associated with *Homo sapiens* at least since Neandertal times. Artifacts found in Neandertal graves have suggested that early people believed in an afterlife. Sculptures of females with ample secondary sex characteristics—which may have been fertility charms—have been found at widely separated archaeological sites. Cave paintings in which the predominant images are animals of the hunt may reflect a belief that the image had some

power over events. Perhaps early humans thought that their hunting could be made more successful if they drew images depicting good fortune in hunting. Megaliths, which were huge monuments of stone usually erected to mark burial sites, have been found in parts of the Middle East and throughout Europe. The details of religions practiced in the far distant past cannot always be recovered. Yet, evidence of ritual treatment of the dead suggests that early people believed in the existence of supernatural spirits and tried to communicate with, and perhaps influence, them.

Since we may reasonably assume the existence of prehistoric religion and we have evidence of the universality of religion in historic times, we can understand why the subject of religion has been the focus of much speculation, research, and theorizing. As long ago as the fifth century B.C., Herodotus made fairly objective comparisons between the religions of the fifty or so societies he visited. He noted many similarities among their gods and pointed out evidence of diffusion of religious worship. During the 2,500 years since Herodotus's time, scholars, theologians, historians, and philosophers have speculated about religion. Some have claimed superiority for their own forms of religion; others have derided the naive simplicity of others' beliefs; and some have expressed skepticism concerning all beliefs.

Speculation about which religion may be superior is not an anthropological concern. What is of interest to anthropologists is why religion is found in all societies. Anthropologists, sociologists, and psychologists have all offered theories to account for the universality of religion. Most of these theories seem to fall into three groups—the psychological, the sociological, and a mixture of the two. The psychological theories generally account for the universality of religion as a way of reducing anxiety or as a means of satisfying a cognitive need for intellectual understanding. The sociological theories usually explain the universality of religion as a reflection of society and its social conditions.

TYLOR'S THEORY

Edward Tylor is generally credited with having constructed the first inclusive theory of religion. He noted the similarities of many contemporary religions, such as Islam and Christianity, to ancient "pagan" religions, especially the widespread belief in the existence of a soul. He assumed that the belief stemmed from speculation about such states as dreams, trances, and death. The dead, the distant, those in the next house, animals—all seem real in dreams and trances. The life-like appearance of these imagined persons and animals suggests a dual existence for all things—a physical, visible body and a psychic, invisible soul. This dual existence formed the basis of a religious belief which Tylor called *animism*.[1] Thus, in Tylor's view, religion may stem from an intellectual curiosity concerning mental states and other things not fully understood.

PSYCHOLOGICAL THEORIES

A number of psychological theories suggest that religion is universal because it helps to reduce the anxiety and uncertainty felt by all individuals. One of these theories, put forth by Malinowski, is that religion is a response to anxieties and uncertainties which affect individuals personally and, as a consequence, threaten to disrupt the social group. The principal disrupter is death itself. But through religion, "man affirms his convictions that death is not real nor yet final, that man is endowed with a personality which persists even after death. . . ."[2]

Psychoanalytic theories suggest that anxiety stems from early childhood experiences. Freud believed that religion springs from the unresolved Oedipus complex, the boy's sexual love for the mother and simultaneous fear and hate for the father. As a result, the feared father

becomes, unconsciously, the feared god. It is the guilt of people who cannot accept their desire and their hatred that leads them to exalt and to fear a god. Freud considered religion a neurotic need which all people would grow out of as mankind matured. Jung, on the other hand, considered religion to be therapeutic. Recognizing the anxieties that people are subject to as a result of their socialization experiences, he suggested that religion provides help for the resolution of inner conflicts and the attainment of maturity.

All psychological theories agree on one thing: whatever its origins or purposes, whatever its beliefs or rituals, religion serves to reduce anxiety and uncertainty, which are common to all people.

SOCIOLOGICAL THEORIES

Sociological theories suggest that religion stems from society and societal needs. Emile Durkheim recognized that it is the society, not the individual, which distinguishes between *sacred* and *profane* things. There is nothing in an object—a piece of wood, a stone, a statue—to make it automatically sacred; it must, therefore, be a symbol. But a symbol of what? Durkheim suggests that a sacred object symbolizes the social fact that society considers something sacred. He cites the symbolic use of totems by the tribes of central Australia as an example of the way religion symbolizes society. The people are organized into clans, with each clan having its own totem. The totem is the focus of the religious rituals of the clan and thus becomes symbolic both of the clan and of the clan's spirits. It is the clan—or the society as a whole—upon which we are dependent for survival, with which we identify, which exercises power over our actions as well as our thoughts, which we must affirm in communal ritual.[3]

Swanson accepts Durkheim's belief that certain aspects or conditions of society generate

---

[1] Edward B. Tylor, "Animism," in *Reader in Comparative Religion,* 3rd ed., ed. W. A. Lessa and E. Z. Vogt (New York: Harper & Row, 1971), pp. 10–19.

[2] Bronislaw Malinowski, "The Group and the Individual in Functional Analysis," *American Journal of Sociology* 44 (May 1939):959.

[3] Emile Durkheim, "The Elementary Forms of the Religious Life," in *Reader in Comparative Religion,* ed. Lessa and Vogt, pp. 28–36.

When the stability of a society is threatened, it may revitalize itself by means of a new cult. Here, New Hebridian tribesmen worship The Red Cross, hoping to bring back the material goods of the World War II American soldiers. (Kal Muller, Woodfin Camp and Associates.)

the responses that we call religious. More explicitly, Swanson suggests that a belief in spirits derives from the kinds of "sovereign" groups in a society. These sovereign groups are those that have original or independent jurisdiction (decision-making powers) over some sphere of life: the family, the clan, the village, the state. Just like sovereign groups in a society, the spirits live longer than people, and they have purposes and goals that supersede those of an individual. In fact, from the point of view of the individual, social groups dictate one's behavior to a great extent. One is born into families, kin groups, and societies. These institutions exert an almost invisible pressure upon the individual to act according to stated and unstated social norms. Swanson suggests that the spirit world which people invent personifies the family and other decision-making groups which are found in society and which have power over them.[4]

OTHER THEORIES

Other theories of the origin of religion combine psychological and sociological approaches to suggest that religion is a response to strain or deprivation which is felt by individuals and which is caused by events in society. Thus, when the society is stable, as it can be for hundreds of years, its efforts and its energy are employed to maintain its equilibrium. But when the stability of a society is threatened, either by internal dissension or by outside force, the society may "revitalize" itself by various means. Perhaps this revitalization is achieved by a new cult, sect, denomination, or religion. Aberle argues that relative deprivation, whether economic or social, is the cause of the stress which generates new religious movements.[5] Wallace suggests that the threat of societal breakdown forces people to examine new ways to survive. It

[4] Guy E. Swanson, *The Birth of the Gods* (Ann Arbor: University of Michigan Press, 1969), pp. 1–31.

[5] David Aberle, "A Note on Relative Deprivation Theory as Applied to Millenarian and Other Cult Movements," in *Reader in Comparative Religion*, ed. Lessa and Vogt, pp. 528–31.

is the hope they gain from these new ways—not deprivation, for people can live for centuries in deprivation—which leads them to revitalize their society.[6]

Variation in Religious Beliefs

There seems to be no general agreement among scholars as to why people need religion, or how they first came to invent spirits, gods, and other supernatural beings and forces. Yet there is general recognition of the enormous variation in the details of religious beliefs and practices. Societies differ in the kinds of supernatural beings or forces which they create and in the character of their supernatural beings. They also differ in the structure or hierarchy of the organization of those beings, in what the beings actually do, and in what happens to people after death. Variation exists also in the ways in which societies interact with the supernatural.

TYPES OF SUPERNATURAL FORCES AND BEINGS

Supernatural Forces Some peoples believe in supernatural forces that have no person-like character. For example, a supernatural, impersonal force called *mana,* after its Malayo-Polynesian name, is thought to inhabit some objects but not others, some people but not others. We can compare mana to the power that a golfer may attribute to some of his clubs but, unhappily, not to all. A ballplayer may think that a certain shirt or pair of socks has supernatural power or force and that more points will be scored when they are worn. A four-leaf clover has mana; a three-leaf clover does not. One farmer in Polynesia places stones around a field; the crops are bountiful; the stones have mana. During a subsequent year the stones may lose their mana and the crops will be poor. People may also possess mana, as, for example, the

chiefs in Polynesia were said to do. However, such power is not necessarily permanently possessed; chiefs who were unsuccessful in war or other activities were said to have lost their mana.

Folktales often refer to an object in which supernatural force—not necessarily mana, sometimes even an evil force—lodges and then acts automatically. The object could be a slipper, a goose, a porridge pot, a lamp, a monkey's paw, a pair of boots. Marrett felt that Tylor's theory of animism advocated a process too sophisticated to have been the first idea of religion. He suggested that *animatism,* a belief in supernatural forces, preceded the creation of spirits.[7]

Wallace distinguishes mana from taboo by pointing out that things containing mana are to be touched, whereas taboo things are not to be touched, for their power can cause harm.[8] Taboos surround food not to be eaten, places not to be entered, animals not to be killed, people not to be touched sexually, people not to be touched at all, and so on. Any person who is the victim of misfortune may unwittingly have violated a taboo. He may have to search his memory for evidence, just as a person who is a victim of neurosis today may search his memory in order to discover the sources of his neurosis. Untouchability is used to separate various castes in India. When a caste taboo is violated, as when a barber cuts the hair of a high-caste man, the high-caste man is then ritually unclean until he performs the rite which cleanses him. The Hebrew tribesmen were forbidden to touch a woman during menstruation or for seven days following. An Australian aborigine could not eat the animal which was his totem, and for many centuries a Catholic could not eat meat on Fridays.

Supernatural Beings Supernatural beings fall within two broad categories: those of non-human origin, such as gods and spirits, and

---

[6] Anthony Wallace, *Religion: An Anthropological View* (New York: Random House, 1966), p. 30.

[7] R. R. Marrett, *The Threshold of Religion* (London: Methuen, 1909).

[8] Wallace, *Religion: An Anthropological View,* pp. 60–61.

those of human origin, such as ghosts and ancestral spirits. Chief among the beings of non-human origin, *gods* are named personalities. They are often anthropomorphic, conceived in the image of a person, although they are sometimes given the shapes of other animals or of celestial bodies such as the sun or moon. Essentially, the gods are believed to have created themselves; but some of these then created, or gave birth to, other gods. While some are seen as creator gods, not all people include the creation of the world as one of the acts of gods.

After their efforts at creation, many creator gods retire. Having set the world in motion, they are not interested in its day-to-day operation. Other creator gods remain interested in the ordinary affairs of human beings, especially the affairs of one small, chosen segment of humanity. Whether a society has a creator god or not, the job of running creation is often left to lesser gods. The Maori of New Zealand, for example, recognize three important gods: a god of the sea, a god of the forest, and a god of agriculture. They call upon each in turn for help and try to get all three gods to share their knowledge of how the universe runs. The gods of the ancient Romans, on the other hand, specialized to a high degree. There were three gods of the plow, one god to help with the sowing, one for weeding, one for reaping, one for storing grain, one for manuring, and so on.

Beneath the gods in prestige, but often closer to people, are multitudes of unnamed spirits. Some may be guardian spirits for people. Some, who become known for particularly efficacious work, may be promoted to the rank of named gods. Some spirits who are known to, but never invoked by, the people are of the hobgoblin type; they delight in mischief and can be blamed for any number of small mishaps. Other spirits take pleasure in deliberately working evil for people.

Ghosts and *ancestor spirits* are among the spirits who were once human. Some cultures believe that everyone has a soul—or several souls—and that the soul survives after death; and there are many varied interpretations of what the soul does after death. Some societies believe that the spirits of the dead remain nearby and continue to be interested in their living kin.

Swanson suggests, and found in his cross-cultural study of fifty societies, that people are likely to believe in active ancestral spirits where kin groups are important decision-making units. The kin group is an entity which exists over time, back into the past as well as forward into the future, despite the deaths of individual members.[9] The dead feel concern for the fortunes, the prestige, and the continuity of their kin group as strongly as the living. As a Lugbara elder put it, "Are our ancestors not people of our lineage? They are our fathers and we are their children whom they have begotten. Those that have died stay near us in our homes and we feed and respect them. Does not a man help his father when he is old?"[10]

The Lugbara recognize two types of dead. The multitude of nameless forebears (including childless members of the clan) by all lines of descent, male and female, are called *a'bi* or ancestors. One shrine embraces them all. Named ancestors—those recently dead and therefore still individually interested in the behavior of living kin—are called *ori*, meaning ancestor spirits or ghosts. Each ghost has a shrine of its own. A man whose father is dead may have the power to "invoke the ghosts" to cause illness or other misfortune to a member of the clan, and especially a younger member, whose behavior threatens clan solidarity. If a man strikes, swears at, deceives, or quarrels with a kinsman, or if he is a poor guardian or a disrespectful heir, the elder of the clan may invoke the ghosts to bring sickness to the deviant clan member. If a woman quarrels with her husband, or strikes him, or denies him sex, she may have the ghosts invoked against her. This veneration of the dead has several effects upon the society. It keeps serious fights from developing within the family. The living may grumble at the behavior of the young, but they leave punishment of

[9] Swanson, *The Birth of the Gods*, pp. 97–108.
[10] John Middleton, "The Cult of the Dead: Ancestors and Ghosts," in *Reader in Comparative Religion*, ed. Lessa and Vogt, p. 488.

In New Guinea, a Gururumba tribesman kills a pig to pacify a ghost. It is believed that the ghost is causing illness in one of the women seated in the foreground. (Courtesy of the American Museum of Natural History.)

389 RELIGION AND MAGIC

that behavior up to the ancestors. The man who eats rich foods and does not invite his kinsman to share, or the man who shows off his agility at a dance and impresses the women while his kinsman stands alone, may not be reproached directly but may have the ghosts invoked against him. The invocation of the ghosts is particularly useful when there is a power struggle for authority within the lineage or clan. The person who wins will claim the favor of the ghosts. If illness is caused by the ghost, a sacrifice is made if the patient recovers. An animal is sacrificed, the family has a small feast, the now-penitent one is anointed and blessed, and the sin is forgotten. Now the former sinner is accepted and, like the prodigal son, he is chastened and restored to the family.[11]

THE CHARACTER OF SUPERNATURAL BEINGS

Whatever types they may be, the gods or spirits venerated in a given culture tend to have certain personality or character traits. They may be unpredictable or predictable, aloof from or interested in human affairs, helpful or punishing. Why do the gods and spirits in a particular culture exhibit certain character traits rather than others?

We have some evidence from cross-cultural studies suggesting that the character of supernatural beings may be related to the nature of child training. Thus, Spiro and D'Andrade suggest that the god/human relationship is a projection of the parent/child relationship, in which case child-training practices might well be relived in dealings with the supernatural. For example, if a child was nurtured by her parents when she cried or waved her arms about or kicked, then she would grow up expecting to be nurtured by the gods when she performed a ritual. On the other hand, if her parents punished her, or sometimes punished and sometimes rewarded her, she would grow up expect-

ing the gods to behave capriciously toward humans.[12] Lambert, Triandis, and Wolf, in another cross-cultural study, found that societies with some hurtful or punitive child-training practices are likely to believe that their gods are aggressive and malevolent. On the other hand, societies with less punitive child training are more likely to believe that the gods are benevolent.[13] It is worth noting, in this context, that some cultures represent the father/child pattern in their own terminology, referring to the god as "father" and to themselves as his "children."

STRUCTURE OR HIERARCHY OF SUPERNATURAL BEINGS

The range of social structures in human societies from egalitarian to highly stratified is matched by a comparable range in the supernatural world. Some societies have a number of gods or spirits with or without any special jurisdictions, and the gods are not ranked. One god has about as much power as another. On the other hand, some societies have gods or spirits that are ranked in prestige and power.

Religions in which there is one high god and all other supernatural beings are subordinate to, or are alternative manifestations of, this supreme being are *monotheistic*. For instance, the Hindu believes in five great gods—Siva, Krishna, Rama, Vishnu, and Lakshmi—who are subordinate to the all-encompassing god, the *One*. Into the One, all humanity is evolving in anticipated spiritual union, or oneness. A *polytheistic* religion recognizes many important gods.

Swanson examined the idea that religions are projections of people's various political systems. He suggests that an association exists between political complexity and monotheism. More specifically, he shows evidence from a cross-cultural study that a belief in a high god is

[11]Ibid., pp. 488–92.

[12]Melford E. Spiro and Roy G. D'Andrade, "A Cross-Cultural Study of Some Supernatural Beliefs," *American Anthropologist* 60 (1958): 456–66.

[13]William W. Lambert, Leigh Minturn Triandis, and Margery Wolf, "Some Correlates of Beliefs in the Malevolence and Benevolence of Supernatural Beings: A Cross-Societal Study," *Journal of Abnormal and Social Psychology* 58 (1959): 162–69.

likely to be found where the political system has three or more levels of decision-making groups. In his study of fifty societies, he discovered that of the twenty which had three or more distinct types of sovereign groups—for instance, the family, clan, and chief—seventeen possessed an idea of a high god. Of the nineteen societies which had fewer than three decision-making groups, only two had a high god.[14] In agreement with Swanson's results are other findings which show that a high god is generally found in societies with higher levels of political development and in societies dependent upon food production rather than upon food collecting.[15]

Also consistent with Swanson's findings, there are societies in which the gods associated with families or clans of high status are themselves awarded high status. In Palauan society, for instance, each clan had its ancestor spirits and acknowledged the existence of all other clans' spirits, which were potentially dangerous. Each clan also worshipped a male and a female god who had names and titles similar to clan titles. The ranking clan in a village was believed to hold its position because of the superiority in rank of its gods, who naturally helped their own clan. Thus, the leading clan's gods were respected by all the clans of the village. Their shrine was given the place of honor in the center of the village and was larger and more elaborately decorated than other shrines.[16]

INTERVENTION OF THE GODS IN HUMAN AFFAIRS

According to Clifford Geertz, it is when faced with ignorance, with pain, and with the unjustness of life that a person explains events by the intervention of the gods.[17] Thus, in Greek religion, the direct intervention of Poseidon as ruler of the seas prevented Odysseus from getting home for ten years. The direct intervention of Yahweh caused the great flood which killed most of the people in the time of Noah. The Trobriand Islanders explain conception as the intervention of the gods. When contemplating pain, illness, and death, the Nyakyusa blames the spirits of the dead, while the Christian says, "it is the will of God." The Maori searches his memory for a violated taboo which has brought him punishment through the spirit's intervention. A Zande looks for some neighbor or relative who might wish to cause him illness or death with the help of some supernatural intervention. The unjustness of things, the knowledge that the good suffer and the evil prosper, is explained by the Christians. They believe that the good will get their reward after death and the evil will then be punished; the projected intervention comes after death. The Greek gods intervened to bring bad fortune to Oedipus, which was undeserved because he did not know that he was breaking two fundamental taboos—murder of a near relative and incest. The intervention of evil spirits is apparent in witchcraft beliefs and in cases of demonic possession.

The brief accounts we have listed above are samples of unasked-for divine interference, with the exception of cases of witchcraft. There are numerous examples of requests for divine intervention, either for good for oneself and friends or for evil for others. Gods are asked to intervene in the weather and make the crops grow, to send fish to the fisherman and game to the hunter, to find lost things, and to accompany travelers and prevent accidents. They are asked to stop the flow of lava down the side of a volcano, to remove the pimples from an adolescent's face, to stop a war, and so on. Generally, as science presents more and more rationally acceptable causes for things—high pressure areas, germs, earth faults, gravity—then educated people see fewer events as due to the intervention of the gods. But isolated villages, small towns, and peasant communities, no matter what religions they profess, still see the intervention of gods as an everyday possibility.

[14] Swanson, *The Birth of the Gods*, pp. 55–81.

[15] Robert B. Textor, comp., *A Cross-Cultural Summary* (New Haven: HRAF Press, 1967).

[16] H. G. Barnett, *Being a Palauan* (New York: Holt, Rinehart and Winston, 1960), pp. 79–85.

[17] Clifford Geertz, "Religion as a Cultural System," in *Anthropological Approaches to the Study of Religion*, ed. Michael Banton, Association of Social Anthropologists Monograph no. 3 (London: Tavistock Publications, 1965).

The gods do not intervene in all societies. To be sure, in some they intervene in human affairs; in others, they are not the slightest bit interested; and in still others they interfere only occasionally. We have little research on why gods are believed to interfere in some societies and not in others. However, we have some evidence as to the kinds of societies in which the gods take an interest in the morality of human behavior.

Swanson's study suggests that a relationship exists between the intervention of the gods in the moral behavior of people and varying degrees of wealth within the society. In a society in which wealth is unequally distributed, the gods are likely to intervene in human affairs by creating sanctions against behavior which threatens the status quo of the society.[18] It may be that supernatural support of moral behavior is particularly useful in societies which have inequalities that tax the ability of the political system to maintain social order and minimize social disorder.

LIFE AFTER DEATH

It is comforting for many people to believe that life is somehow more than the body, that the body possesses a soul which continues its life after the body has died. In cultures with a belief in the soul, there is considerable variation in what happens to the soul after death. The Lugbara see the dead joining the ancestors of the living and staying near the family homesite. They retain an interest in the behavior of the living, both rewarding and punishing them. The Zuni think that the dead join the past dead, known as the Katcinas at a Katcina village at the bottom of a nearby lake. There they lead a life of singing and dancing and bring rain to the living Zuni. They are also swift to punish the priest who fails in his duty or the people who impersonate them in masks during the dance ceremonies.[19] The Chamulas have merged the ancient Mayan worship of the sun and moon with the Spanish conquerors' Jesus and Mary. Their vision of life after death contains a blending of the two cultures. All souls go to the underworld where they live a humanlike life except that they are incapable of sexual intercourse. After the sun travels over the world, it travels under the underworld, so that the dead also have sunlight. Only murderers and suicides are punished, being burned by the Christ/sun on their journey. Life after death is then an inverted form of life: life is up, death is down; life produces new life, death is sterile. Also, daylight and darkness are inverted for the dead; the sun travels counterclockwise for the living, clockwise for the dead.[20]

Christians separate their dead after death, sending the unsaved to everlasting punishment and the saved to everlasting reward. Accounts differ, but hell is often associated with torture by fire and heaven with mansions. Several societies see the dead returning to earth to be reborn. The Hindus use this pattern of reincarnation to justify one's caste in this life and to promise eventual release from the pain of life through the attainment of *Nirvana*, inclusion into "the One."

Variation in Religious Practice

Beliefs are not the only elements of religion that vary from society to society. There is also variation in how people deal with the supernatural. There may or may not be intermediaries between god and people. Also, the manner of approach to the supernatural varies from supplication (requests, prayers, and so on) to manipulation.

In all religions, it is permissible for an individual to approach the supernatural. But in some societies, the contact with the supernatural is on a more individual basis than in others.

[18]Swanson, *The Birth of the Gods*, pp. 153–74.
[19]Ruth Benzel, "The Nature of Katcinas," in *Reader in Comparative Religion*, ed. Lessa and Vogt, pp. 493–95.

[20]Gary H. Gossen, "Temporal and Spatial Equivalents in Chamula Ritual Symbolism," in *Reader in Comparative Religion*, ed. Lessa and Vogt, pp. 135–40.

For instance, before reaching manhood the young Crow Indian would seek contact with a spirit which would become his own guardian spirit. He could choose one of several methods of seeking such contact. He could fast on a hilltop for several days and perhaps also cut off a finger joint as an offering. Or he could have his back or breast pierced and a rope looped through the opening; the rope would then be tied to a stick around which he would run all day. Through such deprivations, the warrior would seek a vision or revelation. The giver of the revelation would then become the guardian spirit of the man, bringing him success in warfare and sometimes in marriage. This spirit might have been previously unknown—a snake, a white eagle, an old couple—but the Crow belief in the diffusion of divine power throughout the universe allows that power to crop up in the most unexpected places.[21]

RELIGIOUS INTERMEDIARIES

The Shaman   Religious intermediaries may be part-time or full-time specialists. The *shaman*, or curer, is one kind of intermediary, usually part-time. Under the name of witch doctor, he has been much maligned by ethnocentric Western reports. Below, there is an account of the making of a Kwakiutl shaman on the American Northwest Pacific Coast, followed by the history of a Washo shaman of this century.

The Kwakiutl, Quesalid, was initially a skeptic who wanted to expose the tricks of the shamans. He began to associate with them in order to spy on them and was taken into their group. In his first lessons, he learned

a curious mixture of pantomime, prestidigitation, and empirical knowledge, including the art of simulating fainting and nervous fits, the learning of sacred song, the technique for inducing vomiting, rather precise notions of auscultation or listening to sounds within the body to detect disorders and obstetrics, and the use of ''dreamers,'' that is, spies who listen to private

A Bushman shaman, in a trance, puts his arms around a patient. (Courtesy of Irven DeVore/Anthro-Photo.)

conversations and secretly convey to the shaman bits of information concerning the origins and symptoms of the ills suffered by different people. Above all, he learned the *ars magna*. . . . The shaman hides a little tuft of down in the corner of his mouth, and he throws it up, covered with blood, at the proper moment—after having bitten his tongue or made his gums bleed—and solemnly presents it to his patient and the onlookers as the pathological foreign body extracted as a result of his sucking and manipulations.[22]

His suspicions were confirmed, but his first curing was a success. The patient had heard that Quesalid had joined the shamans and believed

---

[21] Robert H. Lowie, *The Crow Indians* (New York: Rinehart, 1956), pp. 237–55.

[22] Claude Lévi-Strauss, "The Sorcerer and His Magic," in *Structural Anthropology* (New York: Basic Books, 1963), p. 169.

A Gururumba tribesman of New Guinea has assembled magical leaves for a curing ceremony. (Courtesy of the American Museum of Natural History.)

that only he would heal him. Quesalid remained with the shamans for the four-year apprenticeship during which he could take no fee, and he became increasingly aware that his methods worked. He visited other villages, competed with other shamans in curing hopeless cases and won, and finally seemed convinced that his curing system was more valid than those of other shamans. Instead of denouncing the trickery of shamans, he continued to practice as a renowned shaman.[23]

In 1964, the last Washo shaman, Henry Rupert, was still practicing and still learning new techniques at the age of seventy. He recalls the background to his becoming a shaman, including childhood and mystical experiences. He was never severely disciplined at home and spent much of his time either with his uncle or his sister's husband, both shamans. He had several vivid dreams, one of them prophetic, and learned from his family a great deal of Washo lore and tradition. At eight, he was taken to the harsh U.S. Army school for a ten-year stretch of "forced acculturation." He was strong enough to accept what he needed of the new culture—the lessons in academic subjects and in a trade—and to reject its regimentation and harshness, its alcohol, and its Christianity. At seventeen, he had his "power dream" which confirmed his call as a shaman. Over the next ten years he learned hypnotism, performed a few cures, and began training under an old shaman. His cures at first took four nights of ritual during which he prayed, chanted, washed the patient's face with cold water, and blew smoke on the patient. Then he sprinkled water on the patient's paraphernalia and finally sought to attract the sickness into his own body by blowing a whistle. During the years, Rupert modified his treatments as he learned new techniques. Finally he refused to visit patients but had the patients come to him for a curing which he had shortened to a few hours, or in some cases a few minutes. By the age of seventy, he had discarded chants, whistles, smoke, and water and had added a Hawaiian spirit helper. Rupert dismissed traditional beliefs in evil spirits as the cause of illness and eventually summarized his beliefs as "we help nature, and nature does the rest."[24]

After working with witch doctors in Africa, E. Fuller Torrey, a psychiatrist and anthropologist, concludes that witch doctors use the same mechanisms and techniques to cure patients as psychiatrists use and achieve about the same results. He isolates four categories used by healers the world over:

[23] Franz Boas, *The Religion of the Kwakiutl*, Columbia University Contributions to Anthropology, vol. 10, pt. II (New York: 1930), pp. 1–41, as reported in Lévi-Strauss, *Structural Anthropology*, pp. 169–73.

[24] Don Handelman, "The Development of a Washo Shaman," *Ethnology* 6 (October 1967): 444–61.

1. The naming process. If a disease has a name—"neurasthenia" or "phobia" or "possession by an ancestral spirit" will do—then it is curable; the patient realizes that the doctor understands his case.
2. The personality of the doctor. Those who demonstrate some empathy, nonpossessive warmth, and genuine interest in the patient get results.
3. The patient's expectations. One way of raising the patient's expectations of being cured is the trip to the doctor; the longer the trip—to the Mayo Clinic, Menninger Clinic, Delphi, or Lourdes—the easier the cure. An impressive setting (the Medical Center) and impressive paraphernalia (the stethoscope, the couch, attendants in uniform, the rattle, the whistle, the drum, the mask) also raise the patient's expectations. The healer's training is also important: the Ute Indian has his dreams analyzed; the Blackfoot Indian has a seven-year training course; the American psychiatrist spends four years in medical school and three in hospital training and has diplomas on his wall. High fees also help to raise a patient's expectations. (The Paiute doctors always collect their fees before starting a cure; if they don't, it is believed that they will fall ill.)
4. Curing techniques. Drugs, shock treatment, conditioning techniques, and so on, have been used for some time in different parts of the world.[25]

The Priest Another kind of intermediary is the priest, a full-time specialist. Priests are sometimes marked by their special clothing or hair style as being different from other people. The training of a priest can be vigorous and long, including fasting, praying, and physical labor, as well as learning the dogma and the ritual of his religion. Or a person can set himself up as a priest of his own sect with no training at all. Priests in America generally complete four years of theological school and sometimes serve first as apprentices under established priests. The priest generally does not receive a fee for each of his services but is supported by donations from his parishioners or followers. Since priests often have some political power as a result of their office—the chief priest is sometimes also the head of state, or is a close councillor to the chief of state—their material well-being is a direct reflection of their position in the priestly hierarchy. It is the dependence upon memorized ritual that both marks and protects the priest. If a shaman repeatedly fails to effect a cure, he will probably lose his following, for he has obviously lost the support of the spirits. However, if a priest performs his ritual perfectly, and the gods choose not to respond, the priest will usually retain his position and the ritual will preserve its assumed effectiveness. The nonresponse of the gods will be explained in terms of the people's unworthiness of supernatural favor.

Other kinds of intermediaries exist among the dead, when there is a hierarchy of spirits and gods and the chief gods must not be approached directly. Leach distinguishes the Great Gods of India as *deva* and the lesser gods as *devata*, or intermediaries between men and the Great Gods. The mother goddess, or Parvati, and other lesser deities perform this intermediary role in Hinduism. The saints, the Virgin Mary, and Jesus act as intermediaries to God the Father in many Christian sects.[26]

Why is there more of an emphasis on intermediaries in some societies than in others? Generally, it seems that societies with religious intermediaries are more complex societies in which there is greater specialization. Textor reports that societies with full-time religious specialists (i.e., priests) are likely to be dependent upon food production rather than upon food collecting. They are also likely to have economic exchange involving the use of money, class

[25] E. Fuller Torrey, *The Mind Game: Witchdoctors and Psychiatrists* (New York: Emerson Hall, n.d.).

[26] Edmund R. Leach, "Pulleyar and the Lord Buddha: An Aspect of Religious Syncretism in Ceylon," in *Reader in Comparative Religion,* ed. Lessa and Vogt, pp. 302–6.

stratification, and high levels of political integration. These are all features indicative of cultural complexity.[27]

BEHAVIOR AFFECTING THE SUPERNATURAL

How to get in touch with the supernatural has proved to be a universal problem. Wallace suggests twelve types of activities which are used in religions the world over—though not necessarily all together. These are: prayer, music, physiological experience, exhortation, reciting the code, simulation, mana or taboo, feasts, sacrifices, congregation, inspiration, and symbolism.[28]

1. Prayer. Either as thanksgiving, request, or demand, prayer generally is distinguished from ordinary use of language by a special stance, gesture, or tone of voice, and perhaps by special, often archaic, speech patterns.

Prayer can be spontaneous or memorized, private or public, silent or aloud. The Lugbara do not say the words of a prayer aloud, for that would be too powerful; they simply think about the things that are bothering them. The gods know all languages.

2. Music. Musical instruments, singing, chanting, and dancing are variously used for their integrating effect upon the people as well as upon the spirits.

Needham was surprised by the numerous reports of drums, rattles, sticks, bells, and gongs used in religions throughout the world as devices to attract the attention of the supernatural. Further research led him to the supposition that percussion is used universally to mark the transition of a person from one state to another. The tin cans tied to the car of newlyweds in America, and firecrackers tied to the cart in China, both mark a transition from the unmarried to the married state. The passage from unnamed to named, from state of sin to state of grace, from life to death, from sick to well, and so on, is usually indicated by some percussive instrument.[29]

3. Physiological experience. Drugs (peyote, the magic mushroom), sensory deprivation, mortification of the flesh (by the wearing of hair shirts or chains, self-flagellation, prolonged sleeplessness, piercing of the flesh, amputation of a finger joint, running till exhausted), and deprivation of food or water are methods known to religions as means of producing a trance or a feeling of euphoria.

4. Exhortation or preaching. The person who acts as intermediary between a person and the gods acts in two directions. Since he is closer to the gods than ordinary persons, he both receives messages from the gods and passes them on to the people. He tells the people what the gods expect and informs them what behavior is pleasing, what is displeasing.

5. Reciting the code. Many religions have myths which relate the activities of the gods and describe codes of moral behavior expected by the gods. Some divine literature may be considered as dictated by the gods themselves, while some may be seen as the work of especially favored people.

6. Simulation. Voodoo employs simulation, or imitating things. Dolls are made in the likeness of an enemy and then are maltreated in hopes that the original enemy will also experience pain and even death.

Divination, or foretelling the future, is a rather widespread form of simulation, found in Asian, African, and European societies. Shakespeare's Julius Caesar scorned his wife's prophetic dream of death and was killed in the Senate. Many people today have their fortunes read in crystal balls, tea leaves, Ouija boards, cards, their palms, or their horoscopes. Or they may

---

[27] Textor, *A Cross-Cultural Summary*.

[28] Anthony Wallace, *Religion: An Anthropological View*, pp. 52–67. Copyright © 1966 by Random House, Inc. Used by permission.

[29] Rodney Needham, "Percussion and Transition," in *Reader in Comparative Religion*, ed. Lessa and Vogt, pp. 391–98.

choose a course of action by a toss of a coin or a throw of dice. All are variations of methods used in other cultures.

Lucy Mair distinguishes between three kinds of divination. One is do-it-yourself divination: an object answers questions automatically; no interpreter is needed. For example, a rubbing board used by the Azande of central Africa gives a direct "yes" or "no" answer. A second kind of divination requires interpretation of the object or objects used. For this, a diviner must depend somewhat upon his or her knowledge of local gossip, ability to assess people by their gestures and tone of voice, and intuition in grasping the answer desired by the questioner. A third type offers the diviner as a medium who receives messages from the spirit world. The medium must sometimes go into a trance before the spirit will reveal its answer.

The ostensible purpose of divination is to learn something which only the supernatural powers know. The Yombe, who live near the mouth of the Congo River, believe that death is caused by the sorcery of an enemy or by a relative or friend who is angry. Therefore, part of the funeral ritual is an attempt to discover who caused the death. They send a man out to kill a duiker (a small African antelope). If he kills a male, then the man's side of the family is responsible for the death. If he kills a female, then the woman's side is responsible. A more common means of divining uses a number of small objects made of wood or ivory and carrying symbolic designs. The diviner finds the answer in the way the objects fall when they are thrown to the ground or shaken in a bowl.

In divination, then, a person has a problem and tries to find out the cause and the solution. No matter with what degree of skepticism a person consults a diviner, this skepticism generally centers around the individual diviner, not against divination as a principle. Divination remains an acceptable method of seeking information in any society which believes that the supernatural is concerned about people and actually gets in touch with them from time to time.

It is quite apparent that the methods of diviners are in no way connected with the actual results they achieve. For instance, the cracks in a bone simply do not tell anyone where game is plentiful that day. Moore has suggested that societies would abandon these ineffective techniques unless there were other reasons for continuing them, some "positive latent function" in divination apart from the ostensible problem and solution. He suggests that, in some cases, a random strategy might be more adaptive than a strategy based on experience. For example, the Naskapi, hunters of Labrador, consult the diviner every three or four days when they have no luck in hunting. The diviner holds a caribou bone over the fire and the burns and cracks which appear in the bone indicate where the group should hunt. The device functions as a fairly sophisticated method of assuring a random way of choosing where to hunt. Since humans are likely to develop customary patterns of action, they might be likely to look for game according to some plan. But game might learn to avoid hunters who operate according to a plan. Thus, any method of assuring against patterning or predictable plans may be an advantage to the hunting society. Divination provides such a random strategy. It also relieves any individual of the responsibility of deciding where to hunt, a decision which might arouse anger if the hunt failed.

Moore suggests then that divination resembles games of chance, in which problems are solved by knowing the statistical probabilities of success for competing strategies. To solve problems such as where to find game, which involve the element of chance, a society might more often be successful if the strategy employed is also a chance one. It is possible, then, that the Naskapi and other societies have adopted divination as a way of solving some of their recurring problems. A chance or random strategy, as provided by divination, is the best strategy for problems involving chance.[30]

[30] Omar Khayyam Moore, "Divination—A New Perspective," *American Anthropologist* 59 (1957): 69–74.

7. Mana/taboo. The idea that power can reside in things which should be touched, *mana*, and things which should be avoided, *taboo*, has already been discussed. Relics, good luck symbols, sacred stones, the Blarney stone, and the hem of Jesus' garment are items that should be touched to transmit some of their power to the individual. Certain objects, foods, and people should not be touched to avoid the effects of their power.

8. Feasts. The eating of a sacred meal—for instance, Holy Communion as a simulation of the Last Supper—is found in many religions.

The Australian aborigines, forbidden to eat their totem animal, have one totem feast a year at which they eat the totem, presumably as a gesture of symbolic cannibalism. The feast is a part of marriage and funeral ceremonies, as well as a fringe benefit of the sacrifice of food to the gods.

9. Sacrifices. Some societies make sacrifices to a god in order to influence the god's action, either to divert his anger or to attract his goodwill.

The things sacrificed vary from society to society; a blood sacrifice is sometimes required. The Greeks' arrangement for the sacrifice served two purposes—offerings for the gods and feasts for the people. The Nayar are vegetarians, so they assume that their clan spirits are also vegetarians and make vegetarian offerings. Personal sacrifice such as abstaining from particular foods, drinks, tobacco, or sexual intercourse may be made in an effort to please one's god. Money is the usual Western sacrifice. Some societies feel that the god is obligated to act on their behalf if they make the appropriate sacrifice. Others use the sacrifice in an attempt to persuade the god, without any guarantee that the attempt will be successful.

10. Congregation. Although anyone may perform a religious act in private, the main function of religion is social. People meet together to address the gods or to watch the shaman or the priest address the gods.

11. Inspiration. The gods pick favored people to communicate with. States of ecstasy, possession, conversion, and revelation are recognized as marking the presence of the supernatural. The states are spontaneous or self-induced.

12. Symbolism. Religious symbols can be direct representations of deities in the form of paintings, icons, statues, and masks.

The Eskimos sew small amulets containing symbols of spirits—bits of shellfish, small pebbles—onto their clothing. Early Easter Islanders carved massive stone heads and West Coast Africans carved small wooden dolls as fertility symbols. Iroquois Indians made masks to represent the Great World Rim Dweller. The mandala and associated forms, the cross and the swastika, appear in various religions as symbols of partition and reintegration. That the symbol sometimes is believed to contain the power of the god is apparent from the reverence with which the symbol is often treated.

Magic and Religion All of the modes of interacting with the supernatural can be categorized in various ways. One dimension of variation is how much people in a society rely on pleading or asking or trying to persuade the supernatural being (or force) to act on their behalf, as opposed to whether they believe they can compel such behavior by certain acts. For example, prayer is asking; performing voodoo is presumably compelling. When people believe their action can compel the supernatural to act in some particular and intended way, anthropologists often refer to the belief and related practice as *magical*.

Magic may involve manipulation of the supernatural for good or for evil purposes. Many societes have magical rituals to ensure good crops, the replenishment of game, the fertility of domestic animals, and the avoidance and cure of illness in humans. As we have seen, the witch doctor and the shaman often employ magic to effect a cure. But perhaps the use of magic to bring about harm has evoked the most interest.

Two Gururumba tribesmen perform a magic rite to ward off an impending rainstorm. They circle the group of people assembled for food distribution, carrying a stick and calling out to the ghosts of the recently dead. They ask the ghosts to fence in the rain, just as they are fencing in the group by walking around it with the stick. (Courtesy of the American Museum of Natural History.)

Sorcery and Witchcraft Sorcery and witchcraft are attempts to invoke the spirits to work harm against people. Although the words *sorcery* and *witchcraft* are often used interchangeably, they are also often distinguished. Sorcery may include the use of materials, objects, and medicines to invoke the supernatural. In some societies, sorcery may be used by anyone. Other societies have secret part-time specialists called sorcerers, who must be enlisted to invoke supernatural malevolence. Since sorcerers know how to invoke the supernatural to cause illness, injury, and death, they are feared (although they might be entreated to use their knowledge for some good purpose). Since they use materi-

als, evidence of sorcery can actually be found. Therefore, a person can be accused of sorcery because some objects or medicines were found in his or her house. But witchcraft may be said to accomplish the same ills by means of thought and emotion alone. Evidence of witchcraft can never be found. This lack of visible evidence makes an accusation of witchcraft both harder to prove and harder to disprove.

Attributes of witches vary from society to society, but they are generally disagreeable. The Madari believe that witches rub feces on articles to harm the owner and that they dance on the graves of their victims. The Lugbara believe that witches dance naked. The Ganda believe in

Basezi, people who also dance naked and who feast on corpses. Dinka witches have tails. Amba witches hang by their feet from trees and eat salt when they are thirsty.[31]

Two motivations for organizing witch-hunts are recognized. The society may wish to challenge, and thereby frighten, all witches in a village so that they will abandon their activities; or it may wish actually to accuse certain persons and demand either their death or repentance. The Nupe dance ceremony could serve either function. A secret society called *ndakó gboyá* organizes a masked dance at the request of the authorities but without telling the people. A dancer draped in white cloth and carrying a long pole with a basket top (also draped in white) appears in the village at dawn. All the women of the village are herded into the marketplace and the masked dancer swoops and sways over them. The dancer leaves suddenly, but another dancer appears and continues the dance. Either the second dancer will leave and the village will be considered cleansed, or he will accuse one woman directly. She will be taken into the forest and made to dig into the earth with her fingernails. If blood comes, she is a witch and has to make a payment to clear herself. One of the functions of the witch hunt may be to rid the village of the unpleasant or unconventional person.[32]

To the Azande, witchcraft is part of everyday living. It is not used to explain events for which the cause is known, such as carelessness or violation of a taboo, but is used to explain the otherwise unexplainable. A man is gored by an elephant; he must have been bewitched because he had not been gored on the many other elephant hunts he had been on. A man goes to his beer hut at night, lights some straw, and holds it aloft to look at his beer. The thatch catches fire and the hut burns down. The man has been bewitched, for huts did not catch on fire on hundreds of other nights when he and others

did the same thing. Some people are sitting in the cool shade under a granary and it collapses on them, injuring them. They are bewitched because, although the Azande admit that termites eating through the wooden posts caused the granary to collapse, witchcraft made it collapse at the precise moment on those particular people. Some of the pots of a skilled potter break; some of the bowls of a skilled carver crack. Witchcraft: other pots, other bowls treated exactly the same have not broken. The Azande blame many of their failures and accidents on witchcraft. Their anger—and anger is their reaction, not awe or dread—is then directed outward, often to unnamed people, sometimes directly at others. Their wrath is never against members of their own family. One effect of this procedure is that hostility is avoided within the extended family.[33]

The witch craze in Europe and in Salem, Massachusetts, reminds us that the fear of others, which the belief in witchcraft presumably represents, is not lacking in civilized societies. There had always been witchcraft beliefs in Europe, especially in rural areas; witchcraft accusations were usually directed against old women and unpopular people in general. But no official action was taken against witches. In fact, the early popes declared that a belief in witchcraft was un-Christian, since witches did not exist. However, when feudal authorities went into areas in Europe which resisted the establishment of feudalism, the Church declared the inhabitants of these regions to be heretics. The civil authorities thereupon accused these people of secret meetings with the devil and had them killed. Following the Reformation, first Protestant, then Catholic, missionaries found this method of attacking heretics useful, though they changed the name of the heresy. The new heresy was called witchcraft and, instead of being used against *groups* that resisted the spread of the new culture, it could be used

---

[31] Lucy Mair, *Witchcraft* (New York: World University Library, 1969), pp. 40–42.

[32] Ibid., pp. 65–75.

[33] E. E. Evans-Pritchard, "Witchcraft Explains Unfortunate Events," in *Reader in Comparative Religion*, ed. Lessa and Vogt, pp. 440–44.

against *individuals* who were nonconformist. Protestants could kill Catholic witches; Catholics could kill Protestant witches; and they both could kill pagan witches, all under the name of heresy, or thinking unorthodox thoughts. The witch craze was led by the intellectuals but, in a time of social upheaval, it fed on widespread fear and unrest.[34]

Beatrice Whiting has suggested that sorcery or witchcraft will be found in societies that lack formal procedures or judicial authorities to deal with crime and other offenses. The theory is that all societies need some form of social control—some way of deterring most would-be offenders and of dealing with actual offenders. In the absence of specialized judicial officials who, if present, would also deter and deal with antisocial behavior, the only thing that might tend to prevent such behavior would be the fear of others who might invoke sorcery. The cross-cultural evidence seems to support this theory.[35]

Religion and Adaptation

Following Malinowski, anthropologists often take the view that religions are generally adaptive because they reduce anxieties and uncertainties to which all people are subject. We do not really know that religion is the only means of reducing anxiety and uncertainty, or even that individuals or societies *have* to reduce their anxiety and uncertainty. Still, it seems very likely that certain religious beliefs and practices have directly adaptive consequences.

For example, the Hindu belief in the sacred cow has seemed to many to be the very opposite of a useful or adaptive custom. Their religion does not permit Hindus to slaughter cows. Why

do the Hindus retain such a belief? Why do they allow all those cows to wander around freely, defecating all over the place, and not slaughter any of them? The contrast with our own use of cows could hardly be greater. However, Marvin Harris has suggested that the Hindus' use of cows may have beneficial consequence that some other use of cows would not have. In short, what may appear bizarre to us may not actually be so bizarre in other environments and may even be the best way available to handle some situation, like the keeping of cows.

Harris points out that there may be a sound economic reason for not slaughtering cattle in India. The cows (and the males they produce) provide a number of resources that could not easily be provided otherwise. At the same time, their wandering around to forage is no strain on the food-producing economy. The resources provided by the cows are varied. First, oxen are necessary for traction—a team of oxen and a plow are essential for the many small farms in India. The Indians could produce oxen with fewer cows, but to do so they would have to devote some of their food production to the feeding of those fewer cows. In the present system, they do not feed the cows; and even though this makes the cows relatively infertile, males (which are castrated to make oxen) are still produced at no cost to the economy. Second, cow dung is essential as cooking fuel and fertilizer. The National Council of Applied Economic Research estimates that dung equivalent to 45,000,000 tons of coal is burned annually. Moreover, it is delivered practically to the door each day at no cost. Alternative sources of fuel, such as wood, are scarce or costly. In addition, about 340,000,000 tons of dung are used as manure, essential in a country which is obliged to derive three harvests a year from its intensively cultivated land. Third, although Hindus do not eat beef, the cattle which die naturally or are butchered by non-Hindus are eaten by the lower castes who, without the upper-caste taboo against eating beef, might not get this needed protein. Fourth, the hides and horns of the cattle

[34]H. R. Trevor-Roper, "The European Witch-Craze of the Sixteenth and Seventeenth Centuries," in *Reader in Comparative Religion*, ed. Lessa and Vogt, pp. 444–49.

[35]Beatrice B. Whiting, *Paiute Sorcery*, Viking Fund Publications in Anthropology, no. 15 (New York: Wenner-Gren Foundation, 1950), pp. 36–37; also Swanson, *The Birth of the Gods*, p. 151.

Hindu sacred cow. (Ylla, Rapho/Photo Researchers.)

gions or new sects. The appearance of new religions is one of the things that may happen when cultures are disrupted by contact with dominant societies. Various classifications have been suggested for these religious movements—cargo cults, nativistic movements, messianic movements, millenarian cults. Earlier, we noted that Aberle relates new religious movements to the stress arising from economic or social deprivation. But Wallace suggests that they are all examples of *revitalization movements*, efforts to save a culture by infusing it with new purpose and new life.

Furthermore, it is attractive to speculate that all religions and religious productions, such as myths and rituals, come into existence as parts of the program or code of religious revitalization movements. Such a line of thought leads to the view that religious belief and practice always originate in situations of social and cultural stress and are, in fact, an effort on the part of the stress-laden to construct systems of dogma, myth, and ritual which are internally coherent as well as true descriptions of a world system and which thus will serve as guides to efficient action.[37]

The Seneca Indians, an Iroquois tribe, faced such a situation following the American Revolution. They had lost their lands and were confined to isolated reservations amid an alien people. They were in a state of despondency when a man named Handsome Lake received a vision from God which led him to stop drinking and to preach a new religion that would revitalize the Seneca. This was not the first such movement among the Iroquois. In the fifteenth century, they were an unorganized people, warring against each other and being warred upon by other tribes. Hiawatha, living as a highwayman and a cannibal, was visited by the god Dekanawidal. He became God's spokesman in persuading the five tribes to give up their feuding and to unite as the League of the Iroquois. The Condolence Ritual was adopted, which precluded feuding and blood revenge. The rad-

which die are used in India's enormous leather industry. Therefore, since the sacred cows do not themselves consume resources needed by people, and since it would be impossible to provide traction, fuel, and fertilizer as cheaply by other means, the taboo against slaughtering cattle may be quite adaptive.[36]

RELIGIOUS CHANGE AS REVITALIZATION

The long history of religion includes periods of strong resistance to change as well as periods of radical change. Anthropologists have been especially interested in the founding of new reli-

[36]Marvin Harris, "The Cultural Ecology of India's Sacred Cattle," *Current Anthropology* 7, no. 1 (February 1966): 51–63.

[37]Wallace, *Religion: An Anthropological View*, p. 30.

ical new movement which had united and revitalized the Iroquois settled into a belief which conserved their integrity.[38]

Central to such movements is the link formed between the old ways and the new, a fusion of what is seen as the best of both worlds. Thus the Ghost Dance of the Paiute picked elements of Indian culture, such as games and ceremonies, as symbols of identity and unity. It also accepted elements of the white culture, such as weapons and tools. As another example, the Peyote Way blends traditional kinds of singing and drumming and individual religious experience with some Christian doctrines. It introduces a drug/mystical experience which provides a philosophical acceptance of the harmony of existence. Melanesian cargo cults promised the arrival of boats and planes laden with abundant Western goods for the use of natives alone. The Fiji Tuka Cult of about 1885 predicted that the world would be turned upside down, which would leave the old religion and native people superior to the new religion and the alien white people. Yet the new order would be maintained with European efficiency and weapons. Indians in Mexico kept the ancient worship of Our Mother, Tonantzin, and united her with the Virgin Mary in the form of Our Lady of Guadalupe. This union revitalized them and gave them the faith that they were accepted as human by the Spanish conquerors. It also gave them the hope that they would one day be able to throw out the Spanish overlords.

Wallace looks to the future of religion with some apprehension, aware that the discoveries of science are rapidly leading to a disbelief in things supernatural. "Belief in supernatural beings and supernatural forces that affect nature without obeying nature's laws will erode and become an interesting historical memory."[39] He sees two possible directions. One, which he fears, is that the reverence which has formerly

been applied to the supernatural will be shifted to the state and its leaders. The other is a nontheistic revitalization movement with humanity as the entity to be respected and problems such as population control, technological unemployment, and intergroup conflict as the stimulus for a new affirmation of the worth of living.

Summary

1. Religion is any set of attitudes, beliefs, and practices pertaining to supernatural power. Such beliefs may vary within a culture as well as among societies, and they may change over time.

2. Religious beliefs are evident in all known cultures and are inferred from artifacts associated with *Homo sapiens* since Neandertal times.

3. Various theories have arisen about the origin of religious beliefs. Tylor suggested that religion stemmed from speculation about such states as dreams, trances, and death. Malinowski proposed that, faced with anxieties primarily relating to death, people create rituals to affirm their social unity in the face of social disruption. Freud suggested that religion reflects a neurotic Oedipal need, and Jung regarded religion as a therapeutic solution to inner conflicts. All psychological theories agree that religion serves to reduce individual anxieties. Sociological theories suggest that religion stems from society and societal needs, and religion symbolizes what society considers sacred. Swanson suggests that the spirit world we invent personifies the family and other decision-making groups in society which have power over us. Other theories relate religion to a strain felt by people and caused by events in society.

4. There are wide variations in religious beliefs and practices. Societies vary in the number and kinds of supernatural entities in which they believe. There may be dis-

---

[38]Ibid., pp. 31–34.
[39]Anthony Wallace, "Revitalization Movements," *American Anthropologist* 58 (1956): 265.

embodied supernatural forces; there may be supernatural beings of nonhuman origin (gods or spirits); and there may be supernatural beings of human origin (ghosts of ancestral spirits). The religious belief system of a society may include any or all such supernatural entities.

5. In some societies, all gods are equal in rank; in others, there is a hierarchy of prestige and power among gods and spirits, just as among humans.

6. A monotheistic religion is one in which there is one high god and all other supernatural beings are either subordinate to, or function as alternative manifestations of, this god. A high god is generally found in societies with a high level of political development.

7. Faced with ignorance, pain, and injustice, people frequently explain events by claiming intervention by the gods. Such intervention has also been sought by people to help them achieve their own ends.

8. Among cultures with a belief in the soul, there are many different beliefs about what happens to the soul after death.

9. Various methods have been used to attempt communication with the supernatural. Among them have been prayer, music, physiological experience (drugs, fasting, mortification of the flesh), exhortation or preaching, reciting the code (divine literature), simulation (voodoo, divination), and sacrifice. In some societies, intermediaries, such as shamans or priests, communicate with the supernatural on behalf of others. Societies with religious intermediaries tend to be more complex and have greater specialization; religious specialization seems to be part of this general specialization.

10. When people believe their actions can compel the supernatural to act in a particular and intended way, anthropologists refer to the belief and related practice as "magical."

11. Sorcery and witchcraft are attempts to make the spirits work harm against people.

12. The history of religion includes periods of strong resistance to change and periods of radical change. One explanation is that religious practices always originate during periods of stress. Religious movements may also be examples of revitalization movements, efforts to save a culture by infusing it with new purpose and new life.

Suggested Readings

Banton, M., ed. *Anthropological Approaches to the Study of Religion.* Association of Social Anthropologists of the Commonwealth, Monograph no. 3. New York: Praeger, 1966.

A group of papers, all with the aim of establishing explanatory principles of a general nature. Of the five papers, two are essentially critical evaluations of social anthropology. The other three are descriptive papers on African tribal social structure. Among the topics covered are religion as a cultural system and problems of explanation and description.

Lessa, W. A., and Vogt, E. Z., eds. *Reader in Comparative Religion: An Anthropological Approach.* 3rd ed. New York: Harper & Row, 1971.

A collection of readings balancing the more theoretical trends and the descriptive field reports of the anthropological study of religion. The editors' general introduction gives a broad outline of the main issues, problems, and theoretical positions, as well as defining for the student the concept of "religion" from an anthropological point of view.

Malefjit, A. deW. *Religion and Culture: An Introduction to the Anthropology of Religion.* New York: Macmillan, 1968.

A general introduction to the study of religion. The work begins by introducing and defining the anthropological study of religion, followed by a historical survey of the study of religion from the ancient Greeks to the present. Included is a discussion of the evidence for prehistoric religious practice.

Malinowski, B. *Magic, Science and Religion and Other Essays.* Garden City, N.Y.: Doubleday, 1954.

A collection of papers representing some of Malinowski's work on ritual and religious behavior, and the nature of primitive cults, magic, and faith.

Swanson, G. E. *The Birth of the Gods: The Origin of Primitive Beliefs.* Ann Arbor: University of Michigan Press, 1969.

A cross-cultural study which explores the origins of religious beliefs and examines how various aspects of religion may be related to social and political organization.

The Arts

21

In virtually all cultures, people experience the need to express their feelings, fears, or thoughts in what we might call an artistic medium. A Melanesian stripes his house with vertical bands; an American farmer paints a hex sign on his barn. A Hopi Indian performs a rain dance; the Plains Indians perform a sun dance. Giant stone heads are implanted in the earth on Easter Island; inch-long ivory mice are delicately carved by Chinese artists. What these activities have in common is that they involve a strong *emotional component.* Indeed, one can say that the expression of feeling is the central function of art, music, dance, and folklore. For this reason, anthropologists and other social scientists refer to these activities as forms of *expressive behavior.*

Expressive activities are in part cultural endeavors, involving shared and learned patterns of behavior, belief, and feeling. Although in our society we require that artists be unique and innovative, the art they produce must still fall within some range of acceptable variation. Artists must communicate to us in a way that we can relate to, or at least learn to relate to. Often, they must follow certain current styles of expression which have been set by other artists or by critics, if they hope to have their art accepted by the public. These requirements demonstrate that, even allowing for the high value we place upon originality, art in our society remains in part a cultural activity.

The fact that our artistic activities are mainly cultural is made evident when we compare what is artistic in different cultures. For example, Americans share the value of decorating the interiors of their homes with pictures, either by hanging paintings or by painting directly on the walls; but they do not share the value of painting pictures on the outside walls of their houses, as some peoples do. Earlier in this century, young German men shared the value of a fencing scar, a slash on the cheek; so valued was this scar that it was sometimes self-inflicted. Yet the fencers would have rejected decorative scarring as it is practiced in some African societies.

21

Cultural Variations in Expressive Behavior

Some types of expressive behavior, such as music and decoration, are apparently *universal.* Yet shared values—and with them, the forms and styles of artistic expression—vary from society to society. For example, while body decoration may be an art in many societies, the actual form of the decoration depends upon cultural traditions. Thus, body ornamentation includes the pierced noses of some women in India, the elongated necks of the Mangebetu of Central Africa, the tattooing of American males, the body painting of the Caduveo of South America, and the varying ornaments (jewelry, feathers, belts, and so on) found in almost every culture.

Not only is there cultural variation in forms of expression, but there is also differentiation in style. Thus, while music is universally an expressive behavior, some societies produce music that is very rhythmic, while others produce music having a freer, less regular beat. In some societies, music tends to repeat the same elements over and over again, while in other societies it does not. Recently, there has been an acceleration of research on what may account for differences in form and style of expressive behavior.

To illustrate the variation that exists in expressive behavior, we shall examine the art of body decoration and adornment.

Body Decoration and Adornment

The body was one of the first objects of art— that is, an object of nature which people, by the addition of symbols, transformed into an object of culture. Many societies decorate or adorn the human body. The decorations may be permanent—in the form of scars, tattoos, changes in the shape of a body part. Or they may be temporary—in the form of paintings or objects such

Body decoration often has ceremonial significance. Here, a masked New Guinea dancer represents a clan ancestor in a pageant of the creation of the world. (Courtesy of the American Museum of Natural History.)

as feathers, metals, skins, and, in cases where it is not strictly utilitarian, clothing. Much of this decoration seems to be motivated by aesthetic considerations which, of course, may vary from culture to culture.

However, in addition to satisfying aesthetic needs, body decoration or adornment may be used to delineate social position, rank, sex, occupation, or religion within a society. Along with social stratification come visual means of declaring status. The symbolic halo (i.e., the crown) on the king's head, the scarlet hunting jacket of the English gentleman, the eagle feathers of the Indian chief's bonnet, the gold-embroidered jacket of the Indian rajah—each mark of high status is recognized in its own society.

In our own society, body decoration often signifies religious affiliation. Jewelry in the shape of a cross or the Star of David indicates Christian or Jewish inclinations. Clothes may set apart the priest or the nun, or the member of a sect such as the Amish or the Chasidic Jews. The ceremonial significance of body painting has been noted for a number of societies. In each case, religious content is conveyed through symbols attached to the body. The Sun Dance of the Cheyenne presents a woman who personifies morning; she is painted red, with two blue suns on her face, a blue morning star on her chest, and a blue crescent moon on her right shoulder. Various sky symbols appear on other dancers in the ceremony, during which the power of the sun is sought for the men of the tribe.[1] The mystical significance of much of ancient body decoration is lost to us, but the assumption remains that much of the body adornment had religious meaning.

The erotic significance of some body decoration is also apparent. Women draw attention to erogenous zones of the body by painting, as on the lips, and by attaching some object: an earring, a flower behind the ear, a necklace, bracelet, brooch, anklet, or belt. The Basuto of Basutoland in southern Africa devise a love potion for men and women by rubbing an ointment containing some of the beloved's sweat or blood or hair into open wounds. The resulting scars are evidence of love.[2] Among the Ila-speaking peoples of northern Rhodesia (now Zambia), women practice scarification to heighten arousal during sexual intercourse. They repeatedly cut and reopen vertical lines on their loins and inner thighs; the marks are hidden by their skirts during the day and are revealed only to their husbands.[3] Body adornment for erotic purposes is not peculiar to non-West-

Face painting is also practiced in Western societies. This clown has decorated his face for a European carnival. (Courtesy of Francisco Hidalgo, Woodfin Camp and Associates.)

ern cultures. We have only to follow the fashion trends of Europe and America during the past 300 years, with their history of pinched waists, ballooned hips, bustled rumps, exaggerated breasts, painted faces, and exposed bosoms, to realize the significance of body adornment for sexual provocation.

Special body decoration to mark the initiation of youth into adulthood is a form of sexual and status adornment in some cultures, for it is the sexual maturity of the young person which marks him as ready for social maturity. Many societies circumcise adolescents. In the Poro initiation ceremony as practiced by the Kpelle of Liberia, the circumcised boys spend a period of seclusion in the forest with the older men. They return with scars down their backs, symbolic tooth marks indicative of their close escape from *namu*, the Great Masked Figure, which ate the child but disgorged the young adult.[4] Clitoridectomy (removal of the clitoris)

---

[1] Peter V. Powell, *Sweet Medicine*, vol. 2, (Norman: University of Oklahoma Press, 1969), pp. 842–44.

[2] Hugh Ashton, *The Basuto*, 2d ed. (London: Oxford University Press, 1967), p. 303.

[3] Edwin W. Smith and Andrew Murray Dale, *The Ila-speaking Peoples of Northern Rhodesia* (New Hyde Park, N.Y.: University Books, 1968), p. 96. Originally published in 1920 as *Ethnocentric British Colonial Attitudes*.

[4] James L. Gibbs, Jr., "The Kpelle of Liberia," in *Peoples of Africa* (New York: Holt, Rinehart and Winston, 1965), p. 222.

elongated ears and necks, shaped heads, pierced ears and necks, filed teeth. But what leads some members of our society to transfer body decoration to their animals? Why the shaped hair of the poodle, the braided manes of some horses, and diamond collars, painted toenails, coats, hats, and even boots for some pets? And why, for example, do different societies adorn, paint, or otherwise decorate different parts of the body for sexual (or other) reasons?

EXPLAINING VARIATION IN EXPRESSIVE BEHAVIOR

Many people would agree that expressive behavior, such as music or art, is the area of culture most free to vary. Apparently, the particular style of the art or music of a society has no effect upon the society's survival or success. Therefore, it might seem that any form or style of expression could occur at any time and at any place. This assumption about the freedom of artistic expression to vary may also arise from our own experience in observing rapid changes in popular music and dance, films, and graphic art, in the apparent absence of equally rapid changes in current life-styles and social conditions. However, we must realize that what looks like rapid change to us may merely be slight variation within what a foreign observer would see as a more or less constant form or style. For example, the dominant style of dancing among young people may have changed from the fox trot to rock, but we still generally see couples dancing—not individuals dancing in isolation. Furthermore, our popular music still has a beat (or combination of beats) and is generally made by the same kinds of instruments as were used in the past.

Although expressive form and style may not generally *affect* how an individual lives, there is still the possibility that it *reflects* how that individual lives. Much of the recent research on variation in expressive behavior supports this possibility. Just as some aspects of religion seem to be projections of people's feelings and conflicts, so some forms of expressive behavior, too,

A modern mask of the Iroquois Indian False Face Society of curers. The mask is worn to ward off evil spirits. (Courtesy of the American Museum of Natural History.)

marks the sexual maturity of girls in some societies.

The tendency to decorate the human body is probably universal. We have noted some of the various methods people have used to adorn themselves in different societies. We are aware also of body-decoration practices which raise questions to which we have no ready answers. Perhaps vanity explains adornment of the body and such practices as scarification, bound feet,

The same material may be used artistically in different societies. A Japanese monk rakes sand into traditional patterns. A Navajo Indian creates a sand painting to help heal a sick child. (Left, Burt Glinn, Magnum Photos. Right, Courtesy of the American Museum of Natural History.)

may be ways of ventilating or vicariously revealing the conflicts and feelings of most people in society.

Perhaps the most obvious way that artistic creations reflect how we live is by mirroring the environment—the materials and technologies that are available to a culture. Stone, wood, bones, tree bark, clay, sand, charcoal, berries for staining, and a few mineral-derived ochers are generally available materials. In addition, depending upon the locality, other resources become accessible: shells, horns, tusks, gold, copper, and silver. The different uses to which societies put these materials are of interest to anthropologists, who may ask, for example, why a people choose to use clay and not copper, when both items are available. Although we have no conclusive answers as yet, such questions have important ramifications. The way in which a society views its environment is sometimes apparent in its choice and use of artistic materials. The use of certain revered metals, for example, may be reserved for ceremonial objects of special importance. Or the belief in the supernatural powers of a stone or tree may cause the sculptor to be sensitive to that particular material.[5]

What is particularly meaningful to anthropologists is the realization that, although the materials available to a society may to some extent limit or influence what it can do artistically, the materials by no means determine what is done. Why does the artist in Japanese society make sand into patterns, the artist in Navajo society paint sand, and the artist in Roman society melt sand to form glass? Moreover, even

[5] James J. Sweeney, "African Negro Culture," in *African Folktales and Sculpture*, ed. Paul Radin, (New York: Pantheon, 1952), p. 335.

when the same material is used in the same way by members of different societies, the form or style of the work varies enormously from culture to culture.

A society may choose to represent objects or phenomena that are especially critical to its population. An examination of the art of the Middle Ages tells us something about the medieval preoccupation with theological doctrine. In addition to revealing the primary concerns of a society, the content of its art may also reflect the culture's social stratification. Authority figures may be represented in rather obvious ways. In the art of ancient Sumerian society, the sovereign was portrayed as being much larger than his followers, and the most prestigious gods were given oversized eyes. Also, as we have seen, differences in clothing and jewelry styles within a society usually reflect social stratification.

Certain possible relationships between the art of a society and other aspects of its culture have always been recognized by art historians. Much of this attention has been concentrated on the content of art, since European art has been representational for such a long time. But the style of the art may reflect other aspects of culture. Fischer, for example, has examined the stylistic features of art with the aim of discovering "some sort of regular connection between some artistic feature and some social situation."[6] He argues that all expressive behavior is a form of social fantasy. In other words, in a stable society, artists will respond to those conditions in the society which bring them, and the society, security or pleasure.

Assuming that "pictorial elements in design are, on one psychological level, abstract, mainly unconscious representations of persons in the society,"[7] Fischer reasoned that egalitarian societies would tend to have different stylistic elements in their art than stratified societies. Egalitarian societies are generally composed of

[6]John Fischer, "Art Styles as Cultural Cognitive Maps," *American Anthropologist* 63 (1961): 80.
[7]Ibid., p. 81.

TABLE 1   Artistic Differences in Egalitarian and Stratified Societies

Egalitarian Society	Stratified Society
Repetition of simple elements	Integration of unlike elements
Much empty or "irrelevant" space	Little empty space
Symmetrical design	Asymmetrical design
Unenclosed figures	Enclosed figures

small, self-sufficient communities, which are structurally similar and have little differentiation between persons. Stratified societies, on the other hand, generally have larger and more interdependent (and dissimilar) communities, with great differences among persons in prestige, power, and access to economic resources. Fischer hypothesized, and found in a cross-cultural study, that certain elements of design were strongly related to the presence of social hierarchy. His findings are summarized in Table 1.

Let us see how Fischer's findings apply to the art of some particular societies. For example, repetition of a simple design is found in the art of the Ojibwa, an egalitarian hunting-gathering people around the Great Lakes with little political organization and few authority positions. If each design element unconsciously represents individuals within a society, and the Ojibwa gain security from the essential sameness of people and their refusal to compete for a superior or outstanding position, then it seems that there is a connection between the Ojibwa's social patterns and their expressive behavior. Conversely, the combining of different design elements in a complex pattern in Indian art may be seen as a reflection of the caste system of India. Each individual is well aware of the cultural regulations and the distinctive behavior which effectively separate him from every other level of Indian society.

According to Fischer, the egalitarian society's empty space around a design represents the society's relative isolation. Because egalitarian communities are usually small and self-suffi-

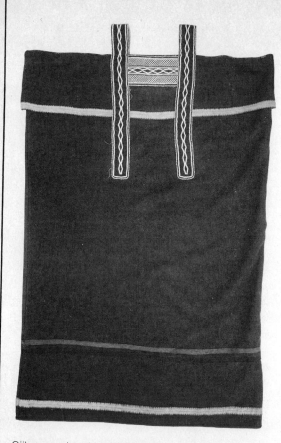

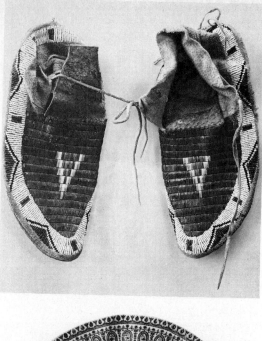

Ojibwa woolen shirt displays the repetition of a simple design; Sioux moccasins have a repetitious central design surrounded by empty space. These designs may reflect an egalitarian social structure. The intricate textile design from India may reflect that country's highly stratified society. (Above and top right, Courtesy of the American Museum of Natural History. Right, Raghubir Singh, Black Star.)

cient, they tend to shy away from foreigners, preferring to find security within their own group. Sioux designs for the toes of moccasins present a strongly integrated, repetitious central design surrounded by empty space, suggesting a relatively egalitarian society that normally has (or tries to have) little contact with surrounding peoples.

On the other hand, the art of India is generally crowded. The hierarchical society does not seek to isolate individuals or communities within the group since they must be interdependent, each social level furnishing services for those above it and help for those beneath it. As Fischer suggests, we can, in general, discern a lack of empty space in the designs of those societies where, instead of security being sought by avoiding the stranger, "security is produced by incorporating strangers into the hierarchy, through dominance or submission as the relative power indicates. In fantasy the hierarchical society seeks to encompass the universe."[8]

Symmetry, the third stylistic feature related to type of society, is similar to the first. Symmetry may suggest likeness or an egalitarian society; asymmetry suggests difference and perhaps stratification. The fourth feature of interest here, the presence or absence of enclosures or boundaries, may indicate the presence or absence of hierarchically imposed rules circumscribing individual behavior. Sioux beadwork presents an unenclosed symmetrical design; elements are not separated from each other. In fact, Sioux society allows free access to most property, and the fencing off of a piece of property for the use of only one person is unknown. In the art of India, the presence of boundaries is more marked. Such definite separations between figures in art may be seen as a reflection of the distinctions between persons in Indian society, which is filled with symbolic boundaries indicated by differences in dress, occupation, type of food allowed, and manners.

Studies like Fischer's offer anthropologists possible new tools with which to evaluate ancient societies that are known only by a few pieces of pottery or a few tools or paintings. If art reflects aspects of a culture, then the study of whatever art of a people has been preserved may provide a means of testing the accuracy of the guesses we make about their culture on the basis of more prosaic archaeological materials.

Music

Apes have been observed having large-scale musical sessions in the jungles. Apparently without warning and for no particular reason, an ape will seize a stick and begin beating on the branch of a tree. Others will join in, beating rhythmically and shrieking a bit, until fifty or so apes are performing. The musicale usually lasts about half an hour.

Not our kind of music, we say, hardly realizing that, like the expressive behavior of apes, "our kind" of music has been programmed into us by our culture. We are limited to the same kinds of acceptable variations in music as in art. Even a trained musicologist, listening for the first time to music of a different culture, will not be able to hear the subtleties of tone and rhythmical structure that members of that culture hear with ease. His or her predicament is similar to that of the linguist who, exposed to a foreign language, cannot at first distinguish phonemes, morphemes, and other regular patterns of speech.

Not only do instruments vary, but music itself varies widely in style from society to society. For example, in some societies people prefer music with a regularly recurring beat; in others they prefer changes in rhythm. There are also variations in singing styles. For example, in some places it is customary to have different vocal lines for different people; in other places people all sing together.

EXPLAINING VARIATIONS IN MUSIC

Is variation in music, as in the other arts, related to other aspects of culture? On the basis of a cross-cultural study of more than 3,500 folk songs from a sample of the world's societies, Alan Lomax found certain relationships between cultural traits and song performance.[9] He asserts that a society's song styles vary with

1. its level of food production
2. its degree of political development
3. its degree of social stratification
4. the severity of its sexual mores
5. the division of labor by sex
6. the level of social cohesiveness.

Certain features of song style appear to be

[8] Ibid., p. 83.

[9] Alan Lomax, *Folk Song Style and Culture,* American Association for the Advancement of Science Publication no. 88 (Washington, D.C.: 1968), p. x.

In Beech Creek, North Carolina, a woman plays the hen fiddle. She is playing a jig while her friends dance a clog dance in the background. (Arthur Tress, Magnum Photos.)

associated with cultural complexity. (The societies Lomax classified as more complex tend to have higher levels of food-production technology, social stratification, and a number of levels of political jurisdiction.) For example, wordiness and clearness of enunciation were found to be associated with cultural complexity. The association is a reasonable one: the more a society depends upon verbal information, as in giving complex instructions for a job or in explaining different points of law, the more strongly will clear enunciation in the transmitting of information be a mark of its culture. Thus, hunter-gatherer bands, in which people know their productive role and perform it without ever being given complex directions, are more likely than we are to base much of their singing on lines of nonwords, such as our refrain lines, "Tra-la-la-la-la." Their songs are characterized by lack of explicit information, by sounds that

give pleasure in themselves, by much repetition, and by relaxed, slurred enunciation.[10]

Examples of the progression from repetition or nonwords to wordy information are found within our society. The most obvious (and universal) example of a song made entirely of repetition is the relaxed lullaby of a mother repeating a comforting syllable to her baby, while improvising her own tune. However, this type of song is not characteristic of our own society. Although our songs sometimes have single lines of nonwords, it is rare for an entire song to be made of them. Usually, the nonwords act as respites from information:

Zippity do dah
Zippety ay
My o my
What a wonderful day

In associating variation in music with cultural complexity, Lomax also found that elaboration of song parts corresponds to the complexity of a society. Societies in which leadership is informal and temporary seem to symbolize their social equality by an "interlocked" style of singing; each person sings independently but within the group, and no one singer is differentiated from the others. Rank societies, in which there is a leader with prestige but no real power, are characterized by a song style in which one "leader" may begin the song, but the others soon drown out his voice. In stratified societies, where leaders have the power of force, choral singing is generally marked by a clear-cut role for the leader and a secondary "answering" role for the others. Societies which are marked by elaborate stratification show singing parts which are differentiated and in which the soloist is deferred to by the other singers.

Lomax also found a relationship between polyphony (two or more melodies sung simultaneously) and a high degree of female participation in food getting. In those societies in which women's work is responsible for at least

[10]Ibid., pp. 117–28.

half of the food, songs are likely to contain more than one simultaneous melody, with the higher tunes usually sung by women.

Counterpoint was once believed to be the invention of European high culture. In our sample it turns out to be most frequent among simple producers, especially gatherers, where women supply the bulk of the food. Counterpoint and perhaps even polyphony may then be very old feminine inventions. . . . Subsistence complementarity is at its maximum among gatherers, early gardeners, and horticulturalists. It is in such societies that we find the highest occurrence of polyphonic singing.[11]

In societies in which women do not contribute much to production, the singing is more likely to reflect the single dominance of the male.[12]

In some societies, survival and social welfare are based upon a unified group effort; in these cultures, singing tends to be marked by cohesiveness. That is, cohesive work parties, teams of gatherers or harvesters, and kin groups who work voluntarily for the good of the family or community seem to express their interconnectedness in song by blending both tone and rhythm.

RELATIONSHIPS OF CHILDREARING PRACTICES TO VARIATIONS IN MUSIC

Some variations in music may be explained as a consequence of variation in childrearing practices. For example, researchers are beginning to explore childrearing practices as a way to explain why some societies respond to, and produce, regular rhythm in their music, while others enjoy free rhythm which has no regular beat but rather approximates the rhythm of speech.

One hypothesis is that a regular beat in music is a simulation of the regular beat of the heart. For nine months in the womb, the fetus feels the mother's regular eighty or so heartbeats a minute. Moreover, mothers generally employ rhythmic tactics in quieting crying infants—patting their backs or rocking them. But the fact that children respond positively to an even tempo does not mean that the regular heartbeat is completely responsible for their sensitivity to rhythm. In fact, if the months in the womb were sufficient to establish a preference for rhythm, then every child would be affected in exactly the same manner by a regular beat, and every society would have the same rhythm in its music.

Barbara Ayres suggests that the importance of regular rhythm in the music of a culture is related to its "acquired reward value"—that is, its associations with feelings of security or relaxation. In a cross-cultural study exploring this possibility, Ayres found a strong correlation between a society's method of carrying infants and the type of musical rhythm the society produced. In some societies, the mother or an older sister continually carries the child, sometimes for two or three years, in a sling, pouch, or shawl, so that the child is in bodily contact with her at all times and experiences the motion of her rhythmic walking. Ayres discovered that such societies tend to have a regularly recurring beat in their songs. Those societies in which the child is put into a cradle or is strapped to a cradleboard tend to have music that is based either on irregular rhythm or on free rhythm. Ayres does not claim that the carrying practices necessarily give rise to a regular beat in music, but that the relationship is strong enough to warrant further study.[13]

The question of why some societies have great tonal ranges in music whereas others do not has also been researched by Ayres, who suggests that this, too, might be explained by certain childrearing practices. Ayres theorized that painful stimulation of infants before weaning might result in bolder, more exploratory behavior in adulthood, which would be apparent in the musical patterns of the culture. This hypothesis was suggested to her by laboratory

---

[11] Ibid., pp. 166–67.
[12] Ibid., pp. 117–69.

[13] Barbara C. Ayres, "Effects of Infant Carrying Practices on Rhythm in Music," *Ethos* #1 (1973): 387–404.

Two children from the Bagabo tribe in the Philippines are playing bamboo musical instruments. (Courtesy of the American Museum of Natural History.)

experiments with animals. Contrary to expectations, those animals which were given electric shocks or were handled before weaning showed greater than usual physical growth and more exploratory behavior when placed in new situations as adults. Ayres equated the range of musical notes (from low to high) with the exploratory range of animals, and forcefulness of accent in music with boldness in animals. The kinds of stress she looked for in ethnographic reports were those which would be applied to all children or to all of one sex: for example, scarification; piercing of the nose, lips, or ears; binding, shaping, or stretching of feet, head, ears, or any limb; inoculation; circumcision; or cauterization. The results showed that in those societies in which infants are stressed before the age of two, music is marked by a wider tonal range than in those societies in which children are not stressed or are stressed only at a later age. Also, a firm accent or beat is characteristic

of music more often in societies which stress children than in societies which do not stress their young.[14]

The culture's emphasis on obedience or independence in children is another variable which may explain some aspects of musical performance. In those societies in which children are generally trained for compliance, cohesive singing predominates. Conversely, in societies where children are encouraged to be assertive, singing is mostly individualized. Moreover, assertive training of children is associated with a raspy voice or harsh singing. A raspy voice seems to be an indication of assertiveness and is most often a male voice quality. Interestingly enough, in societies in which women's work predominates in subsistence production, the women sing with harsher voices.

Other voice characteristics may also be associated with elements of culture. For example, sexual restrictions in a society seem to be associated with voice restrictions, especially with a nasalized or narrow, squeezed tone. These voice qualities are associated with anxiety and are especially noticeable in sounds of pain, deprivation, or sorrow. Restrictive sexual practices may be a source of pain and anxiety, and the nasal tone in song may reflect such emotions.[15]

Folklore

Folklore is all the lore—myths, fairytales, superstitions, riddles, and games—of all the people of a culture. Generally, folklore is orally transmitted, but it may also be written. Because all types of folklore cannot be covered here, we shall limit our discussion to orally transmitted myths and folktales.

All societies have a repertoire of stories with which they entertain each other and teach their children. Examples of our folktales include

---

[14]Barbara C. Ayres, "Effects of Infantile Stimulation on Musical Behavior," in Lomax, *Folk Song Style and Culture*, pp. 211–21.
[15]Lomax, *Folk Song Style and Culture*, pp. 190–97.

Grimm's fairytales and the anecdotes we tell about our so-called folk heroes, such as George Washington's confessing to chopping down a cherry tree. It seems that we tell such stories, particularly to children, to illustrate or teach certain values.

In an attempt to arrive at the meaning of myth—and to discover how, and why, myths differ from society to society—interpreters of myth have often been as fanciful as the myth-makers themselves. For example, Max Muller spent about fifty years reducing most myths to a version of the solar myth (Cinderella is the sun because she starts in the ashes of a fire but ends in a blaze of glory).[16] And Andrew Lang spent about forty years in refuting Muller and offering his own interpretation of "savage" mythology. Such debates point up the fact that it is very easy for people to read different meanings into the same myth. For example, consider the myth that the Hebrews told of a paradise in which only a man was present until Eve, the first woman, arrived and ate the forbidden fruit of knowledge. One might conclude that the men in that society had some traditional grudge against women. If the interpreter were a psychoanalyst, he or (especially) she might assume that the myth reflected the male's deeply hidden fears of female sexuality. A historian might believe that the myth reflected actual historical events, and that men were living in blissful ignorance until women invented agriculture (the effect of Eve's "knowledge" led to a life of digging rather than gathering).

Several recurrent themes in myth and folklore have been examined by Clyde Kluckhohn. He concluded that there are five themes which are universal. They are: catastrophe, generally through flood; the slaying of monsters; incest; sibling rivalry, generally between brothers; and castration, sometimes actual but more usually "symbolic castration."[17]

The theme of the flood is found in myth in many cultures. Fragments of the Babylonian Gilgamesh epic date from about 2000 B.C. Gilgamesh was the favorite of the god Ut-Napishtim and was given instructions to build a boat, in which he saved himself and some animals from a destructive flood. The story of Noah, written later than the Gilgamesh epic, is similar enough to be seen as a case of diffusion. But diffusion cannot account for equally ancient flood myths of Asian and American origin. The theme of destruction and renewal seems to be universal, perhaps because people in many areas of the world have experienced, and been terrified by, floods.

The slaying of monsters is part of the general category of hero myths. Different reasons for the slaying may be given. Hercules must slay some monsters as punishment for having killed his wife and children. Bellerophon and Perseus of Greek mythology are told to slay a monster by kings who hope the two will be killed in the attempt. In some African (Bantu) myths, a hero slays a monster in order to restore the people (all except his father) whom the monster has killed.[18] In North America, a Cree legend relates how a man named Wee-sa-kay-jac slew a monster as revenge for the monster's having killed his younger brother. But Wee-sa-kay-jac did not restore the brother to life (even though in related myths he seems to have had that power).[19]

The incest theme is a general one in which brother-sister incest seems to be the most popular type.[20] Absalom of the Hebrew tradition killed his brother when he learned that the brother had slept with their sister. But with this success behind him, Absalom next attempted to take his father David's throne and was in turn killed for this insolence. In Greek mythology, Zeus and Hera, who were brother and sister, were also husband and wife.

---

[16] Richard Dorson, "The Eclipse of Solar Mythology," in *The Study of Folklore*, ed. Alan Dundes (Englewood Cliffs, N.J.: Prentice-Hall, 1965), pp. 57–83.

[17] Clyde Kluckhohn, "Recurrent Themes in Myths and Myth-making," in *The Study of Folklore*, ed. Dundes, pp. 158–68.

[18] Ibid., p. 163.

[19] James Stevens, *Sacred Legends of the Sandy Lake Cree* (Toronto: McClelland and Stewart, 1971), pp. 22–23.

[20] Kluckhohn, "Recurrent Themes in Myths and Myth-making," p. 163.

Sibling rivalry is apparent in the stories of Absalom and of Wee-sa-kay-jac. It is perhaps most widely known to us in the Hebrew stories of Cain and Abel, and Jacob and Esau. Sister-sister rivalry is a theme of the Greek story of Psyche and appears as jealousy between step-sisters in the story of Cinderella. The castration theme generally appears disguised, as in the warning given to little boys: if you suck your thumb, the butcher will cut it off.

As we have seen earlier, George O. Wright attempted to link the content of folktales to patterns of childrearing.[21] In a cross-cultural study of folktales from thirty-three societies, Wright found that more intense aggression appeared in the folktales of societies that severely punished children for aggression than in the stories of societies which were more tolerant of aggression. The Wright study suggests that folklore, and perhaps other forms of expressive behavior, may reflect the anxieties and conflicts felt by most members of a society, as well as the society's social and political organization.

Some anthropologists have concentrated their attention on the *form* or *structure* of folklore, rather than on its content alone. In these investigations, the emphasis is on how folklore may reflect cognition, or styles of thinking, in a society, not just social and political organization or personality patterns. Alan Dundes isolated two types of structure in the American Indian folktale. One is the movement from disequilibrium. Equilibrium is the desirable state; having too much or too little of anything is a condition which should be rectified as soon as possible. Dundes's structural model is of a folktale which first exhibits disequilibrium, which he calls "lack," and then shows how the lack is corrected.[22] Thus, the Cree version of the flood begins with disequilibrium—too much water, a decided lack of land. But by the efforts of three diving animals, Wee-sa-kay-jac obtains a bit of clay which he boils and the overflow becomes land. The same structure is repeated in the creation story: there is a lack of people, a situation which Wee-sa-kay-jac corrects by molding clay figures.[23]

Another type of myth structure which Dundes isolated is a sequence of interdiction, violation, consequence, and perhaps attempted escape. Thus, in a Lillooet (southern British Columbia) folktale, some children are warned not to call a whale mockingly. The whale comes and swallows them. The children escape when the people cut open the whale.[24] The same sequence is familiar in the Hebrew Garden of Eden tale. The couple is warned not to eat the fruit of a tree; they eat the fruit; they are cast out of their paradise. The Greek Icarus is warned not to fly too high or too low. He flies too high; the sun melts the wax that holds his feathered wings, and he falls and drowns.

The structural analysis of myths, used in conjunction with content analysis, is advocated by anthropologists who are seeking a framework with which to approach the rich and varied folklore of the world's societies. We do not know as yet which structures in myth are universal and which may be found only in certain societies. Nor do we know much as yet about the causes of such variation.

Summary

1. Because of the arts' strong emotional content, anthropologists often refer to them as *expressive behavior*. Expressive activities are partly cultural activities, involving shared and learned patterns of behavior, belief, and feeling.

2. The body was one of the first objects used for decoration and has been adorned by peoples in many different ways, both temporary and permanent. In addition to satisfying aes-

[21] George O. Wright, "Projection and Displacement: A Cross-Cultural Study of Folktale Aggression," *Journal of Abnormal and Social Psychology* 49 (1954): 523–28.

[22] Alan Dundes, "Structural Typology in North American Indian Folktales," in *The Study of Folklore*, pp. 206–15.

[23] Stevens, *Sacred Legends of the Sandy Lake Cree*, pp. 23–25.

[24] Dundes, *The Study of Folklore*, p. 209.

thetic needs, body decoration may be used to delineate social position, sex, or occupation. It may also have an erotic significance—for example, to draw attention to erogenous zones of the body.

3. The materials used to produce art objects, the way those materials are used, and the natural objects which the artist chooses to represent—all these vary from society to society and reveal much about a society's relation to its environment. Some studies indicate a correlation between artistic design and social structure.

4. Like the visual arts, music is subject to a remarkable amount of variation from society to society. Some studies suggest that there are correlations between musical styles and other cultural patterns. Other research shows links between childrearing practices and a society's preference for certain rhythmical patterns, tonal ranges, and voice quality.

5. Folklore, another form of expressive behavior, is a very broad category including such things as myths, fairytales, superstitions, riddles, and games, most of which are transmitted orally. Some anthropologists have identified basic themes in myths. These include catastrophe, slaying of monsters, incest, sibling rivalry, and castration. Myths may reflect a society's deepest preoccupations.

Suggested Readings

Dundes, A, *The Study of Folklore*. Englewood Cliffs, N.J.: Prentice-Hall, 1965.
A collection of theoretical and analytical papers dealing with folklore from a variety of perspectives: humanistic, literary, psychological, historical, and geographical. The essays explore such topics as the origins, processes, and forms of transmission of folklore.

Jacobs, M., and Greenway, J., eds. *The Anthropologist Looks at Myth*. American Folklore Society Bibliographical and Special Series, vol. 17. Austin: University of Texas Press, 1966.
A group of papers representing several varied approaches to the analysis of folklore. Most of the essays discuss the relation of folklore to other cultural norms and goals.

Lomax, A. *Folk Song Style and Culture*. Washington, D.C.: American Association for the Advancement of Science Publication no. 88, 1968.
Describes a method of analyzing the stylistic elements of folksongs from societies around the world. Known as the Cantometrics Project, the data compiled were used to test hypotheses about the relationship of song style to other aspects of culture.

Merriam, A. P. *The Anthropology of Music*. Evanston, Ill.: Northwestern University Press, 1964.
This book attempts to present music as a form of social behavior and thus subject to study by anthropological methods.

Munro, T. *Evolution of the Arts and Other Theories of Culture*. Cleveland: Cleveland Museum of Art, 1963.
The author discusses major problems in the study of art, such as the development of styles and traditions, complication and simplification in art, regressive trends, and cumulative changes in art.

Wingert, P. S. *Primitive Art: Its Traditions and Styles*. New York: Oxford University Press, 1962.
In this introduction to "primitive" art, the author discusses the function, motivation, and meaning of art in simpler societies.

Culture and Anthropology in the Modern World

IV

Culture Change

22

Heraclitus, a Greek philosopher of the sixth century B.C., noted, in going daily to his favorite bathing place at a river, that people can never put their feet twice in the same water. Each time they return to the water's edge, the current has flowed on. Change, he concluded, is a constant factor in a person's experience.

Culture, too, is ever changing. Since culture consists of learned patterns of behavior and belief, cultural traits can be "unlearned" and learned anew as human needs change. Thus, no specific cultural pattern remains impervious to change, just as no specific item of learning is necessarily immortal. In our own society in recent years, members of exclusive, all-male clubs have come to learn that the admission of women does not mean the end of the world, though it does mark the end of an era. On a larger scale, the cultural patterns of twentieth-century New York City are very much altered from those of seventeenth-century New Amsterdam. Most people in our society are aware that "times have changed" and with them people's attitudes and ways of life. Anthropologists wish to understand how and why "times" change—that is, how and why cultures change.

How Cultures Change

DISCOVERY AND INVENTION

Discoveries and inventions may stimulate culture change. The new element may be an object—the wheel, the plow, the computer; or it may be an idea—Christianity, Islam, Communism. According to Linton, a discovery is "any addition to knowledge."[1] The distinction between a discovery and an invention has to do with whether or not the new knowledge is used in some practical way. Thus, a person might discover that children can be persuaded to eat nourishing food if the food is associated with an imaginary character who appeals to them. The

[1] Ralph Linton, *The Study of Man* (New York: Appleton-Century-Crofts, 1936), p. 306.

discovery, however, merely adds to that individual's personal store of knowledge. Yet, suppose that individual exploits the discovery by developing the character of Popeye and creates a series of animated cartoons in which the hero acquires miraculous strength by devouring cans of spinach in a variety of dramatic situations. If the created character stimulates spinach sales on a national level, the individual may then take credit for the character's invention.

"Unconscious Invention" In discussing the process of invention, we should differentiate between varying types of inventions. One type is the consequence of a society's setting itself a specific goal, such as eliminating tuberculosis or placing a man on the moon. Another type emerges less intentionally. This second process of invention is often referred to as "accidental juxtaposition," or "unconscious invention." Ralph Linton has suggested that some inventions, especially those of prehistoric days, were probably the consequences of literally dozens of tiny initiatives by "unconscious" inventors. These inventors made their small contributions, perhaps over many hundreds of years, without being aware of the part they were playing in bringing one invention, such as the wheel or a better form of hand ax, to completion.[2] Consider the example of children playing on a fallen log, which rolls as they walk and balance on it, coupled with the need at a given moment to move a slab of granite from a cave face. The children's play may have suggested the use of logs as rollers and thereby set in motion a series of developments which culminated in the making of the wheel.

In reconstructing the process of invention in prehistoric times, however, we should be careful not to look back upon our ancestors with a smugness born of our more highly developed technology. We have become accustomed to turning to the science sections of our magazines and newspapers and finding, almost daily, reports of miraculous new discoveries and inven-

[2]Ibid., pp. 310–11.

Culture is constantly changing. At times the old and new cultural elements can present a sharp contrast. Here, a Kikuyu tribesman takes his first ride on a double-decker bus during a visit to Nairobi. (Marc and Evelyne Bernheim, Woodfin Camp and Associates.)

tions. From our point of view, then, it is difficult to imagine such a simple invention as the wheel taking so many centuries to come into being. We are tempted to surmise that early humans were less intelligent than we are. However, since human brain capacity has been the same for perhaps 100,000 years, there is no evidence that the inventors of the wheel were less intelligent than we are. Perhaps the accelerating rate of invention today has to do with our having had more time to accumulate knowledge. Perhaps the more knowledge people accumulate, the more often they can produce inventions.

Intentional Invention The history of the last 100 years or so offers us a biased perspective with regard to inventors and their importance. We tend to think that societies have always accepted inventors and their work and welcomed them as full-time specialists constantly in pursuit of social betterment. However, if intentional invention is defined as the deliberate attempt by an individual to produce a new idea or object, then for much of recent history the inventor has been the butt of suspicion rather than the recipient of acclaim. This was true of Galileo in the early seventeenth century; he was forced by the Church to deny that the earth revolved around the sun. Even today, certain developments may cause concern or dismay. Consider public reactions to the ideas that people should be guaranteed an annual income or that nuclear reactors should be used to supply energy.

What motivates the inventor in a complex society? In part, he or she responds to a need, either self-perceived or publicly proclaimed. Henry Ford is an example of an inventor who perceived a future need. He believed that a market existed for a cheap, reliable automobile and invented the mass-production process required to supply it. Richard Arkwright, in late eighteenth-century England, is an example of an inventor who responded to an existing public demand. At the time, new mechanical looms were quite efficient. Textile manufacturers were clamoring for quantities of spun yarn so large that cottage laborers, working with foot-operated spinning wheels, could not meet the demand. Arkwright, realizing that prestige and financial rewards would accrue to the person who invented a water- or machine-powered method of spinning, set about the task and developed the spinning jenny.

Arkwright demonstrates another motivation behind invention in advanced societies: economic reward. Specialization, the expansion of markets, and the growth of competition are some of the factors that cause groups within societies to employ, and to encourage, inventors in the hope that their efforts will increase prof-

its. Encouragement in modern times usually means either the payment of large salaries or the offer of very large sums for the rights to an invention. Another factor motivating inventors in complex societies is prestige, which may be obtained by winning awards such as the Nobel Prize.

Inventions, of course, do not necessarily lead to culture change. If an inventor or the invention is ignored, then no change in culture results. It is only when society accepts an invention and uses it regularly that we can begin to speak of culture change. Unfortunately, we know little as yet about why inventions are accepted or rejected by a society. When we say that a culture was "ready" for a particular invention, we have not come any closer to knowing *why* it was ready.

DIFFUSION

The source of new cultural elements in a society may be another society. The process by which cultural elements are borrowed from another society and incorporated into the culture of the recipient group is called *diffusion.* Borrowing sometimes enables a group to bypass stages or mistakes in the development of a process or institution. For example, Germany was able to accelerate its program of industrialization in the nineteenth century. It avoided some of the errors made by its English and Belgian competitors by taking advantage of technological borrowing. Japan did the same somewhat later.

Diffusion is extremely common. Linton has set its impact at the rate of 90 percent. That is, not more than 10 percent of the traits of most cultures can be attributed to each society's own, unaided efforts. In a well-known passage, Linton conveys the far-reaching effects of diffusion by considering the first few hours in the day of an American man. This man

awakens in a bed built on a pattern which originated in the Near East but which was modified in Northern Europe before it was transmitted to America. He throws back covers made from cotton, domesticated in India, or linen, domesticated in the Near East, or silk, the use of which was discovered in China. All of these materials have been spun and woven by processes invented in the Near East. . . . He takes off his pajamas, a garment invented in India, and washes with soap invented by the ancient Gauls. He then shaves, a masochistic rite which seems to have derived from either Sumer or ancient Egypt.

Before going out for breakfast he glances through the window, made of glass invented in Egypt, and if it is raining puts on overshoes made of rubber discovered by the Central American Indians and takes an umbrella, invented in southeastern Asia. . . .

On his way to breakfast he stops to buy a paper, paying for it with coins, an ancient Lydian invention. . . . His plate is made of a form of pottery invented in China. His knife is of steel, an alloy first made in southern India, his fork a medieval Italian invention, and his spoon a derivative of a Roman original. . . . After his fruit (African watermelon) and first coffee (an Abyssinian plant) . . . he may have the egg of a species of bird domesticated in Indo-China, or thin strips of the flesh of an animal domesticated in Eastern Asia which have been salted and smoked by a process developed in northern Europe. . . .

While smoking (an American Indian habit) he reads the news of the day, imprinted in characters invented by the ancient Semites upon a material invented in China by a process invented in Germany. As he absorbs the accounts of foreign troubles he will, if he is a good conservative citizen, thank a Hebrew deity in an Indo-European language that he is 100 percent American.[3]

Patterns of Diffusion *Direct Contact* Elements of a society's culture may be first taken up by neighboring societies and then gradually spread farther and farther afield. The spread of the manufacture of paper is a good example of extensive diffusion by direct contact. The invention of paper is attributed to the Chinese Ts'ai Lun in A.D. 105. Within fifty years, paper was being made in many places in central

[3]Ibid., pp. 326–27.

China. By 264 it was found in Chinese Turkestan, and from then on the successive places of manufacture were: 751, Samarkand; 793, Baghdad; about 900, Egypt; about 1100, Morocco; 1189, France; 1276, Italy; 1391, Germany; 1494, England. Generally, the pattern of accepting the borrowed invention was the same in each case. Paper was first imported into each area as a luxury, then in ever-expanding quantities as a staple product. Finally, and usually within one to three centuries, the local manufacture of paper was begun.

Another example of diffusion is the spread of tobacco. Tobacco was introduced into England from the New World in 1586 by Sir Walter Raleigh and into Spain in 1558 by Francisco Fernandez. From these twin European bases, the habit of smoking diffused rapidly. English medical students took the custom to Holland around 1590. English and Dutch sailors introduced tobacco throughout the Baltic in such quantities that by 1634 Russian authorities considered it a sufficient nuisance for laws to be enacted against its use. From Spain and Portugal, the use of tobacco spread throughout the Mediterranean countries and the Near East. In 1605, the Sultan of Turkey legislated against its use. At that date, too, the Japanese restricted the acreage which could be set aside for tobacco cultivation.

Intermediate Contact Diffusion by intermediate contact occurs through the agency of third parties. Frequently, traders carry a cultural trait from the society which originated it to another group. As an example of diffusion through intermediaries, Phoenician traders spread the alphabet, which was invented by another Semitic group, to Greece. At times, soldiers serve as intermediaries in spreading a culture trait. European crusaders, such as the Knights Templar and the Knights of St. John, acted as intermediaries in two ways, by carrying Christian culture to Muslim societies of North Africa and bringing Arab culture back to Europe. Today, Western missionaries in all parts of the world encourage natives to wear Western clothing.

The influence of Western societies can be seen in many different parts of the world. This New Guinea girl has made decorative use of the light bulb, which serves a very different function in industrialized societies. (Courtesy of the American Museum of Natural History.)

The result is that in Africa, in the Pacific Islands, and elsewhere, native people can be found wearing khaki shorts, suit jackets, shirts, ties, and other typically Western articles of clothing.

Stimulus Diffusion　In stimulus diffusion, knowledge of a trait belonging to another culture stimulates the invention or development of a local equivalent. A classic example of stimulus diffusion is the Cherokee syllabic writing system created by an Indian named Sequoya so that his people could write down their language. Sequoya received the initial idea from his contact with Europeans. Yet he did not adopt the English writing system; indeed, he did not even learn to write English. What he did was to utilize some English alphabetic symbols, alter a number of others, and invent new ones. All the symbols he used represented Cherokee sylla-

bles and in no way echoed English alphabetic usage. In other words, Sequoya took English alphabetic ideas and gave them a new Cherokee form. The stimulus originated with Europeans; the end result was peculiarly Cherokee.

The Selective Nature of Diffusion　While there is a temptation to view the dynamics of diffusion as similar to a stone sending concentric ripples over still water, this would be an oversimplification of the way diffusion actually occurs. Not all cultural traits are borrowed as readily as the ones we have mentioned, nor do they usually expand in neat, ever-widening circles. Rather, diffusion is a selective process. The Japanese, for instance, accepted much from Chinese culture, but they also rejected many traits. Rhymed tonal poetry, civil service examinations, and foot-binding, which were favored by the Chinese, were never adopted in Japan. The poetry form was unsuited to the structure of the Japanese language; the examinations were unnecessary in view of the entrenched power of the Japanese aristocracy; foot-binding was repugnant to a people who abhorred body mutilation of any sort. Muslim societies offer another example of selective acceptance of cultural diffusion. Originally, the basic test of acceptability in Muslim societies was compatibility with the Koran. Hence, the practices of drinking wine and coffee, gambling, smoking, playing cards, and printing—all prohibited by the Koran—failed to diffuse into Muslim cultures.

In addition, diffusion is selective because cultural traits differ in the extent to which they can be communicated. Elements of material culture, such as mechanical processes and techniques, and other traits, such as physical sports and the like, are not especially difficult to demonstrate. Consequently, they are accepted or rejected on their merits. But the moment we move out of the material context, we encounter real difficulties. Linton has explained the problem in these words:

Although it is quite possible to describe such an element of culture as the ideal pattern for marriage . . . it is much less complete than a description of basketmaking. . . . The most thorough verbalization has difficulty in conveying the series of associations and conditioned emotional responses which are attached to this pattern [marriage] and which give it meaning and vitality within our own society. . . . This is even more true of those concepts which . . . find no direct expression in behavior aside from verbalization. There is a story of an educated Japanese who after a long discussion on the nature of the Trinity with a European friend . . . burst out with: "Oh, I see now, it is a committee." [4]

Finally, diffusion is selective because the overt form of a particular trait, rather than its function or meaning, seems frequently to determine how the trait will be received. For example, the enthusiasm for bobbed hair which swept through feminine America in the 1920s never caught on among the Indians of northwestern California. To American women, short hair was a symbolic statement of their freedom. To Indian women, who traditionally cut their hair short when in mourning, it was a reminder of death.[5]

A society accepting a foreign cultural trait is likely to adapt it in a new way that effectively harmonizes the new trait with the group's own cultural traditions. This process of reinterpretation frequently occurs when religions diffuse. Thus, a little church in an ancient Greek city in southern Italy has an image of Aphrodite which for centuries has been revered as the Virgin Mary. And, in Haiti, Legba and Damballa, the trickster and rainbow gods derived from Dahomey in West Africa are identified with Saint Anthony and Saint Patrick, respectively.[6]

In the process of diffusion, then, we can identify a number of different patterns. We know that cultural borrowing is selective rather than automatic, and we can describe how a particular borrowed trait has been modified by the recipient culture. But we cannot specify

when one or another of these outcomes will occur, under what conditions diffusion will occur, and why it occurs the way it does.

ACCULTURATION

When a group or society is in contact with a more powerful society, the weaker group is often obliged to acquire cultural elements from the dominant group. This process of extensive borrowing in the context of superordinate-subordinate relations between societies is usually called *acculturation.* In contrast to diffusion, which involves the voluntary borrowing of culture elements, acculturation, or the wholesale borrowing of culture traits, comes about as a result of some sort of external pressure. The external pressure can take various forms. In the extreme form, under conditions of conquest, direct force is used by the dominant group to effect cultural change in the conquered group. For example, in the conquest of Mexico by the Spanish, the conquerors forced many of the Indian groups to accept Catholicism. Although such direct force is not always exerted in conquest situations, dominated peoples often have little choice but to change. Examples of such indirectly forced change abound in the history of Indian-white relations in the United States. Although the federal government made few direct attempts to force Indians to adopt American culture, it did drive many Indian groups from their lands. This obliged them to give up many aspects of their traditional ways of life. In order to survive, they had no choice but to adopt many of the white man's traits. When Indian children were required to go to American schools which taught the white man's values, the process was accelerated. Finally, a subordinate society may acculturate to a dominant society even in the absence of direct or indirect force. The dominated people may elect to adopt cultural elements from the dominant society in order to survive in their changed world. Or, perceiving that members of the dominant society enjoy more secure living conditions, the dominated people may identify with the domi-

[4] Ibid., pp. 338–39.
[5] George M. Foster, *Traditional Cultures and the Impact of Technological Change* (New York: Harper & Row, 1962), p. 26.
[6] Ibid., p. 27.

During colonial rule, many African societies were under pressure to adapt Western beliefs, values, and life-styles. In the Lagos cemetery in Nigeria the tomb of a black man bears witness to the process of acculturation. (Marc and Evelyne Bernheim, Woodfin Camp and Associates.)

nant culture in the hope that by doing so they may be able to share some of its benefits.

As in the case of diffusion, acculturation is a selective process. The dominated group does not adopt everything in the dominant culture. For example, the recipient group may be very receptive to technological innovations but more resistant to changes in religion or social organization. But there may be an additional reason why the culture of the donor society is not completely incorporated by the recipient society. Foster suggests that the donor society itself may simplify or screen its customs, so that the cultural elements it exhibits to the subordinate

society are neither all it has to offer nor exact replicas of its own cultural traits.

This screening process can be either formal or informal. Formal screening processes are those which are deliberately guided and planned by civil, military, or religious institutions. The Catholic Church of Spain, for example, intentionally reduced the Catholic ritual calendar before imposing it on Latin America. While it preserved the important ritual observances such as Epiphany, Candlemas, Lent, Holy Week, Christmas, Easter, and so forth, it eliminated most of the colorful, local celebrations which had grown up in Spain. Screening of cultural elements can also be informal. It can consist of "those unplanned mechanisms whereby personal habits of emigrants, their food preferences, superstitions, popular medicine, folklore, . . . beliefs, hopes and aspirations are selected and maintained in the new country."[7] Both of these processes combine to simplify the complexity and variety of the original customs.

REBELLION AND REVOLT

Perhaps the most drastic and rapid way a culture can change is as a result of violent replacement of the society's rulers. Historical records, as well as our daily newspapers, indicate that there have always been revolts and rebellions. Such events occur primarily in state societies, where there is usually a distinct ruling elite; and they take the form of struggles between rulers and ruled, between conquerors and conquered, or between representatives of an external colonial power and segments of the native society. However, not all peoples who are suppressed, conquered, or colonialized eventually revolt or rebel against established authority. Why this is so, and why rebellions and revolts are not always successful in bringing about culture change, are still open questions requiring further research.

A particularly interesting question is why rebellions and revolutions sometimes (perhaps

[7]Ibid., p. 12.

even usually) fail to measure up to the high hopes of the people who initiate them. When revolts succeed in replacing the ruling elite, the result is often the institution of a military dictatorship even more restrictive and repressive than the government which existed before. Spain after the Civil War of 1936 is one example of such a reversal. In the eyes of many, the new ruling establishment seemed merely to substitute one set of repressions for another, rather than to bring any real change to the nation. On the other hand, some revolutions have resulted in fairly drastic overhauls of societies.

The idea of rebellion and revolt has been one of the central myths and inspirations of many groups in the past and present. The colonial empire-building of countries such as England and France created a world-wide situation in which revolution became nearly inevitable. In numerous technologically underdeveloped lands, which have been exploited by more powerful countries for their natural resources and cheap labor, a deep resentment has developed against the foreign ruling classes. Where the ruling classes refuse to be responsive to these feelings, rebellion or revolution becomes the only alternative. In many areas it has emerged as a way of life.

One historian, who has closely examined four revolutions of the past—English, American, French, and Bolshevik—suggests some conditions that may give rise to rebellion and revolt:

1. Loss of prestige of established authority, often as a result of the failure of foreign policy, financial difficulties, dismissals of popular ministers, or alteration of popular policies. France in the eighteenth century lost three major international conflicts, with disastrous results for her diplomatic standing and internal finances.
2. Threat to recent economic improvement. In France, as in Russia, those sections of the population (professional classes and urban workers) whose economic fortunes had only shortly before taken an upward swing were "radicalized" by unexpected setbacks such as steeply rising food prices and unemployment.
3. Indecisiveness of government, as exemplified by lack of consistent policy, which gives the impression of being controlled by, rather than in control of, events. The frivolous arrogance of Louis XVI's regime and the bungling of George III's prime minister, Lord North, with respect to the problems of the American colonies, are examples of this.
4. Loss of support of the intellectual class. Such a loss deprived the prerevolutionary governments of France and Russia of any avowed philosophical support and led to their unpopularity with the literate public.[8]

Apart from resisting internal authority, as happened in the English, French, and Russian revolutions, many revolutions in modern times have been struggles against an externally imposed authority. Such resistance usually takes the form of independence movements which wage campaigns of armed defiance against colonial powers. A brief examination of the Franco-Algerian confrontation offers a typical example.

In Algeria, the conditions leading to the outbreak of the rebellion against France in 1954 resembled those in most colonial environments, namely, resentment of, and inability to alter, certain conditions. These conditions were: loss of land, subjection to alien laws inequitably administered, severe taxation, humiliation and degradation of the indigenous population, and the use of force to expropriate and punish. Two factors emerged which spurred the independence struggle. They were the rise of a reformist Islamic movement and the growth of a large body of disadvantaged workers, mostly former sharecroppers who had been freed from bondage to the land by the new French legal code and who were forced "to bear all the stigmata of a growing economic insecurity."[9]

The *Badissia*, as the Islamic movement was called, established numerous country-wide so-

---

[8] Crane Brinton, *Anatomy of a Revolution* (Englewood Cliffs, N.J.: Prentice-Hall, 1938).
[9] Eric R. Wolf, *Peasant Wars of the Twentieth Century* (New York: Harper & Row, 1969), p. 231.

cieties. Its members affirmed the slogan, "Arabic is my language, Algeria is my country, Islam is my religion."[10] The *Badissia* received much of its support in rural areas from the middle-class peasantry, small-town merchants, businessmen, and teachers. It was especially popular for its opposition to the orthodox Muslim insistence on traditional religious feasts (expenditures for which weighed heavily upon the peasantry) and for its demand that the French return all religious property.

Rural and urban workers had been forced by population growth and rural unemployment to seek jobs in Algerian cities and also in cities in France. There they suffered from insufficient earnings, insecurity, and labor mobility. "Proletarianization" brought with it political awareness; this was especially true of Algerians who had absorbed radical socialist ideas in major French cities. In fact, in addition to their dedication to reformist Islam, most of the leaders of the independence movement were of rural birth and had been educated in urban environments.

The resistance movement was accelerated by a series of events, generally typical of modern independence movements. These were France's failure to institute reforms; the collapse of French military resistance in 1940 and the impact of German propaganda; France's loss of Indochina; political instability in postwar France and the weakness of successive governments in their relations with the military and French settlers. These events, then, gradually led to revolt on the part of the colonized people.

The seven-and-one-half-year conflict that followed was not so much won by the Algerians as lost by the French. The very thoroughness, brutality, and ruthlessness of the French civil and military response to the guerrillas alienated large numbers of Algerians who were not previously committed to independence and hardened the resolve of those who were. Simultaneously, mounting costs, weariness, and disillusionment (accelerated by the loss of Indochina), and resentment at the refusal of the

settlers (*colons*) to compromise, all contributed to a change of attitude in France. In 1962, the French army seemed to be in a strong position—but the French people had had enough, and Algeria gained its independence.

Culture Change in the Modern World

Societies all over the world are changing rapidly. Many of the changes have been caused, directly or indirectly, by the dominance and expansion of Western societies. Thus, much of culture change in the modern world has been externally induced. (This is not to say that cultures are only changing now because of external pressures. It is that these externally induced changes have been the most frequently studied.) The study of culture change in the modern world may ultimately help us to understand not only processes of change in the present but also parallel processes of change in the past.

COMMERCIALIZATION

One of the principal changes resulting from the expansion of Western culture is the increasing dependence of much of the world upon commercial exchange. This includes the proliferation of buying and selling in markets, accompanied by the use of money as a medium of exchange. The borrowed custom of buying and selling may at first be supplementary to traditional means of distributing goods in a society. But as the new commercial customs take hold, the economic base of the receiving society alters. Inevitably, this alteration is accompanied by other changes, with broad social, political, and even psychological ramifications.

In examining contemporary patterns of change, however, we should bear in mind that the process of commercialization has occurred in many parts of the world in the past. The Chinese, Persians, Greeks, Romans, Arabs, Phoenicians, and Hindus were some of the early state societies that pushed commercial enter-

[10] Ibid., p. 228.

Here some Nepalese are fascinated by an electric razor, used by an American mountain climber. (George Holton, Rapho/Photo Researchers.)

prises in other areas. We are probably casting some light upon how and why earlier cultures changed when we consider several questions. How, and why, does a contemporary society change from a subsistence to a commercial economic base? What are the resultant cultural changes? Why do they occur?

Migratory Labor One way commercialization can occur is for members of a community to move to a place nearby that offers the possibility of working for wages. This has happened in the last thirty years to Tikopia, an island near the Solomon Islands in the South Pacific. In 1929, when Raymond Firth first made a study of

the island, its economy was still essentially noncommercial—simple, self-sufficient, and largely self-contained.[11] Some Western goods were known and available but, with the exception of iron and steel in limited quantities, were not sought after. Their possession and use were associated solely with Europeans. This isolated situation changed dramatically with World War II. During the war, military forces occupied neighboring islands, and people from Tikopia migrated to those islands to find employment.

[11] Descriptive material based on Raymond Firth, *Social Change in Tikopia* (New York: Macmillan, 1959), chaps. 5, 6, 7, and 9, passim.

In the period following the war, several large commercial interests extended their activities in the Solomons, thus creating a continued demand for labor. As a result, when Firth revisited Tikopia in 1952, the economic situation was significantly altered.

Over 100 Tikopians had left the island to work for varying periods of time. The migrants wanted to earn money because they aspired to standards of living previously regarded as appropriate only to Europeans. Already, living conditions on Tikopia were changing. Western-type cooking and water-carrying utensils, mosquito nets, kerosene storm lamps, and so forth, had come to be regarded as normal items in a Tikopia household.

The introduction of money into the economy of Tikopia not only altered the economic system but also affected a number of other areas of life. As compared with the situation in 1929, land was under more intensive cultivation in 1952, with manioc and sweet potatoes supplementing the principal taro crop. The pressures on the food supply resulting from improved living standards and an increased population seem to have weakened the ties of extended kinship. For example, the nuclear families comprising the extended family (the landholding and land-using unit in 1929) were not cooperating as much in 1952. In many cases, in fact, the land had actually been split up among the constituent nuclear families. In short, land rights had become more individualized. People were no longer as willing to share with members of their extended family, particularly with respect to the money and goods acquired by working in the Solomons.

Nonagricultural Commercial Production Commercialization can also occur when a simple, self-sufficient hunting or agricultural society comes more and more to depend upon trading for its livelihood. Such a change is exemplified by the Mundurucu of the Amazon Basin, who largely forsook general horticulture for commercial rubber production. A similar change may also be seen in the Montagnais of north-eastern Canada, who increasingly came to depend upon commercial fur trapping, rather than hunting, for subsistence. Murphy and Steward found that when modern goods from industrialized areas became available through trade, both of these societies devoted their energies to making specialized cash crops and other trade items. They did this to obtain more of the industrially made objects.[12] The primary socioeconomic change that occurred among the Mundurucu and Montagnais was a shift from a condition of cooperative labor and community autonomy to one of individualized economic activity and a dependence upon an external market.

Among the Mundurucu, for example, prior to the establishment of close trading links, the native population and the Europeans had been in contact for some eighty years without the Mundurucu's way of life being noticeably altered. The men did, indeed, relinquish their independently inspired warlike activities in order to perform as mercenaries for the whites, but they continued to maintain their horticultural economy. Some trading took place with whites, with the chief acting as agent for the village. Barter was the method of exchange. Traders first distributed their wares, ranging from cheap cottons to iron hatchets, trinkets, and so on; they returned about three months later to collect manioc, india rubber, and beans from the Indians. At this time (1860), however, rubber was only a secondary item of commerce.

The rapidly growing demands for rubber from the 1860s onward increased the importance of Mundurucu-trader relationships. Traders now openly began to appoint agents, called *capitoes*, whose job it was to encourage, in every way possible, greater rubber production. As encouragement, *capitoes* were given economic privileges and, hence, power, both of which began to undercut the position of the traditional chief. In addition, the process of rubber collection itself began to alter Mundurucu social pat-

---

[12] Robert F. Murphy and Julian H. Steward, "Tappers and Trappers: Parallel Process in Acculturation," *Economic Development and Cultural Change* 4 (July 1956): 353.

One way that commercialization can occur is when members of a simple agricultural community find cash-paying jobs in a nearby industry. These Bolivian women are employed at the Milluni Mine, 15,000 feet high in the Andes Mountains. (Courtesy of the United Nations.)

terns, moving people away from their jungle-based communities.

Wild rubber trees are found only along rivers, which are often a considerable distance from the jungle habitat of the Mundurucu, and can be exploited only during the dry season (late May to December). So the Mundurucu man who elected to gather rubber had to separate himself from his family for about half of the year. Furthermore, rubber collecting is a solitary activity. Each tapper must work his territory, consisting of about 150 trees, daily; and he must live close to his trees because the work lasts all day. Therefore, the tapper usually lives alone or in a very small group, except during the rainy season when he returns to his village.

At this stage in the commercialization process, the Mundurucu became increasingly dependent upon goods supplied by the trader. Firearms were useless without regular quantities of powder and lead; clothing required needles and thread for repairs. But these items could only be earned through increased rubber production which, in turn, led to greater dependency upon the outside world. Inevitably, the ability to work with traditional materials and the desire to maintain traditional crafts disappeared. Metal pots took the place of clay ones, and manufactured hammocks replaced homemade ones. Gradually the village agricultural cycle ceased to be adhered to by all in the community (because rubber production would suffer). In the same way, the authority of the traditional chiefs was weakened as that of the *capitoes* was enhanced.

The point of no return was reached when significant numbers of Mundurucu abandoned the villages for permanent settlements near their individual territories of trees. These new settlements lacked the unity, the sense of community, of former village life. Property was held by nuclear families and was carefully maintained in the interest of productivity. The revenue obtained from the rubber trade was used to support a raised standard of living.

Supplementary Cash Crops A third way commercialization occurs is when those cultivating the soil produce a surplus above their subsistence requirements, which is then sold for cash. In many cases, this cash income must be used to pay rent or taxes. Under such circumstances, commercialization may be said to be associated with the formation of a peasantry. Peasants are rural people who produce food for their own subsistence. But they must also contribute or sell their surpluses to others (in towns and cities) who do not produce their own food.

Peasants first appeared with the emergence of the state and urban civilizations about 5,000–6,000 years ago, and they have been associated with civilization ever since.[13] To say that peasants are associated with urban societies (state societies having cities) perhaps needs some qualification. The contemporary, highly industrialized urban society has little need of peasants. Their scale of production is small and their use of land "uneconomic." A highly industrialized society with a large population of nonfood producers requires a mechanized agriculture. As a result, the peasant has passed, or is

passing, out of all but the most peripheral existence in industrial countries. It is the preindustrial city, and the social organization it represents, which generates and maintains peasants. They cultivate land; they furnish the required quantity of food, rent, and profit upon which the remainder of society (particularly the people in the city) depends.

What changes does the development of a peasantry entail? In some respects there is little disturbance to the cultivator's (now peasant's) former way of life. The peasant still has to produce enough food to meet family needs, to replace that which has been consumed, to cover a few ceremonial obligations as, for example, the marriage of a child, village festivals, and funerals. But, in other respects the peasant's situation is radically altered. For in addition to the traditional obligations—indeed often in conflict with them—the peasant now has to produce extra crops to meet the requirements of a group of "outsiders," who are landlords or officials of the state. For instance, these "outsiders" expect to be paid rent or taxes (in produce or currency), and they are able to enforce their expectations because they control the military and the police. The change from near autonomy as a local community to a position of dependence upon a larger society brings the peasant face to face with a situation as novel as it is unpleasant. According to Eric Wolf, the peasant is now "forced to maintain a balance between [the local community's] . . . demands and the demands of the outsiders, and will be subject to tensions produced by this struggle to keep the balance. The outsider sees the peasant primarily as a source of labor and goods with which to increase his fund of power. But the peasant is at once both an economic agent and the head of a household. His holding is both an economic unit and a home."[14]

While no two peasant cultures are quite alike, there are similarities between them in form. Peasants the world over are faced with the problem of balancing the demands of an exter-

[13] Eric Wolf, *Peasants* (Englewood Cliffs, N.J.: Prentice-Hall, 1966), pp. 3–4.

[14] Ibid., p. 13.

nal world against those of an internal society. Their response generally involves increasing production, curtailing domestic consumption, or both. In response to its dealings with the outside urban center, a peasantry tends to develop adaptive social organizations. One such social response is the development of the village council or its equivalent. The Russian *mir* (common before the revolution of 1917), for example, held title to all village land and could reapportion acreages as family size changed. It was also the clearinghouse for local grievances and could unite the village in its dealings with the outside world.

The production of supplementary crops for cash has developed in some societies more or less voluntarily. The Arusha of East Africa are an example. The Arusha came into being as a cultural group in the 1800s when some refugees settled in an enclave in Masai territory. The Arusha were largely self-sufficient cultivators, although they carried on some barter trade with the Masai, whose economy was largely pastoral. However, during the period from 1940 to 1960, the Arusha began to feel the twin pressures of increasing population and decreasing availability of land for cultivation. As a result, they were obliged to abandon their "conservative attachment to traditional institutions and values, and to adopt new economic practices and attitudes." [15] The new attitudes and practices meant abandoning self-sufficient production in favor of the cultivation of cash crops such as coffee and wheat. The income from the cultivation could be utilized to purchase needed goods.

Trade by barter is therefore being replaced among the Arusha with market exchange involving currency. Markets are being established all over the country, not just along the border with the Masai. The possession of money is coming to be regarded as equivalent to wealth. Indeed, many Arusha are clearly prepared to spend money to achieve a higher standard of living.

They are becoming more profit and cash oriented, investing their incomes in goods and services formerly considered unnecessary. The Arusha, then, may have been obliged by circumstances to sell crops for cash; but, unlike the peasants, they were not externally forced by the state or landlords to engage in such market transactions.

Introduction of Commercial and Industrial Agriculture Another way in which commercialization can come about is through the introduction of commercial agriculture. In commercial agriculture, *all* of the cultivated commodities are produced for sale rather than for personal consumption. Along with this change, the system of agriculture may be "industrialized." In other words, some of the production processes, such as plowing, weeding, irrigation, and harvesting, are done by machine. Commercial agriculture is, in fact, often as mechanized as any manufacturing industry. Land is worked for the maximum return it will yield, and labor is hired and fired with impersonality equal to that which occurs in other industries.

E. J. Hobsbawm has noted some of the developments accompanying the introduction of commercial agriculture as it occurred in eighteenth-century England and in continental Europe somewhat later. [16] The close, near-familial relationship between farmer and farm laborer disappeared, as did the once personal connection between landlord and tenant. Land was regarded as a source of profit rather than a way of life. Fields were merged into single units and enclosed, and local grazing and similar privileges were reduced. Labor was hired at market rates and paid increasingly in wages. Eventually, machines began to replace farm laborers, as the emphasis on large-scale production for a mass market increased.

In general, the introduction of commercial agriculture brings several important social consequences. Gradually, a class polarization develops. Farmers and landlords become increas-

[15] P. H. Gulliver, "The Arusha: Economic and Social Change," in *Markets in Africa*, ed. Paul Bohannan and George Dalton (New York: Doubleday, 1965), p. 269.

[16] E. J. Hobsbawm, *Age of Revolution* (New York: Praeger, 1970).

ingly separated from laborers and tenants, just as in the town the employer becomes socially separated from his employee. Gradually, too, manufactured items of all sorts are introduced into rural areas. Laborers migrate to urban centers in search of employment, often meeting even less sympathetic conditions there than exist in the country.

The changeover to commercial agriculture may result in an improved standard of living in the short and long run. But sometimes the switch is followed by a decline in the standard of living if the market price for the commercial crop declines. For example, when the farmer-herders of the arid *sertão* region of northeastern Brazil switched after 1940 to producing sisal (a plant whose fibers can be made into twine and rope), it seemed like a move that could provide a more secure living in their arid environment. But when the world price for sisal dropped, and the wages of sisal workers declined, it seems that many workers were forced to curtail the caloric intakes of their children. The poorer people seem to have been obliged to save their now more limited food supplies for the money-earners, at the expense of the children.[17]

RELIGIOUS CHANGE

The growing influence of Western societies has also led to religious change in many parts of the world. In many cases, the change has been brought about intentionally through the efforts of missionaries. Frequently, missionaries have been among the first Westerners to travel to interior regions and out-of-the-way places. Of course, they have not met with equal success in all parts of the world. In some places, large portions of the native population have converted to the new religion with great zeal. In others, missionaries have been ignored, forced to flee, or even killed. We do not as yet fully understand why missionaries have been successful in some societies and not in others. Yet in many parts of the world, Western missionary activity has been a potent force for all kinds of cultural, and particularly religious, change.

But aside from the direct effects of missionary work, contact with Westerners has probably produced religious change in more indirect ways. In some native societies, contact with Westerners has led to a breakdown of social structure and the growth of feelings of helplessness and spiritual demoralization. Revitalization movements have arisen as apparent attempts to restore the societies to their former confidence and prosperity. Such revitalization movements have usually been started by native prophets who may have visions informing them of new ways of life. The success of a prophet in attracting a following, however, seems to be directly attributable to the amount of demoralization or deprivation brought about through Western contact.

As an example of religious conversion brought about by direct contact with missionaries, we shall examine the process of conversion on the island of Tikopia. As an example of a revitalization movement, we shall examine the case of the Seneca Indians of New York State. They managed, with the help of a Christian-like religion taught by a native prophet named Handsome Lake, to restore some of the tribal morale which had been lost as a result of contact with the whites.

Christianity on Tikopia   Tikopia was one of the last Polynesian societies to retain its traditional religious system into the first decades of the twentieth century. An Anglican mission was first established on the island in 1911, with the permanent residence of a deacon and the founding of two schools for about 200 pupils. By 1929, approximately half the population had converted, and in the early 1960s almost all of Tikopia gave at least nominal allegiance to Christianity.[18]

[17] Daniel R. Gross and Barbara A. Underwood, "Technological Change and Caloric Costs: Sisal Agriculture in Northeastern Brazil," *American Anthropologist* 73 (1971): 725–40.

[18] Discussion based on Raymond Firth, *Rank and Religion in Tikopia* (Boston: Beacon Press, 1970).

The dominance and expansion of Western societies has led to religious change in many parts of the world. On the door of a Catholic church in Nigeria, a Yoruba artist has used native figures to depict biblical scenes. (Marc and Evelyne Bernheim, Woodfin Camp and Associates.)

Traditional Tikopian belief was pantheistic, with a great number of gods and spirits of various ranks inhabiting the sky, the water, and the land. One god in particular—the original creator and shaper of the culture—was given a place of special importance, but he was in no way comparable to the all-powerful God of Christianity. Unlike Christianity, Tikopian religion made no claim to universality. The Tikopian gods did not rule over all creation, only over Tikopia. It was thought that if one left Tikopia, one left one's gods behind.

The people of Tikopia interacted with their gods and spirits primarily through religious leaders who were also the heads of descent groups. Clan chiefs presided over rituals centering around the everyday aspects of island life, such as house construction, fishing, planting, and harvesting. The chief was expected to intercede with the gods on the people's behalf, to persuade them to bring happiness and prosperity to the group. Indeed, when conditions were good it was assumed that the chief was doing his job well. Conversely, when disaster struck, the prestige of the chief often fell in proportion. Why did the Tikopia convert to Christianity? Firth has suggested a number of contributing factors.

First, the mission offered the people the prospect of acquiring new tools and consumer goods. Although conversion by itself did not provide such benefits, attachment to the mission was believed to make them more attainable. Later, it became apparent that education, particularly in reading and writing English, was helpful in getting ahead in the outside world. Then, mission schooling became valued and provided a further incentive for adopting Christianity.

Second, conversion may have been facilitated by the ability of chiefs, as religious and political leaders, to bring over their entire kin groups to Christianity. Should a chief decide to transfer his allegiance to Christianity, the members of his kin group usually followed him, since social etiquette required that they do so. Such a situation actually did develop in 1923 when Tafua, chief of the Faea district of Tikopia, converted to the new religion. He brought with him his entire group—which amounted to nearly half the population of the island. However, the ability of the chiefs to influence their kin groups was both an asset and a hindrance, since some chiefs steadfastly resisted conversion.

A final blow to traditional Tikopian religion appeared to come in 1955, when a severe epidemic killed at least 200 people in a population of about 1,700. According to Firth, "the epidemic was largely interpreted as a sign of divine discrimination," since three of the outstanding non-Christian religious leaders died.[19] Subsequently, the remaining non-Christian chiefs voluntarily converted to Christianity and so did their followers. By 1966 all of Tikopia, with the exception of one rebellious old woman, had converted to the new faith.

Although many Tikopians feel that their conversion to Christianity has been a unifying, revitalizing force, the changeover from one religion to another has not been without problems. Christian missionaries on Tikopia have discouraged and, in fact, have succeeded in eliminating the traditional Tikopia population control devices of abortion, infanticide, and male celibacy. It is very possible that the absence of these controls will continue to intensify population pressure. The island, with its limited capacity to support life, can ill afford this. Firth sums up the situation which Tikopian society must now face.

In the history of Tikopia complete conversion of the people to Christianity was formerly regarded as a solution to their problems; it is now coming to be realized that the adoption and practice of Christianity itself represents another set of problems. As the Tikopia themselves are beginning to see, to be Christian Polynesians in the modern technologically and industrially dominated world, even in the Solomon Islands, poses as many questions as it supplies answers.[20]

[19]Ibid., p. 387.
[20]Ibid., p. 418.

The Seneca and the Religion of Handsome Lake The Seneca reservation of the Iroquois on the Allegheny River in New York State was a place of "poverty and humiliation" by 1799.[21] Demoralized by whiskey and dispossessed from their traditional lands, unable to compete with white technology because of illiteracy and lack of training, the Seneca were at an impasse. In this setting, Handsome Lake, the fifty-year-old brother of a chief, had the first of a number of visions. In them, he met with emissaries of the Creator who showed him heaven and hell and commissioned him to revitalize Seneca religion and society. This he set out to do for the next decade-and-a-half. He used as his principal text the *Gaiwiio*, or "good word," a gospel which contains statements about the nature of religion and eternity and a code of conduct for the righteous. The *Gaiwiio* is interesting both for the influence of Quaker Christianity it clearly reveals[22] and for the way the new material has been merged with traditional Iroquois religious concepts.

The first part of the "good word" has three main themes, one of which is the concept of an apocalypse. Handsome Lake offered many signs by which the faithful could recognize impending, cosmic doom. Great drops of fire would rain from the skies and a veil would be cast over the earth. False prophets would appear, witch women would openly cast spells, and poisonous creatures from the underworld would seize and kill those who had rejected the *Gaiwiio*. Second, the *Gaiwiio* emphasized sin. The great sins were disbelief in the "good way," drunkenness, witchcraft, and abortion. Sins had to be confessed and repented. Finally, the *Gaiwiio* offered salvation. Salvation could be won by following a code of conduct, attending certain important traditional rites, and performing public confession.

The second part of the *Gaiwiio* sets out the code of conduct. This code seems to orient the

Indians toward advantageous white practices without separating them from their culture. The code has five main sections:

1. Temperance. All Seneca leaders were fully aware of the social disorders arising out of abuse of liquor. Handsome Lake went to great lengths to illustrate and explain the harmfulness of alcohol.
2. Peace and social unity. Seneca leaders were to cease their futile bickering, and all Indians were to be united in their approach to whites.
3. Preservation of tribal lands. Handsome Lake, fearing the "piecemeal" alienation of Seneca lands, was far ahead of his Seneca contemporaries in demanding a halt in land sales to the whites.
4. Pro-acculturation. Though individual property and trading for profit were prohibited, the acquisition of literacy in English was encouraged so that Indians would be able to read and understand treaties written by the whites and avoid being cheated.
5. Domestic morality. Sons were to obey their fathers, mothers should avoid interfering with daughters' marriages, husbands and wives should respect the sanctity of their marriage vows.

Handsome Lake's teaching seems to have led to a renaissance among the Seneca. Temperance was widely accepted, as were white schooling and farming methods. By 1801, corn yields had increased tenfold, new crops had been introduced (oats, potatoes, flax), and public health and hygiene had improved considerably. Handsome Lake himself acquired great power among his people. He spent the remainder of his life fulfilling administration duties, acting as a representative of the Iroquois in Washington, and preaching his gospel to neighboring tribes. By the time of Handsome Lake's death in 1815, the Seneca had clearly undergone a dramatic rebirth, attributable at least in part to the new religion. Later in the century, some of Handsome Lake's disciples founded a church in his name which, despite occasional setbacks and political disputes, survives to this day.

[21] Anthony F. C. Wallace, *The Death and Rebirth of the Seneca* (New York: Alfred A. Knopf, 1970), p. 239.
[22] The Quakers, long-time neighbors and trusted advisers of the Seneca, were at pains not to interfere with Seneca religion, principles, and attitudes.

Unfortunately, not all native peoples have made the transition to Christianity as painlessly as the Tikopia, nor succeeded in revitalizing their culture as well as the Seneca. In fact, in most cases the record is a good deal more dismal. All too frequently missionary activity tends to destroy a society's culture and self-respect. It offers nothing in return but an alien, repressive system of values which is ill adapted to the people's real needs and aspirations. Phillip Mason, a critic of white evangelists in Africa, points out some of the psychological damage inflicted by missionary activity.[23] The missionaries repeatedly stressed sin and guilt; they used the color black to represent evil and the color white to signify good; and they showed hostility toward pagan culture. Most damaging of all was the missionaries' promise that the black person, provided he or she adopted the white person's ways, would gain access both to the white person's heaven and to white society. But no matter how diligently the blacks attempted to follow missionary precepts or climb the white socioeconomic ladder, they were soon blocked from entry into white homes, clubs, and even churches and seminaries.

Commercialization and religious change are by no means the only types of changes brought about by Western expansion. Political changes have come about directly through the imposition of a foreign system of government and administration, and indirectly through the changing economic structure of a society. Western influence has brought about changes in dress, music, art, and attitudes throughout the world. Of course, many nations (not just Western ones) have extended their influence in other parts of the globe. Hopefully, future research on the on-going processes of culture change will increase our understanding of how and why these changes are occurring.

[23]Phillip Mason, *Prospero's Magic* (London: Oxford University Press, 1962).

Summary

1. Culture is ever changing. Because culture consists of learned patterns of behavior and belief, cultural traits can be unlearned and learned anew as human needs change.

2. Discoveries and inventions may stimulate culture change. A discovery may be defined as any addition to knowledge, while an invention involves a practical application of knowledge. Some inventions are deliberate attempts to produce something new. Other inventions are "unconscious." They are probably the result of dozens of tiny, perhaps accidental, initiatives over a period of many years by persons who are unaware of the part they are playing in bringing a single invention to completion.

3. The process by which cultural elements are borrowed from another society, and incorporated into the culture of the recipient group is called diffusion. Several patterns of diffusion may be identified: diffusion by direct contact, in which elements of culture are first taken up by neighboring societies and then gradually spread farther and farther afield; diffusion by intermediate contact, in which third parties, frequently traders, carry a cultural trait from the society originating it to another group receiving it; and stimulus diffusion, in which knowledge of a trait belonging to another culture stimulates the invention or development of a local equivalent.

4. Not all cultural traits are as readily borrowed as others. Rather, diffusion is a selective process. A society accepting a foreign cultural trait is likely to adapt it in a way that effectively harmonizes the new trait with the society's own cultural traditions.

5. When a group or society is in contact with a more powerful society, the weaker group is often obliged to acquire cultural elements from the dominant group. This process of extensive borrowing in the context of

superordinate-subordinate relations between societies is usually called acculturation. In contrast to diffusion, acculturation comes about as a result of some sort of external pressure which can take various forms.

6. Perhaps the most drastic and rapid way a culture can change is as a result of violent replacement of the society's rulers. Revolts and rebellions occur primarily in state societies, where there is usually a distinct ruling elite. However, not all peoples who are suppressed, conquered, or colonialized eventually revolt or rebel against established authority.

7. Many of the cultural changes observed in the modern world have been generated, directly or indirectly, by the dominance and expansion of Western societies. One of the principal changes resulting from the expansion of Western culture is the increasing dependence of much of the world upon commercial exchange—that is, the proliferation of buying and selling in markets, accompanied by the use of money as a medium of exchange. The borrowed custom of buying and selling may at first be supplementary to traditional means of distributing goods; but as the new commercial customs take hold, the economic base of the receiving society alters. Inevitably, this alteration is accompanied by other changes, with broad social, political, and even psychological ramifications.

8. One way commercialization can occur is for members of a community to become migratory workers, traveling to a place nearby that offers the possibility of working for wages. Commercialization can also occur when a simple, self-sufficient hunting or agricultural society comes more and more to depend upon trading for its livelihood. A third way commercialization occurs is when those cultivating the soil produce a surplus over and above their subsistence requirements, which is then sold for cash. In many instances, this cash income must be used to pay rent or taxes; and under such circumstances, commercialization may be said to be associated with the formation of a peasantry. A fourth way in which commercialization can come about is through the introduction of commercial agriculture, in which *all* of the cultivated commodities are produced for sale rather than for personal consumption. Along with this change, the system of agriculture may be "industrialized," with some of the production processes being done by machine.

9. The growing influence of Western societies has also led to religious change in many parts of the world. In many societies, such change has been brought about intentionally through the efforts of missionaries. In some societies, where contact with Westerners has produced a breakdown of social structure, with feelings of helplessness and spiritual demoralization, revitalization movements have arisen as apparent attempts to restore the society to its former confidence and prosperity.

Suggested Readings

Geertz, C. *Peddlers and Princes.* Chicago: University of Chicago Press, 1963.
    An analysis of social and economic change in two Indonesian towns, one Balinese, the other Javanese, based upon the author's fieldwork. He sees Indonesian society as existing in a transitional stage, having lost many of its traditional customs but not yet fully developed into an industrial society.

Hunter, M. *Reaction to Conquest.* 2d ed. New York: Oxford University Press for the International African Institute, 1961.
    A study of culture change in an African society. The author describes the process in both urban areas and traditional tribal territories.

Little, K. *West African Urbanization.* New York:

Cambridge University Press, 1965.

This study outlines social problems in an African colony prior to independence. Little constructs a model for explaining certain aspects of social change. His study of voluntary associations suggests that such organizations appear in times of transition and upheaval of traditional social networks, binding together otherwise heterogeneous groups.

Spicer, E. H., ed. *Perspectives in American Indian Culture Change.* Chicago: University of Chicago Press, 1961.

A collection of case studies of various American Indian groups, describing and analyzing cultural changes in each group since the arrival of Europeans.

Tax, S., et al. *Heritage of Conquest: The Ethnology of America.* 2d ed. New York: Cooper Square Publishers, 1968.

Concentrating mainly on rural peasants of Mexico and Central America, this treatment of acculturation in the Americas includes an historical summary of the process as it has been going on for the past 400 years, from the arrival of the Spaniards in the sixteenth century to the present day.

Wallerstein, I., ed. *Social Change: The Colonial Situation.* New York: John Wiley and Sons, 1966.

A comprehensive selection of essays with the colony as the basic unit of study. Most of the articles deal with Africa, India, or Indonesia, although other regions are represented. The forty-four articles deal with various topics, such as sociocultural consequences of labor migration, the role of traditional authorities in the past and present, the rise of ethnic associations and nationalist movements, the process of Westernization, and cultural revivals by the native populations.

Applied
Anthropology

23

All cultures are continually changing. Some of these changes happen quickly, others more slowly. Cultural changes can be accidental—as when entire groups of people are uprooted because of natural disasters, are forced to move, and therefore must alter many of their customs. But cultural changes can also be planned. For example, the technical and health aid programs administered by such agencies as UNESCO or the Peace Corps often involve a deliberate attempt to change a culture in some particular way. Anthropologists are sometimes involved in the planning or the carrying out of such directed changes. The branch of anthropology that concerns itself with planned cultural change, when it is presumably an application of anthropological knowledge, is called *applied anthropology.*

As an academic discipline, cultural anthropology is primarily concerned with recording and analyzing the cultures of other peoples. Anthropologists might enter the field to live with, and write about, the culture of a particular society, but they would try to interfere in that culture as little as possible. Under no circumstances would they consciously attempt to change it. On the other hand, in applied anthropology, the purpose of fieldwork is to introduce a particular change into a society's way of life—generally a new kind of diet, a sanitation system, a health care program, or an agricultural process. Applied anthropology, therefore, is to anthropology what engineering is to physical science. Just as engineering depends for its effectiveness upon physical scientists' understanding of the laws of nature, so applied anthropology depends for its effectiveness upon anthropologists' understanding of the laws of cultural variation and change.

The Acceptance of Applied Anthropology

At the present time, relatively few anthropologists are doing applied work. Perhaps one reason is that the international and governmental agencies which plan cultural changes and have the money to implement them have not often felt the need to consult or employ anthropologists. Traditionally, anthropologists and administrators have not worked well together. Generally, the administrators feel that the anthropologists are working too slowly, submit reports which are too technical to be useful, and are too sympathetic to the problems of the people under study. Similarly, the anthropologists tend to see administrators as unconcerned bureaucrats, who want to implement change too quickly, expect unreasonable results, and are insensitive to the problems of the people to be affected.[1] Many anthropologists interested in applied anthropology think that some of the difficulties and confusion so often encountered by persons attempting to introduce change into a culture different from their own—whether these "agents of change" are religious missionaries, private businessmen, or government officials—would be greatly reduced through the employment of competent anthropologists familiar with the area being affected.

Another reason for the limited amount of applied anthropological work under way today is the reluctance of many anthropologists to participate in planned change. Some anthropologists would say that anthropological knowledge about particular areas and peoples is not yet sufficient to justify its application. In addition, many anthropologists refuse to engage in applied work because they feel it is not right for them or for any other well-intentioned individuals to interfere in the lives of other people. Realistically, of course, everyone's life is interfered with to some extent. The typical American is "interfered with" by a lengthy succession of people—parents, teachers, government officials, and so on—all of whom are seeking to introduce some form of change into his or her life. But according to some anthropologists, it is quite a different matter to interfere in the lives of a group of people whose culture differs from one's own and on whom the effects of such interference can only be guessed.

THE ETHICS OF APPLIED ANTHROPOLOGY

The ethics of applied anthropology is a complicated and much debated issue. The question of ethics seldom arises in normal anthropological fieldwork, since there is generally no reason to suspect that merely living with people, and observing their life-style, will change or harm them in any significant way. But specifically planning and implementing change introduces the ethical question: Will the change benefit the target population? In the early days of the discipline, anthropologists adhered to an unwritten, informally established ethical code. But soon the field expanded, technology advanced, and the negative, as well as the positive, potential of fieldwork became apparent. Therefore, in May 1946, the Society for Applied Anthropology set up a committee on ethics to draw up a specific code by which professional applied anthropologists could work. After many meetings and revisions, the final version of the code was adopted by the Society in 1948.

This code of ethics serves essentially the same purpose for applied anthropologists as the Hippocratic oath does for doctors or as oaths of office do for public officials. That is, it is to be used as a guide, in addition to the anthropologists' own personal codes of ethics, so that the scientists will take appropriate precautions in their work. This is extremely important, because "it is clear that an applied anthropologist could create a great deal of harm if his investigative efforts . . . endangered the people among whom he worked."[2] The code specifies the responsibilities of applied anthropologists toward various people affected by their work. It stresses in particular that the anthropologists

---

[1] George M. Foster, *Applied Anthropology* (Boston: Little, Brown, 1969), p. 155.

[2] "Ethics in Applied Anthropology," *Human Organization* 10, no. 2 (Summer 1951): 4.

must always keep the names of their informants secret. In some societies, the use of informants' real names, particularly in a publication, can cause them real harm. The code further states that applied anthropologists must agree to conduct their investigations scientifically and to inform their scientific colleagues of their findings. In addition, they are pledged to uphold the dignity and general well-being of the people among whom they work and not to intentionally jeopardize those people's safety. Finally, individual anthropologists "must take responsibility for the effects of their recommendations, never maintaining that they are merely technicians unconcerned with the ends toward which their applied scientific skills are directed."[3] Thus, applied anthropologists are held directly responsible for everything they do and are considered indirectly responsible for the way in which their employers eventually use their findings.

A major ethical consideration is whether or not a project of planned change will actually benefit the target population. This is a problem which bureaucratic agencies sometimes ignore, but it is of great concern to anthropologists. After all, anthropologists are pledged to the principle of cultural relativity and the respect for other cultures which that principle fosters. Often, governmental agencies wish to employ anthropologists only to help "sell" the intended changes to the target population. Furthermore, when they work with government agencies, the anthropologists may be hampered in their work, or in the final reports of their results, by political sensitivities. Obviously, no governmental agency is going to be happy to pay a scientist for research which yields results that are critical of that agency.

On the other hand, some anthropologists believe that applied anthropology is justified—and even required—by the problems of the modern world. They would argue that, although they may not have sufficient information yet, still they know more about cultural variation

A Colombian government-sponsored cooking class tries to teach the women of the Cauca region how to change their eating habits and hygiene. (Courtesy of the United Nations.)

and culture change than those not trained in anthropology. The problems of the modern world, they contend, demand as much expert attention as possible. Clearly, even if an applied anthropologist should refuse to participate in a particular project, the agency or company in charge of the project would undoubtedly go ahead with it anyway, using another, and considerably less "expert," consultant.

There is the further argument, advanced by proponents of applied anthropology, that it is unethical *not* to participate in, or comment on, programs of directed culture change, for the programs exist and are part of the human condition studied by anthropologists. Particularly in areas such as preventive medicine, it is difficult ethically to justify *not* providing vaccine against smallpox or other such diseases to societies which are prone to those diseases and do not have adequate medical treatment.

THE DEVELOPMENT OF APPLIED ANTHROPOLOGY

According to George Foster, "applied anthropology enjoys less prestige than does theoretically oriented anthropology."[4] The two most

[3] Ibid.

[4] Foster, *Applied Anthropology*, p. ix.

important reasons Foster gives for the lower status currently enjoyed by applied anthropology involve the questions of cultural relativity and of individual freedom.[5] First, many anthropologists feel that it is extremely important in all aspects of anthropology to retain one's sense of cultural relativity—to avoid making value judgments about another people's culture and acting in terms of such judgments. However, when an anthropologist participates in an applied program, obviously it is nearly impossible to follow this pronouncement completely. Second, anthropologists are likely to value highly their freedom as individual scientific researchers. As university professors, anthropologists have a kind of academic, personal, and professional freedom that is generally missing in applied work, where they must be careful always to act in accordance with the wishes and demands of whatever agency employs them. The debate over when, or if, anthropologists should participate in planned social change will undoubtedly continue for many years.

The early history of the use of applied anthropology also has something to do with its present status. Applied anthropology was first used by officials from some of the larger countries of Europe in their colonial administrations. Such officials were generally not anthropologists, but their work required them to gain at least a basic understanding of the people whose lives they had come to administer. Unfortunately, this knowledge, once gained, was so frequently used to undermine the needs and wishes of the native people that applied anthropology began its career with a questionable reputation.

Today, however, new techniques are often introduced at the request of the host country—for example, when a nation requests aid in industrialization or birth control. Of course, such requests almost always come from the country's ruling elite, who may or may not be as exploitative as their former colonial masters. As a result, applied anthropologists are often compelled to deal with resistance or antagonism in the segment of the population to which the program of directed change is addressed. "When a change that is to be applied to the common man, usually a village peasant, has been agreed upon by a member of the ruling elite and the overseas specialist, the problem is how to convince this common man to accept the new ideas without using force."[6]

Applied anthropologists in the United States were called upon for advice during the second World War, when perplexed American military men wanted to understand why their Japanese enemies refused to behave like "normal" people. One of the practices that most distressed American military leaders was the tendency of Japanese soldiers captured in battle to try to kill themselves, rather than allow themselves to be taken prisoner by the Americans. Certainly, American prisoners of war did not behave in this manner. Eventually, to help them understand the Japanese code of honor, the military hired a number of anthropologists as consultants to the Foreign Morale Analysis Division of the War Office's Information Department. After working with the anthropologists, the American military men learned that a major reason for the "strange" behavior of the Japanese prisoners was the Japanese belief that to surrender in a wartime situation, even to greatly superior odds, or to be taken prisoner when injured and unconscious and therefore unable to avoid capture, was a grave disgrace. The Japanese further believed that the American soldiers killed all prisoners. Thus, it is hardly surprising that so many captured Japanese soldiers preferred honorable death by their own hands. Once the Americans learned what the Japanese thought, they made efforts to explain to them that they would not be executed if captured, with the result that far more Japanese surrendered. Some prisoners even gave military information to the Americans—not to act

---

[5] Ibid., pp. 131–37.

[6] Conrad M. Arensberg and Arthur H. Niehoff, *Introducing Social Change: A Manual for Americans Overseas* (Chicago: Aldine, 1964), p. 66.

In a medical clinic in the Congo in 1963, thousands of people were vaccinated against smallpox. Even such clearly humanitarian programs, however, may at times have unforeseen, negative consequences in the long run. (Courtesy of the United Nations.)

against their own country, but rather to try and establish new lives for themselves, since the disgrace of being captured prevented them from resuming their former lives.

Since World War II, applied anthropologists have concentrated upon more traditional types of projects—introducing health care and housing improvements, teaching Peace Corps trainees about the areas they are to work in, and so forth. But even these apparently simple projects are far more complex than they seem.

Determining the Overall Benefits of Planned Change

The first problem that applied anthropology faces in approaching a new project is how to decide whether or not some proposed change would be beneficial to the target population.

And, surprisingly, this decision is not always easy to make. In certain cases, such as where improved medical care is involved, the benefits offered to the target group would seem to be unquestioned. We all feel sure that health is better than illness, but even this may not always be true. Consider a public health innovation such as inoculation against disease. Although it would undoubtedly have a beneficial effect upon the survival rate of a population, a reduction in the mortality rate might have unforeseen consequences that would, in turn, produce new problems. Once the inoculation program were begun, the number of children surviving would probably increase. But if the rate of food production could not be proportionately increased, given the level of technology, capital, and land resources possessed by the target population, then the death rate, this time from starvation, might rise to its previous level and perhaps even exceed it. In such a case, the inoculation program would merely be changing the cause of death, at least in the long run. The point of this example is that, even if a program of planned change has beneficial consequences in the short run, a great deal of thought and investigation has to be given to its effects over a long period of time. One of the most important, and most difficult, problems for applied anthropology is the need to anticipate all the effects that are likely to result from the single cultural change that is proposed.

A population's health can actually be harmed when foreign health care is introduced into a culture without provision for other related customs. An example of this can be seen in a program that was attempted in a West African rural community. In that community, the women traditionally continued to work in the fields during pregnancy. Then, in an attempt to improve prenatal care, pregnant women were kept from their work. However, because the people who effected this change neglected to encourage the West African women to adopt a substitute program of proper physical activity, the women actually suffered *increased* chances of ill health and infant mortality.[7]

Where the long-range consequences of a proposed cultural change are obviously detrimental, anthropologists may determine that the change is not worth the cost to the community, even if the people desire it. Accordingly, the anthropologists would advise that the program be dropped. In the Gezira part of the Sudan, for example, agricultural production had always been extremely low because of insufficient water. An extensive program of crop irrigation was proposed to increase the crop yield. The program was started and the crops did improve greatly. However, the increased quantities of water near areas where the natives lived, and the local population's greater contact with this water, created a major health hazard. A parasitic disease called *bilharziasis*, which is seldom fatal but which greatly weakens its victims, occurred only occasionally in the Sudan before the irrigation canals were built. Afterward, about 80 percent of the local children were found to have the disease. The larger amounts of water in the area had provided greater breeding opportunities for the organism that carries bilharziasis. Also, since a higher proportion of the population worked near this water, the disease's toll increased. It was decided that until the cycle of the disease could be broken—by eliminating the snail which was the carrier of the parasite—the crop irrigation program would have to be halted.[8]

To determine the overall benefits of planned changes, we must also understand the basic aspects of a society's culture which will probably be influenced by such programs. Cities are likely to show results first, since the upper classes of a target population are frequently the first to adopt new techniques and ideas. Changes then appear in family organization, as the economic basis of earning a livelihood is altered by the introduction of new technical processes. Generally, in places where the emphasis has traditionally been on the extended family, kin-group ties tend to weaken. As cash crops are introduced into a technologically simple society, and as money becomes more important in the people's lives, traditional rural cooperative work patterns are also altered. For example, in Haiti and in parts of West Africa, fieldwork was traditionally performed by large numbers of people, who were entertained as they worked by groups of singers and drummers. The music both helped increase the productivity and provided an extremely important social outlet. However, once money was introduced into the economic system, the landowners had to pay for each person out in the fields and they were unwilling to pay the musicians. Thus, a long-standing work tradition was ended.

Dietary deterioration is yet another unfortunate, but common, side effect of planned cultural change. Once people have been convinced

---

[7] Ibid., pp. 80–81.

[8] Foster, *Applied Anthropology*, pp. 79–80.

that certain foreign foodstuffs have greater nutritional value, prestige, or flavor than local products and hence are more desirable, they may often find that they cannot afford ample quantities of the new foods. Also, rapid culture change is often accompanied by an increase in village factionalism and divisiveness. In many developing countries, rural residents are quick to resent the acquisition by one of their neighbors of a new latrine or an article of clothing, because their traditional rules of sharing and reciprocity lead them to think that people cannot prosper without taking something away from their neighbors.[9]

The Difficulties of Instituting Planned Change

Before an attempt can be made at cultural innovation, the innovators must determine whether or not the target population is aware of the benefits of the proposed change. In many situations where significant health problems exist, target populations are not always aware of these problems. Their lack of awareness can become a major barrier to solving the problems. For example, health workers have often had difficulty convincing scientifically unsophisticated people that they were becoming ill because something was wrong with their water supply. Many people do not understand the nature of disease and do not believe it can be transmitted through an agent such as water. At other times, the target population is perfectly well aware of the problem. A case in point is that of certain Taiwanese women who were introduced to family planning methods in the 1960s. The Taiwanese women knew they were having more children than they wanted or could easily afford, and they wanted to control their birth rate. They offered no resistance—they merely had to be given the proper devices and instructions and the birth

rate fell quite quickly to a more desirable, and more manageable, level.[10]

RESISTANCE TO PLANNED CHANGE AMONG THE TARGET POPULATION

Even when a target population is aware of the possible benefits of a proposed change, it is not always a simple task to get the local people to accept an innovation or to change their behavior. And an innovation rejected by the target population is useless. Because of the uncertainty of acceptance or rejection, the future success or failure of a project of planned change is often difficult to ascertain.

Directed culture change goals are dual, almost always involving changes both in the physical environment and in the behavior of people. . . . Environmental modification, which means design and construction, is often looked upon as the heart of national development and modernization, and the achievement of physical goals symbolizes the successful completion of each project. Yet if the appropriate changes in behavior do not accompany environmental modification, a project is of dubious merit.[11]

In other words, where the aim of a project is to install some kind of new facilities, the mere physical installation of those facilities is not sufficient to call the project successful. To be completely successful, those new facilities must actually be used by the people for whom they were intended. Similarly, when a project aims to introduce an agricultural innovation such as a higher-yield crop, after local residents have become acquainted with the new crop, they must also continue to grow it if the project is to be considered a success. For example, after a few years of growing an improved breed of hybrid corn introduced by an agricultural extension agent, a group of Spanish-American farmers in Arizona suddenly rejected it, returning to the

[9]George M. Foster, *Traditional Cultures and the Impact of Technological Change* (New York: Harper & Row, 1962), pp. 29–43.

[10]Arthur H. Niehoff, *A Casebook of Social Change* (Chicago: Aldine, 1966), pp. 255–67.
[11]Foster, *Applied Anthropology*, p. 5.

An agricultural advisor is about to demonstrate to some farmers in southern India how to use an insecticide sprayer for rice fields. (Marc and Evelyne Bernheim, Woodfin Camp and Associates.)

old variety. After questioning the farmers, the innovator found that the project had ultimately failed because the farmers' wives felt the new corn was too hard to grind into tortillas and because they preferred the taste of the older type of corn.[12]

A society's resistance to planned cultural change is often based upon factors that the planners seldom anticipate—for example, a lack of understanding of various symbols used to describe the innovation. Even the symbols that seem totally unambiguous to us can be interpreted in many different ways by different peoples.

In many U.S. foreign aid programs, for instance, the symbol of a pair of hands clasped in friendship is displayed on trucks, walls, and other highly visible areas to demonstrate that our intentions in these various local projects are entirely honorable, even friendly. Apparently, it never occurred to the designers of that symbol that it could be interpreted differently. But in

certain areas, it has been pointed to as proof that the Americans go to other countries only in order to pull the native peoples into slavery (hence, the two hands, coming from opposite directions). To local people in Thailand, the symbol suggests the spirit world, because disembodied hands do not appear in the real world. Another case of mistaken symbol identification took place in Rhodesia, where European health officials, wishing to emphasize to local villagers the great dangers inherent in tuberculosis, distributed posters in which tuberculosis was personified as a dangerous crocodile. The linking of tuberculosis (which was not even recognized as a disease by the natives) to the crocodile (long recognized as the natives' chief deadly enemy) did not work out as planned. Instead of learning to fear tuberculosis and therefore to do something about it by participating in the European-run health programs, the natives assumed that crocodiles *caused* tuberculosis. Thus, the posters gave the villagers still another reason to fear the reptiles but did not encourage them to attend health clinics.[13]

Problems associated with differential perception of symbols are hardly confined to technologically underdeveloped regions, where the language and customs differ greatly from those of the authorities initiating programs of planned change. A similar difficulty was reported some years ago by an English company that wished to advertise that one of its food products was used by the upper classes as well as by working people. (Apparently, the company felt that if this impression could be conveyed to the working-class people in England, they would be more eager to buy the product, in an attempt to emulate their class superiors.) To indicate that the product was used by upper-class families, the company ran an ad showing the product on a table on which rested some lighted candles, which were presumed to be symbols of gracious dining. However, to people in the working class of northwestern England, this ad gave exactly

---

[12] Arensberg and Niehoff, *Introducing Social Change*, p. 80.

[13] Foster, *Applied Anthropology*, pp. 10–11.

the opposite impression. They interpreted the candles as being required by the family using the product, who were obviously working-class people like themselves whose gas had been cut off for nonpayment of the bill, an all too common occurrence.[14]

Even in cases where the possibility of misinterpreting a particular symbol is not crucial, there are other factors which may act as barriers to planned cultural change. Such factors can be divided roughly into three categories: *cultural* barriers, *social* barriers, and *psychological* barriers. These categories, however, may sometimes appear to overlap.

Cultural barriers have to do with shared behaviors, attitudes, and beliefs that tend to impede the acceptance of an innovation. For example, members of different societies may view gift giving in different ways. Particularly in commercialized societies, things received for nothing are often believed to be worthless. When the government of Colombia instituted a program of giving seedling orchard trees to farmers in order to increase their fruit production, the farmers showed virtually no interest in the seedlings, many of which died as a result of neglect. However, when the government realized that the experiment had apparently failed, it began to charge each farmer a nominal fee for the seedlings. Soon the seedlings became immensely popular and fruit production increased.[15] The farmers' demand for the seedlings may have increased because they were charged a fee and therefore came to value the trees. Or perhaps the greater demand for the seedlings was a response to other new conditions of which we have no knowledge, such as an increase in the market demand for fruit.

Religious beliefs and practices may also hinder the acceptance of a planned change. Thus, in 1940, health workers encountered religious barriers while trying to help contain an epidemic of pulmonary tuberculosis among the Zulu tribesmen of South Africa. The natives

there had already become more susceptible to the disease, because of widespread malnutrition and bad health conditions. Despite the many changes which had already occurred in the Zulu family structure, clothing style, and so forth, as a result of contact with Western cultures, treating the epidemic was difficult. The natives had retained their belief that "all natural phenomena, including crop failures, lightning and storms, as well as sickness, are caused by witchcraft and sorcery." When foreign doctors suggested that an infected girl be hospitalized, her father refused, since allowing this to be done would be admitting that his daughter could spread disease and was therefore a witch.[16]

Social barriers to planned change may arise when traditional patterns of interpersonal relations or traditional social institutions conflict with the innovation being introduced. The structure of authority within the family, for example, is sometimes a factor hindering the acceptance of a planned program of change. In many places, such as parts of Korea and Mexico, and among the Navajo Indians, people cannot be hospitalized or receive extended medical help simply at their own request. Their entire family, which often includes a great many people, must consent, even in emergency cases. Obviously, this process frequently requires a great deal of time and sometimes results in the death of a patient whose physical condition cannot accommodate so much delay.[17]

When planned change is introduced into a society, acceptance may also depend upon psychological factors—that is, how the individuals perceive the innovation. A psychological barrier caused rural Venezuelan mothers to reject the innovation of powdered milk for their infants. Although government officials were distributing the milk without cost at rural clinics, surveys showed that many mothers refused to give it to their children. The women perceived the new

[14]Ibid., p. 111.
[15]Ibid., pp. 122–23.

[16]Benjamin D. Paul, *Health, Culture, and Community: Case Studies of Public Reactions to Health Programs* (New York: Russell Sage Foundation, 1955), p. 18.
[17]Ibid., pp. 106–7.

Medical teams have initiated child-care clinics in hundreds of rural villages in India. A European doctor, however, must guard against imposing his own attitudes and values on the Indian mothers. (Courtesy of the United Nations.)

milk as a threat to their own role as mothers. Many viewed the program as a deliberate attempt to say that mothers' milk was no longer good enough for infants.[18]

Psychological reactions to an innovation are, of course, affected by the way in which the innovation is portrayed. In some situations, planners cannot be sure that the people with whom they are working completely understand the nature or purpose of the change being introduced. Agents of change may think they have effectively communicated to their subjects the details of a process, when this is not really the case. Some common examples of such misunderstanding are in the fields of birth control and medical instructions. Typically, a public health nurse or other type of fieldworker will explain to the mother of a sick infant, for instance, that she must give the baby medicine every three hours. The mother may appear to

[18]Foster, *Applied Anthropology*, pp. 8–9.

understand; but later the worker may discover that the mother gave the child the medicine at each of three consecutive hours, or that she gave it at irregular intervals because she had no clock and did not live by a concept of time that included ideas such as "every three hours." Of course, this problem of faulty communication may have arisen because the public health nurse did not realize that she and the mother spoke different languages or dialects and thus had to make a special effort in translating from one language to the other.

THE PROBLEMS FACING THE INNOVATOR

As we have seen, many factors within the target population may cause it to reject cultural changes which have been planned and introduced by outsiders. But the procedures followed by the outsider, or agent of change, also have an impact on the success or failure of a program. Often such agents must make a conscious effort to overcome certain of their own natural tendencies which would otherwise prevent a program from being successful.

The Importance of Effective Follow-Through Programs

One important problem facing the cultural innovator is the necessity for an effective follow-through program for whatever project is being introduced. That is, the innovator must take into consideration the fact that the native population does not already possess the skills necessary to maintain a project requiring relatively advanced technical knowledge. Of course, the natives can easily learn these skills; but the innovator must specifically and carefully teach such skills to them, before leaving them to their own devices. For example, it makes little sense for a group of technical experts to introduce a system of wells to provide a safe water supply for an area if they do not also make sure to teach the local people how to maintain these wells. Otherwise, whenever all the wells in the area break down, if no adequately trained mechanics are available to fix them the project will simply disappear. The people will return to their old ways of drawing and storing water, as though the wells had never been built.

The Problem of Ethnocentrism

Agents of planned change must also attempt to guard against problems created by their own ethnocentrism. Because many of these agents have been trained in America, according to American rules, beliefs, and values, they often try to ensure the success of their projects by transplanting American-style behavior to whatever country they are working in, whether or not that style applies there. An example of this type of insensitivity to cultural variations is the "technical expert" who designed a series of shower baths to improve the health conditions for a group of people in Iran. This expert did not bother to learn that Iranian men in that area did not like to be seen naked by other people, even other males. Because he did not know this, the innovator designed the shower baths like a typical American men's gymnasium shower, with-

out partitions between the stalls. Needless to say, this design was not popular with the Iranian men, who simply ignored the showers.[19]

This same American ethnocentrism has shown up in several programs meant to help improve nutrition in various technologically underdeveloped regions. The diets of many technologically simple peoples are, in fact, rather good from a nutritional standpoint. Many people substitute, for our traditional selections from the "five food groups," such things as wild berries, roots, nuts, animal fat or hide, and many other perfectly good sources of vitamins, minerals, and proteins. Even Vitamin C can be derived from sources other than citrus fruits. But many change agents do not study the beneficial aspects of a people's traditional diet and attempt to find a way to supplement its nutritional value by using locally available foods. Instead, they spend their time and energy encouraging people from other cultures to consume such typically American foodstuffs as orange juice, eggs, and bacon—which are nutritionally unnecessary in most cases, unavailable in almost all cases, and often repulsive to the target people.

The Danger of "Pseudoimprovements"

One further pitfall which the cultural innovator must guard against is the introduction of "pseudoimprovements." These are new techniques or processes which appear to help raise the quality of life among a group of people, but in reality do not. For example, early American-style wood-burning stoves were introduced to some parts of northern Rhodesia in recent years, as one type of housing improvement. Traditionally, local women had cooked outdoors on raised clay hearths. Once the "improved" stoves were built, it was found that the Rhodesian women did not like them. Although the new stoves looked more modern and therefore seemed to be more efficient, in reality they were not. With the old-style hearths it was easier to regulate the heat, and wood of any size could be

[19] Foster, *Traditional Cultures*, pp. 179–80.

Recognizing the need to use local channels of influence, a government health worker asks permission of a local curer in a Ghana village before spraying the hut with DDT to help fight malaria. (Marc and Evelyne Bernheim, Woodfin Camp and Associates.)

used. The new stoves required that the wood be broken up into pieces of a certain size; their heat was harder to regulate; and the cook had to remain indoors alone, away from one of her primary forms of social contact, around the outdoor cooking fires. Clearly, these new stoves were not really an improvement at all and, needless to say, their life expectancy was short.[20]

Discovering and Utilizing Local Channels of Influence In planning a project involving cultural change, the administrator of the project should find out what the normal channels of influence are in the target population. In most communities, there are preestablished networks for communication, as well as persons of high prestige

or influence who are looked to for everyday guidance and direction. An understanding of such channels of influence is extremely valuable when deciding how to introduce a program of planned change into an area. In addition, it is useful to know at what times, and in what sorts of situations, one channel is likely to be more effective in spreading information and approval than another.

An example of the effective use of local channels of influence occurred when an epidemic of smallpox broke out in the Kalahandi district of Orissa state in India some years ago. The efforts of health workers to vaccinate villagers against the disease were consistently resisted. The villagers, naturally suspicious and fearful of these strange men with their equally strange medical equipment, were unwilling to offer themselves, and particularly their babies,

[20]Foster, *Applied Anthropology*, pp. 7–8.

to whatever peculiar experiments the strangers wished to perform. Afraid of the epidemic, the villagers appealed for help to their local priest, whose opinions on such matters they trusted. The priest went into a trance, explaining that the illness was the result of the goddess Thalerani's anger with the people. She could only be appeased, he continued, by massive feasts, offerings, and other demonstrations of the villagers' worship of her. Realizing that the priest was the village's major opinion leader, at least in medical matters, the frustrated health workers tried to get the priest to convince his people to undergo vaccination. At first, the priest refused to cooperate with the strange men; but when his favorite nephew fell ill, in desperation he decided to try every means available to cure the boy. The priest thereupon went into another trance, telling the villagers that the goddess also wished all her worshippers to be vaccinated. Fortunately, the people agreed, and the epidemic was largely controlled.[21] Agents of change, then, are well advised to identify, and work through, the existing channels of influence in their target populations.

Considering the powerful barriers to change which may exist in many societies, as well as the many difficulties that agents of change may make for themselves, how do cultures ever come to accept planned innovations? In some situations, most of the members of the target population may simply and consciously *want* to change. In such cases, the natives' own desire to adopt the innovations being offered is the most powerful "stimulant" to cultural change. In other situations, however, there may be certain cultural, social, or psychological factors that favor change, even though the target population does not actively seek it. But at the present time, not much is known about why some societies, or segments of societies, seem to be more generally predisposed to change than others.

[21]Niehoff, *A Casebook of Social Change*, pp. 219–24.

Summary

1. All cultures are continually changing, either quickly or slowly, and either accidentally (because of natural disasters or other uncontrollable factors) or as part of a program of planned cultural change directed by a governmental agency, a missionary group, or a private business. Applied anthropologists enter the field, not merely to observe a culture as it is, but to help introduce some specifically planned innovation, such as health care programs or housing improvements.

2. There are relatively few applied anthropologists, partly because the agencies which plan and finance cultural change do not generally seek the advice of anthropologists, and partly because many anthropologists themselves do not choose to do applied work. Some anthropologists feel their knowledge of other cultures is insufficient to be applied effectively; others believe they have no right to interfere in the lives of others. Still others, however, feel obligated to share whatever knowledge they have. The ethics of applied anthropology is a complicated and highly debated issue.

3. Applied anthropology has a lower status than its theoretical counterpart, because many anthropologists feel they cannot retain their sense of cultural relativity or their individual freedom in applied fieldwork. Because applied anthropology was first used by the exploitative colonial administrations of the European nations, its initial reputation was questionable.

4. The first problem to be faced in approaching a new applied project is to determine whether or not the proposed change will benefit the target population. The effect of this change on the entire culture of that population, both in the short and in the long run, must be considered.

5. Even if a planned change will prove beneficial to its target population, the people may not accept it. And if the proposed innovation is not utilized by the intended target, the project cannot be considered a success. Target populations may reject a proposed innovation for various reasons: because they are unaware of the need for the change; because they prefer their traditional way of living; because they misinterpret the symbols used to explain the change or fail to understand its real purpose; because their customs and institutions conflict with the change; or because they are afraid of it.

6. Innovators must overcome certain difficulties if their projects are to succeed. They must institute an effective follow-through program; they must guard against their own ethnocentrism and the lure of "pseudo-improvements"; and they must discover, and use, the traditional channels of influence for introducing their projects to the target population.

Suggested Readings

Arensberg, C. M., and Niehoff, A. H. *Introducing Social Change: A Manual for Americans Overseas.* Chicago: Aldine, 1964.

A manual written for American "change agents" but also useful for the beginning student. It is intended to improve understanding of cultural patterns, problems, and change and to increase the change agent's ability to interact with other cultures. The authors begin with a definition of culture and a description of unplanned and planned changes. They then analyze the culture patterns common to most developing nations and evaluate American culture patterns that may affect those working in such areas.

Foster, G. M. *Applied Anthropology.* Boston: Little, Brown, 1969.

A discussion of the historical and contemporary relationship between theoretical and applied anthropology in terms of the involvement of applied anthropology in social and cultural change. Applied anthropology is defined and illustrated with case studies of planned change. Emphasis is on the problems related to this area of anthropology and the reasons for its importance.

Foster, G. M. *Traditional Cultures and the Impact of Technological Change.* New York: Harper & Row, 1962.

An examination of the effect of technology on cultures throughout the world and of the way that an understanding of past efforts will help solve current problems. Based upon the author's experiences in Latin America, Asia, and North America, this book is an analysis of the factors that hinder, and help to create, cultural changes.

Niehoff, A. H., ed. *A Casebook of Social Change.* Chicago: Aldine, 1966.

A collection of papers on attempts to bring about cultural change in the major underdeveloped areas of the world. The editor critically analyzes each case in terms of its social, economic, and technological success. He believes that the key to faster culture change in these areas is an understanding of the process of change, the reasons for the different rates of change, and the sociocultural elements which may impede change.

Paul, B. D., ed. *Health, Culture, and Community: Case Studies of Public Reactions to Health Programs.* New York: Russell Sage Foundation, 1955.

A collection of papers that deal with health problems throughout the world, the reactions to them, and their possible solutions. Topics include diphtheria control in a Thai community, nutrition programs in Guatemala, and a comprehensive health program among the South African Zulu.

The Effect of the Modern World on Anthropology

In many respects, the world of today is a shrinking one. It is not, of course, physically shrinking, but it is shrinking in the sense that it takes a shorter time to travel around it and even a shorter time to communicate around it—witness the worldwide network of TV satellites. Today it is possible to fly halfway around the globe in the time it took preindustrial humans to visit a nearby town. Newspapers, radio, television, and movies have done much to make different cultures more familiar and accessible to one another.

The world is shrinking culturally too, in the sense that more people are drawn each year into the world market economy, buying and selling similar things, and, as a consequence, altering the patterns of their lives. Perhaps the most obvious illustration of what is happening to the world culturally is the appearance of Coca-Cola, razor blades, steel tools, and even drive-in movies in places that not too long ago lacked such things. But the diffusion of these items is only a small part of the picture. More important than the spread of material goods has been the introduction of selling and buying and wage labor—conditions of life that make it possible for peoples all over the world to acquire the technological "goodies" they now see and hear about. The diffusion of market exchange throughout the world reflects the expansion of certain nations' spheres of influence over the last century. In some places as a result of colonization or conquest, in others as a result of economic and military aid programs, and in still others because of a desire to emulate dominant cultures (American, British, Chinese, and so on), the hundreds of different cultures that survive in the world have become more similar over the last hundred years.

Aside from whether or not these changes are desirable, from our point of view or from the point of view of the peoples experiencing them, we might ask how the shrinking cultural

Epilogue

world affects the field of anthropology, particularly, of course, cultural anthropology.

Some cultural anthropologists have worried about the possible demise of their discipline because of the virtual disappearance of the "primitive" or noncommercial world, which in the past "provided the discipline with most of its data as well as the major inspiration for its key concepts and theoretical ideas."[1] Some of the societies known to ethnography have completely disappeared because of depopulation produced by the introduction of foreign infectious diseases. Others have been so altered by contact with dominant societies that their cultures now retain few of the characteristics that made them unique. To be sure, there are still some cultures in the world (in the interior of New Guinea and a few other large Melanesian islands, and in the back areas of Brazil, Peru, and Venezuela) that have not yet drastically changed. But most of these have changed somewhat, largely under the impact of commercialization, and they will probably continue to change.

Some of those who are worried about the future of cultural anthropology foresee the disappearance of their discipline because it has traditionally focused on cultural variation, and that variation is diminishing. Cultural anthropology, for these people, is synonymous with the ethnographic study of exotic, out-of-the-way cultures not previously described. Nowadays it is difficult to find cultures that have been preserved in such an undescribed and unaltered state. Thus, it is said, we are running out of subject matter because we are running out of new cultures to describe, in part because many have already been described, in part because many have disappeared, and in part because many have so drastically altered as to be indistinguishable from others. Some of the more pessimistic cultural anthropologists envision a time when the last ethnography has been written and the last native has been handed a bottle of Coca-Cola, and the death knell rings upon cultural anthropology as a discipline. Evidence suggests, however, that such a view may be mistaken.

There is no reason to believe that cultural variation, of at least some sorts, will ever disappear. The development of commonly held ideas, beliefs, and behaviors—in other words, culture—depends upon the existence of groups of people relatively separate from one another. After all, most people in their daily lives are isolated from individuals at the opposite ends of the earth, or even down the road, and inasmuch as this continues to be so, they will invariably develop some cultural differences. Although it may be that modern techniques of transportation and communication facilitate the spread of cultural characteristics to all parts of the globe with great rapidity, thus diminishing cultural variability, it is unlikely that all parts will become alike. Thus, although a native of Melanesia and a native of the United States may hear the same song on the same transistor radio, this does not mean that their cultures will not retain some of their original characteristics or will not develop some distinctive adaptations. People in different parts of the world are confronted with different physical and social environments (different climates, soil conditions, natural resources, contacts, and opportunities), and, hence, the chances are that some aspects of their cultures will always be different, assuming that cultures generally consist of common responses that are adapted to particular environmental requirements.

Although cultural variability has undoubtedly decreased recently, it may also be true that much of what we see in the way of cultural variation depends upon what groups we choose to look at and when we look at them. If we move our perspective back in time, we may find (and justifiably, it seems, on the basis of present evidence) that there was less cultural variability in the Lower Paleolithic, when humans were solely dependent upon hunting and gathering, than in the beginning of the Neolithic. In some

---

[1] David Kaplan and Robert A. Manners, "Anthropology: Some Old Themes and New Directions," *Southwestern Journal of Anthropology* 27 (Spring 1971): 71.

areas of the world 10,000 years ago, people were dependent upon agriculture and domesticated animals; in other areas they were dependent upon sedentary food-collection; and in still other areas they were still dependent upon nomadic hunting and gathering. With the spread of agriculture, cultural variability may have again decreased as hunting and gathering began to disappear.

We might expect, then, that whenever a generally adaptive cultural pattern develops and spreads over the globe, cultural variability decreases, at least for a time. Hence, with the recent spread of commercial exchange, and even more significant, with the ongoing diffusion of industrial culture, we may be witnessing a temporary diminution of cultural variability, as humanity experiences another great cultural change. But there is no reason to believe that further and differential cultural change, stemming from varying physical and social environmental requirements, will not occur in different parts of the world.

In short, it does not seem likely that cultural anthropology, the study of cultural variation, will soon run out of variability to study. The same thing can be said for physical anthropology, archaeology, and linguistics. With respect to physical anthropology, there is no reason to expect variation in biological characteristics between human populations to disappear in the future, as long as physical and social environments continue to vary. It will be a long time before the whole of mankind lives under identical environmental conditions, in one great "greenhouse." Moreover, there will always be that great depository of human variability to explore and study—the fossil and more recent human paleontological records. Similarly, archaeologists will always have the remains of past cultures to study and explain. And, with respect to linguistics, even if all linguistic variation disappears from the earth, we shall always have the descriptive data on past languages to study, with all the variability in those records still to be explained.

Yet, a larger question remains. Why should we study simpler cultures at all, either those that exist today or have existed in the past? What conceivable bearing could such studies have on the problems that beset us as we enter the closing decades of the twentieth century? To answer this question we must remind ourselves that humans, whatever culture they may belong to, are still human, and, as a species, share certain significant needs and characteristics in common. If we are to discover laws that account for human behavior, then, all cultures past and present are equally important. As Claude Lévi-Strauss has recently said:

> The thousands of societies that exist today, or once existed on the surface of the earth, constitute so many experiments, the only ones we can make use of to formulate and test our hypotheses, since we can't very well construct or repeat them in the laboratory as physical and natural scientists do. These experiments, represented by societies unlike our own, described and analyzed by anthropologists, provide one of the surest ways to understand what happens in the human mind and how it operates. That's what anthropology is good for in the most general way and what we can expect from it in the long run.[2]

New Directions in Cultural Anthropology

As we have seen, cultural anthropologists have in the past focused mainly on the cultures of the noncommercial world. Now that most of these cultures have disappeared or have drastically changed, many anthropologists are turning their attention to societies that are more in the mainstream of technological and economic development. Such societies (the nations of Europe and Asia or the developing countries of the Third World) have in former times been studied by other disciplines such as economics and political science. Now anthropologists have begun to use some of the techniques developed in the

[2] *New York Times*, 21 January 1972, p. 41; reprinted from *Diacritics*, Cornell University.

study of simpler cultures to study more complex ones. Urban anthropology, for example, a branch of cultural anthropology which is very much a part of this trend, offers possibilities for new research and has begun to attract many younger students who feel that the study of people in cities may yield valuable insights into current problems.

In addition to the new interest in complex societies, cultural athropologists have become interested in aspects of culture which ethnographers have previously neglected. For example, many anthropologists have begun to study unconscious cultural patterns—all those mental and physical habits which are shared by members of a culture but which manifest themselves below the level of conscious awareness. How people position themselves in various situations, how they sit, what they do with their arms and legs, whether they avoid or seek eye contact while speaking—all are aspects of this emerging field of study. The new interest in unconscious cultural patterns also involves an interest in the different ways in which people perceive, order, and describe the world around them. (This interest is the main focus of cognitive and sym-

bolic anthropology.) Most of these new investigations of unconscious cultural patterning are still essentially descriptive in orientation. Their intent is to find out how unconscious patterns vary, not so much yet why they vary. However, even the relatively few studies that have been done so far reveal fascinating similarities and differences in human behavior which, though not yet explainable in terms of tested and validated theory, are nonetheless extremely suggestive and promise much interesting work to come.

Finally, more and more comparative studies are being conducted which make use of descriptive data collected by other anthropologists in an effort to discover possible causal explanations of variable cultural characteristics. Just as we have the fossil and archaeological records, we have an enormous body of ethnographic data on different peoples, which will never disappear. There are many questions to be asked—and possibly many answers that can be gained—from the data we already have. The challenge of uncovering more definitive answers to how and why populations vary—in the past, present, and future—will always be with us.

Glossary

absolute dating method *see* chronometric dating method.

acculturation process of extensive borrowing in the context of superordinate-subordinate relations between societies; usually occurs as the result of external pressure.

Acheulean toolmaking tradition generally associated with *Homo erectus*, characterized by large cutting instruments such as handaxes and cleavers.

achieved qualities those qualities that a person acquires by doing something.

adaptation the ongoing consequence of natural selection whereby populations change in response to changes in their particular environments.

Aegyptopithecus Oligocene ape, about 29 million years old, from the Fayum area of Egypt; possibly an ancestor of modern apes and of humans too.

affinal kin one's relatives by marriage.

age grade category of persons who happen to fall within a particular, culturally distinguished age range.

age-set a group of persons of similar age and sex who move together through some or all of life's stages.

age-village village occupied by members of an age-set and their dependents.

allele one member of a pair of genes.

Allen's rule rule stating that protruding body parts (particularly arms and legs) are relatively shorter in the cooler areas of a species's range than in the warmer areas.

ambilineal descent rule of descent that affiliates an individual with groups of kinsmen related to him or her through men *or* women.

amok mental disorder that occurs in Malaya, Indonesia, and New Guinea, in which the afflicted person becomes depressed, withdrawn, and finally runs berserk.

ancestor spirits supernatural beings who are the ghosts of dead relatives.

animatism a belief in supernatural forces.

animism term used by Tylor to describe a belief in a dual existence for all things—a physical, visible body and a psychic, invisible soul.

anthropoids one of the two suborders of primates; includes monkeys, apes, and humans.

anthropology the study of variations, both biological and cultural, in human populations. Anthropology is concerned with typical biological and cultural characteristics of human populations in all periods and in all parts of the world.

Apidium   short-faced Oligocene monkey from the Fayum area of Egypt whose teeth many believe resemble those of certain modern New World monkeys.

applied anthropology   branch of anthropology that concerns itself with planned cultural change, when it is presumably an application of anthropological knowledge.

archaeology   the study of prehistoric and historic cultures through the analysis of material remains.

association   organization that has membership based on commonly shared characteristics or interests.

Aterian   Upper Paleolithic culture of North Africa dating from about 37,000 years ago; its flaking technique probably derived from the Mousterian tradition.

atlatl   Aztec word for spear thrower.

Aurignacian   Upper Paleolithic culture, dated between 35,000 and 20,000 B.C.; burins used for carving wood, bone, and ivory were widely used tools of the period; Aurignacian peoples are credited with producing the earliest cave paintings in western Europe.

Australopithecus   genus of Pliocene and Pleistocene hominids.

Australopithecus africanus   erect bipedal hominid that lived during the late Pliocene through the early Pleistocene; dentally similar to modern humans, had a rounded brain case with cranial capacity of 428–485 cc, weighed between 50 and 70 lbs.

Australopithecus habilis   *see Homo habilis.*

Australopithecus robustus   fossil hominid similar to *A. africanus*, but larger, with a body weight of 100–150 lb.; also called *Paranthropus.*

avunculocal residence   pattern of residence in which a married couple settles with or near the husband's mother's brother.

balanced reciprocity   giving with the expectation of a straightforward immediate or limited-time trade.

band   a fairly small, self-sufficient, autonomous group of people, usually nomadic.

Bergmann's rule   rule stating that smaller-sized subpopulations of a species inhabit the warmer parts of its geographical range, and larger-sized subpopulations inhabit the cooler areas.

bifacial tool   a tool worked or flaked on two sides.

bilateral descent   rule of descent that affiliates an individual more or less equally with his or her mother's and father's relatives.

bilocal residence   pattern of residence in which a married couple lives with or near either the husband's parents or the wife's parents.

bipedalism   pattern of locomotion in which an animal walks on its two hind legs.

blade   a thin flake whose length is usually more than twice its width. In the blade technique of toolmaking, a core is prepared by shaping it with hammerstones into a pyramidal or cylindrical form and then blades are struck off until the core is used up.

boreal forest   sparsely-wooded, mainly coniferous, Northern hemisphere forest.

brachiation   pattern of arboreal locomotion in which the animal swings from branches, supporting its weight by its hands and arms.

bride price (or bride wealth)   a substantial gift of money or goods which is given to the bride's kin by the groom or his kin at or before the marriage.

bride service   work performed by the groom for his bride's family for a varying length of time either before or after the marriage is finalized.

burin   a chisel-like stone tool used for carving and for making such artifacts as bone and antler needles, awls, and projectile points.

canines   cone-shaped teeth immediately behind the incisors; used in most primates to seize food and in fighting and display.

carbon^{14} (or C^{14})   a radioactive isotope of carbon used to date organic material. *See* radiocarbon dating.

cash crop   cultivated commodity which is raised for sale rather than for personal consumption by the cultivator.

caste system   a hierarchical system of groups with differential access to prestige and economic resources; in such a system, an individual's position in society is completely determined at birth.

catarrhines   group of sharp-nosed anthropoids including Old World monkeys, apes, and humans.

catastrophism   theory that extinct life forms were destroyed by cataclysms and upheavals and were replaced by new divine creations.

cercopithecoids Old World monkeys.

cerebral cortex "grey matter" of the brain; center of speech and other higher mental activities.

chief a person who exercises authority usually on behalf of a multicommunity political unit. This role is generally found in rank societies and is usually permanent and often hereditary.

chiefdom a political unit within a society, with a chief at its head, integrating more than one community.

chromosomes paired rod-shaped structures within a cell nucleus containing the genes that transmit traits from one generation to the next.

chronometric dating method method of dating fossils in which the actual age of a deposit or specimen is measured; also known as absolute dating method.

civilization urban society, from the Latin word for "city-state."

clan (or sib) a set of kin whose members believe themselves to be descended from a common ancestor or ancestress but cannot specify the links back to that ancestor; often designated by a totem.

class a category of persons who have about the same opportunity to obtain economic resources and prestige.

class/caste society a society having socially structured unequal access to both economic resources and prestige.

classificatory terms kinship terms that merge or equate relatives who are genealogically distinct from one another; the same term is used for a number of different kinsmen.

cloning the exact reproduction of an individual from cellular tissue.

cognates words or morphemes in different languages with similar sounds and meanings.

commercial agriculture system of agriculture in which all of the cultivated commodities are produced for sale rather than for personal consumption.

commercialization increasing dependence on buying and selling, using money as the medium of exchange.

comparative (or historical) linguistics the study of the emergence of language, how languages change over time, and how languages may be related.

complementary opposition at times, the uniting of various segments of a segmentary lineage system in opposition to similar segments.

coniferous forest forest of cone-bearing evergreen trees.

consanguineal kin one's biological relatives; relatives by birth.

continental drift theory theory that states that the major continental land masses were not separated as they are today, but instead formed a single large supercontinent surrounded by seas. In recent geological times, the supercontinent is thought to have broken up and the continents drifted apart into the configuration they have today.

corvée a system of required labor.

Cretaceous geologic epoch 135 to 65 million years ago, during which dinosaurs and other reptiles ceased to be the dominant land vertebrates, and mammals and birds began to become important.

crime violence not considered legitimate that occurs within a political unit.

Cro-Magnons early *Homo sapiens sapiens* who lived in western Europe 30,000–35,000 years ago; differed from Neandertals in their higher foreheads, thinner and lighter bones, smaller faces and jaws, protruberant chins, and slight or nonexistent bony ridges on the skull.

cross-cousins children of siblings of the opposite sex; i.e., one's cross-cousins are father's sisters' and mother's brothers' children.

cultivation the planting and raising of plant crops.

cultural anthropology the study of cultural variation.

cultural relativity the attitude that a society's customs and ideas should be viewed within the context of that society's culture and environment.

culture the set of values, behaviors, and attitudes, as well as the products of human activity, that are characteristic of a particular society or population.

cuneiform wedge-shaped writing invented by the Sumerians around 3000 B.C.

cusp point on the chewing surface of a tooth.

Dabban blade industry contemporary with the Aterian but confined to the Mediterrean coast of North Africa.

daughter language a language derived from a protolanguage. For example, English and French are two of the daughter languages of Proto-Indo-European.

dendrochronology tree-ring dating; uses master charts of tree-ring growth patterns for a particular area to date absolutely wooden cultural remains.

descriptive (or structural) linguistics the study of how languages are constructed and used.

descriptive terms kinship terms used to refer to genealogically distinct relatives; a different term is used for each relative.

dialect a variety of a language spoken in a particular area or by a particular social group.

divination foretelling the future by trying to contact the supernatural by any one of several means: drawing straws, reading palms, trance states, or rubbing-boards, etc.

DNA deoxyribonucleic acid; a long two-stranded molecule in the genes that directs the making of an organism according to the instructions in its genetic code.

domestication the cultivation or raising of plants and animals that are different from wild varieties.

dominant the allele of a gene pair that is always phenotypically expressed in the heterozygous form.

double descent (or double unilineal descent) system that affiliates an individual for some purposes with a group of matrilineal kinsmen, and for other purposes with a group of patrilineal kinsmen.

dowry a substantial transfer of goods or money from the bride's family to the married couple or to the groom's family.

Dryopithecus genus of Oligocene-Miocene fossil apes which inhabited Africa and Eurasia, and of which several species are known.

ecology the study of the interrelationships between organisms and their environment.

econiche ecological niche; small, specialized parts of the whole habitat that provide different resources and opportunities for adaptation.

egalitarian society society in which all persons of a given age-sex category have equal access to economic resources and prestige.

ego in the reckoning of kinship, the central reference point; the focal member.

enculturation *see* socialization.

endogamy rule specifying marriage to a person within one's own (kin, caste, community) group.

Eocene geologic epoch $53\frac{1}{2}$–38 million years ago.

epicanthic fold a bit of skin overlapping the eyelid.

estrus period of ovulation or sexual receptivity in female Old World monkeys signaled by reddening and swelling of the sexual skin.

ethnic association association, usually located in urban centers, composed of members of a particular ethnic group.

ethnocentrism the attitude that other societies' customs and ideas can be judged in the context of one's own culture.

ethnographic analogy a method of inferring how a particular tool was used in the past by observing how that tool is used by members of contemporary societies, preferably societies with subsistence activities and environments similar to those of the ancient toolmakers.

ethnography a description of a society's customary behaviors, beliefs, and attitudes.

ethnohistorian an ethnologist who uses historical documents to study how a particular culture has changed over time.

ethnolinguistics the study of the relationships between language and culture.

ethnology the study of how and why cultures differ and are similar.

exchange of females custom whereby a sister or other female relative of the groom is exchanged for the bride.

exogamy rule specifying marriage to a person from outside one's own (kin or community) group.

expressive behavior activities such as art, music, dance, and folklore, which presumably express thoughts and feelings.

extended family a family consisting of two or more monogamous, polygynous, or polyandrous families linked by a blood tie.

extensive (or shifting) cultivation a type of horticulture in which the land is worked for short periods and then left to regenerate for some years before being used again.

family a social unit consisting minimally of a married couple and their children.

family of orientation the family into which a person is born.

family of procreation the family that a person forms by marrying.

feuding a state of recurring hostility between families or groups of kinsmen, usually motivated by a desire to avenge an offense against a member of the group.

fission-track dating a chronometric dating method used to date crystal, glass, and many uranium-rich materials contemporaneous with fossils or deposits that are from 20 years to 5 billion years old. This dating method entails counting the tracks or paths of decaying uranium isotope atoms in the sample, and then comparing the number of tracks with the uranium content of the sample.

fluorine analysis　method of relative dating used to determine if two specimens found together are of the same age; measures the amount of fluorine absorbed from ground water as the specimen lies in the ground; *see* F-U-N tests.

fluted point　projectile point that has had a flake removed down the center of the point to the base; unique to the New World.

folklore　all the lore (myths, fairytales, superstitions, riddles, and games) of a culture; generally orally transmitted, but may also be written.

Folsom　culture of the southwestern and western United States dating from about 9000 to 7000 B.C.; the Folsom tool kit consisted of fluted points and other stone and bone tools.

food collection　the form of subsistence technology in which food getting is dependent upon naturally occurring resources, i.e., wild plants and animals.

food production　form of subsistence technology in which food getting is dependent upon the cultivation and domestication of plants and animals.

foramen magnum　hole in the base of the skull through which the spinal cord passes en route to the brain.

forced observation　a concept that describes certain features of the grammar of a language which seem to compel its speakers to express reality in a particular way.

fossil　the preserved remains of plants and animals that lived in the past.

founder effect　form of genetic drift that occurs when a small population recently derived from a larger one expands in relative isolation. Because the founders of the new population carry only a small sample of the gene pool of the original population, the gene frequencies of the two populations may differ.

"1470" skull　fossil skull with a cranial capacity of over 800 cc, which may be an early *Homo* contemporaneous with australopithecines.

fraternal polyandry　marriage of a woman to two or more brothers at one time.

F-U-N tests　fluorine (F), uranium (U), and nitrogen (N) tests for relative dating. All three minerals are present in ground water. The older a fossil is, the higher will be its fluorine or uranium content, and the lower its nitrogen content.

gene　chemical unit of heredity.

gene flow　process by which genes pass from the gene pool of one population to that of another through mating and reproduction.

gene pool　all of the genes possessed by the members of a given population.

generalized reciprocity　gift giving without any immediate return or conscious thought of return.

generation-set　a combination of a number of age-set units covering a certain number of years.

genetic drift　the various random processes that affect gene frequencies in small, relatively isolated populations.

genitor　one's biological father.

genotype　the total complement of inherited traits or genes of an organism.

genus　a group of related species; pl. genera.

geographical race　a set of at least once-neighboring populations which has certain distinctive trait frequencies.

gestation　period of development before birth; pregnancy.

ghosts　supernatural beings who were once human; the souls of dead people.

gift exchange　marriage custom in which the two kin groups about to be linked by marriage exchange gifts of about equal value.

Gloger's rule　rule stating that populations of birds and mammals living in warm, humid climates have more melanin (and, therefore, darker skin, fur, or feathers) than populations of the same species living in cooler, drier areas.

glottochronology　a method of establishing a date for the divergence between two languages by examining changes in the languages over a period of time.

gods　supernatural beings of nonhuman origin, who are named, often anthropomorphic, personalities.

grammar　description of the possible ways in which morphemes are combined to form words, and words are arranged to form phrases and sentences.

Gravettian　Upper Paleolithic culture centered primarily in eastern and central Europe dating from 22,000 to 18,000 B.C.; characterized by oval hut or skin tent dwellings, mammoth hunting, and geometrically patterned pins, beads, pendants, and figurines.

group marriage   marriage in which more than one man is married to more than one woman at the same time. This is not customary in any known human society.

half-life   the time it takes one-half of the atoms of a radioactive substance to decay into new atoms.

headman   person who holds a powerless but symbolically unifying position in an egalitarian society; may exercise authority but has no power to impose sanctions.

herbivore   animal whose diet consists mainly of seeds, nuts, fruits, leaves, and other vegetable matter.

heterosis   production of healthier and more numerous offspring as a result of matings between individuals with different genetic characteristics; also known as hybrid vigor.

heterozygous   possessing differing genes or alleles in corresponding locations on a pair of chromosomes.

hieroglyphics   "picture writing" as in ancient Egypt and Mayan sites in Mesoamerica.

Hominidae   family of hominids composed of humans and their direct ancestors. It contains at least two and perhaps three genera: *Homo, Australopithecus,* and *Ramapithecus.*

hominids   group of hominoids consisting of humans and their direct ancestors.

hominoid   a member of the *Hominoidea.*

Hominoidea   group of catarrhines which includes both apes and humans.

homiothermic   warm-blooded; having a body temperature that remains at a constant level in spite of fluctuating external temperature.

Homo   genus to which modern humans and their ancestors belong.

Homo erectus   species of early human who lived in Africa, Europe, and Asia during the Pleistocene; cranial capacity of 900–1200 cc; associated with the Acheulean tool tradition and the first use of fire by humans.

Homo habilis   designation for the skeletal remains of several hominids found at Olduvai Gorge (Tanzania) which date from about 1.8 million years ago; cranial capacity about 650 cc; may have been a tool maker. Also known as *Australopithecus habilis.*

Homo sapiens   the species of animal to which modern (and extinct) humans belong. Technically, modern humans are referred to as *Homo sapiens sapiens.*

Homo sapiens sapiens   modern humans.

homozygous   possessing two identical genes or alleles in corresponding locations on a pair of chromosomes.

horticulture   plant cultivation carried out with relatively simple tools and methods.

human paleontology   the study of the emergence of humans and their later physical evolution.

hunter-gatherers   peoples who subsist on the collection of naturally occurring plants and animals.

hybrid vigor   *see* heterosis.

hypoxia   oxygen deficiency.

incest taboo   prohibition of sexual intercourse or marriage between mother and son, father and daughter, and brother and sister.

incisors   the front teeth; used for holding or seizing food, and preparing it for chewing by the other teeth.

initiation ceremony   ceremony symbolizing changed status, usually the passage from childhood to adulthood.

insectivore   an animal that eats insects.

intensive agriculture   food production characterized by the use of the plow, draft animals or machines, fertilizers, irrigation, water-storage techniques, and other complex agricultural techniques.

International Phonetic Alphabet (IPA)   alphabet used by linguists which provides a symbol for every sound that occurs in every known language.

ischial callosities   sitting pads of tough or hardened skin located on the buttocks of Old World monkeys and gibbons.

K⁴⁰   radioactive isotope of potassium used in potassium-argon dating. *See* potassium-argon (or K-Ar) dating.

kindred   a group of close bilateral relatives.

kitchen midden   pile of refuse, often shells, in an archaeological site.

knuckle walking   locomotor pattern of primates such as the chimpanzee and gorilla in which the weight of the upper part of the body is supported on the thickly padded knuckles of the hands.

Kula **ring**   a ceremonial exchange of valued shell

ornaments in the Trobriand Islands, in which white shell armbands are traded around the islands in a counterclockwise direction and red shell necklaces are traded in a clockwise direction.

kwashiorkor   protein deficiency disease common to tropical areas.

lactase deficiency   condition in which an individual lacks the enzyme lactase which is necessary for the digestion of lactose, or milk sugar. Without lactase, the drinking of milk produces digestive disorders.

law   set of rules stipulating what is permissible and what is not; codified law is written (and therefore explicit) law.

lemuriformes   suborder of prosimians whose members include lemurs and their relatives, the indris and the aye-aye. All members of this group are found only on Madagascar and the Comoro Islands.

Levalloisian   tool tradition developed during the Acheulean period whereby flake tools of a predetermined size could be produced from a shaped core with a prepared striking platform.

levirate   custom whereby a man is obliged to marry his brother's widow.

lineage   a set of kin whose members trace descent from a common ancestor through known links.

Llano   toolmaking culture of the United States dating from about 9500 to 7000 B.C.; the Llano tool kit is associated with both large and small herd animals and includes Clovis fluted points and other stone and bone tools.

local race   a breeding population or local group whose members usually interbreed with one another.

lorisiformes   suborder of prosimians found in both Southeast Asia and sub-Saharan Africa; includes the lorises and the galagos (bushbabies).

lumbar curve   curve formed by the lower part of the vertebral column in erect walkers; found only in hominids.

Lupemban   Upper Paleolithic culture of sub-Saharan Africa. *See* Sangoan.

Magdalenian   late Upper Paleolithic culture of western Europe, dating from 15,000 to 8000 B.C.; during this period, microliths, barbed harpoons of bone and antler, and atlatl were made, and the high point of multicolored cave paintings and tool decoration seems to have been reached.

magic   the performance of certain rituals which are believed to compel the supernatural powers to act in particular ways.

Maglemosian   Mesolithic culture of northern Europe characterized by stone axes and adzes for woodworking, canoes, paddles, large-timbered houses, fishhooks, the bow and arrow, and amber and stone pendants and figurines.

mana   a supernatural, impersonal force inhabiting certain objects or people, which is believed to confer success and/or strength.

manioc   cassava; a tropical plant with large starchy roots which are made into flour or beer.

manumission   the granting of freedom to a slave.

manuports   collections of natural stones found in archaeological sites.

market exchange   distribution of goods and services by means of monetary or commercial exchange.

marriage   a socially approved sexual and economic union between a man and a woman which is presumed, both by the couple and others, to be more or less permanent, and which subsumes reciprocal rights between spouses and between spouses and their future children.

matriclan   a clan tracing descent through the female line.

matrilineage   a kin group whose members trace descent through known links in the female line from a common ancestress.

matrilineal descent   rule of descent that affiliates an individual with kinsmen related to him or her through *women* only.

matrilocal residence   pattern of residence in which a married couple lives with or near the wife's parents.

megaliths   huge stone monuments, generally used to mark burial sites, erected in parts of the Middle East and throughout Europe.

Meganthropus   name given to the fossil fragments of the teeth and jaws of a large hominid found in Asia, which may be an Asian australopithecine.

meiosis   the process by which reproductive cells are formed. In this process of division, the number of chromosomes in the new-formed cells is reduced by half, so that when fertilization occurs the resulting organism will have the normal number of chromosomes appropriate to its species, rather than double that number.

melanin   dark brown pigment in the outer layer of skin that absorbs ultraviolet radiation.

Mendelian population population which breeds mostly within itself.

Mesolithic the archaeological period in the Old World beginning about 12,000 B.C., during which preagricultural villages were founded.

microlith a small, razor-like blade fragment that was probably attached to wooden or bone handles to form a cutting edge.

military association association that unites members through common military purposes or experiences.

Miocene geologic epoch 22½ to 5 million years ago, during which the first hominids probably appeared.

mitosis the process of cellular reproduction or growth involving the duplication of chromosome pairs.

modal personality composite of those personality characteristics that occur with the highest frequency in a society; a "typical" personality in a particular society.

moiety a unilineal descent group, when the society is divided into two such maximal groups; there may be smaller unilineal descent groups as well.

molars the large teeth behind the premolars and at the back of the jaw; used for chewing and grinding of food.

Mongoloid spot dark patch of skin at the base of the spine which disappears as a person grows older.

monogamy marriage between only one man and only one woman at a time.

monotheism belief that there is only one high god, and all other supernatural beings are subordinate to, or are alternative manifestations of, this supreme being.

morph smallest unit of a language that has meaning.

morpheme one or more morphs with the same meaning.

morphology the ways in which morphemes are combined to forms words.

Mousterian Middle Paleolithic toolmaking tradition associated with Neandertals; prepared core and percussion flaking techniques were used to produce flakes which were then retouched to make specialized tools.

mutation change in the molecular structure or DNA code of genes. Mutations usually occur randomly and are generally harmful or lethal to the organism and/or its descendants.

natural selection process by which those members of a particular species which are better adapted to their environment survive longer and produce more offspring than the poorer-adapted; in time the better-adapted species survives and evolves in its particular environment.

Neandertals archaic *Homo sapiens* found as early as 100,000 years ago in Europe, Asia, and Africa; cranial capacity averaged 1450 cc; generally associated with Mousterian toolmaking tradition.

negative reciprocity giving and taking that attempts to take advantage of another for one's own self-interest.

Neolithic the archaeological period, characterized by plant and animal domestication, beginning in the Near East about 8000 B.C., in southeast Asia at 6800 B.C., in sub-Saharan Africa by 4000 B.C., and in the New World from 5600 to 5000 B.C.

neolocal residence pattern of residence whereby a married couple lives separately from the kin of either spouse, usually some distance from both sets of in-laws.

nonfraternal polyandry marriage of a woman to two or more men who are not brothers.

nonsororal polygyny marriage of a man to two or more women who are not sisters.

norm the ideal cultural pattern that represents what most members of a society say they ought to do or feel in a particular situation.

nuclear family family consisting of a married couple and their young children.

oasis fertile, well-watered area in an arid region.

oath the act of calling upon a deity to bear witness to the truth of what one says.

obsidian volcanic glass which can be used to make mirrors or sharp-edged tools.

Oldowan term designating cultural materials found in Bed I (lower Pleistocene) levels at Olduvai Gorge, Tanzania.

Oligocene geologic epoch 38 to 22½ million years ago, during which the ancestors of monkeys and apes began to evolve.

omnivores animals that eat both meat and vegetation.

open language system of communication, like all known human languages, in which utterances can be combined to produce new meanings.

opposable thumb thumb that can touch the tips of all the other fingers.

ordeal a means used to determine guilt or innocence by submitting the accused to dangerous or painful tests believed to be under supernatural control.

Paleocene geologic epoch 65 to 53½ million years ago, during which mammal forms (including the early primates) began to diverge extensively.

Paleolithic the "Old Stone Age" dating from 5 million to 14 thousand years ago. The cultures of the early hominids and *Homo erectus* are known collectively as the Lower Paleolithic; the Mousterian tradition of the Neandertals comprises the Middle Paleolithic; and the cultures of early *Homo sapiens sapiens* are known collectively as Upper Paleolithic.

paleontology study of past life through plant and animal fossils.

parallel-cousins children of siblings of the same sex; i.e., one's parallel-cousins are father's brothers' and mother's sisters' children.

Paranthropus *See Australopithecus robustus.*

Parapithecus small monkey-like Oligocene animal found in the Fayum area of Egypt; may possibly be an ancestor of modern Old World monkeys.

pastoralism a relatively rare form of subsistence technology in which food getting is based largely upon the maintenance of large herds of animals.

pater one's socially recognized father.

patriclan a clan tracing descent through the male line.

patrilineage a kin group whose members trace descent through known links in the male line from a common ancestor.

patrilineal descent rule of descent that affiliates an individual with kinsmen of both sexes related to him or her through *men* only.

patrilocal residence pattern of residence in which a married couple lives with or near the husband's parents.

peasants rural people who produce food for their own subsistence, but who must also contribute or sell their surpluses to others (in towns and cities) who do not produce their own food.

peer group group of people who are of the same rank, status, or level.

Peking man name for *Homo erectus* found near Choukoutien, China.

percussion flaking toolmaking technique in which one stone is struck with another to remove a flake.

personality distinctive way an individual thinks, feels, and behaves.

personality integration of culture the theory that personality or psychological processes may account for connections between certain aspects of culture.

phenotype the external and observable physical appearance of an organism which may or may not reflect its genotype or total genetic constitution.

phone a speech sound in a language.

phoneme a set of slightly varying sounds which do not make any difference in meaning to the speakers of the language.

phonology the study of the sounds in a language and how they vary and are combined.

phratry a unilineal descent group composed of a number of supposedly related clans (sibs).

physical anthropology the study of humans as physical organisms, dealing with the emergence and evolution of humans and with contemporary biological variations among human populations.

pibloktoq a mental disorder that occurs among some Eskimo adults of Greenland, usually women, who become oblivious to their surroundings and act in agitated, eccentric ways.

Plano culture of the southwestern United States dating from 7000 to 6500 B.C.; the Plano tool kit consisted of unfluted lancelike knives and points as well as other stone and bone tools and milling stones.

platyrrhines group of flat-nosed anthropoids that includes the monkeys of South and Central America—the cebids and marmosets.

Pleistocene geologic epoch which started 1.8 million years ago and some say continues into the present; during this period, glaciers have often covered much of the earth's surface and humans became the dominant life form.

Plesiadapis Paleocene primate found in Europe and North America.

Pliocene geologic epoch 5 to 1.8 million years ago during which the earliest definite hominids appeared.

pollen analysis microscopic identification of pollen grains from plants; used to describe the vegetation in the area involved. Also a relative dating method when master charts of pollen proportions over the years in a particular area are consulted.

polyandry marriage of one woman to more than one man at a time.

polygamy plural marriage; marriage to more than one spouse simultaneously.

polygyny marriage of one man to more than one woman at a time.

polyphony two or more melodies sung simultaneously.

polytheism belief in many gods, none of which is believed to be superordinate.

pongids hominoids whose members include both the living and extinct apes.

Poro secret society, with membership open to all males, contingent upon passing a series of grueling physical tests; exists among many tribes in west Africa.

postpartum sex taboo prohibition of sexual intercourse between a couple after the birth of their child.

potassium-argon (or K-Ar) dating a chronometric dating method which uses the rate of decay of a radioactive form of potassium (K^{40}) into argon (A^{40}) to date samples from 5,000 years to 3 billion years old. The K-Ar method dates the minerals and rocks in a deposit, not the fossils themselves.

potlatch a feast among northwest Pacific coast Indians at which great quantities of food and goods are given to the guests in order to gain prestige for the host(s).

prairie grassland with taller, better-watered grass cover than that of the steppe.

prehensile adapted for grasping objects.

premolars the teeth immediately behind the canines; used in chewing, grinding and shearing food.

pressure flaking tool-making technique whereby small flakes are struck off by pressing against the core with a bone, antler, or wood tool.

priest full-time religious intermediary between humans and gods.

primary institutions the sources of early experiences, such as family organization and subsistence techniques, that presumably help form the basic or modal personality.

primate a member of the mammalian order Primates, divided into the two suborders prosimian and anthropoid.

prognathism a facial construction characterized by the forward projection of the lower jaw and lower part of the face.

projective tests tests (such as the Rorschach ink blot and the Thematic Apperception tests) which utilize ambiguous stimuli; test subjects must project their own personality traits in order to structure the ambiguous stimuli.

Propliopithecus Oligocene ape, dating from about 32 million years ago, found in the Fayum area of Egypt; possibly the ancestor of *Aegyptopithecus*.

prosimian one of the two suborders of primates; includes lemurs, lorises, and tarsiers.

Proto-Indo-European the protolanguage of many modern European, Near Eastern, and Indic languages.

protolanguage hypothesized ancestral language from which two or more languages seem to have descended.

Purgatorius fossil dating from the late Cretaceous that is thought to be the earliest known primate.

quadrupedalism pattern of locomotion involving walking or running on all fours.

quern a large, flat stone upon which grain can be ground.

race a subpopulation of a single species that differs somewhat in gene frequencies from other members of the species but can interbreed with them and produce fertile and viable offspring.

rachis seed-bearing part of the stem of a plant.

radiocarbon (or C^{14}) dating a chronometric dating method which uses carbon 14 to date organic remains up to 70,000 years old.

raiding a short-term use of force, generally preplanned and organized, to realize a limited objective.

Ramapithecus genus of Miocene primates dating from 14 to 12 million years ago, found in Europe, Asia, and Africa; the oldest suspected hominid.

rank society a society having no socially structured unequal access to economic resources, but having socially structured unequal access to status positions and prestige.

recessive an allele which is phenotypically suppressed in the heterozygous form and only expressed in the homozygous form.

reciprocity giving and taking (not politically arranged) without the use of money.

redistribution the accumulation of goods by a particular person, or in a particular place, for the purpose of subsequent distribution.

regional association club which brings together migrants from a common geographical background; often composed of rural settlers in urban centers.

relative dating method method of dating fossils that determines the age of a specimen or deposit relative to another known specimen or deposit.

religion any set of attitudes, beliefs, and practices pertaining to supernatural power, whether that power be forces, gods, spirits, ghosts, or demons.

revitalization movement new religious movement that may be an effort to save a culture by infusing it with new purpose and life.

RNA ribonucleic acid; a single-stranded molecule that copies the genetic instructions from DNA and transmits them to structures in the cytoplasm of a cell.

Rorschach test projective test that consists of asking subjects to describe what they see in the various ink blots on a series of cards.

rules of descent rules that affiliate individuals with various sets of kin.

Sangoan Upper Paleolithic culture of sub-Saharan Africa dating from about 44,000 to 38,600 B.C.; Sangoan culture and its later form, the Lupemban, were core tool—primarily handaxe and pick—traditions probably adapted to forest conditions.

savanna tropical grassland.

secondary institutions aspects of culture such as religion, music, art, folklore, and games that presumably reflect or are projections of basic or modal personality.

secret society association characterized principally by limited membership and secret rituals.

sedentarism settled life.

segmentary lineage system hierarchy of more and more inclusive lineages, which usually functions only in conflict situations.

shaman religious intermediary, usually part-time, whose primary function is to cure people by using sacred songs, pantomime, and other means; sometimes called "witch doctor" by Westerners.

sib *see* clan.

siblings a person's brothers and sisters.

sickle cell anemia (or sicklemia) condition in which red blood cells assume a crescent (sickle) shape when deprived of oxygen instead of the normal (disk) shape. Severe anemia, painful circulatory problems, enlargement of the heart, brain cell atrophy, and early death may result.

sister language one of two or more languages derived from a common ancestral language. For example, German is a sister language to English.

slash-and-burn a form of shifting horticulture in which the natural vegetation is cut down and burned off. The cleared ground is used for a short time and then is left to regenerate.

slaves a class of persons who do not own their own labor or the products thereof.

socialization (or enculturation) the development, through the influence of parents and others, of patterns of behavior in children that conform to the standards deemed appropriate by the culture.

sociolinguistics (or ethnolinguistics) the study of cultural and subcultural patterns of speaking in different social contexts.

Solutrean Upper Paleolithic culture in France and Spain which dates between 18,000 and 15,000 B.C.; known for finely made stone tools, particularly laurel leaf blades, and for bone tools and eyed needles.

sorcery the use of certain materials to harm people through the manipulation of supernatural powers.

sororal polygyny marriage of a man to two or more sisters at the same time.

sororate custom whereby a woman is obliged to marry her deceased sister's husband.

special-purpose money objects of value for which only some goods and services can be exchanged.

speciation the development of a new species.

species a population which consists of organisms able to interbreed and produce fertile and viable offspring.

spirits unnamed supernatural beings of nonhuman origin, who are beneath the gods in prestige but closer to the people; may be helpful, mischievous, or evil in nature.

state a political unit with centralized decision-making affecting a large population. Most states have cities with public buildings; full-time craft and religious specialists; an "official" art style; a hierarchical social structure topped by an elite class; and a governmental monopoly on the legitimate use of force to implement policies.

status prestige position in a society.

steppe grassland with a dry, low grass cover.

structural (or descriptive) linguistics the study of how languages are constructed and used.

subculture the shared customs of a subgroup within a society.

subsistence technology the methods humans use to procure food and other things which are necessary for the maintenance of life.

supernatural a force that is believed to be not human or subject to the laws of nature.

syntax the ways in which words are arranged to form phrases and sentences.

taboo a prohibition which, if violated, is believed to arouse supernatural punishment.

tarsier nocturnal, tree-living prosimian found on the islands of Southeast Asia, named from their elongated tarsal bones (the bones of the ankle).

taxonomy the study of the classification of extinct and living organisms.

Tetonius an Eocene primate.

Thematic Apperception Test (TAT) projective test using a set of drawings that depict ambiguous life situations; subjects are asked to say what is happening in the pictures.

thermoluminescence method of dating pottery by measuring the amount of light rays released when the object is heated. The older the piece of fired pottery, the more electrons are trapped in it and the more light rays it will release.

totem a plant or animal name given to a clan (sib) which provides group identification and may have other special significance for the group.

transformational grammar an approach to grammar, originated by Noam Chomsky, that attempts to examine the surface structure (the appearance of a sentence) in order to discover the deep structure (the underlying relationships which presumably determine how the sentence was formulated).

tribe egalitarian group with associations that can informally and temporarily integrate more than one local group into a large whole.

Triceratops large horned dinosaur of the late Cretaceous.

tundra treeless plains characteristic of subarctic and arctic regions.

unifacial tool a tool worked or flaked on one side only.

unilineal descent affiliation with a group of kinsmen through descent links of one sex only.

unilocal pattern of residence nonoptional pattern of residence that specifies just one set of relatives that the married couple lives with or near (i.e., patrilocal, matrilocal, or avunculocal).

unisex association an association that restricts its membership to one sex, most often male.

universally ascribed qualities those qualities (age, sex) that a person acquires at birth and that he or she shares with all members of his or her same age-sex category.

variably ascribed qualities those qualities that a person acquires at birth but which differ among persons of a given age-sex category (like ethnicity or region of birth).

varve analysis dating method based on the fact that varves, annually deposited layers of silt remaining in lake basins from the run-off of melting glacial ice, can be counted and used to date sites up to 17,000 years ago.

vertical clinging and leaping locomotor pattern characteristic of several primates including tarsiers and galagos. The animal normally rests by clinging to a branch in a vertical position, and moves by leaping from one branch to land vertically on another.

warfare violence between political entities such as communities, districts, or nations.

wattle-and-daub construction technique that consists of plastering mud over a framework of sticks.

Wiitiko psychosis a form of mental disorder found mostly among males in some North American Indian tribes, in which the afflicted individual has the delusion that he is possessed by the spirit of a Wiitiko (a cannibal giant) and has delusions and cannibalistic impulses.

witchcraft the practice of attempting to harm people by supernatural means, but through the emotions and thought processes alone, not by using any tangible objects.

Bibliography

Aberle, David. "A Note on Relative Deprivation Theory as Applied to Millenarian and Other Cult Movements," in W. A. Lessa and E. Z. Vogt, eds., *Reader in Comparative Religion*, 3rd ed. New York: Harper & Row, 1971.

Aberle, David F., et al. "The Incest Taboo and Mating Patterns of Animals," *American Anthropologist*, vol. 65 (1963), pp. 253–65.

Adams, Robert M. "The Origin of Cities." *Scientific American*, September 1960, p. 153.

Allison, Anthony C. "Sickle Cells and Evolution," *Scientific American*, August 1956, p. 87.

Arensberg, Conrad M., and Arthur H. Niehoff. *Introducing Social Change: A Manual for Americans Overseas*. Chicago: Aldine, 1964.

Armstrong, W. E. "Rossel Island Money: A Unique Monetary System," *Economic Journal*, vol. 34 (September 1924), pp. 423-29.

Asch, Solomon. "Studies of Independence and Conformity: A Minority of One against a Unanimous Majority," *Psychological Monographs*, vol. 70 (1956), pp. 1–70.

Ashton, Hugh. *The Basuto*, 2nd ed. London: Oxford University Press, 1967.

Ayres, Barbara C. "Effects of Infant Carrying Practices on Rhythm in Music," *Ethos*, vol. 1 (1973), pp. 387–404.

Ayres, Barbara C. "Effects of Infantile Stimulation on Musical Behavior," in Alan Lomax, *Folk Song Style and Culture*, American Association for the Advancement of Science, Publication no. 88, Washington, D.C., 1968.

Barnett, H. G. *Being a Palauan*. New York: Holt, Rinehart and Winston, 1960.

Barnouw, Victor. *Culture and Personality*. Homewood, Ill.: Dorsey Press, 1963.

Barry, Herbert, III, Margaret K. Bacon, and Irvin L. Child. "A Cross-Cultural Survey of Some Sex Differences in Socialization," *Journal of Abnormal and Social Psychology*, vol. 55 (1957), pp. 327–332.

Barry, Herbert, III, Irvin L. Child, and Margaret K. Bacon. "Relation of Child Training to Subsistence Economy," *American Anthropologist*, vol. 61 (1959), pp. 51–63.

Barth, Fredrik. "Nomadism in the Mountain and Plateau Areas of South West Asia," in *The Problems of the Arid Zone*. Paris: UNESCO, 1960.

Barth, Fredrik. *Nomads of South Persia*. Boston: Little, Brown, 1968 (originally published in 1964).

Bartram, William. *The Travels of William Bartram* (ed., Francis Harper). New Haven: Yale University Press, 1958.

Bateson, Gregory, and Margaret Mead. *Balinese Character: A Photographic Analysis,* Special Publication of the New York Academy of Sciences, New York, 1942.

Beadle, George, and Muriel Beadle. *The Language of Life.* Garden City, N.Y.: Doubleday, 1966.

Beattie, John. *Bunyoro: An African Kingdom.* New York: Holt, Rinehart and Winston, 1960.

Benzel, Ruth. "The Nature of Katcinas," in W. A. Lessa and E. Z. Vogt, eds., *Reader in Comparative Religion,* 3rd ed. New York: Harper & Row, 1971.

Berlin, Brent, and Paul Kay. *Basic Color Terms: Their Universality and Evolution.* Berkeley: University of California Press, 1969.

Bernardi, B. "The Age-System of the Nilo-Hamitic Peoples," *Africa,* vol. 22 (1952), pp. 316–32.

Binford, Lewis R. "Post-Pleistocene Adaptations," in Lewis R. Binford and S. R. Binford, eds., *New Perspectives in Archaeology.* Chicago: Aldine, 1968.

Binford, Lewis R. "Post-Pleistocene Adaptations," in Stuart Struever, ed., *Prehistoric Agriculture.* Garden City, N.Y.: Natural History Press, 1971.

Blanton, Richard. "The Origins of Monte Albán," in C. Cleland, ed., *Cultural Continuity and Change.* New York: Academic Press, 1976.

Boas, Franz. *Central Eskimos,* Bureau of American Ethnology, Annual Report no. 6, Washington, D.C., 1888.

Boas, Franz. *Geographical Names of the Kwakiutl Indians.* New York: Columbia University Press, 1934.

Boas, Franz. *The Religion of the Kwakiutl,* Columbia University Contributions to Anthropology, vol. 10, pt. II. New York: 1930.

Bogoras, Waldemar. "The Chukchee," Pt. 3, *Memoirs of the American Museum of Natural History,* vol. 2, 1909. In William N. Stephens, *The Family in Cross-Cultural Perspective.* New York: Holt, Rinehart and Winston, 1963.

Bohannan, Laura, and Paul Bohannan. *The Tiv of Central Nigeria.* London: International African Institute, 1953.

Bohannan, Paul. "The Migration and Expansion of the Tiv," *Africa,* vol. 24 (1954), p. 3.

Bordaz, Jacques. *Tools of the Old and New Stone Age.* Garden City, N.Y.: Natural History Press, 1970.

Bordes, F. H. *The Old Stone Age* (trans., J. E. Anderson). Toronto: World University Library, 1968.

Bornstein, Marc H. "The Psychophysiological Component of Cultural Difference in Color Naming and Illusion Susceptibility," *Behavior Science Notes,* vol. 8 (1973), pp. 41–101.

Boserup, Ester. *The Conditions of Agricultural Growth: The Economics of Agrarian Change under Population Pressures.* Chicago: Aldine, 1965.

Brace, C. Loring. "Sexual Dimorphism in Human Evolution," in C. Loring Brace and James Metress, eds., *Man in Evolutionary Perspective.* New York: John Wiley and Sons, 1972.

Braidwood, Robert J. "The Agricultural Revolution," *Scientific American,* September 1960, p. 130.

Braidwood, Robert J., and Gordon R. Willey. "Conclusions and Afterthoughts," in Robert J. Braidwood and Gordon R. Willey, eds., *Courses Toward Urban Life: Archaeological Consideration of Some Cultural Alternatives,* Viking Fund Publications in Anthropology, no. 32. Chicago: Aldine, 1962.

Brinton, Crane. *Anatomy of a Revolution.* Englewood Cliffs, N.J.: Prentice-Hall, 1938.

Brodey, Jane E. "Effects of Milk on Blacks Noted," *New York Times,* October 15, 1971, p. 15.

Brown, Judith K. "A Note on the Division of Labor by Sex," *American Anthropologist,* vol. 72 (1970), p. 1074.

Brown, Roger. *Social Psychology.* New York: Free Press, 1965.

Brown, Roger, and Marguerite Ford. "Address in American English," *Journal of Abnormal and Social Psychology,* vol. 62 (1961), pp. 375–85.

Buettner-Janusch, John. *Origins of Man.* New York: John Wiley and Sons, 1966.

Buettner-Janusch, John. *Physical Anthropology: A Perspective.* New York: John Wiley & Sons, 1973.

Burling, R. *Man's Many Voices.* New York: Holt, Rinehart and Winston, 1970.

Burton, Roger V., and John W. M. Whiting. "The Absent Father and Cross-Sex Identity," *Merrill-Palmer Quarterly,* vol. 7, no. 2 (1961), pp. 85–95.

Butzer, Karl W. "Another Look at the Australopithecine Cave Breccias of the Transvaal," *American Anthropologist,* vol. 73 (1971), pp. 1197–1201.

Byers, D. S. "Comments on R. Mason's *The Paleo Indian Tradition in Eastern North America,*" *Current Anthropology,* vol. 3 (1962), pp. 247–48.

Campbell, Bernard G. *Human Evolution: An Introduction to Man's Adaptations,* rev. ed. Chicago: Aldine, 1974.

Campbell, C. B. G. "On the Phyletic Relationships of the Tree Shrews," *Mammal Review,* vol. 4, no. 4 (1974), pp. 125–43.

Campbell, Donald T. "Variation and Selective Retention in Socio-Cultural Evolution," in Herbert Barringer, George Blankstein and Raymond

Mack, eds., *Social Change in Developing Areas: A Re-Interpretation of Evolutionary Theory*. Cambridge, Mass.: Schenkman, 1965.

Carneiro, Robert L. "Slash-and-Burn Cultivation among the Kuikuru and its Implications for Cultural Development in the Amazon Basin," *Antropologica*, Supplement no. 2 (September 1961).

Carneiro, Robert L. "A Theory of the Origin of the State," *Science*, August 21, 1970, pp. 733–38.

Carpenter, C. R. "A Field Study in Siam of the Behavior and Social Relations of Gibbons, Hylobateslar," *Comparative Psychology Monographs*, vol. 16, no. 15 (1940), pp. 1–212.

Carroll, John B., ed. *Language, Thought, and Reality: Selected Writings of Benjamin Lee Whorf*. New York: John Wiley and Sons, 1956.

Casagrande, Joseph B. "Comanche Baby Talk," *International Journal of American Linguistics*, vol. 14 (1948), pp. 11–14.

Chagnon, Napoleon A. *Yanomamö, the Fierce People*. New York: Holt, Rinehart and Winston, 1968.

Chang, Kwang-Chih. *The Archaeology of Ancient China*. New Haven: Yale University Press, 1968.

Chang, Kwang-Chih. "The Beginnings of Agriculture in the Far East," *Antiquity*, vol. 44, no. 175 (September 1970), pp. 175–85.

Chard, Chester S. *Man in Prehistory*. New York: McGraw-Hill, 1969.

Child, I. L., T. Storm, and J. Veroff. "Achievement Themes in Folktales Related to Socialization Practice," in J. W. Atkinson, ed., *Motives in Fantasy, Action and Society*. Princeton, N.J.: Van Nostrand, 1958.

Childe, V. Gordon. *Man Makes Himself*. New York: Mentor Books, New American Library, 1951.

Childe, V. Gordon. "The New Stone Age," in Harry L. Shapiro, ed., *Man, Culture and Society*. New York: Oxford University Press, 1956.

Clark, Grahame, and Stuart Piggot. *Prehistoric Societies*. New York: Alfred A. Knopf, 1965.

Clark, J. Desmond. *The Prehistory of Africa*. New York: Praeger, 1970.

Coale, Ansley J. "The History of the Human Population," *Scientific American*, September 1974, pp. 40–51.

Coe, Michael D. *The Maya*. New York: Praeger, 1966.

Collier, Stephen, and J. Peter White. "Get Them Young? Age and Sex Inferences on Animal Domestication in Archaeology," *American Antiquity*, vol. 41 (1976), pp. 96–102.

Coon, Carleton. Quoted in Fred T. Adams, *The Way to Modern Man*. New York: Columbia University Press, 1968, p. 250.

Coult, Allan D., and Robert W. Habenstein. *Cross Tabulations of Murdock's World Ethnographic Sample*. Columbia: University of Missouri Press, 1965.

Crabtree, Don E., and B. Robert Butler. "Notes on Experiment in Flint Knapping: 1. Heat Treatment of Silica Materials," *Tebiwa*, vol. 7, no. 1 (January 1964), pp. 1–6.

Curtis, G. H., et al. "Age of KBS Tuff in Koobi Fora Formation, East Rudolf, Kenya," *Nature*, vol. 258 (1975), pp. 395–98.

Dalton, George. "Primitive Money," *American Anthropologist*, vol. 67 (1965), pp. 44–65.

Damon, Albert. "Stature Increase among Italian-Americans: Environmental, Genetic, or Both?" *American Journal of Physical Anthropology*, vol. 23 (1965), pp. 401–8.

Dart, Raymond. "Australopithecus Africanus: The Man-Ape of South Africa," *Nature*, vol. 115 (1925), p. 195.

Darwin, Charles. *On the Origin of Species* (ed., Thomas H. Huxley). Ann Arbor: University of Michigan Press, 1968.

Davenport, William. "Nonunilineal Descent and Descent Groups," *American Anthropologist*, vol. 61 (1959), pp. 557–72.

Davenport, William. "Sexual Patterns and Their Regulation in a Society of the Southwest Pacific," in Frank A. Beach, ed., *Sex and Behavior*. New York: John Wiley and Sons, 1965.

Davis, Allison, Burleigh B. Gardner, and Mary R. Gardner. *Deep South: A Social-Anthropological Study of Caste and Class*. Chicago: University of Chicago Press, 1941.

Davis, Kingsley, and Wilbert Moore. "Some Principles of Stratification," in Celia Heller, ed., *Structured Social Inequality: A Reader in Social Stratification*. New York: Macmillan, 1969.

de Lumley, Henry. "A Paleolithic Camp at Nice," *Scientific American*, May 1969, pp. 42–50.

Divale, William T. "Migration, External Warfare, and Matrilocal Residence," *Behavior Science Research*, vol. 9 (1974), pp. 75–133.

Dobzhansky, Theodosius. *Mankind Evolving: The Evolution of the Human Species*. New Haven: Yale University Press, 1962.

Dohlinow, Phyllis Jay, and Naomi Bishop. "The Development of Motor Skills and Social Relationships among Primates through Play," in Phyllis Jay Dohlinow, ed., *Primate Patterns*. New York: Holt, Rinehart and Winston, 1972.

Dorson, Richard. "The Eclipse of Solar Mythology," in Alan Dundes, ed., *The Study of Folklore.* Englewood Cliffs, N.J.: Prentice-Hall, 1965.

Dowling, John H. "Property Relations and Productive Strategies in Pastoral Societies," *American Ethnologist,* vol. 2 (1975), pp. 419–26.

Drucker, Philip. *Cultures of the North Pacific Coast.* San Francisco: Chandler, 1965.

Drucker, Philip. "The Potlatch," in George Dalton, ed., *Tribal and Peasant Economies.* Garden City, N.Y.: Natural History Press, 1967.

Du Bois, Cora. *The People of Alor: A Social-Psychological Study of an East Indian Island.* Minneapolis: University of Minnesota Press, 1944.

Dundes, Alan. "Structural Typology in North American Indian Folktales," in Alan Dundes, ed., *The Study of Folklore.* Englewood Cliffs, N.J.: Prentice-Hall, 1965.

Dundes, Alan, ed. *The Study of Folklore.* Englewood Cliffs, N.J.: Prentice-Hall, 1965.

Durkheim, Emile. "The Elementary Forms of the Religious Life," in W. A. Lessa and E. Z. Vogt, eds., *Reader in Comparative Religion,* 3rd ed. New York: Harper & Row, 1971.

Durkheim, Emile. *The Rules of Sociological Method,* 8th ed. (trans., Sarah A. Soloway and John H. Mueller; ed., George E. E. Catlin). Glencoe, Ill.: Free Press, 1936.

Dyson-Hudson, Neville. *Karimojong Politics.* Oxford: Clarendon Press, 1966.

Eggan, Fred. *The Social Organization of the Western Pueblos.* Chicago: University of Chicago Press, 1950.

Eiseley, Loren C. "The Dawn of Evolutionary Theory," in Loren C. Eiseley, *Darwin's Century: Evolution and the Men Who Discovered It.* Garden City, N.Y.: Doubleday, 1958.

Eisenstadt, S. N. "African Age Groups," *Africa,* vol. 24 (1954), p. 102.

Elwin, Verrier. *The Religion of an Indian Tribe.* London: Oxford University Press, 1955.

Ember, Carol R., and Melvin Ember. "The Conditions Favoring Multilocal Residence," *Southwestern Journal of Anthropology,* vol. 28 (1972), pp. 382–400.

Ember, Carol R., Melvin Ember, and Burton Pasternak. "On the Development of Unilineal Descent," *Journal of Anthropological Research,* vol. 30 (1974), pp. 69–94.

Ember, Melvin. "The Conditions that May Favor Avunculocal Residence," *Behavior Science Research,* vol. 9 (1974), pp. 203–9.

Ember, Melvin. "The Emergence of Neolocal Residence," *Transactions of the New York Academy of Sciences,* vol. 30 (1967), pp. 291–302.

Ember, Melvin. "The Nonunilinear Descent Groups of Samoa," *American Anthropologist,* vol. 61 (1959), pp. 573–77.

Ember, Melvin. "On the Origin and Extension of the Incest Taboo," *Behavior Science Research,* in press.

Ember, Melvin. "The Relationship between Economic and Political Development in Nonindustrialized Societies," *Ethnology,* vol. 2 (1963), pp. 228–48.

Ember, Melvin. "Warfare, Sex Ratio, and Polygyny," *Ethnology,* vol. 13 (1974), pp. 197–206.

Ember, Melvin, and Carol R. Ember. "The Conditions Favoring Matrilocal versus Patrilocal Residence," *American Anthropologist,* vol. 73 (1971), pp. 571–94.

"Ethics in Applied Anthropology," *Human Organization,* vol. 10 (Summer 1951), p. 4.

Evans-Pritchard, E. E. "Nuer Modes of Address," *Uganda Journal,* vol. 12 (1948), pp. 166–71.

Evans-Pritchard, E. E. "The Nuer of the Southern Sudan," in M. Fortes and E. E. Evans-Pritchard, ed., *African Political Systems.* New York: Oxford University Press, 1940.

Evans-Pritchard, E. E. "Witchcraft Explains Unfortunate Events," in W. A. Lessa and E. Z. Vogt, eds., *Reader in Comparative Religion,* 3rd ed. New York: Harper & Row, 1971.

"Evolution Before Life," *Time,* November 17, 1958, p. 64.

Fagan, Brian. *In the Beginning.* Boston: Little, Brown, 1972.

Feldman, M. W., and R. C. Lewontin. "The Heritability Hang-Up," *Science,* December 19, 1975, pp. 1163–68.

"The First Dentist," *Newsweek,* March 5, 1973, p. 73.

Firth, Raymond. *Rank and Religion in Tikopia.* Boston: Beacon Press, 1970.

Firth, Raymond. *Social Change in Tikopia.* New York: Macmillan, 1959.

Fischer, John. "Art Styles as Cultural Cognitive Maps," *American Anthropologist,* vol. 63 (1961), pp. 80–83.

Fischer, John L. "Social Influences on the Choice of a Linguistic Variant," *Word,* vol. 14 (1958), pp. 47–56.

Flannery, Kent V. "The Cultural Evolution of Civilizations," *Annual Review of Ecology,* vol. 3 (1972).

Flannery, Kent V. "The Ecology of Early Food Production in Mesopotamia," *Science,* March 12, 1965, pp. 1247–56.

Flannery, Kent V. "Origins and Ecological Effects of Early Domestication in Iran and the Near East," in Stuart Struever, ed., *Prehistoric Agriculture.* Garden City, N.Y.: Natural History Press, 1971. (Originally published in Peter J. Ucko and G. W. Dimbleby, eds., *The Domestication and Exploitation of Plants and Animals.* Chicago: Aldine, 1969.)

Flannery, Kent V. "The Origins of Agriculture," *Annual Review of Anthropology,* vol. 2 (1973).

Flannery, Kent V. "The Origins of the Village as a Settlement Type in Mesoamerica and the Near East: A Comparative Study," in Ruth Tringham, ed., *Territoriality and Proxemics.* Andover, Mass.: Warner Modular Publications, 1973.

Fleischer, Robert L., and Howard R. Hart, Jr. "Fission-Track Dating: Techniques and Problems," in W. A. Bishop and J. A. Miller, eds., *Calibration of Hominid Evolution.* Toronto: University of Toronto Press, 1972.

Fleischer, Robert L., P. B. Price, R. M. Walker, and L. S. B. Leakey. "Fission-Track Dating of Bed I, Olduvai Gorge," *Science,* April 2, 1965, pp. 72–74.

Ford, Clellan S. *Smoke from Their Fires.* New Haven: Yale University Press, 1941.

Ford, Clellan S., and Frank A. Beach. *Patterns of Sexual Behavior.* New York: Harper & Row, 1951.

Fortes, M. *The Web of Kinship among the Tallensi.* New York: Oxford University Press, 1949.

Foster, George M. *Applied Anthropology.* Boston: Little, Brown, 1969.

Foster, George M. *Traditional Cultures and the Impact of Technological Change.* New York: Harper & Row, 1962.

Fowler, Melvin L. "A Pre-Columbian Urban Center on the Mississippi," *Scientific American,* August 1975, pp. 92–101.

Frake, Charles O. "The Eastern Subanum of Mindanao," in G. P. Murdock, ed., *Social Structure in Southeast Asia,* Viking Fund Publications in Anthropology, no. 29. Chicago: Quadrangle Books, 1960.

Fried, Morton H. *The Evolution of Political Society.* New York: Random House, 1967.

Friedl, Ernestine. *Vasilika: A Village in Modern Greece.* New York: Holt, Rinehart and Winston, 1962.

Frisch, K. von. "Dialects in the Language of the Bees," *Scientific American,* August 1962, pp. 78–87.

Gardner, R. Allen, and Beatrice T. Gardner. "Teaching Sign Language to a Chimpanzee," *Science,* August 15, 1969, pp. 664–72.

Garn, Stanley M. *Human Races,* 3rd ed. Springfield, Ill.: Charles C. Thomas, 1971.

Geertz, Clifford. "Religion as a Cultural System," in Michael Banton, ed., *Anthropological Approaches to the Study of Religion,* Association of Social Anthropologists, Monograph no. 3. London: Tavistock, 1965.

Geertz, Clifford. *The Religion of Java.* Glencoe, Ill.: Free Press, 1960.

Gentner, W., and H. J. Lippolt. "The Potassium-Argon Datings of Upper Tertiary and Pleistocene Deposits," in Don Brothwell and Eric Higgs, eds., *Science in Archaeology.* New York: Basic Books, 1963.

Gibbs, James L., Jr. "The Kpelle of Liberia," in James L. Gibbs, Jr., ed., *Peoples of Africa.* New York: Holt, Rinehart and Winston, 1965.

Gibbs, James L., Jr., ed. *Peoples of Africa.* New York: Holt, Rinehart and Winston, 1965.

Glass, H. Bentley. "The Genetics of the Dunkers," *Scientific American,* August 1953, pp. 76–81.

Goldstein, Melvyn C. "Stratification, Polyandry, and Family Structure in Central Tibet," *Southwestern Journal of Anthropology,* vol. 27 (1971), pp. 64–74.

Goodall, Jane. "My Life among Wild Chimpanzees," *National Geographic,* August 1963, pp. 272–308.

Goode, William J. *The Family.* Englewood Cliffs, N.J.: Prentice-Hall, 1964.

Goode, William J. *World Revolution and Family Patterns.* New York: Free Press, 1963.

Goodenough, Ward H. *Property, Kin and Community on Truk.* New Haven: Yale University Press, 1951.

Goodrich, L. Carrington. *A Short History of the Chinese People,* 3rd ed. New York: Harper & Row, 1959.

Goody, Jack. "Cousin Terms," *Southwestern Journal of Anthropology,* vol. 26 (1970), pp. 125–42.

Gorer, Geoffrey, and John Rickman. *The People of Great Russia: A Psychological Study.* New York: Chanticleer, 1950.

Gorman, Chester. "The Hoabinhian and After: Subsistence Patterns in Southeast Asia During the Late Pleistocene and Early Recent Periods," *World Archaeology,* vol. 2 (1970), pp. 315–19.

BIBLIOGRAPHY

Gossen, Gary H. "Temporal and Spatial Equivalents in Chamula Ritual Symbolism," in W. A. Lessa and E. Z. Vogt, eds., *Reader in Comparative Religion*, 3rd ed. New York: Harper & Row, 1971.

Gough, Kathleen. "Nayar: Central Kerala," in David M. Schneider and Kathleen Gough, eds., *Matrilineal Kinship*. Berkeley: University of California Press, 1961.

Gough, Kathleen. "The Nayars and the Definition of Marriage," *Journal of the Royal Anthropological Institute*, vol. 89 (1959), pp. 23–24.

Gould, Richard A. *Yiwara: Foragers of the Australian Desert*. New York: Charles Scribner's Sons, 1969.

Graburn, Nelson H. *Eskimos without Igloos*. Boston: Little, Brown, 1969.

Gross, Daniel R., and Barbara A. Underwood. "Technological Change and Caloric Costs: Sisal Agriculture in Northeastern Brazil," *American Anthropologist*, vol. 73 (1971), pp. 725–40.

Gulliver, P. H. "The Arusha: Economic and Social Change," in Paul Bohannan and George Dalton, eds., *Markets in Africa*. Garden City, N.Y.: Doubleday, 1965.

Gumperz, John J. "Speech Variation and the Study of Indian Civilization," *American Anthropologist*, vol. 63 (1961), pp. 976–88.

Gunders, S., and J. W. M. Whiting. "Mother-Infant Separation and Physical Growth," *Ethnology*, vol. 7 (1968), pp. 196–206.

Haas, Mary R. "Men's and Women's Speech in Koasati," *Language*, vol. 20 (1944), pp. 142–49.

Hahn, Emily. "Chimpanzees and Language," *New Yorker*, April 24, 1971, p. 54 ff.

Haldane, J. B. S. "Human Evolution: Past and Future," in Glenn L. Jepsen, Ernst Mayr and George Gaylord Simpson, eds., *Genetics, Paleontology, and Evolution*. New York: Atheneum, 1963.

Hall, Edward T. *The Hidden Dimension*. Garden City, N.Y.: Doubleday, 1966.

Hall, K. R. L. "Aggression in Monkey and Ape Societies," in P. C. Day, ed., *Primates*. New York: Holt, Rinehart and Winston, 1968.

Hallam, A. "Alfred Wegener and the Hypothesis of Continental Drift," *Scientific American*, February 1975, pp. 88–97.

Handelman, Don. "The Development of a Washo Shaman," *Ethnology*, vol. 6 (1967), pp. 444–61.

Harlan, Jack R. "A Wild Wheat Harvest in Turkey," *Archaeology*, vol. 20 (1967), pp. 197–201.

Harlow, H. F., et al. "Maternal Behavior of Rhesus Monkeys Deprived of Mothering and Peer Association in Infancy," *Proceedings of the American Philosophical Society*, vol. 110 (1966), pp. 58–66.

Harner, Michael J. *The Jivaro*. Garden City, N.Y.: Anchor Books, 1973.

Harner, Michael J. "Population Pressure and the Social Evolution of Agriculturalists," *Southwestern Journal of Anthropology*, vol. 26 (1970), pp. 67–86.

Harner, Michael J. "Scarcity, the Factors of Production, and Social Evolution," in Steven Polgar, ed., *Population, Ecology, and Social Evolution*. The Hague: Mouton, 1975.

Harris, Marvin. *Cows, Pigs, Wars and Witches*. New York: Vintage, 1975.

Harris, Marvin. "The Cultural Ecology of India's Sacred Cattle," *Current Anthropology*, vol. 7 (1966), pp. 51–63.

Harrison, Gail G. "Primary Adult Lactase Deficiency: A Problem in Anthropological Genetics," *American Anthropologist*, vol. 77 (1975), pp. 812–35.

Helms, Mary W. *Middle America*. Englewood Cliffs, N.J.: Prentice-Hall, 1975.

Henry, William E. *The Thematic Apperception Technique in the Study of Culture-Personality Relations*, Genetic Psychology Monograph, no. 35 (1947).

Herskovits, M. J. *Dahomey: An Ancient West African Kingdom*. New York: Augustin, 1938.

Hewes, Gordon W. "Food Transport and the Origin of Hominid Bipedalism," *American Anthropologist*, vol. 63 (1961), pp. 687–710.

Hiatt, L. R. "Ownership and Use of Land among the Australian Aborigines," in Richard B. Lee and Irven DeVore, eds., *Man the Hunter*. Chicago: Aldine, 1968.

Hickey, Gerald Cannon. *Village in Vietnam*. New Haven: Yale University Press, 1964.

Hobsbawm, E. J. *Age of Revolution*. New York: Praeger, 1970.

Hock, Raymond J. "The Physiology of High Altitude," *Scientific American*, February 1970, pp. 52–62.

Hockett, C. F., and R. Ascher. "The Human Revolution," *Current Anthropology*, vol. 5 (1964), pp. 135–68.

Hoebel, E. Adamson. *The Cheyenne: Indians of the Great Plains*. New York: Holt, Rinehart and Winston, 1960.

Hoebel, E. Adamson. *The Law of Primitive Man*. New York: Atheneum, 1968 (originally published in 1954).

Hoijer, Harry. "Cultural Implications of Some Navaho Linguistic Categories," *Language,* vol. 27 (1951), pp. 111–20.

Hole, Frank, and Robert F. Heizer. *An Introduction to Prehistoric Archeology,* 2nd ed. New York: Holt, Rinehart and Winston, 1969.

Hollis, A. C. *The Nandi: Their Language and Folklore.* Oxford: Clarendon Press, 1909.

Holloway, Ralph L. "The Casts of Fossil Hominid Brains," *Scientific American,* July 1974, pp. 106–15.

Honigmann, John J. *Personality in Culture.* New York: Harper & Row, 1967.

Howard, B. D. *Life with Trans-Siberian Savages.* London: Longmans, Green, 1893.

Howell, F. Clark. "Observations on the Earlier Phases of the European Lower Paleolithic (Torralba-Ambrona)," in *Recent Studies in Paleoanthropology. American Anthropologist,* Special Publication, April 1966.

Howell, F. Clark. "Remains of Hominidae from Pliocene/Pleistocene Formation in the Lower Omo Basin, Ethiopia," *Nature,* vol. 223 (1969), pp. 1234–39.

Huntingford, G. W. B. *The Nandi of Kenya: Tribal Control in a Pastoral Society.* London: Routledge and Kegan Paul, 1953.

Huxley, Julian. *Evolution in Action.* New York: Mentor Books, 1957.

Isaac, Glynn. "The Diet of Early Man: Aspects of Archaeological Evidence from Lower and Middle Pleistocene Sites in Africa," *World Archeology,* vol. 2 (1971), pp. 277–99.

Isaac, Glynn. "Studies of Early Culture in East Africa," *World Archeology,* vol. 1 (1969), p. 11.

Isaac, Glynn, Richard E. F. Leakey, and Anna K. Behrensmeyer. "Archeological Traces of Early Hominid Activities, East of Lake Rudolf, Kenya," *Science,* September 17, 1971, pp. 1129–33.

Itani, Jun'ichiro. "The Society of Japanese Monkeys," *Japan Quarterly,* vol. 8 (1961), pp. 421–30.

Itkonen, T. I. "The Lapps of Finland," *Southwestern Journal of Anthropology,* vol. 7 (1951), pp. 32–68.

James, Preston E. *A Geography of Man,* 3rd ed. Waltham, Mass.: Blaisdell, 1966.

Janzen, Daniel H. "Tropical Agroecosystems," *Science,* December 21, 1973, pp. 1212–19.

Jenness, Diamond. *The People of the Twilight.* Chicago: University of Chicago Press, 1959.

Jennings, L. *Prehistory of North America.* New York: McGraw-Hill, 1968.

Jensen, Arthur. "How Much Can We Boost IQ and Scholastic Achievement?" *Harvard Educational Review,* vol. 29 (1969), pp. 1–123.

Jolly, Alison. *The Evolution of Primate Behavior.* New York: Macmillan, 1972.

Jolly, Clifford J. "The Seed-Eaters: A New Model of Hominid Differentiation Based on Baboon Analogy," *Man,* vol. 5 (1970), pp. 5–24.

Kaplan, David. "The Mexican Marketplace Then and Now," in June Helm, ed., *Essays in Economic Anthropology,* Proceedings of the Annual Spring Meeting of the American Ethnological Society, 1965.

Kaplan, David, and Robert A. Manners. "Anthropology: Some Old Themes and New Directions," *Southwestern Journal of Anthropology,* vol. 27 (1971), pp. 19–40.

Kardiner, Abram. *The Individual and His Society.* New York: Golden Press, 1946.

Kasarda, John D. "Economic Structure and Fertility: A Comparative Analysis," *Dermography,* vol. 8 (1971), pp. 307–18.

Keller, Helen. *The Story of My Life.* New York: Dell (originally published in 1902).

Kennedy, Kenneth A. R. *Neanderthal Man.* Minneapolis: Burgess, 1975.

Klein, Richard G. "Ice-Age Hunters of the Ukraine," *Scientific American,* June 1974, pp. 96–105.

Klein, Richard G. *Man and Culture in the Late Pleistocene.* San Francisco: Chandler, 1969.

Klein, Richard G. Personal communication. In David Pilbeam, *The Ascent of Man.* New York: Macmillan, 1972.

Klineberg, Otto. *Characteristics of the American Negro.* New York: Harper & Row, 1944.

Klineberg, Otto. *Negro Intelligence and Selective Migration.* New York: Columbia University Press, 1935.

Kluckhohn, Clyde. "As an Anthropologist Views It," in A. Deutsch, ed., *Sex Habits of American Men.* Englewood Cliffs, N.J.: Prentice-Hall, 1948.

Kluckhohn, Clyde. "Recurrent Themes in Myths and Myth-Making," in Alan Dundes, ed., *The Study of Folklore.* Englewood Cliffs, N.J.: Prentice-Hall, 1965.

Kohn, Melvin L. "Social Class and Parent-Child Relationships: An Interpretation," *American Journal of Sociology,* vol. 68 (1963), pp. 471–80.

Kramer, Samuel Noel. *The Sumerians.* Chicago: University of Chicago Press, 1963.

Kummer, Hans. *Primate Societies: Group Techniques on Ecological Adaptation.* Chicago: Aldine, 1971.

Kuper, Hilda. *A South African Kingdom: The Swazi.* New York: Holt, Rinehart and Winston, 1963.

Kuper, Hilda. "The Swazi of Swaziland," in James L. Gibbs, Jr., ed., *Peoples of Africa.* New York: Holt, Rinehart and Winston, 1965.

Lambert, William W., Leigh Minturn Triandis, and Margery Wolf. "Some Correlates of Beliefs in the Malevolence and Benevolence of Supernatural Beings: A Cross-Societal Study," *Journal of Abnormal and Social Psychology,* vol. 58 (1959), pp. 162–69.

Lancaster, Jane B. *Primate Behavior and the Emergence of Human Culture.* New York: Holt, Rinehart and Winston, 1975.

Landauer, Thomas K., and John W. M. Whiting. "Infantile Stimulation and Adult Stature of Human Males," *American Anthropologist,* vol. 66 (1964), p. 1008.

Landes, Ruth. "The Abnormal among the Ojibwa," *Journal of Abnormal and Social Psychology,* vol. 33 (1938), pp. 14–33.

Leach, Edmund. "Pulleyar and the Lord Buddha: An Aspect of Religious Syncretism in Ceylon," in W. A. Lessa and E. Z. Vogt, eds., *Reader in Comparative Religion,* 3rd ed. New York: Harper & Row, 1971.

Leakey, L. S. B. "Finding the World's Earliest Man," *National Geographic,* September 1960, p. 424.

Leakey, Mary D. "A Review of the Oldowan Culture from Olduvai Gorge, Tanzania," *Nature,* vol. 210 (1966), p. 466.

Leakey, Richard E. F. "Evidence for an Advanced Plio-Pleistocene Hominid from East Rudolf, Kenya," *Nature,* vol. 242 (1973), pp. 447–50.

Lee, Richard B. "Population Growth and the Beginnings of Sedentary Life among the !Kung Bushmen," in Brian Spooner, ed., *Population Growth: Anthropological Implications.* Cambridge, Mass.: MIT Press, 1972.

Lee, Richard B. "What Hunters Do for a Living, or, How to Make Out on Scarce Resources," in Richard B. Lee and Irven DeVore, eds., *Man the Hunter.* Chicago: Aldine, 1968.

Lee, Richard B., and Irven DeVore, eds. *Man the Hunter.* Chicago: Aldine, 1968.

Lees, Susan H., and Daniel G. Bates. "The Origins of Specialized Nomadic Pastoralism: A Systemic Model," *American Antiquity,* vol. 39 (1974), pp. 187–93.

Lenski, Gerhard. *Power and Privilege.* New York: McGraw-Hill, 1966.

Leroi-Gourhan, André. "The Evolution of Paleolithic Art," *Scientific American,* February 1968, pp. 58–70.

LeVine, Robert A., and Barbara B. LeVine. "Nyansongo: A Gusii Community in Kenya," in Beatrice B. Whiting, ed., *Six Cultures.* New York: John Wiley and Sons, 1963.

Lévi-Strauss, Claude. "The Sorcerer and His Magic," in Claude Lévi-Strauss, *Structural Anthropology.* New York: Basic Books, 1963.

Lévi-Strauss, Claude. *Totemism.* Boston: Beacon Press, 1962.

Lewis, I. M. *A Pastoral Democracy.* New York: Oxford University Press, 1961.

Lewis, Oscar. *Life in a Mexican Village: Tepoztlan Revisited.* Urbana: University of Illinois Press, 1951.

Lewis, Oscar (with· the assistance of Victor Barnouw). *Village Life in Northern India.* Urbana: University of Illinois Press, 1958.

Linton, Ralph. *The Cultural Background of Personality.* New York: Appleton-Century-Crofts, 1945.

Linton, Ralph. *The Study of Man.* New York: Appleton-Century-Crofts, 1936.

Little, Kenneth. "The Political Function of the Poro," *Africa,* vol. 35 (1965), pp. 349–65; vol. 36 (1966), pp. 62–71.

Little, Kenneth. "The Role of Voluntary Associations in West African Urbanization," *American Anthropologist,* vol. 59 (1957), pp. 582–93.

Little, Kenneth. *West African Urbanization.* New York: Cambridge University Press, 1965.

Livingston, Frank B. "Malaria and Human Polymorphisms," *Annual Review of Genetics,* vol. 5 (1971).

Lomax, Alan. *Folk Song Style and Culture,* American Association for the Advancement of Science, Publication no. 88, Washington, D.C., 1968.

Loomis, W. Farnsworth. "Skin-Pigment Regulation of Vitamin-D Biosynthesis in Man," *Science,* August 4, 1967, pp. 501–6.

Lovejoy, Owen, Kingsbury Heiple, and Albert Bernstein. "The Gait of *Australopithecus,*" *American Journal of Physical Anthropology,* vol. 38 (1973), pp. 757–79.

Lowie, Robert H. *The Crow Indians.* New York: Rinehart, 1956.

Lynd, Robert S., and Helen Merrell Lynd. *Middletown.* New York: Harcourt, Brace, 1929.

Lynd, Robert S., and Helen Merrell Lynd. *Middletown in Transition.* New York: Harcourt, Brace, 1937.

McCarthy, Frederick D., and Margaret McArthur. "The Food Quest and the Time Factor in Aboriginal Economic Life," in C. P. Mountford, ed., *Records of the Australian-American Scientific Expedition to Arnhem Land* (vol. 2, *Anthropology and Nutrition*). Melbourne: Melbourne University Press, 1960.

McClelland, David C. *The Achieving Society.* New York: Van Nostrand, 1961.

McCracken, Robert D. "Lactase Deficiency: An Example of Dietary Evolution," *Current Anthropology,* vol. 12 (1971), pp. 479–500.

McKern, Sharon S., and Thomas W. McKern. *Tracking Fossil Man.* New York: Praeger, 1970.

MacNeish, Richard S. "The Evaluation of Community Patterns in the Tehuacán Valley of Mexico and Speculations about the Cultural Processes," in Ruth Tringham, ed., *Ecology and Agricultural Settlements.* Andover, Mass.: Warner Modular Publications, 1973.

Mair, Lucy. *Witchcraft.* New York: World University Library, 1969.

Malinowski, Bronislaw. "The Group and the Individual in Functional Analysis," *American Journal of Sociology,* vol. 44 (1939), pp. 938–64.

Malinowski, Bronislaw. "*Kula:* The Circulating Exchange of Valuables in the Archipelagoes of Eastern New Guinea," *Man,* vol. 51 (1920), pp. 97–105.

Malinowski, Bronislaw. *The Sexual Life of Savages in North-Western Melanesia.* New York: Halcyon House, 1932.

"Man Traced 3.75 Million Years by Fossils Found in Tanzania," *New York Times,* October 31, 1975, pp. 1, 43.

Mangin, William P. "The Role of Regional Associations in the Adaptation of Rural Migrants to Cities in Peru," in Dwight B. Heath and Richard N. Adams, eds., *Contemporary Cultures and Societies of Latin America.* New York: Random House, 1965.

Maniatis, Tom, and Mark Ptashne. "A DNA Operator-Repressor System," *Scientific American,* January 1976, pp. 64–76.

Mann, Alan. "Hominid and Cultural Origins," *Man,* vol. 7 (1972), pp. 379–86.

Marrett, R. R. *The Threshold of Religion.* London: Methuen, 1909.

Marshall, Lorna. "!Kung Bushmen Bands," in Ronald Cohen and John Middleton, eds., *Comparative Political Systems.* Garden City, N.Y.: Natural History Press, 1967.

Marshall, Lorna. "Sharing, Talking and Giving: Relief of Social Tensions among !Kung Bushmen," *Africa,* vol. 31 (1961), pp. 239–42.

Martin, Paul S. "The Discovery of America," *Science,* March 9, 1973, pp. 969–74.

Martin, R. D. "Strategies of Reproduction," *Natural History,* November 1975, p. 50.

Mason, Phillip. *Prospero's Magic.* London: Oxford University Press, 1962.

Mathiassen, Therkel. *Material Culture of the Iglulik Eskimos.* Copenhagen: Gyldendalske, 1928.

Mazess, Richard B. "Human Adaptation to High Altitude," in Albert Damon, ed., *Physiological Anthropology.* New York: Oxford University Press, 1975.

Mead, Margaret. *Coming of Age in Samoa,* 3rd ed. New York: William Morrow, 1961 (originally published in 1928).

Mead, Margaret. *Growing Up in New Guinea.* London: Routledge & Kegan Paul, 1931.

Meek, C. K. *Land Law and Custom in the Colonies.* London: Oxford University Press, 1940.

Meggitt, M. J. "Male-Female Relationships in the Highlands of Australian New Guinea," *American Anthropologist,* Special Issue, 1964, pp. 204–24.

Meillassoux, Claude. *Urbanization of an African Community.* Seattle: University of Washington Press, 1968.

Mellaart, J. "A Neolithic City in Turkey," *Scientific American,* April 1964, pp. 94–104.

Mellaart, J. "Roots in the Soil," in S. Piggott, ed., *The Dawn of Civilization.* London: Thames and Hudson, 1961.

Middleton, John. "The Cult of the Dead: Ancestors and Ghosts," in W. A. Lessa and E. Z. Vogt, eds., *Reader in Comparative Religion,* 3rd ed. New York: Harper & Row, 1971.

Middleton, Russell. "Brother-Sister and Father-Daughter Marriage in Ancient Egypt," *American Sociological Review,* vol. 27 (1962), p. 606.

Millon, René. "Teotihuacán," *Scientific American,* June 1967, pp. 38–48.

Miner, Horace. "Body Rituals among the Nacirema," *American Anthropologist,* vol. 58 (1956), pp. 504–5.

Minturn, Leigh, and John T. Hitchcock. *The Rājpūts of Khalapur, India.* New York: John Wiley and Sons, 1966.

Minturn, Leigh, and William W. Lambert. *Mothers of Six Cultures: Antecedents of Child Rearing.* New York: John Wiley and Sons, 1964.

Montagu, Ashley. Introduction to Thomas H. Huxley, "Man's Place in Nature," in Louise B. Young, ed., *Evolution of Man.* New York: Oxford University Press, 1970.

Moore, Omar Khayyam. "Divination—A New Perspective," *American Anthropologist,* vol. 59 (1957), pp. 69–74.

Morris, Laura Newell, ed. *Human Populations, Genetics, Variation, and Evolution.* San Francisco: Chandler, 1971.

Motulsky, Arno. "Metabolic Polymorphisms and the Role of Infectious Diseases in Human Evolution," in Laura Newel Morris, ed., *Human Populations, Genetics, Variation, and Evolution.* San Francisco: Chandler, 1971.

Murdock, George Peter. *Social Structure.* New York: Macmillan, 1949.

Murdock, George Peter, and Caterina Provost. "Factors in the Division of Labor by Sex: A Cross-Cultural Analysis," *Ethnology,* vol. 12 (1973), pp. 203–25.

Murphy, Robert F., and Julian H. Steward. "Tappers and Trappers: Parallel Process in Acculturation," *Economic Development and Cultural Change,* vol. 4 (July 1956), p. 353.

Musil, Alois. *The Manners and Customs of Rwala Bedouins,* American Geographical Society, Oriental Exploration Studies no. 6, New York, 1928.

Nadel, S. F. *A Black Byzantium: The Kingdom of Nupe in Nigeria.* London: Oxford University Press, 1942.

Nadel, S. F. "Nupe State and Community," *Africa,* vol. 8 (1935), pp. 257–303.

Napier, J. "The Antiquity of Human Walking," *Scientific American,* April 1967, pp. 56–66.

Napier, J. R., and P. H. Napier. *A Handbook of Living Primates.* New York: Academic Press, 1967.

Napier, J. R., and A. C. Walker. "Vertical Clinging and Leaping—A Newly-Recognized Category of Locomotor Behaviour of Primates," *Folia Primatologica,* vol. 16, nos. 3–4 (1976), pp. 204–19.

Naroll, Raoul. "Two Solutions to Galton's Problem," *Philosophy of Science,* vol. 28 (January 1961), pp. 15–39.

Nash, Manning. *Primitive and Peasant Economic Systems.* San Francisco: Chandler, 1966.

Needham, Rodney. "Percussion and Transition," in W. A. Lessa and E. Z. Vogt, eds., *Reader in Comparative Religion,* 3rd ed. New York: Harper & Row, 1971.

Newman, Marshall T. "The Application of Ecological Rules to the Racial Anthropology of the Aboriginal New World," *American Anthropologist,* vol. 55 (1953), pp. 311–27.

Niehoff, Arthur H. *A Casebook of Social Change.* Chicago: Aldine, 1966.

Nimkoff, M. F., and Russell Middleton. "Types of Family and Types of Economy," *American Journal of Sociology,* vol. 66 (1960), pp. 215–25.

Nissen, Henry W. "Axes of Behavioral Comparison," in Anne Roe and George Gaylord Simpson, eds., *Behavior and Evolution.* New Haven: Yale University Press, 1958.

Norbeck, Edward. "Continuities in Japanese Social Stratification," in Leonard Plotnicov and Arthur Tuden, eds., *Essays in Comparative Social Stratification.* Pittsburgh: University of Pittsburgh Press, 1970.

Oakley, Kenneth. "Analytical Methods of Dating Bones," in Don Brothwell and Eric Higgs, eds., *Science in Archaeology.* New York: Basic Books, 1963.

Oakley, Kenneth. "On Man's Use of Fire, with Comments on Tool-Making and Hunting," in S. L. Washburn, ed., *Social Life of Early Man.* Chicago: Aldine, 1964.

Oliver, Douglas. *A Solomon Island Society.* Cambridge: Harvard University Press, 1955.

Parker, Seymour. "The Wiitiko Psychosis in the Context of Ojibwa Personality and Culture," *American Anthropologist,* vol. 62 (1960), pp. 603–23.

Pasternak, Burton. *Introduction to Kinship and Social Organization.* Englewood Cliffs, N.J.: Prentice-Hall, 1976.

Pasternak, Burton, Carol R. Ember, and Melvin Ember. "On the Conditions Favoring Extended Family Households," *Journal of Anthropological Research,* in press.

Patterson, Thomas C. *America's Past: A New World Archaeology.* Glenview, Ill.: Scott, Foresman & Co., 1973.

Patterson, Thomas C. "Central Peru: Its Population and Economy," *Archaeology,* vol. 24 (1971), pp. 316–21.

Paul, Benjamin D. *Health, Culture, and Community: Case Studies of Public Reactions to Health Programs.* New York: Russell Sage Foundation, 1955.

Pfeiffer, John E. *The Emergence of Man,* rev. and enl. ed. New York: Harper & Row, 1972.

Pilbeam, David. *The Ascent of Man.* New York: Macmillan, 1972.

Pilbeam, David, and Stephen Jay Gould. "Size and

Scaling in Human Evolution," *Science*, December 6, 1974, pp. 892–900.

Poirier, Frank E. *Fossil Man: An Evolutionary Journey.* St. Louis: C. V. Mosby, 1973.

Polanyi, Karl. "The Economy of Instituted Process," in Karl Polanyi, Conrad M. Arensberg, and Harry W. Pearson, eds., *Trade and Market in the Early Empires.* Glencoe, Ill.: Free Press, 1957.

Polanyi, Karl, Harry W. Pearson, and Conrad M. Arensberg, eds. *Trade and Market in the Early Empires.* Glencoe, Ill.: Free Press, 1957.

Pospisil, Leopold. *The Kapauku Papuans of West New Guinea.* New York: Holt, Rinehart and Winston, 1963.

Powell, Peter V. *Sweet Medicine*, vol. 2. Norman: University of Oklahoma Press, 1969.

Premack, Ann James and David Premack. "Teaching Language to an Ape," *Scientific American*, October 1972, pp. 92–99.

Radcliffe-Brown. A. R. *The Andaman Islanders: A Study in Social Anthropology.* London: Cambridge University Press, 1922.

Radinsky, Leonard. "The Oldest Primate Endocast," *American Journal of Physical Anthropology*, vol. 27 (1967), pp. 385–88.

Rathje, William L. "The Origin and Development of Lowland Classic Maya Civilization," *American Antiquity*, vol. 36 (1971), pp. 275–85.

Renfrew, Colin. "Trade and Culture Process in European History," *Current Anthropology*, vol. 10 (1969), pp. 156–69.

Riesenfeld, Alphonse. "The Effect of Extreme Temperatures and Starvation on the Body Proportions of the Rat," *American Journal of Physical Anthropology*, vol. 39 (1973), pp. 427–59.

Ritter, Madeline Lattman. *The Conditions Favoring Age-Set Organization.* M. A. thesis, Hunter College of the City University of New York, January 1974.

Roberts, D. F. "Body Weight, Race, and Climate," *American Journal of Physical Anthropology*, vol. 2 (1953), pp. 533–58.

Roberts, John M. "Oaths, Autonomic Ordeals, and Power," in Clellan S. Ford, ed., *Cross-Cultural Approaches: Readings in Comparative Research.* New Haven: HRAF Press, 1967.

Roberts, John M., and Brian Sutton-Smith. "Child Training and Game Involvement," *Ethnology*, vol. 1 (1962), pp. 166–85.

Robinson, J. T. "Adaptive Radiation in the Australopithecines and the Origin of Man," in F. C.

Howell and F. Boulière, *African Ecology and Human Evolution.* Chicago: Aldine, 1963.

Rose, M. Observation cited in Alison Jolly, *The Evolution of Primate Behavior.* New York: Macmillan, 1972.

Rosen, S. I. *Introduction to the Primates: Living and Fossil.* Englewood Cliffs, N.J.: Prentice-Hall, 1974.

Rowell, Thelma E. "Forest-Living Baboons in Uganda," *Journal of Zoology*, vol. 149 (1966), pp. 344–63.

Rumbaugh, Duane M. "Learning Skills of Anthropoids," in L. A. Rosenblum, ed., *Primate Behavior*, vol. 1. New York: Academic Press, 1970.

Rumbaugh, Duane M., Timothy V. Gill, and E. C. von Glasersfeld. "Reading and Sentence Completion by a Chimpanzee (Pam)," *Science*, November 16, 1973, pp. 731–33.

Ruskin, John. "Of King's Treasuries," in John D. Rosenberg, ed., *The Genius of John Ruskin: Selections from His Writings.* New York: George Braziller, 1963.

Russel, D. E. "Les Mammiferes Paleocenes," *Mémoires du Muséum d'Histoire Naturelle*, vol. 13 (1964), pp. 1–324.

Saban, R. "Les Restes Humains de Rabat (Kébibat)," *Annales de Paléontologie (Vertébrés)*, vol. 61 (1975), pp. 196–97.

Sade, D. S. "Some Aspects of Parent-Offspring and Sibling Relationships in a Group of Rhesus Monkeys, with a Discussion of Grooming," *American Journal of Physical Anthropology*, vol. 23 (1965), pp. 1–17.

Sagan, Carl. "A Cosmic Calendar," *Natural History*, December 1975, pp. 70–73.

Sahlins, Marshall D. *Moala: Culture and Nature on a Fijian Island.* Ann Arbor: University of Michigan Press, 1962.

Sahlins, Marshall D. "On the Sociology of Primitive Exchange," in Michael Banton, ed., *The Relevance of Models for Social Anthropology.* London: Tavistock, 1965.

Sahlins, Marshall D. "The Segmentary Lineage: An Organization of Predatory Expansion," *American Anthropologist*, vol. 63 (1961), pp. 332–45.

Sahlins, Marshall D. *Social Stratification in Polynesia.* Seattle: University of Washington Press, 1958.

Sanders, William T. "Hydraulic Agriculture, Economic Symbiosis, and the Evolution of States in Central Mexico," in Betty J. Meggers, ed., *Anthropological Archaeology in the Americas.* Wash-

BIBLIOGRAPHY

ington, D.C.: Anthropological Society of Washington, 1968.

Sanders, William T., and J. Marino. *New World Prehistory.* Englewood Cliffs, N.J.: Prentice-Hall, 1970.

Sanders, William T., and Barbara J. Price. *Mesoamerica.* New York: Random House, 1968.

Sapir, Edward. *Conceptual Categories in Primitive Languages.* Paper presented at the Autumn meeting of the National Academy of Sciences, New Haven, Conn., November 1931. See *Science,* vol. 74 (1931), p. 578.

Sarich, Vincent M. "The Origin of Hominids: An Immunological Approach," in S. L. Washburn and Phyllis C. Jay, eds., *Perspectives on Human Evolution,* vol. 1. New York: Holt, Rinehart and Winston, 1968.

Sarich, Vincent M., and Allan C. Wilson. "Quantitative Immunochemistry and the Evolution of Primate Albumins: Micro-Component Fixations," *Science,* December 23, 1966, pp. 1563–66.

Schaller, G. B. Referred to in Edward O. Wilson, *Sociobiology.* Cambridge, Mass.: Belknap Press, 1975, p. 504.

Schaller, George. *The Mountain Gorilla.* Chicago: University of Chicago Press, 1963.

Schaller, George. *The Year of the Gorilla.* Chicago: University of Chicago Press, 1964.

Schneider, David M. "The Distinctive Features of Matrilineal Descent Groups," in David M. Schneider and Kathleen Gough, eds., *Matrilineal Kinship.* Berkeley: University of California Press, 1961.

Schneider, David M. "Truk," in David M. Schneider and Kathleen Gough, eds., *Matrilineal Kinship.* Berkeley: University of California Press, 1961.

Semenov, S. A. *Prehistoric Technology* (trans., M. W. Thompson). Bath, England: Adams and Dart, 1970.

Service, Elman R. *The Hunters.* Englewood Cliffs, N.J.: Prentice-Hall, 1966.

Service, Elman R. *Origins of the State and Civilization: The Process of Cultural Evolution.* New York: W. W. Norton, 1975.

Service, Elman R. *Primitive Social Organization: An Evolutionary Perspective.* New York: Random House, 1962.

Service, Elman R. *Profiles in Ethnology.* New York: Harper & Row, 1963.

Simmons, Leo W. *Sun Chief.* New Haven: Yale University Press, 1942.

Simons, Elwyn L. "The Earliest Apes," *Scientific American,* December 1967, pp. 28–35.

Simons, Elwyn L. *Primate Evolution: An Introduction to Man's Place in Nature.* New York: Macmillan, 1972.

Simpson, George Gaylord. *The Meaning of Evolution.* New York: Bantam Books, 1971.

Simpson, S. P., and Ruth Feld. "Law and the Social Sciences," *Virginia Law Review,* vol. 32 (1946), p. 858.

Smith, Edwin W., and Andrew Murray Dale. *The Ila-Speaking Peoples of Northern Rhodesia.* New Hyde Park, N.Y.: University Books, 1968 (originally published in 1920 as *Ethnocentric British Colonial Attitudes*).

Smith, Michael G. "Pre-Industrial Stratification Systems," in Neil J. Smelser and Seymour Martin Lipset, eds., *Social Structure and Mobility in Economic Development.* Chicago: Aldine, 1966.

Solecki, Ralph S. "Shanidar Cave," *Scientific American,* November 1957, pp. 58–64.

Southworth, Franklin C., and Chandler J. Daswani. *Foundations of Linguistics.* New York: Free Press, 1974.

Spencer, Baldwin, and F. J. Gillen. *The Arunta: A Study of a Stone Age People,* vol. 1. London: Macmillan, 1927.

Spencer, Robert F. "Spouse-Exchange among the North Alaskan Eskimo," in P. Bohannan and J. Middleton, eds., *Marriage, Family, and Residence.* Garden City, N.Y.: Natural History Press, 1968.

Speth, John D., and Dave D. Davis. "Seasonal Variability in Early Hominid Predation," *Science,* April 30, 1976, pp. 441–45.

Spiro, Melford E., and Roy G. D'Andrade. "A Cross-Cultural Study of Some Supernatural Beliefs," *American Anthropologist,* vol. 60 (1958), pp. 456–66.

Stebbins, G. Ledyard. *Processes of Organic Evolution,* 2nd ed. Englewood Cliffs, N.J.: Prentice-Hall, 1971.

Steegman, A. T., Jr. "Cold Response, Body Form and Craniofacial Shape in Two Racial Groups in Hawaii," *American Journal of Physical Anthropology,* vol. 37 (1972), pp. 193–221.

Steegman, A. T., Jr. "Human Adaptation to Cold," in Albert Damon, ed., *Physiological Anthropology.* New York: Oxford University Press, 1975.

Stephens, William N. *The Family in Cross-Cultural Perspective.* New York: Holt, Rinehart and Winston, 1963.

Stern, Curt. *Principles of Human Genetics*, 3rd ed. San Francisco: Freeman, 1973.

Stevens, James. *Sacred Legends of the Sandy Lake Cree*. Toronto: McClelland and Steward, 1971.

Steward, Julian H. *Theory of Culture Change*. Urbana: University of Illinois Press, 1955.

Steward, Julian H., and Louis C. Faron. *Native Peoples of South America*. New York: McGraw-Hill, 1959.

Stini, William A. *Ecology and Human Adaptation*. Dubuque, Iowa: Wm. C. Brown, 1975.

Straus, W. L., and A. J. E. Cave. "Pathology and Posture of Neanderthal Man," *Quarterly Review of Biology*, vol. 32 (1957), pp. 348–63.

Struever, Stuart, and Kent D. Vickery. "The Beginnings of Cultivation in the Midwest-Riverine Area of the United States," *American Anthropologist*, vol. 75 (1973), pp. 1197–1220.

Sussman, Robert. "Child Transport, Family Size, and the Increase in Human Population Size During the Neolithic," *Current Anthropology*, vol. 13 (1972), pp. 258–67.

Swanson, Guy E. *The Birth of the Gods*. Ann Arbor: University of Michigan Press, 1969.

Sweeney, James J. "African Negro Culture," in Paul Radin, ed., *African Folktales and Sculpture*. New York: Pantheon, 1952.

Szalay, Frederick S. "The Beginnings of Primates," *Evolution*, vol. 22 (1968), pp. 19–36.

Szalay, Frederick S. "Hunting-Scavenging Proto-hominids: A Model for Hominid Origins," *Man*, vol. 10 (1975), pp. 420–29.

Talmon, Yonina. "Mate Selection in Collective Settlements," *American Sociological Review*, vol. 29 (1964), pp. 491–508.

Tattersall, Ian. *Man's Ancestors*. London: John Murray, 1970.

Teleki, Geza. "The Omnivorous Chimpanzee," *Scientific American*, January 1973, pp. 32–42.

Textor, Robert B., comp. *A Cross-Cultural Summary*. New Haven: HRAF Press, 1967.

Thieme, Paul. "The Comparative Method for Reconstruction in Linguistics," in Dell Hymes, ed., *Language in Culture and Society*. New York: Harper & Row, 1964.

Thomas, Elizabeth Marshall. *The Harmless People*. New York: Alfred A. Knopf, 1959.

Thompson, Elizabeth Bartlett. *Africa, Past and Present*. Boston: Houghton Mifflin, 1966.

Thurnwald, R. C. "Pigs and Currency in Buin: Observations about Primitive Standards of Value and Economics," *Oceania*, vol. 5 (1934), p. 125.

Tobias, Philip. "New Developments in Hominid Paleontology in South and East Africa," *Annual Review of Anthropology*, vol. 2 (1973).

Torrey, E. Fuller. *The Mind Game: Witchdoctors and Psychiatrists*. New York: Emerson Hall, n.d.

Trevor-Roper, H. R. "The European Witch-Craze of the Sixteenth and Seventeenth Centuries," in W. A. Lessa and E. Z. Vogt, eds., *Reader in Comparative Religion*, 3rd ed. New York: Harper & Row, 1971.

Trinkaus, Erik. "A Reconsideration of the Fontéchevade Fossils," *American Journal of Physical Anthropology*, vol. 39 (1973), pp. 25–35.

Turner, B. L. "Population Density in the Classic Maya Lowlands: New Evidence for Old Approaches," *Geographical Review*, vol. 66, no. 1 (January 1970), pp. 72–82.

Tylor, Edward B. "Animism," in W. A. Lessa and E. Z. Vogt, eds., *Reader in Comparative Religion*, 3rd ed. New York: Harper & Row, 1971.

Ucko, Peter J., and Andrée Rosenfeld. *Paleolithic Cave Art*. New York: McGraw-Hill, 1967.

Van Lawick-Goodall, Jane. *In the Shadow of Man*. Boston: Houghton Mifflin, 1971.

Vayda, Andrew P. "Pomo Trade Feasts," in George Dalton, ed., *Tribal and Peasant Economies*. Garden City, N.Y.: Natural History Press, 1967.

Vayda, Andrew P., Anthony Leeds, and David B. Smith. "The Place of Pigs in Melanesian Subsistence," in Viola E. Garfield, ed., *Patterns of Land Utilization and Other Papers*. Proceedings of the Annual Spring Meeting of the American Ethnological Society, Symposium, 1961.

Wallace, Alfred Russell. "On the Tendency of Varieties to Depart Indefinitely from the Original Type," *Journal of the Proceedings of the Linnaean Society*, August, 1858. Reprinted in Louise B. Young, ed., *Evolution of Man*. New York: Oxford University Press, 1970.

Wallace, Anthony. *The Death and Rebirth of the Seneca*. New York: Alfred A. Knopf, 1970.

Wallace, Anthony. "A Possible Technique for Recognizing Psychological Characteristics of the Ancient Maya from an Analysis of their Art," *American Imago*, vol. 7 (1950), p. 245.

Wallace, Anthony. *Religion: An Anthropological View*. New York: Random House, 1966.

Wallace, Anthony. "Revitalization Movements," *American Anthropologist*, vol. 58 (1956), p. 265.

Warner, W. Lloyd. *A Black Civilization*. New York: Harper & Row, 1937.

Warner, W. Lloyd, and Paul S. Lunt. *The Social Life of*

a Modern Community. New Haven: Yale University Press, 1941.

Washburn, Sherwood. "Tools and Human Evolution," *Scientific American,* September 1960, pp. 62–75.

Weber, Max. *The Theory of Social and Economic Organization* (trans., A. M. Henderson and Talcott Parsons). New York: Oxford University Press, 1947.

Weiss, Mark L., and Alan E. Mann. *Human Biology and Behavior.* Boston: Little, Brown, 1975.

Wheatley, Paul. *The Pivot of the Four Quarters.* Chicago: Aldine, 1971.

Whitaker, Ian. *Social Relations in a Nomadic Lappish Community.* Oslo: Utgitt av Norsk Folksmuseum, 1955.

White, Benjamin. "Demand for Labor and Population Growth in Colonial Java," *Human Ecology,* vol. 1 (1973), pp. 217–36.

White, Leslie A. "The Expansion of the Scope of Science," in Morton H. Fried, ed., *Readings in Anthropology,* 2nd ed., vol. 1. New York: Thomas Y. Crowell, 1968.

White, Leslie A. "A Problem in Kinship Terminology," *American Anthropologist,* vol. 41 (1939), pp. 569–70.

White, Leslie A. *The Science of Culture.* New York: Farrar, Straus and Cudahy, 1949.

Whiting, Beatrice B. *Paiute Sorcery,* Viking Fund Publications in Anthropology, no. 15. New York: Wenner-Gren Foundation, 1950.

Whiting, Beatrice B., and John W. M. Whiting. "Methods for Observing and Recording Behavior," in Raoul Naroll and Ronald Cohen, eds., *A Handbook of Methods in Cultural Anthropology.* Garden City, N.Y.: Natural History Press, 1970.

Whiting, Beatrice B., and John W. M. Whiting (in collaboration with Richard Longabaugh). *Children of Six Cultures: A Psycho-Cultural Analysis.* Cambridge: Harvard University Press, 1975.

Whiting, John W. M. *Becoming a Kwoma.* New Haven: Yale University Press, 1941.

Whiting, John W. M. "Cultural and Sociological Influences on Development," in *Growth and Development of the Child in His Setting.* Maryland: Maryland Child Growth and Development Institute, 1959.

Whiting, John W. M. "Effects of Climate on Certain Cultural Practices," in Ward H. Goodenough, ed., *Explorations in Cultural Anthropology.* New York: McGraw-Hill, 1964.

Whiting, John W. M., and Irvin L. Child. *Child Training and Personality: A Cross Cultural Study.* New Haven: Yale University Press, 1953.

Wilson, Monica. *Good Company: A Study of Nyakyusa Age-Villages.* Boston: Beacon Press, 1963.

Wittfogel, Karl. *Oriental Despotism: A Comparative Study of Total Power.* New Haven: Yale University Press, 1957.

Wolf, Arthur. "Adopt a Daughter-in-Law, Marry a Sister: A Chinese Solution to the Problem of the Incest Taboo," *American Anthropologist,* vol. 70 (1968), pp. 864–74.

Wolf, Eric. *Peasant Wars of the Twentieth Century.* New York: Harper & Row, 1969.

Wolf, Eric. *Peasants.* Englewood Cliffs, N.J.: Prentice-Hall, 1966.

Wolpoff, Milford H. "Competitive Exclusion among Lower Pleistocene Hominids: The Single Species Hypothesis," *Man,* vol. 6 (1971), pp. 601–13.

Woodburn, James. "An Introduction to Hadza Ecology," in Richard B. Lee and Irven DeVore, eds., *Man the Hunter.* Chicago: Aldine, 1968.

Wright, Gary A. "Origins of Food Production in Southwestern Asia: A Survey of Ideas," *Current Anthropology,* vol. 12 (1971), pp. 447–78.

Wright, George O. "Projection and Displacement: A Cross-Cultural Study of Folk Tale Aggression," *Journal of Abnormal and Social Psychology,* vol. 49 (1954), pp. 523–28.

Wright, Henry T., and Gregory A. Johnson. "Population, Exchange, and Early State Formation in Southwestern Iran," *American Anthropologist,* vol. 77 (1975), pp. 267–77.

Young, Louise B., ed. *Evolution of Man.* New York: Oxford University Press, 1970.

Young, T. Cuyler, Jr. "Population Densities and Early Mesopotamian Urbanism," in P. J. Ucko, R. Tringham, and G. W. Dimbleby, eds., *Man, Settlement, and Urbanism.* Cambridge, Mass.: Schenkman, 1972.

Zohary, Daniel. "The Progenitors of Wheat and Barley in Relation to Domestication and Agricultural Dispersal in the Old World," in Peter J. Ucko and G. W. Dimbleby, eds., *The Domestication and Exploitation of Plants and Animals.* Chicago: Aldine, 1969.

Sub-ject Index

Geology, 7
German language:
  historical development, 207 and *f*,
    208
  morphology, 205
Germany:
  fencing scars, 406
  Nazi officials, "normalcy" of, 374
  technological borrowing, 426
Ghana:
  city-state of, 135, 136, 173
  early civilization, 135, 136, 173
  insecticide program, 457*p*
  occupational clubs, 334
Ghost Dance (Paiute Indians),
    402
Ghosts, 387, 389
Gibbons, 43, 55
  early evolution, 71
  life expectancy, 52*f*
Gift exchange:
  balanced reciprocity, 250–51
  cultural barriers, 454
  generalized reciprocity, 248
  marriage ceremonies, 285
Gilgamesh epic, 417
Giraffes, evolution of, 25, 27, 28*p*
Glaciations, interglacial periods, 101*f*,
    104. *See also* Upper Paleolithic
    cultures
  and Mesolithic cultures, 142,
    144–45
Gloger's rule, 129
Glottochronology, 207–8
Gods, 386–87. *See also* Religion
Gorillas, 44, 49*p*
  early evolution, 71–72, 72*p*
  knuckle-walking, 44
Grammar, 204–5
  borrowing between languages, 209
  children's acquisition of, 202
  cultural influences, 210–11
    forced observation hypothesis,
      211–12
  morphology, 204, 205
  syntax, 204
  transformational grammar, 205
Grasslands, and agriculture, 230
Gravettian culture, 116
Great Britain:
  advertising, 453–54
  agriculture, commercialization of,
    437
  class system, 267
  incest taboo, 286*p*
  voluntary military duty, 326

Greece, ancient:
  agriculture, 224–25
  mythology, 417, 418
  religion, 383, 390
  sacrifices, 397
  slavery, 270
Grimm's fairy tales, 417
Group marriage, 291
Guadalupe, Our Lady of, 402
Guayaki society (Brazil), band
    organization, 343
Günz glacial period, 101*f*
Gurubumba society (New Guinea):
  amok illness, 376
  ghosts, belief in, 388*p*
  magic rites, 398*p*
Gusii society (Kenya):
  bride price, 284
  marriage ceremonies, 283

Hadza society (Tanzania), land use,
    239
Haiti:
  African gods, 429
  work traditions, 451
Harappa (India), 171
Hausa tribe, postpartum intercourse
    taboo, 293
Hawaii:
  kin terminology, 320–21
  royal incest, 286, 288
Healing. *See* Illness
Health care. *See* Preventive medicine
Hebrew religion:
  myths, 417, 418
  taboos, 386
  Yahweh, 390
Herding. *See* Pastoralism
Heredity. *See* Genetics
Hero myths, 417
Heterosis, 128
Hieroglyphic writing, 169
High altitude, adaptation to,
    129–30
Hindu religion:
  intermediary gods, 394
  monotheistic aspect, 389
  reincarnation, 391
  sacred cows, 400–401
Historical linguistics, 205–9
  comparative methods, 206–7
  divergence in languages, 208–9
  glottochronology, 207–8
Homestead Act (1862), 242
Hominids, 72–76, 80–97
  food-sharing, 91, 92

Hominids, (*cont.*)
  Miocene epoch, 72–76
    characteristic traits, 72
    dentition, 74–76
    diet, 75–76
    fossil evidence, 61, 63
    vs. hominoids, 72
  Pliocene epoch, 80–97
    australopithecines, 86–89
    bipedalism, 81, 82–85
    environmental changes, 80–81
    fossil evidence, 85–86
    Homo erectus, 92–97
    life-styles, 91–92
    tool traditions, 89–91
Hominoidea, 42–45
  blood likenesses, 42–43
  chimpanzees, 44–45. *See also*
    Chimpanzees
  gibbons, siamangs, 43, 52*f*, 71
  gorillas, 44, 49*p*, 71–72
  hominids (humans), 45. *See also*
    Hominids; *Homo*, genus of
  orangutans, 43–44, 45, 47*p*
Homo, genus of, 72, 80
  and the australopithecines, 89, 93
  fossil evidence, 85–86
  "1470" skull, 89
Homo erectus, 82*f*, 86, 89, 92–97, 100
  age, 92, 93, 94*p*
  campsites, 96*f*, 96–97
  cannibalism, 95
  cranial capacity, 83, 84 and *f*, 92,
    94
  fire use, 94–95, 96
  hunting, 95–96
  physical characteristics, 93–94, 95*p*
  tool traditions, 94
Homo habilis, 86, 88–89
Homo sapiens, emergence of, 100–119
  first appearance, 22
  fossil remains, 100–101, 103
  Neandertals, 103–9
  New World cultures, 117–19
  Upper Paleolithic cultures, 109–17
Homo sapiens sapiens, 120*f*, 109. *See*
    also Upper Paleolithic cultures
  and generalized Neandertals, 105
Homozygous, heterozygous traits, 30
Hopi Indians:
  bride price, 284
  childhood sexuality, 277
  childrearing practices, 365
  clans, 315
  mesa settlements, 193 and *p*
  "private" wives, 276

Anthropology

Carol R. Ember
Melvin Ember

Hunter College of the City University of New York